Business Communication

Building Critical Skills

Second Edition

Kitty O. Locker
The Ohio State University

Stephen Kyo Kaczmarek
Columbus State Community College

 Irwin

Boston   Burr Ridge, IL   Dubuque, IA   Madison, WI   New York
San Francisco   St. Louis   Bangkok   Bogotá   Caracas   Kuala Lumpur
Lisbon   London   Madrid   Mexico City   Milan   Montreal   New Delhi
Santiago   Seoul   Singapore   Sydney   Taipei   Toronto

BUSINESS COMMUNICATION: BUILDING CRITICAL SKILLS
Published by McGraw-Hill/Irwin, a business unit of The McGraw-Hill Companies, Inc. 1221 Avenue of the
Americas, New York, NY 10020. Copyright ' 2004, 2001 by The McGraw-Hill Companies, Inc. All
rights reserved. No part of this publication may be reproduced or distributed in any form or by
any means, or stored in a database or retrieval system, without the prior written consent of The
McGraw-Hill Companies, Inc., including, but not limited to, in any network or other electronic
storage or transmission, or broadcast for distance learning.
Some ancillaries, including electronic and print components, may not be available to customers
outside the United States.

This book is printed on acid-free paper.
domestic   2 3 4 5 6 7 8 9 0 QWV/QWV 0 9 8 7 6 5 4 3
international   2 3 4 5 6 7 8 9 0 QWV/QWV 0 9 8 7 6 5 4 3

ISBN 0-07-256219-6

Publisher: *John E. Biernat*
Senior sponsoring editor: *Andy Winston*
Senior developmental editor: *Sarah Reed*
Senior marketing manager: *Ellen Cleary*
Producer, media technology: *Jennifer Barrick*
Project manager: *Natalie J. Ruffatto*
Manager, new book production: *Melonie Salvati*
Designer: *Matthew Baldwin*
Photo research coordinator: *Judy Kausal*
Photo researcher: *Inge King*
Supplement producer: *Betty Hadala*
Senior digital content specialist: *Brian Nacik*
Cover design: *Jenny El-Shammy*
Typeface: *10.5/12 Palatino*
Compositor: *Carlisle Communications, Ltd.*
Printer: *Quebecor World Versailles Inc.*

Library of Congress Cataloging-in-Publication Data

Locker, Kitty O.
    Business communication: building critical skills / Kitty O. Locker, Stephen Kyo
Kaczmarek. 2nd ed.
        p. cm.
    Includes bibliographical references and index.
    ISBN 0-07-256219-6 (alk.) ISBN 0-07-121484-4 (international)
    1. Business communication. I. Kaczmarek, Stephen Kyo. II. Title.
HF5718 .L633 2004
651.7 dc21   2002035595

INTERNATIONAL EDITION ISBN 0-07-121484-4
Copyright ' 2004. Exclusive rights by The McGraw-Hill Companies, Inc. for manufacture and export.
This book cannot be re-exported from the country to which it is sold by McGraw-Hill.
The International Edition is not available in North America.

www.mhhe.com

To my husband, Bob Mills, with love.

—Kitty O. Locker

For my father, who always believed in me.

—Stephen Kyo Kaczmarek

About the Authors

Kitty O. Locker is an Associate Professor of English at The Ohio State University, where she teaches courses in workplace discourse and research methods. She has taught as Assistant Professor at Texas A&M University and the University of Illinois at Urbana.

She received her BA from DePauw University and her MA and PhD from the University of Illinois at Urbana.

She has also written *Business and Administrative Communication* (6th ed., McGraw-Hill/Irwin, 2003) and The *Irwin Business Communication Handbook: Writing and Speaking in Business Classes* (1993), and co-edited *Conducting Research in Business Communication* (1988).

Her consulting clients include URS Greiner, Abbott Laboratories, the Ohio Civil Service Employees Association, AT&T, and the American Medical Association. She developed a complete writing improvement program for Joseph T. Ryerson, the nation's largest steel materials service center.

In 1994–95, she served as President of the Association for Business Communication (ABC). From 1997 to 2000, she edited ABC's *Journal of Business Communication*. She received ABC's Outstanding Researcher Award in 1992 and ABC's Meada Gibbs Outstanding Teacher Award in 1998.

Stephen Kyo Kaczmarek is an Assistant Professor at Columbus State Community College. He teaches business and technical communication, composition, creative writing, journalism, public relations, freshman experience, and courses in film and literature he's designed. He's taught public relations at Ohio Dominican University and business communication at The Ohio State University.

He received an MA in English and BAs in journalism and English from Ohio State.

Steve has presented papers at conferences of the Association for Business Communication, Conference on College Composition and Communication, Northeast Modern Language Association, and the College English Association of Ohio. He co-advises Phi Theta Kappa at Columbus State.

His consulting clients have included Nationwide Insurance, The Ohio Historical Society, The Ohio Association of Historical Societies and Museums, The Ohio Museums Association, United Energy Systems, The Thomas Moyer for Chief Justice of Ohio Campaign, and Van Meter and Associates.

Prior to joining Columbus State, Steve managed staff development and information for the Franklin County, Ohio, Commissioners. He received an Award of Excellence from the National Association of County Information Officers.

A movie buff, Steve's also appeared in educational videos and television commercials.

August 20, 2003

Dear Student:

Business Communication: Building Critical Skills helps you build the writing, speaking, and listening skills that are crucial for success in the 21st-century workplace.

As you read,

- Look for the answers to the opening questions. Check your memory with the **Instant Replays** and your understanding with the **Summary of Key Points** at the end of the chapter.

- Note the terms in bold type and their definitions. Use the **rewind** and **fast forward** icons to go to discussions of terms.

- Read the **Building a Critical Skill** boxes carefully. Practice the skills both in assignments and on your own. These skills will serve you well for the rest of your work life.

- Use items in the lists when your prepare your assignments or review for tests.

- Use the examples, especially the paired examples of effective and ineffective communication, as models to help you draft and revise. Comments in red ink signal problems in an example; comments in blue ink note things done well.

- Read the **Site to See** and **FYI** boxes in the margins to give you more resources on the Internet and interesting facts about business communication.

When you prepare an assignment,

- Review the PAIBOC questions in Module 1. Some assignments have "Hints" to help probe the problem. Some of the longer assignments have preliminary assignments analyzing the audience or developing reader benefits or subject lines. Use these to practice portions of longer documents.

- If you're writing a letter or memo, read the sample problems in Modules 10, 11, and 12 with a detailed analysis, strong and weak solutions, and a discussion of the solutions to see how to apply the principles in this book to your own writing.

August 20, 2003
Page 2

- Use the **Polishing Your Prose** exercises to make your writing its best.

- Remember that most problems are open-ended, requiring original, critical thinking. Many of the problems are deliberately written in negative, ineffective language. You'll need to reword sentences, reorganize information, and think through the situation to produce the best possible solution to the business problem.

- Learn as much as you can about what's happening in business. The knowledge will not only help you develop reader benefits and provide examples but also make you an even more impressive candidate in job interviews.

- Visit the *Online Learning Center* (http://www.mhhe.com/bcs2e) to see how the resources presented there can help you. You will find updated articles, résumé and letter templates, links to job hunting Web sites, and much more.

- Access the *BComm Skill Booster* to complete interactive lessons related to the text module.

Communication skills are critical to success in both the new economy and the old. *Business Communication: Building Critical Skills* can help you identify and practice the skills you need. Have a good term—and a good career!

Cordially,   Cordially,

Kitty O. Locker   Stephen Kyo Kaczmarek
locker.1@osu.edu   kazbcs2@yahoo.com

August 20, 2003

Dear Professor:

Business Communication: Building Critical Skills (BCS) is here to help make your job teaching business communication a little bit easier.

Its modular design makes adapting *BCS* to 5–, 8–, 10–, or 15–week courses simpler. And, with videos, new media tools, and supplements, it is easy to adapt to Internet courses. The features teachers and students find so useful are also here: anecdotes and examples, easy-to-follow lists, integrated coverage of international business communication, analyses of sample problems, and a wealth of in-class exercises and out-of-class assignments.

But *BCS* takes these features a step further. In each module you'll also find

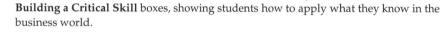
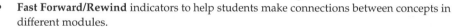
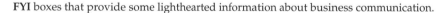

- **Polishing Your Prose** boxes, featuring straightforward instructions to help students correct common writing errors, as well as exercises to test what they know.
- **Building a Critical Skill** boxes, showing students how to apply what they know in the business world.
- **Site to See** boxes that invite students to use the Internet to get timely information available in cyberspace.
- **Instant Replays** to reinforce concepts students are reading.
- **Fast Forward/Rewind** indicators to help students make connections between concepts in different modules.
- **FYI** boxes that provide some lighthearted information about business communication.

This second edition is thoroughly updated based on the latest research in business communication. You'll find many new problems and examples, new Polishing Your Prose exercises, and new Sites to See. Your students will benefit from timelines that identify the steps in planning, writing, and revising everything from 7-minute e-mail messages to memos taking 6 hours to reports taking 30 business days. Cases for Communicators at the end of each unit provide individual and group activities. And each module identifies BComm Skill Booster exercises that can be sent directly to the student's computer to allow extra practice in course concepts.

BCS also includes a comprehensive package of supplements to help you and your students.

- An *Instructor's Resource Manual* with sample syllabi, an overview of each module, suggested lecture topics, in-class exercises, examples and transparency masters, discussion and quiz questions, and solutions to problems.
- A *Test Bank* featuring hundreds of questions for use in quizzes, midterms, and final examinations—with answers. The *Test Bank* is also available in a computerized format (Mac or Windows) that allows you to create and edit your own tests.
- An *Instructor's Presentation CD-ROM,* which includes the print supplements and **PowerPoint presentations,** in a format that allows you to create your own custom presentations.

August 20, 2003
Page 2

- *Videos* showing real managers reacting to situations dealing with cultural differences, active listening, working in teams, and the virtual workplace.
- An *Online Learning Center* (http://www.mhhe.com/bcs2e) with self-quizzes for students, a bulletin board to communicate with other professors, current articles and research in business communication, downloadable supplements, links to professional resources, and more.

You can get more information about teaching business communication from the meetings and publications of The Association for Business Communication (ABC). Contact

Professor Robert J. Myers, Executive Director
Association for Business Communication
Baruch College–CUNY
Communication Studies Department, Box B8–240
One Bernard Baruch Way
New York, NY 10010
Voice: 646-312-3726; Fax: 646-349-5297;
E-mail: ABCRJM@cs.com
Web: www.businesscommunication.org

We've done our best to provide you with the most comprehensive but easy-to-use teaching tools we can. Tell us about your own success stories using *BCS*. We look forward to hearing from you!

Cordially,

Kitty O. Locker
locker.1@osu.edu

Cordially,

Stephen Kyo Kaczmarek
kazbcs2@yahoo.com

Acknowledgments

All writing is in some sense collaborative. This book in particular builds upon the ideas and advice of teachers, students, and researchers. The people who share their ideas in conferences and publications enrich not only this book but also business communication as a field.

People who contributed directly to the formation of this second edition include the following:

Linda Landis Andrews, *University of Illinois at Chicago*
Mary Lou Bertrand, *SUNY Jefferson*
Bill Chapel, *Michigan Technological University*
Missie Cotton, *North Central Missouri College*
Ronald Dunbar, *University of Wisconsin – Baraboo/Sauk County*
Jeff Goddin, *Kelley School of Business*
Geraldine Harper, *Howard University*
Jeanette Heidewald, *Kelley School of Business*
Paula Kaiser, *University of North Carolina – Greensboro*
Luchen Li, *Kettering University*
Richard Malamud, *California State University, Dominguez Hills*
Kenneth Mayer, *Cleveland State University*
Susan Smith McClaren, *Mt. Hood Community College*
Elwin Myers, *Texas A&M University – Corpus Christi*
Judy O'Neill, *University of Texas at Austin*
Brenda Rhodes, *Northeastern Junior College*
Carol Smith, *Fort Lewis College*
Charlene Sox, *Appalachia State University*
Robert Stubblefield, *North Carolina Wesleyan University*
Scott Troyan, *University of Wisconsin – Madison*
Deborah Valentine, *Emory University*
Jie Wang, *University of Illinois at Chicago*

In addition, the book continues to benefit from the contributions of the following people:

Focus group participants
Terese Butler, *Long Beach City College*
Marilyn Harris, *El Camino College*
Dana Loewy, *California State University – Fullerton*
Richard Malamud, *California State University – Dominquez Hills*
John Marino, *St. Charles County Community College*
Mary Nerburn, *Moraine Valley Community College*
Dolores Reja, *Fullerton College*
Deb Richey, *Owens Community College*

Diane Seilo, *Golden West College*
Margaret Taylor, *Coastline Community College*
Lisa Tyler, *Sinclair Community College*

Reviewers and survey participants
Michael Alexander, *Chaffey College*
Ashley Alfaro, *Tarrant County Junior College*
Mable Almond, *Wayne Community College*
James Bennett, *California State University, Northridge*
Ellen Benowitz, *Mercer County Community College*
Joyce Birch, *Normandale Community College*
Cathy Bishop, *Parkland College*
Melanie Boesen, *Ivy Tech State College*
Wally Borgen, *Concordia College*
Patricia Borosky, *Trident Technical College*
Kay Bradley, *University of Alaska, Anchorage*
Martin Brodey, *Montgomery College*
Jennifer China, *Midlands Technical College*
Connie Clark, *Lane Community College*
Roberta Cornelius, *Coastal Bend College*
Anthony J. Cotterell, *University of Nevada at Reno*
Wayne Cox, *Anderson College*
Gary Cruice, *Delgado Community College*
Lake Davis, *Navarro College*
Judith DeRosa, *Red Rocks Community College*
Lorena Edwards, *Belmont University*
H. C. Eichmeier, *Clinton Community College*
Linda Ejda, *North Seattle Community College*
Donna Everett, *Morehead State University*
Molly Floyd, *Tarrant County Junior College*
Judith Graham, *Holyoke Community College*
Saundra Granger, *Louisiana State University*
Greg Green, *Suomi College*
Doris Grear, *Florida Community College at Jacksonville*
Robert Haight, *Kalamazoo Valley Community College*
Susan Haigler, *Portland Community College*
Lynn Hamilton, *University of Virginia*
Jeffrey Hunt, *San Antonio College*
Ron Kapper, *College of DuPage*
Douglas Kleim, *Lansing Community College*
Gary Kohut, *University of North Carolina at Charlotte*
Shirley Kuiper, *University of South Carolina*
Bill Lacewell, *Westark College*
Julie Landgraf Johnson, *South Plains College*
Mary E. Leslie, *Grossmont College*
Victor Lopez, *State University of New York*
Julie McDonald, *Northwestern State University*
Pat McMahon, *South Suburban College*
Rose Marie Lynch, *Illinois Valley Community College*
Billie Miller-Cooper, *Cosumnes River College*

John Marino, *St. Charles County Community College*
Candyce Miller, *Ricks College*
Shirley Mixon, *East Central University*
Josef Moorehead, *California State University*
Patricia Murranka, *Arizona State University*
Valerie Perotti, *Ohio University*
John Parrish, *Tarrant County Junior College*
Jeanne Newhall, *Middlesex Community College*
Gloria Nicosia, *Kingsborough Community College*
Cyndi Phillips, *Sheridan College*
Erin Porter, *University of Texas at Austin*
Catherine Rahmes, *Cincinnati State Technical & Community College*
Camille Reale, *Sacred Heart University*
Ruth Riley, *Texas A&M University*
Marlene Rinnier, *Wor-Wic Community College*
Lorraine Robinson, *East Carolina University*
Lynda Rogerson, *University of Colorado, Colorado Springs*
Harold Rouse, *Lurleen B. Wallace State Junior College*
Jim Rucker, *Fort Hays State University*
Lynne Smith, *State University of New York – Delhi*
Ken Stover, *Manatee Community College*
Jan Tovey, *East Carolina University*
Anna Trexler, *Southern Arkansas University*
Mary Tucker, *Ohio University*

For providing encouragement and assistance, we also thank

Donna Kienzler, Iowa State University
Alisha Rohde, The Ohio State University

And, we thank Kitty's husband, Robert S. Mills, who continues to provide a sounding board for ideas, encouragement, and, when deadlines are tight, weekly or nightly rides to Federal Express.

Steve thanks for encouragement over the years friends and colleagues too numerous to mention in their entirety here. Of special note are Bruce Ardinger, Carol Baker, Daniel Barnes, Saretta Burke, J. D. Britton, Lucy Caswell, Jen Chapman, Laura Dachenbach, Elizabeth Dellapa, Ann Frazier, Janet Gething, Kate Hancock, David Hockenberry, Charlie Hottel, Marilyn Howard, Sheila Kapur, Lisa Mackall-Young, Valeriana Moeller, Susan Moran, Donna Pydlek, Crystal Robinson, Maggie Sanese, Bud Sawyer, Wilma Schneider, David Smith, Mike Snider, Jim Strider, Joe Taleroski, and, of course, his co-author, friend, and mentor, Kitty O. Locker. Special thanks also go to his mother, Myo, and sister, Susan, for love, strength, and guidance—and for putting up with him in ways that can only be described as truly remarkable.

Guided Tour

The 2nd edition of *Business Communication: Building Critical Skills* reinforces the essential skills of good communication. The contents consist not of chapters but of 30 skill-centered modules that can be taught in any order.

Please take a moment to page through the highlights of this 2nd edition to see the helpful tools that reinforce this flexible approach to business communication education.

Module Openers

Modules open with down-to-earth questions that map the module and motivate students to learn the material.
The module then answers these critical questions and teaches real-world skills important in business.

Module 2

Adapting Your Message to Your Audience

To learn how to

• Continue to analyze your audiences.
• Begin to adapt your message to your audiences.
• Begin to understand what your organization wants.

Start by asking these questions:

• Who is my audience?
• Why is my audience so important?
• What do I need to know about my audience(s)?
• Now that I have my analysis, what do I do with it?

• What if my audiences have different needs?
• How do I reach my audience(s)?

Understanding your audience is fundamental to the success of any message. You need to adapt your message to fit the audience's goals, interests, and needs.

Analyzing your audience and adapting your message can be done in a cynical, manipulative way. It can also be done in a sensitive, empathic, ethical way. Audiences have a keen sense for messages that try to manipulate them; empathic analysis and adaptation are almost always more successful, as well as being more ethical.

Some students pride themselves on their "honesty" in not adapting their discourse to anyone and in criticizing their bosses as sharply as they might younger brothers and sisters. But almost all organizations expect deference to people in authority. And customers have enough options to deal only with companies that treat them respectfully.

Building a Critical Skill

Using Positive Emphasis Ethically

Several of the methods to achieve positive emphasis can be misused.

Consider omission.

A bank notified customers that checking account fees were being "revised" but omitted the amounts. Customers had to go into the bank and copy down the new (higher) fees themselves.

In another case, a condominium resort offered an "all-terrain vehicle" as a prize for visiting. (Winners had to pay $29.95 for "handling, processing, and insurance.") The actual "prize" was a lawn chair with four wheels that converted into a wheeled cart. The company claims it told the truth: "It is a vehicle. It's a four-wheel cart you can take anywhere—to the beach, to the pool. It may not be motorized, but [we] didn't say it was motorized."

In both cases, full disclosure might have affected decisions: Some customers might have chosen to change banks; some customers would have declined the condominium visit. It isn't ethical to omit information that people need to make decisions.

Presenting information compactly can also go too far. A credit card company mailed out a letter with the good news that the minimum monthly payment was going down. But a separate small flyer explained that interest rates (on the charges not repaid) were going up. The print was far too small to read: 67 lines of type were crowded into five vertical inches of text.

Source: Carmela M. Padilla, "It's a . . . a . . . a . . . . All-Terrain Vehicle. Yeah, That's It. That's the Ticket," *The Wall Street Journal*, July 17, 1987, 17; and Donna S. Kienzler, "Visual Ethics," *The Journal of Business Communication* 34 (1997), 175–76.

Negative: We cannot sell computer disks in lots of less than 10.

Loophole: To keep down packaging costs and to help you save on shipping and handling costs, we sell computer disks in lots of 10 or more.

Building a Critical Skill

Building a Critical Skill boxes explain 30 skills necessary for job success. Topics include Dealing with Discrimination, Thinking Critically, and Negotiating Salary and Benefits.

FYI

Raises are usually set as a percentage of your current salary. If you work for 40 years, getting an extra $2,000 in salary on your first job could yield $15,000 of extra income in compounded raises.

Source: Christina Larson, "Why the Wage Gap?" *Executive Female*, April/May 2002, 27.

How to Get There

If you're going to a place you haven't been before, do a practice run at the same time of day your interview is scheduled for. Check out bus transfers or parking fees. On the day of the interview, leave early enough so that you'll get to the interview 15 minutes early. Use the extra time to check your appearance in the restroom mirror and to thumb through the company publications in the waiting room. If an accident does delay you, call to say you'll be late.

Should I practice before the interview?

Absolutely!

Your interviewing skills will improve with practice. Rehearse everything you can: put on the clothes you'll wear and practice entering a room, shaking hands, sitting down, and answering questions. Ask a friend to interview you. Saying answers out loud is surprisingly harder than saying them in your head.

Some campuses have videotaping facilities so that you can watch your own sample interview. Videotaping is more valuable if you can do it at least twice, so you can modify behavior the second time and check the tape to see whether the modification works.

FYI

FYI sidebars in each module include fun factoids such as which messages busy executives notice, errors that spell checkers won't catch, and even the effect of group experience on win/loss records of NBA teams.

Site to See

Site to See boxes show Web sites that provide more information about topics in the modules. You'll find The Home for Abused Apostrophes, Word Games on the Web, How to Use Parliamentary Procedure, and Before and After Versions of PowerPoint Slides.

 Site to See

**Go to
www.quality.nist.gov**
You-attitude, positive emphasis, and bias-free language build goodwill with words, just as service, quality, and reliability build goodwill with actions. The Baldridge National Quality Program encourages and recognizes quality in U.S. businesses.

can't be exact, give your reader the information you do have: "UPS shipment from California to Texas normally takes three days." If you have absolutely no idea, give the reader the name of the carrier, so the reader knows whom to contact if the order doesn't arrive promptly.

2. Don't Talk about Feelings, Except to Congratulate or Offer Sympathy.

Lacks you-attitude: We are happy to extend you a credit line of $5,000.

You-attitude: You can now charge up to $5,000 on your American Express card.

In most business situations, your feelings are irrelevant and should be omitted. The reader doesn't care whether you're happy, bored stiff at granting a routine application, or worried about granting so much to someone who barely qualifies. All the reader cares about is the situation from his or her point of view.

It *is* appropriate to talk about your own emotions in a message of congratulation or condolence.

You-attitude: Congratulations on your promotion to district manager! I was really pleased to read about it.

You-attitude: I was sorry to hear that your father died.

---

president of public relations at CNBC, suggests that applicants find out what employees wear "and notch it up one step":

If the dress is jeans and a T-shirt, wear slacks and an open collar shirt. . . . If it's slacks and an open collar shirt, throw on a sport coat. If it's a sport coat, throw on a suit. At least match it and go one step up, but don't go three steps down.[3]

Choose comfortable shoes. You may do a fair amount of walking during an onsite interview.

Take care of all the details. Check your heels to make sure they aren't run down; make sure your shoes are shined. Have your hair cut or styled conservatively. Jewelry and makeup should be understated. Personal hygiene must be impeccable. If you wear cologne or perfume, keep it to a minimum.

What to Bring to the Interview

Bring extra copies of your résumé. If your campus placement office has already given the interviewer a data sheet, present the résumé at the beginning of the interview: "I thought you might like a little more information about me."

Bring something to write on and something to write with. It's OK to bring in a small notepad with the questions you want to ask on it.

Bring copies of your work or a portfolio: an engineering design, a copy of a memo you wrote on a job or in a business writing class, an article you wrote for the campus paper. You don't need to present these unless the interview calls for them, but they can be very effective.

Bring the names, addresses, and phone numbers of references if you didn't put them on your résumé. Bring complete details about your work history and education, including dates and street addresses, in case you're asked to fill out an application form.

If you can afford it, buy a briefcase to carry these items. At the start of your career, an inexpensive briefcase is acceptable.

Instant Replay

Interview Strategy
Plan an interview strategy based on these three questions:
1. What two to five facts about yourself do you want the interviewer to know?
2. What disadvantages or weaknesses do you need to overcome or minimize?
3. What do you need to know about the job and the organization to decide whether or not you want to accept this job if it is offered to you?

Instant Replay

Instant Replay sidebars in the margins of each module reinforce key concepts presented earlier in the module. Topics include Criteria for Effective Messages, Guidelines for Page Design, Organizing Bad News to Superiors, Responding to Criticism, and How to Create a Summary of Qualifications for a Résumé.

BComm Skill Booster

To apply the concepts in this module, complete lessons 12 and 14 on page design and presentation slides. You can access the BComm

Skill Booster through the text Web site at www.mhhe.com/bcs2e.

Cases for Communicators

Hello, Gateway?

Proofreading—making sure that your document is free from typographical errors—is the final step in the writing process. While always important, proofreading is perhaps even more critical in our electronic age, as the reuse of digital information, data, and images is becoming a common practice.

The ability to leverage existing materials is a significant advantage of the digital age, but it can also lead to more errors if the original information is inaccurate. How severe can this problem become? Just ask computer giant Gateway Computers, which was recently hit with a $3.6 million jury verdict—the final outcome in a series of events that began with a small typing error.

The problem began when an employee typed 800, rather than 888, as the prefix for the company's toll-free customer service line. This single error, however, was replicated in the company's internal materials, on its Web site, in its Internet billings, and, finally, on a form distributed to more than 100,000 Gateway customers. As a result, the actual owner of the toll-free number incurred substantial costs and disruption in its own business activities, because its telephone lines were overrun with Gateway customers.

More importantly, though the mistake was identified a mere six days after calls began, it took more than two years for Gateway to correct the error in all of its business materials. Consider the number of business hours involved in correcting this one mistake, which could, and likely should, have been fixed in a

thorough proofreading of the original document. Those business costs, combined with the long-term revenue loss from unhappy customers and the $3.6 million, add up to one expensive mistake!

Source: "Wrong Phone Number Costs Gateway," Associated Press, July 19, 2002. Accessed on Yahoo! News on July 21, 2002.

Individual Activity

Imagine that you are a Communications Manager at Gateway, and it is your responsibility to craft a message to those 100,000 customers who received mailings with the incorrect toll-free number. Because the letter will be such an important part of the company's efforts to restore customer confidence, the Vice-President of Communications will be reviewing the message before it is sent out.

In addition to accepting full responsibility for the incorrect toll-free number, the company has decided to take three actions designed to underscore its ongoing commitment to customer service:

1. Hire more telephone representatives in order to shorten the wait time on the customer service and technical support telephone lines.

2. Create a dedicated message board on the company's Web site that will allow customers to communicate their problems and concerns more quickly and easily.

3. Develop and advertise a new marketing effort: "Have your complaint addressed in 24 hours or less, or get a free $50 Gateway gift certificate."

Cases for Communicators

Unit-ending cases provide both individual and team activities to solve communication challenges faced by real-world companies and organizations. Topics include typos in marketing materials, pop-up ads on the Web, and corporate training programs.

Polishing Your Prose

Making Subjects and Verbs Agree

Make sure the subjects and verbs in your sentences agree. Subjects and verbs agree when they are both singular or both plural:

Correct: The laser printer no longer works.

Correct: The nonworking laser printers are in the store room.

Often, subject-verb errors occur when other words come between the subject and verb. Learn to correct errors by looking for the subject—who or what is doing the principal action—and the verb—the action itself:

Correct: A team of marketing researchers is reviewing our promotional campaign.

Correct: The four-color brochures, which cost about $1,000 to print and ship, were sent to our St. Louis affiliate.

U.S. usage treats company names and the words *company* and *government* as singular nouns. In England and countries adopting the British system, these nouns are plural:

Correct: Nationwide Insurance is
(U.S.) headquartered in Columbus, Ohio.

Correct: Lloyds of London are
(U.K.) headquartered in London.

Use a plural verb when two or more singular subjects are joined by *and*.

Correct: Mr. Simmens, Ms. Lopez, and Mr. Yee were in Seoul for a meeting last week.

Use a singular verb when two or more singular subjects are joined by *or, nor,* or *but.* Follow this rule when using *neither/nor* and *either/or* combinations. However, when one of the subjects is plural, choose the verb based on the subject nearest the verb.

Correct: Neither Crandall nor the Panzinis want to play on the department's softball team this year.

Correct: Either the Panzinis or Crandall needs to help keep score.

Correct: Neither Dr. Hroscoe nor Mr. Jamieson is in today.

When the sentence begins with *There* or *Here,* make the verb agree with the subject that follows the verb:

Correct: There were blank pages in the fax we received.

Correct: Here is the information on the job candidate you requested.

Some words that end in *s* are considered singular and require singular verbs:

Correct: The World Series features advertisements of our product in the stadium.

For some nouns, singular and plural forms can be spelled the same. Examples are *data, deer,* and *fish.* Choose a verb based on how you are using the word—singular or plural.

When you encounter situations that don't seem to fit the rule, or when following the rules produces an awkward sentence, rewrite the sentence to avoid the problem:

Problematic: The grant coordinator in addition to the awarding agency (is, are?) happy with the latest proposal we submitted.

Better: The grant coordinator and the awarding agency are happy with the latest proposal we submitted.

Exercises

Choose the correct verb or rewrite the sentence.

Polishing Your Prose

Polishing Your Prose exercises conclude each module. They may be assigned in any order throughout the term (see the handy list with page numbers on the inside front cover of this book). Students can do the odd-numbered exercises for practice and check the answers at the end of the book. Answers to even-numbered exercises, which can be assigned for homework or used for quizzes, are included in the *Instructor's Resource Manual.*

4. I wish you all the best in your new job. I know you'll do well!

5. Pertaining to the party of the first part, hereafter called "party first," and excepting any and all objections from the party of the second part, hereafter called "party second," this amendment shall be considered null and void with proper written notice three (3) days prior to the execution of the original agreement.

10. We better do something about this soon. I mean, what if we're not ready in time? What if the supplier doesn't fulfill our order? What will we do then? Well? I'm telling you, we need to get moving on this *now.*

Check your answers to the odd-numbered exercises at the back of the book.

BComm Skill Booster

To apply the concepts in this module, complete lessons 21, 22, 23, 25, and 26 on persuasive messages, direct requests, problem-solving

messages, and credibility. You can access the BComm Skill Booster through the text Web site at www.mhhe.com/bcs2e.

BComm Skill Booster References

At the end of each module, you'll see which lessons in the BComm Skill Booster apply to that module. See p. xvii for more information about the Skill Booster.

Supplements

Instructor's Resource Manual

The Instructor's Resource Manual is an excellent tool for veterans as well as new teachers. It includes sample syllabi for 5-, 8-, 10-, and 15-week courses; overviews of each module; key lecture points supported with teaching tips, in-class exercises, and notes for using the PowerPoint slides and transparency masters; answers to the textbook assignments; and answers to the even-numbered Polishing Your Prose exercises.

Test Bank

The Test Bank includes nearly 1,000 true-false, multiple-choice, and fill-in-the-blank questions with answers.

PowerPoint Presentations

PowerPoint Presentations feature 10–15 slides for each module outlining lecture material as well as expanding key concepts in the module. Instructors can customize these slides for their own courses.

Videos

Four Manager's Hot Seat videos available with this book show real managers reacting live and without scripts to situations dealing with negotiation and cultural differences, active listening, working in teams, and communication in the virtual workplace. These videos provide a good foundation for classroom discussion, as you evaluate what the manager could have done differently, or what he or she did well.

Instructor's Resource CD-ROM

The Instructor's Resource CD-ROM includes the Instructor's Resource Manual, PowerPoint slides, transparency masters, Test Bank, and the computerized Test Bank.

Supplements

www.mhhe.com/bcs2e

The Online Learning Center (OLC) is a Web site that follows the text module-by-module, with additional materials and resources to enhance the classroom experience. Instructors can download new exercises and Web site addresses and find transparency masters and PowerPoint slides. Students can take online module quizzes for review, see sample letters and résumés, read about business communication in the news, review key terms, work on additional exercises, and find job hunting resources in the Career Corner.

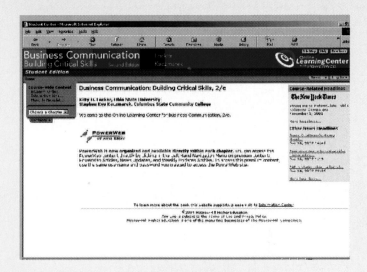

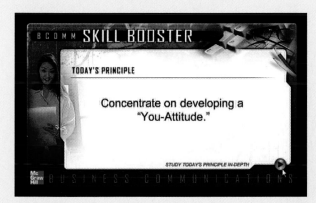

BComm Skill Booster

Access to the BComm Skill Booster is included with each new copy of the text with a registration card/password. The Internet-based Skill Booster delivers interactive lessons to students' computers so students can practice course concepts. Each lesson includes three action steps to help master the skill, reinforced through quizzes, FixIt! exercises, tips, and Web links. Access the Skill Booster through the OLC at www.mhhe.com/bcs2e.

Business Communication Online

Students can evaluate and improve their skills with online activities. Topics include audience analysis, bad news messages, positive emphasis, and résumés. Business Communication Online can be accessed through the OLC.

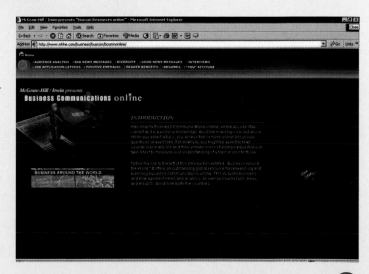

How Can the Internet Help Me Keep My Course Up to Date?

Keeping your course current is a job, and McGraw-Hill/Irwin can help. Extend the learning experience beyond the core textbook with PowerWeb. You'll find all of the latest news and developments pertinent to your course, brought to you via the Internet without all the clutter and dead links of a typical online search.

PowerWeb is a robust Web site that offers these *course-specific* features:

- Current articles related to business communication.
- Daily and weekly updates with assessment tools.
- Informative and timely world news qualified by a content expert and professor.
- Refereed Web links.
- Online handbook for researching, evaluating, and citing online sources.

In PowerWeb, you'll find a trove of helpful learning aids, including self-grading quizzes, interactive glossaries, and exercises. Students may also access study tips, conduct online research, and learn about different career paths.

Visit the PowerWeb site at **www.dushkin.com/powerweb** and see firsthand what PowerWeb can mean to your course.

How Can I Easily Create an Online Course?

To educate your students online, you can use McGraw-Hill/Irwin's *Business Communication* content for complete online courses, which use the most popular delivery platforms currently available. These platforms are designed for instructors who want complete control over course content and how it is presented to students. You can customize the *Business Communication* Online Learning Center content and author your own course materials. It's entirely up to you.

Products like WebCT and Blackboard expand the reach of your course. Online discussion and message boards will now complement your office hours. Thanks to a sophisticated tracking system, you will know which students need more attention—even if they don't ask for help. That's because online testing scores are recorded and automatically placed in your grade book, and if a student is struggling with coursework, a special alert message lets you know.

Remember, *Business Communication's* content is flexible enough to use with any platform currently available. If your department or school is already using a platform, we can help.

PageOut

McGraw-Hill's Course Management System

PageOut is the easiest way to create a Web site for your management course.

There's no need for HTML coding, graphic design, or a thick how-to book. Just fill in a series of boxes with simple English and click on one of our professional designs. In no time, your course is online with a Web site that contains your syllabus!

If you need assistance in preparing your Web site, we can help. Our team of product specialists is ready to take your course materials and build a custom Web site to your specifications. Just contact a McGraw-Hill/Irwin PageOut specialist to start the process. Best of all, PageOut is free when you adopt *Business Communication: Building Critical Skills*. To learn more, please visit **www.pageout.net.**

Brief Contents

Contents

Unit One

Building Blocks for Effective Messages

Module 1

Business Communication, Management, and Success

Start by asking these questions:

- Will I really have to write?
- Don't I know enough about communication?
- What does communication accomplish?
- How much does correspondence cost?
- What makes a message effective?
- How should I analyze business communication situations?

Work requires communication. People communicate to plan products and services; hire, train, and motivate workers; coordinate manufacturing and delivery; persuade customers to buy; and bill them for the sale. For many business, nonprofit, community, and government organizations, the "product" is information or a service rather than something tangible. Information and services are created and delivered by communication. In every organization, communication is the way people get their points across, get work done, and get recognized for their contributions.

Unless you have a fairy godmother, you'll need to know how to communicate.

Communication takes many forms. **Verbal communication,** or communication that uses words, includes

- Face-to-face or phone conversations
- Meetings
- E-mail and voice-mail messages
- Letters and memos
- Reports.

Nonverbal communication does not use words. Examples include

- Pictures
- Company logos
- Gestures and body language
- Who sits where at a meeting
- How long someone keeps a visitor waiting.

Even in your first job, you'll communicate. You'll read information; you'll listen to instructions; you'll ask questions; you may solve problems with other workers in teams. In a manufacturing company, hourly workers travel to a potential customer to make oral sales presentations. In an insurance company, clerks answer customers' letters. Even "entry-level" jobs require high-level skills in reasoning, mathematics, and communicating.[1]

At the Federal Reserve Bank of Minneapolis, Richard Todd tries to find people who can write and read critically:

> Good writing is one of two key abilities I focus on when hiring; the other is the ability to read critically. I can train people to do almost anything else, but I don't have time to teach this.[2]

Communication becomes even more important as you advance. Annette Gregorich, Vice President of Human Resources for Multiple Zones International, says,

> I've actually seen people lose promotions because they couldn't write a proposal or stand in front of the management team and make a presentation.[3]

As a result, good writers earn more. Linguist Stephen Reder has found that among people with two- or four-year degrees, workers in the top 20% of writing ability earn, on average, more than three times as much as workers whose writing falls into the worst 20%.[4]

Will I really have to write?

Yes. A lot.

Claims that people can get by without writing are flawed.

Claim 1: Secretaries will do all my writing.
Reality: Downsizing and voice mail have cut support staffs nationwide. Of the secretaries who remain, 71% are administrative assistants whose duties are managerial, not clerical.[5]

Claim 2: I'll use form letters or templates when I need to write.
Reality: A **form letter** is a prewritten fill-in-the-blank letter designed to fit standard situations. Using a form letter is OK if it's a good letter. But form letters cover only routine situations. The higher you rise, the more frequently you'll face situations that aren't routine and that demand creative solutions.

Claim 3: I'm being hired as an accountant, not a writer.
Reality: Almost every entry-level professional or managerial job requires you to write e-mail messages, speak to small groups, and write paper documents. People who do these things well are more likely to be promoted beyond the entry level.

Claim 4: I'll just pick up the phone.
Reality: Important phone calls require follow-up letters, memos, or e-mail messages. People in organizations put things in writing to make themselves visible, to create a record, to convey complex data, to make things convenient for the reader, to save money, and to convey their own messages more effectively. "If it isn't in writing," says a manager at one company, "it didn't happen." Writing is an essential way to make yourself visible, to let your accomplishments be known.

FYI

In a national survey of adult workers, 87% rated communication skills as "very important" in doing their jobs. Computer skills, in contrast, were "very important" to only 50% of respondents.

MBA alumni ranked one-on-one communication as the most important skill they used. Listening also ranked highly.

Sources: "Making the Grade: What American Workers Think Should Be Done to Improve Education," The John J. Heldrich Center for Workforce Development, Rutgers University, and the Center for Survey Research Analysis, University of Connecticut, June 2000; www.heldrich.rutgers.edu/worktrends/ACFC7.pdf; visited site July 27, 2002; and Andy Raskin, "What's an MBA Really Worth?" *Business 2.0,* July 2002, 43.

Don't I know enough about communication?

Business communication differs from other school writing.

Although both business communication and other school writing demand standard edited English, in other ways the two are very different.

Purpose

- The purpose of school writing is usually to show that you have learned the course material and to demonstrate your intelligence.
- The purpose of business communication is to meet an organizational need. No one will pay you to write something that he or she already knows.

Audience

- The audiences for school writing are limited: usually just the instructor and the other students. The real audience is "an educated person." Even if the instructor disagrees with your views, if they are well-supported, the paper can earn a good grade. The instructor is paid, in part, to read your papers and will read them even if they are boring.
- The audiences for business communication include people both inside and outside the organization (◀|▶ Module 2). Real audiences pay attention to messages only if they seem important, relevant, and interesting.

Information

- Information in school writing may be new to you but is rarely new to your instructor.
- Information in business communication is usually new to your reader. (If it isn't, you have to work extra hard to make it interesting.)

Organization

- School writing often follows the traditional essay form, with a thesis statement up front, paragraphs of evidence, and a final concluding paragraph.
- Business communication is organized to meet the psychological needs of the reader. Most often, the main point comes up front (◀|▶ Modules 10–12).

Style

- The style for school writing is often formal. Big words and long sentences and paragraphs are often rewarded.
- The style for business communication is friendly, not formal. Short words and a mix of sentence and paragraph lengths are best (◀|▶ Modules 15 and 16).

Document Design

- School writing often rewards long paragraphs. Papers are often double spaced, with no attention to visual design.

- Business people want to be able to skim documents. Headings, lists, and single-spaced paragraphs with double spacing between paragraphs help readers find information quickly (◁ ▶ Module 5).

Visuals

- Except for math, construction, and engineering, few classes expect writing to contain anything other than words.
- Business writers are expected to choose the most effective way to convey information. Even a one-page memo may contain a table, graph, or other visual. You'll be expected to be able to use computer programs to create graphs, visuals, and slides for presentations (◁ ▶ Modules 5, 20, and 25).

What does communication accomplish?

Management happens through communication.

According to Henry Mintzberg, managers have three basic jobs: to collect and convey information, to make decisions, and to promote interpersonal unity—that is, to make people want to work together to achieve organizational goals.[6] All of these jobs happen through communication. Effective managers are able to use a wide variety of media and strategies to communicate. They know how to interpret comments from informal channels such as the company grapevine; they can speak effectively in small groups and in formal presentations; they write well.

Communication—oral, nonverbal, and written—goes to both internal and external audiences. **Internal audiences** (Figure 1.1) are other people in the same organization: subordinates, superiors, peers. **External audiences** (Figure 1.2) are people outside the organization: customers, suppliers, unions, stockholders, potential employees, government agencies, the press, and the general public.

Site *to* See

Go to
www1.fubu.com
Word-of-mouth rather than traditional advertising has fueled FUBU's success.

The Importance of Listening, Speaking, and Interpersonal Communication

Informal listening, speaking, and working in groups are just as important as writing formal documents and giving formal oral presentations. As a newcomer in an organization, you'll need to listen to others both to find out what you're supposed to do and to learn about the organization's values and culture. Informal chitchat, both about yesterday's game and about what's happening at work, connects you to the **grapevine,** an informal source of company information. You may be asked to speak to small groups, either inside or outside your organization.[7] Networking with others in your office and in town and working with others in workgroups will be crucial to your success.

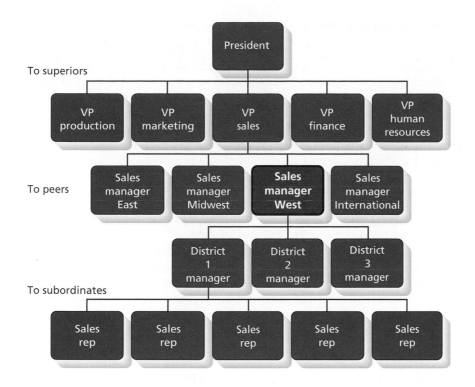

Figure 1.1
The Internal Audiences of the Sales Manager—West

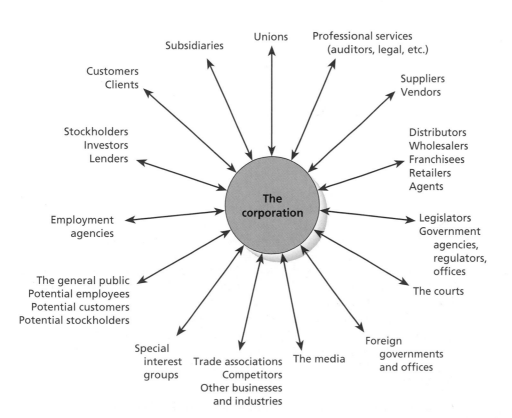

Figure 1.2
The Corporation's External Audiences

Source: Daphne A. Jameson

The Purposes of Messages in Organizations

Messages in organizations have one or more of **three basic purposes:** to inform, to request or persuade, and to build goodwill. When you **inform,** you explain something or tell readers something. When you **request or persuade,** you want the reader to act. The word *request* suggests that the action will be easy or routine; *persuade* suggests that you will have to motivate and convince the reader to act. When you **build goodwill,** you create a good image of yourself and of your organization—the kind of image that makes people want to do business with you.

Most messages have multiple purposes.

- When you answer a question, you're informing, but you also want to build goodwill by suggesting that you're competent and perceptive and that your answer is correct and complete.
- In a claims adjustment, whether your answer is *yes* or *no,* you want to suggest that the reader's claim has been given careful consideration and that the decision is fair, businesslike, and justified.
- To persuade, a résumé gives information to prove that you're qualified for the job and uses layout to emphasize your strong points and build a good image of you.

How much does correspondence cost?

$80 a page—even more if it doesn't work.

Instant Replay

Internal and External Audiences

Internal audiences are other people in the same organization: subordinates, superiors, peers.

External audiences are people outside the organization: customers, suppliers, unions, stockholders, potential employees, government agencies, the press, and the general public.

Writing costs money. In 1996, according to the Dartnell Institute, a 10-minute message cost between $13.60 and $20.52, depending on how it is produced.[8] Dartnell no longer calculates the cost, but it seems unlikely to have fallen. But most messages take more than 10 minutes to write. A consultant who surveyed employees in seven industries found that most of them spent 54 minutes planning, composing, and revising a one-page letter.[9] Her respondents, then, each spent more than $85 at 1996 prices to create a one-page letter. One company in Minneapolis writes 3,000 original letters a day. If each of those letters can be written in less than an hour, it spends at least $252,000 a day just on outgoing correspondence.

In many organizations, all external documents must be approved before they go out. A document may **cycle** from writer to superior to writer to another superior to writer again 3 or 4 or even 11 times before it is finally approved. The cycling process increases the cost of correspondence.

Longer documents can involve large teams of people and take months to write. An engineering firm that relies on military contracts for its business calculates that it spends $500,000 to put together an average proposal and $1 million to write a large proposal.[10]

Poor correspondence costs even more. When writing isn't as good as it could be, you and your organization pay a price in wasted time, wasted efforts, and lost goodwill.

Bad writing wastes time by

- Taking more time to read.
- Requiring more time to revise and more rounds of revision.

- Confusing ideas so that discussions and decisions are needlessly drawn out.
- Delaying action while the reader asks for more information or tries to figure out the meaning.

Ineffective messages don't get results. A reader who has to guess what the writer means may guess wrong. A reader who finds a letter or memo unconvincing or insulting simply won't do what the message asks. Thus second and third and fourth requests are necessary.

Whatever the literal content of the words, every letter, memo, and report serves either to enhance or to damage the image the reader has of the writer. Poor messages damage business relationships.

Good communication is worth every minute it takes and every penny it costs. In fact, in a survey conducted by the International Association of Business Communicators, CEOs said that communication yielded a 235% return on investment.[11]

What makes a message effective?

Good messages meet five criteria.

Good business and administrative writing

- **Is clear.** The meaning the reader gets is the meaning the writer intended. The reader doesn't have to guess.
- **Is complete.** All of the reader's questions are answered. The reader has enough information to evaluate the message and act on it.
- **Is correct.** All of the information in the message is accurate. The message is free from errors in punctuation, spelling, grammar, word order, and sentence structure.
- **Saves the reader's time.** The style, organization, and visual impact of the message help the reader to read, understand, and act on the information as quickly as possible.
- **Builds goodwill.** The message presents a positive image of the writer and his or her organization. It treats the reader as a person, not a number. It cements a good relationship between the writer and the reader (◁ ▶ Modules 6–8).

Whether a message meets these five criteria depends on **the interactions among the writer, the audience, the purposes of the message, and the situation.** No single set of words will work in all possible situations.

Better writing helps you to

- **Save time.** Reduce reading time, since comprehension is easier. Eliminate the time now taken to rewrite badly written materials. Reduce the time taken asking writers, "What did you mean?"
- **Make your efforts more effective.** Increase the number of requests that are answered positively and promptly—on the first request. Present your points—to other people in your organization; to clients, customers, and suppliers; to government agencies; to the public—more forcefully.

Instant Replay

Documents' Purposes

Documents in organizations have three basic purposes: to inform, to request or persuade, and to build goodwill.

Most documents have more than one purpose.

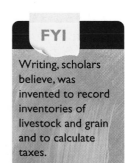

FYI

Writing, scholars believe, was invented to record inventories of livestock and grain and to calculate taxes.

Source: Denise Schmandt-Besserat, "The Earliest Precursor of Writing," *Scientific American,* 238, no. 6 (1978): 50–59.

- **Communicate your points more clearly.** Reduce the misunderstandings that occur when the reader has to supply missing or unclear information. Make the issues clear, so that disagreements can surface and be resolved more quickly.
- **Build goodwill.** Build a positive image of your organization. Build an image of yourself as a knowledgeable, intelligent, capable person.

How should I analyze business communication situations?

Try PAIBOC.

Before you write or speak, you need to understand the situation. Ask yourself the following questions:

- **What's at stake—to whom?** Think not only about your own needs but about the concerns your boss and your readers will have. Your message will be most effective if you think of the entire organizational context— and the larger context of shareholders, customers, and regulators. When the stakes are high, you'll need to take into account people's emotional feelings as well as objective facts.
- **Should you send a message?** Sometimes, especially when you're new on the job, silence is the most tactful response. But be alert for opportunities to learn, to influence, to make your case. You can use communication to build your career.
- **What channel should you use?** Paper documents and presentations are formal and give you considerable control over the message. E-mail, phone calls, and stopping by someone's office are less formal. Oral channels are better for group decision making, allow misunderstandings to be cleared up more quickly, and seem more personal. Sometimes you may need more than one message, in more than one channel.
- **What should you say?** Content for a message may not be obvious. How detailed should you be? Should you repeat information that the audience

People communicate to plan products and services; hire, train, and motivate workers; coordinate manufacturing and delivery; persuade customers to buy; bill them for the sale; and communicate with stakeholders. The Iowa chapter of the Sierra Club honored the Davenport Alcoa plant (whose Shannon Saliard is shown here) for its innovative environmental programs.

Thinking Creatively

Creativity is essential to success in business and business communication. Here are some examples.

- Richard Saul Wurman's *USAtlas* divides the country geographically, not alphabetically. "You don't drive across the country alphabetically," he says.
- To persuade customers to switch to his storage business, Norm Brodsky needed to offer lower prices than his competitors did. He figured out that he could do that by renting warehouses with unusually high ceilings. Space rents by the square foot, not the cubic foot, but with higher ceilings, he could pack in more boxes.
- As a military spouse, Victoria Parham had to change jobs every time her husband was transferred. In 1997, she formed Virtual Support Services, which provides all of its services by teleconference and computer. Now, all she needs is high-speed Internet access. Where she lives doesn't matter.

Ways to become more creative include brainstorming, working within limits, and consciously seeking problems or dissonances that need work.

IBM's tips for creativity are even more diverse. Some of them include

- Have an argument.
- Brainstorm with someone 10 years older and someone 10 years younger.

Griffin Hospital in Derby, Connecticut, has a patient satisfaction rate of 96%. The hospital changed its culture to give customers everything they asked for (not just the items easiest to implement). Innovations include double beds in the maternity ward, kitchens on every wing of every floor, and musicians in the patient lounge.

- Clean your desk.
- Come in early—enjoy the quiet.
- Leave the office. Sit with just a pencil and a pad of paper. See what happens.

Sources: "Get Dumb and Grow Rich," *Inc.*, May 1997, 61–65; Norm Brodsky, "The Right Stuff," *Inc.*, July 1999, 29–30; Bridget McCrea, "Working Virtually Works for Her," *Black Enterprise*, Feburary 2002, 51. David H. Freedman, "Intensive Care," *Inc.*, February 1999, 72; and Liz Zack, "How IBM Gets Unstuck," *Fast Company*, October 1999, 104.

already knows? The answers will depend upon the kind of document, your purposes, your audiences, and the corporate culture. And you'll have to figure these things out for yourself, without detailed instructions.
- **How should you say it?** How you arrange your ideas—what comes first, what second, what last—and the words you use shape the audience's response to what you say.

When you're faced with a business communication situation, you need to develop a solution that will both **solve the organizational problem and meet the psychological needs of the people involved.** The strategies in this section will help you solve the problems in this book. Almost all of these strategies can also be applied to problems you encounter on the job.

- **Understand the situation.** What are the facts? What additional information might be helpful? Where could you get it?
- **Brainstorm solutions.** Consciously develop several solutions. Then measure them against your audience and purposes: Which solution is likely to work best?

Figure 1.3
PAIBOC Questions for Analysis

Use the PAIBOC questions to analyze business communication problems:

P What are your **purposes** in writing?

A Who is (are) your **audience(s)?** How do members of your audience differ? What characteristics are relevant to this particular message?

I What **information** must your message include?

B What reasons or reader **benefits** can you use to support your position?

O What **objection**(s) can you expect your reader(s) to have? What negative elements of your message must you deemphasize or overcome?

C How will the **context** affect reader response? Think about your relationship to the reader, morale in the organization, the economy, the time of year, and any special circumstances.

• **If you want to add or change information, get permission first.** If you have any questions about ideas you want to use, *ask your instructor.* He or she can tell you *before* you write the message.

When you use this book to create messages on the job, you can't change facts. That is, if it's October, you can't pretend that it's April just because it may be easier to think of reader benefits for that time of year. But it may be possible to change habits that your company has fallen into, especially if they no longer serve a purpose. Check with your supervisor to make sure that your departure from company practice is acceptable.

• **Use the PAIBOC questions in Figure 1.3 to analyze your purpose, your audience, and the situation.**

As Figure 1.3 shows, PAIBOC offers an acronym for the questions you need to answer before you begin composing your message. The following discussion lists specific questions you can answer. See Modules 10, 11, and 12 for examples of answers to these questions for specific situations.

P What are your **purposes** in writing or speaking?

What must this message do to solve the organizational problem? What must it do to meet your own needs? What do you want your readers to do? To think or feel? List all your purposes, major and minor. Specify *exactly* what you want your reader to know, think, or do. Specify *exactly* what kind of image of yourself and of your organization you want to project.

Even in a simple message, you may have several related purposes: to announce a new policy, to make readers aware of the policy's provisions and requirements and to have them think that the policy is a good one, that the organization cares about its employees, and that you are a competent writer and manager.

A Who is (are) your **audience(s)?** How do the members of your audience differ from each other? What characteristics are relevant to this particular message?

How much does your audience know about your topic? How will audience members respond to your message? Some characteristics of your readers will be irrelevant; focus on ones that matter *for this message.* Whenever you write to several people or to a group (like a memo to all employees), try to identify the economic, cultural, or situational differences that may affect how various subgroups respond to what you have to say.

I What **information** must your message include?

Make a list of the points that must be included; check your draft to make sure you include them all. If you're not sure whether a particular fact must be included, ask your instructor or your boss.

To include information without emphasizing it, put it in the middle of a paragraph or document and present it as briefly as possible.

B   What reasons or reader **benefits** can you use to support your position?

Brainstorm to develop reasons for your decision, the logic behind your argument, and possible benefits to readers if they do as you ask. Reasons and reader benefits do not have to be monetary. Making the reader's job easier or more pleasant is a good reader benefit. In an informative or persuasive message, identify at least five reader benefits. In your message, use those that you can develop most easily and most effectively.

Be sure that the benefits are adapted to your reader. Many people do not identify closely with their companies; the fact that the company benefits from a policy will help the reader only if the saving or profit is passed directly on to the employees. That is rarely the case: Savings and profits are often eaten up by returns to stockholders, bonuses to executives, and investments in plants and equipment or in research and development.

O   What **objections** can you expect your reader(s) to have? What negative elements of your message must you deemphasize or overcome?

Some negative elements can only be deemphasized. Others can be overcome. Be creative: Is there any advantage associated with (even though not caused by) the negative? Can you rephrase or redefine the negative to make the reader see it differently?

C   How will the **context** affect the reader's response? Think about your relationship to the reader, morale in the organization, the economy, the time of year, and any special circumstances.

Readers may like you or resent you. You may be younger or older than the people you're writing to. The organization may be prosperous or going through hard times; it may have just been reorganized or may be stable. All these different situations will affect what you say and how you say it.

Think about the news, the economy, the weather. Think about the general business and regulatory climate, especially as it affects the organization specified in the problem. Use the real world as much as possible. Think about interest rates, business conditions, and the economy. Is the industry in which the problem is set doing well? Is the government agency in which the problem is set enjoying general support? Think about the time of year. If it's fall when you write, is your business in a seasonal slowdown after a busy summer? Gearing up for the Christmas shopping rush? Or going along at a steady pace unaffected by seasons?

To answer these questions, draw on your experience, your courses, and your common sense. You may want to talk to other students or read *The Wall Street Journal* or look at a company's annual report. Sometimes you may even want to phone a local business person to get information. For instance, if you needed more information to think of reader benefits for a problem set in a bank, you could call a local banker to find out what kinds of services it offers customers and what its rates are for loans.

The remaining modules in this book will show you how to use this analysis to create business messages that meet your needs, the needs of the reader, and the needs of the organization.

Summary of Key Points

- Communication helps organizations and the people in them achieve their goals. The ability to write and speak well becomes increasingly important as you rise in an organization.

- People put things in writing to create a record, to convey complex data, to make things convenient for the reader, to save money, and to convey their own messages more effectively.

- **Internal documents** go to people inside the organization. **External documents** go to audiences outside: clients, customers, suppliers, stockholders, the government, the media, the general public.

- The three basic purposes of business and administrative communication are **to inform, to request or persuade, and to build goodwill.** Most messages have more than one purpose.

- A one-page message that took an hour to plan, write, and revise cost at least $84 in 1996. Poor writing costs even more since it wastes time, wastes efforts, and jeopardizes goodwill.

- Good business and administrative writing meets five basic criteria: it's **clear, complete, and correct;** it **saves the reader's time;** and it **builds goodwill.**

- To evaluate a specific document, we must know the interactions among the writer, the reader(s), the purposes of the message, and the situation. No single set of words will work for all readers in all situations.

- To understand business communication situations, ask the following questions:
  - What's at stake—to whom?
  - Should you send a message?
  - What channel should you use?
  - What should you say?
  - How should you say it?

- Use the PAIBOC question to analyze business communication problems:

  P   What are your **purposes** in writing?

  A   Who is (are) your **audience(s)?** How do members of your audience differ? What characteristics are relevant to the particular message?

  I   What **information** must your message include?

  B   What reasons or reader **benefits** can you use to support your position?

  O   What **objection(s)** can you expect your reader(s) to have? What negative elements of your message must you deemphasize or overcome?

  C   How will the **context** affect reader response? Think about your relationship to the reader, morale in the organization, the economy, the time of year, and any special circumstances.

- A solution to a business communication problem must both solve the organizational problem and meet the needs of the writer or speaker, the organization, and the audience.

Assignments for Module 1

Questions for Comprehension

1.1   What are the three basic purposes of business messages?

1.2   What are the five basic criteria for effective messages?

1.3   What does PAIBOC stand for?

Questions for Critical Thinking

1.4   Why do you need to understand the purposes, audience, and context for a message to know whether a specific set of words will work?

1.5   Why do writing and speaking become even more important as people rise in the organization?

1.6   If you're just looking for a low-level job, why is it still useful to be able to write and speak well?

1.7   What opportunities do you have in volunteer or student organizations to do real "business writing" while you're in school?

Exercises and Problems

1.8   **Letters for Discussion—Landscape Plants**

Your nursery sells plants not only in your store but also by mail order. Today you've received a letter from Pat Sykes, complaining that the plants (in a $572 order) did not arrive in a satisfactory condition. "All of them were dry and wilted. One came out by the roots when I took it out of the box. Please send me a replacement shipment immediately."

The following letters are possible approaches to answering this complaint. How well does each message meet the needs of the reader, the writer, and the organization? Is the message clear, complete, and correct? Does it save the reader's time? Does it build goodwill?

1.

> Dear Sir:
>
> I checked to see what could have caused the defective shipment you received. After ruling out problems in transit, I discovered that your order was packed by a new worker who didn't understand the need to water plants thoroughly before they are shipped. We have fired the worker, so you can be assured that this will not happen again.
>
> Although it will cost our company several hundred dollars, we will send you a replacement shipment.
>
> Let me know if the new shipment arrives safely. We trust that you will not complain again.

2.

> Dear Pat:
>
> Sorry we screwed up that order. Sending plants across country is a risky business. Some of them just can't take the strain. (Some days I can't take the strain myself!) We'll credit your account for $572.

3.

> Dear Mr. Smith:
>
> I'm sorry you aren't happy with your plants, but it isn't our fault. The box clearly says "Open and water immediately." If you had done that, the plants would have been fine. And anybody who is going to buy plants should know that a little care is needed. If you pull by the leaves, you will pull the roots out. Always lift by the stem! Since you don't know how to handle plants, I'm sending you a copy of our brochure, "How to Care for Your Plants." Please read it carefully so that you will know how to avoid disappointment in the future.
>
> We look forward to your future orders.

4.

> Dear Ms. Sikes:
>
> Your letter of the 5th has come to the attention of the undersigned.
>
> According to your letter, your invoice #47420 arrived in an unsatisfactory condition. Please be advised that it is our policy to make adjustments as per the Terms and Conditions listed on the reverse side of our Acknowledgment of Order. If you will read that document, you will find the following:
>
> ". . . if you intend to assert any claim against us on this account, you shall make an exception on your receipt to the carrier and shall, within 30 days after the receipt of any such goods, furnish us detailed written information as to any damage."
>
> Your letter of the 5th does not describe the alleged damage in sufficient detail. Furthermore, the delivery receipt contains no indication of any exception. If you expect to receive an adjustment, you must comply with our terms and see that the necessary documents reach the undersigned by the close of the business day on the 20th of the month.

5.

> Dear Pat Sykes:
>
> You'll get a replacement shipment of the perennials you ordered next week.
>
> Your plants are watered carefully before shipment and packed in specially designed cardboard containers. But if the weather is unusually warm, or if the truck is delayed, small root balls may dry out. Perhaps this happened with your plants. Plants with small root balls are easier to transplant, so they do better in your yard.
>
> The violas, digitalis, aquilegias, and hostas you ordered are long-blooming perennials that will get even prettier each year. Enjoy your garden!

1.9   Memos for Discussion—Announcing a Web Page

The Acme Corporation has just posted its first Web page. Ed Zeplin in Management Information Systems (MIS), who has created the page, wants employees to know about it.

The following memos are possible approaches. How well does each message meet the needs of the reader, the writer, and the organization? Is the message clear, complete, and correct? Does it save the reader's time? Does it build goodwill?

1.

> Subject: It's Ready!
>
> I am happy to tell you that my work is done. Two months ago the CEO finally agreed to fund a Web page for Acme, and now the work of designing and coding is done.
>
> I wanted all of you to know about Acme's page. (Actually it's over 40 pages.) Now maybe the computerphobes out there will realize that you really do need to learn how to use this stuff. Sign up for the next training session! The job you save may be my own.
>
> If you have questions, please do not hesitate to contact me.
>
> L. Ed Zeplin, MIS

2.

> Subject: Web Page
>
> Check out the company Web page at
>
> > www.server.acme.com/homepage.html

3.

> Subject: Visit Our Web Page
>
> Our Web pages are finally operational. The 100 pages were created using DreamWeaver, a program designed to support HTML creation. Though the graphics are sizeable and complex, interlacing and code specifying the pixel size serve to minimize download time. Standard HTML coding is enhanced with forms, Java animation, automatic counters, and tracking packages to ascertain who visits our site.
>
> The site content was determined by conducting a survey of other corporate Web sites to become cognizant of the pages made available by our competitors and other companies. The address of our Web page is www.server/acme/homepage.html. It is believed that this site will support and enhance our marketing and advertising efforts, improving our outreach to desirable demographic and psychographic marketing groups.
>
> L. Ed Zeplin, MIS
> Voice: 713–555–2879; Fax: 713–555–2880; E-mail: zeplin.1@acme.com
> "Only the wired life is worth living."—Anonymous

4.

> Subject: Web Page Shows Acme Products to the World, Offers Tips to Consumers, and Tells Prospective Employees about Job Possibilities
>
> Since last Friday, Acme's been on the World Wide Web. Check out the page at www.server.acme.com/homepage.html. You can't view the page if you don't have a computer.
>
> I have included pages on our products, tips for consumers, and job openings at Acme in the hope of making our page useful and interesting. Content is the number one thing that brings people back, but I've included some snazzy graphics, too.
>
> When I asked people for ideas for the company pages, almost nobody responded. But if seeing the page inspires you, let me know what else you'd like. I'll try to fit it into my busy schedule.
>
> So check it out. But don't spend too much time on the Web: you need to get your work done, too!
>
> L. Ed Zeplin, MIS
>
> zeplin.1@acme.com
> Today's Joke
> Fun Links

5.

> Subject: How to Access Acme's Web Page
>
> Tell your customers that Acme is now on the Web:
>
> > www.server.acme.com/homepage.html
>
> Web pages offer another way for us to bring our story to the public. Our major competitors have Web pages; now we do, too. Our advertisements and packaging will feature our Web address. And people who check out our Web page can learn even more about our commitment to quality, protecting the environment, and meeting customer needs.
>
> If you'd like to learn more about how to use the Web or how to create Web pages for your unit, sign up for one of our workshops. For details and online registration, see
>
> > www.server.acme.com/training.
>
> If you have comments on Acme's Web pages or suggestions for making them even better, just let me know.
>
> L. Ed Zeplin
> zeplin.1@acme.com

1.10 Discussing Strengths

Introduce yourself to a small group of other students. Identify three of your strengths that might interest an employer.

These can be experience, knowledge, or personality traits (like enthusiasm).

1.11 Introducing Yourself to Your Instructor

Write a memo (at least 1½ pages long) introducing yourself to your instructor. Include the following topics:

- Background: Where did you grow up? What have you done in terms of school, extracurricular activities, jobs, and family life?
- Interests: What are you interested in? What do you like to do? What do you like to think about and talk about?
- Achievements: What achievements have given you the greatest personal satisfaction? List at least five. Include things which gave you a real sense of accomplishment and pride, whether or not they're the sort of thing you'd list on a résumé.

- Goals: What do you hope to accomplish this term? Where would you like to be professionally and personally five years from now?

Use complete memo format with appropriate headings. (See Module 9 for examples of memo format.) Use a conversational writing style; check your draft to polish the style and edit for mechanical and grammatical correctness. A good memo will enable your instructor to see you as an individual. Use specific details to make your memo vivid and interesting. Remember that one of your purposes is to interest your reader!

1.12 Describing Your Experiences in and Goals for Writing

Write a memo (at least 1½ pages long) to your instructor describing the experiences you've had writing and what you'd like to learn about writing during this course.

Answer several of the following questions:

- What memories do you have of writing? What made writing fun or frightening in the past?
- What have you been taught about writing? List the topics, rules, and advice you remember.
- What kinds of writing have you done in school? How long have the papers been?
- How has your school writing been evaluated? Did the instructor mark or comment on mechanics and grammar? Style? Organization? Logic? Content? Audience analysis and adaptation? Have you gotten extended comments on your papers? Have instructors in different classes had the same standards,

or have you changed aspects of your writing for different classes?
- What voluntary writing have you done—journals, poems, stories, essays? Has this writing been just for you, or has some of it been shared or published?
- Have you ever written on a job or in a student or volunteer organization? Have you ever typed other people's writing? What have these experiences led you to think about real-world writing?
- What do you see as your current strengths and weaknesses in writing skills? What skills do you think you'll need in the future? What kinds of writing do you expect to do after you graduate?

Use complete memo format with appropriate headings. (See Module 9 for examples of memo format.) Use a conventional writing style; edit your final draft for mechanical and grammatical correctness.

Polishing Your Prose

Sentence Fragments

A complete sentence has a subject and a verb. If either the subject or the verb is missing, the result is a sentence fragment.

> The job candidates.
> Passed seven rounds of interviews.
> And have taken three tests.

To fix the fragment, join it to other words to make a complete sentence.

> The job candidates passed seven rounds of interviews and have taken three tests.

Sentence fragments also occur when a clause has both a subject and a verb but is unable to stand by itself as a complete sentence.

> Although I read my e-mail
> Because she had saved her work
> If he upgrades his computer

The words *although, because,* and *since* make the clause subordinate, which means the clause cannot stand alone. It must be joined to a main clause.

> Although I read my e-mail, I did not respond to the draft of the proposal.
> Because she had saved her work, Paula was able to restore it after the crash.
> If he upgrades his computer, he will be able to use the new software.

Words that make clauses subordinate are

after	if
although, though	when, whenever
because, since	while, as
before, until	

Even sentences that have a subject and verb and are not subordinate may seem fragmentary in thought.

> The computer is.
> I need.
> She transfers.

Add more information to make the sentence clear.

> The computer is the latest model.
> I need more letterhead.
> She transfers to the logistics department on Tuesday.

Sometimes fragments are OK. For instance, fragments are used in résumés, advertisements, and some sales and fund-raising letters. However, fragments are inappropriate for most business documents. Because they are incomplete, they can confuse or mislead readers.

But the biggest problem with grammatical errors like sentence fragments is that readers sometimes assume that people who make errors are unprofessional or unpromotable (◄ ► Module 14). Of course, using "incorrect" grammar has nothing to do with intelligence, but many people nevertheless use grammar as a yardstick. People who cannot measure up to that yardstick may be stuck in low-level jobs.

Exercises

Make the following sentence fragments into complete sentences.

1. Faxed the contract to the Legal Department for review.

2. The conference call scheduled for 2 p.m.

3. Making our profit margin higher.

4. Two-thirds of the latest shipping report.

5. Our first attempt to make the document more readable.

Continued

6. Résumés and cover letters, making the application complete.

7. But instead completed the report.

8. Because Terrell called us first, though our discussion was brief.

9. Lisa is an ideal employee. Because she meets deadlines and is willing to work overtime to complete projects.

10. We have interviewed many topnotch candidates. Several outstanding ones. At least one who stood out noticeably from the rest. In fact, we're quite pleased with results of our search.

Check your answers to the odd-numbered exercises at the back of the book.

BComm Skill Booster

To apply the concepts in this module, complete lessons 1 and 2 on increasing your job marketability and adapting your communication skills to the situation. You can access the BComm Skill Booster through the text Web site at **www.mhhe.com/bcs2e.**

Module 2

Adapting Your Message to Your Audience

Start by asking these questions:

- Who is my audience?
- Why is my audience so important?
- What do I need to know about my audience(s)?
- Now that I have my analysis, what do I do with it?
- What if my audiences have different needs?
- How do I reach my audience(s)?

Understanding your audience is fundamental to the success of any message. You need to adapt your message to fit the audience's goals, interests, and needs.

Analyzing your audience and adapting your message can be done in a cynical, manipulative way. It can also be done in a sensitive, empathic, ethical way. Audiences have a keen sense for messages that try to manipulate them; empathic analysis and adaptation are almost always more successful, as well as being more ethical.

Some students pride themselves on their "honesty" in not adapting their discourse to anyone and in criticizing their bosses as sharply as they might younger brothers and sisters. But almost all organizations expect deference to people in authority. And customers have enough options to deal only with companies that treat them respectfully.

Understanding What Your Organization Wants

Michelle wondered whether her boss was sexist. Everyone else who had joined the organization when she did had been promoted. Her boss never seemed to have anything good to say about her or her work.

Michelle didn't realize that, in her boss's eyes, she wasn't doing good work. Michelle was proud of her reports; she thought she was the best writer in the office. But her boss valued punctuality, and Michelle's reports were always late.

Just as every sport has rules about scoring, so, too, workplaces have rules about what "counts." Even in the same industry, different organizations and different supervisors may care about different things. One boss circles misspelled words and posts the offending message on a bulletin board for everyone to see. Other people are more tolerant of errors. One company values original ideas, while another workplace tells employees just to do what they're told. One supervisor likes technology and always buys the latest hardware and software; another is technophobic and has to be persuaded to get needed upgrades.

Succeeding in an organization depends first on understanding what "counts" at your organization. To find out what counts in your organization,

- Ask your boss, "What parts of my job are most important? What's the biggest thing I could do to improve my work?"
- Listen to the stories colleagues tell about people who have succeeded and those who have failed. When you see patterns, check for confirmation: "So his real problem was that he didn't socialize with co-workers?" This gives your colleagues a chance to provide feedback: "Well, it was more than never joining us for lunch. He didn't really seem to care about the company."
- Observe. See who is praised, who is promoted.

Who is my audience?

More people than you might think!

In an organizational setting, a message may have five separate audiences.[1]

1. The **primary audience** will decide whether to accept your recommendations or will act on the basis of your message. You must reach the decision maker to fulfill your purposes.
2. The **secondary audience** may be asked to comment on your message or to implement your ideas after they've been approved. Secondary audiences can also include lawyers who may use your message—perhaps years later—as evidence of your organization's culture and practices.
3. The **initial audience** receives the message first and routes it to other audiences. Sometimes the initial audience also tells you to write the message.
4. A **gatekeeper** has the power to stop your message before it gets to the primary audience. A secretary who decides who gets to speak to or see the boss is a gatekeeper. Sometimes the supervisor who assigns the message is also the gatekeeper; however, sometimes the gatekeeper is higher in the organization. In some cases, gatekeepers exist outside the organization.
5. A **watchdog audience,** though it does not have the power to stop the message and will not act directly on it, has political, social, or economic power. The watchdog pays close attention to the transaction between you and the primary audience and may base future actions on its evaluation of your message.

Figure 2.1
The Audiences for a Marketing Plan

Writer	An account executive in an ad agency
Initial audience	Her boss, who asks her to write the plan
Gatekeeper	Her boss, who must approve the plan before it goes to the client
Primary audience	The executive committee of the client company, which will decide whether to adopt the plan
Secondary audiences	The marketing staff of the client company, who will be asked for comments on the plan
The artists, writers, and media buyers who will implement the plan if it is accepted

Figure 2.2
The Audiences for a Consulting Report

Writers	Two workers at a consulting thinktank
Initial audience	A consortium of manufacturers, which hires the thinktank to investigate how proposed federal regulations would affect manufacturing, safety, and cost
Gatekeeper	The consortium. If the consortium doesn't like the report, it won't send it on to the federal government.
Primary audience	The federal government agency that regulates this consumer product. It will set new regulation, based in part (the manufacturers hope) on this report. Within this audience are economists, engineers, and policymakers.
Secondary audiences	The general public
Other manufacturers of the product
Other clients and potential clients of the consulting thinktank
The consulting thinktank's competitors
Watchdog audience	Industry reviewers who read drafts of the report and commented on it. Although they had no direct power over this report, their goodwill was important for the consulting company's image—and its future contracts. Their comments were the ones that authors took more seriously as they revised their drafts.

As the charts in Figures 2.1 and 2.2 show, one person or group can be part of two audiences. Frequently, a supervisor is both the initial audience and the gatekeeper. Sometimes the initial audience is also the primary audience that will act on the message.

Why is my audience so important?

To be successful, messages must meet the audiences' needs.

Good business communication is audience-centered. Audience is central to both PAIBOC and to the communication process.

Audience and PAIBOC

Think about the PAIBOC questions in Module 1 (◀▶ p. 12). Of the six questions, the five in blue relate to audience.

P   What are your **purposes** in writing?

Your purposes come from you and your organization. Your audience determines how you achieve those purposes, but not what the purposes are.

A   Who is (are) your **audience(s)?** How do members of your audience differ? What characteristics are relevant to this particular message?

These questions ask directly about your audience.

I   What **information** must your message include?

The information you need to give depends on your audience. You need to say more when the topic is new to your audience. If your audience has heard something but may have forgotten it, you'll want to protect readers' egos by saying "As you know," or putting the information in a subordinate clause: "Because we had delivery problems last quarter, ..."

B   What reasons or reader **benefits** can you use to support your position?

What counts as a good reason and what is a benefit depends on your audience. For some audiences, personal experience counts as a good reason. Other audiences are more persuaded by scientific studies or by experts. For some people, saving money is a good benefit of growing vegetables. Other people may care less about the money than about avoiding chemicals, growing varieties that aren't available in grocery stores, or working

Carl Caspers understands the market for Harmony Systems' prostheses because he is part of it. Often, however, you'll have to analyze audiences of which you are not a part.

outside in the fresh air. Module 8 ◁▶ gives more information on developing reader benefits.

O What **objection(s)** can you expect your reader(s) to have? What negative elements of your message must you deemphasize or overcome?

> Different audiences will have different attitudes. One audience may object to a price increase. Another audience may expect price changes as routine and not be bothered by them. Module 12 on persuasion ◁▶ gives more information on overcoming objections.

C How will the **context** affect reader response? Think about your relationship to the reader, morale in the organization, the economy, the time of year, and any special circumstances.

> People exist in a context. How well they know you, how they feel about you and your organization, how well the economy is doing, even what's been in the news recently will all influence the way they respond to your message.

Audience and the Communication Process

Audience is also central to the communication process.

The following model of the communication process drastically simplifies what is perhaps the most complex of human activities. However, even a simplified model can give us a sense of the complexity of the communication process. And the model is useful in helping us see where and why miscommunication occurs. Figure 2.3 shows the basic process that occurs when one person tries to communicate ideas to someone else.

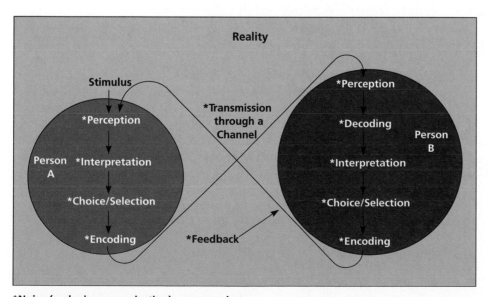

Figure 2.3

A Model of Two-Person Communication with Feedback

*Noise (and miscommunication) can occur here.

Instant Replay

Five Kinds of Audiences

Initial
Is first to receive the message; may assign message.

Gatekeeper
Has the power to stop the message before it gets to primary audience.

Primary
Decides whether to accept recommendations; acts.

Secondary
Comments on message or implements recommendations.

Watchdog
Has political, social, or economic power; may base future actions on its evaluation of your message.

The process begins when Person A (let's call him Alex) **perceives** some stimulus. Here we are talking about literal perception: the ability to see, to hear, to taste, to smell, to touch. Next, Alex **interprets** what he has perceived. Is it important? Unusual? The next step is for Alex to **choose** or **select** the information he wishes to send to Person B (whom we'll call Barbara). Now Alex is ready to put his ideas into words. (Some people argue that we can think only in words and would put this stage before interpretation and choice.) Words are not the only way to convey ideas; gestures, clothing, and pictures can carry meaning nonverbally. The stage of putting ideas into any of these symbols is called **encoding.** Then Alex must **transmit** the message to Barbara using some **channel.** Channels include memos, phone calls, meetings, billboards, TV ads, and e-mail, to name just a few.

To receive the message, Barbara must first **perceive** it. Then she must **decode** it, that is, extract meaning from the symbols. Barbara then repeats the steps Alex has gone through: interpreting the information, choosing a response, and encoding it. The response Barbara sends to Alex is called **feedback.** Feedback may be direct and immediate or indirect and delayed; it may be verbal or nonverbal.

Noise can interfere with every aspect of the communication process. Noise may be physical or psychological. Physical noise could be a phone line with static, a lawn mower roaring outside a classroom, or handwriting that is hard to read. Psychological noise could include disliking a speaker, being concerned about something other than the message, or already having one's mind made up on an issue.

Channel overload occurs when the channel cannot handle all the messages that are being sent. A small business may have only two phone lines; no one else can get through if both lines are in use. **Information overload** occurs when more messages are transmitted than the human receiver can handle. Some receivers process information "first come, first served." Some may try to select the most important messages and ignore others. A third way is to depend on abstracts or summaries prepared by other people. None of these ways is completely satisfactory.

At every stage, both Alex and Barbara could misperceive, misinterpret, choose badly, encode poorly, or choose inappropriate channels. Miscommunication can also occur because different people have different frames of reference. We always interpret messages in light of our personal experiences, our cultures and subcultures, and even the point in history at which we live.

Successful communication depends on the common ground between you and your audience. Choose information that your audience needs and will find interesting. Encode your message in words and other symbols the audience will understand. Transmit the message along a channel that your audience will attend to.

What do I need to know about my audience(s)?

Everything that's relevant to what you're writing or talking about.

Almost everything about your audience is relevant to some message. But for any particular message, only a few facts about your audience will be relevant.

Message/Purpose	Audience	Relevant Factors
Memo announcing that the company will reimburse employees for tuition if they take work-related college courses	All employees	1. Attitudes toward education (some people find courses fun; others may be intimidated) 2. Time available (some may be too busy) 3. Interest in being promoted or in getting cross-training 4. Attitude toward company (those committed to its success will be more interested in program)
Letter offering special financing on a new or used car	College students	1. Income 2. Expectations of future income (and ability to repay loan) 3. Interest in having a new car 4. Attitude toward cars offered by that dealership 5. Knowledge of interest rates 6. Access to other kinds of financing
Letter giving a meeting agenda and saying that you will bring your child along	Client	1. How well the client knows you 2. How much the client likes you 3. How important agenda items are to the client 4. How the client feels about children 5. Physical space for meeting (room for child to play)

Since the factors that matter vary depending on the situation, no one-size-fits-all list of questions for audience analysis exists. In general, you need to use common sense and empathy. **Empathy** is the ability to put yourself in someone else's shoes, to feel with that person. Empathy requires not being self-centered because, in all probability, the audience is *not* just like you. Use what you know about people and about organizations to predict likely responses.

Analyzing Individuals and Members of Groups

When you write or speak to people in your own organization and in other organizations you work closely with, you may be able to analyze your audience as individuals. You may already know your audience; it will usually be easy to get additional information by talking to members of your audience, talking to people who know your audience, and observing your audience.

Go to
www.inside.com/default.asp?
entity=AmericanDemo

American Demographics' Web site offers detailed analyses of major and niche groups. Back issues are available.

In other organizational situations, you'll analyze your audience as members of a group: "taxpayers who must be notified that they owe more income tax," "customers living in the northeast side of the city," or "employees with small children."

Information that is most often helpful includes the following:

- How much the audience knows about your topic
- Demographic factors, such as age, income, number of children, and so forth
- Personality
- Values and beliefs
- Past behavior.

Knowledge

Even people in your own organization won't share all your knowledge. USAA provides insurance to military personnel and their families, but not all the 22,000 people who work there know insurance jargon.[2]

Most of the time, you won't know exactly what your audience knows. Moreover, even if you've told readers before, they may not remember the old information when they read the new message. To remind readers of information in a tactful way,

- Preface statements with "As you know," "As you may know," or a similar phrase.
- Spell out acronyms the first time you use them: "Employee Stock Ownership Plan (ESOP)."
- Give brief definitions in the text: "the principal—the money you have invested—."
- Put information readers should know in a subordinate clause: "Because the renovation is behind schedule, ..."

Demographic Factors

Demographic characteristics are measurable features that can be counted objectively: age, sex, race, religion, education level, income, and so on.

Sometimes demographic information is irrelevant; sometimes it's important. Does age matter? Most of the time, probably not. (Mick Jagger is more than 50 years old, but he probably doesn't subscribe to *Modern Maturity*.) On the other hand, if you were explaining a change in your company's pension plan, you'd expect older workers to be more concerned than younger workers would be.

Business and nonprofit organizations get demographic data by surveying their customers, clients, and donors; by using U.S. census data; or by purchasing demographic data from marketing companies. For many messages, simply identifying subsets of your audience is enough. For example, a school board trying to win support for a tax increase knows that not everyone living in the district will have children in school. It isn't necessary to know the exact percentages to realize that successful messages will need to appeal not only to parents but also to voters who won't directly benefit from the improvements that the tax increase will fund.

Personality

When your primary audience is just one person, his or her personality is relevant. There are many ways to analyze personality. For business, one of the most useful is the **Myers-Briggs Type Indicator,** which uses four dimensions to identify ways that people differ.[3]

- **Introvert–extravert:** where someone gets energy. Introverts get their energy from within; extraverts are energized by interacting with other people.
- **Sensing–intuitive:** how someone gets information. Sensing types gather information step-by-step through their senses. Intuitive types see relationships among ideas.
- **Thinking–feeling:** how someone makes decisions. Thinking types use objective logic to reach decisions. Feeling types make decisions that feel "right."
- **Judging–perceiving:** the degree of certainty someone needs. Judging types like closure. Perceptive types like possibilities.

Figure 2.4 shows how you can use this information to adapt a message to your audience.

Some businesses administer the Myers-Briggs Type Indicator to all employees. Even when you don't have official results, you can often make accurate guesses about someone's type by close observation.

You'll be most persuasive if you play to your audience's strengths. Indeed, many of the general principles of business communication reflect the types most common among managers. Putting the main point up front satisfies the needs of judging types, and some 75% of U.S. managers are judging. Giving logical reasons satisfies the needs of the nearly 80% of U.S. managers who are thinking types.[4]

Values and Beliefs

Psychographic characteristics are qualitative rather than quantitative: values, beliefs, goals, and lifestyles. For example, two families living next door to each other might make about the same amount of money and each have two children. But one family might save every possible penny for college and retirement, taking inexpensive vacations and cooking meals at home rather than eating out. The other family might spend almost everything they made on clothes, cars, vacations, entertainment, and dinners out. One family might do most things together as a family, while in the other, members might spend most of their time on individual activities. The families might have different religious and political beliefs.

If you wanted to persuade each family to do the same thing, you might need to use different reasons and reader benefits; you would have different objections to overcome. Knowing what your audience finds important allows you to organize information in a way that seems natural to your audience and to choose appeals that audience members will find persuasive.

Looking at values may enable a company to identify customer segments. Taco Bell identified two groups of high-potential customers: *penny pinchers,* who visit Taco Bell frequently but don't spend much on a visit, and *speed*

Site *to* **See**

Go to
cluster2.claritas.com/YAWYL

Key in your Zip code to learn which psychographic groups are most common in your neighborhood.

Figure 2.4

Using Myers-Briggs Types in Persuasive Messages

If Your Audience Is	Use This Strategy	Because
An introvert	Write a memo and let the reader think about your proposal before responding.	Introverts prefer to think before they speak. Written documents give them the time they need to think through a proposal carefully.
An extravert	Try out your idea orally, in an informal setting.	Extraverts like to think on their feet. They are energized by people; they'd rather talk than write.
A sensing type	Present your reasoning step-by-step. Get all your facts exactly right.	Sensing types usually reach conclusions step-by-step. They want to know why something is important, but they trust their own experience more than someone else's say-so. They're good at facts and expect others to be, too.
An intuitive type	Present the big picture first. Stress the innovative, creative aspects of your proposal.	Intuitive types like solving problems and being creative. They can be impatient with details.
A thinking type	Use logic, not emotion, to persuade. Show that your proposal is fair, even if some people may be hurt by it.	Thinking types make decisions based on logic and abstract principles. They are often uncomfortable with emotion.
A feeling type	Show that your proposal meets the emotional needs of people as well as the dollars-and-cents needs of the organization.	Feeling types are very aware of other people and their feelings. They are sympathetic and like harmony.
A perceiving type	Show that you've considered all the alternatives. Ask for a decision by a specific date.	Perceiving types want to be sure they've considered all the options. They may postpone coming to closure.
A judging type	Present your request quickly.	Judging types are comfortable making quick decisions. They like to come to closure so they can move on to something else.

Source: Based on Isabel Briggs Myers, "Effects of Each Preference in Work Situations," *Introduction to Type* (Palo Alto, CA: Consulting Pychologists Press, 1962, 1980).

freaks, who are more interested in convenience than price. To attract these consumers, Taco Bell lowered prices on its core menu items and reengineered its production, cutting wait time by 71%. These changes tripled sales and—even with lower prices—raised profits $20 million.[5]

Researcher Mary Modahl's survey of 250,000 households found that online buying depends not on demographics such as age and Zip code but on psychographics: the consumer's attitude toward technology along a continuum from "profoundly suspicious" to "eagerly accepting."[6]

Past Behavior

How people have behaved in the past often predicts how they'll behave in the future. For example, examining records of customer purchases showed Fingerhut that customers who moved made large purchases of furniture and decorations. Fingerhut developed a "mover's catalog" filled with products

Some aspects of corporate culture may no longer serve an obvious purpose.

"I don't know how it started, either. All I know is that it's part of our corporate culture."

likely to appeal to this group—and saved money by not mailing other catalogs to this group right after they moved.[7]

Analyzing People in Organizations

Your reader's reaction is affected not only by his or her personal preferences and feelings but also by the discourse communities to which the reader belongs and by the organizational culture.

A **discourse community** is a group of people who share assumptions about what channels, formats, and styles to use, what topics to discuss and how to discuss them, and what constitutes evidence. Each person is part of several discourse communities, which may or may not overlap.

To analyze an organization's discourse community, ask the following questions:

- What channels, formats, and styles are preferred for communication? Do you write a paper memo, send e-mail, or walk down the hall to talk to someone? How formal or informal are you supposed to be?
- What do people talk about? What is not discussed?
- What kind of and how much evidence is needed to be convincing? Is personal experience convincing? Do you need numbers and formal research?

Procter & Gamble's discourse community requires that recommendations be just one page. So writers create one-page memos—and then add as many pages of "attachments" as they need. In contrast, a Silicon Valley company

expects recommendations to be presented as a PowerPoint slide with a triangle with three words around it.

An **organization's culture** is its values, attitudes, and philosophies. Organizational culture (or **corporate culture,** as it is often called; ◄ ► Module 3) is revealed verbally in the organization's myths, stories, and heroes and nonverbally in the allocation of space, money, and power.

The following questions will help you analyze an organization's culture:

- What are the organization's goals? Making money? Serving customers and clients? Advancing knowledge? Contributing to the community?
- What does the organization value? Diversity or homogeneity? Independence or being a team player? Creativity or following orders?
- How do people get ahead? Are rewards based on seniority, education, being well-liked, making technical discoveries, or serving customers? Are rewards available to only a few top people, or is everyone expected to succeed?
- How formal are behavior, language, and dress?

Two companies in the same field may have very different cultures. FedEx sales representatives court large customers with frequent phone calls. UPS workers send a bid and let that speak for itself—an approach consistent with UPS's culture of humility and modesty.[8] Researcher Jennifer Chatman found that new hires who "fit" a company's culture were more likely to stay with the job, be more productive, and be more satisfied than those who did not fit the culture.[9]

Organizations can have subcultures. For example, manufacturing and marketing may represent different subcultures in the same organization: workers may dress differently and have different values.

You can learn about organizational culture by observing people and by listening to the stories they tell. Here are two of the stories Nike's leaders tell.

Story	Lesson
Coach Bowerman (a company co-founder) decided his team needed better running shoes. So he went into his workshop and poured rubber into the family waffle iron to create a waffle sole.	Nike is committed to innovation.
Steve Prefontaine (a runner and another co-founder) worked to make running a professional sport and to get better-performing equipment.	Nike is committed to helping athletes.

You can also learn about a company's culture by looking at its Web site. Many companies try to describe their cultures, usually as part of the section on employment.

Now that I have my analysis, what do I do with it?

Use it to plan strategy, organization, style, document design, and visuals.

If you know your audience well and if you use words well, much of your audience analysis and adaptation will be unconscious. If you don't know your audience or if the message is very important, take the time to analyze your audience formally and to revise your draft with your analysis in mind.

You can adapt your message's strategy, organization, and style to meet the audience's needs. For paper or electronic documents, you can also adapt the document's design and the photos or illustrations you choose.

Strategy

- Make the action as easy as possible.
- Protect the reader's ego.
- Decide how to balance logic and emotion, what details to use, and whether to use a hard-sell or soft-sell approach based on the specific audience, the organizational culture, and the discourse community.
- Choose appeals and reader benefits that work for the specific audience ◁▶ Module 8).
- Modules 7, 11, and 13 will show you how to emphasize positive aspects, decide how much information to include, and overcome obstacles.

Organization

- Since most managers are intuitive types, it's usually better to get to the point right away. The major exceptions are
  - When we must persuade a reluctant reader.
  - When we have bad news and want to let the reader down gradually.
- Make the organizational pattern clear to the audience. Modules 9, 23, and 24 show you how to use headings and overviews. Module 20 shows how to use overviews and signposts in oral presentations.

The American Legacy Foundation uses irreverent, "guerrilla-style" ads resembling documentaries to persuade young people that smoking isn't cool.

Before their redesign, Olathe Lanes East and West looked alike. But East's customers bowl to relax while West's customers bowl to compete. Now a food court with soothing curves is the center of the East facility, with bowling lanes attached. At West, lanes still dominate, decorated with energetic triangles.

Style

- For most audiences, use easy-to-understand words, a mixture of sentence lengths, and paragraphs with topic sentences (◁ ▷ Modules 15 and 16).
- Avoid words that sound defensive or arrogant.
- Avoid hot buttons or "red-flag" words to which some readers will have an immediate negative reaction: *criminal, un-American, crazy, fundamentalist, liberal.*
- Use the language(s) that your audience knows best. In Quebec, messages are normally presented both in English and in French. In the Southwest United States, messages may be most effective printed in both English and Spanish.
- Use conversational, not "academic," language.

Document Design

- Use lists, headings, and a mix of paragraph lengths to create white space.
- Choices about format, footnotes, and visuals may be determined by the organizational culture or the discourse community.
- See Module 5 for advice about effective document design.

Photographs and Visuals

- Use bias-free photographs.
- Photos and visuals can make a document look more informal or more formal. Think of the difference between cartoons and photos of "high art."
- Some cultures (e.g., France, Japan) use evocative photographs that bear little direct relationship to the text. Most U.S. audiences expect photos that clearly relate to the text.

What if my audiences have different needs?

Focus on gatekeepers and decision makers.

When the members of your audience share the same interests and the same level of knowledge, you can use the principles outlined above for individual readers or for members of homogenous groups. But often different members of the audience have different needs.

When it is not possible to meet everyone's needs, meet the needs of gatekeepers and primary audiences first.

Content and Choice of Details

- Provide an overview or executive summary for readers who just want the main points.
- In the body of the document, provide enough detail for primary audiences and for anyone else who could veto your proposal.
- If the primary audiences don't need details that other audiences will want, provide those details in appendices—statistical tabulations, earlier reports, and so forth.

Organization

- Use headings and a table of contents so readers can turn to the portions that interest them.
- Organize your message based on the primary audiences' attitudes toward it.

Level of Formality

- Avoid personal pronouns. *You* ceases to have a specific meaning when several different audiences use a document.
- If both internal and external audiences will use a document, use a slightly more formal style than you would in an internal document.
- Use a more formal style when you write to international audiences.

Use of Technical Terms and Theory

- In the body of the document, assume the degree of knowledge that primary audiences will have.
- Put background information and theory under separate headings. Then readers can use the headings and the table of contents to read or skip these sections, as their knowledge dictates.
- If primary audiences will have more knowledge than other audiences, provide a glossary of terms. Early in the document, let readers know that the glossary exists.

FYI

Education, not income, correlates most closely with decisions such as wearing 100% cotton clothes and reading *Consumer Reports*.

Source: Ron Feemster, "Going the Distance," *American Demographics*, September 1999, 64.

Instant **Replay**

Organizational Culture

An **organization's culture** is its values, attitudes, and philosophies. Organizational culture (or **corporate culture** as it is also called) is revealed verbally in the organization's myths, stories, and heroes and nonverbally in the allocation of space, money, and power.

How do I reach my audience(s)?

Important messages may require multiple channels.

Communication channels vary in

- Speed
- Accuracy of transmission
- Cost
- Number of messages carried
- Number of people reached
- Efficiency
- Ability to promote goodwill.

Depending on your purposes, the audience, and the situation, one channel may be better than another.

A written message makes it easier to

- Present many specific details of a law, policy, or procedure.
- Present extensive or complex financial data.
- Minimize undesirable emotions.

Messages on paper are more formal than e-mail messages. E-mail messages are appropriate for routine messages to people you already know. Paper is usually better for someone to whom you're writing for the first time.

Oral messages make it easier to

- Answer questions, resolve conflicts, and build consensus.
- Use emotion to help persuade the audience.
- Get immediate action or response.
- Focus the audience's attention on specific points.
- Modify a proposal that may not be acceptable in its original form.

Scheduled meetings and oral presentations are more formal than phone calls or stopping someone in the hall.

Important messages should use more formal channels, whether they're oral or written. Oral and written messages have many similarities. In both, you should

- Adapt the message to the specific audience.
- Show the audience members how they benefit from the idea, policy, service, or product (◄|► Module 8).
- Overcome any objections the audience may have.
- Use you-attitude and positive emphasis (◄|► Modules 6 and 7).
- Use visuals to clarify or emphasize material (◄|► Module 25).
- Specify exactly what the audience should do.

Even when everyone in an organization has access to the same channels, different discourse communities may prefer different ones. When a university updated its employee benefits manual, the computer scientists and librarians wanted the information online. Faculty wanted to be able to read the information on paper. Maintenance workers and carpenters wanted to get answers on voice mail.[10]

The bigger your audience, the more complicated channel choice becomes because few channels reach everyone in your target audience. When possible, use multiple channels. Also use multiple channels for very important messages. For example, talk to key players about a written document before the meeting where the document will be discussed.

Summary of Key Points

- The **primary audience** will make a decision or act on the basis of your message. The **secondary audience** may be asked by the primary audience to comment on your message or to implement your ideas after they've been approved. The **initial audience** routes the message to other audiences and may assign the message. A **gatekeeper** controls whether the message gets to the primary audience. A **watchdog audience** has political, social, or economic power and may base future actions on its evaluation of your message.

- A sender goes through the following steps: **perception, interpretation, choice** or **selection, encoding, transmitting** the message through a **channel.** The receiver perceives the message, **decodes** it, interprets it, chooses a response, encodes the response, and transmits it. The message transmitted to the original sender is called **feedback. Noise** is anything that interferes with communication; it can be both physical and psychological. Miscommunication can occur at every point in the communication process.

- **Channel overload** occurs when a channel cannot handle all the messages being sent. **Information overload** occurs when the receiver cannot process all the messages that arrive. Both kinds of overload require some sort of selection to determine which messages will be sent and which ones will be attended to.

- Common sense and empathy are crucial to good audience analysis.

- A **discourse community** is a group of people who share assumptions about what channels, formats, and styles to use, what topics to discuss and how to discuss them, and what constitutes evidence.

- An **organization's culture** is its values, attitudes, and philosophies. Organizational culture is revealed verbally in the organization's myths, stories, and heroes and nonverbally in the allocation of space, money, and power.

- When you write to multiple audiences, use the primary audience and the gatekeeper to determine level of detail, organization, level of formality, and use of technical terms and theory.

- You can adapt your message's strategy, organization, and style to meet the audience's needs. For paper or electronic documents, you can also adapt the document's design and the photos or illustrations you choose.

- The best channel for a message will depend on the audience, the sender's purposes, and the situation. Channel choice may be shaped by the organizational culture.

- When you communicate to a big audience or about an important topic, use multiple channels.

Assignments for Module 2

Questions for Comprehension

2.1   What are the five kinds of audiences?

2.2   What are ways to analyze your audience?

2.3   What are three ways to adapt your message to your audience?

Questions for Critical Thinking

2.4   Why do internal audiences, especially your boss, sometimes feel more important than primary audiences outside your organization?

2.5   What are your options if your boss's criteria for a document are different than those of the primary audience?

2.6   Emphasizing the importance of audience, marketers frequently say, "The customer is in control." To what extent do you feel in control as a customer, a student, a citizen? What actions could you take to increase your control?

2.7   If you are employed, which aspects of your organization's culture match your own values? What kind of culture would you like to join when you are next on the job market?

Exercises and Problems

2.8   **Identifying Audiences**

In each of the following situations, label the audiences as initial, gatekeeper, primary, secondary, or watchdog.

1. Russell is seeking venture capital so that he can expand his business of offering soccer camps to youngsters. He's met an investment banker whose clients regularly hear presentations from business people seeking capital. The investment banker decides who will get a slot on the program, based on a comprehensive audit of each company's records and business plan.
2. Maria is marketing auto loans. She knows that many car buyers choose one of the financing options presented by the car dealership, so she wants to persuade dealers to include her company in the options they offer.
3. Paul works for the mayor's office in a big city. As part of a citywide cost-cutting measure, a panel has recommended requiring employees who work more than 40 hours in a week to take compensatory time off rather than be paid overtime. The only exceptions will be the Police and Fire Departments. The mayor asks Paul to prepare a proposal for the city council, which will vote on whether to implement the change. Before they vote, council members will hear from (1) citizens, who will have an opportunity to read the proposal and communicate their opinions to the city council; (2) mayors' offices in other cities, who may be asked about their experiences; (3) union representatives, who may be concerned about the reduction in income that will come if the proposal is implemented; (4) department heads, whose ability to schedule work might be limited if the proposal passes; and (5) panel members and good-government lobbying groups. Council members come up for reelection in six months.

2.9 Choosing a Channel to Reach a Specific Audience

Suppose that your business, government agency, or nonprofit group has a product, service, or program targeted for each of the following audiences. What would be the best channel(s) to reach people in that group in your city? Would that channel reach all group members?

1. Renters
2. African–American owners of small businesses
3. People who use wheelchairs
4. Teenagers who work part-time while attending school
5. Competitive athletes
6. Parents whose children play soccer
7. Hispanic Americans
8. People willing to work part-time
9. Financial planners
10. Hunters

2.10 Announcing a New Employee Benefit

Your company has decided to allow employees to pay employees for charity work. Employees can spend one hour working with a charitable or nonprofit group for every 40 they work (one hour a week for people who are on salary rather than paid by the hour; see Problem 10.15). As Vice President of Human Resources, you need to announce this new program. Pick a specific organization you know something about and answer these questions about it.

- What proportion of your employees are already involved in volunteer work?
- Is community service or "giving back" consistent with your corporate mission?
- Some employees won't be able or won't want to participate. What is the benefit for them in working for a company that has such a program?
- Will promoting community participation help your organization attract and retain workers?

2.11 Persuading Students to Use Credit Cards Responsibly

Many college students carry high balances on credit cards, in addition to student and car loans. You want to remind students on your campus to use credit cards responsibly. (See Problem 12.15.)

Answer the following questions about students on your campus.

- What socio-economic groups do students on your campus come from?
- Do students on your campus frequently receive credit card solicitations in the mail? Do groups set up tables or booths inviting students to apply for credit cards?
- What resources exist on campus or in town for people who need emergency funds? For people who are overextended financially?
- What channel will best reach students on your campus?
- What tone will work best to reach the students who are overextended and really need to read the document?

2.12 Announcing Holiday Diversity

To better respect the religious and ethnic diversity of your employees, your organization will now allow employees to take any 10 days off. (See Problem 13.10.) Any religious, ethnic, or cultural holiday is acceptable. (Someone who wants to take off *Cinco de Mayo* or Bastille Day can do so.) As Vice President for Human Resources, you need to announce the policy.

Pick a specific organization you know something about and answer these questions about it.

- What religious and ethnic groups do your employees come from?
- How much do various groups know about each others' holidays?
- What is the general climate for religious and ethnic tolerance? Should the message have a secondary purpose of educating people about less-common holidays?
- Is your organization open every day of the year, or will you be closed on some

holidays (e.g., Christmas, New Year's Day)? If an employee chooses to work on a day when offices or factories are closed, what should he or she do? Work at home? Get a key? (How? From whom?) What kinds of work could a person working alone most profitably do?

2.13 Sending a Question to a Web Site

Send a question or other message that calls for a response to a Web site. (See Problem 13.15.) You could

- Ask a question about a product.
- Apply for an internship or a job (assuming you'd really like to work there).
- Ask for information about an internship or a job.
- Ask a question about an organization or a candidate before you donate money or volunteer.
- Offer to volunteer for an organization or a candidate. You can offer do something small and one-time (e.g., spend an afternoon stuffing envelopes, put up a yard sign), or you can, if you want to, offer to do something more time-consuming or even ongoing.

Pick a specific organization you might use and answer these questions about it.

- Does the organization ask for questions or offers? Or will yours "come out of the blue"?
- How difficult will it be for the organization to supply the information you're asking for or to do what you're asking it to do? If you're applying for an internship or offering to volunteer, what skills can you offer? How much competition do you have?
- What can you do to build your own credibility, so that the organization takes your question or request seriously?

2.14 Analyzing People in Your Organization

1. Analyze your supervisor.
   - Does he or she like short or long explanations?
   - Does he or she want to hear about all the problems in a unit or only the major ones?
   - How important are punctuality and deadlines?
   - How well informed about a project does he or she wish to be?
   - Is he or she more approachable in the morning or the afternoon?
   - What are your supervisor's major hassles?

2. Analyze other workers in your organization.
   - Is work "just a job" or do most people really care about the organization's goals?
   - How do workers feel about clients or customers?
   - What are your co-workers' major hassles?

3. Analyze your customers or clients.
   - What attitudes do they have toward the organization and its products or services?

- What are their major hassles?
- Do education, age, or other factors affect the way they read?

As Your Instructor Directs,
a. Write a memo to your instructor summarizing your analysis.
b. Discuss your analysis with a small group of students.

c. Present your analysis orally to the class.
d. Combine your information with classmates' information to present a collaborative report comparing and contrasting your audiences at work.

2.15 Analyzing a Discourse Community

Analyze the way a group you are part of uses language. Possible groups include

- Work teams
- Sports teams
- Honor organizations and other service or social groups
- Churches, synagogues, temples, and mosques
- Geographic or ethnic groups
- Groups of friends.

Questions to ask include the following:

- What specialized terms might not be known to outsiders?
- What topics do members talk or write about? What topics are considered unimportant or improper?
- What channels do members use to convey messages?
- What forms of language do members use to build goodwill? To demonstrate competence or superiority?

- What strategies or kinds of proof are convincing to members?
- What formats, conventions, or rules do members expect messages to follow?

As Your Instructor Directs,
a. Share your results orally with a small group of students.
b. Present your results in an oral presentation to the class.
c. Present your results in a memo to your instructor.
d. Share your results in an e-mail message to the class.
e. Share your results with a small group of students and write a joint memo reporting the similarities and differences you found.

2.16 Analyzing an Organization's Culture

Interview several people about the culture of their organization. Possible organizations include

- Work teams
- Sports teams
- Honor organizations and other service or social groups
- Churches, synagogues, temples, and mosques
- Geographic or ethnic groups
- Groups of friends.

Questions to ask include those in this module and the following:

1. Tell me about someone in this organization you admire. Why is he or she successful?
2. Tell me about someone who failed in this organization. What did he or she do wrong?
3. What ceremonies and rituals does this organization have? Why are they important?
4. Why would someone join this group rather than a competitor?

As Your Instructor Directs,
a. Share your results orally with a small group of students.
b. Present your results in an oral presentation to the class.
c. Present your results in a memo to your instructor.

d. Share your results in an e-mail message to the class.
e. Share your results with a small group of students and write a joint memo reporting the similarities and differences you found.

2.17 Analyzing the Audiences of Noncommercial Web Pages

Analyze the implied audiences of two Web pages of two noncommercial organizations with the same purpose (combating hunger, improving health, influencing the political process, etc.). You could pick pages of the national organization and a local affiliate, or pages of two separate organizations working toward the same general goal.

Answer the following questions:

• Do the pages work equally well for surfers and for people who have reached the page deliberately?
• Possible audiences include current and potential volunteers, donors, clients, and employees. Do the pages provide material for each audience? Is the material useful? Complete? Up-to-date? Does new material encourage people to return?

• What assumptions about audience do content and visuals suggest?
• Can you think of ways that the pages could better serve their audiences?

As Your Instructor Directs,
a. Share your results orally with a small group of students.
b. Present your results in an oral presentation to the class.
c. Present your results in a memo to your instructor. Attach copies of the Web pages.
d. Share your results with a small group of students and write a joint memo reporting the similarities and differences you found.
e. Post your results in an e-mail message to the class. Provide links to the two Web pages.

 Polishing Your Prose

Comma Splices

In filmmaking, editors *splice,* or connect, two segments of film with tape to create one segment. A *comma splice* occurs when writers try to create one sentence by connecting two sentences with only a comma.

Correct: We shipped the order on Tuesday. It arrived on Wednesday.

Incorrect: We shipped the order on Tuesday, it arrived on Wednesday. (comma splice)

Comma splices are almost always inappropriate in business communication. (Poetry and fiction sometimes use comma splices to speed up action or simulate dialect; some sales letters and advertisements use comma splices for the same effect, though not always successfully.)

Fix a comma splice in one of four ways:

1. If the ideas in the sentences are closely related, use a semicolon:

We shipped the order on Tuesday; it arrived on Wednesday.

2. Add a coordinating conjunction (such as *and*, *or*, or *but*):

   We shipped the order on Tuesday, and it arrived on Wednesday.

3. Make the incorrect sentence into two correct ones:

   We shipped the order on Tuesday. It arrived on Wednesday.

4. Subordinate one of the clauses:

   Because we shipped the order on Tuesday, it arrived on Wednesday.

Exercises

Fix the comma splices in the following sentences.

1. We interviewed two people for the accounting position, we made a job offer to one.

2. I'd rather sacrifice efficiency for quality, we produce better products that way.

3. The Director of Purchasing went to our Main Street warehouse to inspect the inventory, Chuck called him later to ask how things went.

4. Invest in people, your business will prosper.

5. Mr. Margulies gave an audiovisual presentation at our September sales meeting in Terre Haute, it went very well.

6. We didn't receive your résumé in time, your application will be kept on file for the next available job opening.

7. Working weekends is tough, it's part of life in the business world today.

8. Tanya's promotion was approved, the Human Resources Department is sending the paperwork through inter-office mail.

9. Sunil is our most experienced employee, he joined the department in 1982.

10. New accounting regulations take effect next week, make sure our people understand them.

Check your answers to the odd-numbered exercises at the back of the book.

BComm Skills Booster

To apply the concepts in this module, complete lesson 6 on analyzing an audience. You can access the BComm Skill Booster through the text Web site at **www.mhhe.com/bcs2e.**

Module 3

Communicating Across Cultures

To learn how to

- Consider diversity as part of audience analysis.

- Begin to be aware of the values, beliefs, and practices in other cultures.

- Become even more sensitive to verbal and nonverbal behavior.

- Deal with discrimination.

- Use bias-free language and photos.

Start by asking these questions:

- What is "culture"?

- How does culture affect business communication?

- There are so many different cultures! How can I know enough to communicate?

- How can I make my documents bias-free?

In any organization, you'll work with people whose backgrounds differ from yours. Residents of small towns and rural areas have different notions of friendliness than do people from big cities. Californians may talk and dress differently than people in the Midwest. The cultural icons that resonate for baby boomers may mean little to teenagers.

The last 20 years have seen a growing emphasis on diversity, with the "news" that more and more women and people of color are joining the U.S. workforce.[1] But people outside the power structure have always worked. In the past, such people (including non-elite white males) may have been relegated to low-status and low-paying jobs, to agricultural or domestic work, or to staff rather than line work and management.

People often want easy answers about diversity and culture when only guidelines are possible. Human beings are individuals as much as they are part of a group. In many ways, we've only begun to scratch the surface for understanding and respecting the diversity around us; no single discussion can offer all the answers. Because learning about others is an ongoing process, we must find the answers as much through our experiences as through research, using sensitivity and respect. Use this module as a starting point.

"Diversity" in the workplace comes from many sources:

- Gender
- Race and ethnicity
- Regional and national origin
- Social class
- Religion
- Age
- Sexual orientation
- Physical ability.

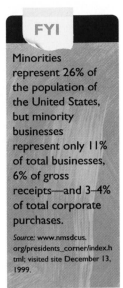

Many young Americans are already multicultural. According to U.S. census figures, a third of Americans aged 17 to 27 are Native Americans or of African, Latino, or Asian descent.[2] One study showed that 80% of teens have a close friend of another race.[3]

Bilingual Canada has long compared the diversity of its people to a "mosaic." But now immigrants from Italy, Greece, and Hong Kong add their voices to the medley of French, English, and Inuit. Radio station CHIN in Toronto broadcasts in 32 languages.[4] The United States has more than 1,100 mosques and Islamic centers, 1,500 Buddhist centers, and 800 Hindu centers.[5] People work in Japanese plants in Peterborough, New Hampshire; Marysville, Ohio; and Smyrna, Tennessee. Employees at the Digital Equipment plant in Boston come from 44 countries and speak 19 languages; the plant's announcements are printed in English, Chinese, French, Spanish, Portuguese, Haitian Creole, and Vietnamese.[6]

Diversity increases in the global marketplace, where your customers, suppliers, subordinates, or bosses may have different cultural values and business practices. Exports are essential to the success both of individual businesses and to a country's economy as a whole. Less technologically advanced countries may offer special opportunities for businesses in mature markets in the United States. For example, the market for buses in Mexico City is greater than the entire bus market in the whole United States.[7] Coca-Cola makes more money in Japan than in the United States.[8]

As many companies have discovered, valuing diversity is good business as well as good social practice. A growing body of literature shows that ethnically diverse teams produce more and higher-quality ideas.[9] One problem with our awareness of difference, however, is that when someone feels shut out, he or she can attribute the negative interaction to prejudice, when other factors may be responsible. A second problem is that members of a dominant group can recognize difference but still expect everyone else to adapt to them, rather than making the effort to understand the preferred communication styles of other workers.

What is "culture"?

Our understanding of acceptable actions and beliefs.

Each of us grows up in a **culture** that provides patterns of acceptable behavior and belief. We may not be aware of the most basic features of our own culture until we come into contact with people who do things differently. For example, we read from left to right. In some countries, text goes from right to left or from bottom to top. In the United States, new acquaintances often ask, "What do you do?" as if our jobs tell people who we are. In many countries, new aquaintances want to know, "Who is your family?" and are more likely to judge people by their family ties.

We can categorize cultures as high-context or low-context.

- In **high-context cultures,** most of the information is inferred from the context of a message; little is "spelled out." Japanese, Arabic, and Latin American cultures are high-context.
- In **low-context cultures,** context is less important; most information is explicitly spelled out. German, Scandinavian, and the dominant U.S. cultures are low-context.

As David Victor points out, high- and low-context cultures value different kinds of communication and have different attitudes toward oral and written channels (Module 2 ◁▶ p. 36).[10] As Figure 3.1 shows, low-context cultures favor direct approaches and may see indirectness as dishonest or manipulative. The written word is seen as more important than oral statements, so contracts are binding but promises may be broken. Details matter. Business communication practices in the United States reflect these low-context preferences.

Figure 3.1
Views of Communication in High- and Low-Context Cultures

	High Context (Examples: Japan, United Arab Emirates)	Low Context (Examples: Germany, Canada, the United States)
Preferred communication strategy	Indirectness, politeness, ambiguity	Directness, confrontation, clarity
Reliance on words to communicate	Low	High
Reliance on nonverbal signs to communicate	High	Low
Importance of written word	Low	High
Agreements made in writing	Not binding	Binding
Agreements made orally	Binding	Not binding
Attention to detail	Low	High

Source: Adapted from David A. Victor, *International Business Communication* (New York: HarperCollins, 1992), 148, 153, 160.

Dealing with Discrimination

Many workers have to deal with discrimination. James Davis, CEO of Davis Safety Supply, says, "When I started my business, I learned that many people didn't want to deal with a black business owner. I said, I've got to think of another way. So I went in as a sales representative for the company rather than CEO—and made sales. Prejudice is an obstacle that you have to overcome like any other objection."

Don't Take Things Personally.

TV host and publisher B. Smith says, "Over and over I have to prove myself, even at this stage. But you can't give up. You can't take it personally and you just have to continue to be the best you can be. You don't win by fighting—you have to outsmart the other party."

Pick Your Battles.

You can't fight everything. And you don't have to fight every battle the same way. Wall Street bond trader Susan Estes didn't complain when her male co-workers made lewd remarks about a woman on CNN. She just wrote down what they said and later read the comments back to them. The men were red-faced but admitted that the "vulgarities sounded silly and were inappropriate." But when a broker at another firm said that a woman could become a broker at his firm only by granting him a sexual favor, Ms. Estes pulled her business from the broker—after checking with her boss. Three years later, Ms. Estes has resumed trading with the broker. She's convinced he has changed, after losing tens of thousands of dollars in commissions. "He's got plenty of sensitivity to the issue now."

Not Everything Is Discrimination.

IBM, AT&T, and Lucent Technologies manager Roland Nolen writes, "As people of color, we don't have

Carmen Jones founded Solutions Marketing Group (www.disability–marketing.com) to help mainstream businesses serve people with disabilities—a group with roughly $1 trillion in spending power.
Source: "Taking the 'Dis' Out of Disability," *Black Enterprise*, March 2002, 102.

ready access to the 'good old boy' network or to powerful mentors who can give us a leg up. But the reality is, not all white males do, either." One woman complained that male clients tested her because she is a woman. But another successful woman pointed out that men test other men, too.

Source: James Davis to Kitty Locker, February 22, 1999; "B. Smith," *Selling Power*, January/February 2000, 73; Anne Fisher, "Ask Annie," *Fortune*, August 16, 1999, 186; Gregory Zuckerman, "Woman on a Bond Desk Deals with Slights and Rises to the Top," *The Wall Street Journal*, November 26, 1999, A1, A6; Roger O. Crockett, "Invisible and Loving It," *Business Week*, October 5, 1998, 124–28 and Harriet Rubin, "The V's' Word," *Fast Company*, March 2001, 44.

How does culture affect business communication?

In every single aspect!

Culture influences every single aspect of business communication: how to show politeness and respect, how much information to give, how to motivate people, how loud to talk, even what size paper to use.

Figure 3.2
National Culture, Organizational Culture, and Personal Culture Overlap.

The discussion that follows focuses on national and regional cultures. But business communication is also influenced by the organizational culture and by personal culture, such as gender, race and ethnicity, social class, and so forth. As Figure 3.2 suggests, all of these intersect to determine what kind of communication is needed in a given situation. Sometimes one kind of culture may be more important than another. For example, in a study of aerospace engineers in Europe, Asia, and the United States, researchers John Webb and Michael Keene found that the similarities of the professional discourse community outweighed differences in national cultures.[11]

Values, Beliefs, and Practices

Values and beliefs, often unconscious, affect our response to people and situations. Most North Americans, for example, value "fairness." "You're not playing fair" is a sharp criticism calling for changed behavior. In some countries, however, people expect certain groups to receive preferential treatment. Most North Americans accept competition and believe that it produces better performance. The Japanese, however, believe that competition leads to disharmony. U.S. business people believe that success is based on individual achievement and is open to anyone who excels. In England and in France, success is more obviously linked to social class. And in some countries, people of some castes or races are prohibited by law from full participation in society.

Many people in the United States value individualism. Other countries may value the group. In traditional classrooms, U.S. students are expected to complete assignments alone; if they get much help from anyone else, they're "cheating." In Japan, in contrast, groups routinely work together to solve problems. In the dominant U.S. culture, quiet is a sign that people are working. In Japan people talk to get the work done.[12]

Values and beliefs are influenced by religion. Christianity coexists with a view of the individual as empowered to make things happen. In some Muslim and Asian countries, however, it is seen as presumptuous to predict the future by promising action by a certain date. The Puritan work ethic legitimizes wealth by seeing it as a sign of divine favor. In other Christian cultures, a simpler lifestyle is considered to be closer to God.

These differences in values, beliefs, and practices lead to differences in what kinds of appeals motivate people. See Figure 3.3.

Nonverbal Communication

Nonverbal communication—communication that doesn't use words—takes place all the time. Body language, the size of an office, or how long someone keeps a visitor waiting—all these communicate pleasure or anger, friendliness or distance, power and status.

Figure 3.3
Cultural Contrasts in Motivation

	United States	Japan	Arab Countries
Emotional appeal	Opportunity	Group participation; company success	Religion; nationalism; admiration
Recognition based on	Individual achievement	Group achievement	Individual status; status of class/society
Material rewards	Salary; bonus; profit sharing	Annual bonus; social services; fringe benefits	Gifts for self/family; salary
Threats	Loss of job	Loss of group membership	Demotion, loss of reputation
Values	Competition; risk taking; freedom	Group harmony; belonging	Reputation; family security; religion

Source: Adapted from Farid Elashmawi and Philip R. Harris, *Multicultural Management 2000: Essential Cultural Insights for Global Business Success* (Houston: Gulf, 1998), 169.

Nonverbal signals can be misinterpreted just as easily as can verbal symbols (words). A young woman took a new idea into her boss, who glared at her, brows together in a frown, as she explained her proposal. The stare and lowered brows symbolized anger to her, and she assumed that he was rejecting her idea. Several months later, she learned that her boss always "frowned" when he was concentrating. The facial expression she had interpreted as anger had not been intended to convey anger at all.

Misunderstandings are even more common in communication across cultures. A European–American teacher sends two African–American students to the principal's office because they're "fighting." European Americans consider fighting to have started when loud voices, insults, and posture indicate that violence is likely. But the African–American culture does not assume that those signs will lead to violence: They can be part of nonviolent disagreements.[13] An Arab student assumed that his U.S. roommate disliked him intensely because the U.S. student sat around the room with his feet up on the furniture, soles toward the Arab roommate. Arab culture sees the foot in general and the sole in particular as unclean; showing the sole of the foot is an insult.[14]

Learning about nonverbal language can help us project the image we want to project and make us more aware of the signals we are interpreting. However, even within a single culture a nonverbal symbol may have more than one meaning.

Body Language

Posture and body movements connote energy and openness. North American **open body positions** include leaning forward with uncrossed arms and legs, with the arms away from the body. **Closed** or **defensive body positions** include leaning back, sometimes with both hands behind the head, arms and legs crossed or close together, or hands in pockets. As the labels imply, open positions suggest that people are accepting and open to new ideas. Closed positions suggest that people are physically or psychologically uncomfortable, that they are defending themselves and shutting other people out.

Instant Replay

High- and Low-Context Cultures

In **high-context cultures,** most of the information is inferred from the context of a message; little is "spelled out."

In **low-context cultures,** context is less important; most information is explicitly spelled out.

People who cross their arms or legs often claim that they do so only because the position is more comfortable. Certainly crossing one's legs is one way to be more comfortable in a chair that is the wrong height. U.S. women are taught to keep their arms close to their bodies and their knees and ankles together. But notice your own body the next time you're in a perfectly comfortable discussion with a good friend. You'll probably find that you naturally assume open body positions. The fact that so many people in organizational settings adopt closed positions may indicate that many people feel at least slightly uncomfortable in school and on the job.

The Japanese value the ability to sit quietly. They may see the U.S. tendency to fidget and shift as an indication of a lack of mental or spiritual balance. Even in North America, interviewers and audiences usually respond negatively to nervous gestures such as fidgeting with a tie or hair or jewelry, tapping a pencil, or swinging a foot.

Eye Contact

North American whites see **eye contact** as a sign of honesty. But in many cultures, dropped eyes are a sign of appropriate deference to a superior. Puerto Rican children are taught not to meet the eyes of adults.[15] The Japanese are taught to look at the neck.[16] In Korea, prolonged eye contact is considered rude. The lower-ranking person is expected to look down first.[17] In Muslim countries, women and men are not supposed to have eye contact.

These differences can lead to miscommunication in the multicultural workplace. Superiors may feel that subordinates are being disrespectful when the subordinate is being fully respectful—according to the norms of his or her culture.

Gestures

Americans sometimes assume that they can depend on gestures to communicate if language fails. But Birdwhistell reported that "although we have been searching for 15 years [1950–65], we have found no gesture or body motion which has the same meaning in all societies."[18]

Gestures that mean approval in the United States may have very different meanings in other countries. The "thumbs up" sign that means "good work" or "go ahead" in the United States and most of Western Europe is a vulgar insult in Greece. The circle formed with the thumb and first finger that means *OK* in the United States is obscene in Southern Italy and can mean "you're worth nothing" in France and Belgium.[19]

In the question period after a lecture, a man asked the speaker, a Puerto Rican professor, if shaking the hands up and down in front of the chest, as though shaking off water, was "a sign of mental retardation." The professor was horrified: in her culture, the gesture meant "excitement, intense thrill."[20] Studies have found that Spanish-speaking doctors rate the mental abilities of Latino patients much higher than do English-speaking doctors. The language barrier is surely part of the misevaluation by English-speaking doctors. Cultural differences in gestures may contribute to the misevaluation. Similarly, European–American supervisors in the workplace may underestimate the abilities of Hispanics because gestures differ in the two cultures.

Space

Personal space is the distance someone wants between himself or herself and other people in ordinary, nonintimate interchanges. Observation and limited experimentation show that most North Americans, North Europeans, and Asians want a bigger personal space than do Latin Americans, French, Italians, and Arabs. People who prefer lots of personal space are often forced to accept close contact on a crowded elevator or subway.

Even within a culture, some people like more personal space than do others. One U.S. study found that men took more personal space than women did.[21] In many cultures, people who are of the same age and sex take less personal space than do mixed-age or mixed-sex groups. Latin Americans will stand closer to people of the same sex than North Americans would, but North Americans stand closer to people of the opposite sex.[22]

Touch

Repeated studies have shown that babies need to be touched to grow and thrive and that older people are healthier both mentally and physically if they are touched. But some people are more comfortable with touch than others. Some people shake hands in greeting but otherwise don't like to be touched at all, except by family members or lovers. Other people, having grown up in families that touch a lot, hug as part of a greeting and touch even casual friends. Each kind of person may misinterpret the other. A person who dislikes touch may seem unfriendly to someone who's used to touching. A toucher may seem overly familiar to someone who dislikes touch.

Studies in the United States have shown that touch is interpreted as power: More powerful people touch less powerful people. When the toucher had higher status than the recipient, both men and women liked being touched.[23]

Most parts of North America allow opposite-sex couples to hold hands or walk arm-in-arm in public but frown on the same behavior in same-sex couples. People in Asia, the Middle East, and South America have the opposite expectation: male friends or female friends can hold hands or walk arm-in-arm, but it is slightly shocking for an opposite-sex couple to touch in public. In Iran, even handshakes between men and women are seen as improper.[24]

People who don't know each other well may feel more comfortable with each other if a piece of furniture separates them. For example, a group may work better sitting around a table than just sitting in a circle. In North America, a person sitting at the head of a table is generally assumed to be the group's leader. However, one experiment showed that when a woman sat at the head of a mixed-sex group, observers assumed that one of the men in the group was the leader.[25]

Spatial Arrangements

In the United States, the size, placement, and privacy of one's office connote status. Large corner offices have the highest status. An individual office with a door that closes connotes more status than a desk in a common area. Japanese firms, however, see private offices as "inappropriate and inefficient," reports Robert Christopher. Only the very highest executives and directors have private offices in the traditional Japanese company, and even they will also have desks in the common areas.[26]

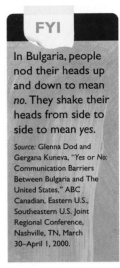

FYI

In Bulgaria, people nod their heads up and down to mean *no*. They shake their heads from side to side to mean yes.

Source: Glenna Dod and Gergana Kuneva, "Yes or *No:* Communication Barriers Between Bulgaria and The United States," ABC Canadian, Eastern U.S., Southeastern U.S. Joint Regional Conference, Nashville, TN, March 30–April 1, 2000.

FYI

Dearborn, Michigan, has 250,000 speakers of Arabic—the third-largest population of Arabic speakers in the world (after Baghdad and Cairo).

Source: David Victor, "Cross-Cultural Issues in Translating Business Communication," Sixth Annual Conference on Teaching Communication, Columbus, OH, July 31, 1999.

Doing business internationally requires an understanding of language and business practices and a sensitivity to cultural differences.

Japanese homes have much smaller rooms than most U.S. homes. The Japanese use less furniture and arrange it differently: A small table will be in the center of the room. In cold weather, a heater is placed under the table; the table-cloth keeps the warm air around the legs and feet of everyone who sits at the table. Even though U.S. homes have more pieces of furniture than the traditional Japanese home, Japanese may see Western rooms as "empty" since Western furniture lines the walls, leaving a large empty space in the middle of the room.[27]

Time

Organizations in the United States—businesses, government, and schools—keep time by the calendar and the clock. Being "on time" is seen as a sign of dependability. Other cultures may keep time by the seasons and the moon, the sun, internal "body clocks," or a personal feeling that "the time is right."

North Americans who believe that "time is money" are often frustrated in negotiations with people who take a much more leisurely approach. Part of the problem is that people in many other cultures want to establish a personal relationship before they decide whether to do business with each other.

The problem is made worse because various cultures mentally measure time differently. Many North Americans measure time in five-minute blocks. Someone who's five minutes late to an appointment or a job interview feels compelled to apologize. If the executive or interviewer is running half an hour late, the caller expects to be told about the likely delay upon arriving. Some people won't be able to wait that long and will need to reschedule their appointments. But in other cultures, 15 minutes or half an hour may be the smallest block of time. To someone who mentally measures time in 15-minute blocks, being 45 minutes late is no worse than being 15 minutes late is to someone who is conscious of smaller units.

Edward T. Hall distinguishes between **monochronic** cultures, which treat time as a resource, and **polychronic** cultures, which emphasize relationships. Researchers see the United States as monochronic. When U.S. managers feel offended because a Latin American manager also sees other people during "their" appointments, the two kinds of time are in conflict.

According to some scholars, Europeans schedule fewer events in a comparable period of time than do North Americans. Perhaps as a result, Germans and German Swiss see North Americans as too time-conscious.[28]

Other Nonverbal Symbols

Many other symbols can carry nonverbal meanings: clothing, colors, age, and height, to name a few.

In the United States and Canada, certain styles and colors of clothing are considered more "professional" and more "credible." In *Dress for Success* and *The Woman's Dress for Success Book,* John T. Molloy tells readers what clothes carry nonverbal messages of success, prestige, and competence. In Japan, clothing denotes not only status but also occupational group. Students wear uniforms. Company badges indicate rank within the organization. Workers wear different clothes when they are on strike than they do when they are working.[29]

Colors can also carry meanings in a culture. In the United States, mourners wear black to funerals, while brides wear white. In pre-Communist China and in some South American tribes, white is the color of mourning. Purple flowers are given to the dead in Mexico.[30] In Korea, red ink is used to record deaths but never to write about living people.[31]

In the United States, youth is valued. Some men as well as some women color their hair and even have face-lifts to look as youthful as possible. In Japan, younger people defer to older people. Americans attempting to negotiate in Japan are usually taken more seriously if at least one member of the team is noticeably gray-haired.

Height connotes status in many parts of the world. Executive offices are usually on the top floors; the underlings work below. Even being tall can help a person succeed. Studies have shown that employers are more willing to hire men over 6 feet tall than shorter men with the same credentials. Studies of real-world executives and graduates have shown that taller men make more money. In one study, every extra inch of height brought in an extra $600 a year.[32] But being too big can be a disadvantage. A tall, brawny football player complained that people found him intimidating off the field and assumed that he "had the brains of a Twinkie."

Oral Communication

Effective oral communication requires cultural understanding. As Figure 3.4 shows, the purpose of and the information exchanged in business introductions differs across cultures.

Figure 3.4

Cultural Contrasts in Business Introductions

	United States	Japan	Arab Countries
Purpose of introduction	Establish status and job identity; network	Establish position in group, build harmony	Establish personal rapport
Image of individual	Independent	Member of group	Part of rich culture
Information	Related to business	Related to company	Personal
Use of language	Informal, friendly; use first name	Little talking	Formal; expression of admiration
Values	Openness, directness, action	Harmony, respect, listening	Religious harmony, hospitality, emotional support

Source: Adapted from Farid Elashmawi and Philip R. Harris, *Multicultural Management 2000: Essential Cultural Insights for Global Business Success* (Houston: Gulf, 1998), 113.

Instant **Replay**

Two Views of Time
Monochronic cultures treat time as a resource. **Polychronic** cultures emphasize relationships.

Deborah Tannen uses the term **conversational style** to denote our conversational patterns and the meaning we give to them: the way we show interest, politeness, and appropriateness.[33] Your answers to the following questions reveal your own conversational style:

- How long a pause tells you that it's your turn to speak?
- Do you see interruption as rude? or do you say things while other people are still talking to show that you're interested and to encourage them to say more?
- Do you show interest by asking lots of questions? or do you see questions as intrusive and wait for people to volunteer whatever they have to say?

Tannen concludes that the following features characterize her own conversational style:

Fast rate of speech
Fast rate of turn-taking
Persistence—if a turn is not acknowledged, try again
Preference for personal stories
Tolerance of, preference for simultaneous speech
Abrupt topic shifting.

Different conversational styles are not better or worse than each other, but people with different conversational styles may feel uncomfortable without knowing why. A subordinate who talks quickly may be frustrated by a boss who speaks slowly. People who talk more slowly may feel shut out of a conversation with people who talk more quickly. Someone who has learned to make requests directly ("please pass the salt") may be annoyed by someone who uses indirect requests ("This casserole needs some salt").

In the workplace, conflicts may arise because of differences in conversational style. Generation Xers often use a rising inflection on statements as well as questions. Xers see this style as gentler and more polite. But baby boomer bosses may see this speech pattern as hesitant, as if the speaker wants advice—which they then proceed to deliver.[34] Thomas Kochman claims that African Americans often use direct questions to criticize or accuse.[35] If Kochman is right, an African–American employee might see a question ("Will that report be ready Friday?") as a criticism of his or her progress. One supervisor might mean the question simply as a request for information. Another supervisor might use the question to mean "I want that report Friday."

Daniel N. Maltz and Ruth A. Borker believe that differences in conversational style may be responsible for the miscommunication that sometimes occurs in male–female conversations. For example, researchers have found that women are much more likely to nod and to say *yes* or *mm hmm* than men are. Maltz and Borker hypothesize that to women, these symbols mean simply, "I'm listening; go on." Men, on the other hand, may decode these symbols as "I agree" or at least "I follow what you're saying so far." A man who receives nods and *mms* from a woman may feel that she is inconsistent and unpredictable if she then disagrees with him. A woman may feel that a man who doesn't provide any feedback isn't listening to her.[36]

Understatement and Exaggeration

Closely related to conversational style is the issue of understatement and overstatement. The British have a reputation for understatement. Someone good enough to play at Wimbledon may say he or she "plays a little tennis." Many people in the United States exaggerate. A U.S. businessman negotiating with a German said, "I know it's impossible, but can we do it?" The German saw the statement as nonsensical: By definition, something that is impossible cannot be done at all. The American saw "impossible" as merely a strong way of saying "difficult" and assumed that with enough resources and commitment, the job could in fact be done.[37]

Compliments

The kinds of statements that people interpret as compliments and the socially correct way to respond to compliments also vary among cultures. The statement "You must be really tired" is a compliment in Japan since it recognizes the other person has worked hard. The correct response is "Thank you, but I'm OK." An

Successful intercultural communicators attempt to understand the communication style the other group prefers.

"Matthews ... we're getting another one of those strange 'aw blah es span yol' sounds."

American who is complimented on giving a good oral presentation will probably say "Thank you." A Japanese, in contrast, will apologize: "No, it wasn't very good."[38]

Statements that seem complimentary in one context may be inappropriate in another. For example, women in business are usually uncomfortable if male colleagues or superiors compliment them on their appearance: The comments suggest that the women are being treated as visual decoration rather than as contributing workers.

Silence

Silence also has different meanings in different cultures and subcultures. Some Americans have difficulty doing business in Japan because they do not realize that silence almost always means that the Japanese do not like the Americans' ideas. Muriel Saville-Troike reports that during a period of military tension, Greek air traffic controllers responded with silence when Egyptian planes requested permission to land. The Greeks intended silence as a refusal; the Egyptians interpreted silence as consent. Several people were killed when the Greeks fired on the planes as they approached the runway.[39]

Different understandings of silence can prolong problems with sexual harassment in the workplace. White women sometimes use silence to respond to comments they find offensive, hoping that silence will signal their lack of appreciation. But some men may think that silence means appreciation or at least neutrality. African–American women may be more likely to "talk tough" in response to unwelcome advances.

Writing to International Audiences

Most cultures are more formal than the United States. When you write to international audiences, use titles, not first names. Avoid contractions, slang, and sports metaphors.

The patterns of organization that work for North American audiences may need to be modified for international correspondence. For most cultures, buffer

Figure 3.5

Cultural Contrasts in Written Persuasive Documents

	United States	Japan	Arab Countries
Opening	Request action or get reader's attention	Offer thanks; apologize	Offer personal greetings
Way to persaude	Immediate gain or loss of opportunity	Waiting	Personal connections; future opportunity
Style	Short sentences	Modesty, minimize own standing	Elaborate expressions; many signatures
Closing	Specific request	Desire to maintain harmony	Future relationship, personal greeting
Values	Efficiency; directness, action	Politeness; indirectness; relationship	Status; continuation

Source: Adapted from Farid Elashmawi and Philip P. Harris, *Multicultural Management 2000: Essential Cultural Insights for Global Business Success* (Houston: Gulf, 1998), 139.

negative messages (◁ ▶ Module 11) and make requests (◁ ▶ Module 12) more indirect. As Figure 3.5 suggests, you may need to modify style, structure, and strategy when you write to international readers. Make a special effort to avoid phrases that could be seen as arrogant or uncaring. Cultural mistakes made orally float away on the air; those made in writing are permanently recorded.

There are so many different cultures! How can I know enough to communicate?

Focus on being sensitive and flexible.

The first step in understanding another culture is to realize that it may do things very differently, and that the difference is not bad or inferior. But people within a single culture differ. The kinds of differences summarized in this module can turn into stereotypes, which can be just as damaging as ignorance. Don't try to memorize the material here as a rigid set of rules. Instead, use the examples to get a sense for the kinds of things that differ from one culture to another. Test these generalizations against your experience. When in doubt, ask.

If you plan to travel to a specific country, or if you work with people from other cultures, read about that country or culture and learn a little of the language. Also talk to people. That's really the only way to learn whether someone is wearing black as a sign of mourning, as a fashion statement, or as a color that slenderizes and doesn't show dirt.

Many developing countries have gone straight to cell phones, skipping the expensive step of laying cables. Many owners of cell phones have become entrepreneurs, allowing people to make calls on their phones for a small fee. Now farmers can call to find out what prices are in the cities, so they aren't at the mercy of what middlemen claim.

Go to
www3.travlang.com
to learn languages for
international travel.

As Brenda Arbeléez suggests, the successful international communicator is

- Aware that his or her preferred values and behaviors are influenced by culture and are not necessarily "right."
- Flexible and open to change.
- Sensitive to verbal and nonverbal behavior.
- Aware of the values, beliefs, and practices in other cultures.
- Sensitive to differences among individuals within a culture.[40]

How can I make my documents bias-free?

Start by using nonsexist, nonracist, and nonagist language.

Bias-free language is language that does not discriminate against people on the basis of sex, physical condition, race, age, or any other category. Bias-free language is fair and friendly; it complies with the law. It includes all readers; it helps to sustain goodwill. When you produce newsletters or other documents with photos and illustrations, choose a sampling of the whole population, not just part of it.

Making Language Nonsexist

Nonsexist language treats both sexes neutrally. Check to be sure that your writing is free from sexism in four areas: words and phrases, job titles, pronouns, and courtesy titles. Courtesy titles are discussed in Module 9 on format. Words and phrases, job titles, and pronouns are discussed in this module.

Figure 3.6

Getting Rid of Sexist Terms and Phrases

Instead of	Use	Because
The girl at the front desk	The woman's name or job title: "Ms. Browning," "Rosa," "the receptionist"	Call female employees *women* just as you call male employees *men*. When you talk about a specific woman, use her name, just as you use a man's name to talk about a specific man.
The ladies on our staff	The women on our staff	Use parallel terms for males and females. Therefore, use *ladies* only if you refer to the males on your staff as *gentlemen*. Few businesses do, since social distinctions are rarely at issue.
Manpower Manhours Manning	Personnel Hours or worker hours Staffing	The power in business today comes from both women and men. If you have to correspond with the U.S. Department of Labor's Division of Manpower Administration, you are stuck with the term. When you talk about other organizations, however, use nonsexist alternatives.
Managers and their wives	Managers and their guests	Managers may be female; not everyone is married.

Words and Phrases

If you find any of the terms in the first column in Figure 3.6 in your writing or your company's documents, replace them with terms from the second column.

Not every word containing *man* is sexist. For example, *manager* is not sexist. The word comes from the Latin *manus*, meaning *hand*; it has nothing to do with maleness.

Avoid terms that assume that everyone is married or is heterosexual.

Biased:　You and your husband or wife are cordially invited to the dinner.

Better:　You and your guest are cordially invited to the dinner.

Job Titles

Use neutral titles which do not imply that a job is held only by men or only by women. Many job titles are already neutral: *accountant, banker, doctor, engineer, inspector, manager, nurse, pilot, secretary, technician,* to name a few. Other titles reflect gender stereotypes and need to be changed.

Instead of	Use
Businessman	A specific title: executive, accountant, department head, owner of a small business, men and women in business, business person
Chairman	Chair, chairperson, moderator
Foreman	Supervisor (from *Job Title Revisions*)
Salesman	Salesperson, sales representative
Waitress	Server
Woman lawyer	Lawyer
Workman	Worker, employee. Or use a specific title: crane operator, bricklayer, etc.

Pronouns

When you write about a specific person, use the appropriate gender pronouns:

In his speech, John Jones said that . . .

In her speech, Judy Jones said that . . .

When you are not writing about a specific person, but about anyone who may be in a given job or position, traditional gender pronouns are sexist.

Sexist:　a. Each supervisor must certify that the time sheet for his department is correct.

Sexist:　b. When the nurse fills out the accident report form, she should send one copy to the Central Division Office.

FYI

More U.S. women work for women-owned businesses than for *Fortune* 500 companies.

Source: Cathy Ologson, "By Women for Women," *Fast Company,* September 1999, 78.

Business writing uses four ways to eliminate sexist generic pronouns: use plurals, use second-person *you,* revise the sentence to omit the pronoun, and use pronoun pairs. Whenever you have a choice of two or more ways to make a phrase or sentence nonsexist, choose the alternative that is the smoothest and least conspicuous.

The following examples use these methods to revise sentences.

1. Use plural nouns and pronouns.

   Nonsexist: a. Supervisors must certify that the time sheets for their departments are correct.

Note: When you use plural nouns and pronouns, other words in the sentence may need to be made plural too. In the example above, plural supervisors have plural time sheets and departments.

Avoid mixing singular nouns and plural pronouns.

   Nonsexist but   a. Each supervisor must certify that the time sheet
   lacks agreement: for their department is correct.

Since *supervisor* is singular, it is incorrect to use the plural *they* to refer to it. The resulting lack of agreement is becoming acceptable orally but is not yet acceptable to many readers in writing. Instead, use one of the four grammatically correct ways to make the sentence nonsexist.

Instant **Replay**

The successful international communicator is

• Aware that his or her preferred values and behaviors are influenced by culture and are not necessarily "right."
• Flexible and open to change.
• Sensitive to verbal and nonverbal behavior.
• Aware of the values, beliefs, and practices in other cultures.
• Sensitive to differences among individuals within a culture.

2. Use *you.*

   Nonsexist: a. You must certify that the time sheet for your department is correct.

   Nonsexist: b. When you fill out an accident report form, send one copy to the Central Division Office.

You is particularly good for instructions and statements of the responsibilities of someone in a given position. Using *you* as the understood subject also shortens sentences, because you write "Send one copy" instead of "You should send one copy." It also makes your writing more direct.

3. Substitute an article (*a, an,* or *the*) for the pronoun, or revise the sentence so that the pronoun is unnecessary.

   Nonsexist: a. The supervisor must certify that the time sheet for the department is correct.

   Nonsexist: b. The nurse will
                              1. Fill out the accident report form.
                              2. Send one copy of the form to the Central Division Office.

4. When you must focus on the action of an individual, use pronoun pairs.

   Nonsexist: a. The supervisor must certify that the time sheet for his or her department is correct.

   Nonsexist: b. When the nurse fills out the accident report form, he or she should send one copy to the Central Division Office.

Making Language Nonracist and Nonagist

Language is **nonracist** and **nonagist** when it treats all races and ages fairly, avoiding negative stereotypes of any group. Use these guidelines to check for bias in documents you write or edit:

- **Give someone's race or age only if it is relevant to your story.** When you do mention these characteristics, give them for everyone in your story—not just the non-Caucasian, non-young-to-middle-aged adults you mention.
- **Refer to a group by the term it prefers. As preferences change, change your usage.** Sixty years ago, *Negro* was preferred as a more dignified term than *colored* for African Americans. As times changed, *black* and *African American* replaced it. Surveys in the mid-1990s showed that almost half of blacks aged 40 and older preferred *black,* but those 18 to 39 preferred *African American.*[41]

  Oriental has now been replaced by *Asian.*

  The term *Latino* is the most acceptable group term to refer to Mexican Americans, Cuban Americans, Puerto Ricans, Dominicans, Brazilians, and other people with Central and Latin American backgrounds. (*Latina* is the term for an individual woman.) Better still is to refer to the precise group. The differences among various Latino groups are at least as great as the differences among Italian Americans, Irish Americans, Armenian Americans, and others descended from various European groups.

  Some native people in Alaska accept the term *Eskimo,* but others prefer native terms such as *Inuit.*

  Older people and *mature customers* are more generally accepted terms than *senior citizens* or *golden agers.*
- **Avoid terms that suggest that competent people are unusual.** The statement "She is an intelligent black woman" suggests that the writer expects most black women to be stupid. "He is an asset to his race" suggests that excellence in the race is rare. "He is a spry 70-year-old" suggests that the writer is amazed that anyone that age can still move.

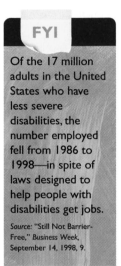

FYI

Of the 17 million adults in the United States who have less severe disabilities, the number employed fell from 1986 to 1998—in spite of laws designed to help people with disabilities get jobs.

Source: "Still Not Barrier-Free," *Business Week,* September 14, 1998, 9.

Talking about People with Disabilities and Diseases

A disability is a physical, mental, sensory, or emotional impairment that interferes with the major tasks of daily living. One in six people in the United States has a disability; the number of people with disabilities will rise as the population ages.[42]

- **People-first language** focuses on the person, not the condition. Use it instead of traditional adjectives used as nouns which imply that the condition defines the person.

Instead of	Use	Because
The mentally retarded	People with mental retardation	The condition does not define the person or his or her potential.
The blind	People with vision impairments	
Cancer patients	People being treated for cancer	

Instant Replay

To eliminate sexist pronouns,

1. Use plurals.
2. Use second-person *you.*
3. Revise the sentence to omit the pronoun.
4. Use pronoun pairs.

- **Avoid negative terms, unless the audience prefers them.** You-attitude takes precedence over positive emphasis: use the term a group prefers. People who lost their hearing as infants, children, or young adults often prefer to be called *deaf.* But people who lose their hearing as older adults often prefer to be called *hard of hearing,* even when their hearing loss is just as great as someone who identifies as part of deaf culture.

Just as people in a single ethnic group may prefer different labels based on generational or cultural divides, so differences exist within the disability community. Using the right term requires keeping up with changing preferences. If your target audience is smaller than the whole group, use the term preferred by that audience, even if the group as a whole prefers another term.

Some negative terms, however, are never appropriate. Negative terms such as *afflicted, suffering from,* and *struck down* also suggest an outdated view of any illness as a sign of divine punishment.

Choosing Bias-Free Photos and Illustrations

When you produce a document with photographs or illustrations, check the visuals for possible bias. Do they show people of both sexes and all races? Is there a sprinkling of various kinds of people (younger and older, people using wheelchairs, etc.)? It's OK to have individual pictures that have just one sex or one race; the photos as a whole do not need to show exactly 50% men and 50% women. But the general impression should suggest that diversity is welcome and normal.

Check relationships and authority figures as well as numbers. If all the men appear in business suits and the women in maids' uniforms, the pictures are sexist even if an equal number of men and women are pictured. If the only blacks and Latinos pictured are factory workers, the photos support racism even when an equal number of people from each race are shown.

In the late 1990s, as Marilyn Dyrud has shown, only 22% of the images of humans in standard clip art files were women, and most of those showed women in traditional roles. An even smaller percent pictured members of minority groups.[43] Don't use biased clip art or stock photos: create your own bias-free illustrations.

Summary of Key Points

- **Culture** provides patterns of acceptable behavior and beliefs.
- In **high-context cultures,** most of the information is inferred from the context of a message; little is explicitly conveyed. In **low-context cultures,** context is less important; most information is explicitly spelled out.

- Nonverbal signals can be misinterpreted just as easily as can verbal symbols (words).
- No gesture has a universal meaning across all cultures. Gestures that signify approval in North America may be insults in other countries, and vice versa.

- **Personal space** is the distance someone wants between him or herself and other people in ordinary, nonintimate interchanges.
- North Americans who believe that "time is money" are often frustrated in negotiations with people who want to establish a personal relationship before they decide whether to do business with each other or who measure time in 15- or 30-minute increments rather than the 5-minute intervals North Americans are used to.
- **Monochronic** cultures treat time as a resource. The United States is classified as monochronic. **Polychronic** cultures emphasize relationships.
- **Conversational style** denotes our conversational patterns and the way we show interest, politeness, appropriateness.

- The successful intercultural communicator is
  - Aware that his or her preferred values and behaviors are influenced by culture and are not necessarily "right."
  - Flexible and open to change.
  - Sensitive to verbal and nonverbal behavior.
  - Aware of the values, beliefs, and practices in other cultures.
  - Sensitive to differences among individuals within a culture.
- Traditional pronouns are sexist when they refer to a class of people, not to specific individuals. Four ways to make the sentence nonsexist are to use plurals, to use *you*, to revise the sentence to omit the pronoun, and to use pronoun pairs.
- Bias-free language is fair and friendly; it complies with the law. It includes all readers; it helps to sustain goodwill.

Assignments for Module 3

Questions for Comprehension

3.1 What sources create diversity in the workplace?

3.2 What is intercultural competence?

3.3 What four methods make a sentence nonsexist?

Questions for Critical Thinking

3.4 It's sexist to always put the male pronoun first in pronoun pairs (e.g., *he/she* rather than *she/he* or *s/he*). Why do the authors of this book recommend that method? Which method do you prefer?

3.5 Suppose that you have an audience that is sexist, racist, or prejudiced in some other

way. To what extent, if any, should you adapt to this aspect of your audience?

3.6 You can't possibly learn what every symbol means in every culture. How can you avoid offending the people you work with?

3.7 What other cultures are you most likely to work with? How could you learn about those cultures?

Exercises and Problems

3.8 Revising Sexist Job Titles

Suggest nonsexist alternatives for each of the following:

cleaning lady   garbage man
Congressman   male nurse

mail boy   repairman
mailman   salesman
night watchman   waitress

3.9 Eliminating Biased Language

Explain the source of bias in each of the following and revise to remove the bias.

1. We recommend hiring Jim Renker and Elizabeth Shuman. Both were very successful summer interns. Jim drafted the report on using rap music in ads, and Elizabeth really improved the looks of the office.
2. All sales associates and their wives are invited to the picnic.
3. Although he is blind, Mr. Morin is an excellent group leader.
4. Unlike many African Americans, Yvonne has extensive experience designing Web pages.
5. Chris Gottlieb
   Pacific Perspectives
   6300 West Coronado Blvd.
   Los Angeles, CA
   Gentlemen:
6. Enrique Torres has very good people skills for a man.
7. *Twenty-First-Century Parenting* shows you how to persuade your husband to do his share of child care chores.
8. Mr. Paez, Mr. O'Connor, and Tonya will represent our office at the convention.
9. Sue Corcoran celebrates her 50th birthday today. Stop by her cubicle at noon to get a piece of cake and to help us sing "The Old Grey Mare Just Ain't What She Used to Be."
10. Because older customers tend to be really picky, we will need to give a lot of details in our ads.

3.10 Identifying Sources of Miscommunication

In each of the following situations, identify one or more ways that cultural differences may be leading to miscommunication.

1. Alan is a U.S. sales representative in Mexico. He makes appointments and is careful to be on time. But the person he's calling on is frequently late. To save time, Alan tries to get right to business. But his hosts want to talk about sightseeing and his family. Even worse, his appointments are interrupted constantly, not only by business phone calls, but also by long conversations with other people and even the customers' children who come into the office. Alan's first progress report is very negative. He hasn't yet made a sale. Perhaps Mexico just isn't the right place to sell his company's products.
2. To help her company establish a presence in Japan, Susan wants to hire a local interpreter who can advise her on business customs. Kana Tomari has superb qualifications on paper. But when Susan tries to probe about her experience, Kana just says, "I will do my best. I will try very hard." She never gives details about any of the previous positions she's held. Susan begins to wonder if the résumé is inflated.
3. Stan wants to negotiate a joint venture with a Chinese company. He asks Tung-Sen Lee if the Chinese people

have enough discretionary income to afford his product. Mr. Lee is silent for a time, and then says, "Your product is good. People in the West must like it." Stan smiles, pleased that Mr. Lee recognizes the quality of his product, and he gives Mr. Lee a contract to sign. Weeks later, Stan still hasn't heard anything. If China is going to be so inefficient, he wonders if he really should try to do business there.

4. Elspeth is very proud of her participatory management style. On assignment in India, she is careful not to give orders but to ask for suggestions. But people rarely suggest anything. Even a formal suggestion system doesn't work. And to make matters worse, she doesn't sense the respect and camaraderie of the plant she managed in the United States. Perhaps, she decides gloomily, people in India just aren't ready for a woman boss.

3.11 Advising a Hasty Subordinate

Three days ago, one of your subordinates forwarded to everyone in the office a bit of e-mail humor he'd received from a friend. Titled "You know you're Southern when . . . ," the message poked fun at Southern speech, attitudes, and lifestyles. Today you get this message from your subordinate:

> Subject: Should I Apologize?
>
> I'm getting flamed left and right because of the Southern message. I thought it was funny, but some people just can't take a joke. So far I've tried not to respond to the flames, figuring that would just make things worse. But now I'm wondering if I should apologize. What do you think?

Answer the message.

3.12 Responding to a Complaint

You're Director of Corporate Communications; the employee newsletter is produced by your office.

Today you get this e-mail message from Caroline Huber:

> Subject: Complaint about Sexist Language
>
> The article about the "Help Desk" says that Martina Luna and I "are the key customer service representatives 'manning' the desk." I don't MAN anything! I WORK.

Respond to Caroline. And send a message to your staff, reminding them to edit newsletter stories as well as external documents to replace biased language.

3.13 Asking about Travel Arrangements

The CEO is planning a trip to visit colleagues in another country (you pick the country). As Executive Assistant to the CEO of your organization, it's your job to make travel plans. At this stage, you don't know anything except dates and flights. (The CEO will arrive in the country at 7 A.M. local time on the 28th of next month, and stay for three days.) It's your job to find out what the plans are and communicate any of the CEO's requirements.

Write an e-mail message to your contact.

Hints:
- Pick a business, nonprofit organization, or government agency you know something about, making

assumptions about the kinds of things its executive would want to do during an international visit.
- How much international traveling does your CEO do? Has he or she ever been to this country before? What questions will he or she want answered?

3.14 Sending a Draft to Japan

You've drafted instructions for a product that will be sold in Japan. Before the text is translated, you want to find out if the pictures will be clear. So you send an e-mail to your Japanese counterpart, Takashi Haneda, asking for a response within a week.

Write an e-mail message; assume that you will send the pictures as an attachment.

3.15 Creating a Web Page

Create a Web page for managers who must communicate across cultures.

Assume that this page can be accessed from the organization's intranet. Offer at least seven links. (More is better.) You may offer information as well as links to other pages with information. At the top of the page, offer an overview of what the page covers. At the bottom of the page, put the creation/update date and your name and e-mail address.

As Your Instructor Directs,
a. Turn in two laser copies of your page(s). On another page, give the URLs for each link.
b. Turn in one laser copy of your page(s) and a disk with the HTML code and .gif files.
c. Write a memo to your instructor (1) identifying the audience for which the page is designed and explaining (2) the search strategies you used to

find material on this topic, (3) why you chose the pages and information you've included, and (4) why you chose the layout and graphics you've used.
d. Post your memo in an e-mail message to the class.
e. Present your page orally to the class.

Hints:
- Limit your page to just one culture or country.
- Try to cover as many topics as possible: history, politics, notable people, arts, conversational style, customs, and so forth. For a culture in another country, also include money, living accommodations, geography, transport, weather, business practices, and so forth.
- Chunk your links into small groups under headings.
- See Module 5 on Web page design.

3.16 Requesting Information about a Country

Use one or more of the following ways to get information about a country. Information you might focus on could include

- Business opportunities
- History and geography
- Principal exports and imports
- Dominant religions
- Holidays
- School system
- Political system.

1. Write to the U.S. & Foreign Commercial Service Office in your

district. (Your instructor has the addresses in the *Instructor's Manual.*)

2. Check the country's trade office, if there is one in your city.
3. Interview someone from that country or someone who has lived there.
4. Read published materials about the country.

As Your Instructor Directs,
a. Share your findings orally with a small group of students.

b. Summarize your findings in a memo to your instructor.
c. Present your findings to the class.
d. E-mail your findings to the class.
e. Join with a group of classmates to write a group report on the country.

3.17 Answering an Inquiry about Photos

You've just been named Vice President for Diversity, the first person in your organization to hold this position. Today, you receive this memo from Sheila Lathan, who edits the employee newsletter.

Subject: Photos in the Employee Newsletter

Please tell me what to do about photos in the monthly employee newsletter. I'm concerned that almost no single issue represents the diversity of employees we have here.

As you know, our layout allows two visuals each month. One of those is always the employee of the month (EM). In the last year, most of those have been male and all but two have been white. What makes it worse is that people want photos that make them look good. You may remember that Ron Olmos was the EM two months ago; in the photo he wanted me to use, you can't tell that he's in a wheelchair. Often the EM is the only photo; the other visual is often a graph of sales or something relating to quality.

Even if the second visual is another photo, it may not look balanced in terms of gender and race. After all, 62% of our employees are men, and 78% are white. Should the pictures try to represent those percentages? The leadership positions (both in management and in the union) are even more heavily male and white. Should we run pictures of people doing important things, and risk continuing the imbalance?

I guess I could use more visuals, but then there wouldn't be room for as many stories—and people really like to see their names in print. Plus, giving people information about company activities and sales is important to maintaining goodwill. A bigger newsletter would be one way to have more visuals and keep the content, but with the cost-cutting measures we're under, that doesn't look likely.

What should I do?

As Your Instructor Directs,
a. Work in a small group with other students to come up with a recommendation for Sheila.
b. Write a memo responding to her.

c. Write an article for the employee newsletter about the photo policy you recommend and how it relates to the company's concern for diversity.

Polishing Your Prose

Using Idioms

Idioms are phrases that have specific meanings different from the meanings for each individual word.

Idiom	Meaning
Cut to the chase	Express your main point immediately.
Read between the lines	Look for a hidden message.

Like idioms, slang changes the definitions of words. *Bad*, a word that is negative, becomes positive when used in slang to denote something good or desirable. Dictionaries often are slow to adapt to slang, which changes constantly.

You need to understand a culture to make sense of its idioms. Because idioms usually violate the rules of standard edited English, they are particularly troublesome for people new to the language.

To learn idioms,

1. Study native speakers in person and on television. When possible, ask native speakers what unfamiliar words and phrases mean.

2. Underline unfamiliar passages in newspapers and magazines. Ask a friend or your instructor to explain their meaning.

3. Practice what you learn with a conversation partner.

Exercises

What do these 10 common idiomatic phrases mean literally? What do they mean in business?

1. From A to Z.

2. Wow them.

3. Catch a plane (or cab).

4. I gave him his walking papers.

5. Sign on the dotted line.

6. Put your nose to the grindstone.

7. In the black/in the red.

8. Burn the midnight oil.

9. Slam the competition.

10. Pay your dues.

Check your answers to the odd-numbered exercises at the back of the book.

BComm Skill Booster

To apply the concepts in this module, complete lessons 31, 33, 69, and 74 on embracing diversity, nonverbal messages, using a conversational style, and communicating cross-culturally. You can access the BComm Skill Booster through the text Web site at **www.mhhe.com/bcs2e.**

Module 4

Planning, Writing, and Revising

Start by asking these questions:

- Does it matter what process I use?
- I don't have much time. How should I use it?
- What planning should I do before I begin writing or speaking?
- What is revision? How do I do it?
- Can a grammar checker do my editing for me?
- I spell check. Do I still need to proofread?
- How can I get better feedback?
- Can I use form letters?
- How can I overcome writer's block and procrastination?

Skilled performances look easy and effortless. In reality, as every dancer, musician, or athlete knows, they're the product of hard work, hours of practice, attention to detail, and intense concentration. Like all skilled performances, writing rests on a base of work.

Planning, writing, and revising include the following activities:

Planning

- Analyzing the problem, defining your purposes, and analyzing the audience; thinking of information, benefits, and objections; choosing a pattern of organization or making an outline; and so on.

- Gathering the information you need—from the message you're answering, a person, a book, or the Web.

Writing

- Putting words on paper or on a screen. Writing can be lists, fragmentary notes, stream-of-consciousness writing, or a formal draft.

Revising

- Evaluating your work and measuring it against your goals and the requirements of the situation and audience. The best evaluation results from *re-seeing* your draft as if someone else had written it. Will your audience understand it? Is it complete? Convincing? Friendly?
- Getting feedback from someone else. Is your pattern of organization appropriate? Does a revision solve an earlier problem? Are there any typos in the final copy?

Editing

- Adding, deleting, substituting, or rearranging. Revision can be changes in single words or in large sections of a document.
- Editing the draft to see that it satisfies the requirements of standard English. Here you'd correct spelling and mechanical errors and check word choice and format. Unlike revision, which can produce major changes in meaning, editing focuses on the surface of writing.
- Proofreading the final copy to see that it's free from typographical errors.

Note the following points about these activities:

- **The activities do not have to come in this order.** Some people may gather information *after* writing a draft when they see that they need more specifics to achieve their purposes.
- **You do not have to finish one activity to start another.** Some writers plan a short section and write it, plan the next short section and write it, and so on throughout the document. Evaluating what is already written may cause a writer to do more planning or to change the original plan.

The most useful feedback evaluates the document in terms of purposes, audiences, information, and context.

- **You may do an activity several times, not just once.** For an important document, you might get feedback, revise, get more feedback, revise yet again, and so on.
- **Most writers do not use all eight activities for all the documents they write.** You'll use more activities when you write a new kind of document, about a new subject, or to a new audience.

Does it matter what process I use?

Using expert processes will improve your writing.

Just as athletes can improve their game by studying videotapes and working on just how they kick a ball or spin during a jump, so writers can improve their writing by studying their own processes. No single writing process works for all writers all of the time. However, expert writers seem to use different processes than novice writers.[1] Expert writers are more likely to

FYI

Direct mail expert Jeffrey Dobkin says, "Write profusely, but edit severely. I write two to three pages to get a one-page letter. Maybe more."

Source: Jeffrey Dobkin, "Hot Tips and-Inside-Secrets in Direct Mail, Part I," *Direct Marketing,* July 1999, 66.

- Realize that the first draft can be revised.
- Write regularly.
- Break big jobs into small chunks.
- Have clear goals focusing on purpose and audience.
- Have several different strategies to choose from.
- Use rules flexibly.
- Wait to edit until after the draft is complete.

Research shows that experts differ from novices in identifying and analyzing the initial problem more effectively, understanding the task more broadly and deeply, drawing from a wider repertoire of strategies, and seeing patterns more clearly. Experts actually composed more slowly than novices, perhaps because they rarely settled for work that was just "OK." Finally, experts were better at evaluating their own work.[2]

Thinking about the writing process and consciously adopting "expert" processes will help you become a better writer.

I don't have much time. How should I use it?

Save two-thirds of your time for planning and revising.

To get the best results from the time you have, spend only a third of your time actually "writing." Spend at least one-third of your time analyzing the situation and your audience, gathering information, and organizing what you have to say. Spend another third evaluating what you've said, revising the draft(s) to meet your purposes and the needs of the audience and the organization, editing a late draft to remove any errors in grammar and mechanics, and proofreading the final typed copy.

When you first get an assignment, think about all the steps you'll need to go through so that you can plan your time for that project. Certainly two writers might need different amounts of time to produce the same quality document. Figure 4.1 shows how a writer might use about 6 hours needed to plan, write, and revise a memo.

Figure 4.1

Allocating Time in Writing a Memo

Planning	1.5 hours
Understand the policy.	
Answer the PAIBOC questions (◀ ▷ Module 1).	
Think about document design (◁ ▶ Module 5).	
Organize the message.	

Revising	3.5 hours
Reread draft.	
Measure draft against PAIBOC questions and against principles of business communication.	
Revise draft.	
Ask for feedback.	
Revise draft based on feedback.	
Edit to catch grammatical errors.	
Run spell check.	
Proof by eye.	
Initial memo.	
Duplicate and distribute document.	

What planning should I do before I begin writing or speaking?

As much as you can!

Instant Replay

How Experts Write

Expert writers

- Realize that the first draft can be revised.
- Write regularly.
- Break big jobs into small chunks.
- Have clear goals focusing on purpose and audience.
- Have several different strategies to choose from.
- Use rules flexibly.
- Wait to edit until after the draft is complete.

Spend at least one-third of your time planning and organizing before you begin to write. The better your ideas are when you start, the fewer drafts you'll need to produce a good document. Start by using the analysis questions from Module 1 to identify purpose and audience. Use the strategies described in Module 2 to analyze audience and in Module 8 to develop reader benefits. Gather information you can use for your document.

If ideas won't come, try the following techniques.

- **Brainstorm.** Think of all the ideas you can, without judging them. Consciously try to get at least a dozen different ideas before you stop. The first idea you have may not be the best.
- **Freewrite.**[3] Make yourself write, without stopping, for 10 minutes or so, even if you must write "I will think of something soon." At the end of 10 minutes, read what you've written and identify the best point in the draft. Get a clean paper or screen and write for another 10 uninterrupted minutes. Read this draft, marking anything that's good and should be kept, and then write again for another 10 minutes. By the third session, you will probably produce several sections that are worth keeping—maybe even a complete draft that's ready to be revised.
- **Cluster.**[4] Write your topic in the middle of the page and circle it. Write down the ideas the topic suggests, circling them, too. (The circles are designed to tap into the nonlinear half of your brain.) When you've filled the page, look for patterns or repeated ideas. Use different colored pens to group related ideas. Then use these ideas to develop

Figure 4.2
Clustering Helps Generate Ideas

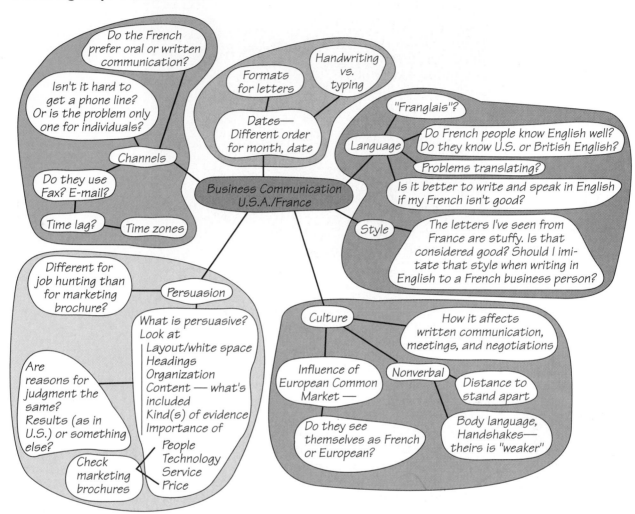

reader benefits in a memo, questions for a survey, or content for the body of a report. Figure 4.2 presents the clusters that one writer created about business communication in the United States and France.

- **Talk to your audiences.** As Rachel Spilka's research shows, talking to internal and external audiences helped writers involve readers in the planning process, understand the social and political relationships among readers, and negotiate conflicts orally rather than depending solely on the document. These writers were then able to think about content as well as about organization and style, appeal to common grounds (such as reducing waste or increasing productivity) which several readers shared, and reduce the number of revisions needed before documents were approved.[5]

Thinking about the content, layout, or structure of your document can also give you ideas. For long documents, write out the headings you'll use. For

Figure 4.3

Customized Planning Guides for Specific Documents

Source: E-mail and proposal guides based on Fred Reynolds, "What Adult Work-World Writers Have Taught Me About Adult Work-World Writing," *Professional Writing in Context: Lessons from Teaching and Consulting in Worlds of Work* (Hillsdale, NJ: Lawrence Erlbaum Associates, 1995), 18, 20.

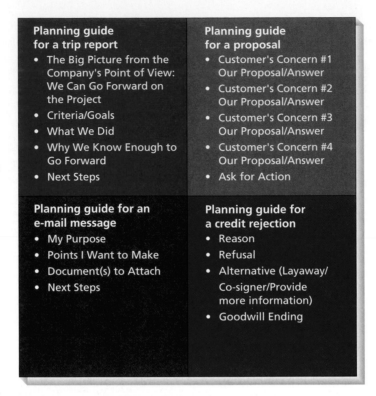

Planning guide for a trip report
- The Big Picture from the Company's Point of View: We Can Go Forward on the Project
- Criteria/Goals
- What We Did
- Why We Know Enough to Go Forward
- Next Steps

Planning guide for a proposal
- Customer's Concern #1 Our Proposal/Answer
- Customer's Concern #2 Our Proposal/Answer
- Customer's Concern #3 Our Proposal/Answer
- Customer's Concern #4 Our Proposal/Answer
- Ask for Action

Planning guide for an e-mail message
- My Purpose
- Points I Want to Make
- Document(s) to Attach
- Next Steps

Planning guide for a credit rejection
- Reason
- Refusal
- Alternative (Layaway/ Co-signer/Provide more information)
- Goodwill Ending

Site *to* See

Go to
www.wisc.edu/writing/ Handbook/Proofreading.html

The University of Wisconsin Writing Center offers tips on proofreading.

anything that's under five pages, less formal notes will probably work. You may want to jot down ideas that you can use as the basis for a draft. For an oral presentation, a meeting, or a document with lots of visuals, try creating a **story-board,** with a rectangle representing each page or unit. Draw a box with a visual for each main point. Below the box, write a short caption or label.

Letters and memos will go faster if you choose a basic organizational pattern before you start. Modules 10, 11, and 12 give detailed patterns of organization for the most common kinds of letters and memos. You may want to customize those patterns with a **planning guide**[6] to help you keep the "big picture" in mind as you write. Figure 4.3 shows planning guides developed for specific kinds of documents.

What is revision? How do I do it?

Revision means "re-seeing" the document.

Good writers make their drafts better by judicious revising, editing, and proofreading.

- **Revising** means making changes that will better satisfy your purposes and your audience.
- **Editing** means making surface-level changes that make the document grammatically correct.

- **Proofreading** means checking to be sure the document is free from typographical errors.

When you're writing to a new audience or have to solve a particularly difficult problem, plan to revise the draft at least three times. The first time, look for content and clarity. The second time, check the organization and layout. Finally, check style and tone, using the information in Modules 15 and 16. Figure 4.4 summarizes the questions you should ask.

Often you'll get the best revision by setting aside your draft, getting a blank page or screen, and redrafting. This strategy takes advantage of the thinking you did on your first draft without locking you into the sentences in it.

As you revise, be sure to read the document through from start to finish. This is particularly important if you've composed in several sittings or if you've used text from other documents. Researchers have found that such documents tend to be well organized but don't flow well.[7] You may need to add transitions, cut repetitive parts, or change words to create a uniform level of formality throughout the document.

If you're really in a time bind, do a light revision (see Figure 4.5). The quality of the final document may not be as high as with a thorough revision, but even a light revision is better than skipping revision.

Figure 4.4
Thorough Revision Checklist

Checklist for
Thorough Revision

Content and Clarity

☐ Does your document meet the needs of the organization and of the reader—and make you look good?

☐ Have you given readers all the information they need to understand and act on your message?

☐ Is all the information accurate?

☐ Is each sentence clear? Is the message free from apparently contradictory statements?

☐ Are generalizations and benefits backed up with adequate supporting detail?

Organization and Layout

☐ Is the pattern of organization appropriate for your purposes, audience, and situation?

☐ Are transitions between ideas smooth? Do ideas within paragraphs flow smoothly?

☐ Does the design of the document make it easy for readers to find the information they need? Is the document visually inviting?

☐ Are the points emphasized by layout ones that deserve emphasis?

☐ Are the first and last paragraphs effective?

Style and Tone

☐ Is the message easy to read?

☐ Is the message friendly and free from biased language?

☐ Does the message build goodwill?

Figure 4.5
Light Revision Checklist

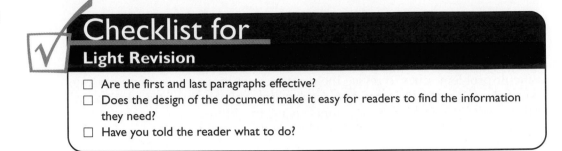

Checklist for
Light Revision

☐ Are the first and last paragraphs effective?
☐ Does the design of the document make it easy for readers to find the information they need?
☐ Have you told the reader what to do?

Instant **Replay**

Revising, Editing, and Proofreading

Revising means making changes that will better satisfy your purposes and your audience.

Editing means making surface-level changes that make the document grammatically correct.

Proofreading means checking to be sure the document is free from typographical errors.

Can a grammar checker do my editing for me?

No. You have to decide whether to make each change.

Grammar checkers are good at finding missing halves. For example, if you open a parenthesis and never close it, a grammar checker will note that a second one is needed. Of course, you have to decide where it goes. In terms of other errors, all a grammar checker can do is to ask you about what you have done. A grammar checker can tell you that you've used a passive verb, and ask if you want to change it. But you have to decide whether the passive is justified. If it finds the word *well*, the grammar checker can tell you that *good* and *well* are sometimes confused. But you have to decide which word fits your meaning (◁ ▶ Module 15). You still need to know the rules so that you can decide which changes to make.

Check to be sure that the following are accurate:

- Sentence structure
- Subject-verb and noun-pronoun agreement
- Punctuation
- Word usage
- Spelling—including spelling of names
- Numbers.

You need to know the rules of grammar and punctuation to edit. Module 14 reviews grammar and punctuation. Module 15 reviews words that are often confused. Most writers make a small number of errors over and over. If you know that you have trouble with dangling modifiers or subject-verb agreement, for example, specifically look for them in your draft. Also look for any errors that especially bother your boss and correct them.

Editing should always *follow* revision. There's no point in taking time to fix a grammatical error in a sentence that may be cut when you clarify your meaning or tighten your style. Some writers edit more accurately when they print out a copy of a document and edit the hard copy. But beware: Laser printing makes a page look good but does nothing to correct errors.

I spell check. Do I still need to proofread?

Yes.

Proofread every document both with a spell checker and by eye to catch the errors a spell checker can't find.

Proofreading is hard because writers tend to see what they know should be there rather than what really is there. Since it's always easier to proof something you haven't written, you may want to swap papers with a proofing buddy. (Be sure the person looks for typos, not for content.)

To proofread,

- Read once quickly for meaning to see that nothing has been left out.
- Read a second time, slowly. When you find an error, correct it and then *reread that line.* Readers tend to become less attentive after they find one error and may miss other errors close to the one they've spotted.
- To proofread a document you know well, read the lines backward or the pages out of order.

Always triple-check numbers, headings, the first and last paragraphs, and the reader's name.

How can I get better feedback?

Ask for the kind of feedback you need.

The process of drafting, getting feedback, revising, and getting more feedback is called **cycling.** Dianna Booher reports that documents in her clients' firms cycled an average of 4.2 times before reaching the intended audience.[8] Susan Kleimann studied a 10-page document whose 20 drafts made a total of 31 stops on the desks of nine reviewers on four different levels.[9] Being asked to revise a document is a fact of life in businesses, government agencies, and nonprofit organizations.

To improve the quality of the feedback you get, tell people which aspects you'd especially like comments about. For example, when you give a reader the outline or planning draft,[10] you might want to know whether the general approach is appropriate. After your second draft, you might want to know whether reader benefits are well developed. When you reach the polishing draft, you'll be ready for feedback on style and grammar. Figure 4.6 lists questions to ask.

It's easy to feel defensive when someone criticizes your work. If the feedback stings, put it aside until you can read it without feeling defensive. Even if you think that the reader has misunderstood what you were trying to say, the fact that the reader complained means the section could be improved. If the reader says "This isn't true" and you know that the statement is true, several kinds of revision might make the truth clear to the reader: rephrasing the statement, giving more information or examples, or documenting the source.

Revising after Feedback

When you get feedback that you understand and agree with, make the change.

If you get feedback you don't understand, ask for clarification.

- Paraphrase: "So you're asking me to give more information?"
- Ask for more information: "Can you suggest a way to do that?"
- Test your inference: "Would it help if I did such and such?"

Sometimes you may get feedback you don't agree with.

- If it's an issue of grammatical correctness, check this book. (Sometimes even smart people get things wrong.)
- If it's a matter of content, recognize that *something* about the draft isn't as good as it could be: something is leading the reader to respond negatively.

- If the reader thinks a fact is wrong (and you know it's right), show where the fact came from. "According to . . . ."
- If the reader suggests a change in wording you don't like, try another option.
- If the reader seems to have misunderstood or misread, think about ways to make the meaning clearer.

Your supervisor's comments on a draft can help you improve that document, help you write better drafts the next time, and teach you about the culture of your organization. Look for patterns in the feedback you receive. Are you asked to use more formal language, or to make the document more conversational? Does your boss want to see an overview before details? Does your company prefer information presented in bulleted lists rather than in paragraphs?

Figure 4.6
Questions to Ask Readers

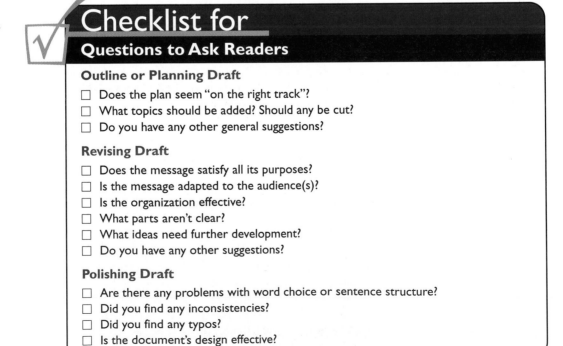

Checklist for
Questions to Ask Readers

Outline or Planning Draft
- [ ] Does the plan seem "on the right track"?
- [ ] What topics should be added? Should any be cut?
- [ ] Do you have any other general suggestions?

Revising Draft
- [ ] Does the message satisfy all its purposes?
- [ ] Is the message adapted to the audience(s)?
- [ ] Is the organization effective?
- [ ] What parts aren't clear?
- [ ] What ideas need further development?
- [ ] Do you have any other suggestions?

Polishing Draft
- [ ] Are there any problems with word choice or sentence structure?
- [ ] Did you find any inconsistencies?
- [ ] Did you find any typos?
- [ ] Is the document's design effective?

Can I use form letters?

Yes. But make sure they're good.

A **form letter** is a prewritten fill-in-the blank letter designed for routine situations. Some form letters have different paragraphs that can be inserted, depending on the situation. For example, a form letter admitting students to college might have additional paragraphs to be added for students who were going to receive financial aid.

Boilerplate is language—sentences, paragraphs, even pages—from a previous document that a writer includes in a new document. In academic papers, material written by others must be quoted and documented. However, because businesses own the documents their employees write, old text may be included without attribution.

In some cases, boilerplate may have been written years ago. For example, many legal documents, including apartment leases and sales contracts, are almost completely boilerplated. In other cases, writers may use boilerplate they themselves have written. For example, a section from a proposal describing the background of the problem could also be used in the final report after the proposed work was completed. A section from a progress report describing what the writer had done could be used with only a few changes in the Methods section of the final report.

Writers use form letters and boilerplate to save time and energy and to use language that has already been approved by the organization's legal staff. However, as Glenn Broadhead and Richard Freed point out, reusing old text creates two problems.[11]

- Using unrevised boilerplate can create a document with incompatible styles and tones.
- Form letters and boilerplate can encourage writers to see situations and audiences as identical when in fact they differ.

Before you use a form letter, make sure that it is well written and that it applies to the situation in which you are thinking of using it.

Before you incorporate old language in a new document,

- Check to see that the old section is well written.
- Consciously look for differences between the two situations, audiences, or purposes that may require different content, organization, or wording.
- Read through the whole document at a single sitting to be sure that style, tone, and level of detail are consistent in the old and new sections.

How can I overcome writer's block and procrastination?

Talk, participate, and practice. Reward yourself for activities that lead to writing.

According to psychologist Robert Boice, a combination of five actions works best to overcome writer's block:[12]

Instant Replay

How to Revise
When you're writing to a new audience or have to solve a particularly difficult problem, plan to revise the draft at least three times. The first time, look for content and clarity. The second time, check the organization and layout. Finally, check style and tone. Do all this **before** you edit and proofread.

- **Participate actively in the organization and the community.** The more you talk to people, the more you interact with some of your audiences, the more you learn about the company, its culture, and its context, the easier it will be to write—and the better your writing will be.
- **Practice writing regularly and in moderation.**
- **Learn as many strategies as you can.** Good writers have a "bag of tricks" to draw on; they don't have to "reinvent the wheel" in each new situation. This book suggests many strategies and patterns. Try them; memorize them; make them your own.
- **Talk positively to yourself:** "I can do this." "If I keep working, ideas will come." "It doesn't have to be wonderful; I can always make it better later."
- **Talk about writing to other people.** Value the feedback you get from your boss. Talk to your boss about writing. Ask him or her to share particularly good examples—from anyone in the organization. Find colleagues at your own level and talk about the writing you do. Do different bosses value different qualities? What aspects of your own boss's preferences are individual and which are part of the discourse community of the organization? Talking to other people expands your repertoire of strategies and helps you understand the discourse community in which you write.

To avoid procrastination, modify your behavior by rewarding yourself for activities that *lead* to writing:

- **Set a regular time to write.** Sit down and stay there for the time you've planned, even if you write nothing usable.
- **Develop a ritual for writing.** Choose tools—paper, pen, computer, chair—that you find comfortable. Use the same tools in the same place every time you write.
- **Try freewriting.** Write for 10 minutes without stopping.
- **Write down the thoughts and fears you have as you write.** If the ideas are negative, try to substitute more positive statements: "I can do this." "I'll keep going and postpone judging." "If I keep working, I'll produce something that's OK."
- **Identify the problem that keeps you from writing.** Deal with that problem; then turn back to writing.
- **Set modest goals** (a paragraph, not the whole document) **and reward yourself for reaching them.**

Summary of Key Points

- Planning, writing, and revising can include analyzing, gathering, writing, evaluating, getting feedback, revising, editing, and proofreading. **Revising** means changing the document to make it better satisfy the writer's purposes and the audience. **Editing** means making surface-level changes that make the document grammatically correct. **Proofreading** means checking to be sure the document is free from typographical errors.

- Processes that help writers write well include expecting to revise the first draft, writing regularly, modifying the initial task if it's too hard or too easy, having clear goals, knowing many different strategies, using rules as guidelines rather than as absolutes, and waiting to edit until after the draft is complete.

- To think of ideas, try brainstorming, **freewriting** (writing without stopping for 10 minutes or so), and **clustering** (brainstorming with circled words on a page).

- You can improve the quality of the feedback you get by telling people which aspects of a draft you'd like comments about. If a reader criticizes something, fix the problem. If you think the reader misunderstood you, try to figure out what caused the misunderstanding and revise the draft so that the reader can see what you meant.

- If the writing situation is new or difficult, plan to revise the draft at least three times.

The first time, look for content and clarity. The second time, check the organization and layout. Finally, check style and tone.

- **Boilerplate** is language from a previous document that a writer includes in a new document. Using form letters and boilerplate can encourage writers to see as identical situations and audiences that in fact differ. Putting boilerplate into a new document can create incompatible styles and tones.

- To overcome writer's block,
  1. Participate actively in the organization and the community.
  2. Follow a regimen. Practice writing regularly and in moderation.
  3. Learn as many strategies as you can.
  4. Talk positively to yourself.
  5. Talk about writing to other people.

- To overcome the tendency to procrastinate, modify your behavior to reward yourself for the activities that lead to writing.

Assignments for Module 4

Questions for Comprehension

4.1 What processes do expert writers use?

4.2 How is revision different from editing? From proofreading?

4.3 What three aspects of a document does thorough revision cover?

Questions for Critical Thinking

4.4 Which processes that expert writers use do you already use? How could you modify your process to incorporate at least one more on the list?

4.5 Of the people who have seen your writing, which one(s) have given you the most useful feedback? What makes it useful?

4.6 In which areas are you best at giving feedback to other people? How could you make your feedback even better?

4.7 Think about the form letters you have received. How do they make you feel? If they have flaws, how could they be improved?

Exercises and Problems

4.8 Giving and Evaluating Feedback

In a group with other students, use the Checklist for Thorough Revision to provide feedback on drafts of letters or memos for this course.

As you give feedback, answer the following questions:

• When you give feedback, do you normally start by looking for places to add, delete, substitute, or change? Or do you normally start by looking for grammatical errors and typos?

• On which aspects is it easiest for you to comment? Which aspects require more thought? Why?

• How many times do you have to read the draft to answer all of the questions in the Checklist?

• Do you tend to suggest mostly big changes, mostly small ones, or a mix?

• How do you tend to word your comments? Are they mostly positive or mostly negative? Do you tend to describe your reaction as a reader, identify why a change is needed, name the change needed, make the change for the writer, or what?

When you read feedback from others, answer the following questions:

• Which comments were new information to you? Which told you something about your draft that you already knew or suspected?

• Did you have any questions that comments did not address?

• What kinds of feedback were most helpful to you? Why?

• Were any comments unclear? Talk to the commenter, and try to figure out what wording would have been clearer to you.

• Did any comments annoy or offend you? Why? Could the commenter have made the same point in a better way?

As Your Instructor Directs,
a. Share your answers with other students in your group. Discuss ways that each of you can make your future feedback even more useful.
b. Organize your answers in a memo to your instructor.

4.9 Interviewing Writers about Their Composing Processes

Interview someone about the composing process(es) he or she uses for on-the-job writing. Questions you could ask include the following:

• What kind of planning do you do before you write? Do you make lists? Formal or informal outlines?

• When you need more information, where do you get it?

• How do you compose your drafts? Do you dictate? Draft with pen and paper? Compose on screen? How do you find uninterrupted time to compose?

• When you want advice about style, grammar, and spelling, what source(s) do you consult?

• Does your superior ever read your drafts and make suggestions?

• Do you ever work with other writers to produce a single document? Describe the process you use.

• Describe the process of creating a document where you felt the final document reflected your best work.

• Describe the process of creating a document which you found difficult or frustrating. What sorts of things make writing easier or harder for you?

As Your Instructor Directs,
a. Share your results orally with a small group of students.

b. Present your results in an oral presentation to the class.

c. Present your results in a memo to your instructor.

d. Post an e-mail message to the class discussing your results.

e. Share your results with a small group of students and write a joint memo reporting the similarities and differences you found.

4.10 Analyzing Your Own Writing Processes

Save your notes and drafts from several assignments so that you can answer the following questions.

- Which of the activities discussed in Module 4 do you use?
- How much time do you spend on each activity?
- What kinds of revisions do you make most often?
- Do you use different processes for different documents, or do you have one process that you use most of the time?
- Which practices of good writers do you follow?
- What parts of your process seem most successful? Are there any places in the process that could be improved? How?

- What relation do you see between the process(es) you use and the quality of the final document?

As Your Instructor Directs,

a. Discuss your process with a small group of other students.

b. Write a memo to your instructor analyzing in detail your process for composing one of the papers for this class.

c. Write a memo to your instructor analyzing your process during the term. What parts of your process(es) have stayed the same throughout the term? What parts have changed?

4.11 Checking Spell and Grammar Checkers

Each of the following paragraphs contains errors in grammar, spelling, and punctuation. Which errors does your spelling or grammar checker catch? Which errors does it miss? Does it flag as errors any words that are correct?

1. Answer to an Inquiry
   Enclosed are the tow copies you requested of our pamphlet, "Using the Internet to market Your products. The pamphelt walks you through the steps of planning the Home Page (The first page of the web cite, shows examples of other Web pages we have designed, and provide a questionnaire that you can use to analyze audience the audience and purposes.

2. Performance Appraisal
   Most staff accountants complete three audits a month. Ellen has completed 21

audits in this past six months she is our most productive staff accountant. Her technical skills our very good however some clients feel that she could be more tactful in suggesting ways that the clients accounting practices could be improved.

3. Brochure
   Are you finding that being your own boss crates it's own problems? Take the hassle out of working at home with a VoiceMail Answering System. Its almost as good as having your own secratery.

4. Presentation Slides
   How to Create a Web résumé Bold
   - Omit home adress and phone number
   - Use other links only if they help an employer evalaute you.
   - ☐ Be Professional.

☐ Carefully craft and proof read the phrase on the index apage.

How to Create a Scannable Résumé
- **Create a 'plain vanilla" document.**

- Use include a "Keywords" section. Include personality trait sas well as accomplishments.
- Be specific and quantifyable.

Polishing Your Prose

Using Spell and Grammar Checkers

Most word-processing programs come with spell and grammar checkers. While these computer tools can be useful, remember that they have limitations.

Spell checkers identify words that don't match their dictionary. If the word is a real word, the spell checker can't tell if it's the right word for the context (e.g., "their" versus "there," as in "We will review the report when we get their.")

Grammar checkers only suggest possible errors and solutions; you must make the final decision. That is, a grammar checker may tell you that you've used passive voice, but the checker can't tell you whether the passive is appropriate in that particular sentence.

Therefore, use spell and grammar checkers as one of several tools to make your writing better. In addition, keep a dictionary, thesaurus, and stylebook handy. Work to improve your command of spelling and grammar; take a class or work with a college writing center for help.

Exercises

Type the following into your word processor. Are all the words or constructions that show up as errors really wrong? Are there any errors that don't show up?

1. The project will have been completed by next Thursday?

2. I cant wait until Mondays meeting.

3. The solution was created in the '90s using a new chemical process.

4. For people called the office today to let's know what is going on. .

5. I call your office because were needed in in the mailroom.

6. Our office in Austin reports they need more stationary.

7. Tom is looking in to buying more property but it won't happen really soon.

8. Theres little reason for they're concern about the contract.

9. This computers spellchecker did a pretty good job.

10. Cheri should bring her calculator and Ill bring the accounting figures.

Check your answers to the odd-numbered exercises at the back of the book.

BComm Skill Booster

To apply the concepts in this module, complete lessons 10 and 11 on brainstorming and revising, editing, and proofreading. You can access the BComm Skill Booster through the text Web site at **www.mhhe.com/bcs2e.**

Module 5

Designing Documents, Slides, and Screens

Start by asking these questions:

- How should I design paper pages?
- How should I design presentation slides?
- How should I design Web pages?
- How do I know whether my design works?
- When should I think about design?

Good document design saves time and money, reduces legal problems, and builds goodwill. A well-designed document looks inviting, friendly, and easy to read. Effective design also groups ideas visually, making the structure of the document more obvious so the document **is** easier to read. Research shows that easy-to-read documents also enhance your credibility and build an image of you as a professional, competent person.[1]

Guidelines for creating effective paper documents are well supported with research and practice. Much less research has been done on effective slides and screens. Moreover, as the population in general becomes more experienced in seeing presentation slides and using the Web, what works may change. Pay attention to the documents, slides and screens you see and to the responses they get from other people in your organization so that you can keep up with evolving standards.

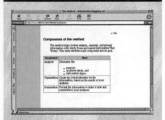
How should I design paper pages?

Follow these five guidelines.

Use the following guidelines to create visually attractive documents.

- Use white space to separate and emphasize points.
- Use headings to group points.
- Limit the use of words set in all capital letters.
- Use no more than two fonts in a single document.
- Decide whether to justify margins based on the situation and the audience.

Use White Space.

White space—the empty space on the page—makes material easier to read by emphasizing the material that it separates from the rest of the text. To create white space,

- Use headings.
- Use a mix of paragraph lengths (most no longer than seven typed lines).
- Use lists.
  - Use tabs or indents—not spacing—to align items vertically.
  - Use numbered lists when the number or sequence of items is exact.
  - Use bullets (large dots or squares like those in this list) when the number and sequence don't matter.

When you use a list, make sure that all of the items in it are parallel and fit into the structure of the sentence that introduces the list.

Faulty: The following suggestions can help employers avoid bias in job interviews:

1. Base questions on the job description.
2. Questioning techniques.
3. Selection and training of interviewers.

Parallel: The following suggestions can help employers avoid bias in job interviews:

1. Base questions on the job description.
2. Ask the same questions of all applicants.
3. Select and train interviewers carefully.

Also parallel: Employers can avoid bias in job interviews by

1. Basing questions on the job description.
2. Asking the same questions of all applicants.
3. Selecting and training interviewers carefully.

Figure 5.1 shows an original typed document. In Figure 5.2, the same document is improved by using shorter paragraphs, lists, and headings. These devices take space. When saving space is essential, it's better to cut the text and keep white space and headings.

Figure 5.1
A Document with Poor Visual Impact

Full capital letters make title hard to read.

MONEY DEDUCTED FROM YOUR WAGES TO PAY CREDITORS

Long para-graph is visually uninviting.

When you buy goods on credit, the store will sometimes ask you to sign a Wage Assignment form allowing it to deduct money from your wages if you do not pay your bill. When you buy on credit, you sign a contract agreeing to pay a certain amount each week or month until you have paid all you owe. The Wage Assignment Form is separate. It must contain the name of your present employer, your social security number, the amount of money loaned, the rate of interest, the date when payments are due, and your signature. The words "Wage Assignment" must be printed at the top of the form and also near the line for your signature. Even if you have signed a Wage Assignment agreement, Roysner will not withhold part of your wages unless all of the following conditions are met: 1. You have to be more than forty days late in payment of what you owe; 2. Roysner has to receive a correct statement of the amount you are in default and a copy of the Wage Assignment form; and 3. You and Roysner must receive a notice from the creditor at least twenty days in advance stating that the creditor plans to make a demand on your wages. This twenty-day notice gives you a chance to correct the problems yourself. If these conditions are all met, Roysner must withhold 15% percent of each paycheck until your bill is paid and give this money to your creditor.

If you think you are not late or that you do not owe the amount stated, you can argue against it by filing a legal document called a "defense." Once you file a defense, Roysner will not withhold any money from you. However, be sure you are right before you file a defense. If you are wrong, you have to pay not only what you owe but also all legal costs for both yourself and the creditor. If you are right, the creditor has to pay all these costs.

Important information is hard to find.

Use Headings.

Headings are words or short phrases that group points and divide your letter, memo, or report into sections.

• Make headings specific.
• Make each heading cover all the material until the next heading.
• Keep headings at any one level parallel: all nouns, all complete sentences, or all questions.

In a letter or memo, type main headings even with the left-hand margin in bold. Capitalize the first letters of the first word and of other

Figure 5.2

A Document Revised to Improve Visual Impact

Money Deducted from Your Wages to Pay Creditors

First letter of each main word capitalized— Title split onto two lines

When you buy goods on credit, the store will sometimes ask you to sign a Wage Assignment form allowing it to deduct money from your wages if you do not pay your bill.

Have You Signed a Wage Assignment Form?

Headings divide document into chunks.

When you buy on credit, you sign a contract agreeing to pay a certain amount each week or month until you have paid all you owe. The Wage Assignment Form is separate. It must contain

- The name of your present employer,
- Your social security number,
- The amount of money loaned,
- The rate of interest,
- The date when payments are due, and
- Your signature.

List with bullets where order of items doesn't matter.

The words "Wage Assignment" must be printed at the top of the form and also near the line for your signature.

When Would Money Be Deducted from Your Wages to Pay a Creditor?

Headings must be parallel. Here, all are questions.

Even if you have signed a Wage Assignment agreement, Roysner will not withhold part of your wages unless all of the following conditions are met:

1. You have to be more than 40 days late in payment of what you owe;

2. Roysner has to receive a correct statement of the amount you are in default and a copy of the Wage Assignment form; and

3. You and Roysner must receive a notice from the creditor at least 20 days in advance stating that the creditor plans to make a demand on your wages. This 20-day notice gives you a chance to correct the problem yourself.

White space between items emphasizes them.

Number list where number, order of items matter.

If these conditions are all met, Roysner must withhold fifteen percent (15%) of each paycheck until your bill is paid and give this money to your creditor.

What Should You Do if You Think the Wage Assignment Is Incorrect?

If you think you are not late or that you do not owe the amount stated, you can argue against it by filing a legal document called a "defense." Once you file a defense, Roysner will not withhold any money from you. However, be sure you are right before you file a defense. If you are wrong, you have to pay not only what you owe but also all legal costs for both yourself and the creditor. If you are right, the creditor has to pay all these costs.

Full capitals hide the shape of a word and slow reading 19%.

FULL CAPITALS HIDE THE SHAPE OF A WORD AND SLOW READING 19%.

Figure 5.3
Full Capitals Hide the Shape of a Word

major words; use lowercase for all other letters. (See Figure 5.2 for an example.) In single-spaced text, triple–space between the previous text and the heading; double–space between the heading and the text that follows.

Limit the Use of Words Set in All Capital Letters.

We recognize words by their shapes.[2] (See Figure 5.3.) In capitals, all words are rectangular; letters lose the descenders and ascenders that make reading go more quickly. Use full capitals sparingly. Instead, make text bold to emphasize it.

Use No More than Two Fonts in a Single Document.

Each font comes in several sizes and usually in several styles (bold, italic, etc.). Typewriter fonts are **fixed;** that is, every letter takes the same space. An *i* takes the same space as a *w*. Courier and Prestige Elite are fixed fonts. Computers usually offer **proportional** fonts as well, where wider letters take more space than narrower letters. Times Roman, Palatino, Helvetica, Geneva, and Arial are proportional fonts.

   Serif fonts have little extensions, called serifs, from the main strokes. (In Figure 5.4, look at the feet on the *t* in Times Roman and the little flicks on the ends of the top bar of the *t*.) Courier, Times Roman, Palatino, and Lucinda Calligraphy are serif fonts. Serif fonts are easier to read since the serifs help the eyes move from letter to letter. Helvetica, Geneva, and Arial are **sans serif** fonts since they lack serifs (*sans* is French for *without*). Sans serif fonts are good for titles, tables, and narrow columns.

   Most business documents use just one font—usually Times Roman, Palatino, Helvetica, or Arial in 11- or 12-point. In a complex document, use bigger type for main headings and slightly smaller type for subheadings and

This sentence is set in 12-point Times Roman.

This sentence is set in 12-point Arial.

This sentence is set in 12-point New Courier.

This sentence is set in 12-point Lucinda Calligraphy.

This sentence is set in 12-point Broadway.

This sentence is set in 12-point Technical.

Figure 5.4
Examples of Different Fonts

The visual design of a message can support or undercut the impact of the words.

Instant Replay

Guidelines for Page Design

• Use white space to separate and emphasize points.
• Use headings to group points.
• Limit the use of words set in all capital letters.
• Use no more than two fonts in a single document.
• Decide whether to justify margins based on the situation and the audience.

text. If you combine two fonts in one document, choose one serif and one sans serif typeface.

Decide Whether to Justify Margins Based on the Situation and the Audience.

Computers allow you to use **full justification,** so that type on both sides of the page is evenly lined up. This paragraph justifies margins. Margins that are justified only on the left are sometimes called **ragged right margins.** Lines end in different places because words are of different lengths. The FYI and Instant Replay boxes use ragged right margins.

Use justified margins when you

• Can use proportional typefaces.
• Want a more formal look.
• Want to use as few pages as possible.
• Write to skilled readers.[3]

Use ragged right margins when you

• Do not have proportional typefaces.
• Want a less formal look.
• Want to be able to revise an individual page without reprinting the whole document.
• Use very short line lengths.

How should I design presentation slides?

Keep slides simple, relevant, and interesting.

As you design slides for PowerPoint and other presentation programs, keep these guidelines in mind.

• Use a big font: 44- or 50-point for titles, 32-point for subheads, and 28-point for examples.
• Use bullet-point phrases rather than complete sentences.

Using Computers to Create Good Design

Standard word-processing programs such as WordPerfect and Word let you control how your page looks. Different versions of each program handle these commands differently. Look up the bolded terms below in a manual, a book about the program, or the online Help menu of your computer program to find out how to use each feature.

Letters and Memos

Choose a businesslike font in 11- or 12-point type. Times Roman, Palatino, Helvetica, and Arial are the most commonly used business fonts.

Use **bold** headings. Avoid having a heading all by itself at the bottom of the page. If you can't have at least one line of text under it, move the heading to the next page. You can check this by eye or set your program to avoid **widows** and **orphans.**

Use **tabs** or **indents** to line up the return address and signature blocks in modified block format (◄ ► Module 9), the To/From/Subject line section of a memo, or the items in a list.

Change your **tab settings** to create good visual impact. A setting at .6" works well for the To/From/Subject line section of memos. Use .4" for paragraphs and .6" for the start of bulleted lists. For lists with 10 or more items, the setting will need to be a bit further to the right—about .65".

Choose the design for **bullets** under Insert or Format. Both WordPerfect and Word will create bulleted or numbered lists automatically. If you have lists with paragraphs, turn off the automatic bullets and create them with the bullets in Symbols. Use **indent** (not tab) to move the whole list in, not just a single line of it.

Use a **header** (in the Insert or View menu) with automatic **page numbering** (pull down Format to Page) for second and subsequent pages. That way, when you delete a paragraph or expand your reader benefits, you don't have to manually move the header. You can either **delay** the header till page 2 or create it on page 2. For best visual impact, make your header one point size smaller than the body type.

For a two-page document, change the top **margin** of the second page to .5" so the header is close to the top of the page.

Use the same side margins as your letterhead. If you aren't using letterhead, use 1" side margins.

On a two-page document, make sure the second page has at least 4 to 6 lines of text for letters and at least 10 lines of text for memos. If you have less, either (1) add details, (2) start the message further down on page one so that there is more text on page two or (3) make the text fit on just one page by (a) tightening your prose, (b) using full justification to save space, or (c) using less white space.

Word processing programs have a **quickcorrect** or **autocorrect** feature that changes *hte* to *the, (c)* to ©, and so forth. Go into the Tools or Format menus to find these features and edit them so they make only the changes you want.

Hyphenation may be under Format or under Language in Tools.

Printing

To save paper, check **print preview** on the File menu. You'll be able to see how your document will look on the page and make minor layout changes before you print.

If you prepare your document on one computer and print it from another, be sure to open the document and check all of it before you print. Different printers may change margins slightly. Even the same size font may differ from printer to printer, so that a document that fit nicely on one page in 11-point on one computer may suddenly take up more room on a different one.

- Use clear, concise language.
- Make only three to five points on each slide. If you have more, consider using two slides.
- Customize your slides with the company logo, charts, and scanned-in photos and drawings.

Use clip art only if the art is really appropriate to your points and only if you are able to find nonsexist and nonracist images. (At the end of the 1990s,

Figure 5.5

Effective and Ineffective Colors for Presentation Slides

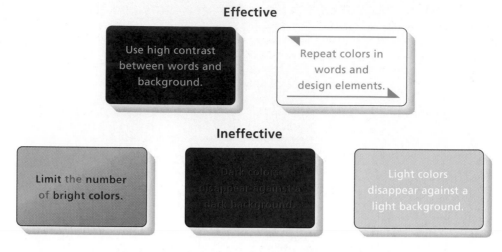

as Marilyn Dyrud has shown, the clip art in major software programs was biased.[4])

Choose a consistent template, or background design, for the entire presentation. Make sure that the template is appropriate for your subject matter. For example, use a globe only if your topic is international business and palm trees only if you're talking about tropical vacations. One problem with PowerPoint is that the basic templates may seem repetitive to people who see lots of presentations made with the program. For a very important presentation, you may want to consider customizing the basic template.

Choose a light background if the lights will be off during the presentation and a dark background if the lights will be on. Slides will be easier to read if you use high contrast between the words and background. See Figure 5.5 for examples of effective and ineffective color combinations.

How should I design Web pages?

Pay attention to content, navigation, and the first screen.

Good Web pages have both good content and an interesting design. You should be able to evaluate the design of a Web page even if you never create one from scratch.

The opening screen is crucial. Jakob Nielsen claims that only 10% of users scroll beyond the first screen.[5] To make it more likely that visitors to your page will scroll down, on the first screen

- Provide an introductory statement orienting the surfing reader to the organization.
- Offer an overview of the content of your page, with links to take readers to the parts that interest them.
- Put information that will be most interesting and useful to most readers.

The rest of the page can contain information that only a limited number of readers will want. When a document reaches four pages or more, think about dividing it into several documents. Specialized information can go on another page, which readers can click on if they want it.

Make it clear what readers will get if they click on a link.

Ineffective phrasing: Employment. <u>Openings and skills levels are determined by each office.</u>

Better phrasing: Employment. Openings listed by <u>skills level</u> and by <u>location.</u>

Minimize the number of links readers have to click through to get to the information they want.

As you design pages,

- Use small graphics; keep animation to a minimum. Both graphics and animation take time to load, especially with a slow modem.
- Provide visual variety. Use indentations, bulleted or numbered lists, and headings.
- Unify multiple pages with a small banner, graphic, or label so surfers know who sponsors each page.
- On each page, provide a link to the home page, the name and e-mail address of the person who maintains the page, and the date when the page was last revised.

Site *to* See

Go to
www.useit.com

Jakob Nielsen's Web site on Web page design is one of the most useful pages on the Web. Nielsen provides classic past columns (such as the Top Ten Mistakes of Web Design) as well as current content.

How do I know whether my design works?

Test it.

A design that looks pretty may or may not work for the audience. To know whether your design is functional, test it with your audience.

- Watch someone as he or she uses the document to do a task. Where does the reader pause, reread, or seem confused? How long does it take? Does the document enable the reader to complete the task accurately?
- Ask the reader to "think aloud" while completing the task, interrupt the reader at key points to ask what he or she is thinking, or ask the reader to describe the thought process after completing the document and the task. Learning the reader's thought processes is important, since a reader may get the right answer for the wrong reasons. In such a case, the design still needs work.
- Test the document with the people who are most likely to have trouble with it: very old or young readers, people with little education, people who read English as a second language.

Instant Replay

Designing PowerPoint Slides

- Use a big font.
- Use bullet-point phrases.
- Use clear, concise language.
- Make only three to five points on each slide.
- Customize your slides.

FYI

People in the United States focus first on the left side of a Web site. Web sites in Arabic and Hebrew orient text, links, and graphics from right to left.

Source: Albert N. Badre, "The Effects of Cross Cultural Interface Design Orientation on World Wide Web User Performance," GVU Technical Report GIT-GVU-01-03, August 31, 2000, 8; www.cc.gatech.edu/gvu/reports/2001, visited site July 27, 2002.

When should I think about design?

At each stage of the writing process.

Document design isn't something to "tack on" when you've finished writing. Indeed, the best documents are created when you think about design at each stage of your writing process(es).

- As you plan, think about your audiences. Are they skilled readers? Are they busy? Will they read the document straight through or skip around in it?
- As you write, incorporate lists and headings. Use visuals to convey numerical data clearly and forcefully.
- Get feedback from people who will be using your document. What parts of the document do they think are hard to understand? Is there additional information they need?
- As you revise, check your draft against the guidelines in this module.

Summary of Key Points

- An attractive document looks inviting, friendly, and easy to read. The visual grouping of ideas also makes the structure of the document more obvious so it is easier to read.
- Good document design can save time, money, and legal problems.
- To create visually attractive documents,
  - Use white space.
  - Use headings.
  - Limit the use of words set in all capital letters.
  - Limit the number of fonts in a single document.
  - Decide whether to justify margins based on the situation and the audience.
- As you design slides for PowerPoint and other presentation programs,
  - Use a big font.
  - Use bullet-point phrases.
  - Use clear, concise language.

- Make only three to five points on each slide.
- Customize your slides.
- Good Web pages have both good content and an interesting design.
  - Orient the surfing reader to the organization.
  - Offer an overview of the content of your page, with links to take readers to the parts that interest them.
  - Make it clear what readers will get if they click on a link.
  - Keep graphics small.
  - Provide visual variety.
  - Unify multiple pages with a small banner, graphic, or label.
  - On each page, provide a link to the home page, the name and e-mail address of the person who maintains the page, and the date when the page was last revised.

- To test a document, observe readers, ask them to "think aloud" while completing the task, interrupt them at key points to ask what they are thinking, or ask them to describe the thought process after completing the document and the task.
- The best documents are created when you think about design at each stage of the writing process.

- As you plan, think about the needs of your audience.
- As you write, incorporate lists, headings, and visuals.
- Get feedback from people who will be using your document.
- As you revise, check your draft against the guidelines in this chapter.

Assignments for Module 5

Questions for Comprehension

5.1 How can you create white space?

5.2 How do you decide whether to use bullets or numbers in a list?

5.3 What are three criteria for good Web pages?

Questions for Critical Thinking

5.4 "Closed captions" for people with hearing impairments are almost always typed in full capital letters. Why is that a bad idea? Are there any advantages to using full capitals? What arguments could you use for changing the practice?

5.5 Suppose that, in one company, a worker says, "We don't need to worry about design. People pay a toll charge to call us, and we make a slight profit on each call. So if they have questions about the product, that's OK. If better design reduced the number of calls, we might actually lose money!" How would you persuade such a person that good document design is worth doing?

5.6 Central Community College is preparing a brochure to persuade prospective students to consider taking classes. The college doesn't have the money for full-scale document testing. What free or almost-free things could it do to make the document as effective as possible?

5.7 Design choices may have ethical implications. Indicate whether you consider each of the following actions ethical, unethical, or a gray area. Which of the actions would you do? Which would you feel uncomfortable doing? Which would you refuse to do?

   a. Putting the advantages of a proposal in a bulleted list, while discussing the disadvantages in a paragraph.
   b. Using a bigger type size so that a résumé visually fills a whole page.
   c. Putting the services that are not covered by your health plan in full caps to make it less likely that people will read the page.

Exercises and Problems

5.8　Evaluating Page Designs

Use the guidelines in Module 5 to evaluate each of the following page designs. What are their strong points? What could be improved?

a.

A Special Report: Living Healthy

Sit amet, con sectetur adipicising elit, sed diam nonnumy nibh euismod tempor inci dunt ut labore et dolore

Lorem ipsum dolor sit amet, con sectetuer adipicising elit, sed diam nonnumy nibh euis-mod tempor inci dunt ut labore et dolore magna ali quam erat volupat. Ut wisi enim as minim veniam, quis nostrud exerci tation ullamcorper suscipit laboris nisl ut aliquip ex ea commodo con sequat. Duis autem vel eum irure dolor in henderit in vulputate velit esse consequat. Lorem ipsum dolor sit amet, con sectetuer adipi-cising elit, sed diam nonnumy nibh euismod tempor inci dunt ut labore et dolore magna ali quam erat volupat. Ut wisi enim as minim veniam, quis nostrud exerci tation ullamcor-per suscipit laboris nisl ut aliquip ex ea con sequat. Duis autem vel eum irure dolor in henderit in vulpu-tate velit esse consequat.

Sit amet, con sectetuer adipi-

cising elit, sed diam nonnumy nibh euismod tempor inci dunt ut labore et dolore magna ali quam erat volupat. Ut wisi enim as minim veniam, quis nostrud exerci tation ullamcor-per suscipit laboris nisl ut aliquip ex ea commodo con sequat. Duis autem vel eum irure dolor in henderit in vulpu-tate velit esse consequat.

Dolor sit amet, con sectetuer adipicising elit, sed diam nonnumy nibh euismod tempor inci dunt ut labore et dolore magna ali quam erat volupat.Duis autem vel eum irure dolor in henderit in vulpu-tate velit esse consequat.

Ipsum dolor sit amet, con sectetuer adipicising elit, sed diam nonnumy nibh euis-mod tempor inci dunt ut labore et dolore magna ali quam erat volupat. Ut wisi enim as minim veniam, quis nostrud exerci

tation ullamcorper suscipit laboris nisl ut aliquip ex ea commodo con sequat. Duis autem vel eum irure dolor in henderit in vulpu-tate velit esse consequat. Lorem ipsum dolor sit amet, con sectetuer adipicising elit, sed diam nonnumy nibh euismod tempor inci dunt ut labore et dolore magna ali quam erat volupat. Ut wisi enim as minim

Sit amet, con sectetur adipicising elit, sed diam nonnumy nibh euismod tempor inci dunt ut labore et dolore

---

A Special Report: Living Healthy

Sit amet, con sectetur adipicising elit, sed diam nonnumy nibh euismod tempor inci dunt ut labore et dolore

Lorem ipsum dolor sit amet, con sectetuer adipicising elit, sed diam nonnumy nibh euis-mod tempor inci dunt ut labore et dolore magna ali quam erat volupat. Ut wisi enim as minim veniam, quis nostrud exerci tation ullamcorper suscipit laboris nisl ut aliquip ex ea commodo con sequat. Duis autem vel eum irure dolor in henderit in vulputate velit esse consequat.

Dolor sit amet, con sectetuer adipicising elit, sed diam nonnumy nibh euismod tempor inci dunt ut labore et dolore magna ali quam erat volupat.Duis autem vel eum irure dolor in henderit in vulpu-tate velit esse consequat.

Sit amet, con sectetuer adipi-cising elit, sed diam nonnumy

nibh euismod tempor inci dunt ut labore et dolore magna ali quam erat volupat. Ut wisi enim as minim veniam, quis nostrud exerci tation ullamcor-per suscipit laboris nisl ut aliquip ex ea commodo con sequat. Duis autem vel eum irure dolor in henderit in vulpu-tate velit esse consequat.

Ipsum dolor sit amet, con sectetuer adipicising elit, sed diam nonnumy nibh euismod tempor inci dunt ut labore et dolore magna ali quam erat volupat. Ut wisi enim as minim veniam, quis nostrud exerci tation ullamcorper suscipit

laboris nisl ut aliquip ex ea commodo con sequat. Duis autem vel eum irure dolor in henderit in vulputate velit esse consequat. Lorem ipsum dolor sit amet, con sectetuer adipi-cising elit, sed diam nonnumy nibh euismod tempor inci dunt ut labore et dolore magna ali quam erat volupat. Ut wisi enim as minim veniam, quis nostrud exerci tation ullamcorper suscipit

Sit amet, con sectetur adipicising elit, sed diam nonnumy nibh euismod tempor inci dunt ut labore et dolore

---

A Special Bulletin: Living Healthy

Counting Calories and Watching Cholesterol

Lorem ipsum dolor sit amet, con sectetuer adipicising elit, sed diam nonnumy nibh euismod tempor inci dunt ut labore et dolore magna ali quam erat volupat. Ut wisi enim as minim veniam, quis nostrud exerci tation ullamcorper suscipit laboris nisl ut aliquip ex ea commodo con sequat. Duis autem vel eum irure dolor in henderit in vulputate velit esse consequat. Sit amet, con sectetuer adipicising elit, sed diam non-numy nibh euismod tempor inci dunt ut labore et dolore magna ali quam erat volupat. Ut wisi enim as minim veniam, quis nostrud exerci tation ullamcorper suscipit laboris nisl ut aliquip ex ea com-modo con sequat. Duis autem vel eum irure dolor in henderit in vulputate velit esse consequat.

Dolor sit amet, con sectetuer adipicising elit, sed diam non-numy nibh euismod tempor inci dunt ut labore et dolore magna ali quam erat volu pat Duis autem vel eum irure dolor in henderit in vulputate velit esse

Exercising and Eating Healthy in a Busy Lifestyle

Ipsum dolor sit amet, con sectetuer adipicising elit, sed diam nonnumy nibh euismod tempor inci dunt ut labore et dolore magna ali quam erat volupat. Ut wisi enim as minim veniam, quis nostrud exerci tation ullamcorper suscipit laboris nisl ut aliquip ex ea commodo con sequat. Duis autem vel eum irure dolor in henderit in vulputate velit esse consequat. Lorem ipsum dolor sit amet, con sectetuer adipicising elit, sed diam nonnumy nibh euismod tempor inci dunt ut labore et dolore magna ali quam erat volupat. Ut wisi

Company Briefs

nim as minim veniam, quis nostrud exerci tation ullamcorper suscipit laboris nisl ut aliquip ex ea commodo con sequat. Duis autem vel eum irure dolor in henderit in vulputate velit esse con-sequat.

Lorem ipsum doler sit amet, con sectetuer adipi-cising elit, sed diam nonnumy nibh euismod ...tempor inci dunt ut labore et dolore magna ali

Managing Your Sleep

quam erat volupat. Ut wisi enim as minim veniam, quis nostrud exerci tation ullamcor-per suscipit laboris nisl ut aliquip ex ea commodo con sequat. Duis autem vel eum irure dolor in vulputate velit esse consequat. Lorem ipsum dolor sit amet, con sectetuer adipicising elit, sed diam nonnumy nibh euismod tempor inci dunt ut labore et dolore magna ali quam erat volupat. Ut wisi enim as minim veniam, quis nostrud exerci tation ullamcorper suscipit laboris nisl ut aliquip ex ea commodo con sequat. Duis au-tem vel eum irure dolor in henderit in vulpu-tate velit esse consequat.

Sit amet, con sectetuer adipi-cising elit, sed diam nonnumy nibh euismod tempor inci dunt ut labore et dolore magna ali quam erat volupat. Ut wisi enim as minim veniam, quis nostrud exerci tation ullamcor-

finis

A Special Bulletin: Living Healthy

Counting Calories and Watching Cholesterol

Lorem ipsum dolor sit amet, con sectetuer adipicising elit, sed diam nonnumy nibh euismod tempor inci dunt ut labore et dolore magna ali quam erat volupat. Ut wisi enim as minim veniam, quis nostrud exerci tation ul-lamcorper suscipit laboris nisl ut aliquip ex ea commodo con sequat. Duis autem vel eum irure dolor in henderit in vulputate velit esse consequat. Lorem ipsum dolor sit amet, con sectetuer adipicising elit, sed diam nonnumy nibh

euismod tempor inci dunt ut labore et dolore magna ali quam erat volupat. Ut wisi enim as minim veniam, quis nostrud exerci tation ul-lamcorper suscipit laboris nisl ut aliquip ex ea commodo con sequat. Duis autem vel eum irure dolor in henderit in vulputate velit esse consequat. Lorem ipsum dolor sit amet, con sectetuer adipicising elit, sed diam nonnumy nibh

Exercising and Eating Healthy in a Busy Lifestyle

Lorem ipsum dolor sit amet, con sectetuer adipicising elit, sed diam nonnumy nibh euismod tempor inci dunt ut labore et dolore magna ali quam erat volupat. Ut wisi enim as minim veniam, quis nostrud exerci tation ul-lamcorper suscipit laboris nisl ut aliquip ex ea commodo con sequat. Duis autem vel eum irure dolor in henderit in vulputate velit esse consequat. Lorem ipsum dolor sit amet, con sectetuer adipicising elit, sed diam nonnumy nibh

euismod tempor inci dunt ut labore et dolore magna ali quam erat volupat. Ut wisi enim as minim veniam, quis

The group will visit many lovely spots

Managing Your Sleep

con sectetuer adipicising elit, sed diam nonnumy nibh euismod tempor inci dunt ut labore et dolore magna ali quam erat volupat. Ut wisi enim as minim veniam, quis nostrud exerci tation ul-lamcorper suscipit laboris nisl ut aliquip ex ea commodo con sequat. Duis autem vel eum irure dolor in henderit in vulputate velit esse consequat. Lorem ipsum dolor sit amet, con sectetuer adipicising elit, sed diam nonnumy nibh euismod tempor inci dunt ut labore et dolore magna ali quam erat volupat. Ut wisi enim as minim veniam, quis nostrud exerci tation ul-lamcorper suscipit laboris nisl ut aliquip ex ea commodo con sequat. Duis autem vel eum irure dolor in henderit in vulputate velit esse consequat.

Sit amet, con sectetuer adipi-cising elit, sed diam nonnumy nibh euismod tempor inci dunt ut labore et dolore magna ali quam erat volupat. Ut wisi

b.

☞ RESIST the TEMPTATION to use **all the fonts** available on your ████████. *Too many* fonts **create** *visual clutter* ☹ and **make a document HARD** to read!! **FONTS** that call *attention* to **themselves** are **NOT** *appropriate* for **BUSINESS** *letters,* memos, and reports.✌ *Even* in a **standard font,** avoid **shadows, outlines,** and ***OVERUSE*** OF **bold** and *italics.* ∞

5.9 Evaluating PowerPoint Slides

Evaluate the following drafts of Power-Point slides.

- Is the background appropriate for the topic?
- Do the slides use words or phrases rather than complete sentences?
- Is the font big enough to read from a distance?
- Is the art relevant and appropriate?
- Is each slide free from errors?

a.

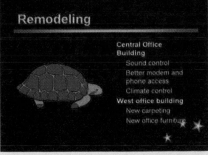
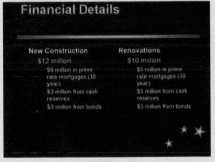

b.

1

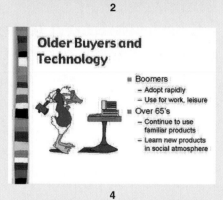

2

3

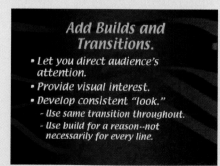

4

c.

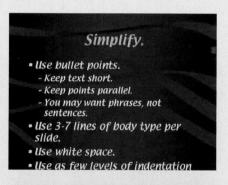

5.10 Using Headings

Reorganize the items in each of the following lists, using appropriate headings. Use bulleted or numbered lists as appropriate.

a. Rules and Procedures for a Tuition Reimbursement Plan
   1. You are eligible to be reimbursed if you have been a full-time employee for at least three months.
   2. You must apply before the first class meeting.
   3. You must earn a "C" or better in the course.
   4. You must submit a copy of the approved application, an official grade report, and a receipt for tuition paid to be reimbursed.
   5. You can be reimbursed for courses related to your current position or another position in the company, or for courses which are part of a degree related to a current or possible job.
   6. Your supervisor must sign the application form.
   7. Courses may be at any appropriate level (high school, college, or graduate school).

b. Activities in Starting a New Business
   - Getting a loan or venture capital
   - Getting any necessary city or state licenses
   - Determining what you will make, do, or sell
   - Identifying the market for your products or services
   - Pricing your products or services
   - Choosing a location
   - Checking zoning laws that may affect the location
   - Identifying government and university programs for small business development
   - Figuring cash flow
   - Ordering equipment and supplies
   - Selling
   - Advertising and marketing

5.11 Analyzing Documents

Collect several documents available to you as a worker, student, or consumer: letters and memos, newsletters, ads and flyers, reports. Use the guidelines in Module 5 to evaluate each of them.

As Your Instructor Directs,
a. Discuss the documents with a small group of classmates.
b. Write a memo to your instructor evaluating three or more of the documents. Include originals or photocopies of the documents you discuss as an appendix to your memo.
c. Write a memo to your supervisor recommending ways the organization can improve its documents.
d. In an oral presentation to the class, explain what makes one document good and another one weak. If possible, use transparencies so that classmates can see the documents as you evaluate them.

5.12 Evaluating Web Pages

Compare three Web pages in the same category (for example, nonprofit organizations, car companies, university departments, sports information). Which page(s) are most effective? Why? What weaknesses do the pages have?

As Your Instructor Directs,
a. Discuss the pages with a small group of classmates.
b. Write a memo to your instructor evaluating the pages. Include URLs of the pages in your memo.

c. In an oral presentation to the class, explain what makes one page good and another one weak. If possible, put the pages on screen so that classmates can see the pages as you evaluate them.

d. Post your evaluation of the pages in an e-mail message to the class. Include hot links to the pages you evaluate.

5.13 Revising a Document

Your state government hires interns for many of its offices. The Director of Human Resources has noticed that few of the interns submit all the needed

paperwork on time and suspects that the problem is the form memo that goes out to interns. You've been asked to revise the memo to make it more effective.

> Subject: Getting Your First Paycheck on Time
>
> So that you can receive your first paycheck on time, please send the following items to the office of Human Resources by the first working day of next month: a copy of your social security card or a copy of your birth certificate; a copy of your driver's license; proof of enrollment in an accredited college (accepted items include a paid fee statement; a letter from the registrar's office; a copy of your college identification card with the term and year on it); and proof of your grade status (e.g., first year, sophomore). Attach one of the following: your latest grade report, your latest transcript; a letter from the registrar's office verifying your grade status; a copy of your college identification card that shows what level you are in. Pay is based on how many quarter or semester hours you have completed. At the end of each term, notify Human Resources. You may be eligible for a pay increase.

Rewrite the message, paying special attention to layout and page design.

5.14 Improving a Financial Aid Form

You've just joined the Financial Aid office at your school. The director gives you the accompanying form and asks you to redesign it.

"We need this form to see whether parents have other students in college besides the one requesting aid. Parents are supposed to list all family members that the parents support—themselves, the person here, any other kids in college, and any younger dependent kids.

"Half of these forms are filled out incorrectly. Most people just list the student going here; they leave out everyone else.

"If something is missing, the computer sends out a letter and a second copy of this form. The whole process starts over. Sometimes we send this form back two or three times before it's right. In the meantime, students' financial aid is

delayed—maybe for months. Sometimes things are so late that they can't register for classes, or they have to pay tuition themselves and get reimbursed later.

"If so many people are filling out the form wrong, the form itself must be the problem. See what you can do with it. But keep it to a page."

As Your Instructor Directs,
a. Analyze the current form and identify its problems.
b. Revise the form. Add necessary information; reorder information; change the chart to make it easier to fill out.

Hints:
• Where are people supposed to send the form? What is the phone number of the financial aid office? Should they need to call the office if the form is clear?

- Does the definition of *half-time* apply to all students or just those taking courses beyond high school?
- Should capital or lowercase letters be used?
- Are the lines big enough to write in?

- What headings or subdivisions within the form would remind people to list all family members whom they support?
- How can you encourage people to return the form promptly?

Please complete the chart below by listing all family members for whom you (the parents) will provide more than half support during the academic year (July 1 through June 30). Include yourselves (the parents), the student, and your dependent children, even if they are not attending college.

EDUCATIONAL INFORMATION, 200_ - 200_						
FULL NAME OF FAMILY MEMBER	AGE	RELATIONSHIP OF FAMILY MEMBER TO STUDENT	NAME OF SCHOOL OR COLLEGE THIS SCHOOL YEAR	FULL-TIME	HALF-TIME* OR MORE	LESS THAN HALF-TIME
STUDENT APPLICANT						

*Half-time is defined as 6 credit hours or 12 clock hours a term.

When the information requested is received by our office, processing of your financial aid application will resume.

Please sign and mail this form to the above address as soon as possible. Your signature certifies that this information and the information on the FAF is true and complete to the best of your knowledge. If you have any questions, please contact a member of the need analysis staff.

_____   _____
Signature of Parent(s)   Date

 ## Polishing Your Prose

Active and Passive Voice

Verbs have "voice": active and passive voice. Business communication generally prefers active voice because it is shorter and clearer.

A verb is active if the grammatical subject acts. Passive voice occurs when the subject is acted upon by someone or something else.

Active: The man bought grapes at the store.

Passive: The grapes were bought by the man at the store.

In the active voice, the subject—the man—is doing the action—bought. In the passive version, *the grapes* is the subject, yet it is the man, not the grapes, that is actually doing the action. It is harder for the reader to follow who or what did the action. In addition, it takes more words to convey the same idea.

To change a passive voice construction into the active voice, start by identifying who or what is doing the action. If no agent ("by ____") is present in the sentence, you will need to supply it. A passive verb is usually accompanied by a helping verb, such as *is*, *are*, or *were*. Rewrite the sentence

Continued

by putting the actor in the role of subject and dropping the helping verb:

Passive: The plan was approved by our clients.

Active: Our clients approved the plan.

Passive: PowerPoint slides have been created.

Active: Susan created the PowerPoint slides.

Passive: It is desired that you back up your work daily.

Active: Back up your work daily.

In business communication, active voice is usually better. However, passive voice is better in three situations:

1. Use passive voice to emphasize the object receiving the action, not the agent.

   Your order was shipped November 15.

   The customer's order, not the shipping clerk, is important.

2. Use passive voice to provide coherence within a paragraph. A sentence is easier to read if "old" information comes at the beginning of a sentence. When you have been discussing a topic, use the word again as your subject even if that requires a passive verb.

   The bank made several risky loans in the late 1990s. These loans were written off as "uncollectible" in 2002.

   Using *loans* as the subject of the second sentence provides a link between the two sentences, making the paragraph as a whole easier to read.

3. Use passive voice to avoid assigning blame.

The order was damaged during shipment.

An active verb would require the writer to specify *who* damaged the order. The passive here is more tactful.

Exercises

Identify whether the passives in the following sentences are acceptable or whether the verb should be changed to active.

1. Two visitors are expected to arrive at headquarters tomorrow.

2. Contracts will need to be signed and delivered by April 30.

3. Outgoing correspondence was collected by the mailroom staff.

4. The audit was approved by the senior partner.

5. The vacation form must be turned in by July 15.

Turn these passive voice constructions into active voice:

6. Ms. Price and Mr. Dobbs were called away for an emergency meeting.

7. In April, budgets were amortized and files created for the project.

8. This experience was gained while interning at Dexter Industries.

9. Packages are to be sent to the mailroom for delivery.

10. Several employee-of-the-month awards were received by Joanne for her outstanding job performance.

Check your answers to the odd-numbered exercises at the end of the book.

BComm Skill Booster

To apply the concepts in this module, complete lessons 12 and 14 on page design and presentation slides. You can access the BComm

Skill Booster through the text Web site at **www.mhhe.com/bcs2e.**

Cases for Communicators

Hello, Gateway?

Proofreading—making sure that your document is free from typographical errors—is the final step in the writing process. While always important, proofreading is perhaps even more critical in our electronic age, as the reuse of digital information, data, and images is becoming a common practice.

The ability to leverage existing materials is a significant advantage of the digital age, but it can also lead to more errors if the original information is inaccurate. How severe can this problem become? Just ask computer giant Gateway Computers, which was recently hit with a $3.6 million jury verdict—the final outcome in a series of events that began with a small typing error.

The problem began when an employee typed 800, rather than 888, as the prefix for the company's toll-free customer service line. This single error, however, was replicated in the company's internal materials, on its Web site, in its Internet billings, and, finally, on a form distributed to more than 100,000 Gateway customers. As a result, the actual owner of the toll-free number incurred substantial costs and disruption in its own business activities, because its telephone lines were overrun with Gateway customers.

More importantly, though the mistake was identified a mere six days after calls began, it took more than two years for Gateway to correct the error in all of its business materials. Consider the number of business hours involved in correcting this one mistake, which could, and likely should, have been fixed in a

thorough proofreading of the original document. Those business costs, combined with the long-term revenue loss from unhappy customers and the $3.6 million, add up to one expensive mistake!

Source: "Wrong Phone Number Costs Gateway," Associated Press, July 19, 2002. Accessed on Yahoo! News on July 21, 2002.

Individual Activity

Imagine that you are a Communications Manager at Gateway, and it is your responsibility to craft a message to those 100,000 customers who received mailings with the incorrect toll-free number. Because the letter will be such an important part of the company's efforts to restore customer confidence, the Vice-President of Communications will be reviewing the message before it is sent out.

In addition to accepting full responsibility for the incorrect toll-free number, the company has decided to take three actions designed to underscore its ongoing commitment to customer service:

1. Hire more telephone representatives in order to shorten the wait time on the customer service and technical support telephone lines.

2. Create a dedicated message board on the company's Web site that will allow customers to communicate their problems and concerns more quickly and easily.

3. Develop and advertise a new marketing effort: "Have your complaint addressed in 24 hours or less, or get a free $50 Gateway gift certificate."

As a first step in creating the letter, you need to carefully analyze this business communication problem. Use PAIBOC to make sure that you understand the purpose, audience, and situation.

Ask yourself the following questions:

P: What is the purpose of this letter? (Remember, there may be more than one!)

A: Who are the initial, primary, gate-keeper, secondary, and watchdog audiences for my letter?

I: What information should this letter include?

B: What reader benefits can I highlight?

O: What objections should I expect? What negative elements should I deemphasize?

C: How will the readers' relationship to Gateway affect their response to my letter?

Write your thoughts down so you can refer to them later. Be as thorough as possible in your answers.

Final thought: If this information were placed on the company's Web site as a general note to customers, how would your analysis of this business communication problem change? For example, would the audience for your message change? If so, how?

Group Activity

Imagine that, in response to the toll-free number error, Gateway's upper-level management has initiated "The Push for Accuracy," a two-part effort designed to make documents accurate. As one part of this process, the company's technical experts are investigating database tools that would allow them to more easily track the use and reuse of data.

The second, and more critical, part of this initiative involves the creation of a committee responsible for going to the heart of the problem: employees' poor writing habits. Known throughout the management ranks for your excellent communication skills, you and your classmates have been named to this group. Your committee has been charged with developing a "Best Practices" program to establish good revising, editing, and proof-reading habits among Gateway employees. After you've created your plan, you will submit it to upper-level management, who wish to review the plan before formally insti-tuting it.

Working with your fellow committee members, develop an outline of this new Best Practices program. The purpose of your document is to explain to your audience why revising, editing, and proofreading are so important, what the best practices are, and how they can most effectively implement these best practices in their own work.

Consider the following questions:

1. What are the key elements to good writing?

2. How important is quality feedback in the writing process?

3. How can individuals learn to provide quality feedback?

4. What is cycling?

5. What specific steps are involved in editing and proofreading a document?

6. What is a thorough revision?

7. What is a light revision?

Include any other tips that you, as experts, can offer to your audience. Finally, if you have time, provide an example of how your program could be implemented in a specific group in the company (such as marketing, customer service, etc.). Consider the types of documents that this group creates most often.

Unit Two

Creating Goodwill

Module 6

You-Attitude

To learn how to

- Begin building goodwill.
- Continue to adapt your message to the audience.
- Emphasize what the reader wants to know.
- See another point of view.

Start by asking these questions:

- How do I create you-attitude in my sentences?
- Does you-attitude basically mean using the word *you*?

- I've revised my sentences. Do I need to do anything else?

You-attitude is a style of writing that

- Looks at things from the reader's point of view.
- Respects the reader's intelligence.
- Protects the reader's ego.
- Emphasizes what the reader wants to know.

You-attitude is a concrete way to show empathy (◀ ▶ p. 21) and the foundation of persuasion.

You-attitude is a matter of style. That is, revisions for you-attitude do not change the basic meaning of the sentence. However, revising for you-attitude often makes sentences longer since sentences become more specific.

Often, we can create you-attitude by changing words. Sometimes, however, it's necessary to revise organization and content as well as style to create the best document.

FYI

Researcher Jim Collins found that the most financially successful companies put "people first, strategy second."

Source: Jim Collins, "Level 5 Leadership: The Triumph of Humility and Fierce Resolve," *Harvard Business Review,* January 2001, 66–76.

How do I create you-attitude in my sentences?

Talk about the reader—except in negative situations.

To create you-attitude,

1. Talk about the reader, not about yourself.
2. Don't talk about feelings, except to congratulate or offer sympathy.
3. In positive situations, use *you* more often than *I*. Use *we* when it includes the reader.
4. Avoid "you" in negative situations.

1. Talk about the Reader, Not about Yourself.

Readers want to know how they benefit or are affected. When you provide this information, you make your message more complete and more interesting.

Lacks you-attitude: I have negotiated an agreement with Apex Rent-a-Car that gives you a discount on rental cars.

You-attitude: As a Sunstrand employee, you can now get a 20% discount when you rent a car from Apex.

Any sentence that focuses on the writer's work or generosity lacks you-attitude, even if the sentence contains the word *you.* Instead of focusing on what we are giving the reader, focus on what the reader can now do. To do that, you may need to change the grammatical subject.

Lacks you-attitude: We are shipping your order of September 21 this afternoon.

You-attitude: The two dozen Corning Ware starter sets you ordered will be shipped this afternoon and should reach you by September 28.

Emphasize what the reader wants to know. The reader is less interested in when we shipped the order than in when it will arrive. Note that the phrase "should reach you by" leaves room for variations in delivery schedules. If you

Me-attitude can make you seem pompous and self-serving.

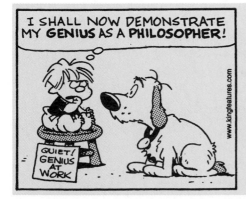

can't be exact, give your reader the information you do have: "UPS shipment from California to Texas normally takes three days." If you have absolutely no idea, give the reader the name of the carrier, so the reader knows whom to contact if the order doesn't arrive promptly.

2. Don't Talk about Feelings, Except to Congratulate or Offer Sympathy.

Lacks you-attitude: We are happy to extend you a credit line of $5,000.

You-attitude: You can now charge up to $5,000 on your American Express card.

In most business situations, your feelings are irrelevant and should be omitted. The reader doesn't care whether you're happy, bored stiff at granting a routine application, or worried about granting so much to someone who barely qualifies. All the reader cares about is the situation from his or her point of view.

It *is* appropriate to talk about your own emotions in a message of congratulation or condolence.

You-attitude: Congratulations on your promotion to district manager! I was really pleased to read about it.

You-attitude: I was sorry to hear that your father died.

In internal memos, it may be appropriate to comment that a project has been gratifying or frustrating. In the letter of transmittal that accompanies a report, it is permissible to talk about your feelings about doing the work. But even other readers in your own organization are primarily interested in their own concerns, not in your feelings.

Don't talk about the reader's feelings, either. It can be offensive to have someone else tell us how we feel—especially if the writer is wrong.

Instant Replay

Definition of You-Attitude

You-attitude is a style of writing that

- Looks at things from the reader's point of view.
- Respects the reader's intelligence.
- Protects the reader's ego.
- Emphasizes what the reader wants to know.

Lacks you-attitude: You'll be happy to hear that Open Grip Walkway Channels meet OSHA requirements.

You-attitude: Open Grip Walkway Channels meet OSHA requirements.

Maybe the reader expects that anything you sell would meet government regulations (OSHA—the Occupational Safety and Health Administration—is a federal agency). The reader may even be disappointed if he or she expected higher standards. Simply explain the situation or describe a product's features; don't predict the reader's response.

When you have good news for the reader, simply give the good news.

Lacks you-attitude: You'll be happy to hear that your scholarship has been renewed.

You-attitude: Congratulations! Your scholarship has been renewed.

3. In Positive Situations, Use *You* More Often than *I*. Use *We* When It Includes the Reader.

Talk about the reader, not you or your company.

Lacks you-attitude: We provide health insurance to all employees.

You-attitude: You receive health insurance as a full-time Procter & Gamble employee.

Most readers are tolerant of the word *I* in e-mail messages, which seem like conversation. Edit paper documents to use *I* rarely if at all. *I* suggests that you're concerned about personal issues, not about the organization's problems, needs, and opportunities. *We* works well when it includes the reader. Avoid *we* if it excludes the reader (as it would in a letter to a customer or supplier or as it might in a memo about what *we* in management want *you* to do).

4. Avoid *You* in Negative Situations.

To avoid blaming the reader, use an impersonal expression or a passive verb. Talk about the group to which the reader belongs so readers don't feel that they're singled out for bad news.

Not you-attitude: You failed to sign your check.

You-attitude (impersonal):   Your check arrived without a signature.

You-attitude (passive):   Your check was not signed.

Impersonal constructions omit people and talk only about things. **Passive verbs** describe the action performed on something, without necessarily saying who did it. (◄ ► See Module 16 for a full discussion of passive verbs.)

In most cases, active verbs are better. But when your reader is at fault, passive verbs may be useful to avoid assigning blame.

Normally, writing is most lively when it's about people—and most interesting to readers when it's about them. When you have to report a mistake or bad news, however, you can protect the reader's ego by using an impersonal construction, one in which things, not people, do the acting.

Lacks you-attitude: You made no allowance for inflation in your estimate.

You-attitude (passive):   No allowance for inflation has been made in this estimate.

You-attitude (impersonal):   This estimate makes no allowance for inflation.

A purist might say that impersonal constructions are illogical: An estimate, for example, is inanimate and can't "make" anything. In the pragmatic world of business writing, however, impersonal constructions often help you convey criticism tactfully.

When you restrict the reader's freedom, talk about the group to which the reader belongs rather than about the reader as an individual.

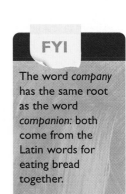

FYI

The word *company* has the same root as the word *companion:* both come from the Latin words for eating bread together.

Goodwill is built with actions as well as with words. Citizens of Arcadia, CA, planned to give the firefighters who had saved their homes a monetary reward–and doughnuts. When Krispy Kreme learned who would receive the 200 dozen doughnuts, the company donated them. Krispy Kreme also donates its products to homeless shelters and food banks.

Lacks you-attitude:	You must get approval from the Director before you publish any articles or memoirs based on your work in the agency.
You-attitude:	Agency personnel must get approval from the Director to publish any articles or memoirs based on their work at the agency.

Does you-attitude basically mean using the word you?

No.

All messages should use you-attitude, but the words to achieve it will change depending on the situation.

Instant Replay

Four Ways to Create You-Attitude

1. Talk about the reader, not about yourself.
2. Don't talk about feelings, except to congratulate or offer sympathy.
3. In positive situations, use *you* more often than *I*. Use *we* when it includes the reader.
4. Avoid *you* in negative situations.

- In a positive message, focus on what the reader can do. "We give you" lacks you-attitude because the sentence focuses on what we are doing.
- Avoid *you* when it criticizes the reader or limits the reader's freedom.
- In a job application letter, create you-attitude by showing how you can help meet the reader's needs, but keep the word *you* to a minimum (◁ ▶ Module 28).

I've revised my sentences. Do I need to do anything else?

Check content and organization, too.
Emphasize what the reader wants to know.

Good messages apply you-attitude beyond the sentence level by using content and organization as well as style to build goodwill.
To create goodwill with content,

- Be complete. When you have lots of information to give, consider putting some details in an appendix that may be read later.
- Anticipate and answer questions the reader is likely to have.

Seeing Another Point of View

Customers were waiting for tables to be cleared at a busy restaurant. The manager pulled rank and told the two dishwashers to clear the tables. They thought the hostess, who was "just standing there," should do the clearing. The manager gave an ultimatum: clear the tables or quit. The dishwashers quit. The tables were still dirty, and now there was no one to wash the dishes.

The manager was unable to resolve the situation constructively because he couldn't see the situation through the eyes of the dishwashers. He had a hierarchical view of work: People do what their superiors tell them to do. A job is what a boss says to do, whether it's in the job description or not.

Another view of work is egalitarian: Everybody pitches in. In particular, the manager and the hostess, who seemed to have the most flexible jobs, should help.

Why did the dishwashers object so strenuously? Were they already planning to quit? Did they feel insulted when the manager didn't give a reason for rejecting their idea? Did the hostess make more than they did? If so, did it seem that she should be the one to do extra work? Did it seem that asking the African–American dishwashers to do extra work while the Caucasian manager and hostess looked on was racist? Had the dishwashers experienced racism there in the past?

Why was the manager inflexible? Did he see the dishwashers as teens "talking back" to an adult? Did he think he knew better than they how to solve the problem? Did he feel that the hostess would soon be busy greeting customers? Had he had problems with the dishwashers before? Was he stressed? Was he aware of the racial overtones?

In this case, neither the dishwashers nor the manager communicated effectively. But it was the manager's responsibility to figure out how to motivate his staff to get the work done and how to solve the immediate problem his restaurant faced.

Various management theories could be invoked to provide solutions to the problem. But the ultimate solution doesn't come from a theory. It comes from the flexibility to see another point of view.

To learn to look beyond your own point of view, start with a situation where you were misunderstood. How did you feel? What resources of yours—time, money, and emotional energy—were wasted? What did you want from the other person?

Now, turn it around. How might the other person answer the same questions? What could you have *given*? The points where concerns overlap are opportunities for compromise.

Resist the temptation to put your needs ahead of others'. Instead, remember that all business is exchange, a form of compromise. Learning to see another point of view is the first step toward a successful exchange.

Source: Linda Flower, "John Dewey, Managers, and Waitresses: Intercultural Interpretations of Workplace Conflict," Conference on College Composition and Communication, Atlanta, GA, March 24–27, 1999.

- When you include information the reader didn't ask for, show why it is important.
- Show readers how the subject of your message affects them.

To organize information to build goodwill,

- Put information readers are most interested in first.
- Arrange information to meet your reader's needs, not yours.
- Use headings and lists so that the reader can find key points quickly.

Consider the letter in Figure 6.1. As the red marginal notes indicate, many individual sentences in this letter lack you-attitude. The last sentence in paragraph 1 sounds both harsh and defensive; the close is selfish. The language is stiff and filled with outdated jargon. Perhaps the most serious problem is that the fact most interesting to the reader is buried in the middle of the first paragraph. Since we have good news for the reader, we should put that information first.

Instant **Replay**

Definitions of Impersonal Constructions

Impersonal constructions omit people and talk only about things.

Passive verbs describe the action performed on something, without necessarily saying who did it.

Figure 6.1

A Letter Lacking You-Attitude

450 INDUSTRIAL PARK   CLEVELAND, OH   44120   (216) 555-4670   FAX: (216) 555-4672

December 11, 2004

Ms. Carol McFarland
Rollins Equipment Corporation
18438 East Night Hawk Way
Phoenix, AZ 85043-7800

Dear Ms. McFarland:

Not you-attitude   *Legalistic*

We are now ready to issue a check to Rollins Equipment in the amount of $14,207.02. To receive said check, you will deliver to me a release of the mechanic's liens in the amount of $14,207.02.   *Sounds dictatorial*

Focuses on negative   *Lacks you-attitude*

Before we can release the check, we must be satisfied that the release is in the proper form. We must insist that we be provided with a stamped original of the lien indicating the document number in the appropriate district court where it is filed. Also, either the release must be executed by an officer of Rollins Equipment, or we must be provided with a letter from an officer of Rollins Equipment authorizing another individual to execute the release.   *Hard to read, remember*

Please contact the undersigned so that an appointment can be scheduled for this transaction.   *Jargon*

Sincerely,

Kelly J. Pickett

Fixing individual sentences could improve the letter. However, it really needs to be rewritten. Figure 6.2 shows a possible revision. The revision is clearer, easier to read, and friendlier.

When you have negatives, third-person is better you-attitude than second-person because third-person shows that everyone is being treated the same way.

Figure 6.2

A Letter Revised to Improve You-Attitude

450 INDUSTRIAL PARK   CLEVELAND, OH   44120   (216) 555-4670   FAX: (216) 555-4672

December 11, 2004

Ms. Carol McFarland
Rollins Equipment Corporation
18438 East Night Hawk Way
Phoenix, AZ 85043-7800

Dear Ms. McFarland:

Let's clear up the lien in the Allen contract.

Starts with main point from the reader's point of view

Rollins will receive a check for $14,207.02 when you give us a release for the mechanic's lien of $14,207.02. To assure us that the release is in the proper form,

Focuses on what reader gets

1. Give us a stamped original of the lien indicating the document's district court number, and

2. Either
   a. Have an officer of Rollins Equipment sign the release
        or
   b. Give us a letter from a Rollins officer authorizing someone else to sign the release.

List makes it easy to see that reader needs to do two things—and that the second can be done in two ways.

Call me to tell me which way is best for you.

Emphasizes reader's choice

Sincerely,

Kelly J. Pickett

Kelly J. Pickett
Extension 5318

Extension number makes it easy for reader to phone.

Summary of Key Points

- You-attitude is a style of writing that
  - Looks at things from the reader's point of view.
  - Respects the reader's intelligence.
  - Protects the reader's ego.
  - Emphasizes what the reader wants to know.
- You-attitude is a matter of style. Revisions for you-attitude do not change the basic meaning of the sentence. However, revising for you-attitude often makes sentences longer since sentences become more specific.

- To create you-attitude in sentences,
  1. Talk about the reader, not about yourself.
  2. Don't talk about feelings, except to congratulate or offer sympathy.
  3. In positive situations, use *you* more often than *I*. Use *we* when it includes the reader.
  4. Avoid *you* in negative situations.
- Apply you-attitude beyond the sentence level by using organization, content, and layout as well as style to build goodwill.

Assignment for Module 6

Questions for Comprehension

6.1   What is you-attitude?

6.2   How can you create you-attitude within sentences?

6.3   How can you create you-attitude beyond the sentence level?

Questions for Critical Thinking

6.4   Why doesn't the word *you* always create you-attitude?

6.5   Why do sentences starting "We give you" lack you-attitude?

6.6   Think of a time when you felt a business cared about you. What words or actions made you feel that way?

6.7   Can you think of situations in which the four strategies would *not* create you-attitude? If so, how would you create you-attitude in those situations?

Exercises and Problems

6.8   **Using Passives and Impersonal Constructions to Improve You-Attitude**

Revise each of these sentences to improve you-attitude, first using a passive verb, then using an impersonal construction (one in which things, not people, do the action). Are both revisions equally good? Why or why not?

1. You did not send us your check.
2. You did not include all the necessary information in your letter.
3. By failing to build a fence around your pool, you have created a health hazard.

4. You did not supply all of the information necessary to process your claim.

5. The credit card number you supplied has expired.

6.9 Improving You-Attitude

Revise these sentences to improve you-attitude. Eliminate any awkward phrasing. In some cases, you may need to add information to revise the sentence effectively.

1. We are pleased to offer you the ability to sign up for health insurance on-line on our intranet.

2. We cannot provide vegetarian meals unless you let us know at least three days in advance.

3. We are pleased to provide free e-mail accounts to students.

4. You'll be happy to know that we have installed an ATM for your convenience.

5. At DiYanni homes, we have more than 30 plans that we will personalize just for you.

6. We have added another employee benefit for you.

7. Today, we shipped the book you ordered.

8. In your report, you forgot to tell how many people you surveyed.

9. I hope that it is obvious to you that we want to give you the very best prices on furniture.

10. You didn't order enough donuts for the meeting.

6.10 Improving You-Attitude

Revise these sentences to improve you-attitude. Eliminate any awkward phrasing. In some cases, you may need to add information to revise the sentence effectively.

1. Starting next month, the company will offer you a choice of three HMOs.

2. We provide health and dental insurance to all full-time employees.

3. We can arrange for our services to reach you within 24 hours.

4. Starting January 1, the company will create a new program that lets full-time employees volunteer one hour a week on company time.

5. I'm very sorry that you were worried. I'm happy to tell you that you qualify for our special offer.

6. You will be happy to learn that you can transfer credits from our Business Associates Program to a four-year school.

7. We give you the following benefits when you join our "Frequent Flier" program.

8. We are pleased to send you a copy of "Investing in Stocks," which you requested.

9. Your audit papers did not convert Canadian revenue into U.S. dollars.

10. Of course we want to give you every possible service that you might need or want.

6.11 Revising a Form Letter for You-Attitude

You've taken a part-time job at a store that sells fine jewelry. In orientation, the manager tells you that the store photographs jewelry it sells or appraises and mails the photo as a goodwill gesture after the transaction. However, when you see the form letter, you know that it doesn't build much goodwill—and you say so. The manager says, "Well, you're in college. Suppose you rewrite it."

Rewrite the letter. Use square brackets for material (like the customer's name) that would have to be inserted in the form letter to vary it for a specific customer. Add information that would help build goodwill.

Dear Customer:

We are most happy to enclose a photo of the jewelry that we recently sold you or appraised for you. We feel that this added service, which we are happy to extend to our fine customers, will be useful should you wish to insure your jewelry.

We trust you will enjoy this additional service. We thank you for the confidence you have shown by coming to our store.

Sincerely,

Your Sales Associate

6.12 Evaluating You-Attitude in Documents That Cross Your Desk

Identify three sentences that use (or should use) you-attitude in documents you see as a worker, consumer, or student. If the sentences are good, write them down or attach a copy of the document(s) marking the sentence(s) in the margin. If the sentences need work, provide both the original sentence and a possible revision.

As Your Instructor Directs,
a. Share your examples with a small group of students.

b. Write a memo to your instructor discussing your examples.
c. Post an e-mail message to the class discussing your examples.
d. Present two or three of your examples to the class in a short presentation.
e. With your small group, write a collaborative short report to your instructor about the patterns you see.

 Polishing Your Prose

It's/Its

With an apostrophe, *it's* is a contraction meaning *it is*. Without an apostrophe, *its* is a possessive pronoun meaning *belonging to it*.
Contractions always use apostrophes:

It is → it's

I have → I've

You will → you'll

They are → they're

Possessive pronouns (unlike possessive nouns) do not use apostrophes:

His / hers / its

My / mine / our / ours

Your / yours

Their / theirs

Since both *it's* and *its* sound the same, you have to look at the logic of your sentence to choose the right word. If you could substitute *it is*, use *it's*.

Decide whether to use contractions (such as *it's, they're, you're, we're, should've,* and so forth) based on audience, purpose, and organizational culture. Some audiences find contractions too informal; others find a lack of contractions off-putting or unfriendly. If the purpose of your document is to persuade while being casual, then contractions make sense. If, however, documents have significant legal ramifications, contractions may seem flip. Your organization may have its own conventions, too—check past correspondence to see what is preferred.

In general, more formal documents such as résumés and long research reports use few (or no) contractions. Contractions are often OK in e-mail, memos, and letters in which you want a conversational tone, such as a fund-raising letter for the local animal shelter.

Exercises

Choose the right word in the set of parentheses.

1. The company projected that (it's / its) profits would rise during the next quarter.

2. (It's / Its) likely that orders will increase in the upcoming quarter.

3. I don't want responsibility for the project unless (it's / its) important.

4. Most people realize that (it's / its) wise to network with other business professionals.

5. I'm not sure whether (it's / its) a good idea to offer a conference.

6. The accounting department is revising (it's / its) estimates for next quarter's earnings.

7. (It's / Its) good that our computer automatically backs up (it's / its) files.

8. We've heard (it's / its) all but certain that the company headquarters will be moved to Miami.

9. (It's / Its) cash reserves protected the company from a hostile takeover.

10. Whether (it's / its) for professional or personal reasons, traveling has (it's / its) good points.

Check your answers to the odd-numbered exercises at the back of the book.

BComm Skill Booster

To apply the concepts in this module, complete lesson 4 on developing a you-attitude. You can access the BComm Skill Booster through the text Web site at **www.mhhe.com/bcs2e.**

Module 7

Positive Emphasis

To learn how to

- Continue building goodwill.
- Emphasize the positive.
- Use positive emphasis ethically.
- Begin to choose an appropriate tone.

Start by asking these questions:

- How do I create positive emphasis?
- Why do I need to think about tone, politeness, and power?
- What's the best way to apologize?

Some negatives are necessary.

- Straightforward negatives build credibility when you have bad news to give the reader: announcements of layoffs, product defects and recalls, price increases.
- Negatives may help people take a problem seriously. Wall Data improved the reliability of its computer programs when it eliminated the term *bugs* and used instead the term *failures*.
- In some messages, such as negative performance appraisals, your purpose is to deliver a rebuke with no alternative. Even here, avoid insults or attacks on the reader's integrity or sanity. Being honest about the drawbacks of a job reduces turnover.
- Sometimes negatives create a "reverse psychology" that makes people look favorably at your product. Rent-a-Wreck is thriving. (The cars really don't look so bad.)[1]

But in most situations, it's better to be positive. Researchers Annette N. Shelby and N. Lamar Reinsch, Jr., found that business people responded more positively to positive rather than to negative language and were more likely to say they would act on a positively worded request.[2] Martin Seligman's research for Met Life found that optimistic salespeople sold 37% more insurance than pessimistic colleagues. As a result, Met Life began hiring optimists even when they failed to meet the company's other criteria. These "unqualified" optimists outsold pessimists 21% in their first year and 57% the next.[3]

Positive emphasis is a way of looking at things. Is the bottle half empty or half full? You can create positive emphasis with the words, information, organization, and layout you choose.

How do I create positive emphasis?

Deemphasize or omit negative words and information.

The following five techniques deemphasize negative information:

1. Avoid negative words and words with negative connotations.
2. Focus on what the reader can do rather than on limitations.
3. Justify negative information by giving a reason or linking it to a reader benefit.
4. If the negative is truly unimportant, omit it.
5. Put the negative information in the middle and present it compactly.

In some messages, especially negative ones (◁ ▶ Module 11), you won't use all five techniques. Practice each of these techniques so that you can use them when they're appropriate.

I. Avoid Negative Words and Words with Negative Connotations.

Figure 7.1 lists some common negative words. If you find one of these words in a draft, try to substitute a more positive word. When you must use a negative, use the *least negative* term that will convey your meaning.

FYI

According to a 30-year study by the Mayo Clinic, optimists live almost 20% longer than pessimists. Optimists are better at coping with stress and have more disease-fighting T-cells.

Source: Donald D. Hensrud, "How to Live Longer (and Love It)," *Fortune*, April 30, 2001, 210.

afraid	except	**Some mis-words:**	worry
anxious	fail	misfortune	wrong
avoid	fault	mistake	
bad	fear	missing	**Many un-words:**
careless	hesitate		unclear
damage	ignorant	neglect	unfair
delay	ignore	never	unfortunate
delinquent	impossible	no	unfortunately
deny		not	unpleasant
difficulty	**Many in-words:**	objection	unreasonable
	inadequate	problem	unreliable
Some dis-words:	incomplete	reject	unsure
disapprove	inconvenient	sorry	
dishonest	insincere	terrible	
dissatisfied	injury	trivial	
		trouble	
eliminate	lacking	wait	
error	loss	weakness	

Figure 7.1

Negative Words to Avoid

Even in a rejection letter, good writers avoid negative words that insult or attack the reader.

The following examples show how to replace negative words with positive words.

Negative: We have failed to finish taking inventory.

Better: We haven't finished taking inventory.

Still better: We will be finished taking inventory Friday.

Negative: If you can't understand this explanation, feel free to call me.

Better: If you have further questions, just call me.

Still better: Omit the sentence.
(Readers aren't shrinking violets. They'll call if they do have questions.)

Omit double negatives.

Negative: Do not forget to back up your disks.

Better: Always back up your disks.

When you must use a negative term, use the least negative word that is accurate.

Negative: Your balance of $835 is delinquent.

Better: Your balance of $835 is past due.

Getting rid of negatives has the added benefit of making what you write easier to understand. Sentences with three or more negatives are very hard to understand.[4]

Beware of **hidden negatives:** words that are not negative in themselves but become negative in context. *But* and *however* indicate a shift, so, after a positive statement, they are negative. *I hope* and *I trust that* suggest that you aren't sure. *Patience* may sound like a virtue, but it is a necessary virtue only when things are slow. Even positives about a service or product may backfire if they suggest that in the past the service or product was bad.

Negative: I hope this is the information you wanted.
[Implication: I'm not sure.]

Better: Enclosed is a brochure about road repairs scheduled for 2005–06.

Still better: The brochure contains a list of all roads and bridges scheduled for repair during 2005–06. Call Gwen Wong at 555–3245 for specific dates when work will start and stop and for alternate routes.

Some stores might say, "Put books you don't want here." But Bookseller Joseph–Beth in Lexington, Kentucky, uses positive emphasis.

Books I'll buy another day...

Negative: Please be patient as we switch to the automated system. [Implication: you can expect problems.]

Better: If you have questions during our transition to the automated system, call Melissa Morgan.

Still better: You'll be able to get information instantly about any house on the market when the automated system is in place. If you have questions during the transition, call Melissa Morgan.

Negative: Now Crispy Crunch tastes better. [Implication: it used to taste terrible.]

Better: Now Crispy Crunch tastes even better.

Removing negatives does not mean being arrogant or pushy.

Negative: I hope that you are satisfied enough to place future orders.

Arrogant: I look forward to receiving all of your future business.

Better: Call Mercury whenever you need transistors.

When you eliminate negative words, be sure to maintain accuracy. Words that are exact opposites will usually not be accurate. Instead, use specifics to be both positive and accurate.

Negative: The exercycle is not guaranteed for life.

Not true: The exercycle is guaranteed for life.

True: The exercycle is guaranteed for 10 years.

Five Ways to Create Positive Emphasis

To deemphasize negative information,

1. Avoid negative words and words with negative connotations.
2. Focus on what the reader can do rather than on limitations.
3. Justify negative information by giving a reason or linking it to a reader benefit.
4. If the negative is truly unimportant, omit it.
5. Put the negative information in the middle and present it compactly.

Definition of Hidden Negatives

Hidden negatives are words that are not negative in themselves but become negative in context.

Negative: Customers under 60 are not eligible for the Prime Time discount.

Not true: You must be over 60 to be eligible for the Prime Time discount.

True: If you're 60 or older, you can save 10% on all your purchases with RightWay's Prime Time discount.

Legal phrases also have negative connotations for most readers and should be avoided whenever possible. The idea will sound more positive if you use conversational English.

Negative: If your account is still delinquent, a second, legal notice will be sent to you informing you that cancellation of your policy will occur 30 days after the date of the legal notice if we do not receive your check.

Better: Even if your check is lost in the mail and never reaches us, you still have a 30-day grace period. If you do get a second notice, you will know that your payment hasn't reached us. To keep your account in good standing, stop payment on the first check and send a second one.

2. Focus on What the Reader Can Do Rather than on Limitations.

Sometimes positive emphasis is a matter of the way you present something: Is the glass half empty or half full? Sometimes it's a matter of eliminating double negatives. When there are limits, or some options are closed, focus on the alternatives that remain.

Negative: We will not allow you to charge more than $1,500 on your VISA account.

Better: You can charge $1,500 on your new VISA card.

or: Your new VISA card gives you $1,500 in credit that you can use at thousands of stores nationwide.

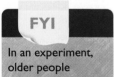

FYI

In an experiment, older people walked faster after they viewed positive words about old age presented subliminally. Says one of the authors of the study, "Self-image is important to quality of life and, perhaps, to physical functioning."

Source: Avery Comarow, "Light of Heart, Swift of Foot," U.S. News and World Report, November 15, 1999, 135.

As you focus on what will happen, **check for you-attitude** (Module 6 ◀▷ p.106). In the last example, "We will allow you to charge $1,500" would be positive, but it lacks you-attitude.

When you have a benefit and a requirement the reader must meet to get the benefit, the sentence is usually more positive if you put the benefit first.

Negative: You will not qualify for the student membership rate of $25 a year unless you are enrolled for at least 10 hours.

Better: You get all the benefits of membership for only $25 a year if you're enrolled for 10 hours or more.

3. Justify Negative Information by Giving a Reason or Linking It to a Reader Benefit.

A reason can help your reader see that the information is necessary; a benefit can suggest that the negative aspect is outweighed by positive factors. Be careful, however, to make the logic behind your reason clear and to leave no loopholes.

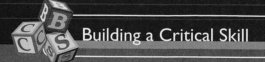

Using Positive Emphasis Ethically

Several of the methods to achieve positive emphasis can be misused.

Consider omission.

A bank notified customers that checking account fees were being "revised" but omitted the amounts. Customers had to go into the bank and copy down the new (higher) fees themselves.

In another case, a condominium resort offered an "all-terrain vehicle" as a prize for visiting. (Winners had to pay $29.95 for "handling, processing, and insurance.") The actual "prize" was a lawn chair with four wheels that converted into a wheeled cart. The company claims it told the truth: "It is a vehicle. It's a four-wheel cart you can take anywhere—to the beach, to the pool. It may not be motorized, but [we] didn't say it was motorized."

In both cases, full disclosure might have affected decisions: Some customers might have chosen to change banks; some customers would have declined the condominium visit. It isn't ethical to omit information that people need to make decisions.

Presenting information compactly can also go too far. A credit card company mailed out a letter with the good news that the minimum monthly payment was going down. But a separate small flyer explained that interest rates (on the charges not repaid) were going up. The print was far too small to read: 67 lines of type were crowded into five vertical inches of text.

Source: Carmella M. Padilla, "It's a . . . a . . . a . . . All-Terrain Vehicle, Yeah, That's It, That's the Ticket," *The Wall Street Journal*, July 17, 1987, 17; and Donna S. Kienzler, "Visual Ethics," *The Journal of Business Communication* 34 (1997): 175–76

Negative: We cannot sell computer disks in lots of less than 10.

Loophole: To keep down packaging costs and to help you save on shipping and handling costs, we sell computer disks in lots of 10 or more.

Suppose the customer says, "I'll pay the extra shipping and handling. Send me seven." If you can't or won't sell in lots of less than 10, you need to write:

Better: To keep down packaging costs and to help customers save on shipping and handling costs, we sell computer disks only in lots of 10 or more.

If you link the negative element to a benefit, be sure that it is a benefit the reader will acknowledge. Avoid telling people that you're doing things "for their own good." They may have a different notion of what their own good is. You may think you're doing customers a favor by limiting their credit so they don't get in over their heads and go bankrupt. They may feel they'd be better off with more credit so they could expand in hopes of making more sales and more profits.

4. If the Negative Is Truly Unimportant, Omit It.

Omit negatives entirely only when

- The reader does not need the information to make a decision.
- You have already given the reader the information and he or she has access to the previous communication.
- The information is trivial.

The following examples suggest the kind of negatives you can omit:

Negative: A one-year subscription to *PC Magazine* is $49.97. That rate is not as low as the rates charged for some magazines.

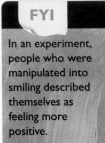
Better:	A one-year subscription to *PC Magazine* is $49.97.
Still better:	A one-year subscription to *PC Magazine* is $49.97. You save 43% off the newsstand price of $87.78.
Negative:	If you are not satisfied with Interstate Fidelity Insurance, you do not have to renew your policy.
Better:	Omit the sentence.

5. Bury the Negative Information and Present It Compactly.

The beginning and end are always positions of emphasis. Put negatives here only if you want to emphasize the negative, as you may in a negative message (◁ ▶ Module 11). To deemphasize a negative, put it in the middle of a paragraph rather than in the first or last sentence, in the middle of the message rather than in the first or last paragraphs.

When a letter or memo runs several pages, remember that the bottom of the first page is also a position of emphasis, even if it is in the middle of a paragraph, because of the extra white space of the bottom margin. (The first page gets more attention since it is on top and the reader's eye may catch lines of the message even when he or she isn't consciously reading it; the tops and bottoms of subsequent pages don't get this extra attention.) If possible, avoid placing negative information at the bottom of the first page.

Giving a topic lots of space emphasizes it. Therefore, you can deemphasize negative information by giving it as little space as possible. Give negative information only once in your message. Don't list negatives vertically on the page since lists take space and emphasize material.

Why do I need to think about tone, politeness, and power?

So you don't offend people by mistake.

No one likes to deal with people who seem condescending or rude. Poorly chosen words can create that sense, whether the sender "meant" to be rude or not. **Tone** is the implied attitude of the writer toward the reader. Tone is tricky because it interacts with power: The words that might seem friendly from a superior to a subordinate may seem uppity if used by the subordinate to the superior. Norms for politeness are cultural and generational. Language that is acceptable within one group may be unacceptable if used by someone outside the group.

The desirable tone for business writing is businesslike but not stiff, friendly but not phony, confident but not arrogant, polite but not groveling. The following guidelines will help you achieve the tone you want.

- **Use courtesy titles for people outside your organization whom you don't know well.** Most U.S. organizations use first names for everyone, whatever their age or rank. But many people don't like being called by their first names by people they don't know or by someone much younger. When you talk or write to people outside your organization, use first names only if you've established a personal relationship. If you don't know someone well, use a courtesy title (◁|▷ Module 9):

Dear Mr. Reynolds:

Dear Ms. Lee:

- **Be aware of the power implications of the words you use.** "Thank you for your cooperation" is generous coming from a superior to a subordinate; it's not appropriate in a message to your superior. Different ways of asking for action carry different levels of politeness.[5]

Order (lowest politeness)	Turn in your time card by Monday.
Polite order (mid-level politeness)	Please turn in your time card by Monday.
Indirect request (higher politeness)	Time cards should be turned in by Monday.
Question (highest politeness)	Would you be able to turn in your time card by Monday?

You need more politeness if you're asking for something that will inconvenience the reader and help you more than the person who does the action. Generally, you need less politeness when you're asking for something small, routine, or to the reader's benefit. Some discourse communities, however, prefer that even small requests be made politely.

Lower politeness: To start the scheduling process, please describe your availability for meetings during the second week of the month.

Higher politeness: Could you let me know what times you'd be free for a meeting the second week of the month?

Higher levels of politeness may be unclear. In some cases, a question may seem like a request for information to which it's acceptable to answer, "No, I can't." In other cases, it will be an order, simply phrased in polite terms.

Generally, requests sound friendliest when they use conversational language.

Poor tone: Return the draft with any changes by next Tuesday.

Better tone: Let me know by Tuesday whether you'd like any changes in the draft.

- **When the stakes are low, be straightforward.** Messages that "beat around the bush" sound pompous and defensive.

Poor tone: Distribution of the low-fat plain granola may be limited in your area. May we suggest that you discuss this matter with your store manager.

Better tone: Our low-fat granola is so popular that there isn't enough to go around. We're expanding production to meet the demand. Ask your store manager to keep putting in orders, so that your grocery is on the list of stores that will get supplies when they become available.

or: Store managers decide what to stock. If your store has stopped carrying our low-fat granola, the store manager has stopped ordering it. Talk to the manager. Managers try to meet customer needs, so if you say something you're more likely to get what you want.

- **When you must give bad news, consider hedging your statement.** John Hagge and Charles Kostelnick have shown that auditors' suggestion letters rarely say directly that firms are using unacceptable accounting practices. Instead, they use three strategies to be more diplomatic: specifying the time ("currently, the records are quite informal"), limiting statements ("it appears," "it seems"), and using impersonal statements that do not specify who caused a problem or who will perform an action.[6]

What's the best way to apologize?

Early, briefly, and sincerely.

When you are at fault, you may build goodwill by admitting that fact forthrightly. However, apologies may have legal implications, so some organizations prefer that apologies not be issued to customers or the public. Think about your audience and the organizational culture in deciding whether to apologize explicitly.

- **No explicit apology is necessary if the error is small and if you are correcting the mistake.**

Negative: I'm sorry the clerk did not credit your account properly.

Better: Your statement has been corrected to include your payment of $263.75.

- **Do not apologize when you are not at fault.** When you have done everything you can and when a delay or problem is due to circumstances beyond your control, you aren't at fault and don't need to apologize. It may be appropriate to include an explanation so the reader knows you weren't negligent. If the news is bad, put the explanation first. If you have good news for the reader, put it before your explanation.

Negative: I'm sorry that I could not answer your question sooner. I had to wait until the sales figures for the second quarter were in.

Better (neutral or bad news)   We needed the sales figures for the second quarter to answer your question. Now that they're in, I can tell you that . . .

Better (good: news)   The new advertising campaign is a success. The sales figures for the second quarter are finally in, and they show that . . .

If the delay or problem is long or large, it is good you-attitude to ask the reader whether he or she wants to confirm the original plan or make different arrangements.

Negative: I'm sorry that the chairs will not be ready by August 25 as promised.

Better: Due to a strike against the manufacturer, the desk chairs you ordered will not be ready until November. Do you want to keep that order, or would you like to look at the models available from other suppliers?

- **When you apologize, do it early, briefly, and sincerely.** Apologize only once, early in the message. Let the reader move on to other, more positive information.

  Even if major trouble or inconvenience has resulted from your error, you don't need to go on about all the horrible things that happened. The reader already knows this negative information, and you can omit it. Instead, focus on what you have done to correct the situation.

  If you don't know whether or not any inconvenience has resulted, don't raise the issue at all.

Negative: I'm sorry I didn't answer your letter sooner. I hope that my delay hasn't inconvenienced you.

Better: I'm sorry I didn't answer your letter sooner.

Summary of Key Points

- **Positive emphasis** means focusing on the positive rather than the negative aspects of a situation.
  1. Avoid negative words and words with negative connotations.
  2. State information positively. Focus on what the reader can do rather than on what you won't or can't let the reader do.
  3. Justify negative information by giving a reason or linking it to a reader benefit.
  4. If the negative is truly unimportant, omit it.
  5. Put the negative information in the middle and present it compactly.

- **Hidden negatives** are words that are not negative in themselves but become negative in context.

- The desirable tone for business writing is businesslike but not stiff, friendly but not phony, confident but not arrogant, polite but not groveling. The following guidelines will help you achieve the tone you want.
  - Use courtesy titles for people outside your organization whom you don't know well.
  - Be aware of the power implications of the words you use.
  - When the stakes are low, be straightforward.

- When you must give bad news, consider hedging your statement.
- Don't apologize if the error is small and if you are correcting the mistake. Don't apologize if you are not at fault. If the delay or problem is long or large, it is good you-attitude to ask the reader whether he or she wants to make different arrangements.
- When you apologize, do it early, briefly, and sincerely. However, apologies may have legal implications, so some organizations prefer that apologies not be issued to customers or the public.

Assignments for Module 7

Questions for Comprehension

7.1   How can you create positive emphasis?

7.2   Which of the following are negative words that you should avoid?

anxious   hesitate
change   hope
eager   necessary
instead   unfortunately

7.3   What are your options when you need to apologize?

Questions for Critical Thinking

7.4   Some negative phrases (such as "please do not hesitate") are business clichés. Why is it better to avoid them?

7.5   Think of a situation when an apology was appropriate. What strategy was actually used? Would another strategy have been better?

7.6   If you work for a company that claims to be egalitarian, do you still need to attend to tone, power, and politeness?

7.7   Can you think of situations in which positive emphasis might backfire or be inappropriate? What strategies would be most likely to meet the audience's needs in those situations?

Exercises and Problems

7.8   Evaluating the Ethics of Positive Emphasis

The first word in each line below is negative; the second is a positive term that is sometimes substituted for it. Which of the positive terms seem ethical? Which seem unethical? Briefly explain your choices.

junk bonds	high-yield bonds
second mortgage	home-equity loan
tax	user fee
tax increase	revenue enhancement
nervousness	adrenaline
problem	challenge
price increase	price change

7.9   Focusing on the Positive

Revise each of the following sentences to focus on the options that remain, not those that are closed off.

1. Housing applications that arrive December 1 or later cannot be processed.

2. You cannot use flextime unless you have the consent of your supervisor.

3. I will be out of the country October 25– November 10 and will not be able to meet with you then.

7.10 Identifying Hidden Negatives

Identify the hidden negatives in the following sentences and revise to eliminate them. In some cases, you may need to add information to revise the sentence effectively.

1. The seminar will help you become a better manager.

2. Thank you for the confidence you have shown in us by ordering one of our products. It will be shipped to you soon.

3. In thinking about your role in our group, I remember two occasions where you contributed something.

7.11 Revising Sentences to Improve Positive Emphasis

Revise the following sentences to improve positive emphasis. In some cases, you may need to add or omit information to revise effectively.

1. The company cannot make its revenue goals without increasing sales in Japan.

2. I'm very sorry that you were worried. I'm happy to tell you that our special offer has not yet expired.

3. You cannot return this item for a full refund if you keep it past 30 days.

4. Although I was only an intern and didn't actually make presentations to major clients, I was required to prepare PowerPoint slides for the meetings and to answer some of the clients' questions.

5. If the above information is unclear, or if further information on this or any other topic is necessary, please do not hesitate to contact me.

6. I have been using e-mail both in my internship and in classes. I realize that almost everyone now does have experience with e-mail, but at least I won't be behind.

7. I am anxious to discuss this problem with you.

8. Medical certification can delay shutoff of electrical service for non-payment of bills. If someone in your home needs electricity to ensure health and well-being, signing up for our Medical certification will delay disconnection for 30 days.

9. I had a difficult time evaluating the Web page. The sheer size of the site made it difficult to weed through. After considerable time, I decided that although it is huge, the site is thorough and well designed.

10. We cannot process your request for a reservation because some information is missing.

7.12 Revising Sentences to Improve Positive Emphasis

Revise the following sentences to improve positive emphasis. In some cases, you may need to add or omit information to revise effectively.

1. Don't drop in without an appointment. Your counselor or caseworker may be unavailable.

2. Once you choose which days you want off, you can't change them after

December 15 unless you have holidays remaining.

3. Next Tuesday will not be a problem. Our service crew is not overbooked and will not have trouble fitting you in.

4. Please notify the publisher of the magazine of your change of address as soon as possible to prevent a disruption of subscription service.

5. I'm sorry you were worried. You did not miss the deadline for signing up for a flexible medical spending account.

6. We are in the process of upgrading our Web site. Please bear with us.

7. I apologize for my delay in answering your inquiry. The problem was that I had to check with our suppliers to see whether we could provide the item in the quantity you say you want. We can.

8. I was Treasurer of the Accounting Club. Of course, we didn't have much money so I didn't have much responsibility, but I was able to put into practice principles I learned in the classroom.

9. If you have any problems using your e-mail account, I will try to explain it so that you can understand.

10. If you submitted a travel request, as you claim, we have failed to receive it.

7.13 Revising a Memo to Improve Positive Emphasis

Revise the following memo to improve you-attitude and positive emphasis.

> Subject: Status of Building Renovations
>
> The renovation of the lobby is not behind schedule. By Monday, October 9, we hope to be ready to open the west end of the lobby to limited traffic.
>
> The final phase of the renovation will be placing a new marble floor in front of the elevators. This work will not be finished until the end of the month.
>
> Insofar as is possible, the crew will attempt to schedule most of the work during the evenings so that normal business is not disrupted.
>
> Please exercise caution when moving through the construction area. The floor will be uneven and steps will be at unusual heights. Watch your step to avoid accidental tripping or falling.

7.14 Identifying Positive Emphasis in Ads and Documents

Look at print advertisements and at documents you receive from your college or university, from your workplace, and from organizations to which you belong. Identify five sentences that either (a) use positive emphasis or (b) should be revised to be more positive.

As Your Instructor Directs,
a. Share your examples with a small group of students.

b. Write a memo to your instructor discussing your examples.
c. Post an e-mail message to the class discussing your examples.
d. Present two or three of your examples to the class in a short presentation.
e. With your small group, write a collaborative short report to your instructor about the patterns you see.

Polishing Your Prose

Singular and Plural Possessives

To show possession when a noun is singular, put the apostrophe right after the word; then add *s*:

Allen's	The manager's
Smith's	The company's

If the possessing noun is plural, put the apostrophe right after the word:

Customers'

Employees'

Companies'

In names that end with *s* or *x*, style books permit either form:

Thomas'	Linux'	Jones'
Thomas's	Linux's	Jones's

Often, the location of the apostrophe tells the reader whether the noun is singular or plural.

Singular Possessive	Plural Possessive
The employee's	The employees'
Product's	Products'

Because the singular and plural possessives sound the same, look at the logic of your sentence to choose the right word. Also note that when you have plural possessive nouns, other words in the sentence will also become plural.

Plural *employees* have plural *opinions*. Plural *products* have plural *prices*.

We listen to our employees' opinions.

You can find all of our products' prices on our Web site.

Exercises

Choose the correct word in each set of parentheses. Indicate if either word is acceptable.

1. The winter holiday season can account for one-fourth to one-half of a (store's/stores') annual profits.

2. The (Morales's/Morales') loan application is on your desk.

3. In order to sell in another country, you need to understand its (people's/peoples') culture.

4. Each division reviews several (department's/departments') monthly sales plans.

5. Two of our (computer's/computers') monitors need to be repaired.

6. During the trip we will visit 11 (city's/cities') chambers of commerce.

7. Employees who have worked as Big Sisters have enjoyed seeing the (girl's/girls') progress.

8. The trucking (company's/companies') bids are all competitive.

9. The (secretary's/secretaries') benefit plan is excellent.

10. (Briton's/Britons') familiarity with English gives them an advantage over other foreign investors in the U.S. market.

Check your answers to the odd-numbered exercises at the back of the book.

BComm Skill Booster

To apply the concepts in this module, complete lesson 5 on accentuating the positive. You can access the BComm Skill Booster through the text Web site at **www.mhhe.com/bcs2e.**

Module 8

Reader Benefits

To learn how to

- Use audience analysis to identify and choose reader benefits.
- Develop reader benefits with logic and details.
- Match the benefit to the audience.

Start by asking these questions:

- Why do reader benefits work?
- How do I identify reader benefits?
- How detailed should each benefit be?
- How do I decide which benefits to use?
- What else do reader benefits need?

Reader benefits are benefits or advantages that the reader gets by

- Using your services.
- Buying your products.
- Following your policies.
- Adopting your ideas.

Reader benefits are important in both informative and persuasive messages. In informative messages, reader benefits give reasons to comply with the policies you announce and suggest that the policies are good ones. In persuasive messages, reader benefits give reasons to act and help overcome reader resistance. Negative messages (◁▶ Module 11) do not use reader benefits.

Good reader benefits are

- Adapted to the audience.
- Based on intrinsic advantages.

- Supported by clear logic and explained in adequate detail.
- Phrased in you-attitude.

Why do reader benefits work?

Reader benefits improve the audience's attitudes and actions.

Reader benefits improve both the attitudes and the behavior of the people you work with and write to. They make people view you more positively; they make it easier for you to accomplish your goals.

Expectancy theory says most people try to do their best only when they believe that they can succeed and when they want the rewards that success brings. Reader benefits tell or remind readers that they can do the job and that success will be rewarded.[1] Thus they help overcome two problems that reduce motivation: People may not think of all the possible benefits, and they may not understand the relationships among efforts, performance, and rewards.[2]

How do I identify reader benefits?

Brainstorm!

Sometimes reader benefits will be easy to think of and to explain. When they are harder to identify, brainstorm. You may want to brainstorm in two steps:

1. Think of the feelings, fears, and needs that may motivate your reader. Then identify features of your product or policy that meet those needs.
2. Identify the objective features of your product or policy. Then think how these features could benefit the audience.

Try to brainstorm at least three to five possible benefits for every informative message and five to seven benefits for every persuasive message. The more benefits you have, the easier it will be to choose good ones rather than settling for something that's so-so.

1. Think of Feelings, Fears, and Needs That May Motivate Your Reader

One of the best-known analyses of needs is Abraham H. Maslow's hierarchy of needs.[3] Physical needs are the most basic, followed by needs for safety and security, for love and a sense of belonging, for esteem and recognition, and finally for self-actualization or self-fulfillment. All of us go back and forth between higher- and lower-level needs. Whenever lower-level needs make themselves felt, they take priority.

Maslow's model is a good starting place to identify the feelings, fears, and needs that may motivate your audience. Figure 8.1 shows organizational motivators for each of the levels in Maslow's hierarchy.

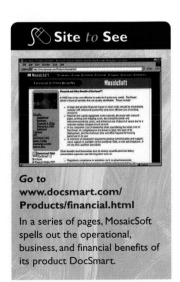

Site *to* See

Go to
**www.docsmart.com/
Products/financial.html**

In a series of pages, MosaicSoft spells out the operational, business, and financial benefits of its product DocSmart.

Figure 8.1

Organizational Motivations for Maslow's Hierarchy of Needs

Self-actualization
- Using your talents and abilities.
- Finding solutions to problems.
- Serving humanity.
- Self-respect and pride.
- Being the best you can be.

Esteem, recognition
- Being publicly recognized for achievements.
- Being promoted or gaining authority.
- Having status symbols.
- Having a good personal reputation.
- Having a good corporate reputation.

Love, belonging
- Having friends, working with people you like.
- Cooperating with other people on a project.
- Conforming to a group's norms.
- Feeling needed.
- Being loyal or patriotic.
- Promoting the welfare of a group you identify with or care about.

Safety, security
- Earning enough to afford a comfortable standard of living.
- Having pleasant working conditions.
- Having good health insurance and pension plans.
- Understanding the reasons for actions by supervisors.
- Being treated fairly.
- Saving time and money.
- Conserving human and environmental resources.

Physical
- Earning enough to pay for basic food, clothing, shelter, and medical care.
- Having safe working conditions.

Often a product or idea can meet needs on several levels. Focus on the ones that audience analysis suggests are most relevant for your audience, but remember that even the best analysis may not reveal all of a reader's needs. For example, a well-paid manager may be worried about security needs if her spouse has lost his job or if the couple is supporting kids in college or an elderly parent.

2. Identify the Features of Your Product or Policy. Then Think How These Features Could Benefit the Audience.

A feature by itself is not a benefit. Often, a feature has several possible benefits.

Feature: Bottled water

Benefits: Is free from chemicals, pollutants

Tastes good

Has no calories

Is easy to carry to class; can be used while biking, driving, hiking

Instant **Replay**

Definition of Reader Benefit

Reader benefits are benefits or advantages that the reader gets by using your services, buying your products, following your policies, or adopting your ideas.

Feature: Closed captions on TV

Benefits: Enables hard-of-hearing viewers to follow dialogue

Helps speakers of English as a second language learn phrases and idioms

Helps small children learn to read

The Rousing Creativity Group sells the solid brass Benefit Finder™ to help salespeople develop benefits for the features of their products or services. See www.rousingcreativity. com/ool_bf_article.html for examples of features and benefits.

Feature: Flextime

Benefits: Enables workers to accommodate personal needs

Helps organization recruit, retain workers

More workers available in early morning and in evening

- Enables office to stay open longer—more service to clients, customers
- Enables workers to communicate with colleagues in different time zones more easily

Different features may benefit different subgroups in your audience. Depending on what features a restaurant offered, you could appeal to one or more of the following subgroups:

Subgroup	Features to meet the subgroup's needs
People who work outside the home	A quick lunch; a relaxing place to take clients or colleagues
Parents with small children	High chairs, child-size portions, and things to keep the kids entertained while they wait for their orders
People who eat out a lot	Variety both in food and in decor
People on tight budgets	Economical food; a place where they don't need to tip (cafeteria or fast food)
People on special diets	Low-sodium and low-calorie dishes; vegetarian food; kosher food
People to whom eating out is part of an evening's entertainment	Music or a floor show; elegant surroundings; reservations so they can get to a show or event after dinner; late hours so they can come to dinner after a show or game

Instant **Replay**

Criteria for Reader Benefits

Good reader benefits are

- Adapted to the audience.
- Based on intrinsic advantages.
- Phrased in you-attitude.

To develop your benefits, think about the details of each one. If your selling point is your relaxing atmosphere, think about the specific details that make the restaurant relaxing. If your strong point is elegant dining, think about all the details that contribute to that elegance. Sometimes you may think of features that do not meet any particular need but are still good benefits. In a

Good reader benefits show how the product, service, or activity meets the audience's needs.

sales letter for a restaurant, you might also want to mention the nonsmoking section, your free coatroom, the fact that you're close to a freeway or offer free parking or a drive-up window, and how fast your service is.

Whenever you're writing to customers or clients about features that are not unique to your organization, it's wise to present both benefits of the features themselves and benefits of dealing with your company. If you talk about the benefits of dining in a relaxed atmosphere but don't mention your own restaurant, people may go somewhere else!

How detailed should each benefit be?

Use strong, vivid details.

You'll usually need at least three to five sentences to give enough details about a reader benefit. If you develop two or three reader benefits fully, you can use just a sentence or two for less important benefits. Develop reader benefits by linking each feature to the readers' needs—and provide details to make the benefit vivid!

Weak: We have placemats with riddles.

Better: Answering all the riddles on Monical's special placemats will keep the kids happy till your pizza comes. If they don't have time to finish (and they may not, since your pizza is ready so quickly), just take the riddles home—or answer them on your next visit.

Make your reader benefits specific.

Weak: You get quick service.

Better: If you only have an hour for lunch, try our Business Buffet. Within minutes, you can choose from a variety of main dishes, vegetables, and a make-your-own-sandwich-and-salad bar. You'll have a lunch that's as light or filling as you want, with time to enjoy it—and still be back to the office on time.

Psychological description is a technique you can use to develop vivid, specific reader benefits. **Psychological description** means creating a scenario rich with sense impressions—what the reader sees, hears, smells, tastes, feels—so readers can picture themselves using your product or service and enjoying its benefits. You can also use psychological description to describe the problem your product will solve. Psychological description works best early in the message to catch readers' attention.

Feature:	Snooze alarm
Benefit:	If the snooze button is pressed, the alarm goes off and comes on again nine minutes later.
Psychological description:	Some mornings, you really want to stay in bed just a few more minutes. With the Sleepytime Snooze Alarm, you can snuggle under the covers for a few extra winks, secure in the knowledge that the alarm will come on again to get you up for that breakfast meeting with an important client. If you don't have to be anywhere soon, you can keep hitting the snooze alarm for up to an additional 63 minutes of sleep. With Sleepytime, you're in control of your mornings.
Feature:	Tilt windows
Benefit:	Easier to clean
Psychological description:	It's no wonder so many cleaners "don't do windows." Balancing precariously on a rickety ladder to clean upper-story windows . . . shivering outside in the winter winds and broiling in the summer sun as you scrub away . . . running inside, then outside, then inside again to try to get the spot that always seems to be on the other side. Cleaning traditional windows really is awful. In contrast, cleaning is a breeze with Tilt-in Windows. Just pull the inner window down and pull the bottom toward you. The whole window lifts out! Repeat for the outer window. Clean them inside in comfort (sitting down or even watching TV if you choose). Then replace the top of the outer window in its track, slide up, and repeat with the inner window. Presto! Clean windows!

In psychological description, you're putting your reader in a picture. If the reader doesn't feel that the picture fits, the technique backfires. To prevent this, psychological description often uses subjunctive verbs ("if you like . . ." "if you were . . .") or the words *maybe* and *perhaps.*

> You're hungry but you don't want to bother with cooking. Perhaps you have guests to take to dinner. Or it's 12 noon and you only have an hour for lunch. Whatever the situation, the Illini Union has a food service to fit your needs. If you want convenience, we have it. If it's atmosphere you're seeking, it's here too. And if you're concerned about the price, don't be. When you're looking for a great meal, the Illini Union is the place to find it.
>
> —*Illini Union brochure*

Instant
Replay

Psychological
Description
Psychological
description means
creating a scenario
rich with sense
impressions—what
the reader sees,
hears, smells, tastes,
feels—so readers
can picture
themselves using
your product or
service and enjoying
its benefits.

How do I decide which benefits to use?

Use the following three principles to decide.

Three principles guide your choice of reader benefits:

1. Use at least one benefit for each part of your audience.
2. Use intrinisic benefits.
3. Use the benefits you can develop most fully.

1. Use at Least One Benefit for Each Part of Your Audience

Most messages go to multiple audiences. In a memo announcing a company-subsidized day care program, you want benefits not only for parents who might use the service but also for people who don't have children or whose children are older. Reader benefits for these last two audiences help convince them that spending money on day care is a good use of scarce funds.

In a letter to "consumers" or "voters," different people will have different concerns. The more of these concerns you speak to, the more persuasive you'll be.

2. Use Intrinsic Benefits.

Intrinsic benefits come automatically from using a product or doing something. **Extrinsic benefits** are "added on." Someone in power decides to give them; they do not necessarily come from using the product or doing the action. Figure 8.2 gives examples of extrinsic and intrinsic rewards for four activities.

Intrinsic rewards or benefits are better than extrinsic benefits for two reasons:

1. There just aren't enough extrinsic rewards for everything you want people to do. You can't give a prize to every customer every time he or she places an order or to every subordinate who does what he or she is supposed to do.

Figure 8.2
Extrinsic and
Intrinsic Rewards

Activity	Extrinsic Reward	Intrinsic Reward
Making a sale.	Getting a commission.	Pleasure in convincing someone; pride in using your talents to think of a strategy and execute it.
Turning in a suggestion to a company suggestion system.	Getting a monetary reward when the suggestion is implemented.	Solving a problem at work; making the work environment a little more pleasant.
Writing a report that solves an organizational problem.	Getting praise, a good performance appraisal, and maybe a raise.	Pleasure in having an effect on an organization; pride in using your skills to solve problems; solving the problem itself.

Matching the Benefit to the Audience

When you write to different audiences, you may need to stress different reader benefits.

Suppose that you manufacture a product and want to persuade dealers to carry it. The features you may cite in ads directed toward customers—stylish colors, sleek lines, convenience, durability, good price—won't convince dealers. Shelf space is at a premium, and no dealer carries all the models of all the brands available for any given product. Why should the dealer stock your product? To be persuasive, talk about the features that are benefits from the dealer's point of view: turnover, profit margin, a national advertising campaign to build customer awareness and interest, special store displays that will draw attention to the product.

Different consumers may want different varieties of the same product. Believing that "retail is detail," Target stocks Jays potato chips in Chicago but Saguaro chips in Phoenix. Customers on the east coast of Florida want bikinis, but the older customers on Florida's west coast prefer one-piece suits.

The Wall Street Journal asked subscribers to renew their subscriptions for two more years rather than just for one. The cost of the second year was 66% of the cost of the first year. The mailing admitted that renewing for two years would tie up the money but presented the cost of the second year as "a 34% tax-free return on your money." The benefit was highly appropriate for an audience concerned about returns on investments and aware of the risk that normally accompanies high returns. *Garbage* magazine urged subscribers to respond to the first renewal notice to save the paper that an additional mailing would take. This logic was appropriate for an audience concerned about the disposal of solid waste.

Even in your own organization, different audiences may care about different things. To create an intranet for Xerox, Cindy Casselman needed

In big cities and rural areas, small banks are thriving by offering superior service: low fees, extended hours, and free services such as investment advice, babysitting, and shoe shines.

support from a variety of divisions. She had to persuade her own supervisor to let her work on the project. He said "yes" but told her she had to raise the $250,000 herself. She got the money and the programming talent she needed by showing other managers how they would benefit from the proposed intranet. The CIO cared about the enormous financial investment the company had already made in its computer infrastructure. She told him that the intranet would put content there. The director of education and training cared about learning at Xerox. Cindy pointed out that the intranet would provide a place for learning to happen. She raised the $250,000 by showing people how her idea would benefit the aspects of the company they cared most about.

Source: Gregory A. Patterson, "Different Strokes: Target 'Micromarkets' Its Way to Success: No 2 Stores Are Alike," *The Wall Street Journal,* May 31, 1995, A1, A9; and Michael Warshaw, "The Good Guy's and Gal's Guide to Office Politics," *Fast Company,* April–May 1998, 156–78.

2. Research suggests that you'll motivate subordinates more effectively by stressing the intrinsic benefits of following policies and adopting proposals.

In a groundbreaking study of professional employees, Frederick Herzberg found that the things people said they liked about their jobs were all *intrinsic* rewards—pride in achievement, an enjoyment of the work itself, responsibility. Extrinsic features—pay, company policy—were sometimes mentioned as things people disliked, but they were never cited as things that motivated or satisfied them. People who made a lot of money still did not mention salary as a good point about the job or the organization.[4] In a 1998 survey of workers all over the United States, Aon Consulting found that the factor most likely to produce employee loyalty and a desire to be productive was management's recognition of employees' personal and family lives. Salary didn't make the top 10. Many family-friendly companies have discovered that a culture of care keeps turnover low. The higher salary that a competitor might pay just doesn't overcome the advantage of working at a supportive, flexible company that values its employees.[5] In the current competitive job market, different candidates want different things. But many accept lower salaries to get flextime, stock options, interesting work, or people they want to work with.[6]

Since money is not the only motivator, choose reader benefits that identify intrinsic as well as extrinsic motivators for following policies and adopting ideas.

3. Use the Benefits You Can Develop Most Fully

One-sentence benefits don't do much. Use the benefits that you can develop in three to five sentences or more.

A reader benefit is a claim or assertion that the reader will benefit if he or she does something. Convincing the reader, therefore, involves two steps: making sure that the benefit really will occur and explaining it to the reader.

If the logic behind a claimed reader benefit is faulty or inaccurate, there's no way to make that particular reader benefit convincing. Revise the benefit to make it logical.

Faulty logic: Using a computer will enable you to write letters, memos, and reports much more quickly.

Analysis: If you've never used a computer, in the short run it will take you *longer* to create a document using a computer than it would to type it. Even after you know how to use a computer and its software, the real time savings comes when a document incorporates parts of previous documents or goes through several revisions. Creating a first draft from scratch will still take planning and careful composing; the time savings may or may not be significant.

Revised reader benefit: Using a computer allows you to revise and edit a document more easily. It eliminates retyping as a separate step and reduces the time needed to proofread revisions. It allows you to move the text around on the page to create the best layout.

If the logic is sound, making that logic evident to the reader is a matter of providing enough evidence and showing how the evidence proves the claim that there will be a benefit. Always provide enough detail to be vivid and concrete. You'll need more detail in the following situations:

- The reader may not have thought of the benefit before.
- The benefit depends on the difference between the long run and the short run.
- The reader will be hard to persuade, and you need detail to make the benefit vivid and emotionally convincing.

Does the following statement have enough detail?

You will benefit if the company saves money.

Readers always believe their own experience. Many readers will know that they didn't get bonuses even during a year that the company did well. In addition to bonuses for top executives, companies could use profits to pay higher dividends to shareholders, to retire debt, or to increase research and development spending. Even spending money on upgrading computers or remodeling the employee lounge may not seem like a strong benefit to some workers. Instead, you'll need to show that money saved will go into one or more specific programs that will benefit employees directly or indirectly. The more indirect the benefit is, the more proof you'll need.

What else do reader benefits need?

Check for you-attitude.

If reader benefits aren't in you-attitude (◀ ▷ p. 106), they'll sound selfish and won't be as effective as they could be. A Xerox letter selling copiers with strong you-attitude as well as reader benefits got a far bigger response than did an alternate version with reader benefits but no you-attitude.[7] It doesn't matter how you phrase reader benefits while you're brainstorming and developing them, but in your final draft, edit for you-attitude.

Lacks you-attitude: We have the lowest prices in town.

You-attitude: At Havlichek Cars, you get the best deal in town.

Summary of Key Points

- **Reader benefits** are benefits or advantages that the reader gets by using your services, buying your products, following your policies, or adopting your ideas. Reader benefits can exist for policies and ideas as well as for goods and services. Reader benefits tell readers that they can do the job and that success will be rewarded.

- Good reader benefits are adapted to the audience, based on intrinsic rather than extrinsic advantages, supported by clear logic and explained in adequate detail, and phrased in you-attitude. Extrinsic benefits

simply aren't available to reward every desired behavior; further, they reduce the satisfaction in doing something for its own sake.

- To create reader benefits,
    1. Identify the feelings, fears, and needs that may motivate your reader.
    2. Show how the reader can meet his or her needs with the features of the policy or product.

- **Psychological description** means creating a scenario rich with sense impressions—

what the reader sees, hears, smells, tastes, feels—so readers can picture themselves using your product or service and enjoying its benefits.

- Brainstorm twice as many reader benefits as you'll need for a message.
  1. Use at least one benefit for each part of your audience.

2. Use intrinsic benefits.
3. Use the benefits you can develop most fully.

- Make sure reader benefits are phrased in you-attitude.

Assignments for Module 8

Questions for Comprehension

8.1 What are reader benefits?

8.2 In a message with reader benefits, how many different benefits should you use?

8.3 What is the difference between intrinsic and extrinsic reader benefits? Which are better? Why?

8.4 What is psychological description?

Questions for Critical Thinking

8.5 If you are writing to multiple audiences with different needs, should you include all the reader benefits you can think of in the message?

8.6 Why do reader benefits need to be in you-attitude?

8.7 How do reader benefits help you achieve your goals?

Exercises and Problems

8.8 Identifying and Developing Reader Benefits

Listed here are several things an organization might like its employees to do.

1. Use less paper.
2. Attend a brown bag lunch to discuss ways to improve products or services.
3. Become more physically fit.
4. Volunteer for community organizations.
5. Ease a new hire's transition into the unit.

As Your Instructor Directs,

a. Identify the motives or needs that might be met by each of the activities.

b. Develop each need or motive as a reader benefit in a full paragraph. Use additional paragraphs for the other needs met by the activity. Remember to use you-attitude!

8.9 Identifying Objections and Reader Benefits

Think of an organization you know something about, and answer the following questions for it.

1. Your organization is thinking of creating a training video. What objec-

tions might people have? What benefits could videos offer your organization? Which people would be easiest to convince?

2. The advisory council of State College recommends that business faculty have

three-month internships with local organizations to learn material. What objections might people in your organization have to bringing in faculty interns? What benefits might your organization receive? Which people would be easiest to convince?

3. Your organization is thinking of buying laptop computers for all employees who travel. What fears or objections might people have? What benefits might your organization

receive? Which people would be easiest to convince?

As Your Instructor Directs,
a. Share your answers orally with a small group of students.
b. Present your answers in an oral presentation to the class.
c. E-mail your answers to class members.
d. Write a paragraph developing the best reader benefit you identified. Remember to use you-attitude.

8.10 Identifying and Developing Reader Benefits for Different Audiences

Assume that you want to encourage people to do one of the following activities:

1. Having a personal trainer
   Audiences: Professional athletes
   Busy managers
   Someone trying to lose weight
   Someone making a major lifestyle change after a heart attack

2. Buying a cellular phone
   Audiences: People who do a lot of big-city driving
   People who do a lot of driving in rural areas
   People who do a lot of flying

3. Getting advice about interior decorating
   Audiences: Young people with little money to spend
   Parents with small children
   People upgrading or adding to their furnishings
   Older people moving from single-family homes into smaller apartments or condominiums

Builders furnishing model homes

4. Getting advice on investment strategies
   Audiences: New college graduates
   People earning more than $100,000 annually
   People responsible for investing funds for a church, synagogue, or temple
   Parents with small children
   People within 10 years of retirement

5. Gardening
   Audiences: People with small children
   People in apartments
   People concerned about reducing pesticides
   People on tight budgets
   Retirees
   Teenagers

6. Buying a laptop computer
   Audiences: College students
   Financial planners who visit clients at home
   Sales representatives who travel constantly

People who make PowerPoint presentations

7. Teaching adults to read

Audiences: Retired workers

Business people

Students who want to become teachers

High school and college students

People concerned about poverty

8. Vacationing at a luxury hotel

Audiences: Stressed-out people who want to relax

Tourists who like to sightsee and absorb the local culture

Business people who want to stay in touch with the office even on vacation

Parents with small children

Weekend athletes who want to have fun

9. Attending a fantasy sports camp (you pick the sport), playing with and against retired players who provide coaching and advice

10. Attending a health spa where clients get low-fat and low-calorie meals, massages, beauty treatments, and guidance in nutrition and exercise

As Your Instructor Directs,

a. Identify needs that you could meet for the audiences listed here. In addition to needs that several audiences share, identify at least one need that would be particularly important to each group.

b. Identify a product or service that could meet each need.

c. Write a paragraph or two of reader benefits for each product or service. Remember to use you-attitude.

d. Develop one or more of the benefits using psychological description.

Hints:

• For this assignment, you can combine benefits or programs as if a single source offered them all.

• Add specific details about particular sports, cities, tourist attractions, activities, etc., as material for your description.

• Be sure to move beyond reader benefits to vivid details and sense impressions.

• Put your benefits in you-attitude.

 Polishing Your Prose

Plurals and Possessives

Singular possessives and plurals sound the same but are spelled differently. A possessive noun will always have an apostrophe. Most possessives of singular nouns are formed by adding 's to the word.

Singular Possessive	Plural
company's	companies
computer's	computers
family's	families
job's	jobs
manager's	managers
team's	team

Because singular possessive nouns and plurals sound the same, you will have to look at the logic of your sentence to choose the right word.

Exercises

Choose the right word in each set of parentheses.

1. We can move your (families/family's) furniture safely and efficiently.

2. Purchase the (refreshments/refreshment's) at the shop in the main lobby for this afternoon's meeting.

3. A (memos/memo's) style can build goodwill.

4. The (supervisors/supervisor's) memo outlines our new purchasing policy.

5. The (companies/company's) benefits plan should be checked periodically to make sure it continues to serve the needs of employees.

6. This (résumés/résumé's) typeface is too small and blocky to read easily.

7. The (managers/manager's) all have open-door policies.

8. We've received several (reports/report's) supporting our plans to expand.

9. Burnout affects a (social workers/social worker's) productivity as well as his or her morale.

10. John says the (consultants/consultant's) fee was reasonable for the (services/service's) provided.

Check your answers to the odd-numbered exercises at the back of the book.

BComm Skill Booster

To apply the concepts in this module, complete lesson 52 on reader benefits. You can access the BComm Skill Booster through the text Web site at **www.mhhe.com/bcs2e.**

Cases for Communicators

Web-Cast, Get Your Web-Cast Here!

When companies first began establishing themselves on the Internet, online advertising was viewed as a veritable gold mine, an endless source of revenues.

Today, Internet advertising is no longer viewed as a prime revenue generator. As a result, many online businesses have begun charging fees for their products and services. For example, many online newspapers now charge customers a monthly access fee, and even some employment search engines require an upfront payment from job seekers. This has not been an easy pill for online consumers to swallow, however, as they were accustomed to receiving these same benefits and services at no cost.

It is in this new, revenue-starved online environment that ABC News finds itself. ABC News provides high-quality, detailed coverage of national and international news <http://www.abcnews.com>. Its news stories, including numerous video clips, had been available free, but that is all about to change. The company has now launched a new online video subscription service, News On Demand, for paying consumers. News On Demand, promoted as "Video news on your schedule," includes audiocasts; video clips from special news segments, such as Exclusives, In the News, and Today's Features; and broadcasts of popular ABC News programs, including 20/20, Nightline, and World News Tonight.

One of ABC's primary competitors, CNN, already charges a fee for its video offerings. Will online users be willing to pay the $4.95 subscription fee, particularly when television broadcasts and the text versions of news stories are still available to them free?

Source: Daniel Sorid, "Livewire: Will Consumers Pay for News Web-Casts?" Reuters, August 2, 2002. Accessed on Yahoo! News, August 2, 2002.

Individual Activity

You work in the marketing department at ABC News and have been selected to work on the advertising campaign being developed to promote News On Demand. ABC News knows that its products are perceived as being high quality, but this will likely not be enough to convince consumers that they should subscribe to the new video service. To achieve this goal, the marketing department has developed a plan to e-mail informational advertisements to prospective subscribers.

The company has gathered e-mail addresses from users who have signed up for News Alerts and other special services. To reach new audiences, the company plans to purchase specialized e-mail databases of potential customers.

Subscribers will receive the following new benefits:

- Personalization tools that will allow each customer to create a unique "video experience"
- An increased number of available video clips
- Versions of the video product that would be accessible via hand-held units such as PDAs and cell phones (The company already provides its news stories via these devices.)
- Improved video quality and content.

Identify the audiences who might respond to these benefits. Consider the following questions:

- What other benefits are inherent to the News On Demand product?

- Who is likely to access these Web-casts and why?
- Why would customers pay for News On Demand rather than a similar product that costs less or is free?
- What types of customers might gain from the product's benefits?
- What feelings or fears might be motivating these users, particularly those who are used to getting this product at no cost?
- What needs may motivate these users?

Identify as many different potential customer groups, or audiences, as you can think of, noting at least one benefit that each of those groups can expect to gain from the News On Demand product.

Give enough detail in your customer descriptions so that the marketing department can use your information to guide its purchase of the e-mail databases!

Group Activity

Plan the e-mail that will be sent out to these potential News On Demand customers. How can you convince ABC News users that they should subscribe to this new offering, in effect paying for a product that they used to receive for free?

Combine the results of your list with those of your classmates to generate a comprehensive list of user benefits and potential audiences. Then, as a group, discuss these audiences and the corresponding benefits, and select the best five on which to focus. Together, develop benefits that can be part of the letter to these potential News On Demand subscribers.

Be sure to

- Include a benefit for each audience.
- Justify negative information, focusing on what the reader can do rather than on limitations.
- Omit unnecessary negative information.
- Use you-attitude.
- Talk about the reader, not the company.

Unit Three

Letters, Memos, and E-Mail Messages

Module 9

Formats for Letters and Memos

To learn how to

- Choose and use standard formats.

- Use nonsexist courtesy titles.

- Create a professional image.

Start by asking these questions:

- How should I set up letters?

- What courtesy titles should I use?

- How should I set up memos?

Letters normally go to people outside your organization; **memos** go to other people in your organization. In very large organizations, corporate culture determines whether people in different divisions or different locations feel close enough to each other to write memos.

Letters and memos do not necessarily differ in length, formality, writing style, or pattern of organization. However, letters and memos do differ in format. **Format** means the parts of a document and the way they are arranged on the page.

Short reports use letter or memo format (see Module 23 ◁ ▷) Long reports can use the formal format illustrated in Module 24. If your organization has its own formats for letters and memos, use them. Otherwise, choose one of the formats in this module. See Module 13 ◁ ▷ for e-mail formats.

How should I set up letters?

Use block or modified block format.

The two most common letter formats are **block,** sometimes called full block (see Figure 9.2), and **modified block** (see Figure 9.3). Your organization may make minor changes from the diagrams in margins or spacing.

Figure 9.1 shows how the formats differ.

Use the same level of formality in the **salutation,** or greeting, as you would in talking to someone on the phone: *Dear Glenn* if you're on a first-name basis, *Dear Mr. Helms* if you don't know the reader well enough to use the first name.

Sincerely and *Cordially* are standard **complimentary closes.** When you are writing to people in special groups or to someone who is a friend as well as a business acquaintance, you may want to use a less formal close. Depending on the circumstances, the following informal closes might be acceptable: *Yours for a better environment,* or even *Ciao* or *Thanks.*

In **mixed punctuation,** a colon follows the salutation and a comma follows the close. In a sales or fund-raising letter, it is acceptable to use a comma after the salutation to make the letter look like a personal letter rather than like a business letter. Most organizations use mixed punctuation. A few organizations use open punctuation, which is faster to type. In **open punctuation,** omit all punctuation after the salutation and the close.

A **subject line** tells what the letter is about. Subject lines are required in memos; they are optional in letters. Good subject lines are specific, concise, and appropriate for your purposes and the response you expect from your reader.

- When you have good news, put it in the subject line.
- When your information is neutral, summarize it concisely in the subject line.
- When your information is negative, use a negative subject line if the reader may not read the message or needs the information to act, or if the negative is your error.
- When you have a request that will be easy for the reader to grant, put either the subject of the request or a direct question in the subject line.
- When you must persuade a reluctant reader, use a common ground, a reader benefit, or a directed subject line (◁ ▶ Module 12) that makes your stance on the issue clear.

Site *to* See

Go to
www.usps.gov/zip4/welcome.htm

If you know the address, the U.S. Post Office page will give you the ZIP + 4 code.

	Block	Modified Block
Date and signature block	Lined up at left margin	Lined up $\frac{1}{2}$ or $\frac{2}{3}$ over to the right
Paragraph indentation	None	Optional
Subject Line	Optional	Rare

Figure 9.1

Differences between Letter Formats

Figure 9.2

Block Format on Letterhead (mixed punctuation; collection letter)

100 Freeway Exchange
Provo, UT 84610

Northwest Hardware Warehouse

(801) 555-4683

Line up everything at left margin.

↑↓ *2–6 spaces depending on length of letter.*

June 20, 2004

Mr. James E. Murphy, Accounts Payable   *Title could be on a separate line.*
Salt Lake Equipment Rentals
5600 Wasatch Boulevard
Salt Lake City, Utah 84121

1″–1½″

Use first name in salutation if you'd use it on the phone.

Dear Jim: *Colon in mixed punctuation*

The following items totaling $393.09 are still open on your account.   *¶ 1 never has a heading.*

Invoice #01R-784391 *Bold heading*

After the bill for this invoice arrived on May 14, you wrote saying that the material had not been delivered to you. On May 29, our Claims Department sent you a copy of the delivery receipt signed by an employee of Salt Lake Equipment. You have had proof of delivery for over three weeks, but your payment has not yet arrived.

⅝″ – 1″

Please send a check for $78.42.   *Single-space paragraphs.*
Double-space between paragraphs.

Triple-space before new heading.

Voucher #59351

The reference line on your voucher #59351, dated June 11, indicates that it is the gross payment for invoice #01G-002345. However, the voucher was only for $1171.25, while the invoice amount was $1246.37. Please send a check for $75.12 to clear this item.

Do not indent paragraphs.

Voucher #55032

Voucher #55032, dated June 15, subtracts a credit for $239.55 from the amount due. Our records do not show that any credit is due on this voucher. Please send either an explanation or a check to cover the $239.55 immediately.

Total Amount Due   *Headings are optional in letters.*

Please send a check for $393.09 to cover these three items and to bring your account up to date.

↓ *2–3 spaces*

Sincerely,

3–4 spaces

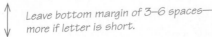

Neil Hutchinson
Credit Representative

cc: Joan Stottlemyer, Credit Manager

↑↓ *Leave bottom margin of 3–6 spaces— more if letter is short.*

Figure 9.3

Modified Block Format on Letterhead (mixed punctuation; letter of recommendation)

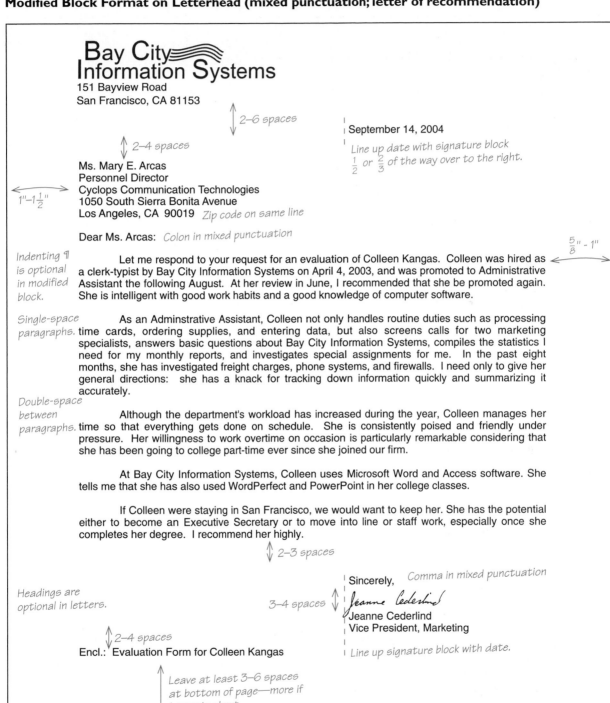

Bay City Information Systems

151 Bayview Road
San Francisco, CA 81153

2–6 spaces

2–4 spaces

September 14, 2004

Line up date with signature block
$\frac{1}{2}$ *or* $\frac{2}{3}$ *of the way over to the right.*

1"–1$\frac{1}{2}$"

Ms. Mary E. Arcas
Personnel Director
Cyclops Communication Technologies
1050 South Sierra Bonita Avenue
Los Angeles, CA 90019 *Zip code on same line*

Dear Ms. Arcas: *Colon in mixed punctuation*

$\frac{5}{8}$ *" – 1"*

Indenting ¶ is optional in modified block.

Let me respond to your request for an evaluation of Colleen Kangas. Colleen was hired as a clerk-typist by Bay City Information Systems on April 4, 2003, and was promoted to Administrative Assistant the following August. At her review in June, I recommended that she be promoted again. She is intelligent with good work habits and a good knowledge of computer software.

Single-space paragraphs.

As an Adminstrative Assistant, Colleen not only handles routine duties such as processing time cards, ordering supplies, and entering data, but also screens calls for two marketing specialists, answers basic questions about Bay City Information Systems, compiles the statistics I need for my monthly reports, and investigates special assignments for me. In the past eight months, she has investigated freight charges, phone systems, and firewalls. I need only to give her general directions: she has a knack for tracking down information quickly and summarizing it accurately.

Double-space between paragraphs.

Although the department's workload has increased during the year, Colleen manages her time so that everything gets done on schedule. She is consistently poised and friendly under pressure. Her willingness to work overtime on occasion is particularly remarkable considering that she has been going to college part-time ever since she joined our firm.

At Bay City Information Systems, Colleen uses Microsoft Word and Access software. She tells me that she has also used WordPerfect and PowerPoint in her college classes.

If Colleen were staying in San Francisco, we would want to keep her. She has the potential either to become an Executive Secretary or to move into line or staff work, especially once she completes her degree. I recommend her highly.

2–3 spaces

Sincerely,   *Comma in mixed punctuation*

Headings are optional in letters.

3–4 spaces

Jeanne Cederlind
Jeanne Cederlind
Vice President, Marketing

Line up signature block with date.

2–4 spaces

Encl.: Evaluation Form for Colleen Kangas

Leave at least 3–6 spaces at bottom of page—more if letter is short.

Creating a Professional Image, I

The way you and your documents look affects the way people respond to you and to them. Every organization has a dress code. One young man was upset when an older man told him he should wear wing-tip shoes. He was wearing leather shoes but not the kind that said "I'm promotable" in that workplace. Dress codes are rarely spelled out; the older worker was doing the young man a favor by being direct. If you have a mentor in the organization, ask him or her if there are other ways you can make your appearance even more professional. If you don't have a mentor, look at the people who rank above you. Notice clothing, jewelry, and hairstyles. If you're on a budget, go to stores that sell expensive clothing to check the kind of buttons, the texture and colors of fabric, and the width of lapels and belts. Then go to stores in your price range and choose garments that imitate the details of expensive clothing.

Rules for documents, like rules for clothing, are sometimes unwritten. To make your document look professional,

- Use good visual impact (◀ ▶ Module 5).
- Edit and proofread to eliminate errors and typos (◀ ▶ Modules 14 and 15).
- Make sure the ink or toner is printing evenly.
- Use a standard format.

For examples of subject lines in each of these situations, see Modules 10, 11, and 12.

A **reference line** refers the reader to the number used on the previous correspondence this letter replies to, or the order or invoice number which this letter is about. Very large organizations, such as the IRS, use numbers on every piece of correspondence they send out so that it is possible to quickly find the earlier document to which an incoming letter refers.

Both formats can use headings, lists, and indented sections for emphasis.

Each format has advantages. Block format is the format most frequently used for business letters; readers expect it; it can be typed quickly since everything is lined up at the left margin. Modified block format creates a visually attractive page by moving the date and signature block over into what would otherwise be empty white space. Modified block is a traditional format; readers are comfortable with it.

The examples of the formats in Figures 9.2 and 9.3 show one-page letters on company letterhead. **Letterhead** is preprinted stationery with the organization's name, logo, address, and phone number. Figure 9.4 shows how to set up modified block format when you do not have letterhead. (It is also acceptable to use block format without letterhead.)

Use the format your reader expects.

Figure 9.4

Modified Block Format without Letterhead (open punctuation; claim letter)

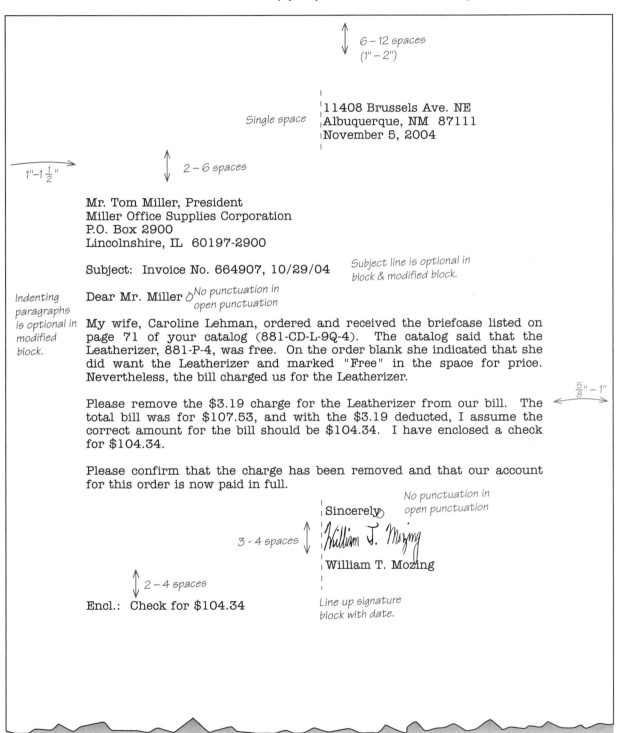

6 – 12 spaces
(1" – 2")

Single space

11408 Brussels Ave. NE
Albuquerque, NM 87111
November 5, 2004

1"–1 ½ "

2 – 6 spaces

Mr. Tom Miller, President
Miller Office Supplies Corporation
P.O. Box 2900
Lincolnshire, IL 60197-2900

Subject: Invoice No. 664907, 10/29/04

Subject line is optional in block & modified block.

Indenting paragraphs is optional in modified block.

Dear Mr. Miller

No punctuation in open punctuation

My wife, Caroline Lehman, ordered and received the briefcase listed on page 71 of your catalog (881-CD-L-9Q-4). The catalog said that the Leatherizer, 881-P-4, was free. On the order blank she indicated that she did want the Leatherizer and marked "Free" in the space for price. Nevertheless, the bill charged us for the Leatherizer.

⅝" – 1"

Please remove the $3.19 charge for the Leatherizer from our bill. The total bill was for $107.53, and with the $3.19 deducted, I assume the correct amount for the bill should be $104.34. I have enclosed a check for $104.34.

Please confirm that the charge has been removed and that our account for this order is now paid in full.

Sincerely

No punctuation in open punctuation

3 - 4 spaces

William T. Mozing

William T. Mozing

2 – 4 spaces

Encl.: Check for $104.34

Line up signature block with date.

When your letter runs two or more pages, use a heading on the second page to identify it. Putting the reader's name in the heading helps the writer, who may be printing out many letters at a time, to make sure the right second page gets in the envelope. Even when the signature block is on the second page, it is still lined up with the date.

Reader's Name
Date
Page Number

or

| Reader's Name | Page Number | Date |

When a letter runs two or more pages, use letterhead only for page 1. (See Figures 9.5 and 9.6.) For the remaining pages, use plain paper that matches the letterhead in weight, texture, and color.

Set side margins of 1″ to 1½″ on the left and ⅝″ to 1″ on the right. If your letterhead extends all the way across the top of the page, set your margins even with the ends of the letterhead for the most visually pleasing page. The top margin should be three to six lines under the letterhead, or 2″ down from the top of the page if you aren't using letterhead. If your letter is very short, you may want to use bigger side and top margins so that the letter is centered on the page.

Many letters are accompanied by other documents. Whatever these documents may be—a multi-page report or a two-line note—they are called **enclosures,** since they are enclosed in the envelope. The writer should refer to the enclosures in the body of the letter: "As you can see from my résumé,. . . ." The enclosure line is usually abbreviated: *Encl.* (see Figure 9.3). The abbreviation reminds the person who seals the letter to include the enclosure(s).

Sometimes you write to one person but send copies of your letter to other people. If you want the reader to know that other people are getting copies, list their names on the last page. The abbreviation *cc* originally meant *carbon copy* but now means *computer copy*. Other acceptable abbreviations include *pc* for *photocopy* or simply *c* for *copy*. You can also send copies to other people without telling the reader. Such copies are called **blind copies.** Blind copies are not mentioned on the original; they are listed on the copy saved for the file with the abbreviation *bc* preceding the names of people getting these copies.

You do not need to indicate that you have shown a letter to your superior or that you are saving a copy of the letter for your own files. These are standard practices.

States with names of more than five letters are frequently abbreviated in letters and memos. The U.S. Postal Service abbreviations use two capital letters with no punctuation. See Figure 9.7.

Figure 9.5

Second Page of a Two-Page Letter, Block Format (mixed punctuation; informative letter)

State
University

4300 Gateway Boulevard
Midland, TX 77205

August 10, 2004

1"–1½"

Ms. Stephanie Voght
Stephen F. Austin High School
1200 Southwest Blvd.
San Antonio, TX 78214

↑ *2 – 3 spaces*

Dear Ms. Voght: *Colon in mixed punctuation.*

Enclosed are 100 brochures about State University to distribute to your students. The brochures describe the academic programs and financial aid available. When you need additional brochures, just let me know.

⅝" – 1"

Videotape about State University

You may also want to show your students the videotape "Life at State University." This 45-

Plain paper for page 2. ↕ *½" – 1"*

Center

Stephanie Voght ← *Reader's name*   2   August 10, 2004

Also OK to line up page number date at left under reader's name.

campus life, including football and basketball games, fraternities and sororities, clubs and organizations, and opportunities for volunteer work. The tape stresses the diversity of the student body and the very different lifestyles that are available at State.

Triple space before each new heading.

Scheduling the Videotape   *Bold headings.*

Same margins as p 1.

To schedule your free showing, just fill out the enclosed card with your first, second, and third choices for dates, and return it in the stamped, self-addressed envelope. Dates are reserved in the order that requests arrive. Send in your request early to increase the chances of getting the date you want.

"Life at State University" will be on its way to give your high school students a preview of the college experience.

Sincerely, *Comma in mixed punctuation.*

3 – 4 spaces ↕

Michael L. Mahler
Director of Admissions

Headings are optional in letters.

↕ *2 – 4 spaces*

Encl.: Brochures, Reservation Form

cc: R. J. Holland, School Superintendent
    Jose Lavilla, President, PTS Association

Figure 9.6

Second Page of a Two-Page Letter, Modified Block Format (mixed punctuation; goodwill letter)

1500 Summit Avenue
Minneapolis, MN 55401

(612) 555-1002
Fax (612) 555-4032

November 8, 2004

Line up date with signature block.

2 – 4 spaces

Mr. Roger B. Castino
Castino Floors and Carpets
418 E. North Street
Brockton, MA 02410

Dear Mr. Castino:

Indenting paragraphs is optional in modified block.

Welcome to the team of Glenarvon Carpet dealers!

Your first shipment of Glenarvon samples should reach you within ten days. The samples include new shades in a variety of weights. With Glenarvon Carpets, your customers can choose matching colors in heavy-duty weights for high-traffic areas and lighter, less expensive weights for less-used rooms.

Plain paper for page 2

½" – 1"

Mr. Roger B. Castino   *Center* 2   *November 8, 2004*

Reader's name

territory. In addition, as a dealer you receive

* Sales kit highlighting product features
* Samples to distribute to customers
* Advertising copy to run in local newspapers
* Display units to place in your store.

Indent or center list to emphasize it.

Use same margins as p 1.

The Annual Sales Meeting each January keeps you up-to-date on new products while you get to know other dealers and Glenarvon executives and relax at a resort hotel.

Make your reservations now for Monterey January 10-13 for your first Glenarvon Sales Meeting!

Cordially, *Comma in mixed punctuation.*

3 – 4 spaces

Barbara S. Charbonneau
Vice President, Marketing

Line up signature block with date in heading and on p 1.

1 – 4 spaces

Encl.: Organization Chart
Product List
National Advertising Campaigns in 2004

1 – 4 spaces

cc: Nancy Magill, Northeast Sales Manager
Edward Spaulding, Sales Representative

3 – 6 spaces — more if second page isn't a full page.

Figure 9.7
Postal Service Abbreviations for States, Territories, and Provinces

State Name	Postal Service Abbreviation	State Name	Postal Service Abbreviation
Alabama	AL	Missouri	MO
Alaska	AK	Montana	MT
Arizona	AZ	Nebraska	NE
Arkansas	AR	Nevada	NV
California	CA	New Hampshire	NH
Colorado	CO	New Jersey	NJ
Connecticut	CT	New Mexico	NM
Delaware	DE	New York	NY
District of Columbia	DC	North Carolina	NC
Florida	FL	North Dakota	ND
Georgia	GA	Ohio	OH
Hawaii	HI	Oklahoma	OK
Idaho	ID	Oregon	OR
Illinois	IL	Pennsylvania	PA
Indiana	IN	Rhode Island	RI
Iowa	IA	South Carolina	SC
Kansas	KS	South Dakota	SD
Kentucky	KY	Tennessee	TN
Louisiana	LA	Texas	TX
Maine	ME	Utah	UT
Maryland	MD	Vermont	VT
Massachusetts	MA	Virginia	VA
Michigan	MI	Washington	WA
Minnesota	MN	West Virginia	WV
Mississippi	MS	Wisconsin	WI
		Wyoming	WY

Territory	Postal Service Abbreviation	Province Name	Postal Service Abbreviation
Guam	GU	Alberta	AB
Puerto Rico	PR	British Columbia	BC
Virgin Islands	VI	Labrador	LB
		Manitoba	MB
		New Brunswick	NB
		Newfoundland	NF
		Northwest Territories	NT
		Nova Scotia	NS
		Ontario	ON
		Prince Edward Island	PE
		Quebec	PQ
		Saskatchewan	SK
		Yukon Territory	YT

What courtesy titles should I use?

Use "Ms." unless a woman has a professional title or prefers a traditional title. Use "Mr." unless a man has a professional title.

Letters require courtesy titles in the salutation *unless* you're on a first-name basis with your reader. Use the first name only if you'd use it in talking to the person on the phone.

When You Know the Reader's Name and Gender

When you know your reader's name and gender, use courtesy titles that do not indicate marital status: *Mr.* for men and *Ms.* for women. There are, however, two exceptions:

1. Use professional titles when they're relevant.

   Dr. Kristen Sorenson is our new company physician.

   The Rev. Robert Townsley gave the invocation.

2. If a woman prefers to be addressed as *Mrs.* or *Miss,* use the title she prefers rather than *Ms.* (You-attitude ◀▶ p. 106] takes precedence over nonsexist language: address the reader as she—or he—prefers to be addressed.)
   To find out if a woman prefers a traditional title,
   a. Check the signature block in previous correspondence. If a woman types her name as *(Miss) Elaine Anderson* or *(Mrs.) Kay Royster,* use the title she designates.
   b. Notice the title a woman uses in introducing herself on the phone. If she says, "This is Robin Stine," use *Ms.* when you write to her. If she says, "I'm Mrs. Stine," use the title she specifies.
   c. Check your company directory. In some organizations, women who prefer traditional titles can list them with their names.
   d. When you're writing job letters or other crucial correspondence, call the company and ask the receptionist which title your reader prefers.

Ms. is particularly useful when you do not know what a woman's marital status is. However, even when you happen to know that a woman is married or single, **you still use *Ms.* unless you know that she prefers another title.**
   In addition to using parallel courtesy titles, use parallel forms for names.

Not parallel	Parallel
Members of the committee will be Mr. Jones, Mr. Yacone, and Lisa.	Members of the committee will be Mr. Jones, Mr. Yacone, and Ms. Melton.
	or
	Members of the committee will be Irving, Ted, and Lisa.

When You Know the Reader's Name but Not the Gender

When you know your reader's name but not the gender, either

1. Call the company and ask the receptionist, or
2. Use the reader's full name in the salutation:

   Dear Chris Crowell:

   Dear J. C. Meath:

When You Know neither the Reader's Name nor Gender

When you know neither the reader's name nor gender, you have three options:

1. Use the reader's position or job title:

   Dear Loan Officer:

   Dear Registrar:

2. Use a general group to which your reader belongs:

   Dear Investor:

   Dear Admissions Committee:

3. Omit the salutation and use a subject line in its place:

   Subject: Recommendation for Ben Wandell

How should I set up memos?

The standard memo format mimics block format but has no salutation, close, or signature.

Memos omit both the salutation and the close. Memos never indent paragraphs. Subject lines are required; headings are optional. Each heading must cover all the information until the next heading. Never use a separate heading for the first paragraph.

Figure 9.8 illustrates the standard memo format typed on a plain sheet of paper. Note that the first letters of the reader's name, the writer's name, and the subject phrase are lined up vertically. Note also that memos are usually initialed by the To/From block. Initialing tells the reader that you have proofread the memo and prevents someone's sending out your name on a memo you did not in fact write.

Some organizations have special letterhead for memos. When *Date/To/From/Subject* are already printed on the form, the date, writer's and reader's names, and subject may be set at the main margin to save typing time. (See Figure 9.9.)

Some organizations alter the order of items in the *Date/To/From/Subject* block. Some organizations ask employees to sign memos rather than simply initialing them. The signature goes below the last line of the memo, starting halfway over on the page, and prevents anyone adding unauthorized information.

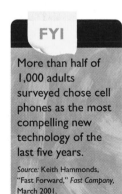

FYI

More than half of 1,000 adults surveyed chose cell phones as the most compelling new technology of the last five years.

Source: Keith Hammonds, "Fast Forward," *Fast Company,* March 2001.

Figure 9.8

Memo Format (on plain paper; direct request)

Everything lined up at left

2 – 4 spaces

October 8, 2004   *Plain paper*

Line up

To: Annette T. Califero

Double-space

From: Kyle B. Abrams **KBA**   *Writer's initials added in ink*

1" – 1½"

Subject: A Low-Cost Way to Reduce Energy Use   *Capitalize first letter of each major word in subject line.*

No heading for ¶ 1

As you requested, I've investigated low-cost ways to reduce our energy use. Reducing the building temperature on weekends is a change that we could make immediately, that would cost nothing, and that would cut our energy use by about 6%.   *⅝" – 1"*

Triple-space before each new heading.

The Energy Savings from a Lower Weekend Temperature   *Bold headings.*

Single-space paragraphs; double-space between paragraphs.

Lowering the temperature from 68° to 60° from 8 p.m. Friday evening to 4 a.m. Monday morning could cut our total consumption by 6%. It is not feasible to lower the temperature on weeknights because a great many staff members work late; the cleaning crew also is on duty from 6 p.m. to midnight. Turning the temperature down for only four hours would not result in a significant heat saving.

Turning the heat back up at 4 a.m. will allow the building temperature to be back to 68° by 9 a.m. Our furnace already has computerized controls which can be set to automatically lower and raise the temperature.

Triple-space

How a Lower Temperature Would Affect Employees   *Capitalize first letter of each major word of heading.*

A survey of employees shows that only 7 people use the building every weekend or almost every weekend. Eighteen percent of our staff have worked at least one weekend day in the last two months; 52% say they "occasionally" come in on weekends.

Do not indent paragraphs.

People who come in for an hour or less on weekends could cope with the lower temperature just by wearing warm clothes. However, most people would find 60° too cool for extended work. Employees who work regularly on weekends might want to install space heaters.

Action Needed to Implement the Change

Would you also like me to check into the cost of buying a dozen portable space heaters? Providing them would allow us to choose units that our wiring can handle and would be a nice gesture towards employees who give up their weekends to work. I could have a report to you in two weeks.

We can begin saving energy immediately. Just authorize the lower temperature, and I'll see that the controls are reset for this weekend.

Memos are initialed by To/From/Subject block — no signature   *Headings are optional in memos.*

Figure 9.9
Memo Format (on memo letterhead; good news)

Kimball,
Walls, and
Morganstern

Date: March 15, 2005   *Line up horizontally with printed Date/To/From/Subject.*

To: Annette T. Califero
                                                               Capitalize first
From: Kyle B. Abrams **KBA** *Writer's initials added in ink*   *letter of each major*
                                                               word in subject line.

Subject: The Effectiveness of Reducing Building Temperatures on Weekends

                  Triple–space

Margin lined up   Reducing the building temperature to 60° on weekends has cut energy
with items in   use by 4% compared to last year's use from December to February and
To/From/Subject   has saved our firm $22,000.
block to save
typing time   This savings is particularly remarkable when you consider that this $\frac{5}{8}" - 1"$
                         winter has been colder than last year's, so that more heat would be   ←——————→
                         needed to maintain the same temperature.

                         Fewer people have worked weekends during the past three months than
                         during the preceding three months, but snow and bad driving
                         conditions may have had more to do with keeping people home than the
                         fear of being cold. Five of the 12 space heaters we bought have
                         been checked out on an average weekend. On one weekend, all 12 were
                         in use and some people shared their offices so that everyone could
                         be in a room with a space heater.

                         Fully 92% of our employees support the lower temperature. I
                         recommend that we continue turning down the heat on weekends
                         through the remainder of the heating season and that we resume the
                         practice when the heat is turned on next fall.

                                        Headings are optional in memos.

     If the memo runs two pages or more, use a heading at the top of the
second and subsequent pages (see Figure 9.10). Since many of your memos
go to the same people, putting a brief version of the subject line will be more
helpful than just using "All Employees."

Figure 9.10

Option 2 for Page 2 of a Memo (direct request)

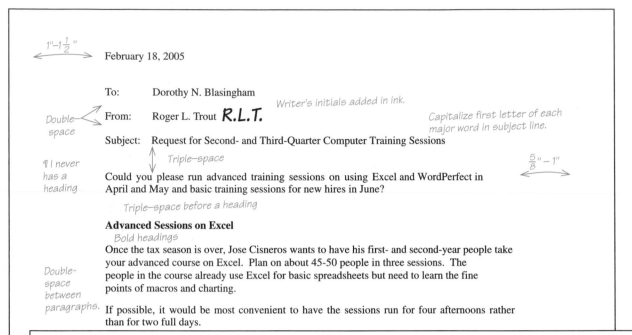

1"–1½"

February 18, 2005

To: Dorothy N. Blasingham

Writer's initials added in ink.

Double-space

From: Roger L. Trout **R.L.T.**

Capitalize first letter of each major word in subject line.

Subject: Request for Second- and Third-Quarter Computer Training Sessions

Triple-space

¶ I never has a heading

Could you please run advanced training sessions on using Excel and WordPerfect in April and May and basic training sessions for new hires in June?

⅝" – 1"

Triple-space before a heading

Advanced Sessions on Excel

Bold headings

Once the tax season is over, Jose Cisneros wants to have his first- and second-year people take your advanced course on Excel. Plan on about 45-50 people in three sessions. The people in the course already use Excel for basic spreadsheets but need to learn the fine points of macros and charting.

Double-space between paragraphs.

If possible, it would be most convenient to have the sessions run for four afternoons rather than for two full days.

Plain paper for page 2

½" – 1"

Dorothy N. Blasingham

Brief subject line or reader's name

2

Page number

February 18, 2005

Also OK to line up page number, date at left under reader's name

Same margins as p 1.

before the summer vacation season begins.

Orientation for New Hires

Capitalize first letter of each major word in heading.

With a total of 16 full-time and 34 part-time people being hired either for summer or permanent work, we'll need at least two and perhaps three orientation sessions. We'd like to hold these the first, second, and third weeks in June. By May 1, we should know how many people will be in each training session.

Would you be free to conduct training sessions on how to use our computers on June 8, June 15, and June 22? If we need only two dates, we'll use June 8 and June 15, but please block off the 22nd too in case we need a third session.

Triple-space before a heading.

Request for Confirmation

Let me know whether you're free on these dates in June, and which dates you'd prefer for the sessions on Excel and WordPerfect. If you'll let me know by February 25, we can get information out to participants in plenty of time for the sessions.

Thanks!

Memos are initialed by To/From/Subject block.

Headings are optional in memos.

Brief Subject Line
Date
Page Number

or

Reader's Name   Page Number   Date

Summary of Key Points

- Block and modified block are the two standard letter formats.

- Use *Ms.* as the courtesy title for a woman, unless she has a professional title, or unless she prefers a traditional title.

- Use *Mr.* as the courtesy title for a man, unless he has a professional title.

- In a list of several people, use parallel forms for names. Use either courtesy titles and last names for everyone, or use first names for everyone. For example, it's sexist to use "Mr." for each man in a document that calls all the women by their first names.

- Memos omit both the salutation and the close. Memos never indent paragraphs. Subject lines are required; headings are optional. Each heading must cover all the information until the next heading. Never use a separate heading for the first paragraph.

Assignments for Module 9

Questions for Comprehension

9.1 When do you send a letter? When do you send a memo?

9.2 What are the differences between block and modified block letter formats?

9.3 What are the differences between block format for letters and the formats for memos?

9.4 What is the Postal Service abbreviation for your state or province?

Questions for Critical Thinking

9.5 Which letter format do you prefer? Why?

9.6 What are the advantages in telling your reader who is getting copies of your message?

9.7 Does following a standard format show a lack of originality and creativity?

Polishing Your Prose

Making Subjects and Verbs Agree

Make sure the subjects and verbs in your sentences agree. Subjects and verbs agree when they are both singular or both plural:

Correct: The laser printer no longer works.

Correct: The nonworking laser printers are in the store room.

Often, subject-verb errors occur when other words come between the subject and verb. Learn to correct errors by looking for the subject—who or what is doing the principal action—and the verb—the action itself:

Correct: A team of marketing researchers is reviewing our promotional campaign.

Correct: The four-color brochures, which cost about $1,000 to print and ship, were sent to our St. Louis affiliate.

U.S. usage treats company names and the words *company* and *government* as singular nouns. In England and countries adopting the British system, these nouns are plural:

Correct: Nationwide Insurance is
(U.S.) headquartered in Columbus, Ohio.

Correct: Lloyds of London are
(U.K.) headquartered in London.

Use a plural verb when two or more singular subjects are joined by *and*.

Correct: Mr. Simmens, Ms. Lopez, and Mr. Yee were in Seoul for a meeting last week.

Use a singular verb when two or more singular subjects are joined by *or, nor,* or *but.* Follow this rule when using *neither/nor* and *either/or* combinations. However, when one of the subjects is plural, choose the verb based on the subject nearest the verb.

Correct: Neither Crandall nor the Panzinis want to play on the department's softball team this year.

Correct: Either the Panzinis or Crandall needs to help keep score.

Correct: Neither Dr. Hroscoe nor Mr. Jamieson is in today.

When the sentence begins with *There* or *Here,* make the verb agree with the subject that follows the verb:

Correct: There were blank pages in the fax we received.

Correct: Here is the information on the job candidate you requested.

Some words that end in *s* are considered singular and require singular verbs:

Correct: The World Series features advertisements of our product in the stadium.

For some nouns, singular and plural forms can be spelled the same. Examples are *data, deer,* and *fish.* Choose a verb based on how you are using the word—singular or plural.

When you encounter situations that don't seem to fit the rule, or when following the rules produces an awkward sentence, rewrite the sentence to avoid the problem:

Problematic: The grant coordinator in addition to the awarding agency (is, are?) happy with the latest proposal we submitted.

Better: The grant coordinator and the awarding agency are happy with the latest proposal we submitted.

Exercises

Choose the correct verb or rewrite the sentence.

1. Lakeland and Associates, the leading management consulting firm in the United States, (operate/operates) offices in all 50 states.

2. We (is/are) going to investigate the cause of last month's shipping delay.

3. Every project team (train/trains) for at least 90 days before projects (is/are) started.

4. Birnham Dunne, Inc., is an expediter that (specialize/specializes) in overnight service.

5. A series of meetings (is/are) planned for February.

6. The parking garage (close/closes) at 10 P.M., so make sure you (leave/leaves) by then.

7. Make it a point to (has/have) your report ready by Monday.

8. Because junk e-mail (clutter/clutters) up our mailboxes, we should (install/installs) filters to screen it out.

9. The offices in Buenos Aries (report/reports) a 19% increase in employee turnover for the past year.

10. Sometimes orders (arrive/arrives) late; we (need/needs) to make sure they (is/are) processed immediately.

Check your answers to the odd-numbered exercises at the back of the book.

BComm Skill Booster

To apply the concepts in this module, complete lesson 53 on formatting messages. You can access the BComm Skill Booster through the text Web site at **www.mhhe.com/bcs2e.**

Module 10

Informative and Positive Messages

Start by asking these questions:

- What's the best subject line for an informative or positive message?
- How should I organize informative and positive messages?
- When should I use reader benefits in informative and positive messages?
- What are the most common kinds of informative and positive messages?
- How can I apply what I've learned in this module?

We categorize messages both by the author's purposes and by the initial response we expect from the reader. In an **informative** or **positive message,** you expect the audience to respond neutrally to the message or to be pleased. Negatives are minor; they are not the main point of the message. You must convey information but are not asking the audience to do anything. However, you may well want the reader to save the information and to act on it later on. You usually do want to build positive attitudes toward the information you are presenting, so in that sense, even an informative message has a persuasive element.

Informative and positive messages include

- Acceptances.
- Positive answers to reader requests.
- Information about procedures, products, services, or options.
- Announcements of policy changes that are neutral or positive.
- Changes that are to the reader's advantage.

Even a simple informative or good news message usually has several purposes:

Primary Purposes:

To give information or good news to the reader or to reassure the reader.

To have the reader read the message, understand it, and view the information positively.

To deemphasize any negative elements.

Secondary Purposes:

To build a good image of the writer.

To build a good image of the writer's organization.

To cement a good relationship between the writer and reader.

To reduce or eliminate future correspondence on the same subject so the message doesn't create more work for the writer.

Good news comes in many forms.

What's the best subject line for an informative or positive message?

One that contains the basic information or good news.

A **subject line** is the title of a document. It aids in filing and retrieving the document, tells readers why they need to read the document, and provides a framework in which to set what you're about to say.

Subject lines are standard in memos. Letters are not required to have subject lines (see Module 9). However, a survey of business people in the Southwest found that 68% of them considered a subject line in a letter to be important, very important, or essential; only 32% considered subject lines to be unimportant or only somewhat important.[1]

A good subject line meets three criteria: it is specific, concise, and appropriate to the kind of message (positive, negative, persuasive).

Making Subject Lines Specific

The subject line needs to be specific enough to differentiate that message from others on the same subject, but broad enough to cover everything in the message.

Too general: Training Sessions

To make this general subject line more specific, identify the particular topic of *this* message.

Better: Dates for 2005 Training Sessions

or: Evaluation of Training Sessions on Conducting Interviews

or: Should We Schedule a Short Course on Proposal Writing?

Making Subject Lines Concise

Most subject lines are relatively short—usually no more than 10 words, often only 3 to 7 words.[2]

Wordy: Survey of Student Preferences in Regards to Various Pizza Factors

Again, the best revision depends on the specific factors you'll discuss.

Better: Students' Pizza Preferences

or: The Feasibility of a Cassano's Branch on Campus

or: What Students Like and Dislike about Cassano's Pizza

If you can't make the subject both specific and short, be specific.

Making Subject Lines Appropriate for the Pattern of Organization

In general, do the same thing in your subject line that you would do in the first paragraph.

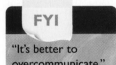
FYI

"It's better to overcommunicate," says [Anu] Shukla, whose Web startup, Rubric, made 65 of her 85 employees millionaires. She created the CEO lunch, inviting six to eight employees at a time to discuss the business with her.

Source: Rochelle Sharpe, "As Leaders, Women Rule," *BusinessWeek,* November 20, 2000, 80.

When you have good news for the reader, build goodwill by highlighting it in the subject line. When your information is neutral, summarize it concisely for the subject line.

Subject: Discount on Rental Cars Effective January 2

Starting January 2, as an employee of Amalgamated Industries you can get a 15% discount on cars you rent for business or personal use from Roadway Rent-a-Car.

Subject: Update on Arrangements for Videoconference with France

In the last month, we have chosen the participants and developed a tentative agenda for the videoconference with France scheduled for March 21.

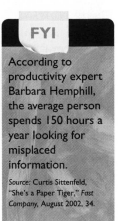

How should I organize informative and positive messages?

Put the good news and a summary of the information first.

The patterns of organization in this module and the modules that follow will work for 70 to 90% of the writing situations most people in business, government, and nonprofit organizations face. Using the appropriate pattern can help you compose more quickly and create a better final product.

- Be sure you understand the rationale behind each pattern so that you can modify the pattern if necessary. (For example, if you write instructions, any warnings should go up front, not in the middle of the message.)
- Not every message that uses the basic pattern will have all the elements listed. The elements you do have will go in the order presented in the pattern.
- Sometimes you can present several elements in one paragraph. Sometimes you'll need several paragraphs for just one element.

Present informative and positive messages in the following order:

1. **Give any good news and summarize the main points.** Share good news immediately. Include details such as the date policies begin and the percent of a discount. If the reader has already raised the issue, make it clear that you're responding.
2. **Give details, clarification, background.** Don't repeat information from the first paragraph. Do answer all the questions your reader is likely to have; provide all the information necessary to achieve your purposes. Present details in the order of importance to the reader.
3. **Present any negative elements—as positively as possible.** A policy may have limits; information may be incomplete; the reader may have to

Figure 10.1

How to Organize an Informative or Positive Message

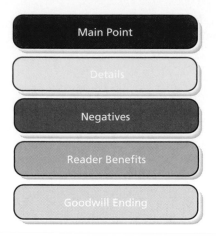

satisfy requirements to get a discount or benefit. Make these negatives clear, but present them as positively as possible.

4. **Explain any reader benefits.** Most informative memos need reader benefits. Show that the policy or procedure helps readers, not just the company. Give enough detail to make the benefits clear and convincing. In letters, you may want to give benefits of dealing with your company as well as benefits of the product or policy.

   In a good news message, it's often possible to combine a short reader benefit with a goodwill ending in the last paragraph.

5. **Use a goodwill ending: positive, personal, and forward-looking.** Shifting your emphasis away from the message to the specific reader suggests that serving the reader is your real concern.

Figure 10.1 summarizes the pattern. Figures 10.2 and 10.3 illustrate two ways that the basic pattern can be applied. (Figures 9.5 and 9.9 ◀▶ also use this pattern.)

The letter in Figure 10.2 authorizes a one-year appointment that the reader and writer have already discussed and describes the organization's priorities. Since the writer knows that the reader wants to accept the job, the letter doesn't need to persuade. The opportunity for the professor to study records that aren't available to the public is an implicit reader benefit; the concern for the reader's needs builds goodwill.

The memo in Figure 10.3 announces a new employee benefit. The first paragraph summarizes the policy. Paragraph 2 gives details. Negative elements are in paragraphs 3 and 4, stated as positively as possible. Paragraphs 5 to 7 give reader benefits and shows that everyone—even part-timers who are not eligible for reimbursement—will benefit from the new program.

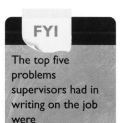

FYI

The top five problems supervisors had in writing on the job were

- Meeting deadlines.
- Deciding what information to include.
- Organizing information.
- Writing clear instructions.
- Summarizing information from other sources.

Source: Mark Mabrito, "Writing on the Front Line: A Study of Workplace Writing," Business Communication Quarterly 60, no. 3 (September 1997): 66.

When should I use reader benefits in informative and positive messages?

When you want readers to view your policies and your organization positively.

Not all informative and positive messages need reader benefits (◀▶ p. 132). You don't need reader benefits when

- You're presenting factual information only.
- The reader's attitude toward the information doesn't matter.
- Stressing benefits may make the reader sound selfish.
- The benefits are so obvious that to restate them insults the reader's intelligence. (See Figure 10.2)

Figure 10.2
A Positive Letter

Interstate
Fidelity
Insurance Company

100 Interstate Plaza
Atlanta, GA 30301
404-555-5000
Fax: 404-555-5270

March 8, 2004

Professor Adrienne Prinz
Department of History
Duke University
Durham, North Carolina 27000

Dear Professor Prinz:

Good news — Your appointment as archivist for Interstate Fidelity Insurance has been approved. When you were in Atlanta in December, you said that you could begin work June 1. We'd like you to start then if that date is still good for you.   *Tactful*

The Board has outlined the following priorities for your work: *Assumes reader's primary interest is the job*

Negative about lighting and security presented impersonally

Details

1. **Organize and catalogue the archives.** You'll have the basement of the Palmer Building for the archives and can requisition the supplies you need. You'll be able to control heat and humidity; the budget doesn't allow special lighting or security measures.

2. **Prepare materials for a 4-hour training session in October** for senior-level managers. We'd like you to cover how to decide what to send to the archives. If your first four months of research uncover any pragmatic uses for our archives (like Wells Fargo's use of archives to teach managers about past pitfalls), include those in the session.

3. **Write an article each month for the employee newsletter** describing the uses of the archives. When we're cutting costs in other departments, it's important to justify committing funds to start an archive program.

These provisions will appeal to the reader

4. **Study the IFI archives to compile** information that (a) can help solve current management problems, (b) could be included in a history of the company, and (c) might be useful to scholars of business history.

5. **Begin work on a corporate history of IFI.** IFI will help you find a publisher and support the book financially. You'll have full control over the content.

Salary is deemphasized to avoid implying that reader is "just taking the job for the money"

Negative that reader will have to reapply presented as normal procedure

Your salary will be $33,000 for six months; your contract can be renewed twice for a total of 18 months. You're authorized to hire a full-time research assistant for $11,000 for six months; you'll need to go through the normal personnel request process to request that that money be continued next year. A file clerk will be assigned full-time to your project. You'll report to me. At least for the rest of this calendar year, the budget for the Archives Project will come from my department.

Figure 10.2

A Positive Letter *(Continued)*

Professor Adrienne Prinz
March 8, 2004
Page 2

IFI offices are equipped with Pentium computers with FoxPro, WordPerfect, and Excel. Is there any software that we should buy for cataloguing or research? Are there any office supplies that we need to have on hand June 1 so that you can work efficiently?

In the meantime,

Goodwill ending

1. Please send your written acceptance right away.

2. Let me know if you need any software or supplies.

3. Send me the name, address, and Social Security number of your research assistant by May 1 so that I can process his or her employment papers.

4. If you'd like help finding a house or apartment in Atlanta, let me know. I can give you the name of a real estate agent.

On June 1, you'll spend the morning in Personnel. Stop by my office at noon. We'll go out for lunch and then I'll take you to the office you'll have while you're at IFI.

Welcome to IFI!

Cordially,

Cynthia Yen

Cynthia Yen
Director of Education and Training

FYI

A majority of all workers—56% of the workforce—gathers, processes, or uses some type of information to conduct their work.

Source: Peter Francese, "The American Work Force," *American Demographics,* February 2002, 40.

You do need reader benefits when

• You are presenting policies.
• You want to shape readers' attitudes toward the information or toward your organization.
• Stressing benefits presents readers' motives positively.
• Some of the benefits may not be obvious to readers.

Messages to customers or potential customers sometimes include a sales paragraph promoting products or services you offer in addition to the product or service that the reader has asked about. Sales promotion in an informative or positive message should be low-key, not "hard sell."

Reader benefits are hardest to develop when you are announcing policies. The organization probably decided to adopt the policy because it

Figure 10.3
A Positive Memo

March 1, 2005

To: All Chamber Employees and Members of the Chamber Insurance Group

From: Lee Ann Rabe, Vice President for Human Resources *LAR*

Subject: Health Care Benefits for Same-Sex Partners

Good news in subject line and first paragraph

Good news Beginning May 1, same-sex partners of employees covered by the Chamber Health Plan will be eligible for the same coverage as spouses.

Details In order to have a partner covered, an employee must sign an affidavit in the Human Resources Department stating that the employee and his or her partner (1) live together, (2) intend to stay together, and (3) are responsible for each other. If the relationship ends, employees must notify the Human Resources Department within 30 days, just as do married couples who divorce.

Negatives presented as positively as possible

Costs and coverage of the Chamber of Health plan remain the same. Dental and vision coverage are also available for a fee; limitations apply and remain the same. For information about the specifics of the Chamber's Health Plan, pick up a brochure in the Human Resources Department.

Negatives

Opposite-sex couples must still marry to receive the spousal coverage.

Extending coverage to same-sex partners of employees shows the Chamber as a progressive, open-minded organization. This in turn portrays Columbus in a positive light.

The new policy will affect not only Chamber employees but also the small businesses that are a part of the Chamber's Health Plan. New businesses may see the change as a reason to join the Chamber–and the Health Plan. Growth in the Health Plan creates a wider base for insurance premiums and helps keep costs as low as possible. Additional Chamber members give us the funds and resources to plan more conferences for members. These conferences, such as the recent "R&D in Ohio's Small Businesses," help Chamber members do business successfully.

Reader Benefits

Making the Health Plan more comprehensive keeps us competitive with other major U.S. cities. As we move out of the recession, businesses are carefully considering possible moves. A policy change like this one shows Columbus' continued goodwill toward minorities in general and will make convincing businesses to relocate here that much easier.

Goodwill ending Selling Columbus as a good place to live and do business has never been easier.

Sharing information is crucial to business success. To drive home that point, Siemens deposited 60 managers from around the world on the shores of a lake south of Munich, Germany, and told them to build rafts. They weren't allowed to talk: They had to write messages and diagrams on flip charts. Back in the office, ShareNet lets employees around the world ask questions and share answers.

appeared to help the organization; the people who made the decision may not have thought at all about whether it would help or hurt employees. Yet reader benefits are most essential in this kind of message so readers see the reason for the change and support it.

When you present reader benefits, be sure to present advantages *to the reader*. Most new policies help the organization in some way, but few workers will see their own interests as identical with the organization's. Even if the organization saves money or increases its profits, workers will benefit directly only if they own stock in the company, if they're high up enough to receive bonuses, if the savings enables a failing company to avoid layoffs, or if all of the savings goes directly to employee benefits. In many companies, any money saved will go to executive bonuses, shareholder profits, or research and development.

To develop reader benefits for informative and positive messages, use the steps suggested in Module 8. Be sure to think about **intrinsic benefits** (◀▶ p. 138) of your policy, that is, benefits that come from the activity or policy itself, apart from any financial benefits. Does a policy improve the eight hours people spend at work?

Instant Replay

Organizing Informative and Positive Messages

1. Give any good news and summarize the main points.
2. Give details, clarification, background.
3. Present any negative elements—as positively as possible.
4. Explain any reader benefits.
5. Use a goodwill ending: positive, personal, and forward-looking.

What are the most common kinds of informative and positive messages?

Transmittals, confirmations, summaries, adjustments, and thank-you notes.

Many messages can be informative, negative, or persuasive depending on what you have to say. A transmittal, for example, can be positive when you're sending glowing sales figures or persuasive when you want the reader to act on the information. A performance appraisal is positive when you evaluate someone who's doing superbly, negative when you want to compile a record to justify firing someone, and persuasive when you want to motivate a satisfactory worker to continue to improve. A collection letter is persuasive; it becomes negative in the last stage when you threaten legal action. Each of these messages is discussed in the module for the pattern it uses most frequently. However, in some cases you will need to use a pattern from a different module.

Transmittals

When you send someone something in an organization, attach a memo or letter of transmittal explaining what you're sending. A transmittal can be as simple as a small yellow Post-it™ note with "FYI" written on it ("For Your Information") or it can be a separate typed document, especially when it transmits a formal document such as a report (◁ ▶ see Module 24).

Organize a memo or letter of transmittal in this order:

1. Tell the reader what you're sending.
2. Summarize the main point(s) of the document.
3. Indicate any special circumstances or information that would help the reader understand the document. Is it a draft? Is it a partial document that will be completed later?
4. Tell the reader what will happen next. Will you do something? Do you want a response? If you do want the reader to act, specify exactly what you want the reader to do and give a deadline.

Frequently, transmittals have important secondary purposes, such as building goodwill and showing readers that you're working on projects they value.

Confirmations

Many informative messages record oral conversations. These messages are generally short and give only the information shared orally; they go to the other party in the conversation. Start the message by indicating that it is a confirmation, not a new message:

As we discussed on the phone today, . . .

As I told you yesterday, . . .

Attached is the meeting schedule we discussed earlier today.

Instant Replay

Use reader benefits when

- You are presenting policies.
- You want to shape readers' attitudes toward the information or toward your organization.
- Stressing benefits presents readers' motives positively.
- Some of the benefits may not be obvious to readers.

Summaries

You may be asked to summarize a conversation, document, or an outside meeting for colleagues or superiors. (Minutes of an internal meeting are usually more detailed. See Module 18 for advice on writing minutes of meetings.)

In a summary of a conversation for internal use, identify

- The people who were present
- The topic of discussion
- Decisions made
- Who does what next.

To summarize a document

1. Start with the main point.
2. Give supporting evidence and details.
3. Evaluate the document, if your audience asks for evaluation.
4. Identify the actions that your organization should take based on the document. Should others in the company read this book? Should

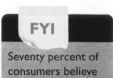

someone in the company write a letter to the editor responding to this newspaper article? Should your company try to meet with someone in the organization that the story is about?

Adjustments and Responses to Complaints

A study sponsored by Travelers Insurance showed that when people had gripes but didn't complain, only 9% would buy from the company again. But when people did complain—and their problems were resolved quickly—82% would buy again.[3]

When you grant a customer's request for an adjusted price, discount, replacement, or other benefit to resolve a complaint, do so in the very first sentence.

> Your Visa bill for a night's lodging has been adjusted to $63. Next month a credit of $37 will appear on your bill to reimburse you for the extra amount you were originally asked to pay.

Don't talk about your own process in making the decision. Don't say anything that sounds grudging. Give the reason for the original mistake only if it reflects credit on the company. (In most cases, it doesn't, so the reason should be omitted.)

Thank-You and Congratulatory Notes

Sending a **thank-you note** will make people more willing to help you again in the future. Thank-you letters can be short but must be prompt. They need to be specific to sound sincere.

Thank-you notes can be written on standard business stationery, using standard formats. But one student noticed that his advisor really liked cats and had pictures of them in her office. So he found a cat card for his thank-you note.

Congratulating someone can cement good feelings between you and the reader and enhance your own visibility. Again, specifics help.

Avoid language that may seem condescending or patronizing. A journalism professor was offended when a former student wrote to congratulate her for a feature article that appeared in a major newspaper. As the professor pointed out, the letter's language implied that the writer had more status than the person being praised. The praiser was "quite impressed," congratulated the professor on reaching a conclusion that the praiser had already reached, and assumed that the professor would have wanted to discuss matters with the praiser. To the reader, "Keep up the good work!" implied that the one cheering her on had been waiting for ages at the finish line.[4]

How can I apply what I've learned in this module?

Plan your activities and answer the PAIBOC questions.

Before you tackle the assignments for this module, examine the following problem. Figure 4.1 (◀▷ p. 72) lists the activities needed to produce a good message. See how the PAIBOC questions probe the basic points required for a solution. Study the two sample solutions to see what makes one unacceptable and the other one good. Note the recommendations for revision that could make the good solution excellent.[5] The checklist at the end of the Module in Figure 10.6 can help you evaluate a draft.

Problem

Interstate Fidelity Insurance (IFI) uses computers to handle its payments and billings. There is often a time lag between receiving a payment from a customer and recording it on the computer. Sometimes, while the payment is in line to be processed, the computer sends out additional notices: past-due notices, collection letters, even threats to sue. Customers are frightened or angry and write asking for an explanation. In most cases, if they just waited a little while, the situation would be straightened out. But policyholders are afraid that they'll be without insurance because the company thinks the bill has not been paid.

IFI doesn't have the time to check each individual situation to see if the check did arrive and has been processed. It wants you to write a letter that will persuade customers to wait. If something is wrong and the payment never reached IFI, IFI would send a legal notice to that effect saying that the policy would be canceled by a certain date (which the notice would specify) at least 30 days after the date on the original premium bill. Continuing customers always get this legal notice as a third chance (after the original bill and the past-due notice).

Prepare a form letter that can go out to every policyholder who claims to have paid a premium for automobile insurance and resents getting a past-due notice. The letter should reassure readers and build goodwill for IFI.

Analysis of the Problem

P What are your **purposes** in writing or speaking?

> To reassure readers: they're covered for 30 days. To inform them they can assume everything is OK *unless* they receive a second notice. To avoid further correspondence on this subject. To build goodwill for IFI: (a) we don't want to suggest IFI is error-prone or too cheap to hire enough people to do the necessary work; (b) we don't want readers to switch companies; (c) we do want readers to buy from IFI when they're ready for more insurance.

A Who is (are) your **audience(s)?** How do the members of your audience differ from each other? What characteristics are relevant to this particular message?

> Automobile insurance customers who say they've paid but have still received a past-due notice. They're afraid they're no longer insured. Since it's a form letter, different readers will have different situations: in some cases payment did arrive late, in some cases the company made a mistake, in some the reader never paid (check lost in mail, unsigned, bounced, etc.)

I What **information** must your message include?

> Readers are still insured. We cannot say whether their checks have now been processed (company doesn't want to check individual accounts). Their insurance will be canceled if they do not pay after receiving the second past-due notice (the legal notice).

B What reasons or reader **benefits** can you use to support your position?

> Computers help us provide personal service to policyholders. We offer policies to meet all their needs. Both of these points would need specifics to be interesting and convincing.

O What **objections** can you expect your reader(s) to have? What negative elements of your message must you deemphasize or overcome?

> Computers appear to cause errors. We don't know if the checks have been processed. We will cancel policies if their checks don't arrive.

C How will the **context** affect the reader's response? Think about your relationship to the reader, morale in the organization, the economy, the time of year, and any special circumstances

> The insurance business is highly competitive—other companies offer similar rates and policies. The customer could get a similar policy for about the same money from someone else. Most people find that money is tight, so they'll want to keep insurance costs low. On the other hand, the fact that prices are steady or rising means that the value of what they own is higher—they need insurance more than ever.

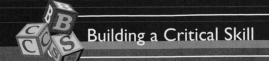

Writing a Goodwill Ending

Goodwill endings focus on the business relationship you share with your reader. When you write to one person, a good last paragraph fits that person specifically. When you write to someone who represents an organization, the last paragraph can refer to your company's relationship to the reader's organization. When you write to a group (for example, to "All Employees") your ending should apply to the whole group.

Possibilities include complimenting the reader for a job well done, describing a reader benefit, or looking forward to something positive that relates to the subject of the message.

For example, consider possible endings for a letter answering the question, "When a patient leaves the hospital and returns, should we count it as a new stay?" For one company, the answer was that if a patient was gone from the hospital overnight or longer, the hospital should start a new claim when the patient was readmitted.

Weak closing paragraph:	Should you have any questions regarding this matter, please feel free to call me.
Goodwill ending:	Many employee-patients appreciate the freedom to leave the hospital for a few hours. It's nice working with a hospital which is flexible enough to offer that option.
Also acceptable:	Omit the paragraph; stop after the explanation.

Some writers end every message with a standard invitation:

If you have questions, please do not hesitate to ask.

That sentence lacks positive emphasis (◀ ▷ p. 119). But saying "feel free to call"—though more positive—is rarely a good idea. Most of the time, the writer should omit the sentence and make the original message clear.

One of the reasons you write is to save the time needed to tell everyone individually. People in business aren't shrinking violets; they will call if they need help. Do make sure your phone number is in the letterhead or is typed below your name. You can also add your e-mail address below your name.

Many insurance companies are refusing to renew policies (car, liability, malpractice insurance). These refusals to renew have gotten lots of publicity, and many people have heard horror stories about companies and individuals whose insurance has been canceled or not renewed after a small number of claims. Readers don't feel very kindly toward insurance companies.

People need car insurance. If they have an accident and aren't covered, they not only have to bear the costs of that accident alone but also (depending on state law) may need to place as much as $50,000 in a state escrow account to cover future accidents. They have a legitimate worry.

Discussion of the Sample Solutions

The solution in Figure 10.4 is unacceptable. The red marginal comments show problem spots. Since this is a form letter, we cannot tell customers we have their checks; in some cases, we may not. The letter is far too negative. The explanation in paragraph 2 makes IFI look irresponsible and uncaring. Paragraph 3 is far too negative. Paragraph 4 is too vague; there are no reader benefits; the ending sounds selfish.

A major weakness with the solution is that it lifts phrases straight out of the problem; the writer does not seem to have thought about the problem or

Figure 10.4

An Unacceptable Solution to the Sample Problem

Need date

Dear Customer:

This explanation makes company look bad.

Relax. We got your check.

Not necessarily true. Reread problem.

There is always a time lag between the time payments come in and the time they are processed. While payments are waiting to be processed, the computer with super-human quickness is sending out past-due notices and threats of cancellation.

Too negative

Need to present this positively

Cancellation is not something you should worry about. No policy would be canceled without a legal notice to that effect giving a specific date for cancellation which would be at least 30 days after the date on the original premium notice.

If you want to buy more insurance, just contact your local Interstate Fidelity agent. We will be happy to help you.

Sincerely,

This paragraph isn't specific enough to work as a reader benefit. It lacks you-attitude and positive emphasis.

about the words he or she is using. Measuring the draft against the answers to the questions for analysis suggests that this writer should start over.

The solution in Figure 10.5 is much better. The blue marginal comments show the letter's strong points. The message opens with the good news that is true for all readers. (Whenever possible, one should use the good news pattern of organization.) Paragraph 2 explains IFI's policy. It avoids assigning blame and ends on a positive note. The negative information is buried in paragraph 3 and is presented positively: The notice is information, not a threat; the 30-day extension is a "grace period." Telling the reader now what to do if a second notice arrives eliminates the need for a second exchange of letters. Paragraph 4 offers benefits for using computers, since some readers may blame the notice on computers, and offers benefits for being insured by IFI. Paragraph 5 promotes other policies the company sells and prepares for the last paragraph.

As the red comments indicate, this good solution could be improved by personalizing the salutation and by including the name and number of the local agent. Computers could make both of those insertions easily. This good letter could be made excellent by revising paragraph 4 so that it doesn't end on a negative note, and by using more reader benefits. For instance, do computers help agents advise clients of the best policies for them? Does IFI offer good service—quick, friendly, nonpresssured—that could be stressed? Are agents well trained? All of these might yield ideas for additional reader benefits.

Figure 10.5
A Good Solution to the Sample Problem

Need date

Dear Customer: *Better: use computer to personalize. Put in name and address of a specific reader.*

Your auto insurance is still in effect.   *Good ¶ 1. True for all readers*

Good to treat notice as information, tell reader what to do if it arrives   Past-due notices are mailed out if the payment has not been processed within three days after the due date. This may happen if a check is delayed in the mail or arrives without a signature or account number. When your check arrives with all the necessary information, it is promptly credited to your account.   *Good you-attitude*

Even if a check is lost in the mail and never reaches us, you still have a 30-day grace period. If you do get a second notice, you'll know that we still have not received your check. To keep your insurance in force, just stop payment on the first check and send a second one.

Benefits of using computers   Computer processing of your account guarantees that you get any discounts you're eligible for: multicar, accident-free record, good student. If you have a claim, your agent uses computer tracking to find matching parts quickly, whatever car you drive. You get a check quickly—usually within three working days—without having to visit dealer after dealer for (time-consuming estimates.)   *Better to put in agent's name, phone number*

Too negative

Need to add benefits of insuring with IFI   Today, your home and possessions are worth more than ever. You can protect them with Interstate Fidelity's homeowners' and renters' policies. Let (your local agent) show you how easy it is to give yourself full protection. If you need a special rider to insure a personal computer, a coin or gun collection, or a fine antique, you can get that from IFI, too.   *Good specifics*

Whatever your insurance needs—auto, home, life, or health—one call to IFI can do it all.   *Acceptable ending*

Sincerely,

Figure 10.6

✓ Checklist for
Informative and Positive Messages

☐ Does the subject line give the good news? Is the subject line specific enough to differentiate this message from others on the same subject?

☐ Does the first paragraph summarize the information or good news? If the information is too complex to fit into a single paragraph, does the paragraph list the basic parts of the policy or information in the order in which the memo discusses them?

☐ Is all the information given in the message? [What information is needed will vary depending on the message, but information about dates, places, times, and anything related to money usually needs to be included. When in doubt, ask!]

☐ In messages announcing policies, is there at least one reader benefit for each segment of the audience? Are all reader benefits ones that seem likely to occur in this organization?

☐ Is each reader benefit developed, showing that the benefit will come from the policy and why the benefit matters to this organization? Do the benefits build on the job duties of people in this organization and the specific circumstances of the organization?

☐ Does the message end with a positive paragraph—preferably one that is specific to the readers, not a general one that could fit any organization or policy?

And, for all messages, not just informative and positive ones,

☐ Does the message use you-attitude and positive emphasis?
☐ Is the style easy to read and friendly?
☐ Is the visual design of the message inviting?
☐ Is the format correct?
☐ Does the message use standard grammar? Is it free from typos?

Originality in a positive or informative message may come from

☐ Creating good headings, lists, and visual impact.
☐ Developing reader benefits.
☐ Thinking about readers and giving details that answer their questions and make it easier for them to understand and follow the policy.

Summary of Key Points

- A **subject line** is the title of a document. A good subject line meets three criteria: it's specific; it's reasonably short; and it's adapted to the kind of message (positive, negative, persuasive). If you can't make the subject both specific and short, be specific.

- The subject line for an informative or positive message should highlight any

good news and summarize the information concisely.

- Informative and positive messages normally use the following pattern of organization:

  1. Give any good news and summarize the main points.

2. Give details, clarification, background.
3. Present any negative elements—as positively as possible.
4. Explain any reader benefits.
5. Use a goodwill ending: positive, personal, and forward-looking.

- Use reader benefits in informative and positive messages when
  - You are presenting policies.
  - You want to shape readers' attitudes toward the information or toward your organization.

- Stressing benefits presents readers' motives positively.
- Some of the benefits may not be obvious to readers.
- Use the PAIBOC questions listed in Module 1 to examine the basic points needed for successful informative and positive messages.

Assignments for Module 10

Questions for Comprehension

10.1 What are the three criteria for good subject lines?

10.2 How should you organize a positive or informative message?

10.3 How do varieties of informative and positive messages adapt the basic pattern?

Questions for Critical Thinking

10.4 What's wrong with the subject line "New Policy"?

10.5 Is it unethical to "bury" any negative elements in an otherwise positive or informative message?

10.6 Why is it important to recognize the secondary as well as the primary purposes of your message?

10.7 Are you more likely to need reader benefits in informative letters or memos? Why?

Exercises and Problems

10.8 **Revising a Positive Message**

As director of purchasing for City College, you maintain a list of approved vendors who must comply with all local, state, and federal laws. You buy only from approved vendors.

You are now responding to a request from Amelia Kemp that her printing company be reinstated on the list. The company was suspended a month ago for paying less than the minimum wage, but she didn't own the business then. A subordinate has prepared this draft for your signature.

> Dear Ms. Kemp:
>
> This is in response to your letter of last week appealing your suspension as a printing vendor for City College because of non-compliance with the prevailing wage requirement.
>
> I have had both our administrative and legal staff review the circumstances surrounding the suspension, and they have recommended that it be reduced to 30 days. Their recommendation is based strongly on the fact that you were not the owner of the business when the violation occurred which resulted in your suspension. In addition, your letter of last week promised that you will be in compliance for all future jobs printed for City College.
>
> Since the letter informing you of the suspension was dated 33 days ago, this means that you are immediately reinstated as an approved vendor. My office, however, reserves the right to review future jobs performed by your company to ensure that you comply with the wage requirements and other requirements.
>
> If you have any questions or concerns about this action, please feel free to contact me.

You know that this is a terrible letter. Both organization and style can be much better.

As Your Instructor Directs,

a. Identify the draft's problems in organization, style, you-attitude, and positive emphasis.

b. Write a new letter to replace this draft.

10.9 Correcting a Misconception

You're an assistant in the Governor's office. Today, the Press Secretary gives you this letter and asks you to answer it.

> I see state employees driving BMWs and sports cars. These cars are a waste of taxpayer money!
>
> Sincerely,
>
> *Rick Shipley*
>
> Rick Shipley

After checking with the Department of Public Safety, you find that some state employees do drive luxury cars. The vehicles were confiscated in criminal investigations, and the state uses them instead of buying other vehicles.

Write to Mr. Shipley, responding to his criticism.

10.10 Accepting Suggestions

Your city government encourages money-saving suggestions to help balance the city budget. The suggestion committee, which you chair, has voted to adopt five suggestions.

1. Direct deposit paychecks to save distribution and printing costs. Suggested by Park Kim Lee, in Recreation and Parks.

2. Buy supplies in bulk. Suggested by Jolene Zigmund, in Maintenance.

3. Charge nearby towns and suburbs a fee for sending their firefighters through the city fire academy. Suggested by Charles Boxell, in Fire Safety.

4. Ask employees to reimburse the city for personal photocopies or phone

calls. Suggested by Maria Echeverria, in Police.

5. Install lock boxes so that meter readers don't have to turn off water valves when people move. This causes wear and tear, and broken valves must be dug up and replaced. Suggested by Travis Gratton, in Water Line Maintenance.

Each suggester gets $100. The Accounting Department will cut checks the first of next month; checks should reach people in interoffice mail a few days later.

As Your Instructor Directs,
a. Write to one of the suggesters, giving the good news.
b. Write to all employees, announcing the award winners.

10.11 Giving Good News

Write to a customer or client, to a vendor or supplier, or to your boss announcing good news. Possibilities include a product improvement, a price cut or special, an addition to your management team, a new contract, and so forth.

10.12 Agreeing to Waive a Fee

You're a customer service representative for a major credit card company. Last week, Naomi Neyens called asking that you waive the annual fee on her account. "I'm getting offers from other companies with no annual fee. I'd like to keep my account, but only if you waive the fee for the life of the account." You agreed to do as she asked, effective immediately. Now, you need to write a letter confirming the conversation.

Write to Ms. Neyens, specifying her 16-digit account number.

10.13 Announcing a Change in Group Life Insurance Rates

Your organization provides group life insurance to your salaried employees, worth 2.5 times the employee's annual salary. Hourly employees who worked 30 hours or more a week in the last year receive life insurance equal to what the person was paid in the last year. The premium that the organization pays has been considered taxable income. The exact value is listed on the pay stub in the box labeled "Employer-Paid Benefits." Now, the Internal Revenue Service has announced a reduction in the rates used to calculate the taxable value of this employer-provided life insurance. As a result, the value of the insurance will be slightly lower, and therefore all of the taxes based on pay will be slightly lower: federal, state, city, medicare hospitalization insurance, and school district taxes. These changes will be effective in the paycheck issued at the end of this month for employees paid monthly and in the paycheck issued 10 days from now for employees paid biweekly.

Write a memo to all employees, explaining the change.

10.14 Announcing an Additional Employee Benefit

To help employees who are caring for elderly relatives, your Human Resources office will provide information and referral services for elder daycare and long-term assisted-living or nursing care and names and addresses of people willing to work part- or full-time as care-givers. In addition, you will sponsor seminars on a number of topics about dealing with elderly parents, ranging from deciding whether to use a nursing facility, when to stop driving, and how to fill out medical forms.

As part of the new policy, the organization will allow employees to use personal time off and sick time to care for any family member. You will also allow employees to take time off during the work day to stay until a nurse arrives or to drive a parent to a doctor's appointment. Employees must notify their supervisors in advance that they will be away and must make up the time sometime during the next 30 days. Employees who need more time can take unpaid leaves of up to 15 months and can return to their present jobs and current salaries.

The policy takes effect the first of next month.

Assume that you're Director of Human Resources, and write a memo to all employees announcing the benefit.

Hints:
- Pick a business, government, or nonprofit organization you know well.
- What age groups do employees represent? How many of them are caring for elderly parents now?
- Specify the topic, date, and place of the first seminar you'll sponsor. If possible, give the schedule for the first three months.
- Be sure to provide reader benefits for employees who do not care for elderly parents as well as those who do.
- How easy is it for your organization to attract and retain skilled workers? Why is it important to your organization that people be alert and be willing to take more responsibility?

10.15 Announcing a New Employee Benefit

Your company has decided to allow employees to spend one hour of "charity" time for every 40 they work (one hour a week for people who are on salary rather than paid by the hour). Employees will be paid for this hour, so their salaries will not fall. People who choose not to participate will work and be paid for the same number of hours as before. Supervisors are responsible for ensuring that essential business services are covered during business hours. Any employee who will be away during regular business hours (either to volunteer or to take off an hour in compensation for volunteering off-shift or on a weekend) will need to clear the planned absence with his or her supervisor. People can work with an organized group or do something informal (such as tutoring at a local

school or coaching kids at a local playground). People can volunteer one hour every week, two hours every other week, or a half-day each month. Volunteer hours cannot be banked from one month to the next; they must be used each month. The program starts January 1 (or June 1). The various groups that people work with will be featured in company publications.

As Vice President of Human Resources, write to all employees announcing this new program.

Hints:
- Pick a business, government, or nonprofit organization that you know something about.
- What proportion of your employees are already involved in volunteer work?

- Is community service or "giving back" consistent with your corporate mission?
- Some employees won't be able or won't want to participate. What is the benefit for them in working for a company that has such a program?
- Will promoting community participation help your organization attract and retain workers?

10.16 Introducing a Wellness Program

The very best way for a company to save money on health insurance costs is to have healthy employees. Studies show that people who smoke, who are moderate or heavy drinkers, who are overweight, and who do not exercise regularly have significantly higher health care costs: They visit doctors more often, need more prescription drugs, and are hospitalized more often and for longer periods of time.

Your company has decided to launch a comprehensive wellness program in an effort to get employees to adopt healthier lifestyles. Employees in your organization pay about 40% of the cost of their health insurance; the organization pays the rest. On January 1 (or July 1) rates are going up, as they have every year for the last nine years. Singles will pay $75 a month; people who also insure a spouse or partner pay $160 a month; the cost for the employee and one child is $150 a month; the family rate is $250 a month.

People who follow good health practices don't have to pay that much. You'll give a $100 rebate (annually) to each employee who doesn't smoke or use chewing tobacco. Employees who don't drink to excess (more than an average of at least 6 ounces of beer or 3 ounces of wine or 1.5 ounces of hard liquor a day) and who don't use illegal drugs can also get $100, as can those whose cholesterol isn't over 150. Employees who exercise at least 30 minutes a day, three times a week will get rebates of $50. Walking and gardening count. Another rebate of $50 is available for a waist-to-hip ratio not over 0.8 for women or 0.95 for men.

As part of the wellness program, the company cafeteria will focus on serving healthier foods and the company will offer twice-yearly heath fairs with free routine immunizations, flu shots, and mammograms for employees and dependents. These parts of the program will begin next month.

Write a memo to all employees informing them about the wellness program and the rates for insurance.

Hints:
- Pick an organization you know well to use for this message.
- Much of the program is described negatively. How can you present it positively?
- Specify when the next health fair is and when the new rates start. If the financial program's start is several months away, suggest that people begin to change habits now.
- If the organization saves money, will employees benefit?
- Why don't people already follow healthy practices? What can you do to overcome these objections?
- Saving money may not motivate everyone. Offer intrinsic benefits as well.

10.17 Announcing an Employee Fitness Center

Your company is ready to open an employee fitness center with on-site aerobics classes, swimming pool, and weight machines. The center will be open 6 A.M. to 10 P.M. daily; a qualified instructor will be on duty at all times.

Employees get first preference; if there is extra room, spouses and children may also use the facilities. Locker rooms and showers will be available.

Your company hopes that the fitness center will help out-of-shape employees get the exercise they need to be more productive. Other companies have gained as many as 762 workdays from shorter hospital stays by fitness center members. People who exercise have medical bills that are 35% lower than people who do not get enough exercise.

Write the memo announcing the center.

Hints:
- Who pays the medical insurance for employees? If the employer pays, then savings from healthier employees will pay for the center. If another payment plan is in effect, you'll need a different explanation for the company's decision to open the fitness center.
- Stress benefits apart from the company's saving money. How can easier access to exercise help employees? What do they do? How can exercise reduce stress, improve strength, and increase their productivity at work?
- What kind of record does the company have of helping employees be healthy? Is the fitness center a new departure for the company, or does the company have a history of company sports teams, stop-smoking clinics, and the like?
- What is the company's competitive position? If the company is struggling, you'll need to convince readers that the fitness center is a good use of scarce funds. If the company is doing well, show how having fit employees can make people even more productive.
- Stress fun as a benefit. How can access to the center make employees' lives more enjoyable?

10.18   Confirming a Reservation

Most travelers phone 13 months in advance to reserve rooms at Signal Mountain Lodge in Grand Teton National Park. Once you process the credit card (payment for the first night), you write to confirm the reservation.

The confirmation contains the amount charged to the credit card, the date on which the reservation was made, the confirmation number, the kind of room (Lakefront Retreat or Mountainview Retreat), and the dates the guest will be arriving and leaving.

The amount of the deposit and the amount quoted per night is the rate for the current calendar year. However, the guest will be charged the rate for the calendar year of the stay, which is likely to increase about 4% to 5%. In addition to paying the new rate for each additional night, the guest will need to pay the difference between the amount of the deposit and the new rate for the first night.

Anyone who wants a refund must cancel the reservation in writing four days prior to the scheduled arrival date. Cancellations may be faxed: The fax number is on the letterhead the letter will be printed on.

Parking is limited. People who bring big motorhomes, boats, or camp trailers may have to park in the main parking area rather than right by their cabins.

All of the rooms are cabin style with three to four rooms in each building. There are no rooms in a main lodge. People will need to walk from their cabins to the restaurants, unless they do their own cooking.

Both Lakefront and Mountainview Retreats have kitchenettes with microwaves, but guests must bring their own cooking utensils, dishes, supplies, and food. The bedroom area (with a king-size bed in the Lakefront Retreats and a queen-size bed in the Mountainview Retreats) has a sliding divider that can separate it from the sitting area, which has a sofa bed.

Since the deposit pays for the first night (less any increase in room rate), the room will be held regardless of the time of arrival. Check-in time is 3 P.M.; earlier room availability cannot be guaranteed. Check-out time is 11 A.M.

All cabins are nonsmoking. Smoking is permitted on the decks of the Lakefront Retreats or the porches of the Mountainview Retreats.

The guest should present the confirmation letter when checking in.

As Your Instructor Directs,

a. Write a form letter that can be used for one type of room (either Lakefront or Mountainview Retreat). Indicate with square brackets material that would need to be filled in for each guest (e.g., "arriving [date of arrival] and departing [date of departure]").

b. Write a letter to Stephanie Simpson, who has reserved a Lakefront Retreat room arriving September 18 and departing September 20. Her credit card is being billed for $183.75 ($175 plus tax—the current rate). Her address is 3122 Ellis Street, Stevens Point, WI 54481.

10.19 Lining up a Consultant to Improve Teamwork

As Director of Education and Training you oversee all in-house training programs. Five weeks ago, Pat Dyrud, Vice President for Human Resources, asked you to set up a training course on teams. You tracked down Sarah Reed, a Business Communication professor at a nearby college.

"Yes, I do workshops on teamwork," she told you on the phone. "I would want at least a day and a half with participants—two full days would be better. They need time to practice the skills they'll be learning. I'm free Mondays and Tuesdays. I'm willing to work with up to five teams at a time, as long as the total number of people is 30 or less. Tell me what kinds of teams they work in, what they already know, and what kinds of things you want me to emphasize. My fee is $2,500 a day. Of course, you'd reimburse me for expenses."

You told her you thought a two-day session would be feasible, but you'd have to get back to her after you got budget approval. You wrote a quick memo to Pat Dyrud explaining the situation and asking about what the session should cover.

Two weeks ago, you received this memo.

I've asked the Veep for budget approval for $5,000 for a two-day session plus no more than $750 for all expenses. I don't think there will be a problem.

We need some of the basics: strategies for working in groups, making decisions, budgeting time, and so forth. We especially need work on dealing with problem group members and on handling conflict—I think some of our people are so afraid that they won't seem to be "team players" that they agree too readily.

I don't want some ivory tower theorist. We need practical exercises that can help us practice skills that we can put into effect immediately.

Attached is a list of 24 people who are free Monday and Tuesday of the second week of next month. Note that we've got a good mix of people. If the session goes well, I may want you to schedule additional sessions.

Today, you got approval from the Vice President to schedule the session and pay Professor Reed the fee and reimburse her for expenses to a maximum of $750. She will have to keep all receipts and turn in an itemized list of expenses to be reimbursed; you cannot reimburse her if she does not have receipts.

You also need to explain the mechanics of the session. You'll meet in the Conference Room, which has a screen and flip charts. You have an overhead projector, a slide projector, a laptop computer for showing Power-Point slides, a video camera, a VCR, and a TV, but you need to reserve these if she wants to use them.

Write to Professor Reed. You don't have to persuade her to come since she's already informally agreed, but you do want her to look forward to the job and to do her best work.

Hints:
- Choose an organization you know something about.
- What do teams do in this organization? What challenges do they face?
- Will most participants have experience working in teams? Will they have bad habits to overcome? What attitudes toward teams are they likely to have?
- Check the calendar to get the dates. If there's any ambiguity about what "the second week of next month" is, "call" Pat to check.

10.20 Answering an International Inquiry

Your business, government, or nonprofit organization has received the following inquiries from international correspondents. (You choose the country the inquiry is from.)

1. Please tell us about a new product, service, or trend so that we can decide whether we want to buy, license, or imitate it in our country.

2. We have heard about a problem [technical, social, political, or ethical] which occurred in your organization. Could you please tell us what really happened and estimate how it is likely to affect the long-term success of the organization?

3. Please tell us about college programs in this field that our managers could take.

4. We are considering setting up a plant in your city. We have already received adequate business information. However, we would also like to know how comfortable our nationals will feel. Do people in your city speak our language? How many? What opportunities exist for our nationals to improve their English? Does your town already have people from a wide mix of nations? Which are the largest groups?

5. Our organization would like to subscribe to an English-language trade journal. Which one would you recommend? Why? How much does it cost? How can we order it?

As Your Instructor Directs,
a. Answer one or more of the inquiries. Assume that your reader either reads English or can have your message translated.
b. Write a memo to your instructor explaining how you've adapted the message for your audience.

Hints:
- Even though you can write in English, English may not be your reader's native language. Write a letter that can be translated easily.
- In some cases, you may need to spell out background information that might not be clear to someone from another country.

10.21 Writing a Thank-You Letter

Write a thank-you letter to someone who has helped you achieve your goals.

As Your Instructor Directs,
a. Turn in a copy of the letter.

b. Mail the letter to the person who helped you.
c. Write a memo to your instructor explaining the choices you made in writing the thank-you letter.

10.22 Evaluating Web Pages

Today you get this e-mail from your boss:

Subject: Evaluating Our Web Page

Our CEO wants to know how our Web page compares to those of our competitors. I'd like you to do this in two steps. First, send me a list of your criteria. Then give me an evaluation of two of our competitors and of our own pages. I'll combine your memo with others on other Web pages to put together a comprehensive evaluation for the next Executive Meeting.

As Your Instructor Directs,
a. List the generic criteria for evaluating a Web page. Think about the various audiences for the page and the content that will keep them coming back, the way the page is organized, how easy it is to find something, the visual design, and the details, such as a creation/update date.
b. List criteria for pages of specific kinds of organizations. For example, a nonprofit organization might want

information for potential and current donors, volunteers, and clients. A financial institution might want to project an image both of trustworthiness and as a good place to work.
c. Evaluate three Web pages of similar organizations. Which is best? Why?

Hint:
Review the information on Web page design in Module 5.

10.23 Announcing a Tuition Reimbursement Program

Your organization has decided to encourage employees to take courses by reimbursing each eligible employee a maximum of $3,500 in tuition and fees during any one calendar year. Anyone who wants to participate in the program must apply before the first class meeting; the application must be signed by the employee's immediate supervisor. The Office of Human Resources will evaluate applications. That office has application forms.

The only courses eligible are those that are related to the employee's current position or to a position in the company that the employee might hold someday, or that are part of a job-related

degree program. Again, the degree may be one that would help the employee's current position or that would qualify him or her for a promotion or transfer in the organization.

Only tuition and fees are covered, not books or supplies. People whose applications are approved will be reimbursed when they have completed the course with a grade of C or better. An employee cannot be reimbursed until he or she submits a copy of the approved application, an official grade report, and a statement of the tuition paid. If someone is eligible for other financial aid (scholarship, veterans' benefits), the company will pay tuition costs not covered by that aid as long as the employee does not receive more than $3,500 and as long as the total tuition reimbursement does not exceed the actual cost of tuition and fees.

Part-time employees are not eligible; full-time employees must work at the company three months before they can apply to participate in the program. Courses may be at any appropriate level (high school, college, or graduate). However, the IRS currently requires workers to pay tax on any reimbursement for graduate programs. Undergraduate and basic education reimbursements of $5,250 a year are not taxed.

As Director of Human Resources, write a memo to all employees explaining this new benefit.

Hints:
- Pick an organization you know something about. What do its employees do? What courses or degrees might help them do their jobs better?
- How much education do employees already have? How do they feel about formal schooling?
- The information in the problem is presented in a confusing order. Put related items together.
- The problem stresses the limits of the policy. Without changing the provision, present them positively.
- How will having a better educated workforce help the organization? Think about the challenges the organization faces, its competitive environment, and so forth.

10.24   Correcting a Mistake

Due to a faulty line in a computer program, your regional Internal Revenue Office sent out letters to hundreds of people in your state saying that because they had defaulted on college loans, their federal income tax refunds would be withheld. You became aware of the error when you got a call from the state Student Aid Commission, saying that in every case it had checked, the loans were in fact repaid.

Now you must send a letter to the people who erroneously received the first letter, telling them that their loans are not delinquent and they will indeed receive their income tax refunds. The checks should follow in 4 to 12 weeks.

You have been asked to write a form letter that can be sent unchanged to everyone.

Your boss also wants you to build support for the IRS-Offset program, which collects defaulted loans by having the IRS withhold the tax refunds of delinquent borrowers. Although an error was made in this case, the program has been effective. Two years ago (the most recent year for which records are complete) the program collected more than $5 million, saving taxpayers the cost of reimbursing banks for these federally guaranteed loans.

Write the letter.

Polishing Your Prose

Dangling Modifiers

Modifiers are words or phrases that give more information about parts of a sentence.

For instance, an adjective is a modifier that usually describes a noun. **Dangling modifiers** make no sense to readers because the word they modify is not in the sentence. If you diagrammed the sentence, the modifier would not be attached to anything; it would dangle.

Dangling: Confirming our conversation, your Hot Springs Hot Tub Spa is scheduled for delivery April 12. (This sentence says that the spa is doing the confirming.)

Dangling: At the age of 10, I bought my daughter her first share of stock.

Correct a dangling modifier in either of these ways:

1. Rewrite the modifier as a subordinate clause.

Correct: As I told you yesterday, your Hot Springs Hot Tub Spa is scheduled for delivery April 12.

Correct: I bought my daughter her first share of stock when she was 10.

2. Rewrite the main clause so its subject or object can be modified correctly.

Correct: Talking on the phone, we confirmed that your Hot Springs Hot Tub Spa is scheduled for delivery April 12.

Correct: At the age of 10, my daughter received the first share of stock I bought for her.

Exercises

Correct the dangling modifiers in these sentences.

1. Using the fax machine, new orders are processed quickly.

2. With little or no work experience, the job market can intimidate newcomers.

3. Working in teams, projects can be completed quickly.

4. Half as expensive, you should fly coach instead of first-class to the trade show.

5. Before joining our company, your résumé shows a good deal of experience with computer software.

6. Like a rocket taking off, I watched our stock prices soar to a record level.

7. A simple notebook filled with thoughts and ideas, you can keep a journal of your business experiences.

8. Already the largest consulting firm in the region, shareholders can expect Key and Associates to go national next year.

9. As a new employee, your supervisor can answer your questions.

10. Making the most of their time, careers with us have no limits for employees.

Check your answers to the odd-numbered exercises at the back of the book.

BComm Skill Booster

To apply the concepts in this module, complete lessons 41 and 55 on presenting information effectively and ending letters on a note of goodwill. You can access the BComm Skill Booster through the text Web site at **www.mhhe.com/bcs2e.**

Module

11

Negative Messages

Start by asking these questions:

- What's the best subject line for a negative message?
- How should I organize negative messages?
- When should I consider using a buffer?

- What are the most common kinds of negative messages?
- How can I apply what I've learned in this module?

In a **negative message,** the basic information is negative; we expect the reader to be disappointed or angry.
Negative messages include

- Rejections and refusals.
- Announcements of policy changes that do not benefit customers or consumers.
- Requests the reader will see as insulting or intrusive.
- Negative performance appraisals and disciplinary notices.
- Product recalls or notices of defects.

A negative message always has several purposes:

Primary Purposes:

- To give the reader the bad news.
- To have the reader read, understand, and accept the message.
- To maintain as much goodwill as possible.

Secondary Purposes:

- To build a good image of the writer.
- To build a good image of the writer's organization.
- To reduce or eliminate future correspondence on the same subject so the message doesn't create more work for the writer.

Even when it is not possible to make the reader happy with the news we must convey, we still want readers to feel that

- They have been taken seriously.
- Our decision is fair and reasonable.
- If they were in our shoes, they would make the same decision.

What's the best subject line for a negative message?

Only use negative subject lines if you think the reader may otherwise ignore the message.

Letters don't require subject lines (◀ ▷ pp. 149 and 168). Omit a subject line in negative letters unless you think readers may ignore what they think is a routine message. (See, for example, Figure 11.2 later in this module).

When you give bad news to superiors, use a subject line that focuses on solving the problem.

Subject: Improving Our Subscription Letter

When you write to peers and subordinates, put the topic (but not your action on it) in the subject line.

Subject: Status of Conversion Table Program

Due to heavy demands on our time, we have not yet been able to write programs for the conversion tables you asked for.

How should I organize negative messages?

It depends on your purposes and audiences.

Choose the pattern based on the situation.

- Letters to people outside your organization should be indirect to build goodwill.
- When you write to superiors, you need to propose solutions, not just report a problem.
- When you write to peers and subordinates, try to get their input in dealing with negative situations.

FYI

Miscommunication hurt their companies, according to 63% of managers polled by the American Management Association. At 55% of the companies, a failure to communicate caused high turnover; 57% said their companies were less effective as organizations.

Source: "Poor Communication," *Black Enterprise,* July 1999, 61.

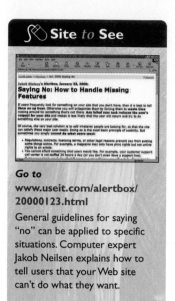

Go to
www.useit.com/alertbox/
20000123.html

General guidelines for saying "no" can be applied to specific situations. Computer expert Jakob Neilsen explains how to tell users that your Web site can't do what they want.

What pattern of organization to use is also influenced by your purposes. The patterns in this section assume that maintaining goodwill is an important purpose. But as you'll see later in the module, on some occasions, maintaining goodwill is less important than giving the negative clearly.

Giving Bad News to Customers and Other People Outside Your Organization

The following pattern helps writers maintain goodwill:

1. **Give the reason for the refusal before the refusal itself when you have a reason that readers will understand and accept.** A good reason prepares the reader to expect the refusal.
2. **Give the negative just once, clearly.** Inconspicuous refusals can be missed, making it necessary to say *no* a second time.
3. **Present an alternative or compromise, if one is available.** An alternative not only gives readers another way to get what they want but also suggests that you care about readers and helping them solve their problems.
4. **End with a positive, forward-looking statement.**

Figure 11.1 summarizes the pattern. Figure 11.2 uses the basic pattern.

Reasons

Make the reason for the refusal clear and convincing. The following reason is inadequate.

Weak reason: The goal of the Knoxville CHARGE-ALL Center is to provide our customers faster, more personalized service. Since you now live outside the Knoxville CHARGE-ALL service area, we can no longer offer you the advantages of a local CHARGE-ALL Center.

If the reader says, "I don't care if my bills are slow and impersonal," will the company let the reader keep the card? No. The real reason for the negative is that the bank's franchise allows it to have cardholders only in a given geographical region.

Figure 11.1
How to Organize a Negative Letter

Figure 11.2
A Negative Letter

Vickers
Insurance Company

3373 Forbes Avenue
Rosemont, PA 19010
(215) 572-0100

Negative information highlighted so reader won't ignore message.

Liability Coverage
Is Being Discontinued—
Here's How to Replace It!

Negative

Alternative

Dear Policyholder:

Negative

When your auto insurance is renewed, it will no longer include liability coverage unless you select the new Assurance Plan. Here's why.

Positive information underlined for emphasis.

Liability coverage is being discontinued. It, and the part of the premium which paid for it, will be dropped from all policies when they are renewed.

This could leave a gap in your protection. But you can replace the old Liability Coverage with Vickers' new Assurance Plan.

No reason is given. The change probably benefits the company rather than the reader, so it is omitted.

Alternative

With the new Assurance Plan, you receive benefits for litigation or awards arising from an accident--regardless of who's at fault. The cost for the Assurance Plan at any level is based on the ages of drivers, where you live, your driving record, and other factors. If these change before your policy is renewed, the cost of your Assurance Plan may also change. The actual cost will be listed in your renewal statement.

To sign up for the Assurance Plan, just check the level of coverage you want on the enclosed form and return it in the postage-paid envelope within 14 days. You'll be assured of the coverage you select.

Forward-looking ending emphasizes reader's choice.

Sincerely,

C. J. Morgan

C. J. Morgan
President

Alternative

P.S. The Assurance Plan protects you against possible legal costs arising from an accident. Sign up for the Plan today and receive full coverage from Vickers.

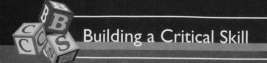

Thinking about the Legal Implications of What You Say

Any message that is recorded—on paper (even a napkin), on a disk or hard drive, on voice mail—can be subpoenaed in a legal case. During the government's months-long case against Microsoft in the late 1990s, e-mail messages figured prominently as evidence. And even an electronic message that has been erased can be reconstituted by experts. In any message you write, however informal or hurried, you need to be sure to say exactly what you mean.

Thinking about the legal implications of what you say is particularly important in negative messages. In an effort to cushion bad news, writers sometimes give reasons that create legal liabilities. For example, as Elizabeth McCord has shown, the statement that a plant is "too noisy and dangerous" for a group tour could be used as evidence against the company in a worker's compensation claim. In another case, a writer telling a job candidate that the firm had hired someone else said that he thought she was the best candidate. She sued and won.

You don't need to be a lawyer to figure out what to say—or not to say. Think about how a reasonable person might interpret your words. If that interpretation isn't what you mean, revise the passage so that it says what you mean.

Source: Elizabeth A. McCord, "The Business Writer, the Law, and Routine Business Communication. A Legal and Rhetorical Analysis," *Journal of Business and Technical Communication* 5, no. 2 (1991): 173–99.

Real reason: Each local CHARGE-ALL Center is permitted to offer accounts to customers in a several-state area. The Knoxville CHARGE-ALL Center serves customers east of the Mississippi. You can continue to use your current card until it expires. When that happens, you'll need to open an account with a CHARGE-ALL Center that serves Texas.

Don't hide behind "company policy": Readers will assume the policy is designed to benefit you at their expense. If possible, show how the readers benefit from the policy. If they do not benefit, don't mention the policy.

Weak reason: I cannot write an insurance policy for you because company policy does not allow me to do so.

Better reason: Gorham insures cars only when they are normally garaged at night. Standard insurance policies cover a wider variety of risks and charge higher fees. Limiting the policies we write gives Gorham customers the lowest possible rates for auto insurance.

Avoid saying that you *cannot* do something. Most negative messages exist because the writer or company has chosen certain policies or cutoff points. In the example above, the company could choose to insure a wider variety of customers if it wanted to do so.

Often you will enforce policies that you did not design. Don't pass the buck by saying, "This is a terrible policy." Carelessly criticizing your superiors is never a good idea. If you really think a policy is bad, try to persuade your superiors to change it. If you can't think of convincing reasons to change the policy, maybe it isn't so bad after all.

If you have several reasons for saying *no*, use only those that are strong and watertight. If you give five reasons and readers dismiss two of them, readers may feel that they've won and should get the request.

Weak reason:	You cannot store large bulky items in the dormitory over the summer because moving them into and out of storage would tie up the stairs and the elevators just at the busiest times when people are moving in and out.
Way to dismiss the reason:	We'll move large items before or after the two days when most people are moving in or out.

If you do not have a good reason, omit the reason rather than use a weak one. Even if you have a strong reason, omit it if it makes the company look bad.

Reason that hurts company:	Our company is not hiring at the present time because profits are down. In fact, the downturn has prompted top management to reduce the salaried staff by 5% just this month, with perhaps more reductions to come.
Better:	Our company does not have any openings now.

Refusals

Deemphasize the refusal by putting it in the same paragraph as the reason, rather than in a paragraph by itself.

Sometimes you may be able to imply the refusal rather than stating it directly.

Direct refusal:	You cannot get insurance for just one month.
Implied refusal:	The shortest term for an insurance policy is six months.

Be sure that the implication is crystal clear. Any message can be misunderstood, but an optimistic or desperate reader is particularly unlikely to understand a negative message. One of your purposes in a negative message is to close the door on the subject. You do not want to have to write a second letter saying that the real answer is *no*.

Alternatives

Giving the reader an alternative or a compromise, if one is available,

- Offers the reader another way to get what he or she wants.
- Suggests that you really care about the reader and about helping to meet his or her needs.
- Enables the reader to reestablish the psychological freedom you limited when you said *no*.
- Allows you to end on a positive note and to present yourself and your organization as positive, friendly, and helpful.

When you give an alternative, give readers all the information they need to act on it, but don't take the necessary steps. Let readers decide whether to try the alternative.

Negative messages limit the reader's freedom. People may respond to a limitation of freedom by asserting their freedom in some other arena. Jack W. Brehm calls this phenomenon **psychological reactance.**[1] Psychological reactance is at work when a customer who has been denied credit no longer buys even on a cash basis or a subordinate who has been passed over for a promotion gets back at the company by deliberately doing a poor job.

Instant Replay

Organizing Letters to Customers

1. Give the reason for the refusal before the refusal itself when you have a reason that readers will understand and accept.
2. Give the negative just once, clearly.
3. Present an alternative or compromise, if one is available.
4. End with a positive, forward-looking statement.

Psychological reactance in action

An alternative allows the reader to react in a way that doesn't hurt you. By letting readers decide for themselves whether they want the alternative, you allow them to reestablish their sense of psychological freedom.

The specific alternative will vary depending on the circumstances. In Figure 11.3, the company is unwilling to quote a price on an item on which it cannot be competitive. In different circumstances, the writer might offer different alternatives.

Endings

If you have a good alternative, refer to it in your ending: "Let me know if you can use A515 grade 70."

The best endings look to the future, as in this letter refusing to continue a charge account for a customer who has moved.

> Wherever you have your account, you'll continue to get all the service you've learned to expect from CHARGE-ALL and the convenience of charging items at over a million stores, restaurants, and hotels in the U.S. and abroad—and in Knoxville, too, whenever you come back to visit!

Avoid endings that seem insincere.

> We are happy to have been of service, and should we be able to assist you in the future, please contact us.

This ending lacks you-attitude and would not be good even in a positive message. In a situation where the company has just refused to help, it's likely to sound sarcastic or mean.

Giving Bad News to Superiors

Your superior expects you to solve minor problems by yourself. But sometimes, solving a problem requires more authority or resources than you have. When you give bad news to a superior, also recommend a way to deal with the problem. Turn the negative message into a persuasive one.

Figure 11.3

A Refusal with an Alternative

ROYSNER
Steel Fabrication

"Serving the needs of America since 1890"
1800 Olney Avenue • Philadelphia, PA 19140 • 215•555•7800 • Fax: 215•555•9803

April 27, 2003

Mr. H. J. Moody
Canton Corporation
2407 North Avenue
Kearney, NE 68847

Subject: Bid Number 5853, Part Number D-40040

Dear Mr. Moody:

Buffer Thank you for requesting our quotation on your Part No. D-40040.

Reason Your blueprints call for flame-cut rings 1/2" thick A516 grade 70. To use that grade, we'd have to grind down from 1" thick material. However, if you can use A515 grade 70, which we stock in 1/2" thick, you can cut the price by more than half.

Quantity	Description	Gross Weight	Price/Each
75	Rings Drawing D-40040, A516 Grade 70 1" thick x 6" O.D. x 2.8" I.D. ground to .5" thick.	12 lbs.	$15.08
75	Rings Drawing D-40040, A515 Grade 70 1/2" thick x 6" O.D. x 2.8" I.D.	6 lbs.	$6.91

Alternative (Depending on circumstances, different alternatives may exist.)

If you can use A515 grade 70, let me know. *Leaves decision up to reader to re-establish psychological freedom*

Sincerely,

Valerie Prynne

Valerie Prynne
VP:wc

Figure 11.4

How to Organize a Negative Memo to Your Superior

1. **Describe the problem.** Tell what's wrong, clearly and unemotionally.
2. **Tell how it happened.** Provide the background. What underlying factors led to this specific problem?
3. **Describe the options for fixing it.** If one option is clearly best, you may need to discuss only one. But if the reader will think of other options, or if different people will judge the options differently, describe all the options, giving their advantages and disadvantages.
4. **Recommend a solution and ask for action.** Ask for approval so that you can go ahead to make the necessary changes to fix the problem.

Figure 11.4 summarizes the pattern.

Giving Bad News to Peers and Subordinates

When you must pass along serious bad news to peers and subordinates, use a variation of the pattern to superiors:

1. **Describe the problem.** Tell what's wrong, clearly and unemotionally.
2. **Present an alternative or compromise, if one is available.** An alternative gives readers another way to get what they want and also suggests that you care about readers and helping them meet their needs.
3. **If possible, ask for input or action.** People in the audience may be able to suggest solutions. And workers who help make a decision are far more likely to accept the consequences.

Figure 11.5 summarizes this pattern.

No serious negative (such as being downsized or laid off) should come as a complete surprise. Managers can prepare for possible negatives by giving full information as it becomes available. It is also possible to let the people

Figure 11.5

How to Organize a Negative Memo to Peers or Subordinates

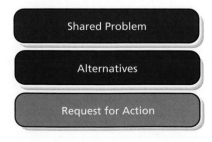

Figure 11.6
A Negative Memo to Subordinates

Memo

Board of County Commissioners
Olentangy County, Nebraska

Date: January 10, 2004

To: All Employees

From: Floyd E. Loer, Dorothy A. Walters, and Stewart Mattson

Subject: Accounting for Work Missed Due to Bad Weather

Reason   Olentangy County Services are always open for our customers, whatever the
                        weather. Employees who missed work during the snowstorm last week may
Refusal,   count the absence as vacation, sick day(s), or personal day(s).
stated as
positively   Hourly workers who missed less than a day have the option of taking the
as   missed time as vacation, sick, or personal hours or of being paid only for the
possible   hours they worked.

One small   Approval of vacation or personal days will be automatic; the normal
positive   requirement of giving at least 24 hours' notice is waived.

Goodwill   Thanks for all the efforts you have made to continue giving our customers
ending   the best possible service during one of the snowiest winters on record.

---

who will be affected by a decision participate in setting the criteria. Someone who has bought into the criteria for awarding cash for suggestions or retaining workers is more likely to accept decisions using such criteria. And in some cases, the synergism of groups may make possible ideas that management didn't think of or rejected as "unacceptable." Some workplaces, for example, might decide to reduce everyone's pay slightly rather than laying off some individuals. Employee suggestions enabled Mentor Training, a San Jose company providing software training, to cut its payroll by 30% without laying off any full-time employees.[2]

When the bad news is less serious, as in Figure 11.6, use the pattern for negative letters unless your knowledge of the reader(s) suggests that another pattern will be more effective.

For memos, the context of communication is crucial. The reader's reaction is influenced by the following factors:

- Do you and the reader have a good relationship?
- Does the organization treat people well?

- Have readers been warned of possible negatives?
- Have readers "bought into" the criteria for the decision?
- Do communications after the negative build goodwill?

When should I consider using a buffer?

When the reader values harmony or when the buffer also serves another purpose.

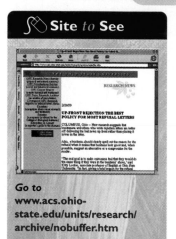

To some writers and readers, the direct patterns used in the previous section may seem too blunt. You may want to begin messages with a buffer when the reader (individually or culturally) values harmony or when the buffer serves another purpose. For example, when you must thank the reader somewhere in the letter, putting the "thank you" in the first paragraph allows you to start on a positive note.

A **buffer** is a neutral or positive statement that allows you to delay the negative. Recent research suggests that buffers do not make readers respond more positively,[3] and good buffers are very hard to write. However in special situations, you may want to use a buffer.

To be effective, a buffer must put the reader in a good frame of mind, not give the bad news but not imply a positive answer either, and provide a natural transition to the body of the letter. The kinds of statements most often used as buffers are good news, facts and chronologies of events, references to enclosures, thanks, and statements of principle.

1. **Start with any good news or positive elements the letter contains.**

> Starting Thursday, June 26, you'll have access to your money 24 hours a day at First National Bank.

Letter announcing that the drive-up windows will be closed for two days while automatic teller machines are installed

2. **State a fact or provide a chronology of events.**

> As a result of the new graduated dues schedule—determined by vote of the Delegate Assembly last December and subsequently endorsed by the Executive Council—members are now asked to establish their own dues rate and to calculate the total amount of their remittance.

Announcement of a new dues structure that will raise most members' dues

3. **Refer to enclosures in the letter.**

> Enclosed is a new sticker for your car. You may pick up additional ones in the office if needed. Please *destroy* old stickers bearing the signature of "L.S. LaVoie."

Letter announcing increase in parking rental rates

4. **Thank the reader for something he or she has done.**

> Thank you for scheduling appointments for me with so many senior people at First National Bank. My visit there March 14 was very informative.

Letter refusing a job offer

5. **State a general principle.**

> Good drivers should pay substantially less for their auto insurance. The Good Driver Plan was created to reward good drivers (those with 5-year accident-free records) with our lowest available rates. A change in the plan, effective January 1, will help keep those rates low.

Letter announcing that the company will now count traffic tickets, not just accidents, in calculating insurance rates—a change that will raise many people's premiums

Buffers are hard to write. Even if you think the reader would prefer to be let down easily, use a buffer only when you can write a good one.

It's better *not* to use a buffer (1) if the reader may ignore a letter with a bland first paragraph, (2) if the reader or the organization prefers "bottom-line-first messages," (3) if the reader is suspicious of the writer, or (4) if the reader "won't take *no* for an answer."

What are the most common kinds of negative messages?

Rejections and refusals, disciplinary notices and negative performance appraisals, and layoffs and firings.

Among the most difficult kinds of negative messages to write are rejections and refusals, disciplinary notices and negative performance appraisals, and layoffs and firings.

Rejections and Refusals

When you refuse requests from people outside your organization, try to use a buffer. Give an alternative if one is available. For example, if you are denying credit, it may still be possible for the reader to put an expensive item on layaway.

Politeness and length help. Graduating seniors at a southwestern university preferred rejection letters that addressed them as *Mr./Ms.* rather than calling them by their first names, that said something specific about their good qualities, that phrased the refusal itself indirectly, and that were longer.[4] An experiment using a denial of additional insurance found that subjects preferred a rejection letter that was longer, more tactful, and more personal. The preferred letter started with a buffer, used a good reason for the refusal, and offered sales promotion in the last paragraph. The finding held both for English-speaking U.S. subjects and for Spanish-speaking Mexican subjects.[5]

When you refuse requests within your organization, use your knowledge of the organization's culture and of the specific individual to craft your message. In some organizations, it may be appropriate to use company slogans, offer whatever help already-established departments can give, and refer to the individual's good work. In less personal organizations, a simple negative without embellishment may be more appropriate.

Disciplinary Notices and Negative Performance Appraisals

Present disciplinary notices and negative performance appraisals directly, with no buffer. A buffer might encourage the recipient to minimize the message's importance—and might even become evidence in a court case that the employee had not been told to shape up "or else." Cite quantifiable observations of the employee's behavior, rather than generalizations or inferences based on it. If an employee is disciplined by being laid off without pay, specify when the employee is to return.

Performance appraisals are discussed in detail in Module 12 on persuasive messages. Performance appraisals will be persuasive when they are designed to help a basically good employee improve. But when an employee violates a company rule or fails to improve after repeated appraisals, the company may discipline the employee or build a dossier to support firing him or her.

Layoffs and Firings

Information about layoffs and firings is normally delivered orally but accompanied by a written statement explaining severance pay or unemployment benefits that may be available. The written statement should start either with the reason or with the decision itself. A buffer would not be appropriate.

If a company is in financial trouble, management needs to communicate the problem clearly long before it is necessary to lay anyone off. Sharing information and enlisting everyone's help in finding solutions may make it possible to save jobs. Sharing information also means that layoff notices, if they become necessary, will be a formality; they should not be new information to employees.

Before you fire someone, double-check the facts. Make sure that the employee has been told about the problem and that he or she will be fired if the problem is not corrected. Give the employee the real reason for the firing. Offering a face-saving reason unrelated to poor performance can create legal liabilities. But avoid broadcasting the reason to other people: to do so can leave the company liable to a defamation suit.[6]

Instant Replay

Effective Buffers

To be effective, a buffer must put the reader in a good frame of mind, not give the bad news but not imply a positive answer either, and provide a natural transition to the body of the letter.

How can I apply what I've learned in this module?

Plan your activities and answer the PAIBOC questions.

Before you tackle the assignments for this module, examine the following problem. Figure 11.7 lists the necessary activities. As in Module 10, the PAIBOC questions probe the basic points required for a solution. Study the two sample solutions to see what makes one unacceptable and the other one good.[7] The checklist at the end of the module in Figure 11.10 can help you evaluate a draft.

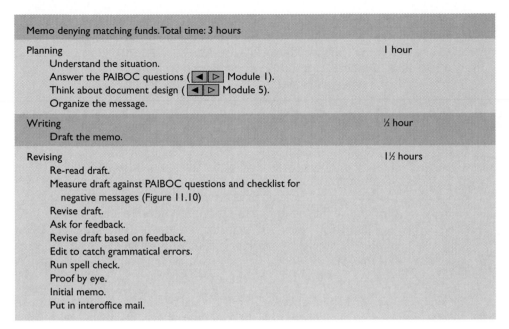

Problem

You're Director of Employee Benefits for a Fortune 500 company. Today, you received the following memo:

From: Michelle Jagtiani

Subject: Getting My Retirement Benefits

Next Friday will be my last day here. I am leaving [name of company] to take a position at another firm.

Please process a check for my retirement benefits, including both the deductions from my salary and the company's contributions for the last three and a half years. I would like to receive the check by next Friday if possible.

You have bad news for Michelle. Although the company does contribute an amount to the retirement fund equal to the amount deducted for retirement from the employee's paycheck, employees who leave with less than five years of employment get only their own contributions. Michelle will get back only the money that has been deducted from her own pay, plus 4% interest compounded quarterly. Her payments and interest come to just over $17,200; the amount could be higher depending on the amount of her last paycheck, which will include compensation for any unused vacation days and sick leave. Furthermore, since the amounts deducted were not considered taxable income, she will have to pay income tax on the money she will receive.

Go to
www.ipsfunds.com/risks.html

IPS Funds offers its Risk
Disclosure in "Legal Boilerplate"
or "Human Language." Scroll
down to the bottom of the page:
"Don't come crying to us if we
lose all your money."

You cannot process the check until after her resignation is effective, so you will mail it to her. You have her home address on file; if she's moving, she needs to let you know where to send the check. Processing the check may take two to three weeks.

Write a memo to Michelle.

Analysis of the Problem

P   What are your **purposes** in writing or speaking?

> To tell her that she will get only her own contributions, plus 4% interest compounded quarterly; that the check will be mailed to her home address two to three weeks after her last day on the job; and that the money will be taxable as income.
>
> To build goodwill so that she feels that she has been treated fairly and consistently. To minimize negative feelings she may have.
>
> To close the door on this subject.

A   Who is (are) your **audience(s)?** How do the members of your audience differ from each other? What characteristics are relevant to this particular message?

> Michelle Jagtiani. Unless she's a personal friend, I probably wouldn't know why she's leaving and where she's going.
>
> There's a lot I don't know. She may or may not know much about taxes; she may or may not be able to take advantage of tax-reduction strategies. I can't assume the answers because I wouldn't have them in real life.

I   What **information** must your message include?

> When the check will come. The facts that the check will be based on her contributions, not her employer's, and that the money will be taxable income. How lump-sum retirement benefits are calculated. The fact that we have her current address on file but need a new address if she's moving.

B   What reasons or reader **benefits** can you use to support your position?

> Giving the amount currently in her account may make her feel that she is getting a significant sum of money. Suggesting someone who can give free tax advice (if the company offers this as a fringe benefit) reminds her of the benefits of working with the company. Wishing her luck with her new job is a nice touch.

O What **objections** can you expect your reader(s) to have? What negative elements of your message must you deemphasize or overcome?

> She is getting about half the amount she expected, since she gets no matching funds.
>
> She might have been able to earn more than 4% interest if she had invested the money herself. Depending on her personal tax situation she may pay more tax on the money as a lump sum than would have been due had she paid it each year as she earned the money.

C How will the **context** affect the reader's response? Think about your relationship to the reader, morale in the organization, the economy, the time of year, and any special circumstances.

> The stock market has been doing poorly; 4% interest is pretty good.

Discussion of the Sample Solutions

The solution in Figure 11.8 is not acceptable. The subject line gives a blunt negative with no reason or alternative. The first sentence has a condescending tone that is particularly offensive in negative messages. The last sentence focuses on what is being taken away rather than what remains. Paragraph 2 lacks you-attitude and is vague. The memo ends with a negative. There is nothing anywhere in the memo to build goodwill.

The solution in Figure 11.9, in contrast, is very good. The policy serves as a buffer and explanation. The negative is stated clearly but is buried in the paragraph to avoid overemphasizing it. The paragraph ends on a positive note by specifying the amount in the account and the fact that the sum might be even higher.

Paragraph 3 contains the additional negative information that the amount will be taxable but offers the alternative that it may be possible to reduce taxes. The writer builds goodwill by suggesting a specific person the reader could contact.

Paragraph 4 tells the reader what address is in the company files (Michelle may not know whether the files are up to date), asks that she update it if necessary, and ends with the reader's concern: getting her check promptly.

The final paragraph ends on a positive note. This generalized goodwill is appropriate when the writer does not know the reader well.

Figure 11.8

An Unacceptable Solution to the Sample Problem

April 20, 2004

To: Michelle Jagtiani

From   Lisa Niaz   *LN*

Subject   Denial of Matching Funds

Give reason before refusal. You cannot receive a check the last day of work and you will get only your own contributions, not a matching sum from the company, because you have not worked for the company for at least five full years.

Better to be specific

This is lifted straight from the problem. The language in problems is often negative and stuffy; information is disorganized. Your payments and interest come to just over $17,200; the amount could be higher depending on the amount of your last paycheck, which will include compensation for any unused vacation days and sick leave. Furthermore, since the amounts deducted were not considered taxable income, you will have to pay income tax on the money you receive.

The check will be sent to your home address. If the address we have on file is incorrect, please correct it so that your check is not delayed. *—— Negative ——*

How will reader know what you have on file? Better to give current address as you have it.

Think about the situation and use your own words to create a satisfactory message.

Figure 11.9
A Good Solution to the Sample Problem

April 20, 2004

To: Michelle Jagtiani

From: Lisa Niaz *LN*

Subject: Receiving Employee Contributions from Retirement Accounts

Good to state reason in third-person to deemphasize negative Employees who leave the company with at least five full years of employment are entitled both to the company contributions and the retirement benefit paycheck deductions contributed to retirement accounts. Those employees who leave the company with less than five years of employment will receive the employee paycheck contributions made to their retirement accounts.

Good to be specific You now have $17,240.62 in your account, which includes 4% interest compounded quarterly. The amount you receive could be even higher since you will also receive payment for any unused sick leave and vacation days.

Good to show how company can help Because you now have access to the account, the amount you receive will be considered taxable income. Beth Jordan in Employee Financial Services can give you information about possible tax deductions and financial investments which can reduce your income taxes.

Good to be specific The check will be sent to your home address on May 16. The address we have on file is 2724 Merriman Road, Akron, Ohio 44313. If your address changes, please let us know so you can receive your check promptly. *Positive*

Good luck with your new job!

Forward-looking

Figure 11.10

√ Checklist for
Negative Messages

☐ Is the subject line appropriate?

☐ If a buffer is used, does it avoid suggesting either a positive or a negative response?

☐ Is the reason, if it is given, presented before the refusal? Is the reason watertight, with no loopholes?

☐ Is the negative information clear?

☐ Is an alternative given if a good one is available? Does the message provide all the information needed to act on the alternative but leave the choice up to the reader?

☐ Does the last paragraph avoid repeating the negative information?

☐ Is tone acceptable—not defensive, but not cold, preachy, or arrogant either?

And, for all messages, not just negative ones,

☐ Does the message use you-attitude and positive emphasis?

☐ Is the style easy to read and friendly?

☐ Is the visual design of the message inviting?

☐ Is the format correct?

☐ Does the message use standard grammar? Is it free from typos?

Originality in a negative message may come from

☐ An effective buffer, if one is appropriate.

☐ A clear, complete statement of the reason for the refusal.

☐ A good alternative, clearly presented, which shows that you're thinking about what the reader really needs.

☐ Adding details that show you're thinking about a specific organization and the specific people in that organization.

Summary of Key Points

- Organize negative letters in this way:
  1. Give the reason for the refusal before the refusal itself when you have a reason that readers will understand and accept.
  2. Give the negative just once, clearly.
  3. Present an alternative or compromise, if one is available.
  4. End with a positive, forward-looking statement.

- Organize negative memos to superiors in this way:
  1. Describe the problem.

  2. Tell how it happened.
  3. Describe the options for fixing it.
  4. Recommend a solution and ask for action.

- When you must pass along serious bad news to peers and subordinates, use a variation of the pattern to superiors:
  1. Describe the problem.
  2. Present an alternative or compromise, if one is available.
  3. If possible, ask for input or action.

- When the bad news is less serious, use the pattern for negative letters unless your knowledge of the reader(s) suggests that another pattern will be more effective.

- A good reason must be watertight. Give several reasons only if all are watertight and are of comparable importance. Omit the reason for the refusal if it is weak or if it makes your organization look bad.

- Giving the reader an alternative or a compromise
  - Offers the reader another way to get what he or she wants.
  - Suggests that you really care about the reader and about helping to meet his or her needs.
  - Enables the reader to reestablish the psychological freedom you limited when you said *no.*
  - Allows you to end on a positive note and to present yourself and your organization as positive, friendly, and helpful.

- People may respond to limits by striking out in some perhaps unacceptable way. This effort to reestablish freedom is called **psychological reactance.**

- When you give an alternative, give the reader all the information he or she needs to act on it, but don't take the necessary steps for the reader. Letting the reader decide whether to try the alternative allows the reader to reestablish a sense of psychological freedom.

- Use a buffer when the reader values harmony or when the buffer serves a purpose in addition to simply delaying the negative. A **buffer** is a neutral or positive statement that allows you to bury the negative message. Buffers must put the reader in a good frame of mind, not give the bad news but not imply a positive answer either, and provide a natural transition to the body of the letter.

- The kinds of statements most often used as buffers are (1) good news, (2) facts and chronologies of events, (3) references to enclosures, (4) thanks, and (5) statements of principle.

- Use the PAIBOC questions listed in Module 1 to examine the basic points needed for successful informative and positive messages.

Assignments for Module 11

Questions for Comprehension

11.1 How should a negative letter to customers or clients be organized?

11.2 Why is giving an alternative or a compromise, if one exists, a good idea?

11.3 What are the most common types of buffers?

11.4 How should a negative memo to a superior be organized?

Questions for Critical Thinking

11.5 How do specific varieties of negative messages adapt the basic pattern?

11.6 How do you use positive emphasis in a negative message?

11.7 How do you decide whether to give the negative directly or to buffer it?

Exercises and Problems

11.8 Revising a Negative Message

Rewrite and reorganize the following negative message to make it more positive. Eliminate any sentences that are not needed.

Dear Renter:

Effective March 1, the rent for your parking space will go up $10 a month. However, our parking lot is still not the most expensive in town.

Many of you have asked us to provide better snow and ice removal and to post signs saying that all spaces are rented so that a car can be towed if it parks in your space. Signs will be posted by March 1, and, if we get any more snow, Acme Company has contracted to have the lot cleared by 7 a.m.

Enclosed is a new parking sticker. Please hang it on your rearview mirror.

Sincerely,

A. E. Jackson

11.9 Rejecting Employees' Suggestions

For years, businesses have had suggestion programs, rewarding employees for money-saving ideas. Now your city government has adopted such a program. But not all of the suggestions are adopted. Today, you need to send messages to the following people. Because their suggestions are being rejected, they will not get any cash.

1. Diane Hilgers, secretary, Mayor's office. Suggestion: Charge for 911 calls. Reason for rejection: "This would be a public relations disaster. We already charge for ambulance or paramedic trips; to charge just for the call will offend people. And it might not save money. It's a lot cheaper to prevent a burglary or murder than to track down the person afterwards—to say nothing of the trauma of the loss or death. Bad idea."

2. Steve Rieneke, building and grounds supervisor. Suggestion: Fire the city's public relations specialists. Reason for rejection: "Positive attitudes toward city workers and policies make the public more willing to support public programs and taxes. We think this is money well spent."

3. Jose Rivera, Accountant I. Suggestion: Schedule city council meetings during the day to save on light bills and staff overtime. Reason for rejection: "Having the meetings in the evening enables more citizens to attend. Open meetings are essential so that citizens don't feel that policies and taxes are being railroaded through."

Write the messages.

11.10 Telling the Boss about a Problem

In any organization, things sometimes go wrong. Tell your supervisor about a problem in your unit and recommend what should be done.

As Your Instructor Directs,
a. Prepare notes for a meeting with your supervisor.

b. Write an e-mail message to your supervisor.
c. Write a memo to your supervisor.
d. Give an oral presentation on the problem.
e. Write a memo to your instructor explaining the problem, the corporate culture, and the reasons for your solution.

11.11 Telling a Potential Subscriber That a Magazine Will Not Be Published

You and a group of investors wanted to launch a magazine called *Endangered Wildlife*. Following industry practice, you conducted a *dry test*. Dry tests allow marketers to determine whether there is an adequate demand for a product before they commit hundreds of thousands of dollars to producing and distributing it.

You mocked up the first three issues. Then you mailed a glossy package with a persuasive sales letter, a brochure with photos, and a response card to 50,000 people who had donated to environmental causes or who subscribe to current wildlife and outdoor activity magazines. Your letter made it clear that

Endangered Wildlife was a new magazine and invited people to become charter subscribers. The order form read, "Yes, I would like to be one of the first to subscribe to *Endangered Wildlife* as soon as it is published. I understand that I will not be billed until after my first issue has arrived."

However, only 137 people were interested in subscribing—far too small a number to make the magazine economically feasible—so you will not, after all, publish the magazine.

Write a letter to these would-be subscribers, telling them about your change in plans.

11.12 Giving the Boss Some Bad News

Your boss is one of the up-and-coming managers in the overnight delivery company for which you work. The boss will go places, and you hope to travel along. One of the brilliant ideas your boss had was to start a magazine for administrative assistants (who choose which overnight delivery company to use) and to survey them to get their reactions to the first three issues. You were assigned to tabulate and analyze the results.

Your boss isn't quite on track. The first three issues have had articles on women's fashions and makeup; readers

want job-related information. Men in the sample said they felt ignored. The survey was titled "Secretarial Attitudes," though that job title is preferred by only 12% of the people who filled out the survey.

The magazine is still a powerful sales tool for your company, but it needs a different content. And future surveys need to be more sensitive to readers' preferences.

Write a memo to your boss.

Hint:
• What topics could the magazine cover that might interest readers?

11.13 Tightening the Limits on Business Expenses

Your firm is forced to save money on business expenses. In the past, your firm has reimbursed employees for all legitimate business expenses. However, starting on the first of next month, the following new limits will apply:

Meals, lodging, and incidental expenses will be limited to

$175 a day in U.S. metropolitan areas whose population is over 2 million.
$125 a day in all other U.S. areas.

Reimbursements for meals for clients cannot exceed
$60 a person in U.S. metropolitan areas whose population is over 2 million.

$40 a person in all other U.S. areas.

No liquor will be reimbursed.

On plane flights, fees for alcohol and in-flight movies are no longer covered.

Employees must submit receipts for all expenses over $10 if they wish to be reimbursed.

Restaurant receipts must be from a cash register; the tabs that a customer fills in are not acceptable.

Where it is impossible to get a register receipt (for example, taxi rides) the employee must submit a bill signed by the person to whom payment is made.

11.14 Telling Retirees They Must Switch to HMOs

Your company has traditionally provided health insurance not only to employees but also to retirees who have worked for the company for at least 20 years at the time of retirement.

Seven years ago, you cut costs for employee health insurance by switching from open-ended insurance to health maintenance organizations (HMOs). At that time, you kept open-ended insurance for retirees because your employees told you that retirees wanted to keep their current doctors. But the high cost of that program gives you no choice: to continue to insure retirees, you must hold down costs, and HMOs offer the best way of doing that.

Under the current plan, the retiree pays 20% of all costs (up to a yearly ceiling of $10,000 and a lifetime ceiling of $100,000) and you pay 80%. In an HMO, more costs will be covered. Routine doctors' visits, for example, charge only a $10 co-payment. Most tests, such as mammograms, X rays, and blood work, are covered 100%. Hospitalization is covered completely, and there's much less paperwork. By presenting one's card when one fills a prescription, one pays only the co-payment, rather than having to pay the entire amount and then filing for partial reimbursement later.

The bad news for retirees is that they have to go to a physician listed with the HMO. If the current physician is not on the list, the retiree will have to switch doctors to retain benefits.

Furthermore, the primary care physician must refer the patient to any other health care providers. That is, someone who wants to see a specialist or go to the emergency room must call the primary care physician first. Primary care physicians always approve such referrals whenever they seem medically advisable, but the requirement does limit the patient's freedom. Further, since HMOs are paid a flat fee and therefore have an incentive to give care that costs less than that fee, some people fear that HMOs will be reluctant to prescribe expensive treatments, even when those treatments are essential.

Your company offers a choice of HMOs. Informational meetings will be held next month for retirees (and anyone else who wishes to attend) to explain the various options. Retirees must return a card within two months, indicating which plan they prefer. The card will be enclosed in the mailing. Anyone who does not return a card will be assigned by the company.

As Vice President for Human Resources, write a form letter to all retirees, explaining the change and telling them how to indicate which HMO they prefer.

Hints:
- Choose a business, government, or nonprofit organization that you know something about.
- About how many retirees do you have? What percentage are "young

old" (under 80, in reasonably good health)? What percentage are "old old" (80 and over, sometimes with more serious health problems)?
• How well educated are your retirees? How easy will it be for them to understand the HMO options?

• What times would be convenient for the retirees to come to meetings? Should you have extra times for them, beyond those you've scheduled for employees?

11.15 Refusing to Waive a Fee

As the licensing program coordinator for your school, you evaluate proposals from vendors who want to make or sell merchandise with the school's name, logo, or mascot. If you find the product acceptable, the vendor pays a $250 licensing fee and then 6.5% of the wholesale cost of the merchandise manufactured (whether it is sold or not).

The licensing fee helps to support the cost of your office; the 6.5% royalty goes into a student scholarship fund. At well-known universities or those with loyal students and alumni, the funds from such a program can add up to hundreds of thousands of dollars a year.

On your desk today is a proposal from a current student, Meg Winston.

> I want to silk screen and sell T-shirts printed with the name of the school, the mascot, and the words, "We're Number One!" (A copy of the design I propose is enclosed.) I ask that you waive the $250 licensing fee you normally require and limit the 6.5% royalty only to those T-shirts actually sold, not to all those made.
>
> I am putting myself through school by using student loans and working 30 hours a week. I just don't have $250. In my marketing class, we've done feasibility analyses, and I've determined that the shirts can be sold if the price is low enough. I hope to market these shirts in an independent study project with Professor Doulin, building on my marketing project earlier this term. However, my calculations show that I cannot price the shirts competitively if just one shirt must bear the 6.5% royalty for all the shirts produced in a batch. I will of course pay the 6.5% royalty on all shirts sold and not returned. I will produce the shirts in small batches (50–100 at a time). I am willing to donate any manufactured but unsold shirts to the athletic program so that you will know I'm not holding out on you.
>
> By waiving this fee, you will show that this school really wants to help students get practical experience in business, as the catalog states. I will work hard to promote these shirts by getting the school president, the coaches, and campus leaders to endorse them, pointing out that the money goes to the scholarship fund. The shirts themselves will promote school loyalty, both now and later when we're alumni who can contribute to our alma mater.
>
> I look forward to receiving the "go-ahead" to market these shirts.

The design and product are acceptable under your guidelines. However, you've always enforced the fee structure across the board, and you see no reason to make an exception now. Whether the person trying to sell merchandise is a student or not doesn't matter; your policy is designed to see that the school benefits whenever it is used to sell something. Students aren't the only ones whose cash flow is limited; many businesses would find it easier to get into the potentially lucrative business of selling clothing, school supplies, and other items with the school name or logo if they got the same deal Meg is asking for. (The policy also lets the school control the kind of items on which its name appears.) Just last week, your office confiscated about 400 T-shirts and shorts made by a company that had used the school name on them without permission; the company has paid the school $7,500 in damages.

Write a letter to Meg rejecting her special requests. She can get a license to produce the T-shirts, but only if she pays the $250 licensing fee and the royalty on all shirts made.

11.16 Turning Down a Faithful Client

You are Midas Investment Services' specialist in estate planning. You give talks to various groups during the year about estate planning. These fees augment your income nicely, and the talks also are marvelous exposure for you and your company.

Every February for the last five years, Gardner Manufacturing Company has hired you to conduct an 8-hour workshop (2 hours every Monday night for four weeks) on retirement and estate planning for its employees who are over 60 or who are thinking of taking early retirement. These workshops are popular and have generated clients for your company. The session last February went smoothly, as you have come to expect.

Today, out of the blue, you got a letter from Hope Goldberger, Director of Employee Benefits at Gardner, asking you to conduct the workshops every Tuesday evening *next* month at your usual fee. She didn't say whether this is an *extra* series, or whether this will replace next February's series.

You can't do it. Your spouse, a microbiologist, is giving an invited paper at an international conference in Paris next month and the two of you are taking your children, ages 13 and 9, on a 3-week trip to Europe. (You've made arrangements with school authorities to have the kids miss three weeks of classes.) Your spouse's trip will be tax-deductible, and you've been looking forward to and planning the trip for the last eight months.

Unfortunately, Midas Investment Services is a small group, and the only other person who knows anything about estate planning is a terrible speaker. You could suggest a friend at another financial management company, but you don't want Gardner to turn to someone else permanently; you enjoy doing the workshops and find them a good way to get leads.

Write the letter to Ms. Goldberger.

11.17 Announcing Cost-Savings Measures

Your company has to cut costs but would prefer to avoid laying off workers. Therefore, you have adopted the following money-saving ideas. Some can be implemented immediately; some will be implemented at renewal dates. The company will no longer pay for

- Flowers at the receptionist's desk and in executive offices.
- Skyboxes for professional sporting events.
- Employees' dues for professional and trade organizations.
- Liquor at business meals.

Only essential business travel will be approved. The company will pay only for the lowest cost of air travel (coach, reservation 7 to 14 days in advance).

The company will no longer buy tables or blocks of tickets for charitable events and will not make any donations to charity until money is less tight.

Counters will be put on the photocopiers. People must have access numbers to make photocopies; personal photocopies will cost $ .10 a page.

As the Chief Financial Officer, write a memo to all employees, explaining the changes.

11.18   Closing Bill-Payment Offices

For many years, City Gas & Electric had five suburban offices to which people could take their payments. On the first of the month following next month, you're closing these offices. On that date, 100 local merchants, such as grocers, will begin to accept utility payments. Closing the freestanding offices will save your company almost $3 million a year. Customers will still be able to mail in payments or have them deducted automatically from their paychecks.

Write a notice that can be inserted in utility bills this month and next month.

11.19   Giving a Customer Less Credit Than She Wants

Yang-Ming Lee applied for your Visa card, asking for a credit limit of $15,000 and a separate card for her husband, Chad Hoang. Her credit references merit granting a credit card. But you generally give new customers only a $7,500 limit, even when the family income is very high, as it is in this case. You might make an exception if your bank had a previous relationship with the client, but no such relationship exists here. While you have no set policy for reviewing and raising credit limits, normally you would expect at least six months of paying the minimum amount promptly.

Write a letter to Ms. Lee, granting her a credit card with a $7,500 limit.

11.20   Rejecting a Member's Request

All nonsupervisory workers in your state are union members. As a paid staff person for the union, you spend about a third of your time writing and editing the monthly magazine, *Public [Your State] Employee*. You receive this letter:

Dear Editor:

Every month, we get two copies of the union magazine—one addressed to me, one to my husband. We have different last names, so your computer may not realize that we're connected, but we are, and we don't need two copies. Sending just one copy will save printing and postage costs and reduce environmental waste. My name is Dorothy Livingston; my husband is Eric Beamer. Please combine our listings to send just one copy.

Sincerely,

Dorothy Livingston

As it happens, two years ago you investigated possible savings of sending just one mailing to couples who both work for the state. Sophisticated computerized merge/purge programs to eliminate duplicates are too expensive for the union's tight budget. And going through the mailing list manually to locate and change duplications would cost more than would be saved in postage. Printing costs wouldn't necessarily drop either, since it actually costs less for each copy to print big runs.

But you want to build goodwill—both to this writer and for the union in general. Extra copies of the magazine (whether a double mailing or simply a copy someone is finished with) could be given to a nonmember or taken to a doctor's or dentist's waiting room or a barber or beauty shop. Such sharing would help spread public support for the union and state workers.

Write a letter to Ms. Livingston, explaining why you can't combine mailings.

Polishing Your Prose

Parallel Structure

Use parallel structure in lists, headings, and subheadings in documents by using the same grammatical form for ideas that have the same relationship in your sentence. Parallel structure is particularly important in business communication, whose bulleted, vertical lists make parallelism errors obvious.

Not parallel: Good reports are factual, logical, and demonstrate clarity.

It may be easier to see faulty parallelism by listing vertically parts that need to be parallel. Check to make sure each component fits with the words that introduce the list.

Not parallel: Good reports are

Factual

Logical

Demonstrate clarity.

Parallel: Good reports are

Factual

Logical

Clear.

Make sure all of the list is horizontal or vertical. Don't start a list horizontally and finish it vertically.

Incorrect: As department manager, I supervised eight employees.
- Wrote the department budget.
- Presented our sales strategy to the Board of Directors.

Correct: As department manager, I supervised eight employees, wrote the department budget, and presented our sales strategy to the Board of Directors.

Also correct: As department manager, I
- Supervised eight employees.
- Wrote the department budget.
- Presented our sales strategy to the Board of Directors.

Headings must be parallel throughout the document, but subheads need only be parallel to other subheads in the same section.

Not parallel: Should Ogden Industries Purchase Blue Chip International?
- Short-Term Costs
- What Are Long-Term Gains?

Parallel: Should Ogden Industries Purchase Blue Chip International?
- Short-Term Costs
- Long-Term Gains

In addition to grammatical parallelism, also check your sentences for logical parallelism.

Incorrect: The group ranges from males and females to people in their 20s, 30s, and 40s.

Better: We interviewed men and women ranging in age from 20 to 50.

Gender is one category; age is another.

Exercises

Rewrite the following sentences or headings to make them parallel.

1. Ask Ms. Liken, Mr. Fitzgerald, Bill Anderson, and Professor Timmons to join us for the meeting.

2. Our trip itinerary includes stops in Los Angeles, California; Chicago, Illinois; Minnesota's Minneapolis; and the City of New York.

3. Make sure benefits announcements get routed to managers, supervisors, and the folks in the Human Resources Department.

4. Additions to our carpool fleet include two Ford Crown Victorias, three Chevrolet Caprices, a Chevy S-10 Pickup, and a pair of Bonnevilles.

5. The project's fixed costs include material, salaries, advertising, bonus packages for anyone who goes above and beyond the call of duty, and the cost of travel to different cities.

6. The report includes the following sections:
   - First-Year Goals
   - Goals for the Second Year
   - Year Three
   - The Year After That

7. The selection committee reviews each job applicant based on education, experience, extracurricular activities, the awards the employee has received, and the strength of the applicant's personal statement.

8. Route this memo to the following departments: Purchasing, Human Resources, the people in Logistics, the Marketing staff, and Shipping.

9. Each agency should estimate

   Annual Costs

   Costs Per Month

   Salaries

   New Equipment Costs

   How Much You Need in a Reserve Fund for Unexpected Expenses

10. For best results, follow these instructions:

    1. Attach the AC adapter to your copier.

    2. Plug the AC adapter into an outlet.

    3. Your copier should be turned on by pressing the blue "Go" button.

    4. Put a test sheet face down on the copier glass.

    5. For a copy, press the "Copy" button, which is green.

    6. Take your test copy out of the output tray.

    7. To adjust copy quality, follow the onscreen directions.

Check your answers to the odd-numbered exercises at the back of the book.

BComm Skill Booster

To apply the concepts in this module, complete lessons 18, 19, and 20 on subject lines and negative messages. You can access the BComm Skill Booster through the text Web site at **www.mhhe.com/bcs2e.**

Module 12

Persuasive Messages

Start by asking these questions:

- What is the best persuasive strategy?
- What is the best subject line for a persuasive message?
- How should I organize persuasive messages?
- How do I identify and overcome objections?
- What other techniques can make my messages more persuasive?
- What are the most common kinds of persuasive messages?
- How can I apply what I've learned in this module?

In the 21st century, businesses depend more and more on persuasion and "buy-in" to get quality work done. You can command people to make widgets. You can't command people to be creative. And even if you're making widgets, just going through the motions isn't enough. You want people to make high-quality widgets while reducing scrap and other costs. Internal commitment is needed to make that happen.

External motivation doesn't last. Some people will buy a certain brand of pizza if they have a "2 for the price of 1" coupon. But if the coupon expires, or if another company offers the same deal, customers may leave. In contrast, if customers like your pizza better—in other words, if they are motivated internally to choose it—then you may keep your customers even if another company comes in with a lower price.

Persuasive messages include

- Orders and requests.
- Proposals and recommendations.
- Sales and fund-raising letters.
- Job application letters.
- Reports, if they recommend action.
- Efforts to change people's behavior, such as collection letters, criticisms or performance appraisals where you want the subordinate to improve behavior, and public-service ads designed to reduce drunken driving, drug use, and so on.

All persuasive messages have several purposes:

Primary Purposes:

- To have the reader act.
- To provide enough information so that the reader knows exactly what to do.
- To overcome any objections that might prevent or delay action.

Secondary Purposes:

- To build a good image of the writer.
- To build a good image of the writer's organization.
- To cement a good relationship between the writer and reader.
- To reduce or eliminate future correspondence on the same subject so the message doesn't create more work for the writer.

What is the best persuasive strategy?

It depends on how much and what kinds of resistance you expect.

Four basic short-term strategies exist: direct request, problem-solving persuasion, sales,[1] and reward and punishment. This book will focus on the first two strategies. Rewards and punishment have limited use, in part because they don't produce permanent change and because they produce psychological reactance (◄ ▷ p. 199). For a major change—such as restoring public confidence in CPA firms and in the stock market—no single message will work. You will need a campaign with a series of messages, preferably from a variety of sources.

Use the **direct request pattern** when

- The audience will do as you ask without any resistance.
- You need a response only from the people who are willing to act.
- The audience is busy and may not read all the messages received.
- Your organization's culture prefers direct requests.

Use the **problem-solving pattern** when

- The audience is likely to object to doing as you ask.
- You need action from everyone.
- You trust the audience to read the entire message.
- You expect logic to be more important than emotion in the decision.

Site *to* See

Go to
www.rice.edu/wetlands
Difficult situations arise when multiple stakeholders in an issue have different—perhaps contradictory—points of view. This Web site, created by faculty and graduate students at Rice University, presents documents, maps, and reports that led to a successful resolution.

The Advertising Council creates public service ads. Here, an ad for the Arab American Institute uses emotional appeal to build a common ground and persuade people to reject hate.

WILL HATE BRING IT ALL BACK? WILL IT BRING BACK THE INNOCENCE? THE SENSE OF SECURITY? WILL IT BRING BACK THE HUSBANDS AND WIVES AND SONS AND DAUGHTERS? WILL HATE MAKE US BETTER THAN THOSE WHO HATE US? OR MERELY BRING US CLOSER TO THEM? WILL HATE HELP US DESTROY OUR ENEMIES? OR WILL IT LAUGH AS WE DESTROY OUR-SELVES? THERE ARE THOSE WHO SAY WE DON'T KNOW WHO OUR ENEMY IS. BUT WE DO. OUR ENEMY IS A NEIGHBORHOOD MOSQUE DEFACED BY VANDALS. AN ARAB AMERICAN STOREKEEPER IN FEAR OF REPRISAL. A SCARED MUSLIM CHILD BULLIED BECAUSE SHE IS DIFFERENT. HATE IS OUR ENEMY. AND WHEN WE START TO HATE OTHER AMERICANS, WE HAVE LOST EVERYTHING. HATE HAS TAKEN ENOUGH FROM US ALREADY. DON'T LET IT TAKE YOU.

AMERICANS STAND UNITED

A strategy that works in one organization may not work somewhere else. James Suchan and Ron Dulek point out that Digital Equipment's corporate culture values no-holds-barred aggressiveness: "Even if opposition is expected, a subordinate should write a proposal in a forceful, direct manner."[2] In another organization with different cultural values, an employee who used a hard sell for a request antagonized the boss.[3]

Corporate culture (◀ ▶ p. 32) isn't written down; it's learned by imitation and observation. What style do high-level people in your organization use? When you show a draft to your boss, are you told to tone down your statements or to make them stronger? Role models and advice are two of the ways organizations communicate their cultures to newcomers.

Different ethnic and national cultures also have different preferences for gaining compliance. In one study, students who were native speakers of American English judged direct statements ("Do this"; "I want you to do this") clearer and more effective than questions ("Could you do this?") or hints ("This is needed"). Students who were native speakers of Korean, in contrast, judged direct statements to be *least* effective. In the Korean culture, the study's authors claim, the more direct a request is, the ruder and therefore less effective it is.[4]

What is the best subject line for a persuasive message?

Instant
Replay

For direct requests, use the request, the topic, or a question.

For problem-solving messages, use a directed subject line or a reader benefit.

In a direct request, put the request, the topic of the request, or a question in the subject line.

Subject: Request for Updated Software

My copy of HomeNet does not accept the aliases for Magnus accounts.

Subject: Status of Account #3548–003

Please get me the following information about account #3548–003.

Subject: Do We Need an Additional Training Session in October?

The two training sessions scheduled for October will accommodate 40 people. Last month, you said that 57 new staff accountants had been hired. Should we schedule an additional training session in October? Or can the new hires wait until the next regularly scheduled session in February?

Use the **direct request pattern** when

• The audience will do as you ask without any resistance.
• You need a response only from the people who are willing to act.
• The audience is busy and may not read all the messages received.
• Your organization's culture prefers direct requests.

Use the **problem-solving pattern** when

• The audience is likely to object to doing as you ask.
• You need action from everyone.
• You trust the audience to read the entire message.
• You expect logic to be more important than emotion in the decision.

When you have a reluctant reader, putting the request in the subject line just gets a quick *no* before you've had a chance to give all your arguments. One option is to use a **directed subject line** that makes your stance on the issue clear.[5] In the following examples, the first is the most neutral. The remaining two increasingly reveal the writer's preference.

Subject: A Proposal to Change the Formula for Calculating Retirees' Benefits

Subject: Arguments for Expanding the Marysville Plant

Subject: Why Cassano's Should Close Its West Side Store

Another option is to use common ground or a reader benefit—something that shows readers that this message will help them.

Subject: Reducing Energy Costs in the New Orleans Office

Energy costs in our New Orleans office have risen 12% in the last three years, even though the cost of gas has fallen and the cost of electricity has risen only 5%.

Although your first paragraph may be negative in a problem-solving message, your subject line should be neutral or positive to show that you are solving a problem, not just reporting one.

Both directed subject lines and benefit subject lines can also be used as report titles.

How should I organize persuasive messages?

In direct requests, start with the request.

In a problem-solving message, start with the problem you share.

Start with the request only when you anticipate ready agreement, when you fear that a busy reader may not read a message whose relevance isn't clear, or when your organization's culture prefers direct requests.

Writing Direct Requests

When you expect quick agreement, save the reader's time by presenting the request directly.

1. **Consider asking immediately for the information or service you want.** Delay the request if it seems too abrupt or if you have several purposes in the message.
2. **Give readers all the information and details they will need to act on your request.** Number your questions or set them off with bullets so the reader can check to see that all of them have been answered.

   In a claim (where a product is under warranty or a shipment was defective), explain the circumstances so that the reader knows what happened. Be sure to include all the relevant details: date of purchase, model or invoice number, and so on.

   In more complicated direct requests, anticipate possible responses. Suppose you're asking for information about equipment meeting certain specifications. Explain which criteria are most important so that the reader can recommend an alternative if no single product meets all your needs. You may also want to tell the reader what your price constraints are and ask whether the item is in stock or must be special ordered.
3. **Ask for the action you want.** Do you want a check? A replacement? A catalogue? Answers to your questions? If you need an answer by a certain time, say so. If possible, show the reader why the time limit is necessary.

Figure 12.1 summarizes this pattern. Figure 12.2 illustrates the pattern as did the claim letter in Figure 9.4. Note that direct requests do not contain reader benefits and do not need to overcome objections: they simply ask for what is needed.

Direct requests should be direct. Don't make the reader guess what you want.

Figure 12.1

How to Organize a Direct Request

Indirect request: Is there a newer version of the 2000 *Accounting Reference Manual?*

Direct request: If there is a newer version of the 2000 *Accounting Reference Manual,* please send it to me.

In some direct requests, your combination of purposes may suggest a different organization. For example, in a letter asking an employer to reimburse you for expenses after a job interview, you'd want to thank your hosts for their hospitality and cement the good impression you made at the

Figure 12.2
A Direct Request

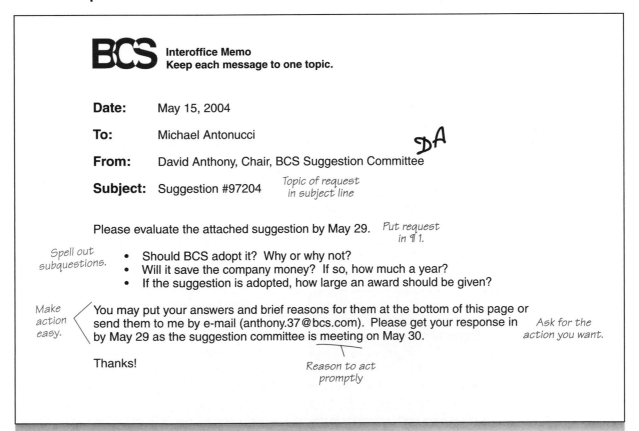

interview. To do that, you'd spend the first several paragraphs talking about the trip and the interview. Only in the last third of the letter (or even in the postscript) would you put your request for reimbursement.

Similarly, in a letter asking about a graduate program, a major purpose might be to build a good image of yourself so that your application for financial aid would be viewed positively. To achieve that goal, provide information about your qualifications and interest in the field as well as ask questions.

Organizing Problem-Solving Messages

Use an indirect approach and the problem-solving pattern of organization when you expect resistance from your reader but can show that doing what you want will solve a problem you and your reader share. This pattern allows you to disarm opposition by showing all the reasons in favor of your position before you give your readers a chance to say *no*.

1. **Describe the problem you both share (which your request will solve).** Present the problem objectively: Don't assign blame or mention personalities.
2. **Give the details of the problem.** Be specific about the cost in money, time, lost goodwill, and so on. You have to convince readers that *something* has to be done before you can convince them that your solution is the best one.
3. **Explain the solution to the problem.** If you know that the reader will favor another solution, start with that solution and show why it won't work before you present your solution.

    Present your solution without using the words *I* or *my*. Don't let personalities enter the picture; don't let the reader think he or she should say *no* just because you've had other requests accepted recently.
4. **Show that any negative elements (cost, time, etc.) are outweighed by the advantages.**

Figure 12.3

How to Organize a Problem-Solving Persuasive Message

Shared Problem

Details

Solution

Negatives

Reader Benefits

Request for Action

5. **Summarize any additional benefits of the solution.** The main benefit—solving the problem—can be presented briefly since you described the problem in detail. However, if there are any additional benefits, mention them.
6. **Ask for the action you want.** Often your reader will authorize or approve something; other people will implement the action. Give your reader a reason to act promptly, perhaps offering a new reader benefit. ("By buying now, we can avoid the next quarter's price hikes.")

Figure 12.3 summarizes the pattern. Figure 12.4 implements the pattern. Reader benefits can be brief in this kind of message because the biggest benefit comes from solving the problem.

Figure 12.4
A Problem-Solving Persuasive Message

Memorandum

February 15, 2006

To: All Staff Members

From: Melissa J. Gutridge *MJG*

Subject: Why We Are Implementing a New Sign-Out System

Directed subject line indicates action writer will ask for to solve the problem.

Shared problem

Successfully mainstreaming our clients into the community is very important, and daily interaction with the public is necessary. Our clients enjoy the times they get to go to the mall or out to lunch instead of remaining here all day.   Recently, however, clients have been taken out on activities without a staff member's knowing where the client is and whom the client is with.

Specific example of problem

We need to know where all clients are at all times because social workers, psychologists, and relatives constantly stop by unannounced. Last week, Janet's father stopped by to pick her up for a doctor's appointment, and she was not here. No one knew where she was or whom she was with. Naturally her father was very upset and wanted to know what kind of program we were running. Staff members' not knowing where our clients are and whom they are with is damaging to the good reputation of our staff and program.

Solution presented impersonally

Additional reader benefit

Starting Monday, February 25, a sign-out board will be located by Betty's desk. Please write down where you and the client are going and when you expect to be back. When signing out, help clients sign themselves out. We can turn this into a learning experience for our clients. Then when a social worker stops by to see someone who isn't here, we can simply look at the sign-out board to tell where the client is and when he or she will return.

Ask for action.

Please help keep up the superb reputation you have helped Weststar earn as a quality center for adults with handicaps. Sign out yourself and clients at all times.

How do I identify and overcome objections?

Talk to your audience. Then try these strategies.

The easiest way to learn about objections your audience may have is to ask knowledgeable people in your organization or your town.

If you can't overcome an objection, admit it. A potential client asked Evonne Weinhaus, "Do you really do anything new in your training?" She looked him in the eye and said, "No, I don't. I just add a twist." After a moment of silence, he said, "That's good. There is nothing new out there, and if you had said 'yes' this lunch would have been over immediately!" They talked about her approach and her "twist" on sales training. The potential client became a real client, signing up for 26 workshops.

FYI

Expert writers show how evidence proves the claims they make, limit their claims, and rebut counterarguments.

Source: Joanna G. Crammond, "The Uses and Complexity of Argument Structures in Expert and Student Persuasive Writing." *Written Communication* 15, no. 2 (April 1998): 230–68.

- **Phrase your questions nondefensively,** in a way that doesn't lock people into taking a stand on an issue: "What concerns would you have about a proposal to do x?" "Who makes a decision about y?" "What do you like best about [the supplier or practice you want to change]?"
- **Ask follow-up questions** to be sure you understand: "Would you be likely to stay with your current supplier if you could get a lower price from someone else? Why?"

People are likely to be most aware of and willing to share objective concerns such as time and money. They will be less willing to tell you that their real objection is emotional. Readers have a **vested interest** in something if they benefit directly from keeping things as they are. People who are in power have a vested interest in retaining the system that gives them their power. Someone who designed a system has a vested interest in protecting that system from criticism. To admit that the system has faults is to admit that the designer made mistakes. In such cases, you'll need to probe to find out what the real reasons are.

The best way to deal with an objection is to eliminate it. To sell Jeep Cherokees in Japan, Mitsuru Sato convinced Chrysler to put the driver's seat on the right side, to make an extra preshipment quality check, and to rewrite the instruction booklet in Japanese style, with big diagrams and cartoons.[6]

If an objection is false or based on misinformation, give the response to the objection without naming the objection. In a persuasive brochure, you can present responses with a "question/answer" format. When objections have already been voiced, you may want to name the objection so that your audience realizes that you are responding to that specific objection. However, to avoid solidifying the opposition, don't attribute the objection to your audience. Instead, use a less personal attribution: "Some people wonder . . ."; "Some citizens are afraid that . . ."

If real objections remain, try one or more of the following strategies to counter objections:

1. Specify how much time and/or money is required—it may not be as much as the reader fears.

> Distributing flyers to each house or apartment in your neighborhood will probably take two afternoons.

2. Put the time and/or money in the context of the benefits they bring.

> The additional $152,500 will (1) allow The Open Shelter to remain open 24 rather than 16 hours a day, (2) pay for three social workers to help men find work and homes, and (3) keep the Neighborhood Bank open, so that men don't have to cash Social Security checks in bars and so that they can save up the $800 they need to have up front to rent an apartment.

Instant Replay

Organizing a Problem-Solving Message

1. Describe a problem you both share (which your request will solve).
2. Give the details of the problem.
3. Explain the solution to the problem.
4. Show that any negative elements (cost, time, etc.) are outweighed by the advantages.
5. Summarize any additional benefits of the solution.
6. Ask for the action you want.

3. Show that money spent now will save money in the long run.

> By replacing the boiler now, we'll no longer have to release steam that the overflow tank can't hold. Depending on how severe the winter is, we could save $100 to $750 a year in energy costs. If energy costs rise, we'll save even more.

4. Show that doing as you ask will benefit some group or cause the reader supports, even though the action may not help the reader directly.

> By being a Big Brother or a Big Sister, you'll give a child the adult attention he or she needs to become a well-adjusted, productive adult.

5. Show the reader that the sacrifice is necessary to achieve a larger, more important goal to which he or she is committed.

> These changes will mean more work for all of us. But we've got to cut our costs 25% to keep the plant open and to keep our jobs.

6. Show that the advantages as a group outnumber or outweigh the disadvantages as a group.

> None of the locations is perfect. But the Backbay location gives us the most advantages and the fewest disadvantages.

7. Turn a disadvantage into an opportunity.

> With the hiring freeze, every department will need more lead time to complete its own work. By hiring another person, the Planning Department could provide that lead time.

What other techniques can make my messages more persuasive?

Build credibility and emotional appeal. Use the right tone, and offer a reason to act promptly.

Persuasive messages—whether short-term or long-term—will be more effective if you build credibility and emotional appeal, use the right tone, and offer a reason to act promptly.

Build Credibility

FYI

Busy executives are most likely to pay attention to messages that

- Are personalized.
- Evoke an emotional response.
- Come from a credible sender.
- Are concise.

Source: Thomas H. Davenport and John C. Beck, "Getting the Attention You Need," *Harvard Business Review*, September–October 2000, 124.

Credibility is the audience's response to you as the source of the message. People are more easily persuaded by someone they see as expert, powerful, attractive, or trustworthy. A sexual abstinence program in Atlanta was effective in large part because the lessons on how to say *no* without hurting the other person's feelings were presented by teenagers slightly older than the students in the program. Adults would have been much less credible.[7]

When you don't yet have the credibility that comes from being an expert or being powerful, build credibility by the language and strategy you use:

- **Be factual.** Don't exaggerate.
- **Be specific.** If you say "X is better," show in detail *how* it is better. Show the reader exactly where the savings or other benefits come from so that it's clear that the proposal really is as good as you say it is.
- **Be reliable.** If you suspect that a project will take longer to complete, cost more money, or be less effective than you originally thought, tell your audience *immediately*. Negotiate a new schedule that you can meet.

Build Emotional Appeal

Emotional appeal means making the reader *want* to do what you ask. People don't make decisions—even business decisions—based on logic alone. J. C. Mathes and Dwight W. Stevenson cite the following example. During his summer job, an engineering student who was asked to evaluate his company's waste treatment system saw a way that the system could be

To persuade, be prepared to appeal to emotions as well as to logic.

redesigned to save the company more than $200,000 a year. He wrote a report recommending the change and gave it to his boss. Nothing happened. Why not? His supervisor wasn't about to send up a report that would require him to explain why *he'd* been wasting more than $200,000 a year of the company's money.[8]

Stories and psychological description (◀ ▶ p. 137) are effective ways of building emotional appeal. Emotional appeal works best when people want to be persuaded. Even when you need to provide statistics or numbers to convince the careful reader that your anecdote is a representative example, telling a story first makes your message more persuasive. Recent research suggests that stories are more persuasive because people remember them.[9]

Use the Right Tone

When you ask for action from people who report directly to you, you have several choices. Even orders ("Get me the Ervin file") and questions ("Do we have the third quarter numbers yet?") will work. When you need action from co-workers, superiors, or people outside the organization, you need to be more forceful but also more polite.

Avoiding messages that sound parental or preachy is often a matter of tone. Saying "Please" is a nice touch, especially to people on your level or outside the organization. Tone will also be better when you give reasons for your request.

Parental: Everyone is expected to comply with these regulations. I'm sure you can see that they are commonsense rules needed for our business.

Better: Even on casual days, visitors expect us to be professional. So leave the gym clothes at home!

When you write to people you know well, humor can work. Just make sure that the message isn't insulting to anyone who doesn't find the humor funny.

Writing to superiors is trickier. You may want to tone down your request by using subjunctive verbs and explicit disclaimers that show you aren't taking a *yes* for granted.

Building Common Ground

A common ground avoids the me-against-you of some persuasive situations and suggests that both you and your audience have a mutual interest in solving the problems you face. To find a common ground, we analyze the audience; understand their biases, objections, and needs; and identify with them so that we can make them identify with us. This analysis can be carried out in a cold, manipulative way. It can also be based on a respect for and sensitivity to the audience's position.

Readers are highly sensitive to manipulation. No matter how much you disagree, respect your audience's intelligence. Try to understand why they believe or do something and why they may object to your position. If you can understand your readers' initial positions, you'll be more effective—and you won't alienate your readers by talking down to them.

The best common grounds are specific. Often a negative—a problem the reader will want to solve— makes a good common ground.

Weak common ground:	This program has had some difficulty finding enough individuals to volunteer their services for the children. As a result, we are sometimes unable to provide the one-on-one mentoring that is our goal.
Improved common ground:	On five Sundays in the last three months, we've had too few volunteers to provide one-on-one mentoring. Last Sunday, we had just two college students to take eight children to the Museum of Science and Industry.

Generalizations are likely to bore the reader. Instead, use the idea behind the generalization to focus on something the reader cares about.

Weak common ground:	We all want this plant to be profitable.
Improved common ground:	We forfeited a possible $186,000 in profits last summer due to a 17% drop in productivity.

In your common ground, emphasize the parts of your proposal that fit with what your audience already does or believes. An employee of 3M wanted to develop laser disks. He realized that 3M's previous products were thin and flat: Scotch tape, Post-it Notes,™ magnetic tape. When he made his presentation to the group that chose new products for development, he held his prototype disk horizontally, so his audience saw a flat, thin object rather than a large, round, recordlike object. Making his project fit with the audience's previous experience was a subtle and effective emotional tool to make it easier for the audience to say yes.

Use audience analysis to evaluate possible common grounds. Suppose you want to install a system to play background music in a factory. To persuade management to pay for the system, a possible common ground would be increasing productivity. However, to persuade the union to pay for the system, you'd need a different common ground. Workers would see productivity as a way to get them to do more work for the same pay. A better common ground would be that the music would make the factory environment more pleasant.

When you want people to change their behavior, don't criticize them. Instead, show that you're on their side and that you and they have a mutual interest in solving a problem.

Arrogant:	Based on this evidence, I expect you to give me a new computer.
Better:	If department funds permit, I would like a new computer.

Passive verbs and jargon sound stuffy. Use active imperatives—perhaps with "Please"—to create a friendlier tone.

Stuffy:	It is requested that you approve the above-mentioned action.
Better:	Please authorize us to create a new subscription letter.

Offer a Reason for the Reader to Act Promptly

The longer people delay, the less likely they are to carry through with the action they had decided to take. In addition, you want a fast response so you can go ahead with your own plans.

Request action by a specific date. Always give people at least a week or two: They have other things to do besides respond to your requests. Set deadlines in the middle of the month, if possible. If you say, "Please return this by March 1," people will think, "I don't need to do this till March." Ask for the response by February 28 instead. If you can use a response even after the deadline, say so. Otherwise, people who can't make the deadline may not respond at all.

Show why you need a quick response:

- **Show that the time limit is real.** Perhaps you need information quickly to use it in a report that has a due date. Perhaps a decision must be made by a certain date to catch the start of the school year, the holiday selling season, or an election campaign. Perhaps you need to be ready for a visit from out-of-town or international colleagues.
- **Show that acting now will save time or money.** If business is slow and your industry isn't doing well, then your company needs to act now (to economize, to better serve customers) in order to be competitive. If business is booming and everyone is making a profit, then your company needs to act now to get its fair share of the available profits.
- **Show the cost of delaying action.** Will labor or material costs be higher in the future? Will delay mean more money spent on repairing something that will still need to be replaced?

What are the most common kinds of persuasive messages?

Orders, collection letters, performance appraisals, and letters of recommendation.

Orders, collection letters, performance appraisals, and letters of recommendation are among the most common varieties of persuasive messages.

Orders

Orders may be written on forms, phoned in, or made by clicking on boxes on the Web. When you write an order,

- Be specific. Give model or page numbers, colors, finishes, and so forth.
- Tell the company what you want if that model number is no longer available.
- Double-check your arithmetic, and add sales tax and shipping charges.

Collection Letters

Most businesses find that phoning rather than writing results in faster payment. But as more and more companies install voice mail systems, you may sometimes need to write letters when leaving messages doesn't work.

Collection letters ask customers to pay (as they have already agreed to do) for the goods and services they have already received. Good credit departments send a series of letters. Letters in the series should be only a week or two apart. Waiting a month between letters implies that you're prepared to wait a long time—and the reader will be happy to oblige you!

Early letters are gentle, assuming that the reader intends to pay but has met with temporary reverses or has forgotten. However, the request should assume that the check has been mailed but did not arrive. A student who had not yet been reimbursed by a company for a visit to the company's office put the second request in the P.S. of a letter refusing a job offer:

> P.S. The check to cover my expenses when I visited your office in March hasn't come yet. Could you check to see whether you can find a record of it? The amount was $490 (airfare $290, hotel room $185; taxi $15).

If one or two early letters don't result in payment, call the customer to ask if your company has created a problem. It's possible that you shipped something the customer didn't want or sent the wrong quantity. It's possible that the invoice arrived before the product and was filed and forgotten. It's possible that the invoice document is poorly designed, so customers set it aside until they can figure it out. If any of these situations apply, you'll build goodwill by solving the problem rather than arrogantly asking for payment.[10]

Middle letters are more assertive in asking for payment. Figure 9.2 (◀ ▶ p. 150) gives an example of a middle letter. Other middle letters offer to negotiate a schedule for repayment if the reader is not able to pay the whole bill immediately, may remind the reader of the importance of a good credit rating (which will be endangered if the bill remains unpaid), educate the reader about credit, and explain why the creditor must have prompt payment.

Unless you have firm evidence to the contrary, assume that readers have some legitimate reason for not yet paying. Even people who are "juggling" payments because they do not have enough money to pay all their bills or people who will put payment off as long as possible will respond more quickly if you do not accuse them. If a reader is offended by your assumption that he or she is dishonest, that anger can become an excuse to continue delaying payment.

Late letters threaten legal action if the bill is not paid. Under federal law, the writer cannot threaten legal action unless he or she actually intends to sue. Other regulations also spell out what a writer may and may not do in a late letter.

Many small businesses find that establishing personal relationships with customers is the best way to speed payment.

Performance Appraisals

At regular intervals, supervisors evaluate, or appraise, the performance of their subordinates. In most organizations, employees have access to their files; sometimes they must sign the appraisal to show that they've read it. The superior normally meets with the subordinate to discuss the appraisal.

Figure 12.5 shows a performance appraisal for a member of a student collaborative group.

Figure 12.5
A Performance Appraisal

February 13, 2004

To: Barbara Buchanan

From: Brittany Papper BAP

Subject: Your Performance Thus Far in Our Collaborative Group

Overall evaluation

You have been a big asset to our group. Overall, our business communication group has been one of the best groups I have ever worked with, and I think that only minor improvements are needed to make our group even better.

What You're Doing Well

Specific observations provide dates, details of performance

You demonstrated flexibility and compatibility at our last meeting before we turned in our proposal on February 12 by offering to type the proposal since I had to study for an exam in one of my other classes. I really appreciated this because I really did not have the time to do it. I will definitely remember this if you are ever too busy with your other classes and cannot type the final report.

Another positive critical incident occurred February 5. We had discussed researching the topic of sexual discrimination in hiring and promotion at Midstate Insurance. As we read more about what we had to do, we became uneasy about reporting the information from our source who works at Midstate. I called you later that evening to talk about changing our topic to a less personal one. You were very understanding and said that you agreed that the original topic was a touchy one. You offered suggestions for other topics and had a positive attitude about the adjustment. Your suggestions ended my worries and made me realize that you are a positive and supportive person.

Other strengths

Your ideas are a strength that you definitely contribute to our group. You're good at brainstorming ideas, yet you're willing to go with whatever the group decides. That's a nice combination of creativity and flexibility.

Areas for Improvement

Two minor improvements could make you an even better member.

Specific recommendations for improvement

The first improvement is to be more punctual to meetings. On February 5 and February 8 you were about 10 minutes late. This makes the meetings last longer. Your ideas are valuable to the group, and the sooner you arrive the sooner we can share in your suggestions.

Specific behavior to be changed

The second suggestion is one we all need to work on. We need to keep our meetings positive and productive. I think that our negative attitudes were worst at our first group meeting February 5. We spent about half an hour complaining about all the work we had to do and about our busy schedules in other classes. In the future if this happens, maybe you could offer some positive things about the assignment to get the group motivated again.

Overall Compatibility

Positive, forward-looking ending

I feel that this group has gotten along very well together. You have been very flexible in finding times to meet and have always been willing to do your share of the work. I have never had this kind of luck with a group in the past and you have been a welcome breath of fresh air. I don't hate doing group projects any more!

FYI

To get paid in a tight economy

• Spell out exactly how much customers will save if they pay promptly.
• Time bills so customers receive them a couple of days after receiving your product or service.
• Call before the due date to be sure the invoice arrived and the accounts payable department has all the documentation it needs. Ask for a commitment to pay on a specific date (not just "next week"). Take notes, and e-mail them to the customer after the conversation.

Source: Ilan Mochari, "30 Ways to Get Paid within 30 Days: How to Collect from Anyone (Even Enron)" *Inc.,* September 2002, 67–72.

As a subordinate, you should prepare for the appraisal interview by listing your achievements and goals. Where do you want to be in a year or five years? What training and experience do you need to reach your goals? Also think about any weaknesses. If you need training, advice, or support from the organization to improve, the appraisal interview is a good time to ask for this help.

Appraisals need to both protect the organization and motivate the employee. These two purposes conflict. Most of us will see a candid appraisal as negative; we need praise and reassurance to believe that we're valued and can do better. But the praise that motivates someone to improve can come back to haunt the company if the person does not eventually do acceptable work. An organization is in trouble if it tries to fire someone whose evaluations never mention mistakes.

Avoid labels (*wrong, bad*) and inferences. Instead, cite specific observations that describe behavior.

Inference: Sam is an alcoholic.

Vague observation: Sam calls in sick a lot. Subordinates complain about his behavior.

Specific observation: Sam called in sick a total of 12 days in the last two months. After a business lunch with a customer last week, Sam was walking unsteadily. Two of his subordinates have said that they would prefer not to make sales trips with him because they find his behavior embarrassing.

Sam might be an alcoholic. He might also be having a reaction to a physician-prescribed drug; he might have a mental illness; he might be showing symptoms of a physical illness other than alcoholism. A supervisor who jumps to conclusions creates ill will, closes the door to solving the problem, and may provide grounds for legal action against the organization.

Be specific in an appraisal.

Too vague: Sue does not manage her time as well as she could.

Specific: Sue's first three weekly sales reports have been three, two, and four days late, respectively; the last weekly sales report for the month is not yet in.

Without specifics, Sue won't know that her boss objects to late reports. She may think that she is being criticized for spending too much time on sales calls or for not working 80 hours a week. Without specifics, she might change the wrong things in a futile effort to please her boss.

Good supervisors try not only to identify the specific problems in subordinates' behavior but also in conversation to discover the causes of the problem. Does the employee need more training? Perhaps a training course or a mentor will help. Does he or she need to work harder? Then the supervisor needs to motivate the worker and help him or her manage distractions. Is a difficult situation causing the problem? Perhaps the situation can be changed. If it can't be changed, the supervisor and the company should realize that the worker is not at fault.

Appraisals are more useful to subordinates if they make clear which areas are most important and contain specific recommendations for improvement. No one can improve 17 weaknesses at once. Which two should the employee work on this month? Is getting in reports on time more important than increasing sales? The supervisor should explicitly answer these questions during the appraisal interview.

Phrase goals in specific, concrete terms. The subordinate may think that "considerable progress toward completing" a report may mean that the project should be 15% finished. The boss may think that "considerable progress" means 50% or 85% of the total work.

Letters of Recommendation

In an effort to protect themselves against lawsuits, some companies state only how long they employed someone and the position that person held. Such bare-bones letters have themselves been the target of lawsuits when employers did not reveal relevant negatives. Whatever the legal climate, there may be times when you want to recommend someone for an award or for a job.

Letters of recommendation must be specific. General positives that are not backed up with specific examples and evidence are seen as weak recommendations. Letters of recommendation that focus on minor points also suggest that the person is weak.

Figure 9.3 (◀ ▶ p. 151) is a letter of recommendation. Either in the first or the last paragraph, summarize your overall evaluation of the person. Early in the letter, perhaps in the first paragraph, show how well and how long you've known the person. In the middle of the letter, offer specific details about the person's performance. At the end of the letter, indicate whether you would be willing to rehire the person and repeat your overall evaluation.

Experts are divided on whether you should include negatives. Some people feel that any negative weakens the letter. Other people feel that presenting but not emphasizing honest negatives makes the letter more convincing.

In many discourse communities, the words "Call me if you need more information" in a letter of recommendation mean "I have negative information that I am unwilling to put on paper. Call me, and I'll tell you what I really think."

How can I apply what I've learned in this module?

Plan your activities and answer the PAIBOC questions.

Before you tackle the assignments for this module, examine the following problem. Figure 12.6 lists the necessary activities. As in Modules 10 and 11, the PAIBOC questions probe the basic points required for a solution. Study the two sample solutions to see what makes one unacceptable and the other one good.[11] The checklists at the end of the module in Figures 12.9 and 12.10 can help you evaluate a draft.

Problem

In one room in the production department of Golden Electronics Company, employees work on computer monitors in conditions that are scarcely bearable due to the heat. Even when the temperature outside is only 75°, it is

Figure 12.6
**Allocating Time
in Writing a
Problem-Solving
Persuasive Memo**

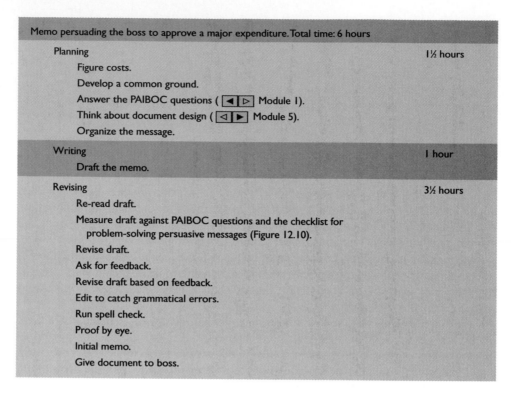

Memo persuading the boss to approve a major expenditure. Total time: 6 hours	
Planning	1½ hours
Figure costs.	
Develop a common ground.	
Answer the PAIBOC questions (◄ ▷ Module 1).	
Think about document design (◁ ► Module 5).	
Organize the message.	
Writing	1 hour
Draft the memo.	
Revising	3½ hours
Re-read draft.	
Measure draft against PAIBOC questions and the checklist for problem-solving persuasive messages (Figure 12.10).	
Revise draft.	
Ask for feedback.	
Revise draft based on feedback.	
Edit to catch grammatical errors.	
Run spell check.	
Proof by eye.	
Initial memo.	
Give document to boss.	

over 100° in the monitor room. In June, July, and August, 24 out of 36 workers quit because they couldn't stand the heat. This turnover happens every summer.

In a far corner of the room sits a quality control inspector in front of a small fan (the only one in the room). The production workers, in contrast, are carrying 20-pound monitors. As Production Supervisor, you tried to get air-conditioning two years ago, before Golden acquired the company, but management was horrified at the idea of spending $500,000 to insulate and air-condition the warehouse (it is impractical to air-condition the monitor room alone).

You're losing money every summer. Write a memo to Jennifer M. Kirkland, Operations Vice President, renewing your request.

Analysis of the Problem

P What are your **purposes** in writing or speaking?

> To persuade Kirkland to authorize insulation and air-conditioning. To build a good image of myself.

A Who is (are) your **audience(s)?** How do the members of your audience differ from each other? What characteristics are relevant to this particular message?

> The Operations Vice President will be concerned about keeping costs low and keeping production running smoothly. Kirkland

may know that the request was denied two years ago, but another person was vice president then; Kirkland wasn't the one who said no.

I   What **information** must your message include?

The cost of the proposal. The effects of the present situation.

B   What reasons or reader **benefits** can you use to support your position?

Cutting turnover may save money and keep the assembly line running smoothly. Experienced employees may produce higher-quality parts. Putting in air-conditioning would relieve one of the workers' main complaints; it might make the union happier.

O   What **objections** can you expect your reader(s) to have? What negative elements of your message must you deemphasize or overcome?

The cost. The time operations will be shut down while installation is taking place.

C   How will the **context** affect the reader's response? Think about your relationship to the reader, morale in the organization, the economy, the time of year, and any special circumstances.

Prices on computer components are falling. The economy is sluggish; the company will be reluctant to make a major expenditure. Filling vacancies in the monitor room is hard—we are getting a reputation as a bad place to work. Summer is over, and the problem is over until next year.

Discussion of the Sample Solutions

Solution 1, shown in Figure 12.7, is unacceptable. By making the request in the subject line and the first paragraph, the writer invites a *no* before giving all the arguments. The writer does nothing to counter the objections that any manager will have to spending a great deal of money. By presenting the issue in terms of fairness, the writer produces defensiveness rather than creating a common ground. The writer doesn't use details or emotional appeal to show that the problem is indeed serious. The writer asks for fast action but doesn't show why the reader should act now to solve a problem that won't occur again for eight months.

Solution 2, shown in Figure 12.8, is an effective persuasive message. The writer chooses a positive subject line. The opening sentence is negative, catching the reader's attention by focusing on a problem the reader and writer share. However, the paragraph makes it clear that the memo offers a solution to the problem. The problem is spelled out in detail. Emotional impact is created by taking the reader through the day as the temperature rises. The solution is presented impersonally. There are no *I*'s in the memo.

Figure 12.7

An Unacceptable Solution to the Sample Problem

Date: October 12, 2004

To: Jennifer M. Kirkland, Operations Vice President

From: Arnold M. Morgan, Production Supervisor *AMM*

Subject: Request for Air-Conditioning the Monitor Room   *Request in subject line stiffens resistance when reader is reluctant.*

Please put air-conditioning in the monitor room. This past summer, 2/3 of our employees quit because it was so hot. It's (not fair) that they should work in unbearable temperatures when management sits in air-conditioned comfort.   *Attacks reader*

Inappropriate emphasis on writer (I) propose that we solve this problem by air-conditioning the monitor room to bring down the temperature to 78°.

Insulating and air-conditioning the monitor room would cost $500,000.

Please approve this request promptly.   *Cost sounds enormous without a context.*

Memo sounds arrogant.
Logic isn't developed.
This attacks reader instead of enlisting reader's support.

The memo stresses reader benefits: the savings that will result once the investment is recovered. The last paragraph tells the reader exactly what to do and links prompt action to a reader benefit. The memo ends with a positive picture of the problem solved.

Figures 12.9 and 12.10 provide checklists for direct requests and problem-solving persuasive messages.

Figure 12.8
A Good Solution to the Sample Problem

Date: October 12, 2004

To: Jennifer M. Kirkland, Operations Vice President

From: Arnold M. Morgan, Production Supervisor   AMM

Subject: Improving Summer Productivity

Reader benefit in subject line

Shared problem
Golden forfeited a possible $186,000 in profits last summer due to a 17% drop in productivity. That's not unusual: Golden has a history of low summer productivity. But we can reverse the trend and bring summer productivity in line with the rest of the year's.

Good to show problem can be resolved

Cause of problem
The problem starts in the monitor room. Due to high turnover and reduced efficiency from workers who are on the job, we just don't make as many monitors as we do during the rest of the year.

Additional reason to solve problem
Both the high turnover and reduced efficiency are due to the unbearable heat in the monitor room. Temperatures in the monitor room average 25° over the outside temperature. During the summer, when work starts at 8, it's already 85° in the tube room. By 11:30, it's at least 105°. On six days last summer, it hit 120°. When the temperatures are that high, we may be violating OSHA regulations.

Production workers are always standing, moving, or carrying 20-lb. monitors. When temperatures hit 90°, they slow down. When no relief is in sight, many of them quit.

We replaced 24 of the 36 employees in the monitor room this summer. When someone quits, it takes an average of five days to find and train a replacement; during that time, the trainee produces nothing. For another five days, the new person can work at only half speed. And even "full speed" in the summer is only 90% of what we expect the rest of the year.

More details about problem
Here's where our losses come from:

Normal production = 50 units a person each day (upd)

Loss due to turnover:
   loss of 24 workers for 5 days =   6,000 units
   24 at ½ pace for 5 days =   3,000 units
    Total loss due to turnover =   9,000 units

Shows detail—Set up like an arithmetic problem

Loss due to reduced efficiency:
   loss of 5 upd x 12 workers x 10 days =   600 units
   loss of 5 upd x 36 x 50 days =   9,000 units
    Total loss due to reduced efficiency = 9,600 units

Total Loss =   18,600 units

Figure 12.8

A Good Solution to the Sample Problem *(concluded)*

Jennifer M. Kirkland　　　　　　2　　　　　　October 12, 2004

According to the accounting department, Golden makes a net profit of $10 on every *Shows where* monitor we sell. And, as you know, with the boom in computer sales, we sell every *numbers in* monitor we make. Those 18,600 units we don't produce are costing us $186,000 a *paragraph 1* year. *come from*

Additional benefit Bringing down the temperature to 78° (the minimum allowed under federal guidelines) from the present summer average of 112° will require an investment of $500,000 to insulate and air-condition the warehouse. Extra energy costs for the air-conditioning will run about $30,000 a year. We'll get our investment back in less than three years. Once the investment is recouped, we'll be making an additional $150,000 a year—all without buying additional equipment or hiring additional workers.

Tells reader what to do By installing the insulation and air-conditioning this fall, we can take advantage of *Reason to act* lower off-season rates. Please authorize the Purchasing Department to request bids *promptly* for the system. Then, next summer, our productivity can be at an all-time high.

Ends on positive note of problem solved, reader enjoying benefit

Figure 12.9

Checklist for
Direct Requests

☐ If the message is a memo, does the subject line indicate the request? Is the subject line specific enough to differentiate this message from others on the same subject?

☐ Does the first paragraph summarize the request or the specific topic of the message?

☐ Does the message give all of the relevant information? Is there enough detail?

☐ Does the message answer questions or overcome objections that readers may have without introducing unnecessary negatives?

☐ Does the last paragraph ask for action? Does it give a deadline if one exists and a reason for acting promptly?

And, for all messages, not just direct requests,

☐ Does the message use you-attitude and positive emphasis?

☐ Is the style easy to read and friendly?

☐ Is the visual design of the message inviting?

☐ Is the format correct?

☐ Does the message use standard grammar? Is it free from typos?

Originality in a direct request may come from

☐ Good lists and visual impact.

☐ Thinking about readers and giving details that answer their questions, overcome any objections, and make it easier for them to do as you ask.

☐ Adding details that show you're thinking about a specific organization and the specific people in that organization.

Figure 12.10

✓ Checklist for
Problem-Solving Persuasive Messages

☐ If the message is a memo, does the subject line indicate the writer's purpose or offer a reader benefit? Does the subject line avoid making the request?

☐ Is the problem presented as a joint problem both writer and reader have an interest in solving, rather than as something the reader is being asked to do for the writer?

☐ Does the message give all of the relevant information? Is there enough detail?

☐ Does the message overcome objections that readers may have?

☐ Does the message avoid phrases that sound dictatorial, condescending, or arrogant?

☐ Does the last paragraph ask for action? Does it give a deadline if one exists and a reason for acting promptly?

And, for all messages, not just persuasive ones,

☐ Does the message use you-attitude and positive emphasis?

☐ Is the style easy to read and friendly?

☐ Is the visual design of the message inviting?

☐ Is the format correct?

☐ Does the message use standard grammar? Is it free from typos?

Originality in a problem-solving persuasive message may come from

☐ A good subject line and common ground.

☐ A clear and convincing description of the problem.

☐ Thinking about readers and giving details that answer their questions, overcome objections, and make it easier for them to do as you ask.

☐ Adding details that show you're thinking about a specific organization and the specific people in that organization.

Summary of Key Points

- Use the **direct request pattern** when
  - The audience will do as you ask without any resistance.
  - You need a response only from the people who are willing to act.
  - The audience is busy and may not read all the messages received.
  - Your organization's culture prefers direct requests.
- Use the **problem-solving pattern** when
  - The audience is likely to object to doing as you ask.

- You need action from everyone.
- You trust the audience to read the entire message.
- You expect logic to be more important than emotion in the decision.

- In a direct request, put the request, the topic of the request, or a question in the subject line. Do not put the request in the subject line of a problem-solving persuasive message. Instead, use a **directed subject line** that reveals your position on the issue or a reader benefit.

Use a positive or neutral subject line even when the first paragraph will be negative.

- In a direct request, consider asking in the first paragraph for the information or service you want. Give readers all the information or details they will need to act on your request. In the last paragraph, ask for the action you want.

- Organize a problem-solving persuasive message in this way:

  1. Describe a problem you both share (which your request will solve).
  2. Give the details of the problem.
  3. Explain the solution to the problem.
  4. Show that any negative elements (cost, time, etc.) are outweighed by the advantages.
  5. Summarize any additional benefits of the solution.
  6. Ask for the action you want.

- Readers have a vested interest in something if they benefit directly from keeping things as they are.

- Use one or more of the following strategies to counter objections:

  - Specify how much time and/or money is required.
  - Put the time and/or money in the context of the benefits they bring.
  - Show that money spent now will save money in the long run.
  - Show that doing as you ask will benefit some group the reader identifies with or some cause the reader supports.
  - Show the reader that the sacrifice is necessary to achieve a larger, more important goal to which he or she is committed.
  - Show that the advantages as a group outnumber or outweigh the disadvantages as a group.
  - Turn the disadvantage into an opportunity.

- To encourage readers to act promptly, set a deadline. Show that the time limit is real, that acting now will save time or money, or that delaying action will cost more.

- Use the PAIBOC questions from Module 1 to analyze persuasive situations.

Assignments for Module 12

Questions for Comprehension

12.1 How do you decide whether to use a direct request or a problem-solving persuasive message?

12.2 How do you organize a problem-solving persuasive message?

12.3 How can you build credibility?

12.4 How do specific varieties of persuasive messages adapt the basic patterns?

Questions for Critical Thinking

12.5 What do you see as the advantages of positive and negative appeals? Illustrate your answer with specific messages, advertisements, or posters.

12.6 Is it dishonest to "sneak up on the reader" by delaying the request in a problem-solving persuasive message?

12.7 Think of a persuasive message (or a commercial) that did not convince you to act. Could a different message have convinced you? Why or why not?

Exercises and Problems

12.8   Asking for Information for an Awards Ceremony

Your community organization recognizes people who have contributed to the community. Julio Moreno, the Chief of Police, sent you names and photos of four officers. But you need more information to introduce them and to write the press release you'll send the paper.

In your files, you find this letter used by the previous program chair:

> Thank you for sending me the names of people to recognize. This will be very helpful. However, you did not give me enough information. I need more than just their names. Please give me more information. I want to know how long each person has worked for your organization. Do they have hobbies? (Provide information.) Supply the names of their spouses and children, if any. It would be helpful also to have the children's ages. Additionally, we plan to send special letters to the City Council Members whose constituents are being recognized. To this end, we need the name or number of the voting ward of each person. It would also be helpful to have the home address of each person because we want to invite both the person to be recognized and his or her spouse or guest to attend the ceremony. What exactly did the person do to deserve recognition? I anxiously await your response at your earliest convenience.

You know this letter is horrible. It's awkward and lacks you-attitude and positive emphasis. The questions aren't arranged or formatted effectively. It doesn't ask for action by a specific date.

As Your Instructor Directs,

a. Identify the problems in this letter.

b. Rewrite the letter, adding information to make it clear and complete.

12.9   Asking for the Right Information

In today's mail, your insurance agency received the following letter:

> When I called last week to find out about insuring my boat, the clerk told me to include a recent photo. Here it is. Please send me a notice telling me that my boat is now insured—I want to take it out sailing!

The writer, Trevor Bishop, included a photo of himself.

Trevor misunderstood what the clerk said: what you need for insurance purposes is a photo of the boat, not its owner. Write to Mr. Bishop to ask for the photo you need—without making him feel stupid for having misunderstood what your clerk meant.

12.10   Getting a Raise for a Deserving Employee

A memo from headquarters announces that the maximum merit increase (i.e., a raise when no promotion is involved) is 6%.

You've got a subordinate who, you feel, deserves a bigger raise. A year ago, Sheila Whitfield was promoted into the pre-label division of your packing department. She quickly became proficient in her duties—so much so that now others ask her for advice. You especially like her positive approach to solving problems. She sees obstacles as challenges and more often than not figures out ways to do what needs to be done within the constraints. On her own initiative, she started a program to make others in the company aware of the expense of labels and shipping to better control costs. The program has been very successful, and the company has saved money while still using clear, informative labels with adequate packaging. She has excellent working relationships with label suppliers and her counterparts in other companies.

In her most recent performance appraisal, Sheila had 14 out of 21 boxes checked "Exceptional" (the other 7 were "Commendable," the next highest category). Her overall ranking was "Exceptional." Indeed, the only two suggestions for improvement were minor ones: "(1) Continue to be aggressive, but temper the aggressiveness with diplomacy; (2) continue to expand responsibility in current position."

Write a memo to the Salary Compensation Committee recommending that an exception to the rules be made so that Sheila can be given an 8% raise.

12.11 Asking for a Raise or Reclassification

Do you deserve a raise? Should your job be reclassified to reflect your increased responsibilities (with more pay, of course)? If so, write a memo to the person with the authority to determine pay and job titles, arguing for what you want.

As Your Instructor Directs,
a. Create a document or presentation to achieve the goal.

b. Write a memo to your instructor describing the situation at your workplace and explaining your rhetorical choices (medium, strategy, tone, wording, graphics or document design, and so forth).

12.12 Writing Collection Letters

You have a small desktop publishing firm. Unfortunately, not all your clients pay promptly.

As Your Instructor Directs,
Write letters for one or more of the following situations.

a. A $450 bill for designing and printing a brochure for Juggles, Inc., a company that provides clowns and jugglers for parties, is now five weeks overdue. You've phoned twice, and each time the person who answered the phone promised to send you a check, but nothing has happened.

b. A $2,000 bill for creating a series of handouts for a veterinarian to distribute to clients. This one is embarrassing: You lost track of the invoice, so you never followed up on the original (and only) bill. The bill is now 72 days overdue.

c. A $3,750 bill for designing and printing a series of ten brochures for Creative Interiors, a local interior decorating shop is three weeks past due. When you billed Creative Interiors, you got a note saying that the design was not acceptable and that you would not be paid until you redesigned it (at no extra charge) to the owner's satisfaction. The owner had approved the preliminary design on which the brochures were based; she did not explain in the note what was wrong with the final product. She's never free when you are; indeed, when you call to try to schedule an appointment, you're told the owner will call you back—but she never does. At this point, the delay is not your fault; you want to be paid.

d. A $100 bill for designing (but not actually creating) a brochure for a cleaning company that, according to its owner, planned to expand into your city. You got the order and instructions by mail and talked to the person on the phone but never met him. You tried to call once since then (as much to try to talk him into having the brochures printed as to collect the $100); the number was "no longer in service." You suspect the owner may no longer be in business, but you'd like to get your money if possible.

12.13   Urging Employees to Handle Routine Calls Courteously

You are manager of the local power company. A recent survey had questions about recipients' attitudes toward the company. On the 7-point "friendly . . . unfriendly" scale, you came out at 2.1—with "1" being the lowest score possible.

The only contact most people have with the power company comes through monthly bills, ads, and phone calls. Many of these calls are about routine matters: whether people can delay payment, how to handle payment when they're away for extended periods of time, how to tell if there's a gas leak, how the budget payment system works. Workers answer these questions over and over and over. But the caller asks because he or she needs to know. To the worker, the caller is just one more faceless voice; to the caller, the worker is the company.

Write a memo to your staff urging them to be patient and friendly when they answer questions.

Hints:
• In your town, does the power company have a monopoly, or do gas and electricity compete for customers? How might competition affect your message?
• What specifically do you want your staff to do? How could they achieve your general goals?
• How can the job be made more interesting for workers?

12.14   Persuading an Organization to Accept Student Interns

At City College, you have more would-be interns than internship positions. As Director of the Internship Program, you'd like to line up more companies to accept your students.

If your school already has an internship program, use the facts about it. If it doesn't, assume that internships

• Are open to students who have completed at least two courses in the area of the internship with grades of "B" or better.
• Can be paid or unpaid.
• Must involve substantive work supervised by someone in the organization.

• Must involve at least 100 hours of on-site work experience during the term.

As Your Instructor Directs,
a. Write a form letter that could be mailed to businesses, urging them to set up one or more internships.
b. Pick an organization you know well. Write to a specific person urging him or her to set up internships in that organization.
c. Write a news release about your school's need for more intern positions.

12.15   Helping Students Use Credit Cards Responsibly

Your college, community college, or university is concerned that some students have high levels of credit card debt and may be using credit cards irresponsibly. Many students—especially those without full-time jobs—pay only part of the bill each month, thus compounding the original amount charged with interest rates that can be 18% annually, or even higher. Nationwide, 20% of students have credit card debt of more than $10,000—and that doesn't count amounts owed for student loans. Excessive credit card debt makes it harder for a student to become financially independent; in extreme cases, students may have to drop out just to pay off the credit card debt.

As Your Instructor Directs,

a. Create a message to urge students on your campus to use credit cards responsibly. Create a document that has the greatest chance of being read and heeded (not just dropped on the ground or in a trash can).

b. Write a memo to your instructor explaining how and when the document would be distributed and why you've chosen the design you have. Show how your decisions fit the students on your campus.

Hints:

• Suggest guidelines for responsible use of credit (limiting the number of credit cards, charging only what one can repay each month except in the case of an emergency, shopping around for a card with the lowest interest rate, and so forth). Suggest a way to test one's own credit savvy.

• Remind students that for continuing expenses, a loan will have a lower interest rate (and may not have to be repaid until after graduation).

• Some students may like the freebies they get with some credit cards (e.g., frequent flyer miles). How can you persuade these students that the freebies aren't worth charging more than they can pay off each month?

• Part of your audience already uses credit responsibly. Be sure the message doesn't offend these people.

• Some students in your audience may already know that they owe too much. What can students do if they already have too much debt?

12.16 Persuading an Organization to Expand Flextime

County government offices are open from 9 A.M. to 5 P.M. Employees have limited flextime: they can come in and leave half an hour early or half an hour late. But some people want to start at 6 A.M. so they can leave at 2 P.M.; others want to work from 11 A.M. to 7 P.M.

Supervisors don't like the idea. "How will we hold staff meetings? How can we supervise people if everyone works different hours? We have to be here for the public, and we won't be if people work whatever hours they please."

But solutions exist. Many firms that use flextime require everyone to be at work (or at lunch) between 10 A.M. and 2 P.M. or 11 A.M. and 2 P.M., so that staff meetings can be scheduled. Right now, when clients call, a representative is frequently on the phone and has to call back. Voice mail and better message forms could solve the problem. And flextime might actually let offices stay open longer hours—say 8 A.M. to 6 P.M., which would be helpful for taxpayers who themselves work 9 A.M. to 5 P.M.

Write a memo to the County Commissioners, persuading them to approve a change in work hours.

Hints:

• Assume that this situation is happening in your own county government. What services does the county offer?

• Use any facts about your county that are helpful (e.g., being especially busy right now, having high turnover, whether tax issues have been voted up or down).

• Use what you know about managing to allay managers' fears.

12.17 Persuading Disability Services to Increase the Handivan's Hours

State University has a "Handivan" that takes students in wheelchairs from their residences or apartments to campus locations and back again. But the van stops at 6 P.M. (even though there are evening classes, lectures, and events).

And it doesn't take people to off-campus restaurants, movies, grocery stores, or shopping centers. Write to the Director of Disability Services, urging that the Handivan's services be increased.

12.18 Handling a Sticky Recommendation

As a supervisor in a state agency, you have a dilemma. You received this e-mail message today:

From: John Inoye, Director of Personnel, Department of Taxation

Subject: Need Recommendation for Peggy Chafez

Peggy Chafez has applied for a position in the Department of Taxation. On the basis of her application and interview, she is the leading candidate. However, before I offer the job to her, I need a letter of recommendation from her current supervisor.

Could you please let me have your evaluation within a week? We want to fill the position as quickly as possible.

Peggy has worked in your office for 10 years. She designed, writes, and edits a monthly statewide newsletter that your office puts out; she designed and maintains the department Web site. Her designs are creative; she's a hard worker; she knows a lot about computers.

However, Peggy is in many ways an unsatisfactory staff member. Her standards are so high that most people find her intimidating. Some find her abrasive. She's out of the office a lot. Some of that is required by her job (e.g., she takes the newsletters to the post office), but some people don't like the fact that she's out of the office so much. They also complain that she doesn't return voice mail and e-mail messages.

You think managing your office would be a lot smoother if Peggy weren't there. You can't fire her: State employees' jobs are secure once they get

past the initial six-month probationary period. Because of budget constraints, you can hire new employees only if vacancies are created by resignations. You feel that it would be pretty easy to find someone better.

If you recommend that John Inoye hire Peggy, you will be able to hire someone you want. If you recommend that John hire someone else, you may be stuck with Peggy for a long time.

As Your Instructor Directs,
a. Write to John Inoye.
b. Write a memo to your instructor listing the choices you've made and justifying your approach.

Hints:
• What are your options? Consciously look for more than two.
• Is it ethical to select facts or to use connotations so that you are truthful but still encourage John to hire

Peggy? Is it certain that John would find Peggy's work as unsatisfactory as you do? If Peggy is hired and

doesn't do well, will your credibility suffer? Why is your credibility important?

12.19 Convincing a Member to Become Active Again

In every organization, one of the ongoing problems is convincing inactive members to become active again. Sometimes members become inactive because of short-term pressures. Sometimes they are offended by something the organization has done or not done. Sometimes they "fall through the cracks" and are not included in events. Whatever the reason, once they've become less active, it's easy for them to drop out entirely. Persuading these members to become active again is important. Because they once supported the organization, it may be easier to persuade them than to seek new members. And if they remain disenchanted with the organization, they may convince other people that the organization has little to offer.

As Your Instructor Directs,
a. Write to someone you know well, urging him or her to become active in the organization again.
b. Write notes for a phone conversation or meeting with your friend.
c. Join with a small group of students to write a form letter to go to inactive members in an organization.

d. Write a memo to your instructor explaining your audience analysis and your choice of strategy and appeals.

Hints:
• Pick a campus, professional, civic, social, or religious organization you know well.
• Be specific about what the organization is doing now, how members can benefit from it, and why the organization needs them.
• If your audience objects to specific things the organization has done or not done, respond to these concerns in your message. Did a misunderstanding occur? Is change already under way? Is change possible if enough people (like your audience, perhaps) work for it?
• What are your audience's priorities? Can you show that this organization will help your audience meet its needs?

12.20 Requesting That an Employee Be Hired on a Permanent Basis

For the last seven months, Luisa Velasquez has been hired on month-to-month contracts in your Division of Editorial and Graphic Services (EGS). She produces the employee newsletter using desktop publishing software. She understands desktop publishing better than anyone else in EGS, she's a good writer and editor, she's smart, and other employees like her.

Yesterday Luisa told you that she's been offered a job at Brown's Business

College teaching desktop publishing. She'd like to stay in your office, but she wants a permanent job where she receives health insurance and can accumulate retirement funds. As a contract employee, she gets $2,800 a month but no benefits.

You called a friend in Personnel and found that a position as Public Information Officer was approved last year but has not been funded or filled for this fiscal year. You talked to the Director of the Budget and found that there is a surplus in the personnel budget—more than enough to hire Luisa.

Normally contract employees are paid a higher monthly salary than are regular employees to compensate them for the lack of benefits and security. However, given Luisa's strong qualifications, you want to continue to pay her

$2,800 a month even when she receives benefits.

You can offer her the job only if your request is approved by your boss, Treg Steels. Write him a memo. You need to make the offer quickly so Luisa doesn't accept the offer from Brown's Business School.

12.21 Asking an Instructor for a Letter of Recommendation

For a job, for a four year school or for graduate school, you need letters of recommendation.

As Your Instructor Directs,

a. Assume that you've orally asked an instructor for a recommendation, and he or she has agreed to write one. "Write up something to remind me of what you've done in the class. Tell me what else you've done, too. And tell me what they're looking for. Be sure to tell me when the letter needs to be in and whom it goes to."

b. Assume that you've been unable to talk with the instructor whose recommendation you want. Write asking for a letter of recommendation.

Hints:

- Be detailed about the points you'd like the instructor to mention.
- How well will this instructor remember you? How much detail about your performance in his or her class do you need to provide?
- Specify the name and address of the person to whom the letter should be written; specify when the letter is due. If there's an intermediate due date (e.g., if you must sign the outside of the envelope to submit the recommendation to law school), say so.

12.22 Recommending Investments*

Recommend whether your instructor should invest in a specific stock, piece of real estate, or other investment. As your instructor directs, assume that your instructor has $1,000, $10,000, or $100,000 to invest.

Hints:

- Pick a stock, property, or other investment you can research easily.
- What are your instructor's goals? Is he or she saving for a house? For

retirement? For kids' college expenses? To pay off his or her own student loans?

- How much risk is your instructor comfortable with?
- Is your instructor willing to put time into the investment (as managing a rental house would require)?

*Based on an assignment created by Cathy Ryan, The Ohio State University.

12.23 Retrieving Your Image

As Director of Business Communication, you get this letter from Sharon Davis, a

member of your college advisory board and a major donor:

My bank received this letter from one of your soon-to-be graduates. It seems as though a closer look at writing skills is warranted.

To Whom It May Concern:

This is in reference to the loan soliciation that I received in the mail. This is the second offer that I am now inquiring about. The first offer sent to my previous address I did not respond. But aftersome careful thought and consideration I think it wise to consolidate my bills. Therefore I hope the information provided is sufficient to complete a successful application. I think the main purpose of this loan is to enable me to repair my credit history. I have had problems in the past because of job status as part-time and being a student. I will be graduating in June and now I do have a full-time job. I think I just need a chance to mend the past credit problems that I have had.

(The next two inches of the letter are blocked out, and neither the signature and typed name can be read.)

As Your Instructor Directs,
Write to
a. The faculty who teach business communication, reminding them that the quality of student writing may affect fund-raising efforts.
b. Ms. Davis, convincing her that indeed your school does make every effort to graduate students who can write.

12.24 **Persuading Tenants to Pay the Rent**

As the new manager of an apartment complex, this message is in the files:

ATTENTION!

DERELICTS

If you are a rent derelict (and you know if you are) this communique is directed to you!

RENT IS DUE THE 5TH OF EACH MONTH AT THE LATEST!

LEASE HAS A 5-DAY GRACE PERIOD UNTIL THE 5TH OF THE MONTH NOT THE 15TH.

If rent is not paid in total by the 5th, you will pay the $25.00 late charge. You will pay the $25.00 late charge when you pay your late rent or your rent will not be accepted.

Half of you people don't even know how much you pay a month. Please read your lease instead of calling up to waste our time finding out what you owe per month! Let's get with the program so I can spend my time streamlining and organizing maintenance requests. My job is maintenance only.

RENT PAYMENT IS YOUR JOB!

If you can show up for a test on time, why can't you make it to the rental office on time or just mail it.

P.S. We don't take cash any longer due to a major theft.

This message is terrible. It lacks you-attitude and may even encourage people not to pay until the 5th.

Write to people who have been slow to pay in the past.

12.25 **Writing a Performance Appraisal for a Member of a Collaborative Group**

During your collaborative writing group meetings, record specific observations of both effective and ineffective things that group members do. Then evaluate the performance of the other members in your group. (If there are two or more other people, write a separate appraisal for each of them.)

In your first paragraph, summarize your evaluation. Then in the body of your memo, give specific details:

- What specifically did the person do in terms of the task? Brainstorm ideas? Analyze the information? Draft the text? Suggest revisions in parts drafted by others? Format the document or create visuals? Revise? Edit? Proofread? (In most cases, several people will have done each of these activities together. Don't overstate what any one person did.) What was the quality of the person's work?
- What did the person contribute to the group process? Did he or she help schedule the work? Raise or resolve conflicts? Make other group members feel valued and included? Promote group cohesion? What roles did the person play in the group?

Support your generalizations with specific observations. The more observations you have and the more detailed they are, the better your appraisal will be.

As Your Instructor Directs,

a. Write a midterm performance appraisal for one or more members of your collaborative group. In each appraisal, identify the two or three things the person should try to improve during the second half of the term.

b. Write a performance appraisal for one or more members of your collaborative group at the end of the term. Identify and justify the grade you think each person should receive for the portion of the grade based on group process.

c. Give a copy of your appraisal to the person about whom it is written.

Polishing Your Prose

Expressing Personality

The words you choose can express personality in speech and writing. What personality do you want in your memos, letters, and reports? Friendly? Assertive? Bureaucratic? Threatening? Confident? These are just a few possibilities.

Consider the personality expressed by billionaire investment guru Warren Buffet in an annual report to the shareholders of Berkshire Hathaway, Inc.:

> Given our gain of 34.1%, it is tempting to declare victory and move on. But last year's performance was no great triumph. Any investor can chalk up large returns when stocks soar, as they did in 1997. In a bull market, one must avoid the error of the preening duck that quacks boastfully after a torrential rainstorm, thinking that its paddling skills have caused it to rise in the world. A right-thinking duck would instead compare its position after the downpour to that of the other ducks in the pond.
>
> So what's our duck rating for 1997? The table on the facing page shows that though we paddled furiously last year, passive ducks that simply invested in the S&P Index rose almost as fast as we did. Our appraisal of 1997's performance then: Quack.

How would you describe the personality of this narrator? Does he sound "folksy"? Fatherly? Grandfatherly? Educated? Confident? How do you know? How does his personality compare to your expectations for someone in the investment field? Someone who is wealthy? Is this someone you would like to know?

Personality is individual. However, we all have control over the words we choose to convey our personalities. To understand your own personality in communication, first see if you can understand the personalities that others convey. Then compare their words and tone to your own.

Exercises

Read the following passages. How would you characterize the narrative voice in each? Which voices seem appropriate for good business communication? Try using your own words to communicate the same basic message.

1. Hi, Mr. Mills! Just stop in to pick up your order when you get a chance. Give us a ring if you want delivery. Thanks!!

2. Don't worry, honey, you just leave everything to me. Don't worry your pretty little head about a thing. I'll take care of it all, sugarpie.

3. Get your act together or you're fired. Got it?

4. I wish you all the best in your new job. I know you'll do well!

5. Pertaining to the party of the first part, hereafter called "party first," and excepting any and all objections from the party of the second part, hereafter called "party second," this amendment shall be considered null and void with proper written notice three (3) days prior to the execution of the original agreement.

6. Please call me about the opportunity to work with you. Please, please, PLEASE! I really need this job. Please!!

7. I QUIT.

8. Your responsibilities are as follows:

   1. Attendance in all supervisory meetings.

   2. Demonstration of knowledge of requisite procedures.

   3. Maintenance of appropriate records.

   4. Distribution of related correspondence.

   Failure to perform adequately in these areas will result in disciplinary action up to and including termination.

9. Nope. This idea won't work. It's not very good. I'm not sure the project is even worth our time anymore. I'm definitely not interested in having a meeting to discuss it. Don't call me unless you eggheads hatch something better.

10. We better do something about this soon. I mean, what if we're not ready in time? What if the supplier doesn't fulfill our order? What will we do then? Well? I'm telling you, we need to get moving on this *now*.

Check your answers to the odd-numbered exercises at the back of the book.

BComm Skill Booster

To apply the concepts in this module, complete lessons 21, 22, 23, 25, and 26 on persuasive messages, direct requests, problem-solving messages, and credibility. You can access the BComm Skill Booster through the text Web site at **www.mhhe.com/bcs2e.**

Module 13

E-Mail Messages

Start by asking these questions:

- How should I set up e-mail messages?
- What kinds of subject lines should I use for e-mail messages?
- Should I write e-mail messages the same way I write paper messages?
- What e-mail "netiquette" rules should I follow?
- How and when should I use attachments?

When you start a new job, you may have a short grace period before you have to write paper documents. But most employers will expect you to "hit the ground running" with e-mail. It's likely that you'll respond to—and perhaps initiate—e-mail messages during your very first week at work.

As you write e-mail messages, keep these guidelines in mind:

- Although e-mail feels informal, it is not private, as a conversation might be. Your employer may legally check your messages. And a message sent to one person can be printed out or forwarded to others without your knowledge or consent. Don't be indiscreet in e-mail.

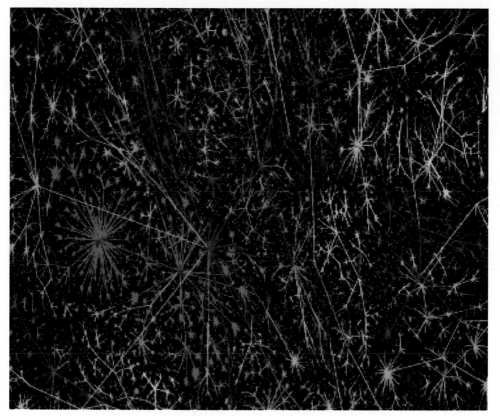

This map shows the shortest path taken by a test message sent in January 2002 from Somerset, NJ, to more than 120,000 registered Internet nodes. Each node may be one computer or many joined in a network. Each color represents a different service provider.

- All the principles of good business writing still apply with e-mail. Remember you-attitude (p. 106) and positive emphasis (p. 119). Use reader benefits (p. 132) when they're appropriate. Use the pattern of organization that fits the purpose of the message.
- Because e-mail feels like talking, some writers give less attention to spelling, grammar, and proofreading. Many e-mail programs have spell checkers; use them. Check your message for grammatical correctness and to be sure that you've included all the necessary information.
- Reread and proofread your message before sending it out.
- E-mail messages have to interest the reader in the subject line and first paragraph. If the message is longer than one screen, the first screen must interest the reader enough to make him or her continue. E-mail messages to people who report directly to you are easy because people will read anything from their supervisors. But writing to people who are not in a direct reporting relationship or to people outside your unit or organization takes more care.

FYI

The average office worker spends 49 minutes a day on e-mail. Top managers spend about four hours a day on e-mail.

Source: Elizabeth Weinstein, "Help! I'm Drowning in E-Mail," *The Wall Street Journal,* January 10, 2002, B1.

How should I set up e-mail messages?

Formats are still evolving.

Most e-mail programs prompt you to supply the various parts of the format. For example, a blank Eudora screen prompts you to supply the name of the person the message goes to and the subject line. *Cc* denotes computer copies; the recipient will see that these people are getting the message. *Bcc* denotes blind computer copies; the recipient does not see the names of these people. Most e-mail programs also allow you to attach documents from other programs. Thus you can send someone a document with formatting, drafts of PowerPoint slides, or the design for a brochure cover. The computer program supplies the date and time automatically. Some programs allow you to write a message now and program the future time at which you want it to be sent.

Some aspects of e-mail format are still evolving. In particular, some writers treat e-mail messages as if they were informal letters; some treat them as memos. Even though the e-mail screen has a "To" line (as do memos), some writers still use an informal salutation, as in Figure 13.1. The writer in Figure 13.1 ends the message with a signature block. You can store a signature block in the e-mail program and set the program to insert the signature block automatically. In contrast, the writer in Figure 13.2 omits both the salutation and his name. When you send a message to an individual or a group you have set up, the "From:" line will have your name and e-mail address. If you post a message to a group someone else has set up, such as a listserv, be sure to give at least your name and e-mail address at the end of your message, as some listservs strip out identifying information when they process messages.

When you hit "reply," the e-mail program automatically uses "Re:" (Latin for *about*) and the previous subject. The original message is set off (see Figure 13.3). You may want to change the subject line to make it more appropriate for your message.

If you prepare your document in a word processor, use two-inch side margins to create short line lengths. If the line lengths are too long, they'll produce awkward line breaks as in Figure 13.3. Use two- or three-space tab settings to minimize the wasted space on the screen.

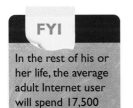

FYI

In the rest of his or her life, the average adult Internet user will spend 17,500 hours—almost 24 months—online.

Source: Karen Star, *Cyber Dialog,* in "Life Span," *Selling Power,* March 2001, 28.

What kinds of subject lines should I use for e-mail messages?

Be specific, concise, and catchy.

Subject lines in e-mail are even more important than those in letters and memos because it's so easy for an e-mail user to hit the delete key. Subject lines must be specific, concise, and catchy. Many e-mail users get so many messages that they don't bother reading messages if they don't recognize the sender or if the subject doesn't catch their interest.

Try to keep the subject line short. If that's difficult, put the most important part into the first few words because some e-mail programs only show the first 28 characters of the subject line.

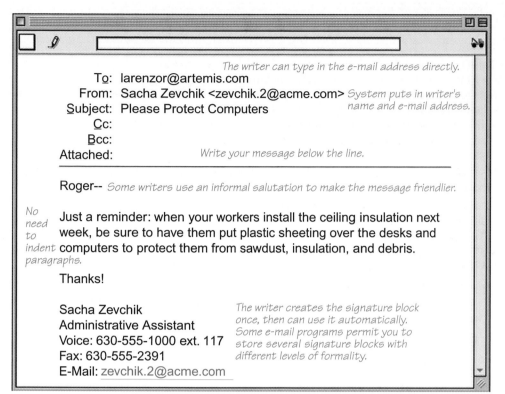

Figure 13.1

A Basic E-Mail Message in Eudora (direct request)

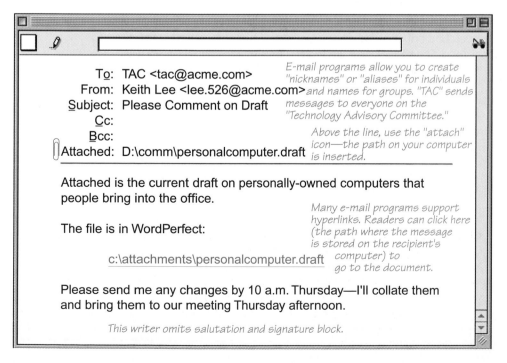

Figure 13.2

An E-Mail Message with an Attachment (direct request)

Figure 13.3

An E-Mail Reply with Copies (response to a complaint)

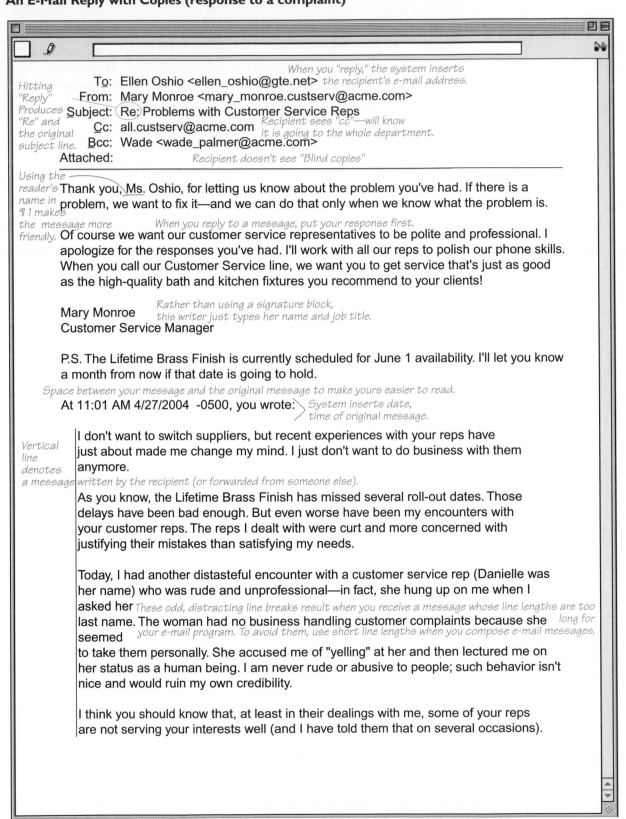

When you "reply," the system inserts

To: Ellen Oshio <ellen_oshio@gte.net> *the recipient's e-mail address.*

Hitting "Reply" Produces "Re" and the original subject line.

From: Mary Monroe <mary_monroe.custserv@acme.com>

Subject: Re: Problems with Customer Service Reps

Cc: all.custserv@acme.com *Recipient sees "cc"—will know it is going to the whole department.*

Bcc: Wade <wade_palmer@acme.com>

Attached: *Recipient doesn't see "Blind copies"*

Using the reader's name in ¶ 1 makes the message more friendly.

Thank you, Ms. Oshio, for letting us know about the problem you've had. If there is a problem, we want to fix it—and we can do that only when we know what the problem is.

When you reply to a message, put your response first.

Of course we want our customer service representatives to be polite and professional. I apologize for the responses you've had. I'll work with all our reps to polish our phone skills. When you call our Customer Service line, we want you to get service that's just as good as the high-quality bath and kitchen fixtures you recommend to your clients!

Mary Monroe *Rather than using a signature block, this writer just types her name and job title.*
Customer Service Manager

P.S. The Lifetime Brass Finish is currently scheduled for June 1 availability. I'll let you know a month from now if that date is going to hold.

Space between your message and the original message to make yours easier to read.

At 11:01 AM 4/27/2004 -0500, you wrote: *System inserts date, time of original message.*

Vertical line denotes a message written by the recipient (or forwarded from someone else).

I don't want to switch suppliers, but recent experiences with your reps have just about made me change my mind. I just don't want to do business with them anymore.

As you know, the Lifetime Brass Finish has missed several roll-out dates. Those delays have been bad enough. But even worse have been my encounters with your customer reps. The reps I dealt with were curt and more concerned with justifying their mistakes than satisfying my needs.

Today, I had another distasteful encounter with a customer service rep (Danielle was her name) who was rude and unprofessional—in fact, she hung up on me when I asked her *These odd, distracting line breaks result when you receive a message whose line lengths are too* last name. The woman had no business handling customer complaints because she *long for* seemed *your e-mail program. To avoid them, use short line lengths when you compose e-mail messages.* to take them personally. She accused me of "yelling" at her and then lectured me on her status as a human being. I am never rude or abusive to people; such behavior isn't nice and would ruin my own credibility.

I think you should know that, at least in their dealings with me, some of your reps are not serving your interests well (and I have told them that on several occasions).

If your message is very short, you may be able to put it in the subject line. "EOM" (end of message) tells your reader that there is no additional information in the body of the message.

Subject: Will Attend 3 p.m. Meeting EOM

Subject: Need Password for Survey EOM

Subject Lines for Informative and Positive E-Mail Messages

If you have good news to convey, be sure it's in the subject line. Be as brief as you can.

The following subject lines would be acceptable for informative and good news e-mail messages:

Subject: Travel Plans for Sales Meeting

Subject: Your Proposal Accepted

Subject: Reduced Prices During February

Subject: Your Funding Request Approved

When you reply to a message, the e-mail system automatically creates a subject line "Re: [subject line of message to which you are responding]." If the subject line is good, that's fine. If it isn't, you may want to create a new subject line. And if a series of messages arises, create a new subject line. "Re: Re: Re: Re: Question" is not an effective subject line.

Subject Lines for Negative E-Mail Messages

When you say "no" to an e-mail request, just hit "reply" and use "Re:" plus whatever the original subject line was for your response. When you write a new message, you will have to decide whether to use the negative in the subject line. The subject line should contain the negative when

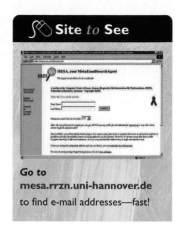

Site *to* See

Go to
mesa.rrzn.uni-hannover.de
to find e-mail addresses—fast!

When you send e-mails just for information, put "FYI" at the end of the subject line.

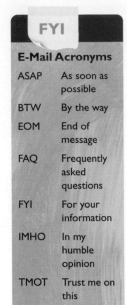

- The negative is serious. Many people do not read all their e-mail messages. A neutral subject line may lead the reader to ignore the message.
- The reader needs the information to make a decision or act.
- You report your own errors (as opposed to the reader's).

Thus the following would be acceptable subject lines in e-mail messages:

Subject: We Lost McDonald's Account

Subject: Power to Be Out Sunday, March 12

Subject: Error in Survey Data Summary

In other situations, a neutral subject line is acceptable.

Subject: Results of 360° Performance Appraisals

Subject Lines for Persuasive E-Mail Messages

The subject line of a persuasive e-mail message should make it clear that you're asking for something. If you're sure that the reader will read the message, something as vague as "Request" may work. Most of the time, it's better to be more specific.

Subject: Move Meeting to Tuesday?

Subject: Need Your Advice

Subject: Provide Story for Newsletter?

Subject: Want You for United Way Campaign

Should I write e-mail messages the same way I write paper messages?

Negative and persuasive messages will be more direct.

Readers read and reply to e-mail quite rapidly. Dealing with 80 to 100 messages in 20 or 30 minutes is normal. Write e-mail messages so that it's easy for readers to understand and act on them quickly. Writing messages so that the reader can deal with them quickly means taking time to plan, revise, and proofread, just as you do with paper messages. Figure 13.4 shows how a writer might allocate time in responding to a simple e-mail request. Figure 13.5 lists the activities needed for a more complex e-mail message.

Writing Positive and Informative E-Mail Messages

E-mail is especially appropriate for positive and informative messages. Figure 13.3 is an example of a positive response to a customer complaint.

Writing Negative E-Mail Messages

Major negatives, such as firing someone, should be delivered in person, not by e-mail. But e-mail is appropriate for many less serious negatives.

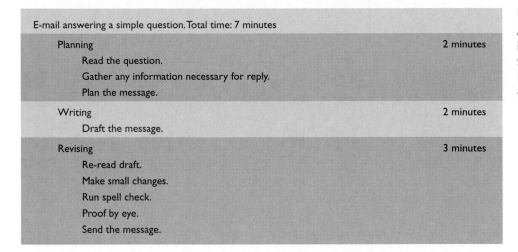

Figure 13.4
Allocating Time in Writing a Simple E-Mail Response (Your time may vary.)

E-mail answering a simple question. Total time: 7 minutes	
Planning	2 minutes
Read the question.	
Gather any information necessary for reply.	
Plan the message.	
Writing	2 minutes
Draft the message.	
Revising	3 minutes
Re-read draft.	
Make small changes.	
Run spell check.	
Proof by eye.	
Send the message.	

Figure 13.5
Allocating Time in Writing a Persuasive E-Mail Message (Your time may vary.)

Persuasive request with attachments. Total time: 3 hours	
Planning	1 hour
Understand the situation.	
Answer the PAIBOC questions (◄ ▷ Module 1).	
Think about document design (◄ ▷ Module 5).	
Organize the message.	
Writing	½ hour
Draft the message and attachments.	
Revising	1½ hours
Re-read draft.	
Measure draft against PAIBOC questions and checklist for problem-solving persuasive messages (◄ ▷ Figure 12.10).	
Revise draft and attachments.	
Ask for feedback.	
Revise draft based on feedback.	
Edit to catch grammatical errors.	
Run spell check.	
Proof by eye.	
Send the message.	

Never write e-mail messages when you're angry. If a message infuriates you, wait till you're calmer before you reply—and even then, reply only if you must. Writers using e-mail are much less inhibited than they would be on paper or in person, sending insults, swearing, name-calling, and making hostile statements.[1] **Flaming** is the name given to this behavior. Flaming does not make you look like a mature, level-headed candidate for bigger things. And since employers have the right to read all e-mail, flaming—particularly if directed at co-workers, regulators, suppliers, or customers—may cause an employee to be fired.

Managing Your Time

Do you need more time? Welcome to the club! Although researchers claim that we have more leisure hours than we did 20 years ago, most of us feel more overworked than ever. And the number of things you'll need to do will only increase as you assume more job responsibilities.

Managing your incoming e-mail is an essential skill for every office worker.

- Create folders, mailboxes, and filters. For example, most e-mail programs allow you to flag messages from your boss in a special color.
- Move items out of your inbox.
- Delete messages after you act on them.
- If you need to save messages, move them to folders on a specific topic or project.
- Create a "delete in 30 days" folder for items you'll need briefly.
- Purge files periodically—at least once a month. (Once a week is better.)

Many workers benefit from managing all their activities (not just their e-mail) more efficiently. To manage your time, divide projects or incoming mail into three piles (real or imaginary). Put urgent items in the *A* pile, important items in the *B* pile, and other items in the *C* pile. Do the *A* items first. Most people find that they never get to their *C* piles.

At the end of the day, make a list of the two most important things you need to do the next day—and leave the paper where you'll see it when you start work the next morning.

If you still don't have enough time to get your *A*s and most of your *B*s done, you're ready for a more systematic approach to time.

1. For at least a week, log how you spend your time. Record what you're doing in 15-minute intervals.
2. Analyze your log to identify patterns, time obligations, time wasters, and frustrations. You may be surprised to find how much time you spend playing computer games. Or you may discover that answering e-mail takes an hour every morning—not the five minutes or so that you'd estimated.
3. Clarify your goals. What do you want to accomplish on the job and in your personal life? What intermediate steps (e.g., taking a course, learning a new skill, or sending out job applications) will you need to do to reach your goals?
4. Set short-term priorities. For the next month, what do you need to accomplish? In addition to goals for school and work, think also about building relationships, meeting personal obligations, and finding time to plan, to relax, and to think.
5. Ask for help or negotiate compromises. Maybe you and another parent can share babysitting so that you each have some time to yourselves. If your responsibilities at work are impossible, talk to your supervisor to see whether some of your duties can be transferred to someone else or whether you should stop trying to be excellent and settle for "good enough." You won't be willing or able to eliminate all your obligations, but sometimes dropping just one or two responsibilities can really help.
6. Schedule your day to reflect your priorities. You don't necessarily have to work on every goal every day, but each goal should appear on your schedule at least three times a week. Schedule some time for yourself, too.
7. Evaluate your new use of time. Are you meeting more of your goals? Are you feeling less stressed? If not, go back to step 1 and analyze more patterns, obligations, time wasters, and frustrations to see how you can make the best use of the time you have.

In the body of the e-mail message, give a reason only if it is watertight and reflects well on the organization. Give an alternative, if one exists.

Edit and proofread your message carefully. An easy way for an angry reader to strike back is to attack typos or other errors.

Remember that e-mail messages, like any documents, can become documents in lawsuits. When an e-mail negative is hard to write, you may want to compose it off-line so that you can revise and even get feedback before you send the message.

Writing Persuasive E-Mail Messages

When you ask for something small or for something that it is part of the reader's job duties to provide, your request can be straightforward. (See Figures 13.1 and 13.2.)

- In the body of the message, give people all the information they need to act.
- At the end of the message, ask for the action you want. Make the action as easy as possible, and specify when you need a response. You may want an immediate response now ("Let me know asap whether you can write a story for the newsletter so that I can save the space") and a fuller one later ("we'll need the text by March 4").

When you ask for something big or something that is not a regular part of that person's duties, the first paragraph must not only specify the request but also make the reader view it positively. Use the second paragraph to provide an overview of the evidence that the rest of the message will provide: Use audience analysis (◀ ▷ p. 22) to find a reason to do as you ask that the reader will find convincing. Everyone is busy, so you need to make the reader *want* to do as you ask. Be sure to provide complete information that the reader will need to act on your request. Ask for the action you want.

Here's why we should do this.

Let me describe the project. Then, if you're willing to be part of it, I'll send you a copy of the proposal.

Major requests that require changes in values, culture, or lifestyles should not be made in e-mail messages.

What e-mail "netiquette" rules should I follow?

Lurk before you leap.

E-mail communities develop their own norms. If possible, lurk a few days—read the messages without writing anything yourself—before you enter the conversation.

Follow these guidelines to be a good "netizen":

- Never send angry messages by e-mail. If you have a conflict with someone, work it out face-to-face, not electronically.
- Use full caps only to emphasize a single word or two. Putting the whole message in caps is considered as rude as shouting.
- Send people only messages they need. Send copies to your boss or CEO only if he or she has asked you to.
- Find out how your recipient's system works and adapt your messages to it. Most people would rather get a separate short message on each of several topics, so that the messages can be stored in different mailboxes.

FYI

In 2000, 51% of respondents to a survey said that the tone of their e-mail messages is sometimes misunderstood.

Source: "Ticker," *Brill's Content,* September 2000, 44.

Instant **Replay**

When Not to Use E-Mail

Major negatives, like firing someone, should be delivered in person, not by e-mail. But e-mail is appropriate for many less serious negatives.

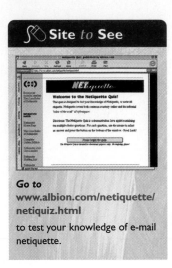

Site *to* See

Go to
**www.albion.com/netiquette/
netiquiz.html**

to test your knowledge of e-mail
netiquette.

But people who pay a fee to download each message may prefer longer messages that deal with several topics.

- When you respond to a message, include only the part of the original message that is essential so that the reader understands your posting. Delete the rest. If the quoted material is long, put your response first, then the original material.
- When you compose a message in your word processor and call it up in e-mail, use short line lengths (set the right margin at 2.5" or 3"). That's the way to avoid the awkward line breaks of Figure 13.3.

How and when should I use attachments?

When the reader expects and needs them.

Any text document can be copied and pasted into the body of your e-mail message. Sending attachments makes most sense when you send

- A long text document.
- A text document with extensive formatting.
- A non-text file (e.g., PowerPoint slides, html file, spreadsheet).

When you send an attachment, tell the reader what program it's in (see Figure 13.2). Word-processing programs can generally open documents in earlier programs but not later ones. Thus WordPerfect 2000 can open documents in Word 97 but not in Word XP.

A computer **virus** is a script that harms your computer or erases your data. You can't get a virus through e-mail, but viruses can infect files that are "attached" to e-mail messages or that you download. To stay virus-free,[2]

- Install an anti-virus program on your computer, and keep it up to date.
- Ask people who send you attachments to include their names in the document titles. Virus titles aren't that specific.
- If you're in doubt about an attachment, don't open it.
- Forward e-mail messages only when you're sure of the source and contents.

Site *to* See

Go to
www.vmyths.com

to learn whether a rumored
virus is real or a hoax.

Summary of Key Points

- All of the principles of good writing apply to e-mail. Use you-attitude, positive emphasis, and reader benefits when you'd use them in paper messages.
- Subject lines for e-mail messages must be specific, concise, and catchy.

- Create e-mail messages that people can read and act on quickly.
- Compose important messages off-line to allow time for thought and revision.

Assignments for Module 13

Questions for Comprehension

13.1 How do subject lines for e-mail messages differ from those for paper messages?

13.2 Should e-mail messages use you-attitude, positive emphasis, and reader benefits?

13.3 What is flaming?

Questions for Critical Thinking

13.4 Why are spelling and punctuation still important in e-mail?

13.5 Why should you compose important e-mail messages off-line?

13.6 Why should negative and persuasive e-mail messages be more direct than their paper counterparts?

13.7 Why is it OK for your boss to send you a message with the subject line "To Do," even though that wouldn't work when you need to ask a colleague to do something?

Exercises and Problems

13.8   **Announcing a New Policy of Compensatory Time Off**

Most of the workers in your office are salaried, so they do not receive overtime pay when they work after 5 P.M. However, the Executive Committee last week decided to institute a policy of compensatory time off. Under this policy, if someone works two or more hours more than the basic 40-hour workweek, he or she can take off the same number of hours on another day while still being paid the full rate. The employee's supervisor must approve the time chosen for compensatory time off; an employee cannot take time off if he or she is needed for an important project. This policy is effective starting the first full week of next month. It is not retroactive; that is, people will not receive compensatory time off for additional hours they may have already worked.

Write a message to all employees announcing the policy.

13.9 **Calming an Angry Co-worker**

You're a member of a self-managed team on a factory assembly line. When you check the team's e-mail, you find this message from the factory's Quality Assurance Manager:

> Subject: Holes in Your Heads?
>
> Yesterday in the scrap bin I found a casting with three times too many holes in it. How could a machinist make such a mistake? What's going on?

The answer is simple. The extra holes come not from crazy machinists but from crafty ones. Your team uses old machines that aren't computerized.

When you make a part on those machines, you have to drill a test piece first to be sure that the alignment and size of the holes are correct. This testing has to be done every time you set up for a new run. Your team has figured out that you can use less material by reusing the test piece until it resembles Swiss cheese, rather than throwing it away

after a single testing. Your team is one of the most efficient in the plant, thanks to creative moves like this one. Write an e-mail response.

13.10   Announcing Holiday Diversity

Your organization has traditionally given employees several holidays off: New Year's; Martin Luther King, Jr., Day; Independence Day; Veterans' Day; Thanksgiving; and Christmas. Employees who celebrate other holidays (e.g., Good Friday, Yom Kippur, Ramadan, Chinese New Year, the Hindu holiday Diwali) have been able to take those days off with the consent of their supervisors. But some employees have complained that it is unfair to depend on the goodwill of supervisors. And now a few other employees have complained that people who honor other holidays are getting "extra" days off since they take those days in addition to the standard holidays.

Therefore, the Executive Committee of your organization has decided to allow employees any 10 days off for holidays; they will have to tell their supervisors which days they plan to take off. People will be asked in December which holidays they want to take off in the following year. People can

change their minds during the year as long as they have not yet taken off the full 10 holidays. Any religious, ethnic, or cultural holiday is acceptable. (Someone who wants to take off *Cinco de Mayo* or Bastille Day can do so.) Vacations, personal days off, and sick days are not affected by this policy.

As Vice President for Human Resources, write an e-mail to all employees, announcing the new policy.

Hints:
- Pick a business, government, or nonprofit organization that you know something about.
- Will the office be "open" every day? If not, do all employees already have keys, or will they need to pick them up so they can get into the office to work days that few other people work?
- See www.holidayfestival.com for a list of holidays in various countries.
- Use your analysis from Problem 2.13.

13.11   Refusing to Provide Graduates' Addresses on Your Web Page

You maintain the Web page for your college or community college depart-

ment. Today, you get the following e-mail message:

Subject: Add Graduates' Names?

I really like your Web site. Could you please add the names and addresses (snail and e-mail) of recent graduates? That would help us keep in touch and would be really useful for networking.

You don't want to do this. Probably someone has this information, but you don't know who. You've got enough to do without tracking down the information, posting it on the Web, and updating it as people move. But you

don't want to offend the person who asked, since recent graduates are asked to help in many ways (sponsor internships, give money, etc.). So you need to say *no* while maintaining goodwill.

Write the message.

13.12 Refusing to Pay an Out-of-Network Bill

Your employees' health insurance allows them to choose from one of three Health Maintenance Organizations (HMOs). Once the employee has selected an HMO, he or she must get all medical care (except for out-of-state emergency care) from the HMO. Employees receive a listing of the doctors and hospitals affiliated with each HMO when they join the company and pick an HMO and again each October when they have a one-month "open enrollment period" to change to another of the three HMOs if they choose.

As Director of Employee Benefits, you've received an angry e-mail from Alvin Reineke. Alvin had just received a statement from his HMO stating that it would not pay for the costs of his hernia operation two months ago at St. Catherine's Hospital in your city. Alvin is furious: One of the reasons he accepted a job with your company six months ago was its excellent health care coverage. He feels the company lied to him and should pay for his (rather large) hospital bill since the HMO refuses to do so.

The HMO that Alvin had selected uses two hospitals, but not St. Catherine's. When Alvin joined the company six months ago, he, like all new employees, received a thick booklet explaining the HMO options. Perhaps he did not take the time to read it carefully. But that's not your fault. Alvin can change plans during the next open enrollment, but even if he switched to an HMO that included St. Catherine's, that HMO wouldn't pay for surgery performed before he joined that HMO.

Write an e-mail message to Alvin giving him the bad news.

Hints:

- What tone should you use? Should you be sympathetic? Should you remind him that this is his own fault?
- Is there any help you can give Alvin (e.g., information about credit-union short-term loans or even information about negotiating payment terms with the hospital)?
- What can you do to make Alvin feel that the company has not lied to him?

13.13 Saying *No* to the Boss

Today, you received this e-mail from your boss.

> Subject: Oversee United Way
>
> I'm appointing you to be the company representative to oversee United Way. You've done a good job the last three years, so this year should be a piece of cake!

It's true that you know exactly what to do. The job wouldn't be hard for you. But that's just the problem. You wouldn't learn anything, either. You'd rather have an assignment that would stretch you, teach you new skills, or enable you to interact with new people. Continuing to grow is your insurance of continued employability and mobility. Three upcoming projects in your division might offer growth: creating videos for a "town meeting" for all employees to be held at the beginning of next quarter, creating an intranet for the company, or serving on the diversity committee. Any of these would be time-consuming, but no more time-consuming than running the United Way campaign.

Write to your boss, asking for something more challenging to do.

13.14 Rejecting a Suggestion

Your company has a suggestion system that encourages workers to submit suggestions that will save the organization money or improve safety, customer service, or morale. If a suggestion is accepted that will save the company money, its proposer gets 10% of the estimated first year's savings. If a suggestion is accepted but will not save money, the proposer gets $25. You chair the committee that makes the decisions.

Today, you must tell Wayne Andersen that the committee has rejected his suggestion to buy a second photocopying machine for the sales department. Wayne pointed out that the sales department occupies a whole floor, yet has only one copier. Although the copier is in the center of the room (by the coffee and vending machines), some people have to walk quite a distance to get to it. Of course, they often stop to talk to the people they pass. Wayne calculated how much time people waste walking to the copier and talking to co-workers multiplied by annual salaries compared to the shorter time needed to walk to one of two copiers, each located to serve half the floor. He calculated that the company could save the cost of a $10,000 machine in just six months, with a further $10,000 savings by the end of the first year.

No one on the committee liked Wayne's idea.

"I don't trust his numbers. After all, lots of people combine trips to the copier with a trip to get a cup of coffee or a cola. They'd do even more walking if they had to make two trips."

"He talks about people waiting in line to use the copier, but I'm in sales, and I know the copier really isn't used that much. Sure, there are some bottle-necks—especially when reports are due—but lots of the time the machine just sits there."

"I'm worried about the economy. I don't think this is the time to spend money we don't have to spend."

"I guess his system would be more efficient. But the real savings comes not from less walking but from less talking. And I think we *want* people to talk to each other. Informal conversations are great for relieving stress, sharing ideas, and strengthening our loyalty to each other and to the company."

"I agree. I think our company is built on informal interchange and a sense that you don't have to account for every single minute. Our people are almost all on salary; they stay overtime without any extra pay. If someone wants to take a break and talk to someone, I think that's OK."

"Well, sometimes we do waste time talking. But his idea isn't really new. Lots of people think we could save money by buying more of every kind of equipment. Even if we get a copier, I don't think he should get any money."

You pointed out that even if a new copier didn't save as much money as Wayne predicted, it would shorten the lines when lots of people have copying to do. You suggested adopting his suggestion but reducing the estimated savings and therefore the award. But the committee rejected your compromise and the suggestion. As chair of the committee, you vote only to break a tie.

Write an e-mail message to Wayne, reporting the committee's decision.

Hints:
- What reason(s) should you give for the committee's decision?

- Should you tell Wayne that you disagreed with the majority?

- How can you encourage Wayne to continue to submit suggestions?

13.15 Sending a Question to a Web Site

Send a question or other message that calls for a response to a Web site. You could

- Ask a question about a product.
- Apply for an internship or a job (assuming you'd really like to work there).
- Ask for information about an internship or a job.
- Ask a question about an organization or a candidate before you donate money or volunteer.
- Offer to volunteer for an organization or a candidate. You can offer to do something small and one-time (e.g., spend an afternoon stuffing envelopes, put up a yard sign), or you can, if you want to, offer to do something more time-consuming or even ongoing.

As Your Instructor Directs,

a. Turn in a copy of your e-mail message and the response you received.
b. Critique messages written by other students in your class. Suggest ways the messages could be clearer and more persuasive.

c. Write a memo evaluating your message and the response, using the checklists for Modules 12 and 10, respectively. If you did not receive a response, did the fault lie with your message?
d. Make an oral presentation to the class, evaluating your message and the response, using the checklists for Modules 12 and 10, respectively. If you did not receive a response, did the fault lie with your message?

Hints:

- Does the organization ask for questions or offers? Or will yours "come out of the blue"?
- How difficult will it be for the organization to supply the information you're asking for or to do what you're asking it to do? If you're applying for an internship or offering to volunteer, what skills can you offer? How much competition do you have?
- What can you do to build your own credibility, so that the organization takes your question or request seriously?

13.16 Asking for a Job Description

Your organization has gone through a lot of changes, and you suspect that the original job descriptions people were hired into are no longer accurate. So you'd like all employees to list their current job duties. You'd also like them to indicate which parts of their jobs they see as most important and how much time they spend on each part of the job.

E-mail all employees, asking for the descriptions.

Hints:

- Pick a real business, government, or nonprofit group you know about.

- When is the next cycle of performance appraisals? Will these descriptions be used then?
- People will be reluctant to tell you they're spending lots of time on things that aren't important, and some people may honestly not know how they spend their time. How can you encourage accurate reporting? (If you ask people to keep logs for a week, be sure also to ask them if that week was typical—it may or may not be.)
- Some people will want to change their job descriptions—that is, to change their duties or the proportion

of time they spend on each. Is that an option in your organization right now? If it isn't (or if it is an option for very few people), how can you make that clear to readers?

13.17 Suggesting a Change in Your Organization's Communication Materials

Your organization has a Web page, but its address isn't on all your business communication materials (stationery, business cards, invoices, product packaging, brochures, catalogs, voice mail announcements, e-mail signatures, promotional items such as pens, coffee cups, and mouse pads). Adding the URL would promote the Web site (and suggest that your organization is up-to-date).

As Your Instructor Directs,

a. Identify the person in your organization with the power to authorize adding the URL to physical materials, and e-mail that person asking him or her to authorize this change.

b. Write an e-mail to all employees, asking them to add the URL and a brief message promoting the organization to their e-mail signature blocks.

Hints:
- Pick a business, nonprofit, or government organization you know something about. What materials does it produce? Which lack the URL?
- Will the reader know you? Has your organization asked for suggestions, or will this come "out of the blue"?
- What should be done with materials already printed or manufactured that lack the Web address? Should they be discarded, or used until they run out?
- Who in your organization has the authority to authorize this change?
- What exactly do you want your reader to do? What information does your reader need?

13.18 Asking for More Time and/or Resources

Today, this message shows up in your e-mail inbox from your boss:

Subject: Fwd: Want Climate Report

This request has come down from the CEO. I'm delegating it to you. See me a couple of days before the Board meeting—the first Monday of next month—so we can go over your presentation.

>I want a report on the climate for underrepresented groups in our organization. A presentation at
>the last Board of Directors' meeting showed that while we do a good job of hiring women and
>minorities, few of them rise to the top. The Directors suspect that our climate may not be
>supportive and want information on it. Please prepare a presentation for the next meeting. You'll
>have 15 minutes.

Making a presentation to the company's Board of Directors can really help your career. But preparing a good presentation and report will take time. You can look at exit reports filed by Human Resources when people leave the company, but you'll also need to interview people—lots of people. And you're already working 60 hours a week on three major projects, one of which is behind schedule. Can one of the projects wait? Can someone else take one of the projects? Can you get some help? Should you do just enough to get by? Ask your boss for advice—in a way that makes you look like a committed employee, not a slacker.

13.19 Asking for Volunteers

You have an executive position with one of the major employers in town. (Pick a business, nonprofit organization, or government office you know something about.) Two years ago, your company "adopted" a local school. You've provided computers and paid for Internet access; a small number of workers have signed up to be mentors. Today you get a call from the school's principal, a friend of yours: "I'd like to talk to you about the mentoring program. You're providing some mentors, and we're grateful for them, but we need 10 times that number."

(You wince. This program has not been one of your successes.) "I know that part of the program hasn't worked out as well as we hoped it would. But people are really busy here. Not all that many people have two or three hours a week to spend with a kid."

"So you think the time it takes is really the problem."

(Maybe your friend will appreciate that you can't force people to do this.) "Pretty much."

"Do you think people would be willing to be mentors if we could find a way for it to take less time?"

"Maybe." (You sense that a hook is coming, and you're wary.)

"Your people spend a lot of time on e-mail, don't they?"

"Yes. Two to three hours a day, for most of them."

"What if we created a new mentoring structure, where people just e-mailed their mentees instead of meeting with them? That way they could still provide advice and support, but they could do it at any time of the day. And it wouldn't have to take long."

(This sounds interesting.) "So people would just have e-mail conversations. That would be a lot easier, and we'd get more people. But can they really have a relationship if they don't meet the kids?"

"Maybe we could have a picnic or go to a game a couple of times a year so people could meet face-to-face."

"And all the kids have computers?"

"Not necessarily at home. But they all have access to e-mail at school. Writing e-mail to professionals will also give them more practice and more confidence. People like to get e-mail."

"Not when they get 200 messages a day, they don't."

"Well, our kids aren't in that category. What do you say?"

"I think it will work. Let's try it."

"Great. Just send me a list of the people who are willing to do this, and we'll match them up with the kids. We'd like to get this started as soon as possible."

Write an e-mail message to all employees asking them to volunteer.

13.20 Persuading People to Register for a Workshop

Your state agency is switching from WordPerfect to Word and has contracted with an outside vendor to provide a class on "Making the Transition from WordPerfect to Word." The fee is $195 a person for 9 or fewer people, and $99 a person for 10 or more. Right now, you have 7 people signed up. Your agency will save money if 3 more people sign up. The session is a week from Wednesday; people need to sign up by next Monday. To sign up, people just need to tell you.

Write a catchy e-mail message designed to persuade at least three more people to register.

Polishing Your Prose

Making Nouns and Pronouns Agree

Pronouns must agree with the nouns to which they refer in two ways: (1) person and (2) number—singular or plural.

	Singular	Plural
First-person	I, my, mine, me, myself	we, our, us, ourselves
Second-person	you, your, yourself	you, your, our, ours, yourselves
Third-person	he, she, it, him, her, his, hers	they, their, them, themselves

Incorrect: In my internship, I learned that you have to manage your time wisely.

Correct: In my internship, I learned to manage my time wisely.

Incorrect: The sales team reached their goal.

Correct: The sales team reached its goal.

U.S. usage treats company names and the words *company* and *government* as singular nouns. In Great Britain and those countries using the British System, these nouns are plural and require plural pronouns:

Correct (U.S.): Nationwide Insurance trains its agents well.

Correct (U.K.): Lloyds of London train their agents well.

Exercises

Correct any noun-pronoun agreement errors, following U.S. style. Note that some sentences do not contain errors.

1. The mayor should give themselves credit for doing a good job.

2. I'm going to get our employee identification card renewed today.

3. Most new employees find that they need to learn a new culture.

4. The research team reached their conclusions after four months of studying the market.

5. The union votes today on whether they will go on strike.

6. Each employee should make sure their personnel information is up-to-date.

7. One of the features of my corporate culture is a willingness to share ideas.

8. Xerox makes sure their sales staff keeps their knowledge of the product line current.

9. Every employee is interested in improving their technical skills.

10. Sotheby's puts its reputation to the test with each auction, regardless of where that auction occurs.

Check your answers to the odd-numbered exercises at the back of the book.

BComm Skill Booster

To apply the concepts in this module, complete lessons 15, 17, 56, 57, and 58 on subject lines and e-mail. You can access the BComm Skill Booster through the text Web site at **www.mhhe.com/bcs2e.**

Cases for Communicators

A Thumbs Down to Pop-Ups

In 2001–02, pop-up advertisements—messages or graphics in small windows that appear on top of the main screen in your browser—became widespread.

However, an iVillage survey found that 92.5% of iVillage's users viewed pop-up advertisements as the most frustrating feature of the World Wide Web. Therefore iVillage announced that it would eliminate all pop-up advertisements from its network of Web sites by the end of the third quarter of 2002. According to Nancy Evans, iVillage's Co-Founder and Editor-in-Chief, "At iVillage we have based everything from our site design and functionality and now to our advertising formats on what we know women want and, more importantly, what works for them."

This is great news for iVillage users, but advertisers may be less enthusiastic. iVillage is currently developing and testing alternate ad formats. The company has already begun working with advertisers to convert their pop-up ads to one of these new formats or to another traditional, but less intrusive, ad format, such as the pop-under ad.

Source: Tobi Elkin, "iVillage Drops Pop-Up Ads, Cites User Complaints for Move," *Ad Age,* July 30, 2002. Accessed on AdAge.com on August 2, 2002; "iVillage To Eliminate Pop-Up Advertising; Proprietary Research Shows Pop-Up Ads as Chief Frustration of Using the Internet Among Women," IVillage News Release, July 29, 2002. Accessed on the iVillage.com on August 7, 2002.

Individual Activity

As an assistant in iVillage's marketing department, you've been asked to prepare a message which can be e-mailed to all registered members of iVillage to tell them about the change in policy. However, a small number of pop-up ads, mostly research and subscription offers, will remain on the site, as will other types of advertisements, including pop-under ads.

You know you must capture the reader's attention early with a good subject line and first paragraph.

As you plan your e-mail, ask yourself the following questions:

- What should the subject line convey?
- How should I organize this positive message?
- Should I include reader benefits in my message?

As you evaluate your draft, consider these questions:

- Is my subject line specific, concise, and catchy?
- Did I organize this message using the pattern for positive messages illustrated below?

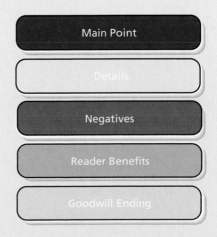

Main Point

Details

Negatives

Reader Benefits

Goodwill Ending

- Did I use PAIBOC (**P**urpose, **A**udience, **I**nformation, **B**enefits, **O**bjections, **C**ontext) to help me write a positive message?
- Did I successfully create you-attitude in this message?

Be sure to check your grammar and proofread the message by eye as well as by spell check!

Group Activity

You want advertisers to continue advertising with iVillage and work with iVillage consultants to develop new formats for their promotional messages.

You have heard from your fellow advertising reps that some companies are already grumbling about the proposed change, while others seem receptive to the idea. Fortunately, the Statistics Department has provided you with two pages of supporting data that you can enclose with your letter. The first page provides solid statistical support for iVillage's decision to eliminate pop-up ads; the second includes graphics that illustrate the efficacy of the new advertising formats developed by the company.

Before you begin your letter, discuss the following issues with your colleagues:

- What should the subject line convey?
- Which persuasive strategy, direct request or problem solving, is appropriate in this situation?
- Which of the following patterns is better?
- What types of possible objections or responses are expected?
- What benefits, if any, could be highlighted?

Use your answers to these questions to outline your letter. Then work together with your group to craft the language for this message.

As you draft the letter, ask yourself these questions:

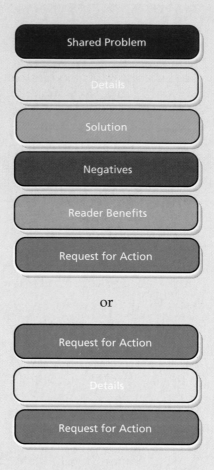

1. Did I include information to negate possible objections or responses to the message?
2. Did I follow the correct organization for the persuasive strategy I am using?
3. Did I offer a reason for the company to respond promptly?
4. Did I use PAIBOC (**P**urpose, **A**udience, **I**nformation, **B**enefits, **O**bjections, **C**ontext) to help me write a persuasive message?
5. Did I successfully create you-attitude in this letter?

Advertising is an important revenue-generating mechanism for iVillage, so be sure to think carefully about the tone of the letter. Remember, these advertisers are your customers!

Unit Four

Polishing Your Writing

Module 14

Editing for Grammar and Punctuation

Start by asking these questions:

- What grammatical errors do I need to be able to fix?
- How can I fix sentence errors?
- Should I put a comma every place I'd take a breath?
- What punctuation should I use inside sentences?
- What do I use when I quote sources?
- How should I write numbers and dates?
- How do I mark errors I find in proofreading?

With the possible exception of spelling, grammar is the aspect of writing that writers seem to find most troublesome. Faulty grammar is often what executives are objecting to when they complain that college graduates or MBAs "can't write."

The modules in this unit gather advice about grammar, punctuation, words, and sentence and paragraph revision. Many of these topics are also treated in the Polishing Your Prose sections at the end of each module. For a list with page numbers, see the inside front cover.

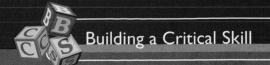

Creating a Professional Image, 2

Grammar and mechanics present a paradox. On the one hand, grammar and punctuation are the least important part of any message: The ideas and their arrangement matter far more.

On the other hand, grammatical "errors" can cause the audience to ignore your ideas. Errors also create a negative image of the writer. Professor Larry Beason found that business people judged the authors of errors to be not only poor writers but also poor business people. Negative judgments included the following:

Careless and hasty

Uncaring (about reader or message)

Problems with thinking and logic

Not a detail person—what will you do with numbers?

Poor oral communicator

Uneducated.

So grammar and punctuation can be the most important part of your message.

Occasionally, errors in grammar and punctuation hide the writer's meaning. More often, it's possible to figure out what the writer probably meant, but the mistake still sends the wrong message (and can be an excuse for a hostile reader or an opposing attorney).

Don't try to fix errors in your first and second drafts. The brain can't attend both to big ideas and to sentence-level concerns at the same time. But do save time to check your almost-final draft to eliminate any errors in grammar, punctuation, and word choice.

Most writers make a small number of grammatical errors repeatedly. Most readers care deeply about only a few grammatical points. Keep track of the feedback you get (from your instructors now, from your supervisors later) and put your energy into correcting the errors that bother the people who read what you write. A command of standard grammar will help you build the credible, professional image you want to create with everything you write.

Source: Larry Beason, "Language Errors in Business Documents: A Study of Business People's Reactions to Error," Southwest Federation of Administrative Disciplines Convention, Dallas, TX, March 4–7, 1998.

What grammatical errors do I need to be able to fix?

Learn how to fix these six errors.

Good writers can edit to achieve subject-verb and noun-pronoun agreement, to use the right case for pronouns, to avoid dangling and misplaced modifiers, and to correct predication errors.

Agreement

Subjects and verbs agree when they are both singular or both plural.

Incorrect: The accountants who conducted the audit was recommended highly.

Correct: The accountants who conducted the audit were recommended highly.

Subject-verb agreement errors often occur when other words come between the subject and the verb. Edit your draft by finding the subject and the verb of each sentence.

U.S. usage treats company names and the words *company* and *government* as singular nouns. British usage treats them as plural:

Correct (U.S.):   State Farm Insurance trains its agents well.

Correct (Great   Lloyds of London train their agents well.
Britain):

Use a plural verb when two or more singular subjects are joined by *and*.

Correct: Larry McGreevy and I are planning to visit the client.

Use a singular verb when two or more singular subjects are joined by *or, nor,* or *but*.

Correct: Either the shipping clerk or the superintendent has to sign the order.

When the sentence begins with *Here* or *There,* make the verb agree with the subject that follows the verb.

Correct: Here is the booklet you asked for.

Correct: There are the blueprints I wanted.

Note that some words that end in *s* are considered to be singular and require singular verbs.

Correct: A series of meetings is planned.

When a situation doesn't seem to fit the rules, or when following a rule produces an awkward sentence, revise the sentence to avoid the problem.

Problematic: The Plant Manager in addition to the sales representative (was, were?) pleased with the new system.

Better: The Plant Manager and the sales representative were pleased with the new system.

Problematic: None of us (is, are?) perfect.

Better: All of us have faults.

Errors in **noun-pronoun agreement** occur if a pronoun is of a different number or person than the word it refers to.

Incorrect: All drivers of leased automobiles are billed $100 if damages to his automobile are caused by a collision.

Correct: All drivers of leased automobiles are billed $100 if damages to their automobiles are caused by collisions.

Incorrect: A manager has only yourself to blame if things go wrong.

Correct: As a manager, you have only yourself to blame if things go wrong.

The following words require a singular pronoun:

everybody	everyone	nobody
each	neither	a person
either		

Correct: Everyone should bring his or her copy of the manual to the next session on changes in the law.

If the pronoun pairs necessary to avoid sexism seem cumbersome, avoid the terms in this list. Instead, use words that take plural pronouns or use second-person *you.*

Each pronoun must refer to a specific word. If a pronoun does not refer to a specific term, add a word to correct the error.

Incorrect: We will open three new stores in the suburbs. This will bring us closer to our customers.

Correct: We will open three new stores in the suburbs. This strategy will bring us closer to our customers.

Hint: Make sure *this* and *it* refer to a specific noun in the previous sentence. If either refers to an idea, add a noun ("this strategy") to make the sentence grammatically correct.

Use *who* and *whom* to refer to people and *which* to refer to objects. *That* can refer to anything: people, animals, organizations, and objects.

Correct: The new Executive Director, who moved here from Boston, is already making friends.

Correct: The audit, which we completed yesterday, shows that the original numbers are incorrect.

Correct: This confirms the price that I quoted you this morning.

Case

Case refers to the grammatical role a noun or pronoun plays in a sentence. Figure 14.1 identifies the case of each personal pronoun.

Use **nominative** pronouns for the **subject** of a clause.

Correct: Shannon Weaver and I talked to the customer, who was interested in learning more about integrated software.

Figure 14.1

The Case of the Personal Pronoun

	Nominative (subject of clause)	Possessive	Objective	Reflexive/ intensive
Singular				
1st person	I	my, mine	me	myself
2nd person	you	your, yours	you	yourself
3rd person	he/she/it	his/her(s)/ its	him/her/it	himself/herself/itself
	one/who	one's/whose	one/whom	oneself/(no form)
Plural				
1st person	we	our, ours	us	ourselves
2nd person	you	your, yours	you	yourselves
3rd person	they	their, theirs	them	themselves

Use **possessive** pronouns to show who or what something belongs to.

Correct: Microsoft Office will exactly meet her needs.

Use **objective** pronouns as **objects** of verbs or prepositions.

Correct: When you send in the quote, thank her for the courtesy she showed Shannon and me.

Hint: Use *whom* when *him* would fit grammatically in the same place in your sentence.

I am writing this letter to (who/whom?) it may concern.

I am writing this letter to him.

Whom is correct.

Have we decided (who, whom?) will take notes?

Have we decided he will take notes?

Who is correct.

Use **reflexive** and **intensive** pronouns (the form with *self* or *selves*) to refer to or emphasize a noun or pronoun that has already appeared in the sentence.

Correct: I nominated myself.

Do not use reflexive pronouns as subjects of clauses or as objects of verbs or propositions.

Incorrect: Elaine and myself will follow up on this order.

Correct: Elaine and I will follow up on this order.

Incorrect: He gave the order to Dan and myself.

Correct: He gave the order to Dan and me.

Note that the first-person pronoun comes after names or pronouns that refer to other people.

Dangling Modifier

Modifiers are words or phrases that give more information about the subject, verb, or object in a clause. A modifier **dangles** when the word it modifies is not actually in the sentence. The solution is to reword the modifier so that it is grammatically correct.

Incorrect: Confirming our conversation, the truck will leave Monday.
[The speaker is doing the confirming. But the speaker isn't in the sentence.]

Incorrect: At the age of eight, I began teaching my children about American business.
[This sentence says that the author was eight when he or she had children who could understand business.]

Correct a dangling modifier in one of these ways:

- Recast the modifier as a subordinate clause.

Correct: As I told you, the truck will leave Monday.

Correct: When they were eight, I began teaching my children about American business.

- Revise the main clause so its subject or object can be modified by the now-dangling phrase.

Correct: Confirming our conversation, I have scheduled the truck to leave Monday.

Correct: At the age of eight, my children began learning about American business.

Hint: Whenever you use a verb or adjective that ends in *-ing*, make sure it modifies the grammatical subject of your sentence. If it doesn't, reword the sentence.

Misplaced Modifier

A **misplaced modifier** appears to modify another element of the sentence than the writer intended.

Incorrect: Customers who complain often alert us to changes we need to make.
[Does the sentence mean that customers must complain frequently to teach us something? Or is the meaning that frequently we learn from complaints?]

Correct a misplaced modifier by moving it closer to the word it modifies or by adding punctuation to clarify your meaning. If a modifier modifies the whole sentence, use it as an introductory phrase or clause; follow it with a comma.

Correct: Often, customers who complain alert us to changes we need to make.

Parallel Structure

Items in a series or list must have the same grammatical structure.

Not parallel: In the second month of your internship, you will
1. Learn how to resolve customers' complaints.
2. Supervision of desk staff.
3. Interns will help plan store displays.

Parallel: In the second month of your internship, you will
1. Learn how to resolve customers' complaints.
2. Supervise desk staff.
3. Plan store displays.

Also parallel: Duties in the second month of your internship include resolving customers' complaints, supervising desk staff, and planning store displays.

Hint: When you have two or three items in a list (whether the list is horizontal or vertical) make sure the items are in the same grammatical form. Put lists vertically to make them easier to see.

Predication Errors

The predicate of a sentence must fit grammatically and logically with the subject.

In sentences using *is* and other linking verbs, the complement must be a noun, an adjective, or a noun clause.

Incorrect: The reason for this change is because the SEC now requires fuller disclosure.

Correct: The reason for this change is that the SEC now requires fuller disclosure.

Make sure that the verb describes the action done by or done to the subject.

Incorrect: Our goals should begin immediately.

Correct: Implementing our goals should begin immediately.

How can I fix sentence errors?

Learn to recognize main clauses.

A **sentence** contains at least one main clause. A **main clause** is a complete statement. A **subordinate** or **dependent clause** contains both a subject and verb but is not a complete statement and cannot stand by itself. A phrase is a group of words that does not contain both a subject and a verb.

Main Clauses

Your order will arrive Thursday.

He dreaded talking to his supplier.

I plan to enroll for summer school classes.

Subordinate Clauses

if you place your order by Monday

because he was afraid the product would be out of stock

although I need to have a job

Phrases

With our current schedule

As a result

After talking to my advisor

A clause with one of the following words will be subordinate:

after	if
although, though	when, whenever
because, since	while, as
before, until	

Using the correct punctuation will enable you to avoid four major sentence errors: comma splices, run-on sentences, fused sentences, and sentence fragments.

Comma Splices

A **comma splice** or **comma fault** occurs when two main clauses are joined only by a comma (instead of by a comma and a coordinating conjunction).

Incorrect: The contest will start in June, the date has not been set.

Correct a comma splice in one of the following ways:

- If the ideas are closely related, use a semicolon rather than a comma. If they aren't closely related, start a new sentence.

Correct: The contest will start in June; the exact date has not been set.

- Add a coordinating conjunction.

Correct: The contest will start in June, but the exact date has not been set.

- Subordinate one of the clauses.

Correct: Although the contest will start in June, the date has not been set.

Remember that you cannot use just a comma with the following transitions.

however	nevertheless
therefore	moreover

Instead, use a semicolon to separate the clauses or start a new sentence.

Incorrect: Computerized grammar checkers do not catch every error, however, they may be useful as a first check before an editor reads the material.

Correct: Computerized grammar checkers do not catch every error; however, they may be useful as a first check before an editor reads the material.

Run-On Sentences

A **run-on sentence** strings together several main clauses using *and, but, or, so,* and *for.* Run-on sentences and comma splices are "mirror faults." A comma splice uses *only* the comma and omits the coordinating conjunction, while a run-on sentence uses *only* the conjunction and omits the comma. Correct a short run-on sentence by adding a comma. Separate a long run-on sentence into two or more sentences. Consider subordinating one or more of the clauses.

Incorrect: We will end up with a much smaller markup but they use a lot of this material so the volume would be high so try to sell them on fast delivery and tell them our quality is very high.

Correct: Although we will end up with a much smaller markup, volume would be high since they use a lot of this material. Try to sell them on fast delivery and high quality.

Fused Sentences

A **fused sentence** results when two or more sentences are *fused* or joined with neither punctuation nor conjunctions. To fix the error, add either punctuation or a conjunction.

Incorrect: The advantages of Intranets are clear the challenge is persuading employees to share information.

Correct: The advantages of Intranets are clear; the challenge is persuading employees to share information.

Also correct: Although the advantages of Intranets are clear, the challenge is persuading employees to share information.

Sentence Fragments

In a **sentence fragment,** a group of words that is not a complete sentence is punctuated as if it were a complete sentence. Sentence fragments often occur when a writer thinks of additional detail that the reader needs. Fragments are acceptable in résumés and sales letters, but they're rarely acceptable in other business documents.

Incorrect: Observing these people, I have learned two things about the program. The time it takes. The rewards it brings.

To fix a sentence fragment, either add whatever parts of the sentence are missing or incorporate the fragment into the sentence before it or after it.

Correct: Observing these people, I have learned that the program is time-consuming but rewarding.

Remember that clauses with the following words are not complete sentences. Join them to a main clause.

after	if
although, though	when, whenever
because, since	while, as
before, until	

Incorrect: We need to buy a new computer system. Because our current system is obsolete.

Correct: We need to buy a new computer system because our current system is obsolete.

Should I put a comma every place I'd take a breath?

No! Commas are not breaths.

Some people have been told to put commas where they'd take breaths. That's bad advice. How often you'd take a breath depends on how big your lung capacity is, how fast and how loud you're speaking, and the emphasis you want. Commas aren't breaths. Instead, like other punctuation, they're road signs.

Punctuation marks are road signs to help readers predict what comes next (see Figure 14.2).

When you move from the subject to the verb, you're going in a straight line; no comma is needed. When you end an introductory phrase or clause, the comma tells readers the introduction is over and you're turning to the main clause. When words interrupt the main clause, like this, commas tell the reader when to turn off the main clause for a short side route and when to return.

What punctuation should I use inside sentences?

Use punctuation to make your meaning clear to your reader.

The good business and administrative writer knows how to use the following punctuation marks: apostrophes, colons, commas, dashes, hyphens, parentheses, periods, and semicolons.

Apostrophe

1. Use an apostrophe in a contraction to indicate that a letter has been omitted.

   We're trying to renegotiate the contract.

   The '90s were years of restructuring for our company.

2. To indicate possession, add an apostrophe and an *s* to the word.

   The corporation's home office is in Houston, Texas.

   Apostrophes to indicate possession are especially essential when one noun in a comparison is omitted.

   This year's sales will be higher than last year's.

Site *to* See

Go to
www.nuff.ox.ac.uk/users/
martin/APOST/Apostrop.htm

The Home for Abused Apostrophes offers visual proof of apostrophe abuse.

Mark	Tells the Reader
Period	We're stopping.
Semicolon	What comes next is closely related to what I just said.
Colon	What comes next is an example of what I just said.
Dash	What comes next is a dramatic example of or a shift from what I just said.
Comma	What comes next is a slight turn, but we're going in the same basic direction.

Figure 14.2
What Punctuation Tells the Reader

Treasure the poor apostrophe.

When a word already ends in an *s*, add only an apostrophe to make it possessive.

> The meeting will be held at New Orleans' convention center.

With many terms, the placement of the apostrophe indicates whether the noun is singular or plural.

Incorrect: The program should increase the participant's knowledge. [Implies that only one participant is in the program.]

Correct: The program should increase the participants' knowledge. [Many participants are in the program.]

Hint: Use *of* in the sentence to see where the apostrophe goes.

> The figures of last year = last year's figures

> The needs of our customers = our customers' needs

Possessive pronouns (e.g., *his, ours*) usually do not have apostrophes. The only exception is *one's.*

> The company needs the goodwill of its stockholders.

> His promotion was announced yesterday.

> One's greatest asset is the willingness to work hard.

3. Use an apostrophe to make plurals that could be confused for other words.

> I earned A's in all my business courses.

However, other plurals do not use apostrophes.

Colon

1. Use a colon to separate a main clause and a list that explains the last element in the clause. The items in the list are specific examples of the word that appears immediately before the colon.

Please order the following supplies:

Printer cartridges

Computer paper (20-lb. white bond)

Bond paper (25-lb., white, 25% cotton)

Company letterhead

Company envelopes.

When the list is presented vertically, capitalize the first letter of each item in the list. When the list is run in with the sentence, you don't need to capitalize the first letter after the colon.

Please order the following supplies: printer cartridges, computer paper (20-lb. white bond), bond paper (25-lb., white, 25% cotton), company letterhead, and company envelopes.

Do not use a colon when the list is grammatically part of the main clause.

Incorrect: The rooms will have coordinated decors in natural colors such as: eggplant, moss, and mushroom.

Correct: The rooms will have coordinated decors in natural colors such as eggplant, moss, and mushroom.

Correct: The rooms will have coordinated decors in a variety of natural colors: eggplant, moss, and mushroom.

If the list is presented vertically, some authorities suggest introducing the list with a colon even though the words preceding the colon are not a complete sentence.

2. Use a colon to join two independent clauses when the second clause explains or restates the first clause.

> Selling is simple: Give people the service they need, and they'll come back with more orders.

Comma

1. Use commas to separate the main clause from an introductory clause, the reader's name, or words that interrupt the main clause. Note that commas both precede and follow the interrupting information.

> R. J. Garcia, the new Sales Manager, comes to us from the Des Moines office.

A **nonessential clause** gives extra information that is not needed to identify the noun it modifies. Because nonessential clauses give extra information, they need extra commas.

Instant **Replay**

Sentence Fragments

In a **sentence fragment,** a group of words that is not a complete sentence is punctuated as if it were a complete sentence.

Sue Decker, who wants to advance in the organization, has signed up for the company training program in sales techniques.

Do not use commas to set off information that restricts the meaning of a noun or pronoun. **Essential clauses** give essential, not extra, information.

Anyone ☐ who wants to advance in the organization ☐ should take advantage of on-the-job training.

Do not use commas to separate the subject from the verb, even if you would take a breath after a long subject.

Incorrect:	Laws requiring anyone collecting $5,000 or more on behalf of another person to be bonded, apply to schools and private individuals as well to charitable groups and professional fund-raisers.
Correct:	Laws requiring anyone collecting $5,000 or more on behalf of another person to be bonded ☐ apply to schools and private individuals as well to charitable groups and professional fund-raisers.

2. Use a comma after the first clause in a compound sentence if the clauses are long or if they have different subjects.

This policy eliminates all sick leave credit of the employee at the time of retirement, and payment will be made only once to any individual.

Do not use commas to join independent clauses without a conjunction. Doing so produces comma splices.

3. Use commas to separate items in a series. Using a comma before the *and* or *or* is not required by some authorities, but using a comma always adds clarity. The comma is essential if any of the items in the series themselves contain the word *and.*

The company pays the full cost of hospitalization insurance for eligible employees, spouses, and unmarried dependent children under age 23.

Dash

Use dashes to emphasize a break in thought.

Ryertex comes in 30 grades—each with a special use.

To type a dash, use two hyphens with no space before or after.

Hyphen

1. Use a hyphen to indicate that a word has been divided between two lines.

Attach the original receipts for lodging, transportation, and registration fees.

Divide words at syllable breaks. If you aren't sure where the syllables divide, look up the word in a dictionary. When a word has several syllables, divide it after a vowel or between two consonants. Don't divide

FYI

A supervisor at a nuclear power plant ordered rods of radioactive material cut into "10 foot long lengths"; he got 10 pieces, each a foot long, instead of the 10-foot lengths required. The loss caused by the missing hyphen was so great it was classified as secret by the federal government.

Source: William E. Blundell, "Confused, Overstuffed Corporate Writing Often Costs Firms Much Time—and Money," *The Wall Street Journal,* August 21, 1980, 21.

words of one syllable (e.g., *used*); don't divide a two-syllable word if one of the syllables is only one letter long (e.g., *acre*).

2. Use hyphens to join two or more words used as a single adjective.

> Order five 10- or 12-foot lengths.

> The computer-prepared Income and Expense statements will be ready next Friday.

The hyphen prevents misreading. In the first example, five lengths are needed, not lengths of 5, 10, or 12 feet. In the second example, without the hyphen, the reader might think that *computer* was the subject and *prepared* was the verb.

Parentheses

1. Use parentheses to set off words, phrases, or sentences used to explain or comment on the main idea.

> For the thinnest Ryertex (.015″) only a single layer of the base material may be used, while the thickest (10″) may contain over 600 greatly compressed layers of fabric or paper. By varying the fabric used (cotton, asbestos, glass, or nylon) or the type of paper, and by changing the kind of resin (phenolic, melamine, silicone, or epoxy), we can produce 30 different grades.

Any additional punctuation goes outside the second parenthesis when the punctuation applies to the whole sentence. It goes inside when it applies only to the words in the parentheses.

> Please check the invoice to see if credit should be issued. (A copy of the invoice is attached.)

2. Use parentheses for the second of two numbers presented both in words and in figures.

> Construction must be completed within two (2) years of the date of the contract.

Period

1. Use a period at the end of a sentence.

2. Use a period after some abbreviations. When a period replaces a person's name, leave one space after the period before the next word. In other abbreviations, no space is necessary.

> R. J. Tebeaux has been named Vice President for Marketing.

> The U.S. division plans to hire 300 new M.B.A.s in the next year.

The tendency is to reduce the use of punctuation. It would also be correct to write

> The US division plans to hire 300 new MBAs in the next year. Use the pattern your organization prefers.

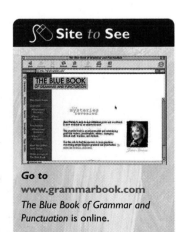

Site *to* See

THE BLUE BOOK
OF GRAMMAR AND PUNCTUATION

Go to
www.grammarbook.com
The Blue Book of Grammar and Punctuation is online.

Semicolon

1. Use semicolons to join two independent clauses when they are closely related.

> We'll do our best to fill your order promptly; however, we cannot guarantee a delivery date.

Using a semicolon suggests that the two ideas are very closely connected. Using a period and a new sentence is also correct but implies nothing about how closely related the two sentences are.

2. Use semicolons to separate items in a series when the items themselves contain commas.

> The final choices for the new plant are El Paso, Texas; Albuquerque, New Mexico; Salt Lake City, Utah; Eureka, California; and Eugene, Oregon.

> Hospital benefits are also provided for certain services such as diagnostic admissions directed toward a definite disease or injury; normal maternity delivery, Caesarean-section delivery, or complications of pregnancy; and in-patient admissions for dental procedures necessary to safeguard the patient's life or health.

Hint: A semicolon could be replaced by a period and a capital letter. It has a sentence on both sides.

What do I use when I quote sources?

Quotation marks, square brackets, ellipses, and underlining or italics.

Quotation marks, square brackets, ellipses, and either underlining or italics are necessary when you use quoted material.

Quotation Marks

1. Use quotation marks around the names of brochures, pamphlets, and magazine articles.

> Enclosed are 30 copies of our pamphlet "Saving Energy."

> You'll find articles like "How to Improve Your Golf Game" and "Can You Keep Your Eye on the Ball?" in every issue.

In U.S. punctuation, periods and commas go inside quotation marks. Colons and semicolons go outside. Question marks go inside if they are part of the material being quoted.

2. Use quotation marks around words to indicate that you think the term is misleading.

> These "pro-business" policies actually increase corporate taxes.

3. Use quotation marks around words that you are discussing as words.

>   Forty percent of the respondents answered "yes" to the first question.

>   Use "Ms." as a courtesy title for a woman unless you know she prefers another title.

It is also acceptable to underline or italicize words instead of using quotation marks. Choose one method and use it consistently.

4. Use quotation marks around words or sentences that you quote from someone else.

>   "The Fog Index," says its inventor, Robert Gunning, is "an effective warning system against drifting into needless complexity."

Square Brackets

Use square brackets to add your own additions to or changes in quoted material.

Senator Smith's statement: "These measures will increase the deficit."

Your use of Smith's statement: According to Senator Smith, "These measures [in the new tax bill] will increase the deficit."

The square brackets show that Smith did not say these words; you add them to make the quote make sense in your document.

Ellipses

Ellipses are spaced dots. In typing, use three spaced periods for an ellipsis. When an ellipsis comes at the end of a sentence, use a dot immediately after the last letter of the sentence for a period. Then add another three spaced dots.

1. Use ellipses to indicate that one or more words have been omitted in the middle of quoted material. You do not need ellipses at the beginning or end of a quote.

>   *The Wall Street Journal* notes that Japanese magazines and newspapers include advertisements for a "$2.1 million home in New York's posh Riverdale section . . . 185 acres of farmland [and] . . . luxury condos on Manhattan's Upper East Side."

2. In advertising and direct mail, use ellipses to imply the pace of spoken comments.

>   If you've ever wanted to live on a tropical island . . . cruise to the Bahamas . . . or live in a castle in Spain . . .

>   . . . you can make your dreams come true with Vacations Extraordinaire.

Underlining and Italics

1. Underline or italicize the names of newspapers, magazines, and books.

   The Wall Street Journal   *The Wall Street Journal*

   Fortune   *Fortune*

   The Wealth of Nations   *The Wealth of Nations*

   Titles of brochures and pamphlets are put in quotation marks.

2. Underline or italicize words to emphasize them.

   Here's a bulletin that gives you, in handy chart form, *workable data* on over 50 different types of tubing and pipe.

   You may also use boldface to emphasize words. Bolding is better than either underlining or italics because it is easier to read.

How should I write numbers and dates?

Usually, spell out numbers under 10 and at the beginning of sentences.

Spell out **numbers** from one to nine. Use figures for numbers 10 and over in most cases. Always use figures for amounts of money.

Spell out any number that appears at the beginning of a sentence. If spelling it out is impractical, revise the sentence so that it does not begin with a number.

   Fifty students filled out the survey.

   In 2002, euro notes and coins entered circulation.

When two numbers referring to different nouns follow each other, use words for the smaller number and figures for the larger number.

In **dates,** use figures for the day and year. The month is normally spelled out. Be sure to spell out the month in international business communication. U.S. usage puts the month first, so that *1/10/04* means *January 10, 2004.* European usage puts the day first, so that *1/10/04* means *October 1, 2004.* Modern punctuation uses a comma before the year only when you give both the month and the day of the month:

   May 1, 2005

but

Summers 2001–04

August 2003

Fall 2006

No punctuation is needed in military or European usage, which puts the day of the month first: 13 July 2005. Do not space before or after the slash used to separate parts of the date: 10/03–5/04.
Use a hyphen to join inclusive dates.

March–August 2005 (**or write out:** March to August 2005)

'03–'04

1999–2004

Note that you do not need to repeat the century in the date that follows the hyphen: 2004–06. But do give the century when it changes: 1999–2001.

How do I mark errors I find in proofreading?

Use these standard proofreading symbols.

Use the proofreading symbols in Figure 14.3 to make corrections when you no longer have access to a computer. Figure 14.4 shows how the symbols can be used to correct a typed text.

✐	delete		[	move to left
⍅	insert a letter		]	move to right
⊍	start a new paragraph here		⊓	move up
(stet)	stet (leave as it was before the marked change)		⊔	move down
(tr) ⟋	transpose (reverse)		#	leave a space
(lc)	lower case (don't capitalize)		⌣	close up
≡	capitalize		‖	align vertically

Figure 14.3
Proofreading Symbols

Figure 14.4
Marked Text

We could cut our travel bill by reimbursing employees only
for the cost of a budget hotel or motel room.

A recent article from *The Wall Street Journal* suggests that
many low-cost hotles and motels are trying to appeal to
business travelers. chains that are actively competing for the business market include

Motel 6
Hampton Inns
Fairfield Inns
Econologde
Super 8

Comfort Inn
Travelodge.

To attract business travelers, some budget chains now offer
free local phone calls, free in-room movies, free continental
breakfasts, and free Computer hookups.

By staying in a budget hotel, the business travelers can
save at least $10 to $20 a night--often much more. For a
company whose employees travel frequently, the savings can
be considerable. Last year Megacorp reimbursed employees
for a total of 4,392 nights in hotels. If each employee had
stayed in a budget hotel, our expenses for travel would been
$44,000 to $88,000 lower. Budget hotels would not be
appropriate for sales meetings since they lack photocopying
facilities or meeting rooms. However, we could and should
use budget hotels and motels for ordinary on-the-road travel.

Assignments for Module 14

Questions for Comprehension

14.1 What words make clauses subordinate
and thus require more than a comma to
join clauses?

14.2 What is parallel structure? When should
you use it?

14.3 What is a sentence fragment? How do
you fix it?

14.4 Why is it better to fix errors in grammar
and punctuation only after you've revised
for content, organization, and style?

Questions for Critical Thinking

14.5 Consuela sees a lot of errors in the
writing of managers at her workplace. If
they don't know or don't care about
correctness, why should she?

14.6 After surveying readers in her workplace (problem 14.15 below), Camilla finds that most of them are not bothered by errors in grammar and punctuation. Does that mean that she doesn't need to fix surface errors?

14.7 Joe knows that his variety of English isn't the privileged variety, but he is afraid that using standard edited English will make him seem "uppity" to people in his home community. Should he try to use standard grammar and pronunciation? Why or why not?

Exercises and Problems

14.8 Making Subjects and Verbs Agree

Identify and correct the errors in the following sentences.

1. Contests are fun for employees and creates sales incentives.

2. Your health and the health of your family is very important to us.

3. Image type and resolution varies among clip art packages.

4. If there's any tickets left, they'll be $17 at the door.

5. I know from my business experience that good communication among people and departments are essential in running a successful corporation.

14.9 Using the Right Pronoun

Identify and correct the errors in the following sentences.

1. The first step toward getting out of debt is not to add any more to it. This means cutting up your old credit card.

2. The higher the position a person has, the more professional their image should be.

3. Employees which lack experience in dealing with people from other cultures could benefit from seminars in international business communication.

4. Chandra drew the graphs after her and I discussed the ideas for them.

5. Please give your revisions to Cindy, Tyrone, or myself by noon Friday.

14.10 Fixing Dangling and Misplaced Modifiers

Identify and correct the errors in the following sentences.

1. Originally a group of four, one member dropped out after the first meeting due to a death in the family.

2. Examining the data, it is apparent that most of our sales are to people on the northwest side of the city.

3. As a busy professional, we know that you will want to take advantage of this special offer.

4. Often documents end up in files that aren't especially good.

5. By making an early reservation, it will give us more time to coordinate our trucks to better serve your needs.

14.11 Creating Parallel Structure

Identify and correct the errors in the following sentences.

1. To narrow a Web search,
   - Put quotation marks around a phrase when you want an exact term.
   - Many search engines have wild cards (usually an asterisk) to find plurals and other forms of a word.
   - Reading the instructions on the search engine itself can teach you advanced search techniques.

2. Men drink more alcoholic beverages than women.

3. Each issue of *Hospice Care* has articles from four different perspectives: legislative, health care, hospice administrators, and inspirational authors.

4. The university is one of the largest employers in the community, brings in substantial business, and the cultural impact is also big.

5. These three tools can help competitive people be better negotiators.

   • Think win-win.

   • It's important to ask enough questions to find out the other person's priorities, rather than jumping on the first advantage you find.

   • Protect the other person's self-esteem.

These three questions can help cooperative people be better at negotiations.

   • Can you developing a specific alternative to use if negotiation fails?

   • Don't focus on the "bottom line." Spend time thinking about what you want and why you need it.

   • Saying "You'll have to do better than that because . . ." can help you resist the temptation to say "yes" too quickly.

14.12 Correcting Sentence Errors

Identify and correct the errors in the following sentences.

1. Members of the group are all experienced presenters, most have had little or no experience using PowerPoint.

2. Proofread the letter carefully and check for proper business format because errors undercut your ability to sell yourself so take advantage of your opportunity to make a good first impression.

3. Some documents need just one pass others need multiple revisions.

4. Entrepreneurs face two main obstacles. Limited cash. Lack of business experience.

5. The margin on pet supplies is very thin and the company can't make money selling just dog food and the real profit is in extras like neon-colored leashes, so you put the dog food in the back so people have to walk by everything else to get to it.

14.13 Providing Punctuation within Sentences

Provide the necessary punctuation in the following sentences. Note that not every box requires punctuation.

1. Office work☐☐ especially at your desk☐☐ can create back☐ shoulder☐ neck☐ or wrist strain.

2. I searched for ☐vacation☐ and ☐vacation planning☐ on Google and Alta Vista.

3. I suggest putting a bulletin board in the rear hallway☐ and posting all the interviewer☐s☐photos on it.

4. Analyzing audiences is the same for marketing and writing☐ you have to identify who the audiences are☐ understand how to motivate them☐ and choose the best channel to reach them.

5. The more you know about your audience☐☐who they are☐ what they buy☐where they shop☐☐the more relevant and effective you can make your ad.

6. The city already has five☐ two☐hundred ☐ bed hospitals.

7. Students run the whole organization☐ and are advised by a

Board of Directors from the community.

8. The company is working on three team☐related issues☐ interaction, leadership, and team size.

9. I would be interesting in working on the committee☐ however I have decided to do less community work so that I have more time to spend with my family.

10. ☐You can create your own future☐☐ says Frank Montaño☐ ☐You have to think about it☐ crystallize it in writing☐ and be willing to work at it☐ We teach a lot of goal☐setting and planning in our training sessions☐☐

14.14 Fixing Errors in Grammar and Punctuation

Identify and correct the errors in the following passages.

a. Company's are finding it to their advantage to cultivate their suppliers. Partnerships between a company and its suppliers can yield hefty payoffs for both company and supplier. One example is Bailey Controls, an Ohio headquartered company. Bailey make control systems for big factories. They treat suppliers almost like departments of their own company. When a Bailey employee passes a laser scanner over a bins bar code the supplier is instantly alerted to send more parts.

b. Entrepreneur Trip Hawkins appears in Japanese ads for the video game system his company designed. "It plugs into the future! he says in one ad, in a cameo spliced into shots of U.S kids playing the games. Hawkins is one of several US celebrities and business people whom plug products on Japanese TV."

c. Mid size firms employing between 100 and 1000 people represent only 4% of companies in the U.S.; but create 33% of all new jobs. One observer attributes their success to their being small enough to take advantage of economic opportunity's agilely, but big enough to have access to credit and to operate on a national or even international scale. The biggest hiring area for midsize company's is wholesale and retail sales (38% of jobs), construction (20% of jobs, manufacturing (19% of jobs), and services (18 of jobs).

14.15 Identifying Audience Concerns about Grammar

Most readers care passionately about only a few points of grammar. Survey one or more readers (including your boss, if you have a job) to find out which kinds of errors concern them. Use a separate copy of this survey for each reader.

Directions: Each of the following sentences contains some error. Please circle Y if the error bothers you a good bit; S if the error bothers you slightly; and N if you would not be bothered by the error (or perhaps even notice it).

Y S N 1. She brung her secretary with her.

Y S N 2. Him and Richard were the last ones hired.

Y S N 3. Wanted to tell you that the meeting will be November 10.

Y S N 4. Each representative should bring a list of their clients to the meeting.

Y S N 5. A team of people from CSEA, Human Services, and Animal Control are preparing the proposal.

Y S N   6. We cannot predict, how high the number of clients may rise.

Y S N   7. He treats his clients bad.

Y S N   8. She asked Darlene and I to give a presentation.

Y S N   9. Update the directory by reviewing each record in the database and note any discrepancies.

Y S N   10. He has went to a lot of trouble to meet our needs.

Y S N   11. She gave the report to Dan and myself.

Y S N   12. I was unable to complete the report. Because I had a very busy week.

Y S N   13. The benefits of an on-line directory are
     a. We will be able to keep records up-to-date;
     b. Access to the directory from any terminal with a modem in the county.
     c. Cost savings.

Y S N   14. By making an early reservation, it will give us more time to plan the session to meet your needs.

Y S N   15. She don't have no idea how to use the computer.

Y S N   16. The change will not effect our service to customers.

Y S N   17. Confirming our conversation, the truck will leave Monday.

Y S N   18. The sessions will begin January 4 we will pass around a sign-up sheet early in December.

Y S N   19. I will be unable to attend the meeting, however I will send someone else from my office.

Y S N   20. Its too soon to tell how many proposals we will receive.

Compare your responses with those of a small group of students.

- Which errors were most annoying to the largest number of readers?
- How much variation do you find in a single workplace? In a single type of business?

As Your Instructor Directs,
a. Present your findings to the class in a short group report.
b. Present your findings to the class in an oral presentation.

Polishing Your Prose

Matters on Which Experts Disagree

Any living language changes. New usages appear first in speaking. Here are five issues on which experts currently disagree:

1. Plural pronouns to refer to *everybody*, *everyone*, and *each*. Standard grammar says these words require singular pronouns: *his or her* rather than *their*.

2. Split infinitives. An infinitive is the form of a verb that contains *to: to understand*. An infinitive is **split** when another word separates the *to* from the rest of an infinitive: *to easily understand, to boldly go*. The most recent edition of the *Oxford English Dictionary* allows split infinitives. Purists disagree.

3. *Hopefully* to mean *I hope that. Hopefully* means "in a hopeful manner." However, a speaker who says "Hopefully, the rain will stop" is talking about the speaker's hope, not the rain's.

4. *Verbal* to mean *oral. Verbal* means "using words." Therefore, both writing and speaking are verbal communication. Nonverbal communication (for example, body language) does not use words.

5. Comma before *and.* In a series of three or more items, some experts require a comma after the next to last item (the item before the *and*); others don't.

Ask your instructor and your boss whether they are willing to accept the less formal usage. When you write to someone you don't know, use standard grammar and usage.

Exercises

Each of the following sentences illustrates informal usage. (a) Which would your instructor or your boss accept? (b) Rewrite each of the sentences using standard grammar and usage.

1. The schedule includes new product information, role plays with common selling situations and awards to the top sales people.

2. The board of directors expects the new strategic plan to quickly catch on with employees and their managers.

3. Prepare to make a brief verbal report on a challenging sales situation.

4. We can choose one of the following options for each laptop computer: a portable DVD drive, a portable CD-ROM drive or a portable inkjet printer.

5. Hopefully, we will have time to work through many of these situations in our role plays.

6. Each employee should make sure their offices are locked at the end of the day to prevent theft.

7. We'll feature verbal quotes from customers in our radio ads.

8. Mr. Lee, Mr. Quinn, and Ms. Leininger plan to thoroughly inspect our Raleigh shipping office on Thursday.

9. Hopefully, the Web page will be live so that we can access it during the meeting.

10. With such a vast selection of options for employee benefits, it's best that I explain them to you verbally.

Check your answers to the odd-numbered exercises at the end of the book.

BComm Skill Booster

To apply the concepts in this module, complete lesson 59 on proper punctuation. You can access the BComm Skill Booster through the text Web site at **www.mhhe.com/bcs2e**.

Module 15

Choosing the Right Word

Start by asking these questions:

- Does using the right word really matter?
- How do words get their meanings?
- Is it OK to use jargon?
- What words confuse some writers?

The best word depends on context: the situation, your purposes, your audience, and the words you have already used. As you choose words,

1. Use words that are accurate, appropriate, and familiar.
   Accurate words mean what you want to say.
   Appropriate words convey the attitudes you want and fit well with the other words in your document.
   Familiar words are easy to read and understand.
2. Use technical jargon only when it is essential and known to the reader. Eliminate business jargon.

Does using the right word really matter?

The right word helps you look good and get the response you want.

Using the right word is part of the way you demonstrate that you're part of a discourse community (◀ ▷ p. 31). Using simple words is part of the way you create a friendly image of yourself and your organization. Using words that are part of standard edited English helps you build credibility and demonstrate your professionalism.

Getting Your Meaning Across

When the words on the page don't say what you mean, the reader has to work harder to figure out your meaning. According to one report, "The western part of Ohio was transferred from Chicago to Cleveland."[1] In fact, Ohio did not move. Instead, a company moved responsibility for sales in western Ohio. Sometimes your audience can figure out what you mean. Sometimes, your meaning will be lost. Sometimes the wrong word can cause you to lose a lawsuit.

Denotation is a word's literal or dictionary meaning. Most common words in English have more than one denotation. The word *pound*, for example, means, or denotes, a unit of weight, a place where stray animals are kept, a unit of money in the British system, and the verb *to hit*. Coca-Cola spends an estimated $20 million a year to protect its brand names so that *Coke* will denote only that brand and not just any cola drink.

When two people use the same word to mean, or denote, different things, **bypassing** occurs. For example, negotiators for Amoco and for the Environmental Protection Agency (EPA) used *risk* differently. At Amoco, *risk* was an economic term dealing with efficiency; for the EPA, the term "was a four-letter word that meant political peril or health risk."[2] Progress was possible only when they agreed on a meaning.

Accurate denotations can make it easier to solve problems. In one production line with a high failure rate, the largest category of defects was *missed operations*. At first, the supervisor wondered if the people on the line were lazy or irresponsible. But some checking showed that several different problems were labeled *missed operations*: parts installed backwards, parts that had missing screws or fasteners, parts whose wires weren't connected. Each of these problems had different solutions. Using accurate words redefined the problem and enabled the production line both to improve quality and cut repair costs.[3]

Getting the Response You Want

Using the right word helps you shape the audience's response to what you say. **Connotation** means the emotional colorings or associations that accompany a word. A great many words carry connotations of approval or disapproval, disgust or delight. Words in the first column on the next page suggest approval; words in the second column suggest criticism.

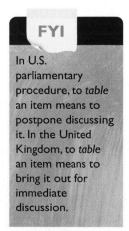

FYI

In U.S. parliamentary procedure, to *table* an item means to postpone discussing it. In the United Kingdom, to *table* an item means to bring it out for immediate discussion.

Positive Word	Negative Word
assume	guess
curious	nosy
negotiate	haggle
cautious	fearful
careful	nit-picking
firm	obstinate
flexible	wishy-washy

A supervisor can "tell the truth" about a subordinate's performance and yet write either a positive or a negative performance appraisal, based on the connotations of the words in the appraisal. Consider an employee who pays close attention to details. A positive appraisal might read, "Terry is a meticulous team member who takes care of details that others sometimes ignore." But the same behavior might be described negatively: "Terry is hung up on trivial details."

Advertisers carefully choose words with positive connotations. Expensive cars are never *used;* instead, they're *pre-owned, experienced,* or even *preloved.* An executive for Rolls-Royce once said, "A Rolls never, never breaks down. Of course," he added, with a twinkle in his eye, "there have been occasions when a car has failed to proceed."[4]

Words may also connote status. Both *salesperson* and *sales representative* are nonsexist job titles. But the first sounds like a clerk in a store; the second suggests someone selling important items to corporate customers.

Use familiar words that are in almost everyone's vocabulary. Try to use specific, concrete words. They're easier to understand and remember.[5] Short, common words sound friendlier.

Stuffy: Please give immediate attention to insure that the pages of all reports prepared for distribution are numbered sequentially and in a place of optimum visibility.[6]

Simple: Please put page numbers on all reports in the top outer corner.

Sales of prunes fell 14% from 1993 to 1999. To stop the slide, the California Prune Board decided to change the product's name (and its own). To do so required approval from the U.S. Food & Drug Administration, which regulates food labels. Now you can't buy prunes; you buy "dried plums."[11]

Prune

Dried Plum

Thinking Critically

Like many terms, critical thinking has more than one meaning.

In its most basic sense, critical thinking means using precise words and asking questions about what you read and hear.

Vague: This *Wall Street Journal* story discusses international business.

Precise: This *Wall Street Journal* story

> tells how Wal-Mart plans to expand into Europe.
>
> challenges the claim that a U.S. company needs a native partner to succeed in international business.
>
> gives examples of translation problems in international business.
>
> compares and contrasts accounting rules in Europe and in Asia.
>
> tells how three women have succeeded in international business.

Questions about a *Wall Street Journal* story might include

- What information is the story based on? Did the reporter interview people on both sides of the issue?
- When was the information collected? Is it still valid?
- Does evidence from other newspapers and magazines and from your own experience tend to confirm or contradict this story?
- How important is this story? Does it call for action on your part?

In a more advanced sense, critical thinking means the ability to identify problems, gather and evaluate evidence, identify and evaluate alternate solutions, and recommend or act on the best choice—while understanding that information is always incomplete and that new information might change one's judgment of the "best" choice.

In its most advanced sense, critical thinking means asking about and challenging fundamental assumptions. For example, stories in *The Wall Street Journal* generally assume that capitalism is good, that a major goal of any business is to make money, and that it's OK for top executives to make much more money than other workers.

Critical thinking in this most advanced sense is evident in the decision of a health maintenance organization (HMO) to give health care decisions back to doctors.

HMOs and other kinds of managed care are based on several assumptions, one of which is that doctors often order expensive but unnecessary tests and treatments. If tests and treatments had to be approved first, the theory went, many would be unnecessary and a great deal of money could be saved.

However, when the United Health Group examined its records, it found that it approved 9 out of 10 decisions. Eliminating the approval process will save about $100 million a year—far more than the cost of the tenth test or treatment that might not have been approved. In addition to saving a significant amount of money, the change will help to repair relations with doctors and patients, neither of whom liked having to get approval, and may have legal advantages. All these benefits came from questioning one of the basic assumptions on which the company—indeed the whole industry—was based.

Source: Carol Roever and Gerry Hines, "Teaching the Two C's Needed for Business Success: Critical Thinking and Creativity," Conference on Teaching Communication, The Ohio State University, July 30–31, 1999; and Milt Freudenheim, "Big H.M.O. to Give Decisions on Care Back to Doctors," *The New York Times*, November 9, 1999, 1.

The following list gives a few examples of short, simple alternatives.

Formal and Stuffy	Short and Simple
ameliorate	improve
commence	begin
enumerate	list
finalize	finish, complete
prioritize	rank
utilize	use
viable option	choice

There are four exceptions to the general rule that "shorter is better."

1. Use a long word if it is the only word that expresses your meaning exactly.
2. Use a long word or phrase if it is more familiar than a short word. *Send out* is better than *emit* and *a word in another language for a geographic place or area* is better than *exonym* because more people know the first item in each pair.
3. Use a long word if its connotations are more appropriate. *Exfoliate* is better than *scrape off dead skin cells.*
4. Use a long word if the discourse community prefers it.

Connotations may differ among cultures. Even within a culture, connotations may change over time. The word *charity* had acquired such negative connotations by the 19th century that people began to use the term *welfare* instead. Now, *welfare* has acquired negative associations. Most states have *public assistance* programs instead.

How positively can we present something and still be ethical? *Pressure-treated lumber* sounds acceptable. But naming the product by the material injected under pressure—*arsenic-treated lumber*—may lead the customer to make a different decision. We have the right to package our ideas attractively, but we have the responsibility to give the public or our superiors all the information they need to make decisions.

How do words get their meanings?

Most meanings depend on usage.

Some dictionaries are *descriptive,* that is, their definitions describe the way people actually use words. In such a dictionary, the word *verbal* might be defined as *spoken, not written,* because many people use the word that way. In a *prescriptive* dictionary, words are defined as they are supposed to be used, according to a panel of experts. In such a dictionary, *verbal* would be defined as *using words*—which of course includes both writing and speaking. Check the introduction to your dictionary to find out which kind it is.

We learn meanings by context, by being alert and observant. Some terms will have a specialized meaning in a social or work group. We learn some

Many words are easily confused.

meanings by formal and informal study: "generally accepted accounting principles" or what the trash can on an e-mail screen symbolizes. Some meanings are negotiated as we interact one-on-one with another person, attempting to communicate. Some words persist, even though the reality behind them has changed. In 9 of the 10 largest U.S. cities, so-called "minorities" are already in the majority.[7] Some people are substituting the term *traditionally underrepresented groups* for *minorities,* but the old term is likely to remain in use for some time.

Some meanings are voted upon. Take, for example, the term *minority-owned business.* For years, the National Minority Supplier Development Council (NMSDC) has defined the term as a business at least 51% of whose owners were members of racial or ethnic minorities. But that made it hard for businesses to attract major capital or to go public, since doing so would give more ownership to European American investors. In 2000, the NMSDC redefined *minority-owned business* as one with minority management and at least 30% minority ownership.[8]

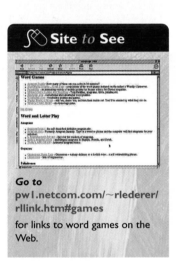

Site *to* See

Go to
**pw1.netcom.com/~rlederer/
rllink.htm#games**

for links to word games on the Web.

Is it OK to use jargon?

If it's essential.

There are two kinds of **jargon.** The first kind of jargon is the specialized terminology of a technical field. *LIFO* and *FIFO* are technical terms in accounting; *byte* and *baud* are computer jargon; *scale-free* and *pickled and oiled* designate specific characteristics of steel. Using technical terms in a job application letter suggests that you're a peer who also is competent in that field. In other messages, use technical jargon only when the term is essential. Define the term when you're not sure whether the reader knows it.

If a technical term has a "plain English" equivalent, use the simpler term:

Jargon: Foot the average monthly budget column down to Total Variable Cost, Total Management Fixed Cost, Total Sunk Costs, and Grand Total.

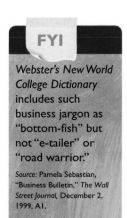

FYI

Webster's New World College Dictionary includes such business jargon as "bottom-fish" but not "e-tailer" or "road warrior."

Source: Pamela Sebastian, "Business Bulletin," *The Wall Street Journal,* December 2, 1999, A1.

Figure 15.1

Getting Rid of Business Jargon

Instead of	Use	Because
At your earliest convenience	The date you need a response	If you need it by a deadline, say so. It may never be convenient to respond.
As per your request; 55 miles per hour	As you requested; 55 miles an hour	*Per* is a Latin word for *by* or *for each*. Use *per* only when the meaning is correct; avoid mixing English and Latin.
Enclosed please find	Enclosed is; Here is	An enclosure isn't a treasure hunt. If you put something in the envelope, the reader will find it.
Forward same to this office	Return it to this office	Omit legal jargon.
Hereto, herewith	Omit	Omit legal jargon.
Please be advised; Please be informed	Omit—simply start your response	You don't need a preface. Go ahead and start.
Please do not hesitate	Omit	Omit negative words.
Pursuant to	According to; or omit	*Pursuant* does not mean *after*. Omit legal jargon in any case.
Said order	Your order	Omit legal jargon.
This will acknowledge receipt of your letter.	Omit—start your response	If you answer a letter, the reader knows you got it.
Trusting this is satisfactory, we remain	Omit	Eliminate *-ing* endings. When you are through, stop.

Better: Add the figures in the average monthly budget column for each category to determine the Total Variable Costs, the Total Management Fixed Costs, and the Total Sunk Costs. Then add the totals for each category to arrive at the Grand Total.

The revision here is longer but better because it uses simple words. The original will be meaningless to a reader who does not know what *foot* means.

The second kind of jargon is **business jargon,** sometimes called **businessese:** *as per your request, enclosed please find, please do not hesitate.* If any of the terms in the first column of Figure 15.1 show up in your writing, replace them with more modern language.

What words confuse some writers?

Words with similar sounds can have very different meanings.

Here's a list of words that are frequently confused. Master them, and you'll be well on the way to using the right word.

1. accede/exceed
   accede: to yield
   exceed: to go beyond, surpass

   I accede to your demand that we not exceed the budget.

2. accept/except
   accept: to receive
   except: to leave out or exclude; but

   > I accept your proposal except for point 3.

3. access/excess
   access: the right to use; admission to
   excess: surplus

   > As supply clerk, he had access to any excess materials.

4. adept/adopt
   adept: skilled
   adopt: to take as one's own

   > She was adept at getting people to adopt her ideas.

5. advice/advise
   advice: (noun) counsel
   advise: (verb) to give counsel or advice to someone

   > I asked him to advise me but I didn't like the advice I got.

6. affect/effect
   affect: (verb) to influence or modify
   effect: (verb) to produce or cause; (noun) result

   > He hoped that his argument would affect his boss' decision, but so far as he could see, it had no effect.

   > The tax relief effected some improvement for the citizens whose incomes had been affected by inflation.

7. affluent/effluent
   affluent: (adjective) rich, possessing in abundance
   effluent: (noun) something that flows out

   > Affluent companies can afford the cost of removing pollutants from the effluents their factories produce.

8. a lot/allot
   a lot: many (informal)
   allot: divide or give to

   > A lot of players signed up for this year's draft. We allotted one first-round draft choice to each team.

9. amount/number
   amount: (use with concepts that cannot be counted individually but can only be measured)
   number: (use when items can be counted individually)

   > It's a mistake to try to gauge the amount of interest he has by the number of questions he asks.

10. are/our
    are: (plural linking verb)
    our: belonging to us

    > Are we ready to go ahead with our proposal?

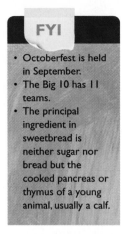

FYI

- Octoberfest is held in September.
- The Big 10 has 11 teams.
- The principal ingredient in sweetbread is neither sugar nor bread but the cooked pancreas or thymus of a young animal, usually a calf.

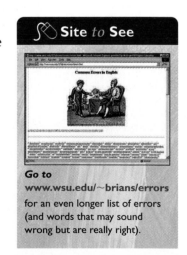

Site *to* See

Go to
www.wsu.edu/~brians/errors
for an even longer list of errors (and words that may sound wrong but are really right).

Two Kinds of Jargon

Technical jargon includes words that have specific technical meanings. Use this kind of jargon in job application letters. Avoid other technical jargon unless it's essential. **Business jargon** or **businessese** are words that do not have specialized meanings. Never use these terms.

11. assure/ensure/insure
    assure: to give confidence, to state confidently
    ensure: to make safe (figuratively)
    insure: to make safe, often by paying a fee against possible risk

    I assure you that we ensure employees' safety by hiring bodyguards.

    The pianist insured his fingers against possible damage.

12. attributed/contributed
    attributed: was said to be caused by
    contributed: gave something to

    The rain probably contributed to the accident, but the police officer attributed the accident to driver error.

13. between/among
    between: (use with only two choices)
    among: (use with more than two choices)

    This year the differences between the two candidates for president are unusually clear.

    I don't see any major differences among the candidates for city council.

14. cite/sight/site
    cite: (verb) to quote
    sight: (noun) vision, something to be seen
    site: (noun) real or virtual location

    She cited the old story of the building inspector who was depressed by the very sight of the site for the new factory.

15. complement/compliment
    complement: (verb) to complete, finish; (noun) something that completes
    compliment: (verb) to praise; (noun) praise

    The compliment she gave me complemented my happiness.

16. compose/comprise
    compose: make up, create
    comprise: consist of, be made up of, be composed of

    The city council is composed of 12 members. Each district comprises an area 50 blocks square.

17. confuse/complicate/exacerbate
    confuse: to bewilder
    complicate: to make more complex or detailed
    exacerbate: to make worse

    Because I missed the first 20 minutes of the movie, I didn't understand what was going on. The complicated plot exacerbated my confusion.

18. describe/prescribe
    describe: list the features of something, tell what something looks like
    prescribe: specify the features something must contain

    The law prescribes the priorities for making repairs. His report describes our plans to comply with the law.

19. discreet/discrete
    discreet: tactful, careful not to reveal secrets
    discrete: separate, distinct

    I have known him to be discreet on two discrete occasions.

20. do/due
    do: (verb) act or make
    due: (adjective) scheduled, caused by

    The banker said she would do her best to change the due date.

    Due to the computer system, the payroll can be produced in only two days for all 453 employees.

21. elicit/illicit
    elicit: (verb) to draw out
    illicit: (adjective) not permitted, unlawful

    The reporter could elicit no information from the Senator about his illicit love affair.

22. eminent/immanent/imminent
    eminent: distinguished
    immanent: dwelling within tangible objects
    imminent: about to happen

    The eminent doctor believed that death was imminent. The eminent minister believed that God was immanent.

23. fewer/less
    fewer: (use for objects that can be counted individually)
    less: (use for objects that can be measured but not counted individually)

    There is less sand in this bucket; there are probably fewer grains of sand, too.

24. forward/foreword
    forward: ahead
    foreword: preface, introduction

    The author looked forward to writing the foreword to the book.

25. good/well
    good: (adjective, used to modify nouns; as a noun, means something that is good)
    well: (adverb, used to modify verbs, adjectives, and other adverbs)

Her words "Good work!" told him that he was doing well.

He spent a great deal of time doing volunteer work because he believed that doing good was just as important as doing well.

26. i.e./ e.g.
    i.e.: (*id est*—that is) introduces a restatement or explanation of the preceding word or phrase
    e.g.: (*exempli gratia*—for the sake of an example; for example) introduces one or more examples

    Although he had never studied Latin, he rarely made a mistake in using Latin abbreviations, *e.g., i.e., etc.*, because he associated each with a mnemonic device (i.e., a word or image used to help one remember something). He remembered *i.e.* as *in effect*, pretended that *e.g.* meant *example given*, and used *etc.* only when *examples to continue* would fit.

27. imply/infer
    imply: suggest, put an idea into someone's head
    infer: deduce, get an idea out from something

    She implied that an announcement would be made soon. I inferred from her smile that it would be an announcement of her promotion.

28. it's/its
    it's: it is, it has
    its: belonging to it

    It's clear that a company must satisfy its customers to stay in business.

29. lectern/podium
    lectern: raised stand with a slanted top that holds a manuscript for a reader or notes for a speaker
    podium: platform for a speaker or conductor to stand on

    I left my notes on the lectern when I left the podium at the end of my talk.

30. lie/lay
    lie: to recline; to tell a falsehood (never takes an object)
    lay: to put an object on something (always takes an object)

    He was laying the papers on the desk when I came in, but they aren't lying there now.

31. loose/lose
    loose: not tight
    lose: to have something disappear

    If I lose weight, this suit will be loose.

32. moral/morale
    moral: (adjective) virtuous, good; (noun: morals) ethics, sense of right and wrong
    morale: (noun) spirit, attitude, mental outlook

Studies have shown that coed dormitories improve student morale without harming student morals.

33. objective/rationale
    objective: goal
    rationale: reason, justification

    The objective of the meeting was to explain the rationale behind the decision.

34. personal/personnel
    personal: individual, to be used by one person
    personnel: staff, employees

    All personnel will get new personal computers by the end of the year.

35. possible/possibly
    possible: (adjective) something that can be done
    possibly: (adverb) perhaps

    It is possible that we will be able to hire this spring. We can choose from possibly the best graduating class in the past five years.

36. precede/proceed
    precede: (verb) to go before
    proceed: (verb) to continue; (noun: proceeds) money

    Raising the money must precede spending it. Only after we obtain the funds can we proceed to spend the proceeds.

37. principal/principle
    principal: (adjective) main; (noun) person in charge; money lent out at interest
    principle: (noun) basic truth or rule, code of conduct

    The Prince, Machiavelli's principal work, describes his principles for ruling a state.

38. quiet/quite
    quiet: not noisy
    quite: very

    It was quite difficult to find a quiet spot anywhere near the floor of the stock exchange.

39. regulate/relegate
    regulate: control
    relegate: put (usually in an inferior position)

    If the federal government regulates the size of lettering on county road signs, we may as well relegate the current signs to the garbage bin.

40. residence/residents
    residence: home
    residents: people who live in a building

    The residents had different reactions when they learned that a shopping mall would be built next to their residence.

41. respectfully/respectively
    respectfully: with respect
    respectively: to each in the order listed

    > When I was introduced to the Queen, the Prime Minister, and the court jester, I bowed respectfully, shook hands politely, and winked, respectively.

42. role/roll
    role: part in a play or script, function (in a group)
    roll: (noun) list of students, voters, or other members; round piece of bread; (verb) move by turning over and over

    > While the teacher called the roll, George—in his role as class clown—threw a roll he had saved from lunch.

43. simple/simplistic
    simple: not complicated
    simplistic: watered down, oversimplified

    > She was able to explain the proposal in simple terms without making the explanation sound simplistic.

44. stationary/stationery
    stationary: not moving, fixed
    stationery: paper

    > During the earthquake, even the stationery was not stationary.

45. their/there/they're
    their: belonging to them
    there: in that place
    they're: they are

    > There are plans, designed to their specifications, for the house they're building.

46. to/too/two
    to: (preposition) function word indicating proximity, purpose, time, etc.
    too: (adverb) also, very, excessively
    two: (adjective) the number 2

    > The formula is too secret to entrust to two people.

47. unique/unusual
    unique: sole, only, alone
    unusual: not common

    > I believed that I was unique in my ability to memorize long strings of numbers until I consulted *Guinness World Records* and found that I was merely unusual: Someone else had equaled my feat in 1997.

48. verbal/oral
    verbal: using words
    oral: spoken, not written

His verbal skills were uneven: His oral communication was excellent, but he didn't write well. His sensitivity to nonverbal cues was acute: He could tell what kind of day I had just by looking at my face.

> **Hint:** Oral comes from the Latin word for mouth, *os.* Think of Oral-B Toothbrushes: For the mouth.
>   Verbal comes from the Latin word for word, *verba.* Nonverbal language is language that does not use words (e.g., body language).

49. whether/weather
    whether: (conjunction) used to introduce possible alternatives
    weather: (noun) atmosphere: wet or dry, hot or cold, calm or storm

    We will have to see what the weather is before we decide whether to hold the picnic indoors or out.

50. your/you're
    your: belonging to you
    you're: you are

    You're the top candidate for promotion in your division.

Summary of Key Points

- Use words that are accurate, appropriate, and familiar.
- **Denotation** is a word's literal or dictionary meaning.
- **Bypassing** occurs when two people use the same word to mean, or denote, different things.
- **Connotation** means the emotional colorings or associations that accompany a word.
- Generally, short words are better. But use a long word when
    1. It is the only word that expresses your meaning exactly.
    2. It is more familiar than a short word.
    3. Its connotations are more appropriate.
    4. The discourse community prefers it.
- Use technical jargon only when it is essential. Eliminate business jargon.

Assignments for Module 15

Questions for Comprehension

15.1 What is the difference between *denotation* and *connotation*?

15.2 What is *bypassing*?

15.3 What are the two kinds of jargon? Which is OK to use at times?

15.4 Why are short, simple words generally best?

Questions for Critical Thinking

15.5 If you were going to buy a new dictionary, would you want a descriptive or a prescriptive one? Why?

15.6 Why is it desirable to use technical jargon in a job letter and a job interview?

15.7 Is it possible to avoid connotations entirely?

Exercises and Problems

15.8 Identifying Words with Multiple Denotations

a. Each of the following words has several denotations. How many do you know? How many does a good dictionary list?

browser   log   court

b. List five words that have multiple denotations.

15.9 Explaining Bypassing

Show how bypassing is possible in the following examples.

a. France and Associates: Protection from Professionals

b. We were not able to account for the outstanding amount of plastic waste generated each year.

c. I scanned the résumés when I received them.

15.10 Evaluating Connotations

a. Identify the connotations of each of the following metaphors for a multicultural nation.
   melting pot
   mosaic

   tapestry
   garden salad
   stew

b. Which connotations seem most positive? Why?

15.11 Evaluating the Ethical Implications of Connotations

In each of the following pairs, identify the more favorable term. Is its use justified? Why or why not?

1. wastepaper   recovered fiber
2. feedback   criticism
3. scalper   ticket reseller
4. budget   spending plan
5. caviar   fish eggs

15.12 Correcting Errors in Denotation and Connotation

Identify and correct the errors in the following sentences.

1. I will take credit for the mistake.

2. The technology for virtual reality looms over the horizon.

3. The three proposals are diametrically opposed to each other.

4. In her search for information, she literally devours *The Wall Street Journal* every day.

5. Approximately 489 customers answered our survey.

15.13 Using Connotations to Shape Response

Write two sentences to describe each of the following situations, one with positive words, the other with negative words.

1. Lee talks to co-workers about subjects other than work, such as last weekend's ball game.

2. Lee spends a lot of time sending e-mail messages and monitoring e-mail newsgroups.

3. As a supervisor, Lee rarely gives specific instructions to subordinates.

15.14 Choosing Levels of Formality

Identify the more formal word in each pair. Which term is better for most business documents? Why?

1. adapted to   geared to

2. befuddled   confused
3. assistant   helper
4. pilot project testing the waters
5. cogitate   think

15.15 Identifying Jargon

How many of these business jargon terms do you know?

1. Sticky Web site
2. Alpha geek
3. Road warrior

15.16 Eliminating Jargon and Simplifying Language

Revise these sentences to eliminate jargon and to use short, familiar words. You may need to rewrite or add information.

1. Computers can enumerate pages when the appropriate keystroke is implemented.

2. Any alterations must be approved during the 30-day period commencing 60 days prior to the expiration date of the agreement.

3. As per your request, the undersigned has compiled a report on claims paid in 1996. A copy is attached hereto.

4. Please be advised that this writer is unable to attend the meeting on the fifteenth due to an unavoidable conflict.

5. Enclosed please find the schedule for the training session. In the event that you have alterations which you would like to suggest, forward same to my office at your earliest convenience.

15.17 Choosing the Right Word

Choose the right word for each sentence.

1. Exercise is (good/well) for patients who have had open-heart surgery.

2. This response is atypical, but it is not (unique/unusual).

3. The personnel department continues its (roll/role) of compiling reports for the federal government.

4. The Accounting Club expects (its/it's) members to come to meetings and participate in activities.

5. Part of the fun of any vacation is (cite/sight/site)-seeing.

6. The (lectern/podium) was too high for the short speaker.

7. The (residence/residents) of the complex want more parking.

8. Please order more letterhead (stationary/stationery).

9. The closing of the plant will (affect/effect) house prices in the area.

10. Better communication (among/between) design and production could enable us to produce products more efficiently.

15.18 Choosing the Right Word

Choose the right word for each sentence.

1. The audit revealed a small (amount/number) of errors.

2. Diet beverages have (fewer/less) calories than regular drinks.

3. In her speech, she (implied/inferred) that the vote would be close.

4. We need to redesign the stand so that the catalog is eye-level instead of (laying/lying) on the desk.

5. (Their/There/They're) is some evidence that (their/there/they're) thinking of changing (their/there/they're) policy.

6. The settlement isn't yet in writing; if one side wanted to back out of the (oral/verbal) agreement, it could.

7. In (affect/effect), we're creating a new department.

8. The firm will be hiring new (personal/personnel) in three departments this year.

9. Several customers have asked that we carry more campus merchandise, (i.e.,/e.g.,) pillows and mugs with the college seal.

10. We have investigated all of the possible solutions (accept/except) adding a turning lane.

15.19 Choosing the Right Word

Choose the right word for each sentence.

1. The author (cites/sights/sites) four reasons for computer phobia.

2. The error was (do/due) to inexperience.

3. (Your/you're) doing a good job motivating (your/you're) subordinates.

4. One of the basic (principals/principles) of business communication is "Consider the reader."

5. I (implied/inferred) from the article that interest rates would go up.

6. Working papers generally are (composed/comprised) of working trial balance, assembly sheets, adjusting entries, audit schedules, and audit memos.

7. Eliminating time clocks will improve employee (moral/morale).

8. The (principal/principle) variable is the trigger price mechanism.

9. (Its/It's) (to/too/two) soon (to/too/two) tell whether the conversion (to/too/two) computerized billing will save as much time as we hope.

10. Formal training programs (complement/compliment) on-the-job opportunities for professional growth.

 Polishing Your Prose

Run-On Sentences

A sentence with too many ideas, strung together by coordinating conjunctions that lack the required commas, is a *run-on*. (Remember that coordinating conjunctions such as *and, or,* and *but* need a comma to connect independent clauses.)

Run-ons confound readers because there are too many ideas competing for attention and because the missing commas make the ideas harder to follow. The effect is similar to listening to a speaker who does not pause between sentences—where does one point begin and another end?

Test for run-ons by looking for more than two main ideas in a sentence and a lack of commas with coordinating conjunctions:

We installed the new computers this morning and they are running fine but there weren't enough computers for everyone so we are going to purchase more on Wednesday and we will install them and then the department will be fully operational.

Count the number of things going on in this sentence. Where are the commas?

Fix a run-on in one of three ways:

1. For short run-ons, add the missing commas:

Incorrect: The Purchasing Department sent order forms but we received too few so we are requesting more.

Correct: The Purchasing Department sent order forms, but we received too few, so we are requesting more.

2. Rewrite the sentence using subordination:

Correct: Because we received too few order forms, we are requesting more from the Purchasing Department.

3. For longer run-ons, break the run-on into two or more sentences, add missing commas, and subordinate where appropriate.

Correct: We installed the new computers this morning. They are running fine, but because there weren't enough computers for everyone, we are going to purchase more on Wednesday. When we install them, the department will be fully operational.

Exercises

Fix the following run-on errors.

1. All online purchases should be itemized based on type and cost so remember to include the appropriate shipping confirmation number.

2. Our subsidiary in Chicago needs more employee handbooks but our subsidiary in Memphis has a surplus and so does the one in Indianapolis.

3. We will take a final product inventory on December 1 and managers will report any lost stock so employees should make sure any broken items are reported and managers should record this information in their computer databases.

4. Mr. Jacobs e-mailed he wants to meet on Tuesday but Ms. Powell said that Tuesday is out so we will have to find a day all of us can meet.

5. John leaves his computer on overnight but Aaron turns his off and Marilyn leaves hers on, too, and so does Tashi.

6. Include references with your job application so that we can contact those who know your work best.

7. The Cleveland office is planning a new marketing campaign so the Atlanta office will help with the promotion but the Detroit office is coordinating the product show.

8. We can install the computer in about half an hour but the peripherals will take longer and we will need to find time to train you.

9. Last week I went to Montreal and Haj went to Miami and this week Tony took a trip to Scottsdale so our travel budget is almost gone.

10. Our best employees come to us with energy and enthusiasm but some of our employees treat their positions simply as paychecks and do as little as possible to keep their jobs.

Check your answers to the odd-numbered exercises at the back of the book.

Module 16

Revising Sentences and Paragraphs

To learn how to

- Build a forceful style.
- Choose between active and passive voice.
- Make your writing tight and concise.
- Vary sentence patterns.
- Use the right tone.

Start by asking these questions:

- What is "good" style?
- Are there rules I should follow?
- What should I look for when I revise sentences?
- What should I look for when I revise paragraphs?
- How does organizational culture affect style?

Revising sentences and paragraphs can make the difference between a not-so-great document and a really effective paper or e-mail message.

In your first round of revision (◀▶ p. 75), when you focus on content and clarity, you'll add, expand, modify, and perhaps delete sentences and paragraphs. In the second round of revision, as you focus on organization and layout, you change the order of sentences and paragraphs to make them flow better or to put earliest the reader benefit (◀▶ p. 132) that will appeal to most readers. The third round of revision focuses on sentences and paragraphs, as you improve style and tone. In *editing*, you'll again check sentences, this time for grammatical corrections (Module 14 ◀▶).

What is "good" style?

It's both businesslike and friendly.

Good business and administrative writing sounds like a person talking to another person. Unfortunately, much of the writing produced in organizations today seems to have been written by faceless bureaucrats rather than by real people.

The style of writing that has traditionally earned high marks in college essays and term papers is arguably more formal than good business and administrative writing. (See Figure 16.1.) However, many professors also like term papers that are easy to read and use good visual impact.

Most people have several styles of talking, which they vary instinctively depending on the audience. Good writers have several styles, too. A memo to your boss complaining about the delays from a supplier will be informal, perhaps even chatty; a letter to the supplier demanding better service will be more formal.

Keep the following points in mind as you choose a level of formality for a specific document:

- Use a friendly, informal style to someone you've talked with.
- Avoid contractions, slang, and even minor grammatical lapses in paper documents to people you don't know. Abbreviations are OK in e-mail messages if they're part of the group's culture.

Figure 16.1
Different Levels of Style

Feature	Conversational Style	Good Business Style	Traditional Term Paper Style
Formality	Highly informal	Conversational; sounds like a real person talking	More formal than conversation would be, but retains a human voice
Use of contractions	Many contractions	OK to use occasional contractions	Few contractions, if any
Pronouns	Uses *I*, first- and second-person pronouns	Uses *I*, first- and second-person pronouns	First- and second-person pronouns kept to a minimum
Level of friendliness	Friendly	Friendly	No effort to make style friendly
How personal	Personal; refers to specific circumstances of conversation	Personal; may refer to reader by name; refers to specific circumstances of readers	Impersonal; may generally refer to *readers* but does not name them or refer to their circumstances
Word choice	Short, simple words; slang	Short, simple words but avoids slang	Many abstract words; scholarly, technical terms
Sentence and paragraph length	Incomplete sentences; no paragraphs	Short sentences and paragraphs	Sentences and paragraphs usually long
Grammar	Can be ungrammatical	Uses standard edited English	Uses standard edited English
Visual impact	Not applicable	Attention to visual impact of document	No particular attention to visual impact

Using the Right Tone

Business writing should be businesslike and friendly. But what exactly does it mean to be "friendly"? Well, it depends. It depends on whom you're dealing with, the culture of your workplace, and even the part of the country where you work.

In the past 50 years, social distance in the United States has decreased. In many, perhaps most, workplaces, most people call each other by their first names, whatever their age or rank. But even in cultures that pride themselves on their egalitarianism, differences in status do exist. When you're a newcomer in an organization, when you're a younger person speaking to someone older, or when you're a subordinate speaking to a superior, you're wise to show your awareness of status in the tone you use.

Tone (◀ ▶ p. 124) is the implied attitude of the speaker or writer toward what the words say. We're usually experts on tone of voice, especially the tones of other people's voices who don't seem to respect us. But sometimes it's harder for us to hear the lack of respect in our own voices as we talk or write to others.

If you're the boss, it's probably OK to e-mail your subordinates, "Let me know when you're free next week for a meeting." But if you're a subordinate trying to line up people on your own level or higher up, politeness pays: "Would you be able to meet next week? Could you let me know what times you have free?"

The difficulty, of course, is that norms for politeness, like those for friendliness, can differ from organization to organization, from group to group, and even in different parts of the country and of the world (◀ ▶ p. 124). Furthermore, the same words that seem polite and friendly coming from a superior to a subordinate can seem pushy or arrogant coming from a subordinate to a superior. "Keep up the good work!" is fine coming from your boss. It isn't, however, something you would say *to* your boss.

As in other communication situations, you have to analyze the situation rhetorically. Who are your audiences (◀ ▶ p. 22)? What are your purposes? How do other people in the organization talk and write? What kind of response do you get? If a customer winces when you return her credit card and say, "Have a nice day, Mary," maybe she doesn't appreciate being called by her first name. Talk to your peers in the organization about communication. What seems to work? What doesn't? And talk to a superior you trust. How do you come across? If you're creating the image you want to create, good. But if people think that you're rude, stuck-up, or arrogant, they may be reacting to your tone. A tone that worked for you in some situations in the past may need to be changed if you're to be effective in a new workplace or a new organization.

- Pay particular attention to your style when you have to write uncomfortable messages: when you write to people you fear or when you must give bad news. Reliance on nouns rather than on verbs and a general deadening of style increase when people are under stress or feel insecure.[1] Confident people are more direct. Edit your writing so that you sound confident, whether you feel that way or not.

Good business style allows for individual variation. Depending on the audience and situation, humor may be acceptable.

Are there rules I should follow?

Most "rules" are really guidelines.

Some "rules" are grammatical conventions. For example, standard edited English requires that each sentence has a subject and verb and that they agree. Business writing normally demands standard grammar, but exceptions exist. Promotional materials such as brochures, advertisements, and sales and fund-raising letters may use sentence fragments to gain the effect of speech.

Other "rules" may be conventions adopted by an organization so that its documents will be consistent. For example, a company might decide to capitalize job titles (*Production Manager*), even though grammar doesn't require the capitals, or always to use a comma before *and* in a series, even though a sentence can be grammatical without the comma. A different company might make different choices.

Still other "rules" are attempts to codify "what sounds good." "Never use *I*" and "use big words" are examples of this kind of "rule." These "rules" are half-truths and must be applied selectively, if at all. Think about your audience ◄|▷ p. 22), the discourse community (◄|▷ p. 31), your purposes, and the situation. If you want the effect produced by an impersonal style and polysyllabic words, use them. But use them only when you want the distancing they produce.

To improve your style,

- Get a clean page or screen, so that you aren't locked into old sentence structures.
- Try WIRMI: *What I Really Mean Is.*[2] Then write the words.
- Try reading your draft out loud to someone sitting at a comfortable personal distance. If the words sound stiff, they'll seem stiff to a reader, too.
- Ask someone else to read your draft out loud. Readers stumble because the words on the page aren't what they expect to see. The places where that person stumbles are places where your writing can be better.
- Read widely and write a *lot.*
- Use the eight techniques in the next two sections.

What should I look for when I revise sentences?

Try these six techniques.

At the sentence level, six kinds of revisions will help make your writing easy to read.

1. Use Active Verbs Most of the Time.

"Who does what" sentences with active verbs make your writing more forceful.

A verb is **active** if the grammatical subject of the sentence does the action the verb describes. A verb is **passive** if the subject is acted upon. Passives are usually made up of a form of the verb *to be* plus a past participle. *Passive* has nothing to do with *past*. Passives can be past, present, or future:

were received	(in the past)
is recommended	(in the present)
will be implemented	(in the future)

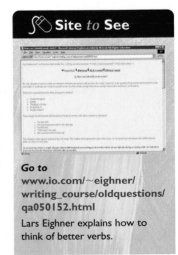

Site *to* See

Go to
www.io.com/~eighner/
writing_course/oldquestions/
qa050152.html

Lars Eighner explains how to think of better verbs.

To spot a passive, find the verb. If the verb describes something that the grammatical subject is doing, the verb is active. If the verb describes something that is being done to the grammatical subject, the verb is passive.

Active	**Passive**
The customer received 500 widgets.	Five hundred widgets were received by the customer.
I recommend this method.	This method is recommended by me.
The state agencies will implement the program.	The program will be implemented by the state agencies.

Verbs can be changed from active to passive by making the direct object (in the oval) the new subject (in the box). To change a passive verb to an active one, you must make the agent ("by _____" in < >) the new subject. If no agent is specified in the sentence, you must supply one to make the sentence active.

Active	**Passive**
The plant manager approved the request.	The request was approved by the <plant manager>.
The committee will decide next month.	A decision will be made next month. No agent in sentence.
[You] send the customer a letter informing her about the change.	A letter will be sent informing the customer of the change. No agent in sentence.

If the sentence does not have a direct object in its active form, no passive equivalent exists.

Active	**No Passive Exists**
I would like to go to the conference.	
The freight charge will be about $1,400.	
The phone rang.	

Passive verbs have at least three disadvantages:

1. If all the information in the original sentence is retained, passive verbs make the sentence longer. Passives take more time to understand.[3]
2. If the agent is omitted, it's not clear who is responsible for doing the action.
3. When many passive verbs are used, or when passives are used in material that has a lot of big words, the writing can be boring and pompous.

Passive verbs are desirable in these situations:

- Use passives to emphasize the object receiving the action, not the agent.

  Your order was shipped November 15.

The customer's order, not the shipping clerk, is important.

- Use passives to provide coherence within a paragraph. A sentence is easier to read if "old" information comes at the beginning of a sentence. When you have been discussing a topic, use the word again as your subject even if that requires a passive verb.

> The bank made several risky loans in the late 1990s. These loans were written off as "uncollectible" in 2004.

Using *loans* as the subject of the second sentence provides a link between the two sentences, making the paragraph as a whole easier to read.

- Use passives to avoid assigning blame.

> The order was damaged during shipment.

An active verb would require the writer to specify *who* damaged the order. The passive here is more tactful.

2. Use Verbs to Carry the Weight of Your Sentence.

Put the weight of your sentence in the verb. When the verb is a form of the verb *to be*, revise the sentence to use a more forceful verb.

Weak: The financial advantage of owning this equipment instead of leasing it is 10% after taxes.

Better: Owning this equipment rather than leasing it will save us 10% after taxes.

Nouns ending in *-ment, -ion,* and *-al* often hide verbs.

make an adjustment	adjust
make a payment	pay
make a decision	decide
reach a conclusion	conclude
take into consideration	consider
make a referral	refer
provide assistance	assist

Use verbs to present the information more forcefully.

Weak: We will perform an investigation of the problem.

Better: We will investigate the problem.

Weak: Selection of a program should be based on the client's needs.

Better: Select the program that best fits the client's needs.

3. Tighten Your Writing.

Writing is **wordy** if the same idea can be expressed in fewer words. Unnecessary words increase typing time, bore your reader, and make your meaning

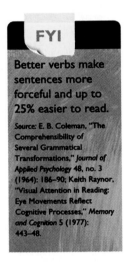

FYI

Better verbs make sentences more forceful and up to 25% easier to read.

Source: E. B. Coleman, "The Comprehensibility of Several Grammatical Transformations," *Journal of Applied Psychology* 48, no. 3 (1964): 186–90; Keith Raynor, "Visual Attention in Reading: Eye Movements Reflect Cognitive Processes," *Memory and Cognition* 5 (1977): 443–48.

more difficult to follow, since the reader must hold all the extra words in mind while trying to understand your meaning.

Good writing is tight. Tight writing may be long because it is packed with ideas. In Modules 6–8, we saw that revisions to create you-attitude and positive emphasis and to develop reader benefits were frequently *longer* than the originals because the revision added information not given in the original.

Sometimes you may be able to look at a draft and see immediately how to tighten it. When wordiness isn't obvious, try the following strategies for tightening your writing.

a. Eliminate words that say nothing.
b. Use gerunds (the *-ing* form of verbs) and infinitives (the *to* form of verbs) to make sentences shorter and smoother.
c. Combine sentences to eliminate unnecessary words.
d. Put the meaning of your sentence into the subject and verb to cut the number of words.

The purpose of eliminating unnecessary words is to save the reader's time, not simply to see how few words you can use. You aren't writing a telegram, so keep the little words that make sentences complete. (Incomplete sentences are fine in lists where all the items are incomplete.)

The following examples show how to use these methods.

a. Eliminate Words That Say Nothing.

Cut words that are already clear from other words in the sentence. Substitute single words for wordy phrases.

Wordy: Keep this information on file for future reference.

Tighter: Keep this information for reference.

or: File this information.

Wordy: Ideally, it would be best to put the billing ticket just below the screen and above the keyboard.

Tighter: If possible, put the billing ticket between the screen and the keyboard.

Phrases beginning with *of*, *which*, and *that* can often be shortened.

Wordy: the question of most importance

Tighter: the most important question

Wordy: the estimate which is enclosed

Tighter: the enclosed estimate

Sentences beginning with *There are* or *It is* can often be tighter.

Wordy: There are three reasons for the success of the project.

Tighter: Three reasons explain the project's success.

Instant Replay

Active and Passive Verbs

If the verb describes something that the grammatical subject is doing, the verb is active. If the verb describes something that is being done to the grammatical subject, the verb is passive.

Wordy: It is the case that college graduates advance more quickly in the company.

Tighter: College graduates advance more quickly in the company.

Check your draft. If you find unnecessary words, eliminate them.

Wordiness
Writing is **wordy** if the same idea can be expressed in fewer words.

b. Use Gerunds and Infinitives to Make Sentences Shorter and Smoother.

A **gerund** is the *-ing* form of a verb; grammatically, it is a verb used as a noun. In the sentence, "Running is my favorite activity," *running* is the subject of the sentence. An **infinitive** is the form of the verb which is preceded by *to: to run* is the infinitive.

In the revision below, a gerund (*purchasing*) and an infinitive (*to transmit*) tighten the revision.

Wordy: A plant suggestion has been made where they would purchase a fax machine for the purpose of transmitting test reports between plants.

Tighter: The plant suggests purchasing a fax machine to transmit test reports between plants.

Even when gerunds and infinitives do not greatly affect length, they often make sentences smoother and more conversational.

c. Combine Sentences to Eliminate Unnecessary Words.

In addition to saving words, combining sentences focuses the reader's attention on key points, makes your writing sound more sophisticated, and sharpens the relationship between ideas, thus making your writing more coherent.

Wordy: I conducted this survey by telephone on Sunday, April 21. I questioned two groups of juniors and seniors—male and female—who, according to the Student Directory, were still living in the dorms. The purpose of this survey was to find out why some juniors and seniors continue to live in the dorms even though they are no longer required by the university to do so. I also wanted to find out if there were any differences between male and female juniors and seniors in their reasons for choosing to remain in the dorms.

Tighter: On Sunday, April 21, I phoned male and female juniors and seniors living in the dorms to find out (1) why they continue to live in the dorms even though they are no longer required to do so, and (2) whether men and women had the same reasons for staying in the dorms.

d. Put the Meaning of Your Sentence into the Subject and Verb to Cut the Number of Words.

Put the core of your meaning into the subject and verb of your main clause. Think about what you *mean* and try saying the same thing in several different ways. Some alternatives will be tighter than others. Choose the tightest one.

Wordy: The reason we are recommending the computerization of this process is because it will reduce the time required to obtain data and will give us more accurate data.

Better: We are recommending the computerization of this process because it will save time and give us more accurate data.

Tight: Computerizing the process will give us more accurate data more quickly.

Wordy: The purpose of this letter is to indicate that if we are unable to mutually benefit from our seller/buyer relationship, with satisfactory material and satisfactory payment, then we have no alternative other than to sever the relationship. In other words, unless the account is handled in 45 days, we will have to change our terms to a permanent COD basis.

Better: A good buyer/seller relationship depends upon satisfactory material and satisfactory payment. You can continue to charge your purchases from us only if you clear your present balance in 45 days.

4. Vary Sentence Length and Sentence Structure.

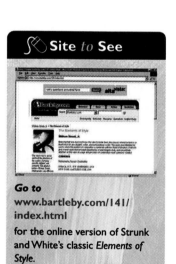

Site *to* See

Go to www.bartleby.com/141/ index.html

for the online version of Strunk and White's classic *Elements of Style.*

Readable prose mixes sentence lengths and varies sentence structure. Most sentences should be 20 words or fewer. A really short sentence (under 10 words) can add punch to your prose. Really long sentences (over 30 or 40 words) are danger signs.

You can vary sentence patterns in several ways. First, you can mix simple, compound, and complex sentences. **Simple sentences** have one main clause:

We will open a new store this month.

Compound sentences have two main clauses joined with *and, but, or,* or another conjunction. Compound sentences work best when the ideas in the two clauses are closely related.

We have hired staff, and they will complete their training next week.

We wanted to have a local radio station broadcast from the store during its grand opening, but the DJs were already booked.

Complex sentences have one main and one subordinate clause; they are good for showing logical relationships.

When the stores open, we will have balloons and specials in every department.

Because we already have a strong customer base in the northwest, we expect the new store to be just as successful as the store in the City Center Mall.

You can also vary sentences by changing the order of elements. Normally the subject comes first.

Energy and enthusiasm are good. Add standard grammar and accuracy to create good sentences.

We will survey customers later in the year to see whether demand warrants a third store on campus.

To create variety, occasionally begin the sentence with some other part of the sentence.

Later in the year, we will survey customers to see whether demand warrants a third store on campus.

To see whether demand warrants a third store on campus, we will survey customers later in the year.

Use these guidelines for sentence length and structure:

- Always edit sentences for tightness. Even a 10-word sentence can be wordy.
- When your subject matter is complicated or full of numbers, make a special effort to keep sentences short.
- Use long sentences

   To show how ideas are linked to each other.

   To avoid a series of short, choppy sentences.

   To reduce repetition.

- Group the words in long and medium-length sentences into chunks that the reader can process quickly.[4]
- When you use a long sentence, keep the subject and verb close together.

Let's see how to apply the last three principles.

Use Long Sentences to Show How Ideas Are Linked to Each Other, to Avoid a Series of Short, Choppy Sentences, and to Reduce Repetition.

The following sentence is hard to read not simply because it is long but also because it is shapeless. Just cutting it into a series of short, choppy sentences doesn't help. The best revision uses medium-length sentences to show the relationship between ideas.

Too long: It should also be noted in the historical patterns presented in the summary that though there were delays in January and February which we realized were occurring, we are now back where we were about a year ago, and that we are not off line in our collect receivables as compared to last year at this time, but we do show a considerable over-budget figure because of an ultraconservative goal on the receivable investment.

Choppy: There were delays in January and February. We knew about them at the time. We are now back where we were about a year ago. The summary shows this. Our present collect receivables are in line with last year's. However, they exceed the budget. The reason they exceed the budget is that our goal for receivable investment was very conservative.

Better: As the summary shows, although there were delays in January and February (of which we were aware), we have now regained our position of a year ago. Our present collect receivables are in line with last year's, but they exceed the budget because our goal for receivable investment was very conservative.

Group the Words in Long and Medium-Length Sentences into Chunks.

The "better" revision above has seven chunks. In the list below, the chunks starting immediately after the numbers are main clauses. The chunks that are indented are subordinate clauses and parenthetical phrases.

1.   As the summary shows,
2.   although there were delays in January and February
3.   (of which we were aware),
4. we have now regained our position of a year ago.
5. Our present collect receivables are in line with last year's,
6. but they exceed the budget
7.   because our goal for receivable investment was very conservative.

The first sentence has four chunks: an introductory phrase (1), a subordinate clause (2) with a parenthetical phrase (3), followed by the main clause of the first sentence (4). The second sentence begins with a main clause (5). The sentence's second main clause (6) is introduced with *but*, showing that it will reverse the first clause. A subordinate clause explaining the reason for the reversal completes the sentence (7). At 27 and 24 words, respectively, these sentences aren't short, but they're readable because no chunk is longer than 10 words.

Any sentence pattern will get boring if it is repeated sentence after sentence. Use different sentence patterns—different kinds and lengths of chunks—to keep your prose interesting.

Keep the Subject and Verb Close Together.

Often you can move the subject and verb closer together if you put the modifying material in a list at the end of the sentence. For maximum readability, present the list vertically.

Instant Replay

Sentence Length and Sentence Structure

Readable prose mixes sentence lengths and varies sentence structure. Most sentences should be 20 words or fewer.

Hard to read: Movements resulting from termination, layoffs and leaves, recalls and reinstates, transfers in, transfers out, promotions in, promotions out, and promotions within are presently documented through the Payroll Authorization Form.

Smoother: The following movements are documented on the Payroll Authorization Form: termination, layoffs and leaves, recalls and reinstates, transfers in and out, and promotions in, out, and within.

Still better: The following movements are documented on the Payroll Authorization Form:
- Termination.
- Layoffs and leaves.
- Recalls and reinstates.
- Transfers in and out.
- Promotions in, out, and within.

Sometimes you will need to change the verb and revise the word order to put the modifying material at the end of the sentence.

Hard to read: The size sequence code that is currently used for sorting the items in the NOSROP lists and the composite stock list is not part of the online file.

Smoother: The online file does not contain the size sequence code that is currently used for sorting the items in the composite stock lists and the NOSROP lists.

5. Use Parallel Structure.

Words or ideas that share the same logical role in your sentence must also be in the same grammatical form. Parallelism is also a powerful device for making your writing smoother and more forceful. See Figure 16.2. Note the parallel portions in the following examples.

Faulty: I interviewed juniors and seniors and athletes.

Parallel: I interviewed juniors and seniors. In each rank, I interviewed athletes and non-athletes.

Faulty

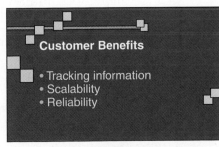
Parallel

Figure 16.2

Use Parallelism to Tighten Your Writing

Figure 16.3
Eliminate Repeated Words in Parallel Lists

PowerPoint Reports
• They work best when the discourse community is well-defined.
• They work best when visuals can carry the message.
• They work best when oral comments can explain and connect ideas.

Wordy

PowerPoint reports work best when
• The discourse community is well-defined.
• Visuals can carry the message.
• Oral comments can explain and connect ideas.

Tight

Faulty: Errors can be checked by reviewing the daily exception report or note the number of errors you uncover when you match the lading copy with the file copy of the invoice.

Parallel: Errors can be checked by reviewing the daily exception report or by noting the number of errors you uncover when you match the lading copy with the file copy of the invoice.

Also Parallel: To check errors, note
1. The number of items on the daily exception report.
2. The number of errors discovered when the lading copy and the file copy are matched.

Note that a list in parallel structure must fit grammatically into the umbrella sentence that introduces the list.

Eliminate repeated words in parallel lists. See Figure 16.3.

6. Put Your Readers in Your Sentences.

Use second-person pronouns (*you*) rather than third-person (*he, she, one*) to give your writing more impact. *You* is both singular and plural; it can refer to a single person or to every member of your organization.

Third-person: Funds in a participating employee's account at the end of each six months will automatically be used to buy more stock unless a "Notice of Election Not to Exercise Purchase Rights" form is received from the employee.

Second-person: Once you begin to participate, funds in your account at the end of each six months will automatically be used to buy more stock unless you turn in a "Notice of Election Not to Exercise Purchase Rights" form.

Be careful to use *you* only when it refers to your reader.

Incorrect: My visit with the outside sales rep showed me that your schedule can change quickly.

Correct: My visit with the outside sales rep showed me that schedules can change quickly.

What should I look for when I revise paragraphs?

Check for topic sentences and transitions.

Paragraphs are visual and logical units. Use them to chunk your sentences.

1. Begin Most Paragraphs with Topic Sentences.

A good paragraph has **unity;** that is, it discusses only one idea, or topic. The **topic sentence** states the main idea and provides a scaffold to structure your document. Topic sentences are not essential, but your writing will be easier to read if you make the topic sentence explicit and put it at the beginning of the paragraph.[5]

Hard to read (no topic sentence): In fiscal 2003, the company filed claims for a refund of federal income taxes of $3,199,000 and interest of $969,000 paid as result of an examination of the company's federal income tax returns by the Internal Revenue Service (IRS) for the years 1999 through 2002. It is uncertain what amount, if any, may ultimately be recovered.

Better (paragraph starts with topic sentence): The company and the IRS disagree about whether the company is liable for back taxes. In fiscal 2003, the company filed claims for a refund of federal income taxes of $3,199,000 and interest of $969,000 paid as a result of an examination of the company's federal income tax returns by the Internal Revenue Service (IRS) for the years 1999 through 2002. It is uncertain what amount, if any, may ultimately be recovered.

A good topic sentence forecasts the structure and content of the paragraph.

Plan B also has economic advantages.
(Prepares the reader for a discussion of B's economic advantages.)

We had several personnel changes in June.
(Prepares the reader for a list of the month's terminations and hires.)

Employees have complained about one part of our new policy on parental leaves.
(Prepares the reader for a discussion of the problem.)

When the first sentence of a paragraph is not the topic sentence, readers who skim may miss the main point. Move the topic sentence to the beginning of the paragraph. If the paragraph does not have a topic sentence, you will need to write one. If you can't think of a single sentence that serves as an "umbrella" to cover every sentence, the paragraph lacks unity. To solve the problem, either split the paragraph into two, or eliminate the sentence that digresses from the main point.

Figure 16.4

Transition Words and Phrases

To Show Addition or Continuation of the Same Idea	To Introduce an Example e.g.	To Show That the Contrast Is More Important Than the Previous Idea	To Show Time after
and	for example	but	as
also	for instance	however	before
first, second, third	indeed	nevertheless	in the future
in addition	to illustrate	on the contrary	next
likewise	namely		then
similarly	specifically	**To Show Cause and Effect**	until
		as a result	when
To Introduce the Last or Most Important Item	**To Contrast**	because	while
finally	in contrast	consequently	
furthermore	on the other hand	for this reason	**To Summarize or End**
moreover	or	therefore	in conclusion

2. Use Transitions to Link Ideas.

Transition words and sentences signal the connections between ideas to the reader. Transitions tell whether the next sentence continues the previous thought or starts a new idea; they can tell whether the idea that comes next is more or less important than the previous thought. Figure 16.4 lists some of the most common transition words and phrases.

How does organizational culture affect style?

Different cultures may prefer different styles.

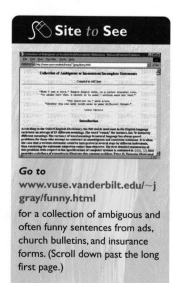

Site *to* See

Go to
www.vuse.vanderbilt.edu/~j gray/funny.html
for a collection of ambiguous and often funny sentences from ads, church bulletins, and insurance forms. (Scroll down past the long first page.)

Different organizations and bosses may legitimately have different ideas about what constitutes good writing. If the style the company prefers seems reasonable, use it. If the style doesn't seem reasonable—if you work for someone who likes flowery language or wordy paragraphs, for example—you have several choices.

- **Use the techniques in this module.** Sometimes seeing good writing changes people's minds about the style they prefer.
- **Help your boss learn about writing.** Show him or her this book or the research cited in the notes to demonstrate how a clear, crisp style makes documents easier to read.
- **Recognize that a style may serve other purposes than communication.** An abstract, hard-to-read style may help a group forge its own identity. James Suchan and Ronald Dulek have shown that Navy officers preferred a passive, impersonal style because they saw themselves as followers. An aircraft company's engineers saw wordiness as the verbal equivalent of backup systems. A backup is redundant but essential to safety,

because parts and systems do fail.[6] When big words, jargon, and wordiness are central to a group's self-image, change will be difficult, since changing style will mean changing the corporate culture.

- Ask. Often the documents that end up in files aren't especially good. Later, other workers may find these documents and imitate them, thinking they represent a corporate standard. Bosses may in fact prefer better writing.

Building a good style takes energy and effort, but it's well worth the work. Good style can make every document more effective; good style can help make you the good writer so valuable to every organization.

Summary of Key Points

- Good style in business and administrative writing is less formal, more friendly, and more personal than the style usually used for term papers.
- To improve your style,
  - Get a clean page or screen, so that you aren't locked into old sentence structures.
  - Try WIRMI: *What I Really Mean Is*. Then write the words.
  - Try reading your draft out loud to someone sitting at a comfortable personal distance. If the words sound stiff, they'll seem stiff to a reader, too.
  - Ask someone else to read your draft out loud. Readers stumble because the words on the page aren't what they expect to see. The places where that person stumbles are places where your writing can be better.
  - Write a lot.
- As you write and revise sentences,
  1. Use active verbs most of the time. Active verbs are better because they are shorter, clearer, and more interesting.
  2. Use verbs to carry the weight of your sentence.

3. Tighten your writing. Writing is **wordy** if the same idea can be expressed in fewer words.
   a. Eliminate words that say nothing.
   b. Use gerunds and infinitives to make sentences shorter and smoother.
   c. Combine sentences to eliminate unnecessary words.
   d. Put the meaning of your sentence into the subject and verb to cut the number of words.
4. Vary sentence length and sentence structure.
5. Use parallel structure. Use the same grammatical form for ideas that have the same logical function.
6. Put your readers in your sentences.

- As you write and revise paragraphs,
  1. Begin most paragraphs with topic sentences so that readers know what to expect in the paragraph.
  2. Use transitions to link ideas.

- Different organizations and bosses may legitimately have different ideas about what constitutes good writing.

Assignments for Module 16

Questions for Comprehension

16.1 What problems do passive verbs create? When are passive verbs desirable?

16.2 List two ways to tighten your writing.

16.3 What is parallel structure?

16.4 How do topic sentences help readers?

Questions for Critical Thinking

16.5 Would your other instructors like the style you're learning to use in this class?

16.6 Can a long document be tight rather than wordy?

16.7 Ask a trusted friend or colleague how your tone comes across in classes and at work. If other people find you shy on the one hand or arrogant on the other, what changes in your tone could you make?

Exercises and Problems

16.8 **Changing Verbs from Passive to Active**

Identify the passive verbs in the following sentences and convert them to active verbs. In some cases, you may need to add information to do so. You may use different words as long as you retain the basic meaning of the sentence. Remember that imperative verbs are active, too.

1. The business plan was written by Tyrone King.

2. The cost of delivering financial services is being slashed by computers, the Internet, and toll-free phone lines.

3. When the vacation schedule is finalized it is recommended that it be routed to all supervisors for final approval.

4. As stated in my résumé, I have designed Web pages for three student organizations.

5. Material must not be left on trucks outside the warehouse. Either the trucks must be parked inside the warehouse or the material must be unloaded at the time of receiving the truck.

16.9 **Using Better Verbs**

Revise each of the following sentences to use better verbs.

1. The advantage of using color is that the document is more memorable.

2. Customers who make payments by credit card will receive a 1% rebate on all purchases.

3. When you make an evaluation of media buys, take into consideration the demographics of the group seeing the ad.

4. We provide assistance to clients in the process of reaching a decision about the purchase of hardware and software.

5. We maintain the belief that Web ads are a good investment.

16.10 Reducing Wordiness

1. Eliminate words that say nothing. You may use different words.
   a. There are many different topics that you will read about on a monthly basis once you subscribe to *Inc.*
   b. With the new organic fertilizer, you'll see an increase in the quality of your tomatoes and the number grown.
   c. As a manager, I am responsible for helping to promote any action or ideas that may help to improve this organization as a whole. One such idea is printing our URL on our business cards and stationery. We could also put the URL on our invoices. I therefore recommend that when we reorder said materials, we imprint our URL on all of them so that our current and prospective customers will be able to access our Web site.

2. Use gerunds and infinitives to make these sentences shorter and smoother.
   a. The completion of the project requires the collection and analysis of additional data.
   b. The purchase of laser printers will make possible the in-house production of the newsletter.
   c. The treasurer has the authority for the investment of assets for the gain of higher returns.

3. Combine sentences to show how ideas are related and to eliminate unnecessary words.
   a. Some buyers want low prices. Other buyers are willing to pay higher prices for convenience or service.
   b. We projected sales of $34 million in the third quarter. Our actual sales have fallen short of that figure by $2.5 million.
   c. We conducted this survey by handing out questionnaires January 10, 11, and 12. Our office surveyed 100 customers. We wanted to see whether they would like to be able to leave voice-mail messages for their representatives. We also wanted to find out if our hours are convenient for them. Finally, we asked whether adequate parking was available.

16.11 Improving Parallel Structure

Revise each of the following sentences to create parallelism.

1. The county will benefit from implementing flextime.
   - Offices will stay open longer for more business.
   - Staff turnover will be lower.
   - Easier business communication with states in other time zones.
   - Increased employee productivity.

2. Newsletters enhance credibility, four times as many people read them as read standard ad formats, and allow soft-sell introduction to prospective customers.

3. When you leave a voice-mail message,
   - Summarize your main point in a sentence or two.
   - The name and phone number should be given slowly and distinctly.
   - The speaker should give enough information so that the recipient can act on the message.
   - Tell when you'll be available to receive the recipient's return call.

16.12 Putting Readers in Your Sentences

Revise each of the following sentences to put readers in them. As you revise, use active verbs and simple words.

1. Mutual funds can be purchased from banks, brokers, financial planners, or from the fund itself.

2. Every employee will receive a copy of the new policy within 60 days after the labor agreement is signed.

3. Another aspect of the university is campus life, with an assortment of activities and student groups to participate in and lectures and sports events to attend.

16.13 Editing Sentences to Improve Style

Revise these sentences to make them smoother, less wordy, and easier to read. Eliminate jargon and repetition. Keep the information; you may reword or reorganize it. If the original is not clear, you may need to add information to write a clear revision.

1. The table provided was unclear due to hard-to-understand headings.

2. By working a co-op or intern position, you may have to be in school an additional year to complete the requirements for graduation, but this extra year is paid for by the income you make in the co-op or intern position.

3. There is a seasonality factor in the workload, with the heaviest being immediately prior to quarterly due dates for estimated tax payments.

4. Informational meetings will be held during next month at different dates and times. These meetings will explain the HMO options. Meeting times are as follows:
   October 17, noon–1 P.M.
   October 20, 4–5 P.M.
   October 23, 2–3 P.M.

5. Listed below are some benefits you get from an HMO:

   1. Routine visits to a doctor will cost only a $10 co-payment.

   2. No hassle of prescription reimbursements later. You only pay the co-payment when you fill your prescription.

   3. Hospitalization is covered 100%.

16.14 Using Topic Sentences

Make each of the following paragraphs more readable by opening each paragraph with a topic sentence. You may be able to find a topic sentence in the paragraph and move it to the beginning. In other cases, you'll need to write a new sentence.

1. At Disney World, a lunch put on an expense account is "on the mouse." McDonald's employees "have ketchup in their veins." Business slang flourishes at companies with rich corporate cultures. Memos at Procter & Gamble are called "reco's" because the model P&G memo begins with a recommendation.

2. The first item on the agenda is the hiring for the coming year. George has also asked that we review the agency goals for the next fiscal year. We should cover this early in the meeting since it may affect our hiring preferences. Finally, we need to announce the deadlines for grant proposals, decide which grants to apply for, and set up a committee to draft each proposal.

3. Separate materials that can be recycled from your regular trash. Pass along old clothing, toys, or appliances to someone else who can use them. When you purchase products, choose those with minimal packaging. If you have a yard, put your yard waste and kitchen scraps (excluding meat and fat) in a compost pile. You can reduce the amount of solid waste your household produces in four ways.

16.15 Writing Paragraphs

Write a paragraph on each of the following topics.

a. Discuss your ideal job.
b. Summarize a recent article from a business magazine or newspaper.
c. Explain how technology is affecting the field you plan to enter.
d. Explain why you have or have not decided to work while you attend college.
e. Write a profile of someone who is successful in the field you hope to enter.

As Your Instructor Directs,

a. Label topic sentences, active verbs, and parallel structure.
b. Edit a classmate's paragraphs to make the writing even tighter and smoother.

 Polishing Your Prose

Commas in Lists

Use commas in lists to separate items:

At the office supply store, I bought pens, stationery, and three-ring binders.

Commas show distinctions between items in a list. Technically, the comma before the coordinating conjunction, such as *and* or *or*, is optional, but the additional comma always adds clarity. Use commas consistently throughout your document. Missing or improperly placed commas confuse readers:

We bought the following items for the staff lounge: television cabinet computer desk refrigerator and microwave oven.

Does *television* describe *cabinet* or is it a separate item? Is *computer desk* one item? Or are *computer* and *desk* two separate things? Inserting commas makes the distinction clear:

We bought the following items for the staff lounge: television, cabinet, computer, desk, refrigerator, and microwave oven.

Semicolons replace commas in lists where the items themselves contain commas:

Our company has plants in Blue Ridge, Kentucky; Boise, Idaho; and Saganaw, Michigan.

Exercises

Use commas to make these lists clearer.

1. At the weekly staff meeting we will be joined by Mr. Loomis Ms. Handelman Ms. Lang and Mr. Kim.

2. Separate the order forms according to whether they arrived in January February March April or May.

3. Buy small medium and large paper clips at the office supply store.

4. Customers can purchase computers in the following colors: blue green orange red or purple.

5. Applicants should send copies of their résumés to Mr. Arthur Bramberger

(continued)

Human Resource Director Ms. Tina Ramos Vice President of Marketing and Ms. Ellen Choi Administrative Assistant in Marketing.

6. Whether we send the message by e-mail snail mail overnight courier or fax, it needs to arrive by the 17th.

7. Interns will be rotated through the receiving claims adjustment customer service and shipping departments.

8. Send our satellite offices in Milan Italy Paris France London England and

Bern Switzerland copies of the spring summer and winter catalogs.

9. We are open until 9 P.M. on Mondays Wednesdays Fridays and Saturdays.

10. Our franchises on Main Broad Long and Front Streets each need updated vendor lists.

Check your answers to the odd-numbered exercises at the back of the book.

BComm Skills Booster

To apply the concepts in this module, complete lesson 9 on making your writing easier to read. You can access the BComm Skill Booster through the text Web site at **www.mhhe.com/bcs2e.**

Cases for Communicators

A Hard Lesson in Grammar

Bad grammar or punctuation can make even the best writer appear to be ill-trained, unprofessional, and even unintelligent. Errors in punctuation and grammar can confuse, mislead, and even cause readers to disregard or ignore an otherwise well-written letter. In some cases, such errors can generate a great deal of unwanted attention, with decidedly negative consequences.

Consider the case of a class of graduating high school seniors from Vorobyovo, Russia. In anticipation of their upcoming graduation party, several members of the class sent a one-page, handwritten letter to Russian President Vladimir Putin, inviting him to their celebration and asking him to send a video camera so they could tape the festivities.

Upon receiving the letter, the Kremlin returned it to the local school district with a request that the authors be identified. When the school officials read the missive, they were horrified! Written on a small, dirty piece of paper, the note had several punctuation and grammatical mistakes, the most egregious of which was an error in the salutation to President Putin. As one school official noted, "This is not what educated and smart people do."

The embarrassed district officials' response was quick and severe. They ordered the director of the school to write an explanatory note and meet with them about the students' letter, and then they examined the school records of the students involved. Two of the seniors had just been awarded special silver medals for their exceptional performance on final exams. The school administrators revoked those medals.

Losing this honor in this manner had severe repercussions for the two students, dashing their hopes for an advanced education and a future outside of their small village. Ironically, the Kremlin itself was unfazed by the errors. It responded to the students' letter by sending the video camera just in time for graduation.

Fortunately, grammatical and punctuation errors do not generally carry such a high penalty as loss of life-long dreams, but these errors can greatly damage others' perception of you as an intelligent, professional business person. As these students learned the hard way, grammar and punctuation can be the most important part of your message!

Source: Michael Wines, "A Letter to the President, a Lesson in Style," *New York Times,* June 23, 2000. Accessed on nytimes.com on August 8, 2002.

Individual Activity

Imagine that you are the principal of the high school where the grammar furor erupted. You know that your students are intelligent, and you pride yourself on the good writing skills that are taught at the school. Unfortunately, as a result of this incident, administrators no longer have the same impression. You need to take action or your job may be in jeopardy!

Write a letter to the superintendent of schools discussing the recent events and describing your philosophy about good grammar and writing skills. To illustrate that you recognize the importance of mastering these skills, be sure to include at least three specific points describing how poor grammar and punctuation can affect the perception of both the writer and an otherwise well-written document.

The school's curriculum is complete and well crafted. You believe it was merely haste and a resulting failure to adequately polish the offending letter rather than ignorance of good grammar and punctuation that created the embarrassing situation. Therefore, you believe that the academic medals should be returned to your students.

Before you begin writing your letter, ask yourself the following question: What do I really mean? (Use WIRMI!)

After you've written your first draft, read it out loud. Then, think about these questions as you polish your letter:

- Did I use active verbs most of the time?
- Did I use verbs to carry the weight of my sentences?
- Did I include any words that mean nothing?
- Can I tighten my writing by combining sentences or using gerunds and infinitives?
- Did I vary sentence length and structure?
- Did I use parallel structure?
- Did I begin most paragraphs with strong topic sentences?
- Did I use transitions to link ideas?

Given the current situation, the superintendent will have no tolerance for errors, so be sure to carefully review your letter for typographical and grammatical errors.

Group Activity

(Note: To prepare for this group activity, print out a new version of your draft, omitting all punctuation and formatting. The end result should be one large block of text without any clear sentence or paragraph structure. Next, break the members of the group into pairs.)

You want to share your draft with the school's teachers. Unfortunately, as you prepare to print out copies for them, your unreliable laptop computer crashes! The only version you can recover is complete but lacks punctuation and formatting. You only have one copy of the final letter, so as you are pressed for time, you decide to distribute this "raw" version.

Exchange unformatted drafts with your partner. Carefully read through the letter and then go back through it and, using the correct proofreading marks, note where the punctuation and paragraph breaks should go.

Before you return the draft to its author, ask yourself the following questions:

- Did I use the correct proofreading marks?
- Does my edited version of the letter make sense and read smoothly?

Give the edited draft back to your partner. Examine your own draft, now copyedited by your partner, and compare it to your original version. As you do this, ask yourself the following questions:

- How does this edited version compare to my draft?
- Are the sentence and paragraph breaks the same?

- Has the meaning or emphasis been changed?
- Did my partner identify any errors in my draft?

Note all differences in meaning and structure that you find.

As a group, share your findings and discuss the ways in which grammar and punctuation affected meaning and structure. What does this tell you about the importance of proper grammar and punctuation in effective business communications?

Unit Five

Interpersonal Communication

Module 17

Listening

To learn how to

- Listen rather than simply hear.
- Listen actively.
- Continue to build goodwill.

Start by asking these questions:

- What do good listeners do?
- What is active listening?
- How do I show people that I'm listening to them?
- Can I use these techniques if I really disagree with someone?

Listening is the form of communication we practice most often. Yet because we rarely have formal training in it, it may be the one that we do most poorly. Listening is even more crucial on the job than it is in classes, but it may also be more difficult.

- In class you're encouraged to take notes. But you can't whip out a notepad every time your boss speaks.
- Many classroom lectures are well organized, with signposts (◁ ▶ Module 20) and repetition of key points to help hearers follow. But conversations usually wander. A key point about when a report is due may be sandwiched in among statements about other due dates for other projects.
- In a classroom lecture you're listening primarily for information. In interchanges with friends and co-workers, you need to listen for feelings, too. Feelings of being rejected or overworked need to be

Polish your listening skills. You'll need them on the job as well as in your personal life.

dealt with as they arise. But you can't deal with a feeling unless you are aware of it.

As Module 2 explains (◀▷ p. 25), to receive a message, the receiver must first perceive the message, then decode it (that is, translate the symbols into meaning), and then interpret it. In interpersonal communication, **hearing** denotes perceiving sounds. **Listening** means decoding and interpreting them correctly.

What do good listeners do?

They consciously follow four practices.

Good listeners pay attention, focus on the other speaker(s) in a generous way rather than on themselves, avoid making assumptions, and listen for feelings as well as for facts.

Pay Attention.

Good listening requires energy. You have to resist distractions and tune out noise (◀▷ p. 25), whether the rumble of a truck going by or your own worry about whether your parking meter is expiring.

Some listening errors happen because the hearer wasn't paying enough attention to a key point. After a meeting with a client, a consultant waited for the client to send her more information that she would use to draft a formal proposal to do a job for the client. It turned out that the client thought the next move was up to the consultant. The consultant and the client had met together, but they hadn't remembered the same facts.

To avoid listening errors caused by inattention,

- Before the meeting, anticipate the answers you need to get. Make a mental or paper list of your questions. When is the project due? What resources do you have? What is the most important aspect of this project from the other person's point of view? During a conversation, listen for answers to your questions.

Numbers can be hard to hear. A hotel ordered five dozen doughnuts. The bakery misheard the order as 5,000 doughnuts—and misheard the order again when a worker called to confirm the order. To avoid such errors, paraphrase, rephrase, or spell out: "That's a total of 60—six zero—doughnuts."

Source: Ty Tagami, "4,940 Extra Doughnuts," *Lexington Herald-Leader,* January 11, 2002, A1.

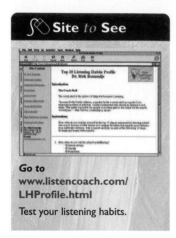

Go to
www.listencoach.com/
LHProfile.html

Test your listening habits.

- At the end of the conversation, check your understanding with the other person. Especially check who does what next.
- After the conversation, write down key points that affect deadlines or how work will be evaluated.

Focus on the Other Speaker(s) in a Generous Way.

Some people listen looking for flaws. They may focus on factors other than the substance of the talk: "What an ugly tie." "She sounds like a little girl." "There's a typo in that slide." Or they may listen as if the discussion were a war, listening for points on which they can attack the other speaker. "Ah hah! You're wrong about *that*!"

Good listeners, in contrast, are more generous. They realize that people who are not polished speakers may nevertheless have something to say. Rather than pouncing on the first error they hear and tuning out the speaker while they wait impatiently for their own turn to speak, good listeners weigh all the evidence before they come to judgment. They realize that they can learn something even from people they do not like.

To avoid listening errors caused by self-absorption,

- Focus on the substance of what the speaker says, not his or her appearance or delivery.
- Spend your time evaluating what the speaker says, not just planning your rebuttal.
- Consciously work to learn something from every speaker.

Avoid Making Assumptions.

Many listening errors come from making faulty assumptions. In 1977, when two Boeing 747 jumbo jets ran into each other on the ground in Tenerife, the pilots seem to have heard the control tower's instructions. The KLM pilot was told to taxi to the end of the runway, turn around, and wait for clearance. But the KLM pilot assumed he didn't need to follow the order to wait. The Pan Am pilot assumed that *his* order to turn off at the "third intersection" meant the third *unblocked* intersection. He didn't count the first blocked ramp, so he was still on the main runway when the KLM pilot ran into his plane at 186 miles an hour. The planes exploded in flames; 576 people died.[1]

Go to
www.esl-lab.com

ESL/EFL speakers can practice listening to English conversations at Randall's ESL Cyber Listening Lab.

In contrast, asking questions can provide useful information. Magazine advertising account representative Beverly Jameson received a phone call from an ad agency saying that a client wanted to cancel the space it had bought. Jameson saw the problem as an opportunity: "Instead of hearing 'cancel,' I heard, 'There's a problem here—let's get to the root of it and figure out how to make the client happy.' " Jameson met with the client, asked the right questions, and discovered that the client wanted more flexibility. She changed some of the markets, kept the business, and turned the client into a repeat customer.[2]

To avoid listening errors caused by faulty assumptions,

- Don't ignore instructions you think are unnecessary. Before you do something else, check with the order giver to see if in fact there is a reason for the instruction.

- Consider the other person's background and experiences. Why is this point important to the speaker? What might he or she mean by it?
- Paraphrase what the speaker has said, giving him or her a chance to correct your understanding.

Listen for Feelings as Well as Facts.

Sometimes, someone just needs to blow off steam, to vent (◁ ▶ p. 362). Sometimes, people just want to have a chance to fully express themselves; "winning" or "losing" may not matter. Sometimes, people may have objections that they can't quite put into words.

To avoid listening errors caused by focusing solely on facts,

- Consciously listen for feelings.
- Pay attention to tone of voice, facial expression, and body language (◁ ▶ p. 49).
- Don't assume that silence means consent. Invite the other person to speak.

What is active listening?

Feeding back the literal meaning, the emotional content, or both.

In **active listening,** receivers actively demonstrate that they've heard and understood a speaker by feeding back either the literal meaning or the emotional content or both. Other techniques in active listening are asking for more information and stating one's own feelings.

Five strategies create active responses:

- **Paraphrase the content.** Feed back the meaning in your own words.
- **Mirror the speaker's feelings.** Identify the feelings you think you hear.
- **State your own feelings.** This strategy works especially well when you are angry.
- **Ask for information or clarification.**
- **Offer to help solve the problem.**

Instead of simply mirroring what the other person says, many of us immediately respond in a way that analyzes or attempts to solve or dismiss the problem. People with problems need first of all to know that we hear that they're having a rough time. Figure 17.1 lists some of the responses that block communication. Ordering and interrogating all tell the other person that the speaker doesn't want to hear what he or she has to say. Preaching attacks the other person. Minimizing the problem suggests that the other person's concern is misplaced. Even advising shuts off discussion. Giving a quick answer minimizes the pain the person feels and puts him or her down for not seeing (what is to us) the obvious answer. Even if it is a good answer from an objective point of view, the other person may not be ready to hear it. And sometimes, the off-the-top-of-the-head solution doesn't address the real problem.

Hearing and Listening
Hearing denotes perceiving sounds. **Listening** means decoding and interpreting them correctly.

To make it clear that you're listening,
- Make eye contact with the speaker.
- Don't do unrelated paperwork.
- Avoid body language (like looking at your watch or shuffling papers) that suggests that you want the conversation to end.

Source: William G. Pagonis, "Leadership in a Combat Zone," *Harvard Business Review,* December 2001, 113.

Figure 17.1

Blocking Responses versus Active Listening

Blocking Response	Possible Active Response
Ordering, threatening "I don't care how you do it. Just get that report on my desk by Friday."	**Paraphrasing content** "You're saying that you don't have time to finish the report by Friday."
Preaching, criticizing "You should know better than to air the department's problems in a general meeting."	**Mirroring feelings** "It sounds like the department's problems really bother you."
Interrogating "Why didn't you *tell* me that you didn't understand the instructions?"	**Stating one's own feelings** "I'm frustrated that the job isn't completed yet, and I'm worried about getting it done on time."
Minimizing the problem "You think *that's* bad. You should see what *I* have to do this week."	**Asking for information or clarification** "What parts of the problem seem most difficult to solve?"
Advising "Well, why don't you try listing everything you have to do and seeing which items are most important?"	**Offering to help solve the problem together** "Is there anything I could do that would help?"

Source: The 5 responses that block communication are based on a list of 12 in Thomas Gordon and Judith Gordon Sands, *P.E.T. in Action* (New York: Wyden, 1976), 117–18.

Active listening takes time and energy. Even people who are skilled active listeners can't do it all the time. Furthermore, as Thomas Gordon and Judith Gordon Sands point out, active listening works only if you genuinely accept the other person's ideas and feelings. Active listening can reduce the conflict that results from miscommunication, but it alone cannot reduce the conflict that comes when two people want apparently inconsistent things or when one person wants to change someone else.[3]

How do I show people that I'm listening to them?

Acknowledge their comments in words, nonverbal symbols, and actions.

Active listening is a good way to show people that you are listening. Referring to another person's comment is another way: "I agree with Diana that. . . ."

Acknowledgment responses—nods, *uh huh's,* smiles, frowns—also help carry the message that you're listening. However, listening responses vary in different cultures. Research has found that European Americans almost always respond nonverbally when they listen closely, but that African Americans respond with words rather than nonverbal cues. This difference in response patterns may explain the fact that some European Americans think that African Americans do not understand what they are saying. For example, in the mid-1970s studies showed that white counselors repeated themselves more often to black clients than to white clients.[4] Similarly, black supervisors may want verbal feedback when they talk to white subordinates who only nod.

Instant Replay

Four Habits of Good Listeners

Good Listeners

- Pay attention.
- Focus on the other speaker(s) in a generous way.
- Avoid making assumptions.
- Listen for feelings as well as for facts.

Leading by Listening

Until January 1999, D. Michael Abrashoff was captain of the U.S.S. *Benfold,* a $1 billion warship in the U.S. Navy. Abrashoff practiced what he called "grassroots leadership": seeing the ship through the eyes of the crew.

"Soon after arriving at this command . . . I realized that my job was to listen aggressively. . . . I decided to interview five people a day . . . ask[ing] three simple questions: What do you like most about the *Benfold*? What do you like least? What would you change if you could? . . .

"I tackled the most demoralizing things first—like chipping and painting. Because ships sit in salt water and rust, . . . my youngest sailors—the ones I wanted most to connect with—were spending entire days sanding down rust and repainting the ship. It was a huge waste of physical effort." Abrashoff had all the metal parts replaced with stainless steel and then painted with a rust inhibitor. "The entire process cost just $25,000, and that paint job is good for 30 years. The kids haven't picked up a paintbrush since. And they've had a lot more time to learn their jobs. . . .

"A lot of them wanted to go to college. But most of them had never had a chance to take the SAT. So I posted a sign-up sheet to see how many would take the test if I could arrange it. Forty-five sailors signed up. I then found an SAT administrator through our base in Bahrain and flew him out to the ship to give the test. That was a simple step for me to take, but it was a big deal for morale. . . .

"Most ships report several family problems during every deployment, and most of those problems result from lack of communication. I created an AOL account for the ship and set up a system for sending messages daily through a commercial satellite. That way, sailors can check in with their families, take part in important decisions, and get a little peace of mind."

In the Navy as a whole, only 54% of sailors sign up for a third tour of duty. Under Abrashoff's command, 100% of career sailors signed on for an

additional tour. Because recruiting and training cost the Navy at least $100,000 a sailor, Abrashoff estimates that the *Benfold*'s retention rate saved the Navy $1.6 million in 1998. Meanwhile, *Benfold* sailors were promoted at twice the rate of the Navy's average. Sailors were so productive that in fiscal 1998 the *Benfold* returned $600,000 of its $2.4 million maintenance budget and $800,000 of its $3 million repair budget to the Navy.

Source: "The Most Important Thing a Captain Can Do Is to See the Ship from the Eyes of the Crew," *Fast Company,* April 1999, 114–26 and "Fast Pack 2000," *Fast Company,* March 2000, 248.

The mainstream U.S. culture shows attention and involvement by making eye contact, leaning forward, and making acknowledgment responses. However, as Module 3 shows (◀ ▶ p. 50), some cultures show respect by looking down. In a multicultural workforce, you won't always know whether a colleague who listens silently as you talk agrees with what you say or disagrees violently but is too polite to say so. The best thing to do is to observe the behavior, without assigning a meaning to it: "You aren't saying much." Then let the other person speak.

Of course, if you go through the motions of active listening but then act with disrespect, people will not feel as though you have heard them. Acting on what people say is necessary for people to feel completely heard.

Instant Replay

Strategies for Active Listening

- Paraphrase the content.
- Mirror the speaker's feelings.
- State your own feelings.
- Ask for information or clarification.
- Offer to help solve the problem.

Can I use these techniques if I really disagree with someone?

Yes!

Most of us do our worst listening when we are in highly charged emotional situations, such as talking with someone with whom we really disagree, getting bad news, or being criticized. At work, you need to listen even to people with whom you have major conflicts.

At a minimum, good listening enables you to find out why your opponent objects to the programs or ideas you support. Understanding the objections to your ideas is essential if you are to overcome those objections.

Good listening is crucial when you are criticized, especially by your boss. You need to know which areas are most important and exactly what kind of improvement counts. Otherwise, you might change your behavior in a way that wasn't valued by your organization.

Listening can do even more. Listening to people is an indication that you're taking them seriously. If you really listen to the people you disagree with, you show that you respect them. And taking that step may enable them to respect you and listen to you.

Summary of Key Points

- **Hearing** denotes perceiving sounds. **Listening** means decoding and interpreting them correctly.

- Good listeners pay attention, focus on the other speaker(s) rather than on themselves, avoid making assumptions, and listen for feelings as well as for facts.

- To avoid listening errors caused by inattention,
  - Be conscious of the points you need to know and listen for them.
  - At the end of the conversation, check your understanding with the other person.

- After the conversation, write down key points that affect deadlines or how work will be evaluated.

- To avoid listening errors caused by self-absorption,
  - Focus on what the speaker says, not his or her appearance or delivery.
  - Spend your time evaluating what the speaker says, not just planning your rebuttal.
  - Consciously work to learn something from every speaker.

- To reduce listening errors caused by misinterpretation,

- Don't ignore instructions.
- Consider the other person's background and experiences. Why is this point important to the speaker?
- Paraphrase what the speaker has said, giving him or her a chance to correct your understanding.
- To avoid listening errors caused by focusing solely on facts,
  - Consciously listen for feelings.
  - Pay attention to tone of voice, facial expression, and body language.

- Don't assume that silence means consent. Invite the other person to speak.
- In **active listening,** receivers actively demonstrate that they've heard and understood a speaker by feeding back either the literal meaning or the emotional content or both. To do this, hearers can
  - Paraphrase the content.
  - Mirror the speaker's feelings.
  - State your own feelings.
  - Ask for information or clarification.
  - Offer to help solve the problem.

Assignments for Module 17

Questions for Comprehension

17.1 What is the difference between hearing and listening?

17.2 What do good listeners do?

17.3 What is active listening?

Questions for Critical Thinking

17.4 Why is listening such hard work?

17.5 How do you show that you are listening?

17.6 What are the people and circumstances in your life where you find it most difficult to listen? Why do you find it difficult?

17.7 Think of a time when you really felt that the other person listened to you, and a time when you felt unheard. What are the differences in the two situations?

Exercises and Problems

17.8 **Identifying Responses That Show Active Listening**

Which of the following responses show active listening? Which block communication?

1. Comment: Whenever I say something, the group ignores me.

   Responses:
   a. That's because your ideas aren't very good. Do more planning before group meetings.
   b. Nobody listens to me, either.
   c. You're saying that nobody builds on your ideas.

2. Comment: I've done more than my share of work on this project. But the people who have been freeloading are going to get the same grade I worked so hard to earn.

   Responses:
   a. Yes, we all get the same grade.
   b. Are you afraid we won't do well on the assignment?
   c. It sounds like you feel resentful.

3. Comment: My parents are going to kill me if I don't have a job lined up at the end of this term.

   Responses:

   a. You know they're exaggerating. They won't *really* kill you.

   b. Can you blame them? I mean, you've been in school for six years.

Surely you've learned something to make you employable!

c. If you act the way in interviews that you do in our class, I'm not surprised. Companies want people with good attitudes and good work ethics.

17.9 Practicing Active Listening

Go around the room. In turn, let each student complain about something (large or small) that really bothers him or her. Then the next student(s) will

a. Offer a statement of limited agreement that would buy time.

b. Paraphrase the statement.

c. Check for feelings that might lie behind the statement.

d. Offer inferences that might motivate the statement.

17.10 Interviewing Workers about Listening

Interview a worker about his or her on-the-job listening. Possible questions to ask include the following:

• Whom do you listen to as part of your job? Your superior? Subordinates? (How many levels down?) Customers or clients? Who else?

• How much time a day do you spend listening?

• What people do you talk to as part of your job? Do you feel they hear what you say? How do you tell whether or not they're listening?

• Do you know of any problems that came up because someone didn't listen? What happened?

• What do you think prevents people from listening effectively? What advice would you have for someone on how to listen more accurately?

As Your Instructor Directs,

a. Share your information with a small group of students in your class.

b. Present your findings orally.

c. Present your findings in a memo to your instructor.

d. Join with other students to present your findings in a group report or presentation.

17.11 Reflecting on Your Own Listening

Keep a listening log for a week. Record how long you listened, what barriers you encountered, and what strategies you used to listen more actively and more effectively. What situations were easiest? Which were most difficult? Which parts of listening do you need to work hardest on?

As Your Instructor Directs,

a. Share your information with a small group of students in your class.

b. Present your findings orally.

c. Present your findings in a memo to your instructor.

d. Join with other students to present your findings in a group report or presentation.

17.12 Reflecting on Acknowledgment Responses

Join at least three conversations involving people from more than one culture. What acknowledgment responses do you observe? Which seem to yield the most positive results? If possible, talk to the other participants about what verbal and nonverbal cues show attentive listening in their cultures.

As Your Instructor Directs,
a. Share your information with a small group of students in your class.

b. Present your findings orally.
c. Present your findings in a memo to your instructor.
d. Join with other students to present your findings in a group report or presentation.

Polishing Your Prose

Combining Sentences

Combining sentences is a powerful tool to make your writing tighter and more forceful.

When too many sentences in a passage have fewer than 10 words and follow the same basic pattern, prose is **choppy.** Choppy prose seems less unified and either robot-like or frenzied in tone. Combining short sentences to create longer, flowing ones can eliminate this problem.

Choppy: I went to the office supply store. I purchased a computer, a fax machine, and a laser printer. I went to my office. I installed the equipment. I became more efficient.

Better: At the office supply store, I purchased a computer, a fax machine, and a laser printer. After installing the equipment, I became more efficient.

Combine sentences in one of four ways.

1. Use **transitions:** words and phrases that signal connections between ideas. Common transitions are *first, second, third, finally, in addition, likewise, for example, however, on the other hand, nevertheless, because, therefore, before, after, then, while,* and *in conclusion.*

Choppy: Neil drove the truck to the warehouse. Charlie loaded it with cement. Phil supervised the work.

Better: First, Neil drove the truck to the warehouse. Then Charlie loaded it with cement while Phil supervised the work.

2. Rewrite sentences using **subordinate clauses.** A clause with one of the following words will be subordinate: *after, although, though, because,* or *since.*

Better: After Neil drove the truck to the warehouse, Charlie loaded it with cement. Phil supervised the work.

3. Join simple sentences with **coordinating conjunctions,** like *and, but,* or *or.* These conjunctions can also function as transitional words. Be sure to use the comma before the conjunction when combining two independent clauses.

Better: Neil drove the truck to the warehouse, Charlie loaded it with cement, and Phil supervised the work.

4. Create a **list** using commas and coordinating conjunctions.

Choppy: Sam put our old files in the storeroom. Sam placed extra copies of the company telephone directory in the storeroom. Sam put boxes of three-ring binders in the storeroom.

Better: Sam put old files, extra copies of the telephone directory, and boxes of three-ring binders in the storeroom.

Exercises

Combine the following sentences to make them easier to read.

1. There are many reasons to choose Armstrong, Locke, Peabody & Associates as your human resources consulting firm. Our company has more than 75 years in the business. We have offices in New York, Chicago, Washington, D.C., Los Angeles, and Seattle. Armstrong, Locke, Peabody & Associates has 140 consultants.

2. The tan lateral file cabinets contain personnel records. The green lateral file cabinets contain contracts. The gray lateral file cabinets contain public relations materials. The lateral file cabinets are located on the first floor. The room also contains black lateral file cabinets with marketing literature.

3. The Development Team members took a plane to Seattle. That was on Friday. They attended a conference. That was on Saturday. They came home. That was on Sunday. On Friday it rained. The team members used umbrellas. The other two days it did not rain. They did not need their umbrellas on those days.

4. Todd Mendes called to let us know that he will miss Monday's staff meeting. Monday's staff meeting is scheduled for 9 A.M. Because his children's day care center is closed for painting, Todd will miss the meeting. He will need to watch his children that day because he could not find a babysitter. Todd is asking for the meeting minutes to be e-mailed to him that day. His e-mail address is TMendes@Scofield.org.

5. In January and February, the sales department plans to push its newest line of replacement toner cartridges. The department also plans to hire two more support people in January. These people will be internal hires, as the clerical pool has more than enough eligible people. In March, the department will assess the success of the sales push. By April, the department will decide whether to repeat the sales push in the fall.

Check your answers to the odd-numbered exercises at the back of the book.

BComm Skill Booster

To apply the concepts in this module, complete lessons 60 and 61 on improving your listening skills. Access the BComm Skill Booster through the text Web site at **www.mhhe.com/ bcs2e**.

Module 18

Working and Writing in Teams

Start by asking these questions:

- What kinds of messages should groups attend to?
- What roles do people play in groups?
- How should we handle conflict?
- How can we create the best co-authored documents?

Teamwork is crucial to success in an organization. Some teams produce products, provide services, or recommend solutions to problems. Other teams—perhaps in addition to providing a service or recommending a solution—also produce documents. **Interpersonal communication** is communication between people. Interpersonal skills such as listening (◄▷ Module 17) and dealing with conflict are used in one-on-one conversations, in problem-solving groups, and in writing groups. These skills will make you more successful on the job, in social groups, and in community service and volunteer work. In writing groups, careful attention to both group process and writing process (◄▷ Module 4) improves both the final product and members' satisfaction with the group.

Teams are often most effective when they explicitly adopt ground rules. Figure 18.1 lists some of the most common ground rules used by workplace teams.

Figure 18.1
Possible Group Ground Rules

- Start on time; end on time.
- Come to the meeting prepared.
- Focus comments on the issues.
- Avoid personal attacks.
- Listen to and respect members' opinions.
- NOSTUESO (No One Speaks Twice Until Everybody Speaks Once)

- If you have a problem with another person, tell that person, not everyone else.
- Everyone must be 70% comfortable with the decision and 100% committed to implementing it.
- If you agree to do something, do it.
- Communicate immediately if you think you may not be able to fulfill an agreement.

Source: Nancy Schullery and Beth Hoger, "Business Advocacy for Students in Small Groups," Association for Business Communication Annual Convention, San Antonio, November 9–11, 1998; "An Antidote to Chronic Cantankerousness," *Fast Company,* February/March 1998, 176; John Grossmann, "We've Got to Start Meeting Like This," *Inc.,* April 1998, 70; Gary Dessler, *Winning Commitment,* quoted in *Team Management Briefings,* preview issue (September 1998), 5; and 3M Meeting Network, "Groundrules and Agreements," www.3M.com/meetingnetwork/readingroom/meetingguide_grndrules.html (September 22, 2002).

What kinds of messages should groups attend to?

Different messages are appropriate at different points in a group's development.

Group messages fall into three categories:

- **Informational** messages focus on content: the problem or challenge, data, and possible solutions.
- **Procedural** messages focus on method and process. How will the group make decisions? Who will do what? When will assignments be due?
- **Interpersonal** messages focus on people, promoting friendliness, cooperation, and group loyalty.

Different messages dominate during the various stages of group development. During **orientation,** when members meet and begin to define their task, groups need to develop some sort of social cohesiveness and to develop procedures for meeting and acting. Interpersonal and procedural comments reduce the tension that exists in a new group. Insistence on information in this first stage can hurt the group's long-term productivity.

During **formation,** conflicts almost always arise when the group chooses a leader and defines the problem. Successful leaders make the procedure clear so that each member knows what he or she is supposed to do. Interpersonal communication is needed to resolve the conflict that surfaces during this phase. Successful groups analyze the problem carefully before they begin to search for solutions.

Coordination is the longest phase, during which most of the group's work is done. While procedural and interpersonal comments help maintain direction and friendliness, most of the comments need to deal with information. Good information is essential to a good decision. Conflict occurs as the group debates alternate solutions.

In **formalization,** the group seeks consensus. The success of this phase determines how well the group's decision will be implemented. In this stage, the group seeks to forget earlier conflicts.

Many businesses use teams. This Merrill Lynch "Six Sigma Process Improvement Team" saved the company more than $1 million a year and strengthened supplier relationships.

What roles do people play in groups?

Roles can be positive or negative.

Positive roles and actions that help the group achieve its task goals include the following:[1]

- **Seeking information and opinions.** Asking questions, identifying gaps in the group's knowledge.
- **Giving information and opinions.** Answering questions, providing relevant information.
- **Summarizing.** Restating major points, pulling ideas together, summarizing decisions.
- **Evaluating.** Comparing group process and products to standards and goals.
- **Coordinating.** Planning work, giving directions, and fitting together contributions of group members.

Positive roles and actions that help the group build loyalty, resolve conflicts, and function smoothly include the following:

- **Encouraging participation.** Demonstrating openness and acceptance, recognizing the contributions of members, calling on quieter group members.
- **Relieving tensions.** Joking and suggesting breaks and fun activities.
- **Checking feelings.** Asking members how they feel about group activities and sharing one's own feelings with others.
- **Solving interpersonal problems.** Opening discussion of interpersonal problems in the group and suggesting ways to solve them.
- **Listening actively.** Showing group members that they have been heard and that their ideas are being taken seriously (p. 349).

Negative roles and actions that hurt the group's product and process include the following:

- **Blocking.** Disagreeing with everything that is proposed.
- **Dominating.** Trying to run the group by ordering, shutting out others, and insisting on one's own way.

FYI

Even in basketball, teams are most effective when members have experience working together. A study of NBA teams showed that teams with low turnover did better the following year than teams that shuffled their rosters.

Source: Gene Koretz, "Chalk It Up to Teamwork," *Business—Week,* March 11, 2002, 22.

Go to
www.workteams.unt.edu
The Center for the Study of
Work Teams offers abstracts of
research reports, newsletter
archives, and an extensive list of
links.

- **Clowning.** Making unproductive jokes and diverting the group from the task.
- **Withdrawing.** Being silent in meetings, not contributing, not helping with the work, not attending meetings.

Some actions can be positive or negative depending on how they are used. Criticizing ideas is necessary if the group is to produce the best solution, but criticizing every single idea raised without ever suggesting possible solutions blocks a group. Jokes in moderation can defuse tension and make the group more fun. Too many jokes or inappropriate jokes can make the group's work more difficult.

Leadership in Groups

You may have noted that "leader" was not one of the roles listed above. Being a leader does *not* mean doing all the work yourself. Indeed, someone who implies that he or she has the best ideas and can do the best work is likely playing the negative roles of blocking and dominating.

Effective groups balance three kinds of leadership, which parallel the three group dimensions:

- **Informational leaders** generate and evaluate ideas and text.
- **Interpersonal leaders** monitor the group's process, check people's feelings, and resolve conflicts.
- **Procedural leaders** set the agenda, make sure that everyone knows what's due for the next meeting, communicate with absent group members, and check to be sure that assignments are carried out.

While it's possible for one person to do all of these responsibilities, in many groups, the three kinds of leadership are taken on by three (or more) different people. Some groups formally or informally rotate or share these responsibilities, so that everyone—and no one—is a leader.

Several studies have shown people who talk a lot, listen effectively, and respond nonverbally to other members in the group are considered to be leaders.[2]

Characteristics of Successful Student Groups

A case study of six student groups completing class projects found that students in successful groups were not necessarily more skilled or more experienced than students in less successful groups. Instead, successful and less successful groups communicated differently in three ways.[3]

1. In the successful groups, the leader set clear deadlines, scheduled frequent meetings, and dealt directly with conflict that emerged in the group. In less successful groups, members had to ask the leader what they were supposed to be doing. The less successful groups met less often, and they tried to pretend that conflicts didn't exist.
2. The successful groups listened to criticism and made important decisions together. Perhaps as a result, everyone in the group could articulate the group's goals. In the less successful groups, a subgroup made decisions and told other members what had been decided.

Leading Without Being Arrogant

Sometimes when groups form, no one wants to "lead." Perhaps that's because we've seen "leaders" who seemed dictatorial, implied that no one else's work would be up to their high standards, and generally antagonized the people unfortunate enough to have to work with them.

You don't have to be arrogant to be a leader. Here are some things that you can do to get your group started on the right track.

- **Smile.** Get to know the other members of your group as individuals. Invite members to say something about themselves, perhaps what job they're hoping to get and one fact about their lives outside school.
- **Share.** Tell people about your own work style and obligation, and ask others to share their styles and obligations. Savvy group members play to each other's strengths and devise strategies for dealing with differences. The earlier you know what those differences are, the easier it will be to deal with them.

- **Suggest.** "Could we talk about what we see as our purposes in this presentation?" "One of the things we need to do is . . ." "One idea I had for a project is. . . ." Presenting your ideas as suggestions gets the group started without suggesting that you expect your views to prevail.
- **Think.** Leaders look at the goal and identify the steps needed to get there. "Our proposal is due in two weeks. Let's list the tasks we need to do in order to write a rough draft."
- **Volunteer.** Volunteer to take notes or to gather some of the data the group will need or to prepare the charts after the data are in. Volunteer not just for the fun parts of the job (such as surfing the Web to find visuals for your PowerPoint presentation) but also for some of the dull but essential work, such as proofreading.
- **Ask.** Bring other people into the conversation. Learn about their knowledge, interests, and skills so that you'll have as much as possible to draw on as you complete your group projects.

3. The successful groups had a higher proportion of members who worked actively on the project. The successful groups even found ways to use members who didn't like working in groups. For example, one student who didn't want to be a "team player" functioned as a "freelancer" for her group, completing assignments by herself and giving them to the leader. The less successful groups had a much smaller percentage of active members and each had some members who did very little on the final project.

Rebecca Burnett has shown that student groups produce better documents when they disagree over substantive issues of content and document design. The disagreement does not need to be angry: A group member can simply say, "Yes, and here's another way we could do it." Deciding among two (or more) alternatives forces the proposer to explain the rationale for an idea. Even when the group adopts the original idea, considering alternatives rather than quickly accepting the first idea produces better writing.[4]

Kimberly Freeman found that the students who spent the most time meeting with their groups had the highest grades—on their individual as well as on group assignments.[5]

Peer Pressure and Groupthink

Groups that never express conflict may be experiencing groupthink. **Groupthink** is the tendency for groups to put such a high premium on agreement that they directly or indirectly punish dissent.

Instant Replay

Positive Roles in Groups

Task Roles
- Seeking information and opinions
- Giving information and opinions
- Summarizing
- Evaluating
- Coordinating

Interpersonal Roles
- Encouraging participation
- Relieving tensions
- Checking feelings
- Solving interpersonal problems
- Listening actively

Groups that "go along with the crowd" and suppress conflict ignore the full range of alternatives, seek only information that supports the positions they already favor, and fail to prepare contingency plans to cope with fore-seeable setbacks. A business suffering from groupthink may launch a new product that senior executives support but for which there is no demand. Student groups suffering from groupthink turn in inferior documents.

The best correctives to groupthink are to

- Consciously search for additional alternatives.
- Test assumptions against those of a range of other people.
- Encourage disagreement, perhaps even assigning someone to be "devil's advocate."
- Protect the right of people in a group to disagree.

How should we handle conflict?

Get at the real issue, and repair bad feelings.

Conflicts will arise in any group of intelligent people who care about the task. Yet many of us feel so uncomfortable with conflict that we pretend it doesn't exist. However, unacknowledged conflicts rarely go away: they fester, making the next interchange more difficult.

To reduce the number of conflicts in a group,

- Make responsibilities and ground rules clear at the beginning.
- Discuss problems as they arise, rather than letting them fester till people explode.
- Realize that group members are not responsible for each others' happiness.

Figure 18.2 suggests several possible solutions to conflicts that student groups often experience. Often the symptom arises from a feeling of not being respected or appreciated by the group. Therefore, many problems can be averted if people advocate for their ideas in a positive way. As Nancy Schullery and Beth Hoger point out, the best time to advocate for an idea is when the group has not yet identified all possible options, seems dominated by one view, or seems unable to choose among solutions. A tactful way to advocate for the position you favor is to recognize the contributions others have made, to summarize, and then to hypothesize: "What if . . . ?" "Let's look six months down the road." "Let's think about *x*."[6]

Steps in Conflict Resolution

Dealing successfully with conflict requires both attention to the issues and to people's feelings. This five-step procedure will help you resolve conflicts constructively.

1. Make Sure That the People Involved Really Disagree.

Sometimes someone who's under a lot of pressure may explode. But the speaker may just be **venting** anger and frustration; he or she may not in fact

Instant **Replay**

Three Kinds of Group Leadership

Informational leaders generate and evaluate ideas and text.

Procedural leaders set the agenda, make sure that everyone knows what's due for the next meeting, communicate with absent group members, and check to be sure that assignments are carried out.

Interpersonal leaders monitor the group's process, check people's feelings, and resolve conflicts.

Figure 18.2

Troubleshooting Group Problems

Symptom	Possible Solutions
We can't find a time to meet that works for all of us.	*a.* Find out why people can't meet at certain times. Some reasons suggest their own solutions. For example, if someone has to say home with small children, perhaps the group could meet at that person's home. *b.* Assign out-of-class work to "committees" to work on parts of the project. *c.* Use e-mail to share, discuss, and revise drafts.
One person just criticizes everything.	*a.* Ask the person to follow up the criticism with a suggestion for improvement. *b.* Talk about ways to express criticism tactfully. "I think we need to think about *x*" is more tactful than "You're wrong." *c.* Value criticism about ideas and writing (not about people). Ideas and documents need criticism if we are to improve them.
People in the group don't seem willing to disagree. We end up going with the first idea suggested.	*a.* Appoint someone to be a "devil's advocate." *b.* Brainstorm so you have several possibilities to consider. *c.* After an idea is suggested, have each person in the group suggest a way it could be improved. *d.* Have each person in the group write a draft. It's likely the drafts will be different, and you'll have several options to mix and match. *e.* Talk about good ways to offer criticism. Sometimes people don't disagree because they're afraid that other group members won't tolerate disagreement.
I seem to be the only one in the group who cares about quality.	*a.* Find out why other members "don't care." If they received low grades on early assignments, stress that good ideas and attention to detail can raise grades. Perhaps the group should meet with the instructor to discuss what kinds of work will pay the highest dividends. *b.* Volunteer to do extra work. Sometimes people settle for something that's just OK because they don't have the time or resources to do excellent work. They might be happy for the work to be done—if they didn't have to do it. *c.* Be sure that you're respecting what each person can contribute. Group members sometimes withdraw when one person dominates and suggests that he or she is "better" than other members.
One person isn't doing his or her fair share.	*a.* Find out what is going on. Is the person overcommitted? Does he or she feel unappreciated? Those are different problems you'd solve in different ways. *b.* Do things to build group loyalty. Get to know each other as writers and as people. Sometimes, do something fun together. *c.* Encourage the person to contribute. "Mary, what do you think?" "Jim, which part of this would you like to draft?" Then find something to praise in the work. "Thanks for getting us started." *d.* If someone misses a meeting, assign someone else to bring the person up to speed. People who miss meetings for legitimate reasons (job interviews, illness) but don't find out what happened may become less committed to the group. *e.* Consider whether strict equality is the most important criterion. Sometimes the best group product results from letting people do different amounts of "work." *f.* Even if you divide up the work, make all decisions as a group: what to write about, which evidence to include, what graphs to use, what revisions to make. People excluded from decisions become less committed to the group.

be angry at the person who receives the explosion. One way to find out if a person is just venting is to ask, "Is there something you'd like me to do?"

2. Check to See That Everyone's Information Is Correct.

Sometimes different conversational styles (◀ ▶ p. 54) or cultural differences (◀ ▶ p. 48) create apparent conflicts when in fact no real disagreement exists. During a negotiation between a U.S. businessman and a Balinese businessman, the Balinese man dropped his voice and lowered his eyes when he discussed price. The U.S. man saw the low voice and breaking of eye contact as an indication of dishonesty. But the Balinese believe that it is rude to mention price specifically. He was embarrassed, but he wasn't lying.[7]

Similarly, misunderstanding can arise from faulty assumptions. A U.S. student studying in Colombia quickly learned that only cold water was available for his evening shower. Since his host family washed dinner dishes in cold water, he assumed that the family didn't have hot water. They did. Colombians turn off the water heater in the morning after everyone has bathed; washing later in the day is done with cold water. He could have had hot water for his showers if he had taken them in the morning.[8]

3. Discover the Needs Each Person Is Trying to Meet.

Sometimes determining the real needs makes it possible to see a new solution. The **presenting problem** that surfaces as the subject of dissension may or may not be the real problem. For example, a worker who complains about the hours he's putting in may in fact be complaining not about the hours themselves but about not feeling appreciated. A supervisor who complains that the other supervisors don't invite her to meetings may really feel that the other managers don't accept her as a peer. Sometimes people have trouble seeing beyond the presenting problem because they've been taught to suppress their anger, especially toward powerful people. One way to tell whether the presenting problem is the real problem is to ask, "If this were solved, would I be satisfied?" If the answer is *no,* then the problem that presents itself is not in fact the real problem. Solving the presenting problem won't solve the conflict. Keep probing until you get to the real conflict.

4. Search for Alternatives.

Sometimes people are locked into conflict because they see too few alternatives. At one data-entry company, productivity fell because women employees took time off to visit their children at day care. Men on the board wanted to solve the problem by "docking" pay. The one woman on the board proposed installing software to let mothers check on their children online. That solved the problem.[9]

5. Repair Bad Feelings.

Conflict can emerge without anger and without escalating the disagreement, as the next section shows. But if people's feelings have been hurt, the group needs to deal with those feelings to resolve the conflict constructively. Only when people feel respected and taken seriously can they take the next step of trusting others in the group.

Responding to Criticism

Conflict is particularly difficult to resolve when someone else criticizes or attacks us directly. When we are criticized, our natural reaction is to defend ourselves—perhaps by counterattacking. The counterattack prompts the critic to defend him- or herself. The conflict escalates; feelings are hurt; issues become muddied and more difficult to resolve.

Just as resolving conflict depends upon identifying the needs each person is trying to meet, so dealing with criticism depends upon understanding the real concern of the critic. Constructive ways to respond to criticism and get closer to the real concern include

- Paraphrasing
- Checking for feelings
- Checking inferences
- Buying time with limited agreement.

Paraphrasing

To **paraphrase,** repeat in your own words the verbal content of the critic's message. The purposes of paraphrasing are (1) to be sure that you have heard the critic accurately, (2) to let the critic know what his or her statement means to you, and (3) to communicate the feeling that you are taking the critic and his or her feelings seriously.

Criticism: You guys are stonewalling my requests for information.

Paraphrase: You think that we don't give you the information you need quickly enough.

Checking for Feelings

When you check the critic's feelings, you identify the emotions that the critic seems to be expressing verbally or nonverbally. The purposes of checking feelings are to try to understand (1) the critic's emotions, (2) the importance of the criticism for the critic, and (3) the unspoken ideas and feelings that may actually be more important than the voiced criticism.

Criticism: You guys are stonewalling my requests for information.

Feeling check: You sound pretty angry.

Always *ask* the other person if you are right in your perception. Even the best reader of nonverbal cues is sometimes wrong.

Checking for Inferences

When you check the inferences you draw from criticism, you identify the implied meaning of the verbal and nonverbal content of the criticism, taking the statement a step further than the words of the critic to try to understand

FYI

Many business students report that they would work better in teams if they improved in the following areas:

Conflict resolution

Public speaking

Leadership

Motivation

Brainstorming

Patience and tolerance of others.

Source: Nancy M. Schullery and Melissa K. Gibson, "Working in Groups: Identification and Treatment of Students' Perceived Weaknesses," *Business Communication Quarterly* 62, no. 2, June 2001.

why the critic is bothered by the action or attitude under discussion. The purposes of checking inferences are (1) to identify the real (as opposed to the presenting) problem and (2) to communicate the feeling that you care about resolving the conflict.

Criticism: You guys are stonewalling my requests for information.

Inference: Are you saying that you need more information from our group?

Inferences can be faulty. In the above interchange, the critic might respond, "I don't need *more* information. I just think you should give it to me without my having to file three forms in triplicate every time I want some data."

Buying Time with Limited Agreement

Go to
http://users.ids.net/~brim/
sdwth.html
The Self Directed Work Team site's "Examples on the Web" links to dozens of examples of effective teams in a wide variety of organizations.

Buying time is a useful strategy for dealing with criticisms that really sting. When you buy time with limited agreement, you avoid escalating the conflict (as an angry statement might do) but also avoid yielding to the critic's point of view. To buy time, restate the part of the criticism that you agree to be true. (This is often a fact, rather than the interpretation or evaluation the critic has made of that fact.) *Then let the critic respond, before you say anything else.* The purposes of buying time are (1) to allow you time to think when a criticism really hits home and threatens you, so that you can respond to the criticism rather than simply reacting defensively, and (2) to suggest to the critic that you are trying to hear what he or she is saying.

Criticism: You guys are stonewalling my requests for information.

Limited agreement: It's true that the cost projections you asked for last week still aren't ready.

DO NOT go on to justify or explain. A "Yes, but . . ." statement is not a time-buyer.

You-Attitude in Conflict Resolution

You-attitude (◀ ▶ p. 106) means looking at things from the audience's point of view, respecting the audience, and protecting the audience's ego. The *you* statements that many people use when they're angry attack the audience; they do not illustrate you-attitude. Instead, substitute statements about your own feelings. In conflict, *I* statements show good you-attitude!

Lacks you-attitude: You never do your share of the work.

You-attitude: I feel that I'm doing more than my share of the work on this project.

Lacks you-attitude: Even you should be able to run the report through a spell checker.

You-attitude: I'm not willing to have my name on a report with so many spelling errors. I did lots of the writing, and I don't think I should have to do the proofreading and spell-checking, too.

How can we create the best co-authored documents?

Talk about your purposes and audience(s).

Discuss drafts and revisions as a group.

Whatever your career, it is likely that some of the documents you produce will be written with a group. Lisa Ede and Andrea Lunsford found that 87% of the 700 professionals in seven fields who responded to their survey sometimes wrote as members of a team or a group.[10] Collaboration is often prompted by one of the following situations:

- The task is too big or the time is too short for one person to do all the work.
- No one person has all the knowledge required to do the task.
- A group representing different perspectives must reach a consensus.
- The stakes for the task are so high that the organization wants the best efforts of as many people as possible; no one person wants the sole responsibility for the success or failure of the document.

Collaborative writing can be done by two people or by a much larger group. The group can be democratic or run by a leader who makes decisions alone. The group may share or divide responsibility for each of the eight stages in the writing process (◀ ▷ p. 71).

Research in collaborative writing is beginning to tell us about the strategies that produce the best writing. Rebecca Burnett found that student groups that voiced disagreements as they analyzed, planned, and wrote a document produced significantly better documents than those that suppressed disagreement, going along with whatever was first proposed.[11] A case study of two collaborative writing teams in a state agency found that the successful group distributed power equally, worked to soothe hurt feelings, and was careful to involve all group members. In terms of writing process, the successful group understood the task as a response to a rhetorical situation, planned revisions as a group, saw supervisors' comments as legitimate, and had a positive attitude toward revision.[12]

Ede and Lunsford's detailed case studies of collaborative teams in business, government, and science create an "emerging profile of effective collaborative writers": "They are flexible; respectful of others; attentive and analytical listeners; able to speak and write clearly and articulately; dependable and able to meet deadlines; able to designate and share responsibility, to lead and to follow; open to criticism but confident in their own abilities; ready to engage in creative conflict."[13]

Planning the Work and the Document

Collaborative writing is most successful when the group articulates its understanding of the document's purposes and audience's and explicitly discusses the best way to achieve these rhetorical goals. Businesses schedule formal planning sessions for large projects to set up a time line specifying intermediate and final due dates, meeting dates, who will attend each

Instant Replay

Responding to Criticism
Constructive ways to respond to criticism and get closer to the real concern include paraphrasing, checking for feelings, checking inferences, and buying time with limited agreement.

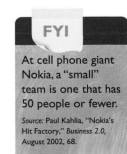

FYI

At cell phone giant Nokia, a "small" team is one that has 50 people or fewer.

Source: Paul Kahlia, "Nokia's Hit Factory," *Business 2.0*, August 2002, 68.

meeting, and who will do what. Putting the plan in writing reduces misunderstandings during the project.

When you plan a collaborative writing project,

- Make your analysis of the problem, the audience, and your purposes explicit so you know where you agree and where you disagree.
- Plan the organization, format, and style of the document before anyone begins to write to make it easier to blend sections written by different authors.
- Consider your work styles and other commitments. A writer working alone can stay up all night to finish a single-authored document. But members of a group need to work together to accommodate each other's styles and to enable members to meet other commitments.
- Build some leeway into your deadlines. It's harder for a group to finish a document when one person's part is missing than it is for a single writer to finish the last section of a document on which he or she has done all the work.

Composing the Drafts

Most writers find that composing alone is faster than composing in a group. However, composing together may reduce revision time later, since the group examines every choice as it is made.

Show that you're willing and able to work in teams.

© 1993 Farcus Cartoons   WAISGLASS/COULTHART

"We've had a few complaints that you're not a team player."

When you draft a collaborative writing project,

- Use word processing to make it easier to produce the many drafts necessary in a collaborative document.
- If the quality of writing is crucial, have the best writer(s) draft the document after everyone has gathered the necessary information.

Revising the Document

Revising a collaborative document requires attention to content, organization, and style. The following guidelines can make the revision process more effective:

- Evaluate the content and discuss possible revisions as a group. Brainstorm ways to improve each section so the person doing the revisions has some guidance.
- Recognize that different people favor different writing styles. If the style satisfies the demands of standard English and the conventions of business writing, accept it even if you wouldn't say it that way.
- When the group is satisfied with the content of the document, one person—probably the best writer—should make any changes necessary to make the writing style consistent throughout.

Editing and Proofreading the Document

Since writers' mastery of standard English varies, a group document needs careful editing and proofreading.

- Have at least one person check the whole document for correctness in grammar, mechanics, and spelling and for consistency in the way that format elements, names, and numbers are handled.
- Run the document through a spell checker if possible.
- Even if you use a computerized spell checker, at least one human being should proofread the document too.

Making the Group Process Work

When you create a co-authored document,

- Give yourselves plenty of time to discuss problems and find solutions. Purdue students who are writing group reports spend six to seven hours a week outside class in group meetings—not counting the time they spend gathering information and writing their drafts.[14]
- Take the time to get to know group members and to build group loyalty. Group members will work harder and the final document will be better if the group is important to members.
- Be a responsible group member. Attend all the meetings; carry out your responsibilities.
- Be aware that people have different ways of experiencing reality and of expressing themselves.
- Because talking is "looser" than writing, people in a group can think they agree when they don't. Don't assume that because the discussion went smoothly, a draft written by one person will necessarily be acceptable.

Summary of Key Points

- Effective groups balance information leadership, interpersonal leadership, and procedural leadership.

- A case study of six student groups completing class projects found that students in successful groups had leaders who set clear deadlines, scheduled frequent meetings, and dealt directly with conflict that emerged in the group; an inclusive decision-making style; and a higher proportion of members who worked actively on the project.

- Students who spent the most time meeting with their groups got the highest grades.

- **Groupthink** is the tendency for groups to put such a high premium on agreement that they directly or indirectly punish dissent. The best correctives to groupthink are to consciously search for additional alternatives, to test one's assumptions against those of a range of other people, and to protect the right of people in a group to disagree.

- To resolve conflicts, first make sure that the people involved really disagree. Next, check to see that everyone's information is correct. Discover the needs each person is trying to meet. The **presenting problem** that surfaces as the subject of dissension may or may not be the real problem. Search for alternatives.

- Constructive ways to respond to criticism include paraphrasing, checking for feelings, checking inferences, and buying time with limited agreement.

- Use statements about the speaker's feelings to own the problem and avoid attacking the audience. In conflict, *I* statements are good you-attitude!

- **Collaborative writing** means working with other writers to produce a single document. Writers producing a joint document need to pay attention not only to the basic steps in the writing process but also to the processes of group formation and conflict resolution.

Assignments for Module 18

Questions for Comprehension

18.1 What are the three kinds of group leadership?

18.2 What is groupthink?

18.3 How do you use you-attitude during conflict?

18.4 What strategies produce the best co-authored documents?

Questions for Critical Thinking

18.5 Why are so many people so afraid of conflict in groups? What can a group do to avoid groupthink?

18.6 Why is it better for groups to deal with conflicts, rather than just trying to ignore them?

18.7 What is the most successful group or team you've been part of? What made it effective?

Exercises and Problems

18.8   Keeping a Journal about a Group

As you work in a collaborative writing group, keep a journal after each group meeting.

- What happened?
- What roles did you play in the meeting?
- What conflicts arose? How were they handled?
- What strategies could you use to make the next meeting go smoothly?
- Record one observation about each group member.

In 18.9 through 18.13, assume that your group has been asked to recommend a solution.

As Your Instructor Directs,

a. Send e-mail messages to group members laying out your initial point of view on the issue and discussing the various options.

b. Meet as a group to come to a consensus.

c. As a group, answer the message.

d. Write a memo to your instructor telling how satisfied you are with

1. The decision your group reached.
2. The process you used to reach it.

e. Write a memo describing your group's dynamics (18.15).

18.9   Recommending a Fair Way to Assign Work Around the Holidays

You are on the Labor-Management Committee. This e-mail arrives from the general manager:

Subject: Allocating Holiday Hours

As you know, lots of people want to take extra time off around holidays to turn three-day weekends into longer trips. But we do need to stay open. Right now, there are allegations that some supervisors give the time off to their friends. But even "fair" systems, such as giving more senior workers first choice at time off, or requiring that workers with crucial skills work, also create problems. And possibly we need a different system around Christmas, when many people want to take off a week or more, than around other holidays, when most people take only an extra day or two.

Please recommend an equitable way to decide how to assign hours.

Write a group response recommending the best way to assign hours and supporting your recommendation.

Hint:
Agree on an office, factory, store, hospital, or other workplace to use for this problem.

18.10   Recommending a Policy on Student Entrepreneurs

Assume that your small group comprises the officers in student government on your campus. You receive this e-mail from the Dean of Students:

As you know, campus policy says that no student may use campus resources to conduct business-related activities. Students can't use college e-mail addresses for business. They can't post business Web pages on the college server.

On the other hand, a survey conducted by the Kauffman Center for Entrepreneurial Leadership showed that 7 out of 10 teens want to become entrepreneurs.

Should campus policy be changed to allow students to use college e-mail addresses for business? (And then what happens when our network can't carry the increased e-mail traffic?) Please recommend what support (if any) should be given to student entrepreneurs.

Write a group report recommending what (if anything) your campus should do for student entrepreneurs and supporting your recommendation.

Hints:
• Does your campus offer other support for entrepreneurs (courses, a business plan competition, a startup incubator)? What should be added or expanded?
• Is it realistic to ask alumni for money to fund student startups?
• Are campus e-mail, phone, and delivery services funded by tax dollars? If your school is a public institution, do state or local laws limit business use?

18.11 Recommending a Dress Policy

Assume that your small group comprises your organization's Labor-Management Committee This e-mail arrives from the CEO:

> In the last 10 years, we became increasingly casual. But changed circumstances seem to call for more formality. Is it time to reinstate a dress policy? If so, what should it be?

Write a group response recommending the appropriate dress for employees and supporting your recommendation.

Hint:
Agree on an office, factory, store, or other workplace to use for this problem.

18.12 Responding to an Employee Grievance

Assume that your small group comprises the Labor-Management committee at the headquarters of a chain of grocery stores. This e-mail arrives from the Vice President for Human Resources:

> As you know, company policy requires that employees smile at customers and make eye contact with them. In the past nine months, 12 employees have filed grievances over this rule. They say they are being harassed by customers who think they are flirting with them. A produce clerk claims customers have propositioned her and followed her to her car. Another says "Let *me* decide who I am going to say hello to with a big smile." The union wants us to change the policy to let workers *not* make eye contact with customers, and to allow workers to refuse to carry groceries to a customer's car at night. My own feeling is that we want to maintain our image as a friendly store that cares about customers, but that we also don't want to require behavior that leads to harassment. Let's find a creative solution.

Write a group response recommending whether to change the policy and supporting your recommendation.

18.13 Planning a Game*

Many companies are using games and contests to solve problems in an enjoyable way. One company promised to give everyone $30 a month extra if they got the error rate below 0.5%. The rate improved immediately. After several successful months, the incentive went to $40 a month for getting it under 0.3% and finally to $50 a month for getting it under 0.2%. Another company offered workers two "well hours" if they got in by 7 A.M. every day for a month. An accounting and financial-services

*Based on John Case, *The Open-Book Experience: Lessons from Over 100 Companies Who Successfully Transformed Themselves* (Reading, MA: Addison-Wesley, 1998), 129–201.

company divided its employees into two teams. The one that got the most referrals and new accounts received a meal prepared and served by the losing team (the firm paid for the food). Games are best when the people who will play them create them. Games need to make business sense and give rewards to many people, not just a few. Rewards should be small.

Think of a game or contest that could improve productivity or quality in your classroom, on campus, or in a workplace you know well.

As Your Instructor Directs,

a. Write a message to persuade your instructor, boss, or other decision maker to authorize the game or contest.

b. Write a message announcing the game and persuading people to participate in it.

18.14 Creating Brochures

In a collaborative group, create a series of brochures for an organization and present your design and copy to the class in a group oral presentation. Your brochures should work well as a series but also be capable of standing alone if a reader picks up just one. They should share a common visual design and be appropriate for your purposes and audience. You may use sketches rather than photos or finished drawings. Text, however, should be as it will appear in the final copy.

As you prepare your series, talk to a knowledgeable person in the organization. For this assignment, as long as the person is knowledgeable, he or she does not have to have the power to approve the brochures.

In a manila folder, turn in

1. Two copies of each brochure.

2. A copy of your approved proposal (◄ ► Module 21).

3. A narrative explaining (a) how you responded to the wishes of the person in the organization who was your contact and (b) five of the choices you made in terms of content, visuals, and design and why you made these choices.

18.15 Analyzing the Dynamics of a Group

Analyze the dynamics of a task group of which you are a member. Answer the following questions:

1. Who was the group's leader? How did the leader emerge? Were there any changes in or challenges to the original leader?

2. Describe the contribution each member made to the group, and the roles each person played.

3. Did any members of the group officially or unofficially drop out? Did anyone join after the group had begun working? How did you deal with the loss or addition of a group member, both in terms of getting the

work done and in terms of helping people work together?

4. What planning did your group do at the start of the project? Did you stick to the plan or revise it? How did the group decide that revision was necessary?

5. How did your group make decisions? Did you vote? Reach decisions by consensus?

6. What problems or conflicts arose? Did the group deal with them openly? To what extent did they interfere with the group's task?

7. Evaluate your group both in terms of its task and in terms of the satisfaction

members felt. How did this group compare with other task groups you've been part of? What made it better or worse?

As you answer the questions,

- Be honest. You won't lose points for reporting that your group had problems or did something "wrong."
- Show your knowledge of good group dynamics. That is, if your group did something wrong, show that you know what *should* have been done. Similarly, if your group worked well, show that you know *why* it worked well.

- Be specific. Give examples or anecdotes to support your claims.

As Your Instructor Directs,

a. Discuss these questions with the other group members.
b. Present your findings orally to the class.
c. Present your findings in an individual memo to your instructor.
d. Join with the other group members to write a collaborative memo to your instructor.

 Polishing Your Prose

Delivering Criticism

None of us likes to be told that our work isn't good. But criticism is necessary if people and documents are to improve.

Depending on the situation, you may be able to use one of these strategies:

1. Notice what's good as well as what needs work.

> The charts are great. We need to make the text as good as they are.

> I really like the builds you've used in the slides. We need to edit the bullet points so they're parallel.

2. Ask questions.

> Were you able to find any books and articles, in addition to sources on the Internet?

> What do you see as the most important revisions to make for the next draft?

3. Refer to the textbook or another authority.

> The module on design says that italic type is hard to read.

Our instructor told us that presentations should have just three main points.

4. Make statements about your own reaction.

> I'm not sure what you're getting at in this section.

> I wouldn't be convinced by the arguments here.

5. Criticize what's wrong, without making global attacks on the whole document or on the writer as a person.

> There are a lot of typos in this draft.

> You begin almost every sentence with *um.*

Exercises

Rewrite each criticism to make it less hurtful. You may add or omit information as needed.

1. My 10-year-old can spell better than you do.

2. Our group project would be going better with someone much less lazy than you.

3. You've used four different fonts in this report. Didn't you read the book? Don't you know that we're not supposed to use more than two?

4. You should straighten up and fly right if you want to succeed.

5. There's no way we'll get a passing grade if we turn this in.

6. This résumé is like bad fastfood: it looks nice but lacks anything really good for a person.

7. This is really creative. You've written the perfect illustration for "How to Fail This Course."

8. I'd explain to you what you did wrong, but what's the point? Each time you get an opportunity to prove yourself, you find a way to blow it.

9. This clip art is sexist. There's no way we should use it.

10. The last time I read something this confusing it was done in crayon by my two-year-old.

Check your answers to the odd-numbered exercises at the back of the book.

BComm Skill Booster

To apply the concepts in this module, complete lessons 64 and 65 on conducting effective meetings. You can access the BComm Skill Booster through the text Web site at **www.mhhe.com/bcs2e.**

Module 19

Planning, Conducting, and Recording Meetings

Start by asking these questions:

- What planning should precede a meeting?

- When I'm in charge, how do I keep the meeting on track?

- What decision-making strategies work well in meetings?

- How can I be an effective meeting participant?

- What should go in meeting minutes?

- How can I use informal meetings with my boss to advance my career?

- Do electronic meetings require special consideration?

Meetings have always taken a large part of the average manager's week. The increased number of teams means that meetings are even more frequent.

Business, nonprofit, and government organizations hold several types of meetings.

- **Parliamentary meetings** are run under strict rules, like the rules of parliamentary procedure summarized in *Robert's Rules of Order.* Parliamentary meetings are often used by Boards of Directors and by legislative bodies such as the U.S. Congress and Senate, but they are rarely part of the day-to-day meetings common in most businesses and nonprofit organizations.

- **Regular staff meetings** are held to announce new policies and products, answer questions, share ideas, and motivate workers. For example, Microsoft Exchange Group's development team meets every morning to review daily software builds and to identify any issues that have come up in the last 24 hours. On Fridays, about 50 Google employees meet for a fast-paced hour to discuss ways to make Google searches better and choose which new ideas to take to the next level of development.[1] A financial services company holds quarterly town-hall meetings for all employees, complete with staging, professional-quality videos, and question-and-answer sessions with the executive team.[2]
- **Team meetings** bring together team members to brainstorm, solve problems, and create documents. Meetings may be called on short notice when a problem arises that needs input from several people.
- **One-on-one meetings** are not always thought of as meetings, but they are perhaps the most common meetings of all. Employees talk by the water cooler or the refrigerator or ride up an elevator together. One person walks into another's office or cubicle to ask a question. A supervisor stops by a line worker to see how things are going and to "manage by walking around." These highly informal meetings can be crucial to your being seen as promotable.

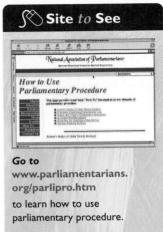

Site *to* See

How to Use Parliamentary Procedure

Go to www.parliamentarians. org/parlipro.htm

to learn how to use parliamentary procedure.

Other kinds of meetings also are held. Many companies hold sales meetings for their sales staff. Conventions bring together workers in the same field from many different employers. Retreats allow a small group to get away for team-building, brainstorming, or long-range planning.

Any of these meetings may be supported with computers. Allstate and McKinsey & Co. are among the organizations that key in comments on a computer hooked up to a large overhead projector for all the participants to see: "People literally see themselves being heard. Related comments are identified, linked, and edited on screen. The digressions and tangents quickly become apparent." The resulting document can be posted on the company intranet for further discussion and comments.[3]

Other organizations use group support software. Each person sits at a workstation. Participants key in their own brainstorming ideas and comments. People can vote by ranking items on a 1-to-10 scale; the software calculates the averages.[4]

Speakerphones and conference calls allow people in different locations to participate in the same conversation. Online meetings, such as those hosted by WebEx (www.webex.com), allow you to bring together five other participants for a simultaneous e-mail conversation in your own private chat room. Some computer systems support video as well as data or audio transmissions. Videoconferences provide high-quality video and audio transmissions.

The length and purposes of the meeting, the number of people who attend, the budget, and the available technology all affect outcomes. However, a number of principles apply to almost all meetings.

What planning should precede a meeting?

Identify the purpose(s) and create an agenda.

Meetings can have at least six purposes:

- To share information.
- To brainstorm ideas.
- To evaluate ideas.
- To make decisions.
- To create a document.
- To motivate members.

FYI

Corporate America spent more than $82.82 billion on nearly 800,000 off–site meetings last year for more than 84 million people.

Source: Ken Liebeskind, "Great Meetings," *Selling Power,* visited Web site August 1, 2002.

When meetings combine two or more purposes, it's useful to make the purposes explicit. For example, in the meeting of a university senate or a company's board of directors, some items are presented for information. Discussion is possible, but the group will not be asked to make a decision. Other items are presented for action; the group will be asked to vote. A business meeting might specify that the first half hour will be time for brainstorming, with the second half hour devoted to evaluation.

Intel's agendas also specify *how* decisions will be made. The company recognizes four different decision-making processes:

- Authoritative (the leader makes the decision alone).
- Consultative (the leader hears group comments, but then makes the decision alone).
- Voting (the majority wins).
- Consensus (discussion continues until everyone can "buy into" the decision).[5]

Specifying how input will be used makes expectations clear and focuses the conversation.

Once you've identified your purposes, think about how you can make them happen. Perhaps participants will need to receive and read materials before the meeting. Perhaps people should bring drafts to the meeting so that creating a document can go more quickly.

To make meetings more fun, the Burrell Communications Group uses giant blue, red, and yellow "relaxation balls" instead of chairs.

For team meetings called on short notice, the first item of business is to create an agenda. This kind of agenda can be informal, simply listing the topics or goals.

For meetings with more lead time, distribute an agenda several days before the meeting. (*Agenda* is Latin for "to be done.") If possible, give participants a chance to comment and revise the agenda in response to those comments. A good agenda indicates

- The time and place of the meeting.
- Whether each item is presented for information, for discussion, or for a decision.
- Who is sponsoring or introducing each item.
- How much time is allotted for each item.

See Figure 19.1 for an example.

Many groups put first routine items on which agreement will be easy. Schedule controversial items early in the meeting, when people's energy level is high, and to allow enough time for full discussion. Giving a controversial item only half an hour at the end of the day or evening makes people suspect that the leaders are trying to manipulate them.

If you're planning a long meeting, for example, a training session or a conference, recognize that networking is part of the value of the meeting. Allow short breaks at least every two hours and generous breaks twice a day so participants can talk informally to each other. If participants will be strangers, include some social functions so they can get to know each other. If they will have different interests or different levels of knowledge, plan concurrent sessions on different topics or for people with different levels of expertise.

Allow for creativity and fun. Each Best Buy store chooses its own way to start monthly staff meetings. The Best Buy in Boca Raton, Florida, opens each 7:30 A.M. meeting with a talent show.[6]

You may want to leave five minutes at the end of the meeting to evaluate it. What went well? What could be better? What do you want to change next time?

Go to
www.3M.com/meetingnet
work/readingroom/meeting
guides.html
See 3M's Meeting Network for guides to running better face-to-face and virtual meetings.

When I'm in charge, how do I keep the meeting on track?

Pay attention both to task and to process.

Your goal as chair is to help participants deal with the issues in a way that is both timely and adequately thorough.

- If many people are new to the group, make the ground rules explicit. Possible team ground rules were presented in Figure 18.1 (◁ ▷ p. 358). Ground rules for a larger meeting might cover whether it is acceptable to check e-mail during the meeting and whether people must stay for the whole meeting or can drop in and out.
- Introduce the person who introduces each issue, recognize people who want to speak, and remind the group of its progress: "We're a bit behind schedule. Let's try to get through the committee reports quickly."

Figure 19.1
Sample Meeting Agenda

Distribute the agenda early.

Marketing Committee Agenda

September 9, 10 A.M.
Conference Room 410

Specify when and where the meeting will be held.

10:00 1. Updates on Projects
       (For information)   Some groups   Everyone!
People don't vote on information items.   approve the agenda
                                             and the minutes of the   Specify who is
10:15 2. Budget Report   last meeting.   responsible for
          (For information)   Tim   presenting each
Realistic time estimates help keep a meeting on track.   item.

10:20 3. Report from the Web Subcommittee   Lori   Agendas don't
          (For <u>decision</u>: choose one of the three prototypes)   have to give this
              decision will be made during meeting   much detail. But
                                                                     referring to
10:45 4. Planning the Subsidiary Web Pages   Lori   documents reminds
          (For decision: brainstorm; then assign responsibility)   participants to
                                                                     bring them to
                                                                     the meeting.
11:00 5. Report from the Diversity Committee   Hiroshi
          (For decision: approve hiring plan)

11:25 6. Report from the Research Committee   Amanda
          (For decision: assign research topics)

11:45 7. Evaluation   Many groups use the last   Some groups leave
                            five minutes to review what   a slot for "new business."
                            went well and what needs to be
11:50 8. Adjourn   improved.

Networking

Getting to know people within and beyond your own organization helps you build a network of contacts, colleagues, and friends.

In your own organization,

- Most days, have lunch with other people in your organization. At least once a month (more often is better), invite someone whom you don't know well. You can go someplace inexpensive or even bring brown-bag lunches. But don't work through lunch more than twice a week. Use the time to widen your circle of acquaintances at the place where you work.
- At a meeting, sit by someone you don't know well. Introduce yourself, and find out something about the other person.

To get to know other business people in your community,

- At events, sit with people you don't yet know. For example, if your company buys a table of 10 seats at a charity luncheon, ask the organizers to put two of you at each of five tables so that you can use the lunch to network.
- Attend meetings of the trade association for your industry and meetings of business people specifically designed to network or to share ideas.

Join a listserv to get to know other people in your field. To find the appropriate listserv, visit www.lsoft.com/catalist.html. As this book goes to press, it links to 61,369 public listservs on the Web.

When you meet new people, suggests Marc Kramer, don't waste your time talking about news, weather, and sports. Instead, talk about business. Ask strangers what they and their companies do. When you know someone's specialty, ask his or her opinion about challenges or events in that industry. After you find out about the other person, give a short, 60-second description of your work and your company. Then probe more deeply into the other person's experience and ideas. Find out what his or her position is. Exchange business cards. And ask for the names of other people in that organization whom you should talk to, depending on your own interests and your job.

Once you've established a contact, you need to nurture it. Some business people like to send a short follow-up message right after the first meeting. In some cases, you may want to set up occasional lunches with people—in your own or in other organizations—who are particularly useful and interesting. The very best follow-up is to send something the other person can truly use—information about a book or article, a URL, the address for a listserv you find useful. Think of networking not just as a way to meet people who can be useful to you but also a way that you can be more useful and visible in your own organization and in the community in which you live and work.

Source: Marc Kramer, *Power Networking: Using the Contacts You Didn't Even Know You Have to Succeed in the Job You Want* (Lincolnwood, IL: VGM Career Horizons, 1998); and L-Soft, www.lsoft.com/catalist.html September 22, 2002.

- Be prepared to summarize issues to shape the discussion when the issues are complex or when members have major disagreements: "We're really talking about two things: whether the change would save money and whether our customers would like it. Does it make sense to keep those two together, or could we talk about customer reaction first, and then deal with the financial issues?"
- If the issue is contentious, ask that speakers for and against a recommendation alternate. If no one remains on one side, then the discussion can stop.
- Pay attention to people and process as well as to task. In small groups, invite everyone to participate.
- If conflict seems to be getting out of hand, focus on ways the group could deal with conflict (◀ ▷ Module 18) before getting back to the substantive issues.

City Year, a Boston-based, nationwide nonprofit service organization, opens meetings with a show of hands. Smaller groups reach their hands in to form a circle. Larger groups raise their hands high. Conversations stop, all is quiet, and group members are physically engaged in a common action.

- If the group doesn't formally vote, summarize the group's consensus after each point so that everyone knows what decision has been made and who is responsible for implementing or following up on each item.

What decision-making strategies work well in meetings?

Try the standard agenda or dot planning.

Probably the least effective decision-making strategy is to let the person who talks first, last, loudest, or most determine the decision. Voting is quick but may leave people in the minority unhappy with and uncommitted to the majority's plan. Coming to consensus takes time but results in speedier implementation of ideas. Two strategies that are often useful in organizational groups are the standard agenda and dot planning.

The **standard agenda** is a seven-step process for solving problems.

Instant Replay

Agenda

A good agenda indicates

- The time and place of the meeting.
- Whether each item is presented for information, for discussion, or for a decision.
- Who is sponsoring or introducing each item.
- How much time is allotted for each item.

1. Understand what the group has to deliver, in what form, by what due date. Identify available resources.
2. Identify the problem. What exactly is wrong? What question(s) is the group trying to answer?
3. Gather information, share it with all group members, and examine it critically.
4. Establish criteria. What would the ideal solution include? Which elements of that solution would be part of a less-than-ideal but still acceptable solution? What legal, financial, moral, or other limitations might keep a solution from being implemented?
5. Generate alternate solutions. Brainstorm and record ideas for the next step.
6. Measure the alternatives against the criteria.
7. Choose the best solution.[7]

Figure 19.2

Dot Planning Allows Groups to Set Priorities Quickly

Here, green dots mean "high priority;" purple dots mean "low priority." One can see at a glance which items have widespread support, which are controversial, and which are low priority.

Source: "The Color-Coded Priority Setter," Inc., June 1995, 70–71.

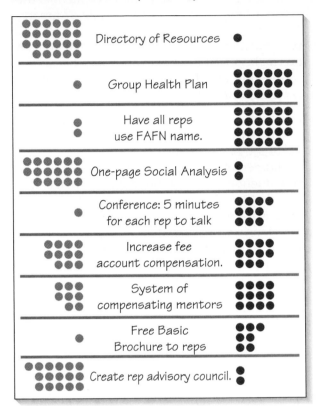

Dot planning offers a way for large groups to choose priorities quickly. First, the group brainstorms ideas, recording each on pages that are put on the wall. Then each individual gets two strips of three to five adhesive dots in different colors. One color represents high priority, the other lower priority. People then walk up to the pages and affix dots by the points they care most about. Some groups allow only one dot from one person on any one item; others allow someone who is really passionate about an idea to put all of his or her dots on it. As Figure 19.2 shows, the dots make it easy to see which items the group believes are most important.

How can I be an effective meeting participant?

Be prepared.

Take the time to prepare for meetings. Read the materials distributed before the meeting and think about the issues to be discussed. Bring those materials

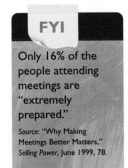

FYI

Only 16% of the people attending meetings are "extremely prepared."

Source: "Why Making Meetings Better Matters," Selling Power, June 1999, 78.

to the meeting, along with something to write on, and with, even if you're not the secretary.

In a small meeting, you'll probably get several chances to speak. Roger Mostvick and Robert Nelson found that the most influential people in a meeting are those who say something in the first five minutes of the meeting (even just to ask a question), who talk most often, and who talk at greatest length.[8]

In a large meeting, you may get just one chance to speak. Make notes of what you want to say so that you can be succinct, fluent, and complete.

It's frustrating to speak in a meeting and have people ignore what you say. Here are some tips for being taken seriously.[9]

- Show that you've done your homework. Laura Sloate, who is blind, establishes authority by making sure her first question is highly technical: "In footnote three of the 10K, you indicate . . ."
- Link your comment to the comment of a powerful person. Even if logic suffers a bit, present your comment as an addition, not a challenge. For example, say, "John is saying that we should focus on excellence, AND I think we can become stronger by encouraging diversity."
- Find an ally in the organization and agree ahead of time to acknowledge each other's contributions to the meeting, whether you agree or disagree with the point being made. Explicit disagreement signals that the comment is worth taking seriously: "Duane has pointed out . . . , but I think that . . ."

What should go in meeting minutes?

Site to See

**Go to
www.bog.frb.fed.us/FOMC/
minutes/**

The Federal Open Market Committee posts its minutes on the Web.

Topics discussed, decisions reached, and who does what next.

Meeting expert Michael Begeman suggests recording three kinds of information:

- Decisions reached.
- Action items, where someone needs to implement or follow up on something.
- Open issues—issues raised but not resolved.[10]

Minutes of formal meetings indicate who was present and absent and the wording of motions and amendments as well as the vote. Committee reports are often attached for later reference. For less formal meetings, brief minutes are fine. The most important notes are the decisions and assignments. Long minutes will be most helpful if assignments are set off visually from the narrative.

> We discussed whether we should switch from road to rail shipment.
>   Action: Sue will get figures on cost for the next meeting.
>   Action: Tyrone will survey current customers online to ask their opinions.

How can I use informal meetings with my boss to advance my career?

Plan scripts to present yourself positively.

You'll see your supervisor several times a week. Some of these meetings will be accidental: you'll meet by the coffeepot or ride up the elevator together. Some of them will be deliberately initiated: your boss will stop by your work-station, or you'll go to your boss's office to ask for something.

You can take advantage of these meetings by planning for them. These informal meetings are often short. An elevator ride, for example, may last about three minutes. So plan 90-second scripts that you can use to give your boss a brief report on what you're doing, ask for something you need, or lay the groundwork for an important issue.

Planning scripts is especially important if your boss doesn't give you much feedback or mentoring. In this case, your boss probably doesn't see you as promotable. You need to take the initiative. Make statements that show the boss you're thinking about ways to work smarter. Show that you're interested in learning more so that you can be even more valuable to the organization.

Instant Replay

Decision-Making Strategies
The **standard agenda** is a seven-step process for solving problems.
Dot planning offers a way for large groups to choose priorities quickly.

Do electronic meetings require special consideration?

Yes. Watch interpersonal communication.

For important projects, build in some face-to-face meetings as well.

When you meet electronically rather than in person, you lose the informal interactions of going to lunch or chatting during a break. Those interactions not only create bonds, so that people are more willing to work together, but also give people a chance to work out dozens of small issues. Listening (◀▶ Module 17), teamwork, and the ability to resolve conflicts construc-tively (◀▶ Module 18) become even more crucial.

Be aware of the limitations of your channel. When you are limited to e-mail, you lose both tone of voice and body language. In addition, e-mail messages are often more brusque than comments in person (◀▶ Module 13). Audio messages provide tone of voice but not the nonverbal signals that tell you whether someone wants to make a comment or understands what you're saying. Even videoconferencing gives you only the picture in the camera's lens. With any of these technologies, you'll need to attend specifi-cally to interpersonal skills.

Technical communicator Aimee Kratts recommends the following tips for making an international teleconference run smoothly:

- Distribute the agenda and other materials well in advance. The call may take place in the middle of the night in some countries. Participants at home may not have printers or even computers and may not be able to receive last-minute documents.

Meetings depend on social interaction as well as on a good agenda.

- Encourage speakers to use standard English with as little slang as possible. If you think participants have misunderstood each other, try to clarify.
- Ask for questions periodically.
- Ask for contributions from people who haven't spoken.
- Listen for disagreements. "I hear Raul saying *X* and Bertine saying *Y*. Is that right?"
- Encourage offline discussions on e-mail to follow up on topics.
- Call participants individually the next day to take the emotional temperature.
- Take and distribute written minutes.[11]

Summary of Key Points

- A good agenda indicates
  - The time and place of the meeting.
  - Whether each item is presented for information, for discussion, or for a decision.
  - Who is sponsoring or introducing each item.
  - How much time is allotted for each item.
- To make meetings more effective,
  - State the purpose of the meeting at the beginning.
  - Distribute an agenda that indicates whether each item is for information, for

  discussion, or for a decision, and how long each is expected to take.
- Allow enough time to discuss controversial issues.
- Pay attention to people and process as well as to the task at hand.
- If you don't take formal votes, summarize the group's consensus after each point. At the end of the meeting, summarize all decisions and remind the group who is responsible for implementing or following up on each item.

- The **standard agenda** is a seven-step process for solving problems. In **dot planning** the group brainstorms ideas. Then each individual affixes adhesive dots by the points or proposals he or she cares most about.

- Minutes should record
  - Decisions reached.
  - Action items, where someone needs to implement or follow up on something.
  - Open issues—issues raised but not resolved.

Assignments for Module 19

Questions for Comprehension

19.1 What should go in an agenda?

19.2 What are the seven steps in the standard meeting agenda?

19.3 When would dot planning be most effective?

19.4 What should go in minutes of a meeting?

Questions for Critical Thinking

19.5 What opportunities do you have to network?

19.6 In the groups of which you're a member (at school, at work, and in volunteer organizations), what kinds of comments are most valued in meetings?

19.7 What is the best meeting you ever attended? What made it so effective?

Exercises and Problems

19.8 Writing an Agenda

Write an agenda for your next collaborative group meeting.

As Your Instructor Directs,
a. Write a memo to your instructor, explaining the choices you made.

b. Compare your agenda with the ones developed by others in your group. Use the agendas as drafts to help you create the best possible agenda.

c. Present your best agenda to the rest of the class in a group oral presentation.

19.9 Taking Minutes

As Your Instructor Directs,
Have two or more people take minutes of each class or collaborative group meeting for a week. Compare the accounts of the same meeting.

- To what extent do they agree on what happened?

- Does one contain information missing in other accounts?
- Do any accounts disagree on a specific fact?
- How do you account for the differences you find?

19.10 Writing a Meeting Manual*

Create a manual for students next term telling them how to have effective meetings as they work on collaborative projects.

*Adapted from Miles McCall, Beth Stewart, and Timothy Clipson, "Teaching Communication Skills for Meeting Management," *1998 Refereed Proceedings*, Association for Business Communication Southwestern United States, ed. Marsha L. Bayless (Nacogdoches, TX), 68.

19.11 Planning Scripts for 3-Minute Meetings

Create a script for a 90-second statement to your boss

1. Describing the progress on a project you're working on.

2. Providing an update on a problem the boss already knows about.

3. Telling about a success or achievement.

4. Telling about a problem and asking approval for the action you recommend.

5. Asking for resources you need for a project.

6. Asking for training you'd like to get.

7. Laying the groundwork for a major request you need to make.

As Your Instructor Directs,

a. Discuss your scripts with a small group of other students.

b. Present your script to the class.

c. Write a memo to your instructor giving your script(s) and explaining the choices you have made in terms of content, arrangement, and word choice.

Polishing Your Prose

Hyphens and Dashes

Hyphens and dashes are forms of punctuation used within sentences.

Use a **hyphen** to

1. Join two or more words used as a single adjective.

   Correct: Order five 10- or 12-foot lengths.

Here, hyphens prevent misreading. Five lengths are needed, not lengths of 5, 10, or 12 feet.

2. Indicate that a word has been divided between two lines.

   Correct: Our biggest competitor announced plans to introduce new models of computers into the European market.

Divide words only at syllable breaks. If you aren't sure where the syllables break, look up the word in a dictionary. When a word has several syllables, divide it after a vowel or between two consonants.

While many word processing programs automatically hyphenate for you, knowing where and when to divide words is important for words the program may not recognize or for special cases. For instance, don't divide words of one syllable (e.g., *used*), and don't divide a two-syllable word if one of the syllables is only one letter long (e.g., *acre*).

Use a **dash** to

1. Emphasize a break in thought.

   Correct: Despite our best efforts— which included sending a design team to Paris and increasing our promotional budget—sales are lagging.

Create a dash by typing the hyphen key twice. With some word processors, this "double hyphen" will automatically be replaced with a longer, single dash, which is acceptable.

Exercises

Supply necessary dashes or hyphens in the following sentences. If no punctuation is needed—if a space is correct—leave the box blank.

1. Our cutting☐edge fashions sell best in French☐Canadian cities like Montreal.

2. The 12 ☐ by ☐ 25 ☐ foot conference room is too small for the meeting; see if we can reserve the 23 ☐ by ☐ 30 ☐ foot conference room instead.

3. Next Monday, *BusinessWeek* ☐ magazine will do a cover story on a thriving new business created by Native ☐ Americans.

4. The three contracts ☐ all signed the same day ☐ nonetheless were mailed on three successive days, and we're investigating why.

5. Our gift certificates come in 5 ☐, 10 ☐, and 15☐dollar denominations.

6. Check the Table ☐ of ☐ Contents in the Anderson report ☐ the one on the top of my desk ☐ to see which sections are included.

7. We need to work on more cost ☐ effective versions of our best ☐ selling software programs.

8. The Data ☐ Processing ☐ Division expects to bring a more user ☐ friendly MIS system online for subsidiaries throughout Western ☐ Europe.

9. Kathy gave us four ☐ options during the sales ☐ meeting on Friday afternoon.

10. The Public Relations Department awarded the two ☐ student essays on business ☐ ethics each a $25 ☐ savings ☐ bond.

Check your answers to the odd-numbered exercises at the back of the book.

BComm Skill Booster

To apply the concepts in this module, complete lessons 35, 36, and 37 on communicating and resolving conflict in group situations. You can access the BComm Skill Booster through the text Web site at **www.mhhe.com/bcs2e.**

Module 20

Making Oral Presentations

Start by asking these questions:

- What decisions do I need to make as I plan a presentation?
- How can I create a strong opener and close?
- How should I organize a presentation?
- What are the keys to delivering an effective presentation?
- How should I handle questions from the audience?
- What are the guidelines for group presentations?

Making a good oral presentation is more than just good delivery: It also involves developing a strategy that fits your audience and purpose, having good content, and organizing material effectively. The choices you make in each of these areas are affected by your purposes, the audience, and the situation.

Giving a presentation is in many ways very similar to writing a message. The other modules in this book—on analyzing your audience, using you-attitude and positive emphasis, developing reader benefits, designing slides, overcoming objections, doing research, and analyzing data—remain relevant as you plan an oral presentation.

Oral presentations have the same three basic purposes that written documents have: to inform, to persuade, and to build goodwill. Like written messages, most oral presentations have more than one purpose.

Informative presentations inform or teach the audience. Training sessions in an organization are primarily informative. Secondary purposes may be to persuade new employees to follow organizational procedures, rather than doing something their own way, and to help them appreciate the organizational culture (◄ ▷ p. 32).

Persuasive presentations motivate the audience to act or to believe. Giving information and evidence is an important means of persuasion. Stories, visuals, and self-disclosure are also effective. In addition, the speaker must build goodwill by appearing to be credible and sympathetic to the audience's needs. The goal in many presentations is a favorable vote or decision. For example, speakers making business presentations may try to persuade the audience to approve their proposals, to adopt their ideas, or to buy their products. Sometimes the goal is to change behavior or attitudes or to reinforce existing attitudes. For example, a speaker at a meeting of factory workers may stress the importance of following safety procedures. A speaker at a church meeting may talk about the problem of homelessness in the community and try to build support for community shelters for the homeless.

Goodwill presentations entertain and validate the audience. In an after-dinner speech, the audience wants to be entertained. Presentations at sales meetings may be designed to stroke the audience's egos and to validate their commitment to organizational goals.

Make your purpose as specific as possible.

Weak: The purpose of my presentation is to discuss saving for retirement.

Better: The purpose of my presentation is to persuade my audience to put their 401(k) funds in stocks and bonds, not in money market accounts and CDs.

or: The purpose of my presentation is to explain how to calculate how much money someone needs to save in order to maintain a specific lifestyle after retirement.

Note that the purpose *is not* the introduction of your talk; it is the principle that guides your decisions as you plan your presentation.

What decisions do I need to make as I plan a presentation?

Choose your main point, the kind of presentation, and ways to involve the audience.

An oral presentation needs to be simpler than a written message to the same audience. Identify the one idea you want the audience to take home. Simplify your supporting detail so it's easy to follow. Simplify visuals so they can be taken in at a glance. Simplify your words and sentences so they're easy to understand.

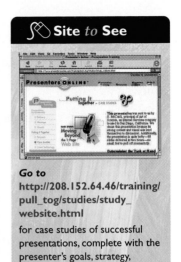

Site *to* See

Go to
**http://208.152.64.46/training/
pull_tog/studies/study_
website.html**

for case studies of successful presentations, complete with the presenter's goals, strategy, outline, and sample slides.

FYI

CEOs face many of the same challenges as other presenters: anxiety, lack of preparation time, and misreading an audience. If a CEO misspeaks or represents his company poorly, the consequences can be severe—from a dip in stock price to lower employee morale.

Source: Julie Hill, "The Big Cheese," *Presentation*, June 12, 2002.

Three Purposes

• **Informative presentations** inform or teach the audience.

• **Persuasive presentations** motivate the audience to act or to believe.

• **Goodwill presentations** entertain and validate the audience.

Most oral presentations have more than one purpose.

Presentation coach Jerry Weissman helped client David Angel simplify his description of his company:[1]

Too complicated: Information Storage Devices provides voice solutions using the company's unique, patented multilevel storage technique.

Simple: We make voice chips. They're extremely easy to use. They have unlimited applications. And they last forever.

Analyze your audience for an oral presentation just as you do for a written message. If you'll be speaking to co-workers, talk to them about your topic or proposal to find out what questions or objections they have. For audiences inside the organization, the biggest questions are often practical ones: Will it work? How much will it cost? How long will it take?[2]

Think about the physical conditions in which you'll be speaking. Will the audience be tired at the end of a long day of listening? Sleepy after a big meal? Will the group be large or small? The more you know about your audience, the better you can adapt your message to the audience.

Choosing the Kind of Presentation

Choose one of three basic kinds of presentations: monologue, guided discussion, or sales.

In a **monologue presentation,** the speaker speaks without interruption; questions are held until the end of the presentation, where the speaker functions as an expert. The speaker plans the presentation in advance and delivers it without deviation. This kind of presentation is the most common in class situations, but it's often boring for the audience. Good delivery skills are crucial, since the audience is comparatively uninvolved.

Linda Driskill suggests that **guided discussions** offer a better way to present material and help an audience find a solution it can "buy into." In a guided discussion, the speaker presents the questions or issues that both speaker and audience have agreed on in advance. Rather than functioning as an expert with all the answers, the speaker serves as a facilitator to help the audience tap its own knowledge. This kind of presentation is excellent for presenting the results of consulting projects, when the speaker has specialized knowledge, but the audience must implement the solution if it is to succeed. Guided discussions need more time than monologue presentations, but produce more audience response, more responses involving analysis, and more commitment to the result.[3]

A **sales presentation** is a conversation, even if the salesperson stands up in front of a group and uses charts and overheads. The sales representative uses questions to determine the buyer's needs, probe objections, and gain temporary and then final commitment to the purchase. Even in a memorized sales presentation, the buyer will talk at least 30% of the time. In a problem-solving sales presentation, the buyer may talk 70% of the time.

Adapting Your Ideas to the Audience

Measure the message you'd like to send against where your audience is now. If your audience is indifferent, skeptical, or hostile, focus on the part of your message the audience will find most interesting and easiest to accept.

To win the plum Domino's account, Deutsch advertising conducted months of research and made numerous presentations. Wearing Domino's clothing was one strategy for making Domino's decision makers feel comfortable with Deutsch.

Don't seek a major opinion change in a single oral presentation. If the audience has already decided to hire an advertising agency, then a good presentation can convince them that your agency is the one to hire. But if you're talking to a small business that has always done its own ads, limit your purpose. You may be able to prove that an agency can earn its fees by doing things the owner can't do and by freeing the owner's time for other activities. A second presentation may be needed to prove that an ad agency can do a *better* job than the small business could do on its own. Only after the audience is receptive should you try to persuade the audience to hire your agency rather than a competitor.

Make your ideas relevant to your audience by linking what you have to say to the audience's experiences and interests. Showing your audience members that the topic affects them directly is the most effective strategy. When you can't do that, at least link the topic to some everyday experience.

> When was the last time you were hungry? Maybe you remember being hungry while you were on a diet, or maybe you had to work late at a lab and didn't get back to the dorm in time for dinner.

speech about world hunger to an audience of college students

Planning Visuals and Other Devices to Involve the Audience

Visuals can give your presentation a professional image. In 1986, a study found that presenters using overhead transparencies were perceived as "better prepared, more professional, more persuasive, more credible, and more interesting" than speakers who did not use visuals. They were also more likely to persuade a group to adopt their recommendations. Colored overhead transparencies were most effective in persuading people to act.[4] In 2000, a study found that in an informative presentation, multimedia (PowerPoint slides with graphics and animation) produced 5% more learning than overheads made from the slides and 16% more learning than text alone. In a sales presentation by two banks, multimedia (PowerPoint slides with graphics, animation, and video) motivated 58% more students to choose that

Instant **Replay**

Simplify
An oral presentation needs to be simpler than a written message to the same audience.

bank compared to overheads and 60% more compared to text alone. Although the two banks offered identical fees and services, students said that the bank represented by the multimedia presentation "was more credible, was more professional, and offered better services and fees."[5]

Use at least 18-point type for visuals you prepare with a word processor. When you prepare slides with PowerPoint, Corel, or another presentation program, use at least 24-point type for the smallest words.

Well-designed visuals can serve as an outline for your talk (see Figure 20.1), eliminating the need for additional notes. Don't try to put your whole talk on visuals. Visuals should highlight your main points, not give every detail.

Use these guidelines to create and show visuals for presentations:

- Make only one point with each visual. Break a complicated point down into several visuals.
- Give each visual a title that makes a point.
- Limit the amount of information on a visual. Use 35 words or less in seven lines or less; use simple graphs, not complex ones.
- Don't put your visual up till you're ready to talk about it. Leave it up until your next point; don't turn the projector or overhead off.

See Module 25 for information on how to present numerical data through visuals.

Visuals work only if the technology they depend on works. When you give presentations in your own office, check the equipment in advance. When you make a presentation in another location or for another organiza-

Figure 20.1
PowerPoint Slides for an Informative Presentation

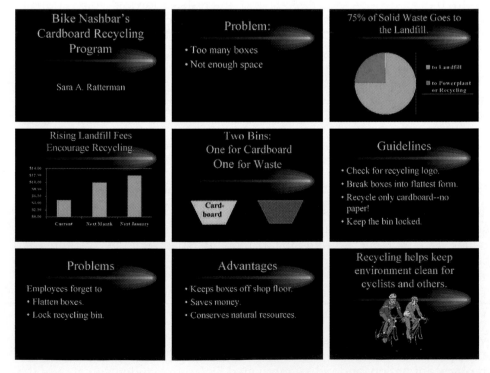

tion, arrive early so that you'll have time not only to check the equipment but also to track down a service worker if the equipment isn't working. Be prepared with a backup plan to use if you're unable to show your slides or videotape.

You can also involve the audience in other ways.

- A student giving a presentation on English-French business communication demonstrated the differences in U.S. and French handshakes by asking a fellow class member to come up to shake hands with her.
- Another student discussing the need for low-salt products brought in a container of Morton salt, a measuring cup, a measuring spoon, and two plates. As he discussed the body's need for salt, he measured out three teaspoons onto one plate: the amount the body needs in a month. As he discussed the amount of salt the average U.S. diet provides, he continued to measure out salt onto the other plate, stopping only when he had 1¼ pounds of salt—the amount in the average U.S. diet. The demonstration made the discrepancy clear in a way words or even a chart could not have done.[6]
- To make sure that his employees understood where money went, the CEO of a specialty printing shop in Algoma, Wisconsin, printed up $2 million in play money and handed out big cards to employees marked *Labor, Depreciation, Interest,* and so forth. Then he asked each "category" to come up and take its share of the revenues. The action was more dramatic than a color pie chart could ever have been.[7]
- Another speaker who was trying to raise funds used the simple act of asking people to stand to involve them, to create emotional appeal, and to make a statistic vivid:

  [A speaker] was talking to a luncheon club about contributing to the relief of an area that had been hit by a tornado. The news report said that 70% of the people had been killed or disabled. The room was set up ten people at each round table. He asked three persons at each table to stand. Then he said, ". . . You people sitting are dead or disabled. You three standing have to take care of the mess. You'd need help, wouldn't you?"[8]

FYI

Good speakers spend one hour of planning and rehearsal time for every minute of presentation time.

Source: Dave Zielinski, "Managing Prep Time," *Presentations,* February 2002, 34.

PowerPoint slides aren't the only or necessarily the best way to involve the audience. Dan Leeber persuaded UPS to swtich to Valeo clutches by completely disassembling the competitor's clutch and showing part by part why Valeo's product was better.

How can I create a strong opener and close?

Brainstorm several possibilities.

The following four modes can help.

The beginning and end of a presentation, like the beginning and end of a written document, are positions of emphasis. Use those key positions to interest the audience and emphasize your key point. You'll sound more natural and more effective if you talk from notes but write out your opener and close in advance and memorize them. (They'll be short: just a sentence or two.)

Brainstorm several possible openers for each of the four modes: startling statement, narration or anecdote, question, or quotation. The more you can do to personalize your opener for your audience, the better. Recent events are better than things that happened long ago; local events are better than events at a distance; people they know are better than people who are only names.

Startling Statement

> Twelve of our customers have canceled orders in the past month.

This presentation to a company's executive committee went on to show that the company's distribution system was inadequate and to recommend a third warehouse located in the southwest.

Narration or Anecdote

> A mother was having difficulty getting her son up for school. He pulled the covers over his head.
> "I'm not going to school," he said. "I'm not ever going again."
> "Are you sick?" his mother asked.
> "No," he answered. "I'm sick of school. They hate me. They call me names. They make fun of me. Why should I go?"
> "I can give you two good reasons," the mother replied. "The first is that you're 42 years old. And the second is *you're the school principal.*"[9]

This speech to a seminar for educators went on to discuss "the three knottiest problems in education today." Educators had to face those problems; they couldn't hide under the covers.

Even better than canned stories are anecdotes that happened to you. The best anecdotes are parables that contain the point of your talk.

Question

> Are you going to have enough money to do the things you want to when you retire?

Don't start a speech with a joke unless it fits the occasion, won't offend anyone, and is really funny.

This presentation to a group of potential clients discusses the value of using the services of a professional financial planner to achieve one's goals for retirement.

Quotation

According to Towers Perrin, the profits of Fortune 100 companies would be 25% lower—they'd go down $17 billion—if their earnings statements listed the future costs companies are obligated to pay for retirees' health care.

This presentation on options for health care for retired employees urges executives to start now to investigate options to cut the future cost.

Your opener should interest the audience and establish a rapport. Some speakers use humor to achieve those goals. However, an inappropriate joke can turn the audience against the speaker. Never use humor that's directed against the audience. In contrast, speakers who can make fun of themselves almost always succeed:

It's both a privilege and a pressure to be here.[10]

Humor isn't the only way to set an audience at ease. Smile at your audience before you begin; let them see that you're a real person and a nice one.

The end of your presentation should be as strong as the opener. For your close, you could do one or more of the following:

• Restate your main point.
• Refer to your opener to create a frame for your presentation.

- End with a vivid, positive picture.
- Tell the audience exactly what to do to solve the problem you've discussed.

The following close from a fund-raising speech combines a restatement of the main point with a call for action, telling the audience what to do.

> Plain and simple, we need money to run the foundation, just like you need money to develop new products. We need money to make this work. We need money from you. Pick up that pledge card. Fill it out. Turn it in at the door as you leave. Make it a statement about your commitment . . . make it a big statement.[11]

When you write out your opener and close, be sure to use oral rather than written style. As you can see in the example close above, oral style uses shorter sentences and shorter, simpler words than writing does. Oral style can even sound a bit choppy when it is read by eye. Oral style uses more personal pronouns, a less varied vocabulary, and more repetition.

How should I organize a presentation?

Start with the main point. Often, one of five standard patterns will work.

Most presentations use a direct pattern of organization, even when the goal is to persuade a reluctant audience. In a business setting, the audience members are in a hurry and know that you want to persuade them. Be honest about your goals, and then prove that your goal meets the audience's needs too.

In a persuasive presentation, start with your strongest point, your best reason. If time permits, give other reasons as well and respond to possible objections. Put your weakest point in the middle so that you can end on a strong note.

Often one of five standard patterns of organization will work.

- **Chronological.** Start with the past, move to the present, and end by looking ahead.
- **Problem-Causes-Solution.** Explain the symptoms of the problem, identify its causes, and suggest a solution. This pattern works best when the audience will find your solution easy to accept.
- **Excluding alternatives.** Explain the symptoms of the problem. Explain the obvious solutions first and show why they won't solve the problem. End by discussing a solution that will work. This pattern may be necessary when the audience will find the solution hard to accept.
- **Pro-Con.** Give all the reasons in favor of something, then those against it. This pattern works well when you want the audience to see the weaknesses in its position.
- **1-2-3.** Discuss three aspects of a topic. This pattern works well to organize short informative briefings. "Today I'll review our sales, production, and profits for the last quarter."

Finding Your Best Voice

A good voice supports and enhances good content. Your best voice will manipulate pitch, intonation, tempo, and volume. Sound energetic and enthusiastic.

Pitch

Pitch measures whether a voice uses sounds that are low (like the bass notes on a piano) or high. Low-pitched voices are usually perceived as being more authoritative, sexier, and more pleasant to listen to than are high-pitched voices. Most voices go up in pitch when the speaker is angry or excited; some people raise pitch when they increase volume. Women whose normal speaking voices are high may need to practice projecting their voices to avoid becoming shrill when they speak to large groups.

To find your best pitch, try humming. The pitch where the hum sounds loudest and most resonant is your best voice.

Intonation

Intonation marks variation in pitch, stress, or tone. Speakers who use many changes in pitch, stress, and tone usually seem more enthusiastic; often they also seem more energetic and more intelligent. Someone who speaks in a monotone may seem apathetic or unintelligent. Non-native speakers whose first language does not use tone, pitch, and stress to convey meaning and attitude may need to practice varying these voice qualities.

Avoid raising your voice at the end of a sentence, however. In English, a rising intonation signals a question. Therefore, speakers who end sentences on higher tones sound as though they're unsure of what they're saying.

Tempo

Tempo is a measure of speed. In a conversation, match your tempo to the other speaker's to build rapport. In a formal presentation, you'll need to speak more slowly and have longer pauses than in an informal conversation. Vary your tempo. Speakers who speak quickly and who vary their volume during the talk are more likely to be perceived as competent.

Volume

Volume is a measure of loudness or softness. Very soft voices, especially if they are also breathy and high-pitched, give the impression of youth and inexperience. People who do a lot of speaking to large groups need to practice projecting their voices so they can increase their volume without shouting.

Source: George B. Ray, "Vocally Cued Personality Prototypes: An Implicit Personality Theory Approach," *Communication Monographs* 53, no. 3 (1986): 266–76, and Jacklyn Boice, "Verbal Impressions," *Selling Power*, March 2000, 69.

Early in your talk—perhaps immediately after your opener—provide an **overview of the main points** you will make.

> First, I'd like to talk about who the homeless in Columbus are. Second, I'll talk about the services The Open Shelter provides. Finally, I'll talk about what you—either individually or as a group—can do to help.

An overview provides a mental peg that hearers can hang each point on. It also can prevent someone missing what you are saying because he or she wonders why you aren't covering a major point that you've saved for later.[12]

Offer a clear signpost as you come to each new point. A **signpost** is an explicit statement of the point you have reached. Choose wording that fits your style. The following statements are four different ways that a speaker could use to introduce the last of three points:

> Now we come to the third point: what you can do as a group or as individuals to help homeless people in Columbus.

So much for what we're doing. Now let's talk about what you can do to help.

You may be wondering, what can I do to help?

As you can see, the Shelter is trying to do many things. We could do more things with your help.

What are the keys to delivering an effective presentation?

Turn your fear into energy, look at the audience, and use natural gestures.

Audience members want the sense that you're talking directly to them and that you care that they understand and are interested. They'll forgive you if you get tangled up in a sentence and end it ungrammatically. They won't forgive you if you seem to have a "canned" talk that you're going to deliver no matter who the listeners are or how they respond. You can convey a sense of caring to your audience by making direct eye contact and by using a conversational style.

Transforming Fear

Feeling nervous is normal. But you can harness that nervous energy to help you do your best work. As one student said, you don't need to get rid of your butterflies. All you need to do is make them fly in formation.

To calm your nerves as you prepare to give an oral presentation,

- Be prepared. Analyze your audience, organize your thoughts, prepare visual aids, practice your opener and close, check out the arrangements.
- Use only the amount of caffeine you normally use. More or less may make you jumpy.
- Avoid alcoholic beverages.
- Use positive emphasis (◄ ▶ Module 7). Instead of saying, "I'm scared," try saying, "My adrenaline is up." Adrenaline sharpens our reflexes and helps us do our best.

Just before your presentation,

- Consciously contract and then relax your muscles, starting with your feet and calves and going up to your shoulders, arms, and hands.
- Take several deep breaths from your diaphragm.

During your presentation,

- Pause and look at the audience before you begin speaking.
- Concentrate on communicating well.
- Use body energy in strong gestures and movement.

Instant Replay

Humor

An inappropriate joke can turn the audience against the speaker. Never use humor that's directed against the audience. In contrast, speakers who can make fun of themselves almost always succeed.

Using Eye Contact

Look directly at the people you're talking to. In one study, speakers who looked more at the audience during a seven-minute informative speech were judged to be better informed, more experienced, more honest, and friendlier than speakers who delivered the same information with less eye contact.[13] An earlier study found that speakers judged sincere looked at the audience 63% of the time, while those judged insincere looked at the audience only 21% of the time.[14]

The point in making eye contact is to establish one-on-one contact with the individual members of your audience. People want to feel that you're talking to them. Looking directly at individuals also enables you to be more conscious of feedback from the audience so that you can modify your approach if necessary.

Standing and Gesturing

Stand with your feet far enough apart for good balance, with your knees flexed. Unless the presentation is very formal or you're on camera, you can walk if you want to. Some speakers like to come in front of the lectern to remove that barrier between themselves and the audience.

If you use slides or transparencies, stand beside the screen so that you don't block it.

Build on your natural style for gestures. Gestures usually work best when they're big and confident.

Using Notes and Visuals

Unless you're giving a very short presentation, you'll probably want to use notes. Even experts use notes. The more you know about the subject, the greater the temptation to add relevant points that occur to you as you talk. Adding an occasional point can help to clarify something for the audience, but adding too many points will destroy your outline and put you over the time limit.

Put your notes on cards or on sturdy pieces of paper. Most speakers like to use 4-by-6-inch or 5-by-7-inch cards because they hold more information. Your notes need to be complete enough to help you if you go blank, so use long phrases or complete sentences. Under each main point, jot down the evidence or illustration you'll use. Indicate where you'll refer to visuals.

Look at your notes infrequently. Most of your gaze time should be directed to members of the audience. Hold your notes high enough so that your head doesn't bob up and down like a yo-yo as you look from the audience to your notes and back again.

If you have lots of visuals and know your topic well, you won't need notes. Put the screen to the side so that you won't block it. Face the audience, not the screen. With transparencies, you can use color marking pens to call attention to your points as you talk. Show the entire visual at once: Don't cover up part of it. If you don't want the audience to read ahead, prepare several visuals that build up. In your overview, for example, the first visual could list your first point, the second the first and second, and the third all three points.

Instant Replay

Overviews and Signposts

Immediately after your opener, provide an **overview of the main points** you will make. Offer a clear signpost as you come to each new point. A **signpost** is an explicit statement of the point you have reached.

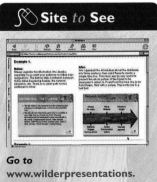

Site *to* See

Go to www.wilderpresentations.com/articles/visual.htm

Presentation expert Claudyne Wilder's *before* and *after* slides show how to express ideas visually in PowerPoint.

Keep the room lights on if possible; turning them off makes it easier for people to fall asleep and harder for them to concentrate on you.

How should I handle questions from the audience?

Anticipate questions that might be asked. Be honest.

Rephrase biased or hostile questions.

Prepare for questions by listing every fact or opinion you can think of that challenges your position. Treat each objection seriously and try to think of a way to deal with it. If you're talking about a controversial issue, you may want to save one point for the question period, rather than making it during the presentation. Speakers who have visuals to answer questions seem especially well prepared.

During your presentation, tell the audience how you'll handle questions. If you have a choice, save questions for the end. In your talk, answer the questions or objections that you expect your audience to have. Don't exaggerate your claims so that you won't have to back down in response to questions later.

During the question period, don't nod your head to indicate that you understand a question as it is asked. Audiences will interpret nods as signs that you agree with the questioner. Instead, look directly at the questioner. As you answer the question, expand your focus to take in the entire group. Don't say, "That's a good question." That response implies that the other questions have been poor ones.

If the audience may not have heard the question or if you want more time to think, repeat the question before you answer it. Link your answers to the points you made in your presentation. Keep the purpose of your presentation in mind, and select information that advances your goals.

If a question is hostile or biased, rephrase it before you answer it. "You're asking whether . . . ." Or suggest an alternative question: "I think there are problems with both the positions you describe. It seems to me that a third solution which is better than either of them is . . . ."

Occasionally someone will ask a question that is really designed to state the speaker's own position. Respond to the question if you want to. Another option is to say, "I'm not sure what you're asking" or even "That's a clear statement of your position. Let's move to the next question now." If someone asks about something that you already explained in your presentation, simply answer the question without embarrassing the questioner. No audience will understand and remember 100% of what you say.

If you don't know the answer to a question, say so. If your purpose is to inform, write down the question so that you can look up the answer before the next session. If it's a question to which you think there is no answer, ask if anyone in the room knows. When no one does, your "ignorance" is vindicated. If an expert is in the room, you may want to refer questions of fact to him or her. Answer questions of interpretation yourself.

At the end of the question period—or at the end of your talk, if there are no questions—take two minutes to summarize your main point once more.

(This can be a restatement of your close.) Questions may or may not focus on the key point of your talk. Take advantage of having the floor to repeat your message briefly and forcefully.

What are the guidelines for group presentations?

In the best presentations, voices take turns within each point.

Plan carefully to involve as many members of the group as possible in speaking roles.

The easiest way to make a group presentation is to outline the presentation and then divide the topics, giving one to each group member. Another member can be responsible for the opener and the close. During the question period, each member answers questions that relate to his or her topic.

In this kind of divided presentation, be sure to

- Plan transitions.
- Enforce time limits strictly.
- Coordinate your visuals so that the presentation seems a coherent whole.
- Practice the presentation as a group at least once; more is better.

The best group presentations are even more fully integrated: together, the members of the group

- Write a very detailed outline.
- Choose points and examples.
- Create visuals.

Then, *within* each point, speakers take turns. This presentation is most effective because each voice speaks only a minute or two before a new voice comes in. However, it works only when all group members know the subject well and when the group plans carefully and practices extensively.

Whatever form of group presentation you use, be sure to introduce each member of the team to the audience at the beginning of the presentation and to use the next person's name when you change speakers: "Now, Jason will explain how we evaluated the Web pages." Pay close attention to who is speaking. If other members of the team seem uninterested in the speaker, the audience gets the sense that that speaker isn't worth listening to.

> **FYI**
>
> Inadequate rehearsal time is the number one problem with team presentations and the main reason teams lose sales.
>
> *Source:* Heather Baldwin, "Team Presentations," *Selling Power*, May 2002, 82.

Summary of Key Points

- **Informative presentations** inform or teach the audience. **Persuasive presentations** motivate the audience to act or to believe. **Goodwill presentations** entertain and validate the audience. Most oral presentations have more than one purpose.

- An oral presentation needs to be simpler than a written message to the same audience.

- In a **monologue presentation,** the speaker plans the presentation in advance and delivers it without deviation. In a **guided**

discussion, the speaker presents the questions or issues that both speaker and audience have agreed on in advance. Rather than functioning as an expert with all the answers, the speaker serves as a facilitator to help the audience tap its own knowledge. A **sales presentation** is a conversation using questions to determine the buyer's needs, probe objections, and gain provisional and then final commitment to the purchase.

- Adapt your message to your audience's beliefs, experience, and interests.

- Use the beginning and end of the presentation to interest the audience and emphasize your key point.

- Using visuals makes a speaker seem more prepared, more interesting, and more persuasive.

- Use a direct pattern of organization. Put your strongest reason first.

- Limit your talk to three main points. Early in your talk—perhaps immediately after your opener—provide an **overview of the main points** you will make. Offer a clear signpost as you come to each new point. A **signpost** is an explicit statement of the point you have reached.

- To calm your nerves as you prepare to give an oral presentation,

    - Be prepared. Analyze your audience, organize your thoughts, prepare visual aids, practice your opener and close, check out the arrangements.

    - Use only the amount of caffeine you normally use.

    - Avoid alcoholic beverages.

- Relabel your nerves. Instead of saying, "I'm scared," try saying, "My adrenaline is up." Adrenaline sharpens our reflexes and helps us do our best.

Just before your presentation,

- Consciously contract and then relax your muscles, starting with your feet and calves and going up to your shoulders, arms, and hands.

- Take several deep breaths from your diaphragm.

During your presentation,

- Pause and look at the audience before you begin speaking.

- Concentrate on communicating well.

- Use body energy in strong gestures and movement.

- Convey a sense of caring to your audience by making direct eye contact with them and by using a conversational style.

- Treat questions as opportunities to give more detailed information than you had time to give in your presentation. Link your answers to the points you made in your presentation.

- Repeat the question before you answer it if the audience may not have heard it or if you want more time to think. Rephrase hostile or biased questions before you answer them.

- The best group presentations result when the group writes a very detailed outline, chooses points and examples, and creates visuals together. Then, within each point, voices trade off.

Assignments for Module 20

Questions for Comprehension

20.1 How are monologue presentations, guided discussions, and sales presentations alike and different?

20.2 What are the four modes for openers?

20.3 What does maintaining eye contact and smiling do for a presentation?

Questions for Critical Thinking

20.4 If you use presentation software, will you automatically have strong visuals?

20.5 Why should you plan a strong close, rather than just saying, "Well, that's it"?

20.6 Why does an oral presentation have to be simpler than a written message to the same audience?

20.7 What are the advantages and disadvantages of using humor?

Exercises and Problems

20.8 Making a Short Oral Presentation

As Your Instructor Directs,
Make a short (2- to 5-minute) presentation, with three to eight slides, on one of the following topics:

a. Explain how what you've learned in classes, in campus activities, or at work will be useful to the employer who hires you after graduation.

b. Profile someone who is successful in the field you hope to enter and explain what makes him or her successful.

c. Describe a specific situation in an organization in which communication was handled well or badly.

d. Make a short presentation based on another problem in this book.

1.10 Discuss three of your strengths.

2.14 Analyze your boss.

11.10 Tell your boss about a problem in your unit and recommend a solution.

26.10 Explain one of the challenges (e.g., technology, ethics, international competition) that the field you hope to enter is facing.

26.11 Profile a company you would like to work for and explain why you think it would be a good employer.

29.10 Explain your interview strategy.

20.9 Making a Longer Oral Presentation

As Your Instructor Directs,
Make a 5- to 12-minute presentation on one of the following. Use visuals to make your talk effective.

a. Show why your unit is important to the organization and either should be exempt from downsizing or should receive additional resources.

b. Persuade your supervisor to make a change that will benefit the organization.

c. Persuade your organization to make a change that will improve the organization's image in the community.

d. Persuade classmates to donate time or money to a charitable organization. (Read Module 12.)

e. Persuade an employer that you are the best person for the job.

f. Use another problem in this book as the basis for your presentation.

2.15 Analyze a discourse community.

2.16 Analyze an organization's corporate culture.

13.10 Explain an international holiday.

23.10 Summarize the results of a survey you have conducted.

24.10 Summarize the results of your research.

20.10 Making a Group Oral Presentation

As Your Instructor Directs,
Make a 5- to 12-minute presentation
using visuals.

3.10 Show how cultural differences can
lead to miscommunication.

5.12 Evaluate the design of three Web
pages.

12.22 Recommend an investment for
your instructor.

18.10 Recommend a policy on student
entrepreneurs.

18.14 Present brochures you have
designed to the class.

24.10 Summarize the results of your
research.

29.8 Share the advice of students
currently on the job market.

Polishing Your Prose

Choosing Levels of Formality

Some words are more formal than others.
Generally, business messages call for a
middle-of-the-road formality, not too formal, but not so casual as to seem sloppy.

Formal and stuffy	Short and simple
ameliorate	improve
commence	begin, start
enumerate	list
finalize	finish, complete
prioritize	rank
utilize	use
viable option	choice

Sloppy	Casual
goofed up	confused
diss	criticize
guess	assume
haggle	negotiate
nosy	curious
wishy-washy	indecisive, flexible

What makes choosing words so challenging is that the level of formality changes
depending on your purposes, the audience,
and the situation. What's just right for a
written report will be too formal for an oral
presentation or an advertisement. The level
of formality that works in one discourse
community may be inappropriate for another.

Listen to the language that people in
your discourse community use. What words
seem to have positive connotations? What
words persuade? As you identify these
terms, use them in your own messages.

Exercises

Choose the better word or phrase in each
pair of square brackets for written documents. Justify your choice.

1. [Starting/Commencing] at 5 P.M., all
   qualifying employees may
   [commence/begin] their [leave
   times/vacations].

2. Tisha [articulated/told us] she is
   [planning/strategizing] a lateral move
   to the Human Resources Department.

3. Call to schedule [some time/a
   meeting] with me to [talk about/delib-
   erate on the issues in] your memo.

4. You should [cease/stop] all [extracur-
   ricular/non-work] activities during
   business hours.

5. Rick has [done his job/performed]
   well as [top dog/manager] of our
   Sales Department.

6. Few people [comprehend/realize] that
   the department supervisor [can/is

empowered to] make policies as
needed.

7. Please [contact/communicate with]
[me/the undersigned] if you [have
questions/desire further information
or knowledge].

8. [Bequeath/Give] Sandy this memo to
type before you [leave/take off].

9. In this report, I have
[guessed/assumed] that the economy
will continue to grow.

10. I [have reservations about/am really
bugged by] the sketchy job descriptions on this [applicant's/guy's]
résumé.

**Check your answers to the odd-numbered
questions at the back of the book.**

BComm Skill Booster

To apply the concepts in this module, complete
lessons 7, 43, 45, and 46 on adapting your
presentation to fit the audience, designing
visuals, and preparing for oral reports. You can
access the BComm Skill Booster through the
text Web site at **www.mhhe.com/bcs2e.**

Cases for Communicators

Whirlpool's Spin on Training and Teamwork

Most companies have training programs to
educate incoming employees and help
maintain high levels of performance among
their current staff. Many programs include
activities that sharpen their workers' communication skills, creativity, and teamwork.

Few companies, however, have developed
training efforts as complex and immersing as
the reality-based program used by Whirlpool,
the household appliance giant. Two or three
times a year, the company selects seven young
people from around the country to live and
learn together for eight weeks in a house
located not far from the company's headquarters in Benton Harbor, Michigan. This
program, modeled after the MTV series "The
Real World," is called "The Real Whirled."

These recruits test and push Whirlpool
products to their limits. In addition, their
knowledge of product specifications and
attributes is tested regularly in quizzes, written
exams, and oral presentations. The training
also develops trust, teamwork, and team spirit.
The diverse group of recruits must create
"rules to live by," resolve group conflicts, share
household responsibilities, and learn to live
and work together as a productive unit.

In visits to local stores, trainees observe
salespeople and interact with customers; they
also go on house calls with repair crews and
visit manufacturing plants. In the course of
these outings, the recruits are exposed to
different peoples' experiences and points of
view—knowledge that is critical to good
communication and teamwork. As one of the
trainees aptly noted, "Business is about relationships anyway."

Source: David Barboza, "Living and Learning at Dishwasher U.; Whirlpool
Trainees Prepare for the Real World," *New York Times,* September 12, 2000.
Accessed on nytimes.com on August 12, 2002.

Individual Activity

As a participant in Whirlpool's live-in training program, "The Real Whirled," you are asked is to create a 15-minute oral presentation on "listening" for other members of your team. Topics that you might cover in your presentation include:

- What is good listening?
- What is active listening?
- What are blocking responses?
- How do people show that they are listening?

Before you begin crafting your presentation, consider the following questions:

- What is the purpose of the presentation? Is it informative, persuasive, or goodwill?
- What type of presentation is this? Is it a monologue, a guided discussion, or a sales presentation?
- How does the type of presentation affect interactions with my audience?
- How can I make my ideas relevant to my audience?
- What is my main point?

Choose an appropriate organization—chronological, problem-causes, solution, excluding alternatives, pro-con, or 1-2-3—and outline your presentation, using enough detail to make the content clear.

Identify possible visuals. Brainstorm at least three different things that you could do to involve your audience.

Finally, craft a good, short opener for your presentation, using one of the four primary opener types: startling statement, narration or anecdote, question, or quotation.

Now you are ready to take a deep breath, find your best voice, and go for it!

Group Activity

Your group has been asked to write a 500-word essay on what makes a good leader. You must create and polish this document as a team.

Plan the work and the document as a team. In this process, discuss the following questions:

- What is the purpose of this document?
- Who is the audience?
- What organization, format, and style should the essay take?

Once the planning is done, begin drafting the essay as a group.

Next, evaluate the content and discuss possible revisions as a group. Remember that business writing can embrace many different styles; keep this point in mind if your revision discussions stall over questions of style.

With a solid revision in hand, you are ready to edit and proofread the document. This stage may be even more important for group writing projects because of the myriad writing styles and levels of expertise involved. With that, in addition to running a spell checker, be sure to have at least one person check the whole document for grammar, mechanics, accuracy, and completeness.

After you have completed the document, discuss the following questions as a team:

- Did the majority of team members work actively on the project?
- Can you identify the positive roles and actions demonstrated during the writing process? (For example, did anyone encourage participation?)
- Can you identify any negative roles and actions demonstrated during the writing process? (For example, did a group member clown or attempt to dominate the group?)
- Can you identify an informational leader, interpersonal leader, and procedural leader in your group?

Finally, if you have time, reflect as a group on the issue of conflict. Did conflict arise during this group project? If so, did you work as a team to identify the source and type of conflict and then follow the appropriate steps to resolve the issue?

Unit Six

Research, Reports, and Visuals

Module 21

Proposals and Progress Reports

Start by asking these questions:

- What is a "report"?
- What should I do before I write a proposal?
- What should go in a proposal?
- What should go in a progress report?

Reports provide the information that people in organizations need to make plans and solve problems.

Writing any report includes five basic steps:

1. Define the problem.
2. Gather the necessary information.
3. Analyze the information.
4. Organize the information.
5. Write the report.

After reviewing the varieties of reports, this module focuses on the first step. Module 22 discusses the second and third steps. Modules 23 and 24 illustrate the fourth and fifth steps.

Other modules that are useful for writing reports are Modules 12, 18, 20, and 25.

What is a "report"?

Many different kinds of documents are called reports.

In some organizations, a report is a long document or a document that contains numerical data. In others, one- and two-page memos are called *reports*. In still others, *reports* consist of PowerPoint slides printed out and bound together. A short report to a client may use a letter format. **Formal reports** contain formal elements such as a title page, a transmittal, a table of contents, and a list of illustrations. **Informal reports** may be letters and memos or even computer printouts of production or sales figures.

Reports can just provide information, both provide information and analyze it, or provide information and analysis to support a recommendation (see Figure 21.1). Reports can be called **information reports** if they collect data for the reader, **analytical reports** if they interpret data but do not recommend action, and **recommendation reports** if they recommend action or a solution.

What should I do before I write a proposal?

Finish at least one-fourth of your research!

As Figure 21.2 suggests, before you draft a proposal, you need not only to do the analysis that you'd do for any message, but you also need to complete part of your research—usually about one-fourth of the total research you'll

Reports Can Provide

Information only

- **Sales reports** (sales figures for the week or month).
- **Quarterly reports** (figures showing a plant's productivity and profits for the quarter).

Information plus analysis

- **Annual reports** (financial data and an organization's accomplishments during the past year).
- **Audit reports** (interpretations of the facts revealed during an audit).
- **Make-good** or **pay-back reports** (calculations of the point at which a new capital investment will pay for itself).

Information plus analysis plus a recommendation

- **Feasibility reports** evaluate two or more alternatives and recommend which alternative the organization should choose.
- **Justification reports** justify the need for a purchase, an investment, a new personnel line, or a change in procedure.
- **Problem-solving reports** identify the causes of an organizational problem and recommend a solution.

Figure 21.1
Three Levels of Reports

Figure 21.2

Allocating Time in Writing a Proposal (Your time may vary.)

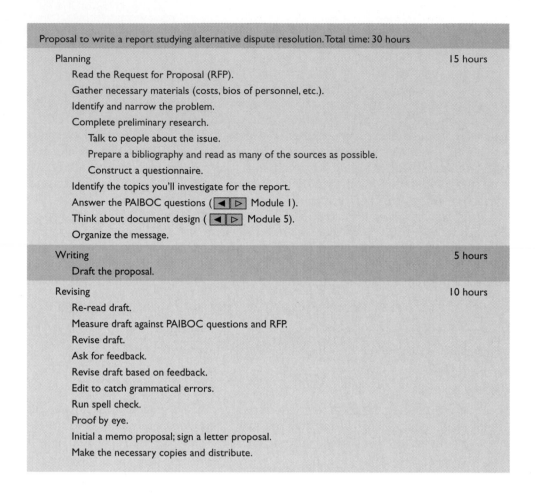

Proposal to write a report studying alternative dispute resolution. Total time: 30 hours

Planning	15 hours
Read the Request for Proposal (RFP).	
Gather necessary materials (costs, bios of personnel, etc.).	
Identify and narrow the problem.	
Complete preliminary research.	
Talk to people about the issue.	
Prepare a bibliography and read as many of the sources as possible.	
Construct a questionnaire.	
Identify the topics you'll investigate for the report.	
Answer the PAIBOC questions (◀ ▷ Module 1).	
Think about document design (◀ ▷ Module 5).	
Organize the message.	
Writing	5 hours
Draft the proposal.	
Revising	10 hours
Re-read draft.	
Measure draft against PAIBOC questions and RFP.	
Revise draft.	
Ask for feedback.	
Revise draft based on feedback.	
Edit to catch grammatical errors.	
Run spell check.	
Proof by eye.	
Initial a memo proposal; sign a letter proposal.	
Make the necessary copies and distribute.	

need to do for a class project. You'll use this research both to define the problem your report will discuss and to identify the topics you'll investigate. Fortunately, if these parts of the proposal are well written, they can be used with minor changes in the report itself.

Narrow your problem. For example, "improving the college experiences of international students studying in the United States" is far too broad. First, choose one college or university. Second, identify the specific problem. Do you want to increase the social interaction between U.S. and international students? Help international students find housing? Increase the number of ethnic grocery stores and restaurants? Third, identify the specific audience that would have the power to implement your recommendations. Depending on the topic, the audience might be the Office of International Studies, the residence hall counselors, a service organization on campus or in town, a store, or a group of investors.

How you define the problem shapes the solutions you find. For example, suppose that a manufacturer of frozen foods isn't making money. If the problem is defined as a marketing problem, the researcher may analyze the product's price, image, advertising, and position in the market. But perhaps the problem is really that overhead costs are too high due to poor inventory management, or that an inadequate distribution system doesn't get the product to its target market. Defining the problem accurately is essential to finding an effective solution.

Once you've defined your problem, you're ready to write a purpose statement. The purpose statement goes both in your proposal and in your final report. A good **purpose statement** makes three things clear:

- The organizational problem or conflict.
- The specific technical questions that must be answered to solve the problem.
- The rhetorical purpose (to explain, to recommend, to request, to propose) the report is designed to achieve.

The following purpose statements have all three elements.

FYI

A research think tank writes proposals to do research for the federal government and private corporations. Proposals used to run 250 pages. Now, clients request 90-minute oral presentations supplemented with 50-page summaries of qualifications.

Source: Ruth Ann Hendrickson to Kitty Locker, March 5, 1997.

> Current management methods keep the elk population within the carrying capacity of the habitat, but require frequent human intervention. Both wildlife conservation specialists and the public would prefer methods that controlled the elk population naturally. This report will compare the current short-term management techniques (hunting, trapping and transporting, and winter feeding) with two long-term management techniques, habitat modification and the reintroduction of predators. The purpose of this report is to recommend which techniques or combination of techniques would best satisfy the needs of conservationists, hunters, and the public.

Report Audience: Superintendent of Yellowstone National Park

> When banner ads on Web pages first appeared in 1994, the initial reponse, or "click-through" rate, was about 10%. However, as ads have proliferated on Web pages, the click-through rate has dropped sharply. Rather than assuming that any banner ad will be successful, we need to ask, What characteristics do successful banner ads share? Are ads for certain kinds of products and services or for certain kinds of audiences more likely to be successful on the Web? The purpose of this report is to summarize the available research and anecdotal evidence and to recommend what Leo Burnett should tell its clients about whether and how to use banner ads.

Report audience: Leo Burnett Advertising Agency

To write a good purpose statement, you must understand the basic problem and have some idea of the questions that your report will answer. Note, however, that you can (and should) write the purpose statement before researching the specific alternatives the report will discuss.

What should go in a proposal?

What you're going to do, how and when you'll do it, and evidence that you'll do it well.

Proposals suggest a method for finding information or solving a problem.[1] (See Figure 21.3.)

Figure 21.3
Relationship among Situation, Proposal, and Final Report

Company's Current Situation	The Proposal Offers to	The Final Report Will Provide
We don't know whether we should change.	Assess whether change is a good idea.	Insight, recommending whether change is desirable.
We need to/want to change, but we don't know exactly what we need to do.	Develop a plan to achieve desired goal.	A plan for achieving the desired change.
We need to/want to change, and we know what to do, but we need help doing it.	Implement the plan, increase (or decrease) measurable outcomes.	A record of the implementation and evaluation process.

Source: Adapted from Richard C. Freed, Shervin Freed, and Joseph D. Romano, *Writing Winning Proposals: Your Guide to Landing the Client, Making the Sale, Persuading the Boss* (New York: McGraw-Hill, 1995), 21.

Instant Replay

Purpose Statements

A good **purpose statement** makes three things clear:

- The organizational problem or conflict.
- The specific technical questions that must be answered to solve the problem.
- The rhetorical purpose the report is designed to achieve.

As Donna Kienzler points out, proposals have two goals: to get the project accepted and to get you accepted to do the job. Proposals must stress reader benefits and provide specific supporting details. Attention to details—including good visual impact and proofreading—helps establish your professional image and suggests that you'd give the same care to the project if your proposal is accepted.

To write a good proposal, you need to have a clear view of the problem you hope to solve and the kind of research or other action needed to solve it. A proposal must answer the following questions convincingly:

- What problem are you going to solve?
- How are you going to solve it?
- What exactly will you provide for us?
- Can you deliver what you promise?
- What benefits can you offer?
- When will you complete the work?
- How much will you charge?

Government agencies and companies often issue Requests for Proposals, known as **RFPs**. Follow the RFP exactly when you respond to a proposal. Competitive proposals are often scored by giving points in each category. Evaluators look only under the heads specified in the RFP. If information isn't there, the proposal gets no points in that category.

Proposals for Class Research Projects

A proposal for a student report usually has the following sections:

1. In your first paragraph (no heading), summarize in a sentence or two the topic and purposes of your report.
2. **Problem.** What organizational problem exists? What is wrong? Why does it need to be solved? Is there a history or background that is relevant?
3. **Feasibility.** Are you sure that a solution can be found in the time available? How do you know?
4. **Audience.** Who in the organization would have the power to implement your recommendation? What secondary audiences might be asked to evaluate your report? What audiences would be affected by your recommendation? Will anyone serve as a gatekeeper, determining

whether your report is sent to decision makers? What watchdog audiences might read the report?

For each of these audiences and for your initial audience (your instructor), give the person's name, job title, and business address and answer the following questions:

- What is the audience's major concern or priority?
- What will the audience see as advantages of your proposal? What objections, if any, is the reader likely to have?
- How interested is the audience in the topic of your report?
- How much does the audience know about the topic of your report?

List any terms, concepts, equations, or assumptions that one or more of your audiences may need to have explained. Briefly identify ways in which your audiences may affect the content, organization, or style of the report.

5. **Topics to Investigate.** List the questions and subquestions you will answer in your report, the topics or concepts you will explain, the aspects of the problem you will discuss. Indicate how deeply you will examine each of the aspects you plan to treat. Explain your rationale for choosing to discuss some aspects of the problem and not others.

6. **Methods/Procedure.** How will you get answers to your questions? Whom will you interview or survey? What published sources will you use? What Web sites will you consult? Give the full bibliographic references.

Make your proposal persuasive by using benefits that your audience finds important.

"Your Majesty, my voyage will not only forge a new route to the spices of the East but also create over three thousand new jobs."

Your Methods section should clearly indicate how you will get the information needed to answer the questions in the topics to investigate section.

7. **Qualifications/Facilities/Resources.** Do you have the knowledge and skills needed to conduct this study? Do you have adequate access to the organization? Do you have access to any equipment you will need to conduct your research (computer, books, etc.)? Where will you turn for help if you hit an unexpected snag?

    You'll be more convincing if you have already scheduled an interview, checked out books, or printed out online sources.

8. **Work Schedule.** List both the total time you plan to spend on and the date when you expect to finish each of the following activities:
   • Gathering information
   • Analyzing information
   • Preparing the progress report
   • Organizing information
   • Writing the draft
   • Revising the draft
   • Preparing the visuals
   • Editing the draft
   • Proofreading the report

   Organize your work schedule either in a chart or in a calendar. A good schedule provides realistic estimates for each activity, allows time for unexpected snags, and shows that you can complete the work on time.

9. **Call to Action.** In your final section, indicate that you'd welcome any suggestions your instructor may have for improving the research plan. Ask your instructor to approve your proposal so that you can begin work on your report.

Figure 21.4 shows a student proposal for a long report using online and library research.

Sales Proposals

To sell expensive goods or services, you may be asked to submit a proposal.

For everything you offer, show the reader benefits (◀ ▷ Module 8) of each feature, using you-attitude (◀ ▷ Module 6). Consider using psychological description (◀ ▷ p. 137) to make the benefits vivid.

Use language appropriate for your audience. Even if the buyers want a state-of-the-art system, they may not want the level of detail that your staff could provide; they may not understand or appreciate technical jargon (◀ ▷ p. 309).

With long proposals, provide a one-page cover letter. Organize the cover letter in this way:

1. Catch the reader's attention and summarize up to three major benefits you offer.
2. Discuss each of the major benefits in the order in which you mentioned them in the first paragraph.
3. Deal with any objections or concerns the reader may have.

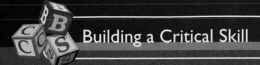
Identifying "Hot Buttons"

In a proposal, as in any persuasive document, it's crucial that you deal with the audience's "hot buttons." **Hot buttons** are the issues to which your audience has a strong emotional response.

Hot buttons sometimes cause people to make what seems like an "illogical" decision—unless you understand the real priorities. A phone company lost a $36 million sale to a university because it assumed that the university's priority would be cost. Instead, the university wanted a state-of-the-art system. The university accepted a higher bid.

When Ernst & Young prepared a proposal to provide professional services to a major automotive company, a team of 15 subject-matter experts spent two intense days working one-on-one with client personnel to learn what issues they cared most about. Reducing work and saving money were concerns, and Ernst & Young proposed redesigning the work to reduce costs and increase return on investment. The focus on value also enabled Ernst & Young to identify an opportunity related to but not part of the original RFP.

But even more important, spending time with the automotive company allowed Ernst & Young to see that a real "hot button" was that the competitor who held the current contract for services seemed to take the automotive company for granted. Ernst & Young exploited this hot button in two ways. First, the proposed work plan included steps to help stakeholders in the company buy into and support the project. Second, the form of the oral presentation of the proposal shouted, "We understand you." Ernst & Young invited the decision makers to come to the Ernst & Young office in Columbus, OH, for the presentation. Personnel wore shirts with the company logo, mirroring the uniforms worn at the automotive company. The presentation took place on an office floor that had been designed to mimic the floor plan at the automotive company.

Not only providing logical evidence but also meeting emotional needs won Ernst & Young a seven-figure contract, with the possibility of even more work.

Source: James Lane to Kitty Locker, March 8, 1999.

4. Mention other benefits briefly.
5. Ask the reader to approve your proposal and provide a reason for acting promptly.

Proposals for Funding

If you need money for a new or continuing public service project, you may want to submit a proposal for funding to a foundation, a corporation, a government agency, or a religious agency. In a proposal for funding, stress the needs your project will meet and show how your project helps fulfill the goals of the organization you are asking to fund it. Every funding source has certain priorities; most post lists of the projects they have funded in the past.

Figuring the Budget and Costs

A good budget is crucial to making the winning bid. Ask for everything you need to do a quality job. Asking for too little may backfire, leading the funder to think that you don't understand the scope of the project.

Read the RFP to find out what is and isn't fundable. Talk to the program officer and read successful past proposals to find out

- What size projects will the organization fund in theory?
- Does the funder prefer making a few big grants or many smaller grants?
- Does the funder expect you to provide in-kind or matching funds from other sources?

Figure 21.4

Proposal for a Student Group Report Using Online and Library Research

October 19, 2004

To: Steve Kaczmarek

In subject line ① indicate that this is a proposal
② specify the kind of report
③ specify the topic.

From: Anwar Abbe, Candice Call, Heather Driscoll, Tony Yang

Subject: Proposal to Study the Feasibility of an Alternative Dispute Resolution Program
for Shepherd Greene Industries

Spell out term the first time you use it, with the abbreviation in
parentheses. Then you can use the abbreviation by itself.

Many private companies and government agencies use Alternative Dispute Resolution
(ADR) programs to resolve disputes with employees. Adopting an ADR program would
save time and money for Shepherd Greene. It would also help reinforce the company's
application to manufacture parts for US Air Force combat aircraft.

Summarize topic and purposes of report.

MLA style omits the periods in "US".

For our report, we plan to research the feasiblility of an ADR program at Shepherd
Greene. We hope to recommend a model ADR program for the company based on an
existing program with demonstrated success.

↑ Triple–space (2 empty spaces)

Background
↕ Double–space (1 empty space) after heading before first paragraph

Founded in 1958, Shepherd Greene Industries is primarily a manufacturer of engine
components for civilian aircraft. Since 1997, the company has also produced engine
components and wing mount assemblies for military reconnaissance aircraft. The
company is privately held.

Bold headings.

Problem

Background gives your reader information
needed to understand the problem.

Shepherd Greene wants an alternative to traditional court remedies, which have mixed
results for the company in the recent past. In 1995, an employee fired for poor attendance
sued, claiming a manger had illegally altered her time cards. After two years in the courts,
Shepherd Greene settled for an undisclosed amount. In 1998, two employees fired for
failing on-the-job drug tests unsuccessfully sued the company to get their jobs back,
appealing the case all the way to the State of Ohio Supreme Court. In 2002, a coalition of
employees sued the company about a management structure that allegedly keeps black
employees in low-level jobs. The suit is still pending.

These lawsuits take months or even years to work through the court systems, costing the
company thousands of dollars, not including any settlement or judgment cost. Although
outside attorneys are also hired, preparing these cases requires hundreds of staff hours and
takes the legal staff away from its primary duty of reviewing bids and contracts with
Shepherd Greene's customers and suppliers.

Shepherd Green has another reason to change the way it handles employment disputes.
The company has submitted a bid to the US Air Force to manufacture replacement parts
for combat aircraft. In addition to adhering to strict manufacturing guidelines and having
highest security clearance, the successful company must demonstrate stability in its labor
and management practices. Programs that minimize employee grievances thus would
enhance Shepherd Greene's application.

If "Problem" section is detailed and well-written,
you may be able to use it unchanged in your report.

Figure 21.4

Proposal for a Student Group Report Using Online and Library Research *(continued)*

Steve Kaczmarek   2   October 19, 2004

Feasibility

Convince your instructor that you have a backup plan if your original proposal proves unworkable.

If our research supports creating an ADR program at Shepherd Greene, we will recommend one based on an existing model. If the research suggests an ADR program is inappropriate for Shepherd Greene, we will recommend the company stay with its current system for handling employee disputes. If our research is inconclusive, we will recommend Shepherd Greene revisit the topic in one year.

Topics to Investigate

Indicate what you'll discuss briefly and what you'll discuss in more detail. This list should match your audience's concerns.

In our report, we will briefly discuss Shepherd Greene's recent litigation history and the general issues in litigating employee grievances. We will focus on the following questions:

All items in list must be grammatically parallel. Here, all are questions.

- What is ADR?
- What organizations use ADR to handle employment disputes?
- How well does ADR work to resolve employment disputes?
- What model ADR programs seem worth imitating?
- What resources are required to create an ADR program?

If it is well-written, "Topics to Investigate" section will become the "Scope" section of the report—with minor revisions.

Audiences

Identify the kinds of audience and the major concerns or priority of each.

Several audiences have a stake in the findings of our research. Our primary audience is Mr. Richard Yang, Director of Legal Services at Shepherd Greene. He is a 17-year employee with the company and has the authority to submit a plan for ADR to Shepherd Greene's top management for approval. A former trial attorney and member of both the Ohio and New York Bar Associations, Mr. Yang favors reforms to help alleviate the glut of lawsuits in our nation's courts. He is especially interested in our group's ability to apply research to the field of law, as one of the group's members is his son and plans to attend law school.

Vary paragraph lengths to provide good visual impact.

You are our initial audience. Your concern is that we produce a report that is timely, logical, thorough, and well written. You have told us that you have taken courses in business law and journalism law, so the report topic should interest you.

Secondary audiences for this proposal will include employees in Shepherd Greene's legal and human resources departments, the company's top executives, and union representatives. Each of these audiences must support an ADR program for it to succeed.

Methods

If you're writing a report based on library research, list 10–15 sources that look relevant. Give full bibliographic citations. Here, MLA style is used.

We will use library research and online research. The following materials on the Web or in the Columbus State Community College Educational Resource Center appear to be useful:

Use hanging indents.

Alternative Dispute Resolution: A Resource Guide. US Office of Personnel Management. 23 Oct. 2004 <http://www.opm.gov/er/adrguide/toc.htm>.

Bedikian, Mary A. "Employment ADR: Current Issues and Methods of Implementation." *The Metropolitan Corporate Counsel* Dec. 2001: 33.4 Oct. 2004 <http://web.lexis-nexis.com>.

Blanchard, Roger, and Joe McDade. Testimony before the US HR Committee on Government Reform Subcommittee on Civil Service. 20 Mar. 2000. 3 Oct. 2004.<http://www.adr.af.mil/ whatsnew/blanchard.htm>.

Divide URL only at a slash.

Figure 21.4

Proposal for a Student Group Report Using Online and Library Research *(continued)*

Steve Kaczmarck   3   October 19, 2004

Bresler, Samuel. "ADR: One Company's Answer to Settling Employee Disputes." *HRFocus* Sept. 2000: 3-5.

Carrel, Michael R., and Christina Heavrin. *Labor Relations and Collective Bargaining: Cases, Practice, and Law.* 5th ed. Upper Saddle River, NJ: Prentice Hall, 1998.

If you'll administer a survey or conduct interviews, tell how many subjects you'll have, how you'll choose them, and what you'll ask them.

Cross, Frank B., and Roger LeRoy Miller. *West's Legal Environment of Business: Text, Cases, Ethical, Regulatory, International, and E-Commerce Issues.* 4th ed. Cincinnati, OH: West/Thomson Learning: 2001.

Longstreth, Andrew. "The Softer Side of Sears." *Corporate Counsel Magazine* 9 (2002): 18. 15 Oct. 2004 *Academic Search Premier Database* Item 6177553.

Phillips, F. Peter. "Current Trends in Employment ADR: CPR Institute for Dispute Resolution." *The Metropolitan Corporate Counsel* (Aug. 2002). 8 Oct. 2004. <http://web.lexis-nexis.com>.

Senger, Jeffrey M. Testimony before the US HR Committee on the Judiciary, Subcommittee on Commercial and Administrative Law. 29 Feb. 2000. 28 Oct. 2004. <http://www.house.gov/judiciary/seng0229.htm>.

Stone, Katherine V. W. "Employment Arbitration under the Federal Arbitration Act." *Employment Dispute Resolution and Worker Rights in the Changing Workplace.* Ed. Adrienne E. Eaton and Jeffrey H. Keefe. Ithaca: Cornell UP, 2000. 27-66.

If possible, we will also use the library at nearby Ohio State University (OSU). The OSU system is one of the largest in the world and houses significantly more resources than does our own library. As students, we can request materials from the library through OHIOLINK; one of our group members is also a student there.

Qualifications and Resources

Cite knowledge and skills from other classes, jobs, and activities that will enable you to conduct the research and interpret your data.

Here are the strengths we bring to this project:

Bulleted list adds visual variety.

- Anwar Abbe's knowledge of the manufacturing industry will help us better understand labor and management practices in such an environment. He is second-year student in the Legal Studies Program and already holds a Bachelor's degree in chemistry from The National Somalian University. Anwar also worked for several years for a paint manufacturer in North Carolina.

- With nearly eight years of experience as a personnel clerk for Franklin County, Candice Call's familiarity with legal issues related to human resources will help us understand the workings of current labor law. She is a second-year student in the Human Resources Technology Program, where she had taken a labor relations course whose text talked briefly about ADR.

- Heather Driscoll's expert knowledge of PowerPoint will be invaluable to creating our oral presentation for this project. A second-year student in Multimedia Technology, she is also an expert at research on the Web.

- Tony Yang's internship in Shepherd Green's management program last summer will help our group understand the company's organizational culture. A junior from OSU who is taking business communication here, Tony is majoring in pre-law/English, plans to specialize in labor law, and has already completed a business law course at OSU. He is

Figure 21.4

Proposal for a Student Group Report Using Online and Library Research *(continued)*

Steve Kaczmarck   4   October 19, 2004

also the son of Richard Yang, the director of Shepherd Greene's legal department, and will have access to the company's legal and human resources staff.

Work Schedule

The following schedule will allow us to complete our report by the due date.

Activity	Responsibility	Total Time	Completion Date
Gathering Information	Anwar, Heather	25 hours	November 15
Preparing the Progress Report	Tony	3 hours	November 19
Analyzing Information	All	10 hours	November 22
Organizing Information	Anwar, Heather	5 hours	November 23
Planning the Draft/Visuals	All	8 hours	November 25
Drafting the Report/Visuals	Tony, Candice	15 hours	November 30
Planning Revisions	All	8 hours	December 2
Revising the Draft/Visuals	Tony, Candice	12 hours	December 7
Editing	Heather	7 hours	December 9
Proofreading	All	3 hours	December 10

Make items in list parallel

Time needed will depend on the length and topic of the report, your knowledge of the topic, and your writing skills.

Allow plenty of time! Good reports need good revision, editing, and proofreading as well as good research.

Call to Action

With Shepherd Greene's legal costs increasing and its bid to the US Air Force under consideration, we urge you to accept this proposal. Let us know if you have suggestions for improving our project. Our team stands ready to begin its research immediately with your approval.

It's tactful to indicate you'll accept suggestions. End on a positive note.

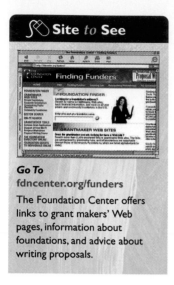
Think about exactly what you'll do and who will do it. What will it cost to get that person? What supplies or materials will he or she need? Also think about indirect costs for using office space, about retirement and health benefits as well as salaries, about office supplies, administration, and infrastructure.

Make the basis of your estimates specific.

Weak: 75 hours of transcribing interviews $1,500

Better: 25 hours of interviews; a skilled transcriber
can complete an hour of interviews in 3 hours;
75 hours @ $20/hour $1,500

Without inflating your costs, give yourself a cushion. For example, if the going rate for skilled transcribers is $20 an hour, but you think you might be able to train someone and pay only $12 an hour, use the higher figure. Then, even if your grant is cut, you'll still be able to do the project well.

What should go in a progress report?

What you've done, why it's important, and what the next steps are.

When you're assigned to a single project that will take a month or more, you'll probably be asked to file one or more progress reports. A progress report reassures the funding agency or employer that you're making progress and allows you and the agency or employer to resolve problems as they arise. Different readers may have different concerns. An instructor may want to know whether you'll have your report in by the due date. A client may be more interested in what you're learning about the problem. Adapt your progress report to the needs of the audience.

Progress reports can do more than just report progress. You can use progress reports to

- **Enhance your image.** Provide details about the number of documents you've read, people you've surveyed, or experiments you've conducted to create a picture of a hardworking person doing a thorough job.
- **Float trial balloons.** Explain, "I could continue to do X [what you approved]; I could do Y instead [what I'd like to do now]." The detail in the progress report can help back up your claim. Even if the idea is rejected, you don't lose face because you haven't made a separate issue of the alternative.
- **Minimize potential problems.** As you do the work, it may become clear that implementing your recommendations will be difficult. In your regular progress reports, you can alert your boss or the funding agency to the challenges that lie ahead, enabling them to prepare psychologically and physically to act on your recommendations.

Christine Barabas's study of the progress reports in a large research and development organization found that poor writers tended to focus on what they had done and said very little about the value of their work. Good writers, in contrast, spent less space writing about the details of what they'd done but much more space explaining the value of their work for the organization.[2]

Subject lines for progress reports are straightforward. Specify the project on which you are reporting your progress.

> Subject: Progress on Developing a Marketing Plan for TCBY

> Subject: Progress on Group Survey on Campus Parking

If you are submitting weekly or monthly progress reports on a long project, number your progress reports or include the time period in your subject line. Include dates for the work completed since the last report and to be completed before the next report.

Make your progress report as positive as you honestly can. You'll build a better image of yourself if you show that you can take minor problems in stride and that you're confident of your own abilities.

Negative: I have not deviated markedly from my schedule, and I feel that I will have very little trouble completing this report by the due date.

Positive: I am back on schedule and expect to complete my report by the due date.

Progress reports can be organized in three ways: to give a chronology, to specify tasks, or to support a recommendation.

Chronological Progress Reports

The following pattern of organization focuses on what you have done and what work remains.

1. **Summarize your progress in terms of your goals and your original schedule.** Use measurable statements.

   Poor: My progress has been slow.

   Better: The research for my report is about one-third complete.

2. **Under the heading Work Completed, describe what you have already done.** Be specific, both to support your claims in the first paragraph and to allow the reader to appreciate your hard work. Acknowledge the people who have helped you. Describe any serious obstacles you've encountered and tell how you've dealt with them.

   Poor: I have found many articles about Procter & Gamble on the Web. I have had a few problems finding how the company keeps employees safe from chemical fumes.

   Better: On the Web, I found Procter & Gamble's home page, its annual report, and mission statement. No one whom I interviewed

Instant Replay

Proposal for a Student Report

Include the following sections:

- Problem
- Feasibility
- Audience
- Topics to Investigate
- Methods
- Qualifications
- Work Schedule
- Call to Action

FYI

Good sales proposals include the following:

1. Budget: How much will it cost?
2. Objective: What is the goal of this proposal?
3. Strategy and Tactics: How will you meet the objective?
4. Schedule: What's the time frame?
5. Results: How will this action benefit the prospect?
6. Closing Arguments: Why should the prospect buy now?

Source: John Fellows, "A Decent Proposal," www.SellingPower.com, August 19, 2002.

could tell me about safety programs specifically at P&G. I have found seven articles about ways to protect workers against pollution in factories, but none mentions P&G.

3. **Under the heading Work to Be Completed, describe the work that remains.** If you're more than three days late (for school projects) or two weeks late (for business projects) submit a new schedule, showing how you will be able to meet the original deadline. You may want to discuss "Observations" or "Preliminary Conclusions" if you want feedback before writing the final report or if your reader has asked for substantive interim reports.

4. **Either express your confidence in having the report ready by the due date or request a conference to discuss extending the due date or limiting the project.** If you are behind your original schedule, show why you think you can still finish the project on time.

The student progress report in Figure 21.5 uses this pattern of organization.

Task Progress Reports

In a task progress report, organize information under the various tasks you have worked on during the period. For example, a task progress report for a group report project might use the following headings:

> Finding Background Information on the Web and in Print
> Analyzing Our Survey Data
> Working on the Introduction of the Report and the Appendices

Under each heading, the group could discuss the tasks it has completed and those that remain.

Recommendation Progress Reports

Recommendation progress reports recommend action: increasing the funding for a project, changing its direction, canceling a project that isn't working out. When the recommendation will be easy for the reader to accept, use the Direct Request pattern of organization from Module 12 (◀▶ p. 226). If the recommendation is likely to meet strong resistance, the Problem-Solving pattern (◀▶ p. 228) may be more effective.

Figure 21.5
A Student Chronological Progress Report

October 29, 2004

To: Kitty O. Locker

From: David G. Bunnel *DGB*

Subject: Progress on CAD/CAM Software Feasibility Study for the Architecture Firm, Patrick and Associates, Inc.

¶ 1: Summarize results in terms of purpose, schedule.

I have obtained most of the information necessary to recommend whether CADAM or CATIA is better for Patrick and Associates, Inc. (P&A). I am currently analyzing and organizing this information and am on schedule.

Work Completed *Underline headings or bold.*

Be very specific about what you've done.

To learn how computer literate P&A employees are, I interviewed a judgment sample of five employees. My interview with Bruce Ratekin, the director of P&A's Computer-Aided Design (CAD) Department on October 15 enabled me to determine the architectural drafting needs of the firm. Mr. Ratekin also gave me a basic drawing of a building showing both two- and three-dimensional views so that I could replicate the drawing with both software packages.

Show how you've overcome minor problems.

I obtained tutorials for both packages to use as a reference while making the drawings. First, I drew the building using CADAM, the package designed primarily for two-dimensional architectural drawings. I encountered problems with the isometric drawing because there was a mistake in the manual I was using; I fixed the problem by trying alternatives and finally getting help from another CADAM user. Next, I used CATIA, the package whose strength is three-dimensional drawings, to construct the drawing. I am in the process of comparing the two packages based on these criteria: quality of drawing, ease of data entry (lines, points, surfaces, etc.) for computer experts and novices, and ease of making changes in the completed drawings. Based on my experience with the packages, I have analyzed the training people with and without experience in CAD would need to learn to use each of these packages.

Work to Be Completed

Indicate changes in purpose, scope, or recommendations. Progress report is a low-risk way to bring the readers on board.

Making the drawings has shown that neither of the packages can do everything that P&A needs. Therefore, I want to investigate the feasibility of P&A's buying both packages.

Specify the work that remains.

As soon as he comes back from an unexpected illness that has kept him out of the office, I will meet with Tom Merrick, the CAD systems programmer for The Ohio State University, to learn about software expansion flexibility for both packages as well as the costs for initial purchase, installation, maintenance, and software updates. After this meeting, I will be ready to begin the first draft of my report.

Whether I am able to meet my deadline will depend on when I am able to meet with Mr. Merrick. Right now, I am on schedule and plan to submit my report by the December 10th deadline.

End on a positive note.

Summary of Key Points

- **Information reports** collect data for the reader; **analytical reports** present and interpret data; **recommendation reports** recommend action or a solution.

- A good purpose statement must make three things clear:
  - The organizational problem or conflict.
  - The specific technical questions that must be answered to solve the problem.
  - The rhetorical purpose (to explain, to recommend, to request, to propose) the report is designed to achieve.

- A proposal must answer the following questions:
  - What problem are you going to solve?
  - How are you going to solve it?
  - What exactly will you provide for us?
  - Can you deliver what you promise?
  - When will you complete the work?
  - How much will you charge?

- In a proposal for a class research project, use the following headings:
  - Problem
  - Feasibility
  - Audience
  - Topics to Investigate
  - Methods
  - Qualifications
  - Work Schedule
  - Call to Action

- Use the following pattern of organization for the cover letter for a sales proposal.

1. Catch the reader's attention and summarize up to three major benefits you offer.
2. Discuss each of the major benefits in the order in which you mentioned them in the first paragraph.
3. Deal with any objections or concerns the reader may have.
4. Mention other benefits briefly.
5. Ask the reader to approve your proposal and provide a reason for acting promptly.

- In a proposal for funding, stress the needs your project will meet. Show how your project helps fulfill the goals of the organization you are asking to fund it.

- To focus on what you have done and what work remains, organize a progress report in this way:
  1. Summarize your progress in terms of your goals and your original schedule.
  2. Under the heading "Work Completed," describe what you have already done.
  3. Under the heading "Work to Be Completed," describe the work that remains.
  4. Either express your confidence in having the report ready by the due date or request a conference to discuss extending the due date or limiting the project.

- Use positive emphasis in progress reports to create an image of yourself as a capable, confident worker.

Assignments for Module 21

Questions for Comprehension

21.1 What three components belong in a purpose statement?

21.2 What is an RFP?

21.3 How does the RFP relate to the organization of the proposal?

Questions for Critical Thinking

21.4 How can you learn your audience's hot buttons?

21.5 What should you do if you have information you want to put in a proposal that the RFP doesn't call for?

21.6 In the budget for a proposal, why isn't it to your advantage to try to ask for the smallest amount of money possible?

21.7 How do you decide whether to write a chronological, task, or recommendation progress report?

Exercises and Problems

21.8 Writing a Proposal for a Student Report

Write a proposal to your instructor to do the research for a formal or informal report. (See Problems 23.9, 23.10, 23.11, 24.8, 24.9, and 24.10.)

The headings and the questions in the section titled "Proposals for Class Research Projects" are your RFP; be sure to answer every question and to use the headings exactly as stated in the RFP. Exception: Where alternate heads are listed, you may choose one, combine the two ("Qualifications and Facilities"), or treat them as separate headings in separate categories.

21.9 Writing a Chronological Progress Report

Write a memo summarizing your progress on your report.

In the introductory paragraph, summarize your progress in terms of your schedule and your goals. Under a heading titled "Work Completed," list what you have already done. (This is a chance to toot your own horn: If you have solved problems creatively, say so! You can also describe obstacles you've encountered that you have not yet solved.) Under "Work to Be Completed," list what you still have to do. If you are more than two days behind the schedule you submitted with your proposal, include a revised schedule, listing the completion dates for the activities that remain.

In your last paragraph, either indicate your confidence in completing the report by the due date or ask for a conference to resolve the problems you are encountering.

As Your Instructor Directs,
Send the e-mail or paper progress report to

a. The other members of your group.
b. Your instructor.

21.10 Writing a Task Progress Report

Write a memo summarizing your progress on your report in terms of its tasks.

As Your Instructor Directs,
Send the e-mail or paper progress report to

a. The other members of your group.
b. Your instructor.

21.11 Writing a Chronological Progress Report for a Group Report

Write a memo to your instructor summarizing your group's progress.

In the introductory paragraph, summarize the group's progress in terms of its goals and its schedule, your own progress on the tasks for which you are responsible, and your feelings about the group's work thus far.

Under a heading titled "Work Completed," list what has already been done. Be most specific about what you yourself have done. Describe briefly the chronology of group activities: number, time, and length of meetings; topics discussed and decisions made at meetings.

If you have solved problems creatively, say so! You can also describe obstacles you've encountered that you have not yet solved. In this section, you can also comment on problems that the group has faced and whether or not they've been solved. You can comment on things that have gone well and have contributed to the smooth functioning of the group.

Under "Work to be Completed," list what you personally and other group members still have to do. Indicate the schedule for completing the work.

In your last paragraph, either indicate your confidence in completing the report by the due date or ask for a conference to resolve the problems you are encountering.

Polishing Your Prose

Mixing Verb Tenses

Normally, verb tenses within a sentence, paragraph, and document should be consistent.

Incorrect: I went to the store yesterday. There, I will buy a new computer, desk, and bookcase. Afterward, I assemble everything and arrange my new home office.

Correct: I went to the store yesterday. There, I bought a new computer, desk, and bookcase. Afterward, I assembled everything and arranged my new home office.

When you have to mix tenses in a document, do so appropriately. The reader must understand the relationship between time and action throughout your document:

Incorrect: By the time you get to the meeting, I drop off the package at FedEx.

Correct: By the time you get to the meeting, I will have dropped off the package at FedEx.

The correct example uses *future perfect tense* to indicate action that has not occurred yet, but will prior to your getting to the meeting (expressed in *simple present tense*).

In general, stick to simple verb tenses in business communication. Standard edited English prefers them. Unless you must indicate specifically when one action takes place with respect to another, the simple tenses work fine.

- Use present tense in résumés and job application letters to describe current job duties; use it in persuasive documents when you want the reader to feel close to the action.

- Use past tense in résumés and job application letters to describe previous job duties; use it in correspondence and reports when action has already occurred.

- Use future tense in messages to describe action that still needs to be completed—in a progress report, any remaining activities; in a résumé or job application letter, when you will graduate from college or complete a job certification program.

Exercises

Fix the verb tense errors in the following sentences.

1. Many of our retirees work for the company for many years.

2. Without a car, I had to delivered the office supplies on foot.

3. The phone rang until I answer it.

4. Two days ago, I will have gone to the meeting in Tulsa.

5. About two hundred résumés come in for the position yesterday.

6. Tom dropped Michelle off at the airport this morning. Then he goes to the Chamber of Commerce to met with its board. Tonight he will spent the evening with the Mayor, discussing our new tax abatement.

7. Before you left for the interview, make sure you have a copy of your employment records. You should also took another copy of your résumé. When you get back, make sure you sent a thank-you letter to everyone you met today.

8. The sales tax increase was create to generate more revenue for the local community college. So far, it had raised more than $2 million to help funded our students. We were pleased because this joint effort between local government and the college was expect to make this region more livable.

9. About a quarter of the employees eligible for telecommuting take advantage of this employee benefit. The rest of the employees felt that they were comfortable with their current schedules. We were debating whether to keep the program or not.

10. I sent the invitations off today. They will have had arrived by next Monday. Once we got the RSVPs, we should get a better sense of how much food to order. This anniversary party for our Texas subsidiary was going to be great!

Check your answers to the odd-numbered exercises at the back of the book.

BComm Skill Booster

To apply the concepts in this module, complete lessons 28, 29, and 42 on writing proposals, progress reports, and formal reports. You can access the BComm Skill Booster through the text Web site at **www.mhhe.com/bcs2e.**

Module 22

Finding, Analyzing, and Documenting Information

Start by asking these questions:

- How can I find information online and in print?
- How do I write questions for surveys and interviews?
- How do I decide whom to survey or interview?
- How should I analyze the information I've collected?
- How should I document sources?

Research for a report may be as simple as getting a computer printout of sales for the last month; it may involve finding online or published material or surveying or interviewing people. **Secondary research** retrieves information that someone else gathered. Library research and online searches are the best known kinds of secondary research. **Primary research** gathers new information. Surveys, interviews, and observations are common methods for gathering new information for business reports.

How can I find information online and in print?

Learn how to do keyword searches.

Keywords are the terms that the computer searches for in a database or on the Web. The *ABI/Inform Thesaurus* lists synonyms and the hierarchies in which information is arranged in various databases.

At the beginning of a search, use all the synonyms and keywords you can think of. For example, the report on alternative dispute resolution (◁▶ Module 24) used the following search terms:

alternative dispute resolution

ADR

mediation

arbitration

employee grievances

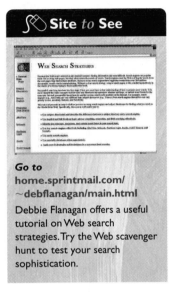

Site *to* See

Go to home.sprintmail.com/ ~debflanagan/main.html

Debbie Flanagan offers a useful tutorial on Web search strategies. Try the Web scavenger hunt to test your search sophistication.

Skim several of the first sources you find; if they use additional or different terms, search for these new terms as well.

Use a Boolean search (Figure 22.1) to get fewer but more useful hits. For example, to study the effect of the minimum wage on employment in the restaurant industry, you might specify

(minimum wage) *and* (restaurant *or* fast food) *and*

(employment rate *or* unemployment)

Without *and,* you'd get articles that discuss the minimum wage in general, articles about every aspect of *restaurants,* and every article that refers to *unemployment,* even though many of these would not be relevant to your topic. The *or* calls up articles that use the term *fast food* but not *restaurant.* An article that used the phrase *food service industry* would be eliminated unless it also used the term *restaurant.*

Use a computer to search for print as well as online sources. Include paper as well as online sources in your research. Information in many periodicals is checked before it goes to print; papers in scholarly journals are reviewed by experts before they are accepted. Thus, print sources are often more credible than Web pages, which anyone can post.

Figures 22.2, 22.3, and 22.4 list some of the many resources available.

Figure 22.1

Examples of a Boolean Search

Figure 22.2
Sources for Electronic Research

These CD-ROM databases are available in many university libraries:
Black Studies on Disc

Business Source Premier (full text for more than 2,800 scholarly business journals in management, economics, finance, accounting, international business, and more)

ComIndex (indexes and abstracts journals in communication)

ERIC (research on education and teaching practices in the United States and other countries)

Foreign Trade and Economic Abstracts

GPO on SilverPlatter (government publications)

Handbook of Latin American Studies

LEXIS/NEXIS Services

Newspaper Abstracts

PAIS International—Public Affairs Information Service

Social Sciences Index

Wilson Business Abstracts

Women's Resources International

Figure 22.3
Sources for Web Research

Web addresses may change. For links to the current URLs, see the BCS Web site.

Subject Matter Directories
AccountingNet
   www.accounting.smartpros.com

Education index
   www.educationindex.com

FINWeb
   www.finweb.com

Human resource management resources on the Internet
   www.nbs.ntu.ac.uk/depts/hrm/hrm_link.htm

International Business Kiosk
   www.calintel.org/kiosk

Management and entrepreneurship
   www.lib.lsu.edu/bus/management.html

The WWW Virtual Library: Marketing
   www.knowthis.com

News Sites
BusinessWeek Online
   www.businessweek.com

CNN/CNNFN
   www.cnn.com (news)
   www.cnnfn.com (financial news)

National Public Radio
   www.npr.org

NewsLink (links to U.S., Canadian, and international newspapers, magazines, and resources online)
   http://newslink.org/

The New York Times
   www.nyt.com

The Wall Street Journal
   www.wsj.com

U.S. Government Information
EDGAR Online (SEC's online database)
   www.edgar-online.com
   www.sec.gov/edgar.shtm

FEDSTATS (links to 70 U.S. government agencies)
   www.fedstats.gov

STAT-USA (fast-breaking statistics on U.S. trade and economy)
   www.stat-usa.gov

U.S. Census (including Data FERRET)
   www.census.gov

U.S. government publications (search databases online)
   www.access.gpo.gov/su_docs

U.S. Small Business Administration
   www.sbaonline.sba.gov

White House Briefing Room (economic issues)
   www.whitehouse.gov/fsbr/esbr.html

Reference Collections
Hoover's Online (information on more than 13,000 public and private companies worldwide)
   www.hoovers.com

Liszt (mailing lists)
   www.liszt.com

My Virtual Reference Desk
   www.refdesk.com

Figure 22.3
Sources for Web Research (*continued*)

Web addresses may change. For links to the current URLs, see the BCS Web site.

FYI

Dead links or inaccurate routing makes 5% of the Web—on as many as 100 million hosts—inaccessible.

Source: "Must Read," *Wired,* March 2002, 48.

Indexes:
   Accountants' Index
   Business Periodicals Index
   Canadian Business Index
   Hospital Literature Index
   Personnel Management Abstracts

Facts, figures, and forecasts (also check the Web):
   Almanac of Business and Industrial Financial Ratios
   Moody's Manuals
   The Statistical Abstract of the U.S.

U.S. Census reports (also available on the Web):
   Census of Manufacturers
   Census of Retail Trade

International business and government:
   Canada Year Book
   Dun and Bradstreet's *Principal International Businesses*
   European Marketing Data and Statistics
   Statistical Yearbook of the United Nations

Figure 22.4
Print Sources for Research

Using the Internet for Research

Most research projects today include the Internet. However, don't rely solely on the Internet for research. Powerful as it is, the Internet's just one tool. Your public or school library, experts in your company, journals and newspapers, and even information in your files are others.

Finding Web Pages

Use root words to find variations. A root word such as *stock* followed by the plus sign (*stock+*) will yield *stock, stocks, stockmarket,* and so forth.

Use quotation marks for exact terms. If you want only sites that use the term "business communication," put quotes around the term.

Uncapitalize words. Capitalizing words limits your search to sites where the word itself is capitalized; if the word doesn't have to be capitalized, don't.

Some search engines group related sites based on keywords. Look for these links at the top of your search engine.

If you get a broken or dead link, try shortening the URL. For example, if www.mirror.com/newinfo/index.html no longer exists, try www.mirror.com. Then check the site map to see whether it has the page you want.

Evaluating Web Pages

Anyone can post a Web site, and no one checks the information for accuracy or truthfulness. By contrast, many print sources, especially academic journals, have an editorial board that reviews manuscripts for accuracy and truthfulness. The review process helps ensure that information meets high standards.

For a list of Web sites about evaluating information, see www.vuw.ac.nz/~agsmith/evaln/evaln.htm.

Use reputable sources. Start with sites produced by universities and established companies or organizations. Be aware, however, that such organizations are not going to post information that makes them look bad. To get "the other side of the story," you may need to monitor listservs or to access pages critical of the organization. (Search for "consumer opinion" and the name of the organization.)

Look for an author. Do individuals take "ownership" of the information? What are their credentials? How can you contact them with questions? Remember that ".edu" sites could be from students not yet expert on a subject.

Check the date. How recent is the information?

Check the source. Is the information adapted from other sources? If so, try to get the original.

Compare the information with other sources. Internet sources should complement print sources. If facts are correct, you'll likely find them recorded elsewhere.

How do I write questions for surveys and interviews?

Test your questions to make sure they're neutral and clear.

A **survey** questions a large group of people, called **respondents** or **subjects.** The easiest way to ask many questions is to create a **questionnaire,** a written list of questions that people fill out. Figure 22.5 shows an example of a questionnaire. An **interview** is a structured conversation with someone who will be able to give you useful information. Surveys and interviews can be useful only if the questions are well designed.

Phrase questions in a way that won't bias the response. Avoid questions that make assumptions about your subjects. The question "Does your spouse have a job outside the home?" assumes that your respondent is married.

Figure 22.5

A Student Questionnaire

In your introductory ¶,
① tell how to return the survey.   **Survey on Internships**
② tell how the information will be used.

Please answer the following questions and return the completed survey to the person who gave it to you. All information will be confidential and used only for a class project examining the feasibility of establishing an internship program for a particular business.

1. Major _____

2. Rank: First Year _____

Start with   Sophomore _____
easy-to-answer   Junior _____
questions.   Senior _____

3. How important it is to you to have one or more internships before you graduate?
   ___ Very important
   ___ Somewhat important   *Put directions in*
   ___ Not important   *parentheses to*
Branch   *separate them from the*
questions   *question itself.*
allow
readers 4. Did you have an internship last summer?
to skip   ___ Yes   ___ No (Skip to Question 6.)
questions.

5. What were the most beneficial aspects of your internship? (Check all that apply.)
   ___ Work related to my major
   ___ Likely to get a job offer/got a job offer
   ___ Chance to explore my interests
   ___ Made connections
   ___ Worked with clients
   ___ Looks good on my résumé
   ___ Other (Please explain.)

6. How much money did you make last summer? (Approximate hourly rate, before taxes)
Give readers
information _____
they need to understand your question.
   ❏ Check here if you did not make any money last summer.

7. For next summer, could you afford to take an unpaid internship?
   ___ Yes   ___ No

8. For next summer, could you afford to take an internship paying only the minimum wage?
   ___ Yes   ___ No

9. How important is each of the following criteria in choosing whether to accept a specific internship?

These abbreviations are OK when
you survey skilled readers.

	Very impt.	Some impt.	Not impt.
a. Money	❏	❏	❏
b. Prestige of company	❏	❏	❏
c. Location near where you live now	❏	❏	❏
d. Quality of mentoring	❏	❏	❏
e. Building connections	❏	❏	❏
f. Chance of getting a job with that company	❏	❏	❏
g. Gaining experience	❏	❏	❏

Make sure to break up the lines. Leaving an extra space makes it more likely that the respondent will check the right line.

10. How interested are you in a career in managed care?
    ___ Very interested
    ___ Somewhat interested
    ___ Not interested

11. Could you take a job in Cleveland next summer?
    ___ Definitely
    ___ Maybe
    ___ No

12. Have you heard of FFI Rx Managed Care?
    ___ Yes
    ___ No

13. I invite any other comments you would like to make regarding internships.

Using columns gets the survey on one side, saving money in copying and eliminating the problem of people missing questions on the back. But it leaves almost no room to write in comments.

Thank you for taking the time to answer this survey. Please return it to the person who gave it to you.

Repeat where to turn in or mail completed surveys.

Poor questions yield poor data.

Use words that mean the same thing to you and to the respondents. Words like *often* and *important* mean different things to different people. Whenever possible, use more objective measures:

Vague: Do you use the Web often?

Better: How many hours a week do you spend on the Web?

Closed questions have a limited number of possible responses. **Open questions** do not lock the subject into any sort of response. Figure 22.6 gives examples of closed and open questions. The second question in Figure 22.6 is an example of a Likert-type scale. Closed questions are faster for subjects to answer and easier for researchers to score. However, since all answers must fit into chosen categories, they cannot probe the complexities of a subject. You can improve the quality of closed questions by conducting a pretest with open questions to find categories that matter to respondents.

When you use multiple-choice questions, make sure that only one answer fits in any one category. In the following example of overlapping categories, a person who worked for a company with exactly 25 employees could check either *a* or *b*. The resulting data would be unreliable.

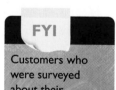

Overlapping categories: Indicate the number of full-time employees in your company on May 16:

    __a. 0–25

    __b. 25–100

    __c. 100–500

    __d. over 500

Discrete categories: Indicate the number of full-time employees in your company on May 16:

    __a. 0–25

    __b. 26–100

    __c. 101–500

    __d. over 500

Figure 22.6

Closed and Open Questions

Closed Questions

Are you satisfied with the city bus service? (yes/no)

How good is the city bus service?
  Excellent 5 4 3 2 1 Terrible

Indicate whether you agree or disagree with each of the following statements about city bus service:

  A D   The schedule is convenient for me.

  A D   The routes are convenient for me.

  A D   The drivers are courteous.

  A D   The buses are clean.

Rate each of the following improvements in the order of their importance to you (1 = most important, 6 = least important)

_____ Buy new buses.

_____ Increase non-rush-hour service on weekdays.

_____ Provide earlier and later service on weekdays.

_____ Increase service on weekends.

_____ Buy more buses with wheelchair access.

_____ Provide unlimited free transfers.

Open Questions

How do you feel about the city bus service?

Tell me about the city bus service.

Why do you ride the bus? (or, Why don't you ride the bus?)

What do you like and dislike about the city bus service?

How could the city bus service be improved?

Branching questions direct different respondents to different parts of the questionnaire based on their answers to earlier questions.

10. Have you talked to an academic advisor this year?
    yes _____ no _____
    (if "no," skip to question 14.)

Use closed multiple-choice questions for potentially embarrassing topics. Seeing their own situation listed as one response can help respondents feel that it is acceptable. However, very sensitive issues are perhaps better asked in an interview, where the interviewer can build trust and reveal information about himself or herself to encourage the interviewee to answer.

Generally, put early in the questionnaire questions that will be easy to answer. Put questions that are harder to answer or that people may be less willing to answer (e.g., age and income) near the end of the questionnaire. Even if people choose not to answer such questions, you'll still have the rest of the survey filled out.

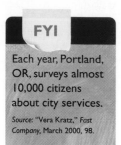

FYI

Each year, Portland, OR, surveys almost 10,000 citizens about city services.

Source: "Vera Kratz," Fast Company, March 2000, 98.

If subjects will fill out the questionnaire themselves, pay careful attention to the physical design of the document. Use indentations and white space effectively; make it easy to mark and score the answers. Include a brief statement of purpose if you (or someone else) will not be available to explain the questionnaire or answer questions. Pretest the questionnaire to make sure the directions are clear. One researcher mailed out a two-page questionnaire without pretesting it. Twenty-five respondents didn't answer the questions on the back of the first page.[1]

How do I decide whom to survey or interview?

Use a random sample for surveys, if funds permit.

Use a judgment sample for interviews.

The **population** is the group you want to make statements about. Depending on the purpose of your research, your population might be all Fortune 1000 companies, all business students at your college, or all consumers.

Defining your population correctly is crucial to getting useful information. For example, Microscan wanted its sales force to interview "customer defectors." At first, salespeople assumed that a "defector" was a former customer who no longer bought anything at all. By that definition, very few defectors existed. But then the term was redefined as customers who had stopped buying *some* products and services. By this definition, quite a few defectors existed. And the fact that each of them had turned to a competitor for some of what they used to buy from Microscan showed that improvements—and improved profits—were possible.[2]

Because it is not feasible to survey everyone, you select a sample. If you take a true random sample, you can generalize your findings to the whole population from which your sample comes. In a **random sample,** each person in the population theoretically has an equal chance of being chosen. When people say they did something *randomly* they often mean *without conscious bias.* However, unconscious bias exists. Someone passing out surveys in front of the library will be more likely to approach people who seem friendly and less likely to ask people who seem intimidating, in a hurry, much older or younger, or of a different race, class, or sex. True random samples rely on random digit tables, generated by computers and published in statistics texts and books such as *A Million Random Digits.*

A **convenience sample** is a group of respondents who are easy to get: students who walk through the student center, people at a shopping mall, workers in your own unit. Convenience samples are useful for a rough pretest of a questionnaire. However, you cannot generalize from a convenience sample to a larger group.

A **judgment sample** is a group of people whose views seem useful. Someone interested in surveying the kinds of writing done on campus might ask each department for the name of a faculty member who cared about writing, and then send surveys to those people. Judgment samples are often good for interviews, where your purpose is to talk to someone whose views are worth hearing.

Sharon Lee's marketing firm, Look-Look, ferrets out youth trends. Her sources include nearly 10,000 14- to 30-year-old volunteers who upload photos, send e-mail reports, and use the message boards on Look-Look's Intranet.

How should I analyze the information I've collected?

Look for answers to your research questions, patterns, and interesting nuggets.

As you analyze your data, look for answers to your research questions and for interesting nuggets that may not have been part of your original questions but emerge from the data. Such stories can be more convincing in reports and oral presentations than pages of computer printouts.

Understanding the Source of the Data

If your report is based upon secondary data from library and online research, look at the sample, the sample size, and the exact wording of questions to see what the data actually measure. Some studies bias results by limiting the alternatives. Ninety percent of students surveyed by Levi Strauss & Co. said Levi's 501 jeans would be the most popular clothes this year. But the Levi's were the only brand of jeans on the list of choices.[3]

Identify the assumptions used in analyzing the data. When studies contradict each other, the explanation sometimes lies in the assumptions. For example, a study that found disposable diapers were better for the environment than cloth diapers assumed that a cloth diaper lasted for 92.5 uses. A study that found that cloth diapers were better assumed that each cloth diaper lasted for 167 uses.[4]

FYI

IBM interviews 40,000 customers a year, in 71 countries and 26 languages.

Source: Robert Hiebeler, Thomas B. Kelly, and Charles Ketterman, *Best Practices: Building Your Business with Customer-Focused Solutions* (New York: Simon & Schuster, 2000), 168.

Evaluating online sources, especially Web pages, can be difficult, since anyone can post pages on the Web or contribute comments to chat groups. Check the identity of the writer: Is he or she considered an expert? Can you find at least one source printed in a respectable newspaper or journal that agrees with the Web page? If a comment appeared in chat groups, did others in the group support the claim? Does the chat group include people who could be expected to be unbiased and knowledgeable? Especially when the issue is controversial, seek out opposing views.

Analyzing Numbers

Many reports analyze numbers—either numbers from databases and sources or numbers from a survey you have conducted.

If you've conducted a survey, your first step is to transfer the responses on the survey form into numbers. For some categories, you'll assign numbers arbitrarily. For example, you might record men as "1" and women as "2"—or vice versa. Such assignments don't matter, as long as you're consistent throughout your project. In these cases, you can report the number and percentage of men and women who responded to your survey, but you can't do anything else with the numbers.

When you have numbers for salaries or other figures, start by figuring the average, or mean, the median, and the range. The **average** or **mean** is calculated by adding up all the figures and dividing by the number of samples. The **median** is the number that is exactly in the middle. When you have an odd number of observations, the median will be the middle number. When you have an even number, the median will be the average of the two numbers in the center. The **range** is the high and low figures for that variable.

Finding the average takes a few more steps when you have different kinds of data. For example, it's common to ask respondents whether they find a feature "very important," "somewhat important," or "not important." You might code "very important" as "3," "somewhat important" as "2," and "not important" as "1." To find the average in this kind of data,

1. For each response, multiply the code by the number of people who gave that response.
2. Add up the figures.
3. Divide by the total number of people responding to the question.

For example, suppose you have surveyed 50 people about the features they want in a proposed apartment complex.

The average gives an easy way to compare various features. If the party house averages 2.3 while extra parking for guests is 2.5, you know that your respondents would find extra parking more important than a party house. You can now arrange the factors in order of importance:

Instant Replay

Three Kinds of Samples

In a **random sample,** each person in the population has an equal chance of being chosen. A **convenience sample** is a group of respondents who are easy to get. A **judgment sample** is a group of people whose views seem useful.

Table 4. "How Important Is Each Factor to You in Choosing an Apartment?" $n = 50$; $3 =$ "Very Important"	
Extra parking for guests	2.5
Party house	2.3
Pool	2.2
Convenient to bus line	2.0

Often it's useful to simplify numerical data: round it off and combine similar elements. Then you can see that one number is about 2½ times another. Charting it can also help you see patterns in your data. Look at the raw data as well as at percentages. For example, a 50% increase in shoplifting incidents sounds alarming—but an increase from two to three shoplifting incidents sounds well within normal variation.

Analyzing Words

If your data include words, try to find out what the words mean to the people who said them. Respondents to Whirlpool's survey of 180,000 households said that they wanted "clean refrigerators." After asking more questions, Whirlpool found that what people really wanted were refrigerators that *looked* clean, so the company developed models with textured fronts and sides to hide fingerprints.[5] Also try to measure words against numbers. When he researched possible investments, Peter Lynch found that people in mature industries were pessimistic, seeing clouds. People in immature industries saw pie in the sky, even when the numbers weren't great.[6]

Look for patterns. If you have library sources, on which points do experts agree? Which disagreements can be explained by early theories or numbers that have now changed? By different interpretations of the same data? Having different values and criteria? In your interviews and surveys, what patterns do you see?

- Have things changed over time?
- Does geography account for differences?
- What similarities do you see?
- What differences do you see?
- What confirms your hunches?
- What surprises you?

Checking Your Logic

Don't confuse causation with correlation. **Causation** means that one thing causes or produces another. **Correlation** means that two things happen at the same time. One might cause the other, but both might be caused by a third.

For example, suppose that you're considering whether to buy cell phones for everyone in your company, and suppose that your surveys show that the people who currently have cell phones are, in general, more productive than people who don't use cell phones. Does having a cell phone lead to higher productivity? Perhaps. But perhaps productive people are more likely to push to get cell phones from company funds, while less productive people are more passive. Perhaps productive people earn more and are more likely to be able to buy their own cell phones if the organization doesn't provide them.

Consciously search for at least three possible causes for each phenomenon you've observed and at least three possible solutions for each problem. The more possibilities you brainstorm, the more likely you are to find good options. In your report, mention all of the possibilities; discuss in detail only those that will occur to readers and that you think are the real reasons and the best solutions.

Analyzing Numbers

The **average** or **mean** is calculated by adding up all the figures and dividing by the number of samples. The **median** is the number that is exactly in the middle. The **range** is the high and low figures for that variable.

When you have identified patterns that seem to represent the causes of the problem or the best solutions, check these ideas against reality. Can you find support in the quotes or in the numbers? Can you answer counter-claims? If you can, you will be able to present evidence for your argument in a convincing way.

If you can't prove the claim you originally hoped to make, modify your conclusions to fit your data. Even when your market test is a failure, you can still write a useful report.

- Identify changes that might yield a different result (e.g., selling the product at a lower price might enable the company to sell enough units).
- Discuss circumstances that may have affected the results.
- Summarize your negative findings in progress reports to let readers down gradually and to give them a chance to modify the research design.
- Remember that negative results aren't always disappointing to the audience. For example, the people who commissioned a feasibility report may be relieved to have an impartial outsider confirm their suspicions that a project isn't feasible.[7]

How should I document sources?

Use MLA or APA format.

The two most widely used formats for endnotes and bibliographies in reports are those of the Modern Language Association (MLA) and the American Psychological Association (APA). Figure 22.7 shows the MLA and APA formats for books, government documents, journal and newspaper articles, online sources, and interviews.

In a good report, sources are cited and documented smoothly and unobtrusively. **Citation** means attributing an idea or fact to its source **in the body of the report.** "According to the 2000 Census . . ." "Jane Bryant Quinn argues that . . ." Citing sources demonstrates your honesty, enhances your credibility, and protects you from charges of plagiarism. **Documentation** means providing the bibliographic information readers would need to go back to the original source. Note that citation and documentation are used in addition to quotation marks. If you use the source's exact words, you'll use the name of the person you're citing and quotation marks in the body of the report; you'll indicate the source in parentheses and a list of References or Works Cited. If you put the source's idea into your own words, or if you condense or synthesize information, you don't need quotation marks, but you still need to tell whose idea it is and where you found it.

Indent long quotations on the left and right to set them off from your text. Indented quotations do not need quotation marks; the indentation shows the reader that the passage is a quote. Since many readers skip quotes, always summarize the main point of the quotation in a single sentence before the quotation. End the sentence with a colon, not a period, since it introduces the quote.

Interrupt a quotation to analyze, clarify, or question it.

Figure 22.7
MLA and APA Formats for Documenting Sources

MLA Format

MLA internal documentation gives the author's last name and page number in parentheses in the text for facts as well as for quotations (Gilsdorf and Leonard 470). If the author's name is used in the sentence, only the page number is given in parentheses. A list of WORKS CITED gives the full bibliographic citation, arranging the entries alphabetically by the first author's last name.

Comma   *Frst name first for*   *Put quotation marks around title*

Article in a Periodical
second author   *of article.*

Capitalize all major words in titles of articles, books, journals magazines, and newspapers.

Gilsdorf, Jeanette, and Don Leonard. "Big Stuff, Little Stuff: A Decennial Measurement of Executives' and Academics' Reactions to Questionable Usage Elements." *The Journal of Business Communication* 38 (2001): 448-75.   *Omit "4" in "475."*

Italicize title of journal, magazine, or newspaper.

Volume number

McCartney, Scott. "Why a Baseball Superstar's Megacontract Can Be Less Than It Seems." *The Wall Street Journal*, 27 Dec. 2000: B1+.

Use a "plus" when pages are discontinuous.

Article from an Edited Book

Give authors', editors' names as printed in the source.

Killingsworth, M. Jimmie, and Martin Jacobsen. "The Rhetorical Construction of Environmental Risk Narratives in Government and Activist Websites: A Critique." *Narrative and Professional Communication*. Ed. Jane M. Perkins and Nancy Blyler. Stamford, CT: Ablex. 167-77.   *Spell out editors' names. Join with "and."*

Give state when city is not well known.

Article from a Publication on the Web

Greengard, Samuel. "Scoring Web Wins." *Business Finance Magazine*. May 2001. 12 July 2001. <http://www.businessfinancemag.com/archives/appfiles/Article.cfm?IssueID=348&ArticleID=13750>.

Don't add any extra hyphens when you break a long Web address.

Put Web address in angle brackets.
End entry with a period.

Book

Cross, Geoffrey A. *Forming the Collective Mind: A Contextual Exploration of Large-Scale Collaborative Writing in Industry*. Creskill, NJ: Hampton Press, 2001.

Put in square brackets information known to you

Book or Pamphlet with a Corporate Author
but not printed in source.

Citibank. *Indonesia: An Investment Guide*. [Jakarta:] Citibank, 1994.

Date after city and publisher

E-Mail Message
Abbreviate long months.

Locker, Kitty O. "Could We Get a New Photo?" E-mail to Rajani J. Kamuth. 17 Dec. 2001.

day month year

Government Document

United States. Sen. Special Committee on Aging. *Long-Term Care: States Grapple with Increasing Demands and Costs*. 107th Cong., 1st sess. Washington: GPO, 2001.

Omit state when city is well known.

Abbreviate "Government Printing Office."

Government Document Available on the Web from the GPO Access Database

United States. General Accounting Office. *Aviation Security: Terrorist Acts Demonstrate Urgent Need to Improve Security at the Nation's Airports*. Testimony before the Committee on Commerce, Science, and Transportation, U.S. Senate (GAO-01-1162T). 20 Sept. 2001. 20 Dec. 2001 <http://www.gao.gov/new.items/d011162t.pdf>.

Figure 22.7

MLA and APA Formats for Documenting Sources *(continued)*

Interview Conducted by the Researcher
Drysdale, Andrew. Telephone interview. 12 Apr. 1999.

Posting to a Listserv   *Date of posting.*
Dietrich, Dan. "Re: Course on Report and Proposal Writing." Online posting. 31 Aug. 2002.
BizCom Discussion Group. 23 Dec. 2001 <bizcom@ebbs.English.vt.edu>. *If discussion group*
                                                              has a Web archive, give the Web address.
Date you
accessed posting   *If it doesn't have a*
Web Site   *Web page, give the*
American Express. *Creating an Effective Business Plan.* 2001. 20 Dec. 2001.   *email address*
<http://home3.americanexpress.com/smallbusiness/tool/biz_plan/index.asp>   *of the list.*

APA Format

APA internal documentation gives the author's last name and the date of the work in parentheses in the text. A comma separates the author's name from the date (Gilsdorf & Leonard, 2001). The page number is given only for direct quotations (Cross, 2001, p. 74). If the author's name is used in the sentence, only the date is given in parentheses. (See Figure 13.9.) A list of REFERENCES gives the full bibliographic citation, arranging the entries alphabetically by the first author's last name.

comma   *last name first*   *No quotes around*
Article in a Periodical   *Year (period outside parenthesis).*   *title of article*
In titles of   Gilsdorf, J., & Leonard, D. (2001). Big stuff, little stuff: A decennial measurement of
articles   executives' and academics' reactions to questionable usage elements. *The Journal of*
and books   *Business Communication, 38*, 439-475. *no "pp." when journal*   *Capitalize all major words in title of*
capitalize only   *Italicize volume.*   *has a volume number*   *journal, magazine, or newspaper.*
① first word,
② first word of   McCartney, S. (2000, December 27). Why a baseball superstar's megacontract can be less
subtitle,   than it seems. *The Wall Street Journal*, p. B1, B3.
③ proper   *Separate discontinuous pages with comma and space.*
nouns. Article in an Edited Book   *Ampersands join names of co-authors, co-editors.*   *Editors'*
Killingsworth, M. J., & Jacobsen, M. (1999). The rhetorical construction of environmental *names*
                risk narratives in government and activist websites: A critique. In J. M. Perkins & N. *have last*
                Blyler (Eds.), *Narrative and professional communication* (pp. 167-177). Stamford, CT: *names*
Editors   Ablex.   *last.*
before book title   *Repeat "1" in 177.*   *Give state when*
Article from a Publication on the Web   *city is not well known.*
Greengard, S. (2001, May). Scoring web wins. *Business Finance Magazine*. p. 37.
        Retrieved July 12, 2001, from http://www.businessfinancemag.com/archives/appfiles/
        Article.cfm? IssueID=348&ArticleID=13750 *no punctuation after URL*

Initials only
Book   *Italicize title of book.*
Cross, G. A. (2001). *Forming the collective mind: A contextual exploration of large-scale*
        collaborative writing in industry. Creskill, NJ: Hampton Press.

                                                          Put in square brackets information known to you
Book or Pamphlet with a Corporate Author   *but not printed in document.*
Citibank. (1994). *Indonesia: An investment guide.* [Jakarta:] Author.
                                Indicates that the organization authoring
                                document also published it

Figure 22.7
MLA and APA Formats for Documenting Sources *(continued)*

E-Mail Message
[Identify e-mail messages in the text as personal communications. Give name of author and as specific a date as possible. Do not list in References.]

Government Document
Senate Special Committee on Aging. (2001). *Long-term care: States grapple with increasing demands and costs.* Hearing before the Special Committee on Aging, Senate, One Hundred Seventh Congress, first session, hearing held in Washington, DC, July 11, 2001 (Doc ID: 75-038). Washington, DC: U.S. Government Printing Office.

No abbreviations

Document number   *APA uses periods for "U.S."*   *Copyright or update date*

Government Document Available on the Web from the GPO Access Database
U.S. General Accounting Office. (2001, September 20.) Aviation security: Terrorist acts demonstrate urgent need to improve security at the nation's airports. Testimony before the Committee on Commerce, Science, and Transportation, U.S. Senate (GAO-01-1162T). Retrieved December 20, 2001, from General Accounting Office Reports Online via GPO Access: http://www.gao.gov/new.items/d011162t.pdf

Date you visited site

Keep "http://"

Interview Conducted by the Researcher
[Identify interviews in the test as personal communications. Give name of interviewee and as specific a date as possible. Do not list in References.]

Posting to a Listserv
[Identify messages on listservs to which one must subscribe in the text as personal communications. Give name of author and as specific a date as possible. Do not list in References.]

Web Site
American Express. (2001). Creating an effective business plan. Retrieved August 31, 2002, from the World Wide Web: http://home3.americanexpress.com/smallbusiness/tool/biz_plan/index.asp

Comma

No punctuation

Break long Web address at a slash or other punctuation mark.

Use square brackets around words you add or change to clarify the quote or make it fit the grammar of your sentence. Omit any words in the original source that are not essential for your purposes. Use ellipses (spaced dots) to indicate omissions.

Summary of Key Points

- To decide whether to use a Web site as a source in a research project, evaluate the site's authors, objectivity, information, and revision date.

- A **survey** questions a large group of people, called **respondents** or **subjects.** A **questionnaire** is a written list of questions that people fill out. An **interview** is a structured conversation with someone who will be able to give you useful information.

- **Closed questions** have a limited number of possible responses. **Open questions** do not lock the subject into any sort of response. **Branching questions** direct different respondents to different parts of the questionnaire based on their answers to earlier questions.

- In a **random sample,** each person in the population theoretically has an equal chance of being chosen. Only in a random sample is the researcher justified in inferring that the results from the sample are also true of the population from which the sample comes. A **convenience sample** is a group of subjects who are easy to get. A **judgment sample** is a group of people whose views seem useful.

- **Causation** means that one thing causes or produces another. **Correlation** means that two things happen at the same time. One might cause the other, but both might be caused by a third.

- **Citation** means attributing an idea or fact to its source in the body of the report. **Documentation** means providing the bibliographic information readers would need to go back to the original source.

Assignments for Module 22

Questions for Comprehension

22.1 What is the difference between open and closed questions?

22.2 What is the difference between the mean and the median?

22.3 What is the difference between correlation and causation?

Questions for Critical Thinking

22.4 Why do you need to know the exact way a question was phrased before using results from the study as evidence?

22.5 How do you decide whether a Web site is an acceptable source for a report?

22.6 Why should you test a questionnaire with a small group of people before you distribute it?

22.7 Why should you look for alternate explanations for your findings?

Exercises and Problems

22.8   Evaluating Survey Questions

Evaluate each of the following questions. Are they acceptable as they stand? If not, how can they be improved?

a. Questionnaire on grocery purchases.
1. Do you *usually* shop at the same grocery store?
   a. Yes
   b. No
2. How much is your average grocery bill?
   a. Under $25
   b. $25–50
   c. $50–100
   d. $100–150
   e. Over $150

b. Survey on technology
1. Would you generally welcome any technological advancement that allowed information to be sent and received more quickly and in greater quantities than ever before?

2. Do you think that all people should have free access to all information, or do you think that information should somehow be regulated and monitored?

c. Survey on job skills

How important are the following skills for getting and keeping a professional-level job in U.S. business and industry today?

	Low				High
Ability to communicate	1	2	3	4	5
Leadership ability	1	2	3	4	5
Public presentation skills	1	2	3	4	5
Selling ability	1	2	3	4	5
Teamwork capability	1	2	3	4	5
Writing ability	1	2	3	4	5

22.9   Evaluating Web Sites

Evaluate seven Web sites related to the topic of your report. For each, consider

- Author(s)
- Objectivity
- Information
- Revision date.

Based on these criteria, which sites are best for your report? Which are unacceptable? Why?

As Your Instructor Directs,
a. Share your results with a small group of students.
b. Present your results in a memo to your instructor.
c. Present your results to the class in an oral presentation.

22.10   Designing Questions for an Interview or Survey

Submit either a one- to three-page questionnaire or questions for a 20- to 30-minute interview AND the information listed below for the method you choose.

Questionnaire
1. Purpose(s), goal(s)
2. Subjects (who, why, how many)

3. How and where to be distributed
4. Rationale for order of questions, kinds of questions, wording of questions

Interview
1. Purpose(s), goal(s)
2. Subject (who and why)

3. Proposed site, length of interview
4. Rationale for order of questions, kinds of questions, wording of questions, choice of branching or follow up questions

As Your Instructor Directs,

a. Create questions for a survey on one of the following topics:

- Survey students on your campus about their knowledge of and interest in the programs and activities sponsored by a student organization.

- Survey workers at a company about what they like and dislike about their jobs.

- Survey people in your community about their willingness to pay more to buy products using recycled materials and to buy products that are packaged with a minimum of waste.

- Survey students and faculty on your campus about whether adequate parking exists.

- Survey two groups on a topic that interests you.

b. Create questions for an interview on one of the following topics:

- Interview an international student about the form of greetings and farewells, topics of small talk, forms of politeness, festivals and holidays, meals at home, size of families and roles of family members in his or her county.

- Interview the owner of a small business about the problems the business has, what strategies the owner has already used to increase sales and profits and how successful these strategies were, and the owner's attitudes toward possible changes in product line, decor, marketing, hiring, advertising, and money management.

- Interview someone who has information you need for a report you're writing.

 Polishing Your Prose

Using MLA Style

Using MLA requires two steps: gathering all the information you need and then applying it correctly. MLA documentation uses

- The full names of all authors; the full names of editors of an edited book.

- The title and subtitle (if any).

- The title of the edited book or journal, for articles within books and journals.

- For books: city of publication (with state if not well known), publisher, and year of publication.

- For articles in popular periodicals: the date of publication, in as much detail as

the periodical gives, and the page on which the article starts.

- For articles in scholarly periodicals: the volume and year and beginning and ending page numbers.

- The specific page(s) on which you find the fact(s) you cite or the sections you quote.

Using MLA style requires that you look closely at the order of words and at punctuation marks. For example, when you use a short quote (39 words or fewer), the period of your sentence goes outside the parentheses with the page number. In a long indented quote (40 words or more), the parentheses with the page number follows the period at the end of the sentence.

For details about how to use MLA style, see Figure 22.7 or <http://owl.english.purdue.edu/handouts/research/r_mla.html>.

Exercises

Identify and correct the errors in MLA format in the following Works Cited items.

1. Environmental Protection Agency. "An Office Building Occupant's Guide to Indoor Air Quality." 19 July 2001. <www.epa.gov/iaq/pubs/occupgd.html>.

2. Nai, A. K. "Squabbles Delay Cure of "Sick" Office Building." *The Wall Street Journal* 26 October 1995: B1+.

3. Locker, K. O. and Kaczmarek, S. K. Business Communication: Building Critical Skills. 2nd ed. McGraw-Hill/Irwin. 2004.

4. Thea Singer. "Can Business Still Save the World?" *Inc.,* April 2001, pp. 58–71.

5. Alison Stein Wellner, "The National Headcount," *American Demographics,* March 2001, s12.

6. James Dubinski, telephone conversation with the author, December 27, 2000.

7. E-mail message from me. September 2003.

8. NCAA. (2000). *Playing rules: Men's and women's basketball rules and interpretations.* Retrieved August 30, 2001, from the World Wide Web: http://www.ncaa.org/library/rules.html

9. Campbell, Kim Sydow, Follender, Saroya I.., and Guy Shane, "Preferred Strategies for Responding to Hostile Questions in Environmental Meetings," *Management Communication Quarterly,* 11 (1998): 401–421.

10. Schryer, Catherine. "Walking a fine line: writing negative letters in an insurance company," *Journal of Business and Technical Communication* 14 (October 2000): 445–97.

Check your answers to the odd-numbered exercises at the back of the book.

BComm Skill Booster

To apply the concepts in this module, complete lessons 40 and 78 on analyzing data and conducting a survey. You can access the BComm Skill Booster through the text Web site at **www.mhhe.com/bcs2e**.

Module 23

Short Reports

Start by asking these questions:

- Do different kinds of reports use different patterns of organization?

- What are the basic strategies for organizing information?

- Should I use the same style for reports as for other business documents?

Whenever you have a choice, write a short report rather than a long one. Never put information in reports just because you have it or just because it took you a long time to find it. Instead, choose the information that your reader needs to make a decision.

One report writer was asked to examine a building that had problems with heating, cooling, and air circulation. The client who owned the building wanted quick answers to three questions: What should we do? What will it cost? When will it pay for itself? The client wanted a three-page report with a seven-page appendix showing the payback figures.[1] When Susan Kleimann studied reply forms for a hotel, its managers said they didn't want to read a report. So Kleimann limited the "report" to an executive summary with conclusions and recommendations. Everything else went into appendixes.[2]

Short reports normally use letter or memo format.

Do different kinds of reports use different patterns of organization?

Yes. Work with the readers' expectations.

Informative, feasibility, and justification reports will be more successful when you work with the readers' expectations for that kind of report.

Informative and Closure Reports

An **informative** or **closure report** summarizes completed work or research that does not result in action or recommendation.

Informative reports often include the following elements:

- **Introductory paragraph** summarizing the problems or successes of the project.
- **Chronological account** of how the problem was discovered, what was done, and what the results were.
- **Concluding paragraph** with suggestions for later action. In a recommendation report, the recommendations would be based on proof. In contrast, the suggestions in a closure or recommendation report are not proved in detail.

Figure 23.1 presents this kind of informative report.

Feasibility Reports

Feasibility reports evaluate several alternatives and recommend one of them. (Doing nothing or delaying action can be one of the alternatives.)

Feasibility reports normally open by explaining the decision to be made, listing the alternatives, and explaining the criteria. In the body of the report, each alternative will be evaluated according to the criteria. Discussing each alternative separately is better when one alternative is clearly superior, when the criteria interact, and when each alternative is indivisible. If the choice depends on the weight given to each criterion, you may want to discuss each alternative under each criterion.

Whether your recommendation should come at the beginning or the end of the report depends on your reader. Most readers want the "bottom line" up front. However, if the reader will find your recommendation hard to accept, you may want to delay your recommendation till the end of the report when you have given all your evidence.

Justification Reports

Justification reports recommend or justify a purchase, investment, hiring, or change in policy. If your organization has a standard format for justification reports, follow that format. If you can choose your headings and organization, use this pattern when your recommendation will be easy for your reader to accept:

1. **Indicate what you're asking for and why it's needed.** Since the reader has not asked for the report, you must link your request to the organization's goals.

Figure 23.1

An Informative Memo Report Describing How Local Government Solved a Problem

JEFFERSON COUNTY COMMISSIONERS

April 20, 2004

Use your organization's culture to decide whether to list titles.

Informal short reports use letter or memo format.

To: Doug Perrin, Human Resources Director

From: Tamalyn Sykes, Staff Training and Development Manager *TS*

Subject: Workplace Violence Awareness Training at the Commissioners' Office

First paragraph summarizes main points.

Three months ago, the Commissioners' Office began to offer workplace violence awareness training to all 1,200 Jefferson County employees under its direct authority. The program was held to reduce employee concerns about the possibility of a hostage situation similar to the one in October at the State Workers' Compensation building next to the county courthouse.

Purpose and scope of report.

In this report, I will explain the need for the program, as well as its structure and cost.

Triple-space before heading.   *Capitalize first letter of major words in heading.*

Need for Workplace Violence Awareness Training

Talking heads tell reader what to expect in each section.

On October 11, 2003, county employees were shocked to learn of a hostage situation at the State Workers' Compensation building. A 41-year-old man, frustrated that his final benefits appeal had been rejected and facing home foreclosure, walked into a 15th-floor office with a handgun and took five people hostage. He demanded to see the account manager who had denied his original claim.

Double-space between paragraphs within heading.

Reason training is needed.

When the account manager stepped out of her office, she was shot twice by the man, who then turned the gun on himself. Both died. Later, questions abounded: How could the man have entered the building with a handgun? What could have been done to prevent violence? What emergency procedures were in place to protect staff? Why did building security fail to respond soon enough to prevent violence?

Specific impact on organization.

In the weeks that followed, many county employees expressed concern to supervisors that they felt vulnerable–after all, if it happened next door, it could happen here. Calls to the county's Employee Assistance Program for counseling tripled. Supervisors also noted drops in employee attendance; one supervisor reported that half of her staff called off work the week after the shooting.

Figure 23.1
An Informative Memo Report Describing How Local Government Solved a Problem (continued)

Short subject (or reader's name)   *Page number*   *Date*
Workplace Violence Awareness Training   2   April 20, 2004

Bold headings.

Structure and Cost of Training

Double–space between paragraphs.

At the November 20 General Session, the Commissioners approved a proposal to initiate workplace violence awareness training to address employee concerns. I then wrote and published the requisite RFP for services, and three training organizations responded with bids. New Horizons Training Services submitted the lowest and best bid.

The Commissioners hired New Horizons to provide 11 training sessions for 100-150 persons each. Sessions were held in the courthouse auditorium twice weekly starting January 7. While managers were allowed to schedule employees for sessions at their discretion, training was mandatory for all 1,200 employees. Employees on vacation or sick leave were required to attend a special "make-up" training session held at New Horizons' headquarters in March.

The two-and-a-half-hour training sessions consisted of three parts:

Indented lists provide visual variety.

- A one-hour video on general issues related to workplace violence.
- A one-hour panel discussion led by New Horizons' staff and featuring members of the county's security department and crisis management team (videotaped for the make-up session.)
- A half-hour question-and-answer session that included a written evaluation of the program.

At the end, the county's "Action Plan" booklet for dealing with workplace violence was distributed. The plan includes emergency telephone numbers, evacuation procedures, an overview of public safety measures at the courthouse, and directions on what to do in a hostage situation.

Be sure to double–check numbers.

The total cost for the sessions was $11,500: $1,000 for each session at the courthouse and $500 for the make-up session held at New Horizons' headquarters.

Employee feedback about the program was overwhelmingly positive.

2. **Briefly give the background of the problem or need.**
3. **Explain each of the possible solutions.** For each, give the cost and the advantages and disadvantages.
4. **Summarize the action needed to implement your recommendation.** If several people will be involved, indicate who will do what and how long each step will take.
5. **Ask for the action you want.**

If the reader will be reluctant to grant your request, use this variation of the problem-solving pattern described in Module 12:

1. **Describe the organizational problem (which your request will solve).** Use specific examples to prove the seriousness of the problem.
2. **Show why easier or less expensive solutions will not solve the problem.**
3. **Present your solution impersonally.**
4. **Show that the disadvantages of your solution are outweighed by the advantages.**
5. **Summarize the action needed to implement your recommendation.** If several people will be involved, indicate who will do what and how long each step will take.
6. **Ask for the action you want.**

How much detail you need to give in a justification report depends on your reader's knowledge of and attitude toward your recommendation and on the corporate culture. Many organizations expect justification reports to be short—only one or two pages. Other organizations may expect longer reports with much more detailed budgets and a full discussion of the problem and each possible solution.

What are the basic strategies for organizing information?

Try one of these seven patterns.

Seven basic patterns for organizing information are useful in reports:

1. Comparison/contrast.
2. Problem-solution.
3. Elimination of alternatives.
4. General to particular or particular to general.
5. Geographic or spatial.
6. Functional.
7. Chronological.

Any of these patterns can be used for a whole report or for only part of it.

I. Comparison/Contrast

Comparison/contrast takes up each alternative in turn, discussing strengths and weaknesses. Feasibility studies usually use this pattern.

A variation of the divided pattern is the **pro and con pattern.** In this pattern, under each specific heading, give the arguments for and against that alternative.

Whatever information comes second will carry more psychological weight. This pattern is least effective when you want to deemphasize the disadvantages of a proposed solution, for it does not permit you to bury the disadvantages between neutral or positive material.

A report recommending new plantings for a university quadrangle uses the pro and con pattern:

Advantages of Monocropping
    High Productivity
    Visual Symmetry
Disadvantages of Monocropping
    Danger of Pest Exploitation
    Visual Monotony

2. Problem-Solution

Identify the problem; explain its background or history; discuss its extent and seriousness; identify its causes. Discuss the factors (criteria) that affect the decision. Analyze the advantages and disadvantages of possible solutions. Conclusions and recommendations can go either first or last, depending on the preferences of your reader. This pattern works well when the reader is neutral.

A report recommending ways to eliminate solidification of a granular bleach during production uses the problem-solution pattern:

Recommended Reformulation for Vibe Bleach
Problems in Maintaining Vibe's Granular Structure
    Solidifying during Storage and Transportation
    Customer Complaints about "Blocks" of Vibe in Boxes
Why Vibe Bleach "Cakes"
    Vibe's Formula
    The Manufacturing Process
    The Chemical Process of Solidification
Modifications Needed to Keep Vibe Flowing Freely

3. Elimination of Alternatives

After discussing the problem and its causes, discuss the *impractical* solutions first, showing why they will not work. End with the most practical solution. This pattern works well when the solutions the reader is likely to favor will not work, while the solution you recommend is likely to be perceived as expensive, intrusive, or radical.

A report on toy commercials eliminates alternatives:

The Effect of TV Ads on Children
Camera Techniques Used in TV Advertisements
Alternative Solutions to Problems in TV Toy Ads
    Leave Ads Unchanged
    Mandate School Units on Advertising
    Ask the Industry to Regulate Itself
    Give FCC Authority to Regulate TV Ads Directed at Children

4. General to Particular or Particular to General

General to particular starts with the problem as it affects the organization or as it manifests itself in general and then moves to a discussion of the parts of

Problem-solving starts with recognizing a problem or need in your organization.

"Call it a hunch, but I'd say it's about time to re-evaluate the company's hiring criteria."

the problem and solutions to each of these parts. Particular to general starts with the problem as the audience defines it and moves to larger issues of which the problem is a part. Both are good patterns when you need to redefine the reader's perception of the problem in order to solve it effectively.

The directors of a student volunteer organization, VIP, have defined their problem as "not enough volunteers." After studying the subject, the writer is convinced that problems in training, the way work is structured, and campus awareness are responsible both for a high drop-out rate and a low recruitment rate. The general to particular pattern helps the audience see the problem in a new way:

Why VIP Needs More Volunteers
Why Some VIP Volunteers Drop Out
 Inadequate Training
 Feeling That VIP Requires Too Much Time
 Feeling That the Work Is Too Emotionally Demanding
Why Some Students Do Not Volunteer
 Feeling That VIP Requires Too Much Time
 Feeling That the Work Is Too Emotionally Demanding
 Preference for Volunteering with Another Organization
 Lack of Knowledge about VIP Opportunities
How VIP Volunteers Are Currently Trained
Time Demands on VIP Volunteers
Emotional Demands on VIP Volunteers

Ways to Increase Volunteer Commitment and Motivation
    Improving Training
    Improving the Flexibility of Volunteers' Hours
    Providing Emotional Support to Volunteers
    Providing More Information about Community Needs and VIP Services

5. Geographic or Spatial

In a geographic or spatial pattern, you discuss problems and solutions by units by their physical arrangement. Move from office to office, building to building, factory to factory, state to state, region to region, etc.

    A sales report uses a geographic pattern of organization:

Sales Have Risen in the European Economic Community
Sales Have Fallen Slightly in Asia
Sales Are Steady in North America

6. Functional

In functional patterns, discuss the problems and solutions of each functional unit. For example, a report on a new plant might divide data into sections on the costs of land and building, on the availability of personnel, on the convenience of raw materials, etc. A government report might divide data into the different functions an office performed, taking each in turn.

    A strategy report for a political party uses a functional pattern of organization:

Current Makeup of the Senate
Senate Seats Open in 2008
    Seats Held by a Democratic Incumbent
        Races in Which the Incumbent Has a Commanding Lead
        Races in Which the Incumbent Is Vulnerable
    Seats Held by a Republican Incumbent
        Races in Which the Incumbent Has a Commanding Lead
        Races in Which the Incumbent Is Vulnerable
    Seats Where No Incumbent Is Running

7. Chronological

A chronological report records events in the order in which they happened or are planned to happen.

    Many progress reports are organized chronologically:

Work Completed in October
Work Planned for November

Instant Replay

Seven Ways to Organize Information

1. Comparison/contrast
2. Problem-solution
3. Elimination of alternatives
4. General to particular or particular to general
5. Geographic or spatial
6. Functional
7. Chronological

Should I use the same style for reports as for other business documents?

Yes, with three exceptions

The advice about style in Modules 15 and 16 also applies to reports, with three exceptions:

1. **Use a fairly formal style, without contractions or slang.**
2. **Avoid the word *you*.** In a document to multiple audiences, it will not be clear who *you* is. Instead, use the company name.
3. **Include in the report all the definitions and documents needed to understand the recommendations.** The multiple audiences for reports include readers who may consult the document months or years from now. Explain acronyms and abbreviations the first time they appear.

   Explain the history or background of the problem. Add as appendixes previous documents on which you build.

The following points apply to any kind of writing, but they are particularly important in reports.

1. Say what you mean.
2. Tighten your writing.
3. Use transitions, topic sentences, and headings to make your organization clear to your reader.

Let's look at each of these principles as they apply to reports.

1. Say What You Mean

Not-quite-right word choices are particularly damaging in reports, which may be skimmed by readers who know very little about the subject. Putting the meaning of your sentence in the verbs will help you say what you mean.

Vague: My report revolves around the checkout lines and the methods used to get price checks when they arise.

Better: My report shows how price checks slow checkout lines and recommends ways to reduce the number of price checks needed.

Sometimes you'll need to completely recast the sentence.

Incorrect: The first problem with the incentive program is that middle managers do not use good interpersonal skills in implementing it. For example, the hotel chef openly ridicules the program. As a result, the kitchen staff fear being mocked if they participate in the program.

Better: The first problem with the incentive program is that some middle managers undercut it. For example, the hotel chef openly ridicules the program. As a result, the kitchen staff fear being mocked if they participate in the program.

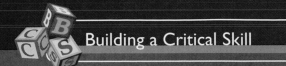
Asking Specific and Polite Questions

Learning to ask the *right* question *the right way* is a critical skill in business. Good business communicators use specificity and politeness.

Specificity

Vague questions often result in vague or rambling answers. Therefore, make sure you ask the right question for the kind of answer you want. To get a short answer,

- Give simple choices:

When you work extra hours, would you prefer overtime pay or comp time (the same number of hours off)?

- Ask the real question.

Not: When do you want to meet?

But: Which day is best for you to meet?

- Ask for a quantifiable or measurable response, such as facts, dates, statistics, and so forth.

What percentage of our customers are repeat business?

When you want longer, more qualitative answers, make your question specific enough for your audience to understand what you're asking:

- Start with one of the five Ws or H: who, what, where, when, why, or how.

- Add concrete language that invites a qualified response:

What reservations do you have about my proposal?

Why do you want to work for this firm?

Politeness

Politeness is a matter of timing, tone, language, and culture (◀ ▶ Module 3). Remember that when and how you ask the question are almost as important as the question itself. To increase your chances of not offending anyone,

- **Use timing.** Don't assault people with questions the moment they arrive or get up to leave. If someone is upset, give him or her time to calm down. Avoid questions when it's obvious someone doesn't want to answer them.

- **Keep questions to a minimum.** Review all the resources at your disposal first to see if the answers are there.

- **Avoid embarrassing or provocative questions.** Even if *you* are comfortable discussing such issues, don't assume other people are.

- **Avoid language that implies doubt, criticism, or suspicion.**

Rude: You don't really think you can handle this project, do you?

Polite: How do you feel about managing this project?

- **Use you-attitude and empathy.** Try to look at situations from the other person's point of view, particularly if a conflict is involved.

Because culture affects the rules of politeness—and culture changes—keep abreast of what is and isn't acceptable in society. Remember that different cultures have different concepts of politeness.

2. Tighten Your Writing

Eliminate unnecessary words, use gerunds and infinitives, combine sentences, and reword sentences to cut the number of words.

Wordy: Campus Jewelers' main **objective** is to increase sales. Specifically, the objective is to double sales in the next five years by becoming a more successful business.

Better: Campus Jewelers' **objective** is to double sales in the next five years.

3. Use Blueprints, Transitions, Topic Sentences, and Headings.

Blueprints are overviews or forecasts that tell the reader what you will discuss in a section or in the entire report. Make your blueprint easy to read by telling the reader how many points there are and numbering them. In the following example, the first sentence in the revised paragraph tells the reader to look for four points; the numbers separate the four points clearly. This overview paragraph also makes a contract with readers, who now expect to read about tax benefits first and employee benefits last.

Paragraph without numbers:	Employee Stock Ownership Programs (ESOPs) have several advantages. They provide tax benefits for the company. ESOPs also create tax benefits for employees and for lenders. They provide a defense against takeovers. In some organizations, productivity increases because workers now have a financial stake in the company's profits. ESOPs are an attractive employee benefit and help the company hire and retain good employees.
Revised paragraph with numbers:	Employee Stock Ownership Programs (ESOPs) provide four benefits. First, ESOPs provide tax benefits for the company, its employees, and lenders to the plan. Second, ESOPs help create a defense against takeovers. Third, ESOPs may increase productivity by giving workers a financial stake in the company's profits. Fourth, as an attractive employee benefit, ESOPs help the company hire and retain good employees.

Transitions are words, phrases, or sentences that tell the reader whether the discussion is continuing on the same point or shifting points.

There are economic advantages, too.
(Tells the reader that we are still discussing advantages but that we have now moved to economic advantages.)

An alternative to this plan is. . . .
(Tells reader that a second option follows.)

These advantages, however, are found only in A, not in B or C.
(Prepares reader for a shift from A to B and C.)

A **topic sentence** introduces or summarizes the main idea of a sentence. Readers who skim reports can follow your ideas more easily if each paragraph begins with a topic sentence.

Hard to read (no topic sentence):	Another main use of ice is to keep the fish fresh. Each of the seven kinds of fish served at the restaurant requires one gallon twice a day, for a total of 14 gallons. An additional 6 gallons a day are required for the salad bar.
Better (begins with topic sentence):	Twenty gallons of ice a day are needed to keep food fresh. Of this, the biggest portion (14 gallons) is used to keep the fish fresh. Each of the seven kinds of fish served at the restaurant requires one gallon twice a day ($7 \times 2 = 14$). An additional 6 gallons a day are required for the salad bar.

Headings are single words, short phrases, or complete sentences that indicate the topic in each section. A heading must cover all of the material under it until the next heading. For example, *Cost of Tuition* cannot include the cost of books or of room and board. You can have just one paragraph under a heading or several pages. If you do have several pages between headings you may want to consider using subheadings. Use subheadings only when you have two or more divisions within a main heading.

Topic headings focus on the structure of the report. As you can see from the following example, topic headings give very little information.

Recommendation
Problem
   Situation 1
   Situation 2
Causes of the Problem
   Background
   Cause 1
   Cause 2
Recommended Solution

Talking heads, in contrast, tell the reader what to expect. Talking or informative heads, like those in the examples in this chapter, provide an overview of each section and of the entire report:

Recommended Reformulation for Vibe Bleach
Problems in Maintaining Vibe's Granular Structure
   Solidifying during Storage and Transportation
   Customer Complaints about "Blocks" of Vibe in Boxes
Why Vibe Bleach "Cakes"
   Vibe's Formula
   The Manufacturing Process
   The Chemical Process of Solidification
Modifications Needed to Keep Vibe Flowing Freely

Headings must be **parallel** (◀ ▷ p. 86), that is, they must use the same grammatical structure. Subheads must be parallel to each other but do not necessarily have to be parallel to subheads under other headings.

Summary of Key Points

- **Comparison/contrast** takes up each alternative in turn. The **pro and con pattern** divides the alternatives and discusses the arguments for and against that alternative. A **problem-solving report** identifies the problem, explains its causes, and analyzes the advantages and disadvantages of possible solutions. **Elimination** identifies the problem, explains its causes, and discusses the least practical solutions first, ending with the one the writer favors. **General to particular** begins with the problem as it affects the organization or as it manifests itself in general, then moves to a discussion of the parts of the problem and solutions to each of these parts. **Particular to general** starts with specific aspects of the problem, then moves to a discussion of the larger implications of the problem for the organization. **Geographical or spatial** patterns discuss the problems and solutions by units. **Functional** patterns discuss the problems and solutions of each functional unit.

- Reports use the same style as other business documents, with three exceptions:
  1. Reports use a more formal style than do many letters and memos.
  2. Reports rarely use the word *you*.
  3. Reports should be self-explanatory.
- To create good report style,
  1. Say what you mean.
  2. Tighten your writing.
  3. Use blueprints, transitions, topic sentences, and headings.
- **Headings** are single words, short phrases, or complete sentences that cover all of the material under it until the next heading. **Informative** or **talking heads** tell the reader what to expect in each section.

Assignments for Module 23

Questions for Comprehension

23.1 What are the seven basic patterns for organizing information?

23.2 What is a blueprint?

23.3 What is a talking head?

Questions for Critical Thinking

23.4 Why shouldn't you put all the information you have into a report?

23.5 Why do reports often use a more formal style than other business documents?

23.6 Why should you avoid *you* in reports?

23.7 Why are topic sentences especially useful in reports?

Exercises and Problems

23.8 **Explaining "Best Practices"**

Write a report explaining the "best practices" of the unit where you work that could also be adopted by other units in your organization.

23.9 **Recommending Action**

Write a report recommending an action that your unit or organization should take. Address your report to the person who would have the power to approve your recommendation. Possibilities include
- Hiring an additional worker for your department.

- Making your organization more family-friendly.
- Making a change that will make the organization more efficient.

- Making changes to improve accessibility for customers or employees with disabilities.

23.10 **Writing up a Survey**

Survey two groups of people on a topic that interests you. Possible groups are men and women, people in business and in English programs, younger and older students, students and townspeople. Non-random samples are acceptable.

As Your Instructor Directs,
a. Survey 40 to 50 people.
b. Team up with your classmates. Survey 50 to 80 people if your group has two members, 75 to 120 people if it has three members, 100 to 150 people if it has four members, and 125 to 200 people if it has five members.
c. Keep a journal during your group meetings and submit it to your instructor.
d. Write a memo to your instructor describing and evaluating your group's process for designing, conducting, and writing up the survey. (◄ ▷ See Module 18 on working and writing in groups.)

As you conduct your survey, make careful notes about what you do so that you can use this information when you write up your survey. If you work with a group, record who does what.

Use complete memo format. Your subject line should be clear and reasonably complete. Omit unnecessary words such as "Survey of." Your first paragraph serves as an introduction, but it needs no heading. The rest of the body of your memo will be divided into four sections with the following headings: Purpose, Procedure, Results, and Discussion.

In your first paragraph, briefly summarize (not necessarily in this

order) who conducted the experiment or survey, when it was conducted, where it was conducted, who the subjects were, what your purpose was, and what you found out.

In your **Purpose** section, explain why you conducted the survey. What were you trying to learn? Why did this subject seem interesting or important?

In your **Procedure** section, describe in detail *exactly* what you did.

In your **Results** section, first tell whether your results supported your hypothesis. Use both visuals and words to explain what your numbers show. (◄ ▷ See Module 25 on how to design visuals.) Process your raw data in a way that will be useful to your reader.

In your **Discussion** section, evaluate your survey and discuss the implications of your results. Consider these questions:

1. Do you think a scientifically valid survey would have produced the same results? Why or why not?

2. Were there any sources of bias either in the way the questions were phrased or in the way the subjects were chosen? If you were running the survey again, what changes would you make to eliminate or reduce these sources of bias?

3. Do you think your subjects answered honestly and completely? What factors may have intruded? Is the fact that you did or didn't know them, were or weren't of the same sex relevant?

4. What causes the phenomenon your results reveal? If several causes together account for the phenomenon, or if it is impossible to be sure

of the cause, admit this. Identify possible causes and assess the likelihood of each.

5. What action should be taken?

The discussion section gives you the opportunity to analyze the significance of your survey. Its insight and originality lift the otherwise well-written memo from the ranks of the merely satisfactory to the ranks of the above-average and the excellent.

23.11   Writing a Report Based on Your Knowledge and Experience

Write a report on one of the following topics.

1. What should a U.S. or Canadian manager know about dealing with workers from _____ [you fill in the country or culture]? What factors do and do not motivate people in this group? How do they show respect and deference? Are they used to a strong hierarchy or to an egalitarian setting? Do they normally do one thing at once or many things? How important is clock time and being on time? What factors lead them to respect someone? Age? Experience? Education? Technical knowledge? Wealth? Or what? What conflicts or miscommunications may arise between workers from this culture and other workers due to cultural differences? Are people from this culture pretty similar in these beliefs and behaviors, or is there lots of variation?

2. Describe an ethical dilemma encountered by workers in a specific organization. What is the background of the situation? What competing loyalties exist? In the past, how have workers responded? How has the organization responded? Have "whistleblowers" been rewarded or punished? What could the organization do to foster ethical behavior?

3. Describe a problem or challenge encountered by an organization where you've worked. Show why it needed to be solved, tell who did what to try to solve it, and tell how successful the efforts were. Possibilities include

   • How the organization is implementing work teams, downsizing, or a change in organizational culture.
   • How the organization uses e-mail or voice mail, statistical process control, or telecommuting.
   • How managers deal with stress, make ethical choices, or evaluate subordinates.
   • How the organization is responding to changing U.S. demographics, the Americans with Disabilities Act, international competition and opportunities, or challenges from dot.com companies.

Polishing Your Prose

Being Concise

Being **concise** in business writing means using only necessary words to make your point, without sacrificing politeness or clarity. Wordy sentences may confuse or slow readers:

Wordy: All of our employees at Haddenfield and Dunne should make themselves available for a seminar meeting on the 5th of August, 2004, at 10 o'clock in the morning. Please make sure you come to the conference room on the 2nd Floor of the Main Complex.

Concise: Please plan to attend a seminar at 10 A.M. August 5 in the Main Complex 2nd Floor conference room.

Being concise does not mean eliminating necessary information. Sometimes you'll have to write longer sentences to be clear.

Nor does tightening your writing mean using short, choppy sentences.

Choppy: We have a new copier. It is in the supply room. Use it during regular hours. After 5 P.M., it will be shut down.

Concise: A new copier is available in the supply room for use before 5 P.M.

Use Concrete Words.

Instead of vague nouns and verbs with strings of modifiers, use specifics.

Vague: The person who drops off packages talked about the subject of how much to charge.

Concrete: The delivery person discussed fees.

Avoid Vague or Empty Modifiers.

Words like *very, some, many, few, much, kind of/sort of,* and so forth usually can be cut.

Cut Redundant Words or Phrases.

Don't say the same thing twice. *Cease* and *desist, first* and *foremost,* the *newest* and *latest, official company* policy, 24 *stories tall, said out loud,* and *return* the form *back* to me are all redundant.

Avoid Unnecessarily Complex Constructions.

Instead of *the bid that won the contract,* use *the winning bid.*

Stick to Simple Verb Tenses.

Standard edited English prefers them. Instead of "I *have been attending* the University of Michigan" use "I *attend* the University of Michigan." Instead of "By 2006, I *will have completed* my junior year" use "I *will be* a senior by 2006."

Exercises

Rewrite the following sentences to make them concise.

1. Our official records show that you are a very responsible person.

2. We are in the process of planning to open another retail store over in the Miami area that will help us to sell our merchandise to customers in Miami.

3. The mainframe computer is located in our subterranean basement.

4. Some people who work for the folks in Human Resources are going to be stopping by the office tomorrow in the morning to look at our files on our employees.

5. We faxed a reproduced copy of the application on the fax machine.

6. We are very, very grateful to have had so many opportunities to work with customers such as you in the past.

7. I enjoyed the presentation very much.

8. The enclosed job application letter that describes me features numerous descriptions of the many jobs I've held, as well as a lot of information about when I worked and where I worked.

9. The guy that runs our advertising department yelled loudly across the parking lot that a delivery truck had left its two headlights on.

10. By this time tomorrow, I will have arrived in London for a meeting on business with members of the staff at our British subsidiary.

Check your answers to the odd-numbered exercises at the back of the book.

Module 24

Long Reports

Start by asking these questions:

- I've never written anything so long. How should I organize my time?

- How do I create each of the parts of a formal report?

Formal reports are distinguished from informal letter and memo reports by their length and by their components. A full formal report may (but does not have to) contain all of the following components:

Cover

Title Page

Letter of Transmittal

Table of Contents

List of Illustrations

Executive Summary

Report Body

Introduction (Usually has subheadings for Purpose and Scope; may also have Limitations, Assumptions, and Methods.)

Background/History of the Problem (Serves as a record for later readers of the report.)

Body (Presents and interprets data in words and visuals. Analyzes causes of the problem and evaluates possible solutions. Specific headings will depend on the topic of the report.)

Conclusions (Summarizes main points of report.)

Recommendations (Recommends actions to solve the problem. May be combined with Conclusions; may be put before body rather than at the end.)

References or Works Cited (Documents or sources cited in the report.)

Appendixes (Provide additional materials that the careful reader may want: transcript of an interview, copies of questionnaires, tallies of all the questions, computer printouts, previous reports.)

I've never written anything so long. How should I organize my time?

Write parts as soon as you can.

Spend most of your time on sections that support your recommendations.

Figure 24.1 shows how you might allocate your time in writing a long report.

To use your time efficiently, think about the parts of the report before you begin writing. Much of the Introduction comes from your proposal with only minor revisions: Purpose, Scope, Assumptions, and Methods.

The bibliography from your proposal can form the first draft of your References or Works Cited.

Save a copy of your questionnaire or interview questions to use as an appendix. As you tally and analyze the data, prepare an appendix summarizing all the responses to your questionnaire, your figures and tables, and a complete list of References or Works Cited.

You can write the title page and the transmittal as soon as you know what your recommendation will be.

One key to writing a good report is to start early and budget your time.

Figure 24.1
Allocating Time in Writing a Report (Your time may vary.)

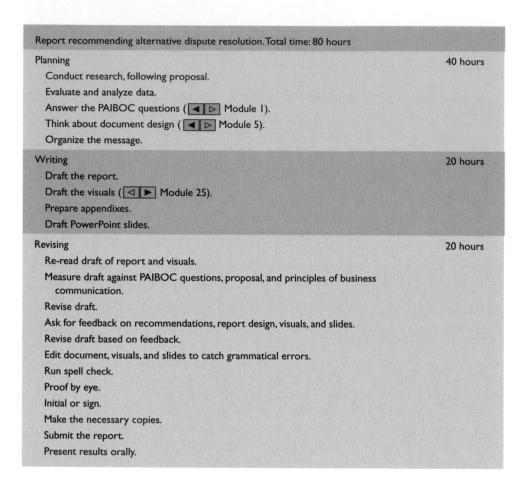

Report recommending alternative dispute resolution. Total time: 80 hours	
Planning	40 hours
Conduct research, following proposal.	
Evaluate and analyze data.	
Answer the PAIBOC questions (◄ ▷ Module 1).	
Think about document design (◄ ▷ Module 5).	
Organize the message.	
Writing	20 hours
Draft the report.	
Draft the visuals (◁ ► Module 25).	
Prepare appendixes.	
Draft PowerPoint slides.	
Revising	20 hours
Re-read draft of report and visuals.	
Measure draft against PAIBOC questions, proposal, and principles of business communication.	
Revise draft.	
Ask for feedback on recommendations, report design, visuals, and slides.	
Revise draft based on feedback.	
Edit document, visuals, and slides to catch grammatical errors.	
Run spell check.	
Proof by eye.	
Initial or sign.	
Make the necessary copies.	
Submit the report.	
Present results orally.	

After you've analyzed your data, write the Executive Summary, the body, and the Conclusions and Recommendations. Prepare a draft of the table of contents and the list of illustrations.

When you write a long report, list all the sections (headings) that your report will have. Mark those that are most important to your reader and your proof, and spend most of your time on them. Write the important sections early. That way, you won't spend all your time on Background or History of the Problem. Instead, you'll get to the meat of your report.

How do I create each of the parts of a formal report?

Follow the example here.

As you read each section below, you may want to turn to the corresponding pages of the long report in Figure 24.2 to see how the component is set up and how it relates to the total report.

Figure 24.2
A Long Report

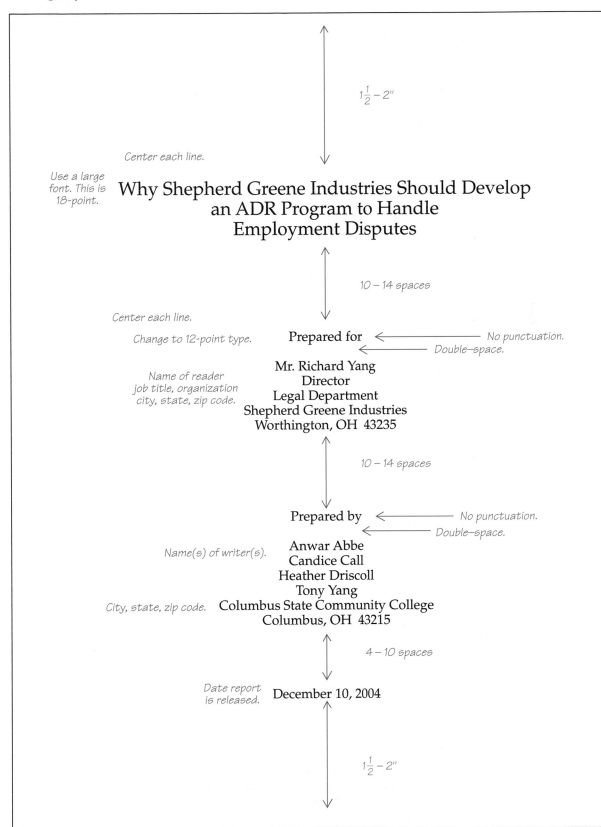

$1\frac{1}{2} - 2''$

Center each line.

Use a large font. This is 18-point.

Why Shepherd Greene Industries Should Develop an ADR Program to Handle Employment Disputes

10 – 14 spaces

Center each line.

Change to 12-point type.

Prepared for ← *No punctuation.*
Double–space.

Name of reader job title, organization city, state, zip code.

Mr. Richard Yang
Director
Legal Department
Shepherd Greene Industries
Worthington, OH 43235

10 – 14 spaces

Prepared by ← *No punctuation.*
Double–space.

Name(s) of writer(s).

Anwar Abbe
Candice Call
Heather Driscoll
Tony Yang

City, state, zip code. Columbus State Community College
Columbus, OH 43215

4 – 10 spaces

Date report is released. December 10, 2004

$1\frac{1}{2} - 2''$

Figure 24.2

A Long Report *(continued)*

You may also design a letterhead for yourself, especially if you're assuming that you are doing the report as a consultant.

550 East Town Street
Apartment 201
Columbus, OH 43210
December 10, 2004

This letter uses block format (see Figure 9.2). Modified block is also acceptable.

Mr. Richard Yang
Director
Legal Department
Shepherd Greene Industries
3241 Corporate Center Way
Worthington, OH 43235

In paragraph 1, release the report. Note when and by whom the report was authorized. Note report's purpose.

Dear Mr. Yang:

Enclosed is the report you requested in October on whether Shepherd Greene Industries should adopt an Alternative Dispute Resolution (ADR) program. We believe it should. An ADR program can

Give recommendations or thesis.

- Clear our cluttered court system of cases which can be settled by other means.
- Reduce costs of litigating employee grievances.
- Reduce the amount of time required to settle disputes.
- Increase employee morale by involving employees in the dispute resolution process.

Shepherd Greene should conduct further research to determine which ADR plan to adopt, involve the union in deciding which plan to use, support the plan financially, and pilot the plan for a year.

The Air Force already uses ADR. Adopting an ADR program will both enhance the stability of Shepherd Greene's workforce and create another point of similarity between the Air Force and Shepherd Greene, making it easier for the Air Force to accept Shepherd Greene's bid to manufacture replacement parts for combat aircraft.

Thank people who helped you.

The information in this report came from print and online sources, as well as interviews with Richard Yang and Chuck Scanlon at Shepherd Greene. We appreciate the time they took from busy schedules to meet with us.

Thank the reader for the opportunity to do the research.

Thank you for the opportunity to conduct this research. We appreciate the chance to apply our knowledge to helping Shepherd Greene achieve its goal of reducing legal costs while providing an effective means to settle employee grievances.

Offer to answer questions about the report. Answers would be included in your fee, if any—no extra charge!

If you have any questions about this report, please ask!

Sincerely,	Sincerely,	Sincerely,	Sincerely,
Anwar Abbe	Candice Call	Heather Driscoll	Tony Yang
aabbe71@hotmail.com	cc_ccsc@yahoo.com	hrdrisco@juno.com	yang.285@cscc.edu

Center page number at the bottom of the page. Use a lower-case Roman numeral.

Figure 24.2
A Long Report *(continued)*

Table of Contents does not list itself.

Table of Contents

Use lower-case Roman numerals for front matter.

Intro begins on page "1".

Indent subheads.

Capitalize first letter of each major word in headings.

Headings or subheadings must be parallel within a section.

Some reports have separate sections for "Conclusions" and "Recommendations"

Line up right margin (justify).

List of Illustrations

Add a "List of Illustrations" at the bottom of the Table of Contents or on a separate page if the report has graphs and other visuals. Omit "List of Illustrations" if you have only tables.

ii

Figure 24.2

A Long Report *(continued)*

Report title. **Why Shepherd Greene Industries Should Develop an ADR Program to Handle Employee Disputes**

The Executive Summary contains the logical skeleton of the report: the recommendation(s) and evidence supporting them.

Executive Summary

Start with recommendations or thesis.

Shepherd Greene Industries should adopt an Alternative Dispute Resolution (ADR) program to handle employee disputes. ADR includes negotiation, in which the parties simply work out a solution together; mediation, in which a third party helps the disputing parties reach an agreement; and arbitration, in which a third party determines a solution which the disputing parties must accept. ADR programs are increasingly common in both private companies and federal agencies.

Lawsuits arising from employee disputes cost the company thousands of dollars and hundreds of staff hours, not including any settlement or judgment costs, and take the legal staff away from its primary duty of reviewing bids and contracts with Shepherd Greene's customers and suppliers. Shepherd Greene has submitted a bid to the US Air Force to manufacture replacement parts for combat aircraft. Programs that minimize employee grievances would enhance Shepherd Greene's application.

ADR programs have a good record of resolving disputes while saving time and money and building goodwill. Organizations using ADR report success rates of more than 60%, sometimes reaching 100%. In some organizations, most of the cases are resolved through informal consultation, before formal mediation or arbitration is necessary. Instead of taking months or years, ADR can settle disputes in as little as a day. The legal costs saved by adopting ADR are substantial. Estimates for processing and legal fees range from $1,795 for a single case (Blanchard and McDade) to $77,000 (Senger). GE estimates that its Early Dispute Resolution program saves $15 million a year (Paquin, Victor, and Villarreal 24).

Document sources in the Executive Summary as you would in the report.

To adopt an ADR program, Shepherd Greene should

Provide brief support for each recommendation.

1. **Do further research to determine which ADR plan to use.** The four-step model used by Science Applications International Corporation (SAIC) offers a possible model, but the company should also talk to faculty in the Dispute Resolution Program at The Ohio State University Moritz College of Law and to the US Air Force, which itself has an award-winning ADR program. *MLA style omits the periods in "US."*

2. **Involve the union in deciding which ADR plan to use.** The union, its president believes, is receptive to ADR. To make the implementation as smooth as possible, union representatives should be involved in researching additional ADR plans and recommending one.

3. **Support ADR financially.** Shepherd Greene should supply funds for
   - Release time for personnel.
   - ADR training.
   - Publicizing the program.
   - Funds to hire mediators and arbitrators.

In some plans, such as SAIC's, employees who seek mediators and arbitrators pay part of the cost of hiring these people.

4. **Pilot the program for a year.** While several organizations now have experience with ADR, many different specifics are possible. It will be easier to get a program started if people know that it can be modified (or even disbanded) later as Shepherd Greene gains experience with ADR. *Language in Executive Summary can come from report. Make sure any repeated language is well-written.*

iii

Figure 24.2
A Long Report *(continued)*

Introduction

Many private companies and government agencies use Alternative Dispute Resolution (ADR) programs to resolve disputes with employees. Adopting an ADR program would save time and money for Shepherd Greene.

Problem

Shepherd Greene wants an alternative to traditional court remedies, which have had mixed results for the company in the recent past. In 1995, an employee fired for poor attendance sued, claiming a manager had illegally altered her time cards. After two years in the courts, Shepherd Greene settled for an undisclosed amount. In 1998, two employees fired for failing on-the-job drug tests unsuccessfully sued the company to get their jobs back, appealing the case all the way to the State of Ohio Supreme Court. In 2002, a coalition of employees sued the company about a management structure that allegedly keeps black employees in low-level jobs. The suit is pending.

These lawsuits take months or even years to work through the court system, costing the company thousands of dollars, not including any settlement or judgment cost. Although outside attorneys are also hired, preparing these cases requires hundreds of staff hours and takes the legal staff away from its primary duty of reviewing bids and contracts with Shepherd Greene's customers and suppliers.

Shepherd Greene has another reason to change the way it handles employment disputes. The company has submitted a bid to the US Air Force to manufacture replacement parts for combat aircraft. In addition to adhering to strict manufacturing guidelines and having the highest security clearance, the successful company must demonstrate stability in its labor and management practices. Programs that minimize employee grievances thus would enhance Shepherd Greene's application.

Purpose and Scope

The purpose of this report is to recommend whether it is feasible for Shepherd Greene to adopt an Alternative Dispute Resolution program for employee disputes.

In this report, we will focus on how ADR can settle employee grievances, the savings in time and money from using ADR, the goodwill gained by using ADR, model ADR programs, and the resources required for Shepherd Greene to develop its own ADR program. We will briefly discuss the effect of using ADR on crowded court dockets and the potential for an ADR program at Shepherd Greene to succeed.

Assumptions

Our recommendation is based on three assumptions:
- The frequency and severity of employee grievances at Shepherd Greene will remain steady or rise.
- Legal costs will remain steady or rise.
- The time required to litigate cases in the courts will remain steady or rise.

Figure 24.2

A Long Report *(continued)*

If you use only library and online sources, you do not need a "Methods" section.

Limitations

If your report has limitations, state them.

This report depends almost entirely on print and online sources. Before adopting a specific ADR system, Shepherd Greene should talk with people experienced with ADR, such as faculty in the Dispute Resolution Program at The Ohio State University Moritz College of Law.

Criteria

These ideas could be presented in a paragraph. But the list provides visual variety and makes it easier for the reader to skim the page.

According to Shepherd Greene's Legal Department Director, Richard Yang, an ADR program must satisfy three criteria:

1. The program must reduce the time and money currently spent on legal remedies.
2. It must be possible to create and implement the program within the existing $1.2 million annual operating budget for Shepherd Greene's Legal Department.
3. The program must be approved not only by Shepherd Greene's management but also by the employee union.

Triple-space (2 empty spaces) before new head. Double-space after head before paragraph.

What ADR Is

Document your sources!

West's Legal Environment of Business defines ADR as "any procedure or device for resolving disputes other than the tradional judicial process" (Cross and Miller 60). ADR includes negotiation, in which the parties simply work out a solution together; mediation, in which a third party helps the disputing parties reach an agreement; and arbitration, in which a third party determines a solution which the disputing parties must accept.

ADR is not limited to employer-employee disputes. Instead, ADR can be used for any dispute that might otherwise result in a lawsuit: as an alternative to divorce litigation, to resolve disputes between companies and customers or suppliers, or even to resolve disputes between states or countries.

Cross and Miller note that formal procedures for ADR have become increasingly common as lawsuits have become more expensive and time-consuming. The huge backlog of court cases means that years can elapse before a case comes to trial. In the early 1990s, Congress "required the federal court cases to develop a plan to cut court costs and reduce delay within the federal judicial system" (60). Today, only 5% to 10% of the lawsuits that are filed actually result in a trial; the rest are dismissed or settled out of court (59). *Period after parentheses when the quotation is short and not indented.*

ADR is now becoming sufficiently common that some writers have dropped the label "alternative" and simply discuss methods of "dispute resolution." Even people who keep the "A" sometimes redesignate it: Attorney General Janet Reno said the ADR stood for "Appropriate Dispute Resolution" (Senger). We will keep the "A" in ADR since the acronym is so widely known.

Using ADR to Resolve Employment Disputes

In essence, any program that allows an aggrieved employee and employer to settle claims without going to court qualifies as ADR. Thus, a simple discussion between the employee and management to arrive at a mutually agreeable solution to a problem that otherwise would go to court is ADR. Formal ADR programs can include mediation, arbitration, mini-trials, fact-finding, private judging, or summary-jury trials (Kelly 4).

Give page numbers for facts, not just quotes, in MLA style.

Figure 24.2

A Long Report *(continued)*

Early Use of ADR in Employment Disputes

Using ADR to resolve disputes between employers and employees is not new. Michael R. Carrell and Christina Heavrin note that the first mention of labor arbitration "dates to a clause in the constitution of the Journeymen Cabinet-Makers of Philadelphia in 1829" while the "earliest recorded arbitration hearing occurred in 1865 when iron workers in Pittsburgh arbitrated their wages" (408). The United States Conciliation Service, part of the Department of Labor, began mediating and arbitrating labor disputes during World War I and continued to do so until after World War II, when it was replaced by Federal Mediation and Conciliation Service (Barrett 40-41).

Page number covers all sentences from citation to number. Eileen Kelly notes that in 2001, the US Supreme Court upheld a company's right to require non-union applicants and employees to use arbitration to settle employee disputes (Circuit City Stores, Inc. v. Adams, 121 S. Ct. 1302). The decision sets a precedent for companies to require non-union employees to use ADR as a mandatory condition of employment. That is, by accepting a job, a candidate agrees not to sue the employer if a dispute arises but to submit to binding arbitration. The Supreme Court decision did not speak to unionized organizations. Presumably, if a union represents employees, the employer and the union must agree in advance to the conditions of ADR, such as binding arbitration (4).

Why ADR Has Become a Popular Way to Settle Employee Disputes

Two factors explain the growing interest in ADR to settle employee disputes: the drastic increase in the number of disputes, and the high costs of settling them with lititgation.

In the 1990s, the number of lawsuits filed by employees against employers skyrocketed. As Katherine Stone reports, in 1996 more than twice as many employment discrimination cases were filed in federal courts as had been filed in 1990 (29). See Figure 1. Today, employment lawsuits comprise 15% of the load of cases in federal courts (Bedikian 33). *Refer to figures in your text.*

Figure 1

Employee Lawsuits against Employers Skyrocket *Tell a story with your Figure title.*

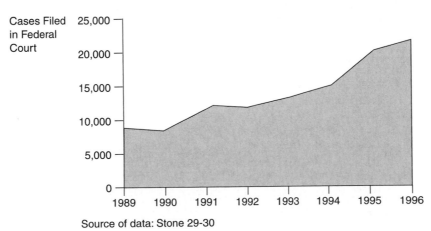

Cases Filed in Federal Court

Source of data: Stone 29-30

Provide a source for data when you get numbers but not the chart from someone else.

Figure 24.2

A Long Report (*continued*)

Use square brackets for your changes in quoted text.

Long quotations are indented, one inch; no quotation marks needed.

The cost of settling these cases also skyrocketed. As Katherine Stone reports, in the period 1989-90, plaintiffs began to win large judgments [. . . which] hit an all-time high in 1990. That year, plaintiffs who prevailed won an astounding *average* recovery of $1,989,300. Of the 254 cases that went to juries, plaintiffs prevailed 38% of the time and recovered an *average* judgment of $2,652,270. (29; emphasis in original)

The judgments Stone cites exclude legal fees.

The period goes before the parenthesis when the quote is long and indented.

The amount losing companies had to pay increased further when, in 1991, Title VII was amended to allow the winning party to collect attorney fees from the losing party and to receive punitive damages as well as money for actual damages (Stone 29). Such fees help explain why Texaco recently paid $176.1 million and Coca-Cola paid $192.5 million to settle race discrimination cases (Kelly 4).

Clearly, it is in employers' interests to find ways to settle employee disputes without going to court.

Organizations Using ADR to Settle Employee Disputes

ADR is an increasingly popular form of dispute resolution. A 1997 survey of Fortune 1000 companies by PricewaterhouseCoopers and Cornell University found that 87% had used forms of ADR in the previous three years (Meade and Zimmerman 60). Companies using ADR include Alcoa, Anheuser-Busch, GE, Halliburton, Johnson & Johnson, Masco, McGraw-Hill, Science Applications International, Sears, UAL, and UBS Paine-Webber (Bresler 3; Longstreth 18; F. Phillips).

Use first initial when two or more authors share a last name.

Acts passed by Congress in 1991 and 1996 and a Presidential Memorandum in 1998 directed all executive federal agencies to use ADR (Blanchard and McDade). The US Office of Personnel Management's Web site, *Alternative Dispute Resolution: A Resource Guide,* links to the ADR programs of 53 federal agencies, including the Air Force, Army, Navy, Defense Logistics Agency, National Aeronautics and Space Administration, and National Security Agency.

Use an acronym only if it will appear more than once; spell out names the first time you use them.

ADR is not limited to disputes between individual employees and their employers. In the late 1990s, a "massive" sexual harassment suit brought against the Mitsubishi company was settled with the aid of a federal mediator (Senger).

Web source, so no page number.

Results of ADR Programs

Heading must cover everything under that heading until the next head or subhead at that level.

ADR programs have a good record of resolving disputes while saving time and money and building goodwill.

List points in the order in which you'll will discuss them.

Resolving Disputes

Begin most paragraphs with topic sentences.

ADR programs work. Of the 13,000 disputes mediated in the US Postal Service's ADR program from 1998 to 2001, 61% were settled; of those 94% were settled without any cash settlement (Bedikian 33). The Air Force's award-winning ADR program resolves 75% of the disputes which use ADR. Some locations have even higher success rates: the Tinker Air Force base has an 85% success rate, and the Los Angeles Air Force base has a 100% success rate (Blanchard and McDade). A study of 20 large ADR programs by the CPR Institute found that "nearly all disputes submitted to systemic [sic] employment dispute programs are resolved by agreement, prior to the arbitration stage" (F. Phillips).

Use square brackets for anything you add in quote. Sic indicates that the error is in the original.

Figure 24.2

**A Long Report (*continued*)

A Northeastern University survey finds that disputes that do not settle fall into two groups: the "Jackpot Syndrome," where plaintiffs are seeking only money, and situations where it is simply not in the financial interests of one party to settle (G. Phillips 66). Shepherd Greene Legal Department Director Richard Yang believes that the company has yet to encounter an aggrieved employee who fits these conditions.

Clearing Court Dockets   *Use talking heads. Note how much more informative this is than "Advantages."*

Since 1960, the number of lawsuits (of all types) in the United States has tripled, but the number of judges and courts has not changed significantly (Cross and Miller 59). The resulting bottleneck contributes to the slow passage of cases through the legal system. As we have seen, employment lawsuits comprise 15% of the load of cases in federal courts (Bedikian 33). If most or all of these cases were resolved through alternate means, court dockets would be less clogged.

Second-level heads are flush with the left margin and bolded. Triple-space before new head; double-space after.

Saving Time   *Quote when the source is especially credible.*

Instead of taking months or years, ADR can settle disputes in as little as a day. According to Jeffrey M. Senger, Deputy Senior Counsel for Alternative Dispute Resolution in the US Department of Justice, at the US Postal Services "[the average mediation takes just four hours, and 81 percent of mediated cases are closed without a formal complaint being filed."

This quote comes from the Web and has no page number.

Saving Money

Begin most paragraphs with topic sentences.

The legal costs saved by adopting ADR are substantial. The Air Force estimated that before adopting ADR, it spent $1,795 to process each informal discrimination complaint and $16,372 to process formal complaints (Blanchard and McDade). The US Postal Service estimated that a "simple" complaint cost at least $5,000 to process, while a "complicated" complaint that goes "all the way through the end of the process" costs $77,000 (Senger). Anastasia Kelly, General Counsel of Sears, estimated that "each litigated case with an employee costs between $50,000 and $75,000" in legal fees. Indeed, before its adoption of an ADR system in 2002, Sears—a company "[w]ith more than 300,000 employees and high turnover rate" spent "more legal dollars on battling its own people than anything else" (Longstreth 18). GE estimates that its Early Dispute Resolution program saves $15 million a year and that the savings continue to increase each year (Paquin, Victor, and Villarreal 24).

Quote when the words of the source are memorable.

Formal ADR systems often employ third-party mediators or arbitrators. Hourly fees run about $150–$250 an hour (Meade and Zimmerman 61). A 2000 Northeastern University survey found median costs of $2,750 for mediation and $11,800 for arbitration (G. Phillips 65). *Not every idea needs a source. Use your knowledge of people and of business.*

Because disputes are settled outside the legal system, it is easier to find creative, non-monetary solutions. Even when the solution does involve money, it is likely to cover only actual damages, not punitive ones. Other sources for savings may also exist: "As an incentive [to adopt ADR], at least one major national insurance company offers a refund in deductibles of up to $25,000 for companies that adopt employment programs" (Meade and Zimmerman 61).

Quote when you can't think of any better words than those in the source.

Building Goodwill

The 1997 Cornell Survey found that resolutions reached thorough ADR maintain more goodwill than would be possible with litigation:

Figure 24.2

A Long Report (continued)

Why Shepherd Greene Should Adopt ADR

Quote to give the exact wording of survey questions so reader can interpret data accurately.

Page 6

No extra space above or below quote.

> 81% of the respondents say their corporations used mediation because it provides "a more satisfactory process" than litigation; 66% say it provides more "satisfactory settlements"; and 59% say it preserves good relationships. (qtd. in G. Phillips 65)

Employees of the US Postal Service who participated in ADR programs were overwhelmingly satisfied with "the amount of control, respect, and fairness of the process." Indeed, the satisfaction rate was twice as high as satisfaction with traditional adversarial systems (see Figure 2). Employees and managers reported equal levels of satisfaction (Senger).

Figure 2

Use a second font for figures.

Satisfaction Doubles with ADR

Percent Satisfied
(US Postal Service)

Make sure bars are of equal width.

Traditional   ADR

Source of data: Senger

Quote when the source is especially credible for the point you want to make.

Simply having a forum to air disagreements helps. After a study in 1997, the Equal Employment Opportunity Commission (EEOC) concluded that *Use ellipses in square brackets when you omit words.*

> a sizable number of disputes [. . .] may not involve discrimination at all. They reflect, rather, basic communications problems in the workplace. Such issues may be brought into the EEO process as a result of a perception that there is no other forum available to air general workplace concerns. (qtd. in Blanchard and McDade)

The source of the quote and where you found it.

Even when the ADR process finds that the employee's concern was justified, mediation makes it possible to resolve issues positively. Roger Blanchard and Joe McDade report the example of a case of alleged racism in the US Air Force:

Indent long quotes 1".

> [D]uring the mediation, it became clear that management regarded the Asian female GS-12 as a skilled and talented worker. Accordingly, as part of the mediated settlement, the Air Force agreed to temporarily detail her into a GS-13 position for which she was qualified. Her subsequent superior performance resulted in her being competitively selected for the GS-13 position when it became vacant. Had this case not resulted in a settlement, the Air Force could have paid compensatory damages and attorneys [sic] fees; office morale and productivity would have suffered greatly; and most importantly, the Air Force would likely have lost the services of a talented employee. *Web source, so no page number.*

Figure 24.2
A Long Report (continued)

12 pt. **Model ADR Programs**

11 pt.   Many models of ADR programs exist. Some have three to five stages, from informal consultation to formal mediation and arbitration; others have only one "stage" that is empowered to do whatever is necessary to resolve the dispute, including hiring mediators or arbitrators. Some organizations use different kinds of structures for different kinds of complaints. For example, some federal agencies use a fact-finding team of a man and a woman to investigate allegations of sexual harassment (Bedikian 33). The best programs focus not simply on avoiding litigation but on resolving conflicts by identifying and resolving the underlying problem that led to the dispute (Bedikian 33; Paquin, Victor, and Villarreal 24). As a result, good programs reduce the number of future disputes.

One of the most detailed programs reported in the literature is the one developed by Science Applications International Corporation (SAIC), a high-tech company that employs 40,000 workers. SAIC's four-stage ADR program allows employees to "take their grievances to a committee of both workers and management that investigates and delivers a binding decision" (Bresler 3). According to the company, more than 90% of disputes are resolved in initial meetings between workers and managers, long before formal mediation or arbitration is necessary.

According to Samuel Bresler, SAIC's corporate vice president and western regional director of human resources, SAIC's program uses the following four steps:

Step 1:   The employee presents an oral or written complaint to management through a hotline or the Ethics Committee. The complaint travels upward through the management structure; if a mutually agreeable resolution is unobtainable (10% of SAIC claims), the process moves to Step 2.

Step 2:   The employee documents the claim in detail, and management drafts a response. Both documents are sent to a five-person committee that reviews the documentation and interviews witnesses, if any. The committee consists of

Vertical lists provide visual variety.
- An employee representative,
- A non-management representative from a large employee focus group,
- The Senior Vice President of Human Resources, who also chairs the committee,
- A senior-level executive from the area where the dispute occurred, and
- A mid-level manager from division operations or a group manager from an area outside the dispute.

The committee recommends a solution. If the employee rejects the solution, the claim may move to Step 3 or 4.

Step 3:   A third-party mediator steps in to negotiate a settlement between the parties in dispute. The employee must pay a $50 filing fee, and both sides may consult attorneys. Because the mediator can only recommend a solution, the employee may reject it and move to Step 4.

Step 4:   An arbitrator reviews the claim and makes a final, binding decision. The employee must pay a $150 filing fee. (4)

SAIC's ADR program is cost-effective, empowers the employee at each step of the process, and has demonstrated a high success rate.

Figure 24.2

A Long Report (continued)

Name items in the order in which you'll discuss them.

Resources Required to Create an ADR Program

Fewer resources are required for ADR than for traditional litigation. Meeting space, training in ADR, financial support, and management and labor participation are the essentials.

Meeting space is available on site at Shepherd Greene. The employee union at Shepherd Greene, the National Fraternal Order of Aviation Workers, Local 111, has also offered meeting space at its union hall in nearby Gahanna, Ohio. Union president Chuck Scanlon noted that this space would be available free to discuss any ADR issue related to Shepherd Greene workers.

Vary sentence length and sentence structure.

ADR works best when all supervisors and managers are trained in conflict resolution. One-shot training sessions may not be enough; long-term training and the opportunity to debrief after resolutions will improve resolution skills. While this training has a cost, both in hiring a consultant and releasing people from work duties to attend, it will more than pay for itself. Indeed, GE's estimated $15 million savings came not from implementing an ADR program but from refining an existing program to try to resolve potential issues before they resulted in conflicts (Paquin, Victor, and Villarreal 24).

Financial support is needed to pay for the cost of the training, the time of the person or people who run the ADR system, the time released for workers and managers to sit on peer review committees, and the fees for hiring outside mediators and arbitrators. While some up-front work will be needed to set up and publicize a system, once it is in place, running it should be no more time-consuming than running the current grievance system. Requiring the employee to pay a filing fee for a mediator or arbitrator reduces the company's costs. Most of these costs will be heaviest during planning and the first year of the program. Most organizations find that successful ADR systems not only resolve disputes without litigation but also make it possible to improve work conditions so that fewer disputes arise in the future.

Support from both management and labor is essential. In general, Shepherd Greene has good managment-labor relations, with joint teams already functioning in many areas. ADR would fit well with the "team" culture of the organization. Union president Chuck Scanlon believes that the company union will be receptive to an ADR program, provided that union representation on any review panels equals that of the Shepherd Greene management.

Conclusions repeat points made in the report.
Recommendations are actions the readers should take.

Conclusions and Recommendations

Our research suggests that an ADR program at Shepherd Greene would resolve employee disputes more economically and quickly while building goodwill. The resources needed to start an ADR program at Shepherd Greene are well within budget guidelines, and the union is receptive. Finally, a model from a high-tech environment exists on which to base the Shepherd Greene ADR program.

1. Do Further Research to Determine Which ADR Plan to Use.

We were able to get detailed information only about SAIC's plan. While the plan seems workable and SAIC, like Shepherd Greene, is a high-tech company, Shepherd Greene should learn about additional plans before proposing one. The two best sources seem to be the faculty in the Dispute Resolution Program at The Ohio State University Moritz College of Law, since it is right in town, and the US Air Force, since Shepherd Greene hopes to do business with it.

Some companies ask for Conclusions and Recommendations at the beginning of reports.

Figure 24.2
A Long Report *(continued)*

*Numbering the issues makes
it easy for readers to discuss them.*

2. Involve the Union in Deciding Which ADR Plan to Use.

The union, its president believes, is receptive to ADR. To make implementation as smooth as possible, union representatives should be involved in researching additional ADR plans and recommending one. The more "buy-in" union members feel in the details of a specific ADR plan, the more quickly it will be approved and the more smoothly implementation will go.

3. Support ADR Financially.

An ADR program will require start-up funds for

Use standard, not gimmicky, bullets.

- Release time for personnel as they research additional ADR plans.
- ADR training.
- Publicizing the program.

Once the program is up and running, continuing funds will be needed for
- Release time for the person who administers the ADR plan.
- Release time for personnel as they meet to resolve disputes.
- On-going ADR training.
- Funds to hire mediators and arbitrators.

While these items are not free, their cost is likely to be much less than the amount Shepherd Greene is currently spending to deal with employee grievances.

Asking employees who seek mediators and arbitrators to pay part of the cost of hiring these people, as SAIC does, is reasonable and would reduce the cost to the company.

4. Pilot the Program for a Year.

The initial agreement should specify that the ADR Plan Shepherd Greene adopts will be tested for one year. At the end of that period, both Shepherd Greene management and union officials should review the success of the program and decide whether to continue. Should the two parties be unable to agree, the program should automatically be discontinued—and an agreement to that effect should be in place before the pilot begins. While several organizations now have experience with ADR, many different specifics are possible. It will easier to get a program started if people know that it can be modified (or even disbanded) later as Shepherd Greene gains experience with ADR.

*Because many readers turn to the "Recommendations" first, provide
a brief rationale for each. The ideas in this section must be logical
extensions of the points made and supported in the body of the report.*

Figure 24.2
A Long Report (continued)

Why Shepherd Greene Should Adopt ADR

List all the printed and online sources Page 10
cited in your report. Do not list sources
you used for background but did not cite.

MLA Style

Works Cited

Italicize title of Web page.

Alternative Dispute Resolution: A Research Guide. US Office of Personnel Management. 23 Nov. 2004 <http://www.opm.gov/er/adrguide/toc.htm>.
Put URL in angle brackets.

Barrett, Jerome T. "Labor-Management Dispute Resolution Is Not as Neanderthal as You've Heard." *Journal of Alternative Dispute Resolution* 2.2 (2000): 40-51.
Use issue number if each issue is paginated separately.

Bedikian, Mary A. "Employment ADR: Current Issues and Methods of Implementation." *The Metropolitan Corporate Counsel* Dec. 2001: 33. 4 Nov. 2004<http://web.lexis-nexis.com>.
Date you visited soure.

Blanchard, Roger, and Joe McDade. Testimony before the US HR Committee on Government Reform, Subcommittee on Civil Service. 20 Mar. 2000. 3 Dec. 2004. <http://www.adr.af.mil/whatsnew/blanchard.htm>.
Divide URL only at a slash.

Bresler, Samuel. "ADR: One Company's Answer to Settling Employee Disputes." *HRFocus* Sept. 2000: 3-5.
Comma after first author's name.

Carrell, Michael R., and Christina Heavrin. *Labor Relations and Collective Bargaining: Cases, Practice, and Law.* 5th ed. Upper Saddle River, NJ: Prentice Hall, 1998.
Give month when each issue is paginated separately.

Cross, Frank B., and Roger LeRoy Miller. *West's Legal Environment of Business: Text, Cases, Ethical, Regulatory, International, and E-Commerce Issues.* 4th ed. Cincinnati, OH: West/Thomson Learning: 2001.
Give state when city is not well known.

Kelly, Eileen P. "Resolving Nonunion Employment Disputes through Arbitration." *Phi Kappa Phi Journal* Fall 2001: 4-5.

Longstreth, Andrew. "The Softer Side of Sears." *Corporate Counsel Magazine* 9 (2002): 18. 15 Nov. 2004 *Academic Search Premier Database* Item 6177553.

Meade, Robert E., and Philip Zimmerman. "Resolving Workplace Disputes through Mediation." CPA Journal 70 (2000): 60.
Last name first only for the first author. Use regular order for other authors' names.

Paquin, Jeffrey, Jennifer Victor, and Elpidio P. D. Villarreal. "GE Proves the Value of Innovative Dispute Resolution." *Corporate Legal Times* Sept. 2001: 24. 17 Oct. 2004. <http://web.lexus-nexus.com>.

Phillips, F. Peter. "Current Trends in Employment ADR: CPR Institute for Dispute Resolution." *The Metropolitan Corporate Counsel* (Aug. 2002). 8 Oct. 2004 <http://web.lexus-nexus.com>

Phillips, Gerald F. "What Your Client Needs to Know about ADR." *Dispute Resolutions Journal* Feb. 2000: 64-68.
No periods in MLA abbreviations.

Senger, Jeffrey M. Testimony before the US HR Committee on the Judiciary, Subcommittee on Commercial and Administrative Law. 29 Feb. 2000. 28 Nov. 2004. <http://www.house.gov/judiciary/seng 0229.htm>.

Stone, Katherine, V. W. Employment Arbitration under the Federal Arbitration Act." *Employment Dispute Resolution and Worker Rights in the Changing Workplace.* Ed. Adrienne E. Eaton and Jeffrey H. Keefe. Ithaca: Cornell UP. 2000. 27-66.
Abbreviate "University Press".
Page numbers of essay in edited book.

Title Page

The Title Page of a report contains four items: the title of the report, whom the report is prepared for, whom it is prepared by, and the release date. Sometimes title pages also contain a brief summary of the contents of the report; some title pages contain decorative artwork.

The title of the report should be as informative as possible.

Poor title: New Office Site

Better title: Why Dallas Is the Best Site for the New Info.com Office

Large organizations that issue many reports may use two-part titles to make it easier to search for reports electronically. For example, U.S. government report titles first give the agency sponsoring the report, then the title of that particular report.

Small Business Administration: Management Practices Have Improved for the Women's Business Center Program
Small Business Administration: Steps Taken to Better Manage Its Human Capital, but More Needs to Be Done
Small Business: SBA Could Better Focus Its 8(a) Program to Help Firms Obtain Contracts

In many cases, the title will state the recommendation in the report: "Why the United Nations Should Establish a Seed Bank." However, the title should omit recommendations when

- The reader will find the recommendations hard to accept.
- Putting all the recommendations in the title would make it too long.
- The report does not offer recommendations.

If the title does not contain the recommendation, it normally indicates what problem the report tries to solve.

Letter or Memo of Transmittal

Use a memo of transmittal if you are a regular employee of the organization for which you prepare the report; use a letter if you are not. The transmittal has several purposes: to transmit the report, to orient the reader to the report, and to build a good image of the report and of the writer.

Organize the transmittal in this way:

1. **Tell when and by whom the report was authorized and the purpose it was to fulfill.**
2. **Summarize your conclusions and recommendations.**
3. **Indicate minor problems you encountered in your investigation and show how you surmounted them. Thank people who helped you.**
4. **Point out additional research that is necessary, if any.**
5. **Thank the reader for the opportunity to do the work and offer to answer questions.** Even if the report has not been fun to do, expressing satisfaction in doing the project is expected.

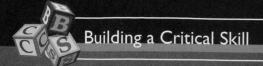
Creating a Professional Image, 3

Even on casual Fridays, most businesses still expect employees to be anything but casual with their work. Attention to detail, organization, accuracy, economy, and courtesy are the norm.

On casual days, don't dress as though you're planning to clean the garage. Instead, wear clothes in good repair that are one or two "notches" below what you'd wear on other days. If suits are the norm, choose blazers and slacks or skirts. If blazers and slacks or skirts are the norm, choose sweaters or knit sport shirts; khakis, simple skirts, or dressier jeans; or simple dresses. Wear good shoes and always be well groomed. Avoid anything that's ill-fitting or revealing.

Other symbols also convey professionalism. Your work area, for instance, says a lot about you. If your organization allows employees to personalize their desks or offices with photographs, knickknacks, and posters, don't display so much that you seem frivolous. And never display offensive photos or slogans, even in an attempt to be funny. One local government supervisor, known for being strict, put a poster of Adolph Hitler on his door to make light of his reputation. He so offended others that he lost his job. The same caution goes for screen savers and radio stations. It isn't professional to play a morning "shock jock" who uses coarse language and offensive stereotypes.

If your organization allows employees to listen to music, keep the volume at a reasonable level. If your organization allows, consider wearing headphones.

Avoid playing computer games, surfing the Web inappropriately, or ordering personal items on company time.

Keep your voicemail message succinct and professional—find out what co-workers say in theirs.

Keep your desk organized. File papers; keep stacks to a minimum. Throw away anything you don't need. Don't store food in your office. Clean periodically. Water your plants.

The volume of your voice can also disturb others. While most people wouldn't shout across an office, many of us don't realize how loud our voices can be when we're excited or happy. Keep personal conversations to a minimum, in person and on the phone.

Learn the culture of your organization and fit into it as much as you can. When in doubt, follow the lead of someone the organization respects.

Table of Contents

In the Table of Contents, list the headings exactly as they appear in the body of the report. If the report is shorter than 25 pages, list all the headings. In a very long report, list the two or three highest levels of headings.

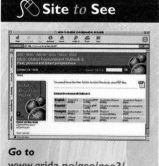

Site *to* See

Go to

www.grida.no/geo/geo3/

Tables of Contents for Web reports can have search boxes and clickable links for chapter titles and headings, as does this United Nations report on the state of the global environment.

List of Illustrations

Report visuals comprise both tables and figures. **Tables** are words or numbers arranged in rows and columns. **Figures** are everything else: bar graphs, pie charts, maps, drawings, photographs, computer printouts, and so forth. Tables and figures are numbered independently, so you may have both a "Table 1" and a "Figure 1." In a report with maps and graphs but no other visuals, the visuals are sometimes called "Map 1" and "Graph 1." Whatever you call the illustrations, list them in the order in which they appear in the report; give the name of each visual as well as its number.

See Module 25 for information about how to design and label visuals.

Executive Summary

An **Executive Summary** tells the reader what the document is about. It summarizes the recommendation of the report and the reasons for the recommendation.

To write an executive summary, you must know the report's recommendations and support.

1. In the first paragraph, identify the report's recommendations or main point (thesis). Often the problem can be stated quite briefly: "To market life insurance to mid-40s urban professionals, Interstate Fidelity Insurance should. . . ." Provide background on the problem only if needed to explain the goal of the recommendations.
2. In the body, identify the major supporting points for your argument. Include all the information decision makers will need. Make the summary clear as a stand-alone document.
3. If you have conducted surveys or interviews, briefly describe your methods.

Introduction

The **Introduction** of the report contains a statement of purpose and scope and may include all the parts in the following list.

- **Purpose.** Identify the organizational problem the report addresses, the technical investigations it summarizes, and the rhetorical purpose (to explain, to recommend).
- **Scope.** Identify the topics the report covers. For example, Company XYZ is losing money on its line of radios. Does the report investigate the quality of the radios? The advertising campaign? The cost of manufacturing? The demand for radios? If the report was authorized to examine only advertising, then one cannot fault the report for not considering other factors.
- **Limitations.** Limitations make the recommendations less valid or valid only under certain conditions. Limitations usually arise because time or money constraints haven't permitted full research. For example, a campus pizza restaurant considering expanding its menu may not have enough money to take a random sample of students and townspeople. Without a random sample, the writer cannot generalize from the sample to the larger population.

Instant Replay

Report Titles
Normally, the title of the report should give the recommendation. Omit the recommendations when

- The reader will find the recommendations hard to accept.
- Putting all the recommendations in the title would make it too long.
- The report does not offer recommendations.

If the title does not contain the recommendation, it normally indicates what problem the report tries to solve.

Two hospitals in Columbus, OH, had helicopter services that were each losing money. They commissioned a feasibility study to see whether the two services could merge. The report found that a merger was feasible. The resulting service, MedFlight, is profitable. Here, a MedFlight helicopter team transports the survivor of an automobile accident.

Many recommendations are valid only for a limited time. For example, a store wants to know what kinds of clothing will appeal to college men. The recommendations will remain in force only for a short time: Three years from now, styles and tastes may have changed.

- **Assumptions.** Assumptions are statements whose truth you assume and which you use to support your conclusions and recommendations. If they are wrong, the conclusion will be wrong too. For example, recommendations about what cars appeal to drivers ages 18 to 34 would be based on assumptions both about gas prices and about the economy. If gas prices radically rose or fell, the kinds of cars young adults wanted would change. If there were a major recession, people wouldn't be able to buy new cars.
- **Methods.** Tell how you chose the people for a survey, focus groups, or interviews and how, when, and where they were interviewed.
  Omit Methods if your report is based solely on library and online research. Instead, simply cite your sources in the text and document them in References or Works Cited. See Module 22 for details.

Background or History

Even though the current audience for the report probably knows the situation, reports are filed and consulted years later. These later audiences will need the background to understand the options that are possible.

In some cases, the History may cover many years. For example, a report recommending that a U.S. hotel chain open hotels in Vietnam will probably give the history of that country for at least the last hundred years. In other cases, the Background or History is much briefer, covering only a few years or even just the immediate situation.

Conclusions and Recommendations

Conclusions summarize points made in the body of the report; **Recommendations** are action items that would solve or partially solve the problem. Number the recommendations to make them easy to discuss. If the recommendations will seem difficult or controversial, give a brief rationale after each recommendation. If they'll be easy for the audience to accept, simply list them without comments or reasons. The recommendations will also be in the Executive Summary and perhaps in the title and the transmittal.

Summary of Key Points

- The Title Page contains the title of the report, whom the report is prepared for, whom it is prepared by, and the release date.
- The title of a report should contain the recommendation unless

- The reader will find the recommendations hard to accept.
- Putting all the recommendations in the title would make it too long.
- The report does not offer recommendations.

- If the report is shorter than 25 pages, list all the headings in the Table of Contents. In a long report, pick a level and put all the headings at that level and above in the Contents.

- Organize the transmittal in this way:
  1. Release the report.
  2. Summarize your conclusions and recommendations.
  3. Mention any points of special interest. Indicate minor problems you encountered in your investigation and show how you surmounted them. Thank people who helped you.
  4. Point out additional research that is necessary, if any.
  5. Thank the reader for the opportunity to do the work and offer to answer questions.

- The **Introduction** of the report contains a statement of Purpose and Scope. The **Purpose** statement identifies the organizational problem the report addresses, the technical investigations it summarizes, and the rhetorical purpose (to explain, to recommend). The **Scope** statement identifies the topics the report covers. The Introduction may also include **Limitations,** problems or factors that limit the validity of the recommendations; **Assumptions,** statements whose truth you assume, and which you use to prove your final point; and **Methods,** an explanation of how you gathered your data.

- A **Background** or **History** section is included because reports are filed and may be consulted years later.

- **Conclusions** summarize points made in the body of the report; **Recommendations** are action items that would solve or partially solve the problem.

Assignments for Module 24

Questions for Comprehension

24.1 What parts of the report come from the proposal, with some revision?

24.2 How do you decide whether to write a letter or memo of transmittal?

24.3 How should you organize a transmittal?

24.4 What goes in the Executive Summary?

Questions for Critical Thinking

24.5 How do you decide what headings to use in the body of the report?

24.6 How do you decide how much background to provide in a report?

24.7 How much evidence do you need to provide for each recommendation?

Exercises and Problems

As Your Instructor Directs,
Turn in the following documents for Problems 24.8 through 24.10:
a. The approved proposal

b. Two copies of the report, including
Cover
Title Page
Letter or Memo of Transmittal

Table of Contents
List of Illustrations
Executive Summary
Body (Introduction, all information, recommendations). Your instructor may specify a minimum length, a minimum number or kind of sources, and a minimum number of visuals.
References or Works Cited
Appendixes, if useful or relevant
c. Your notes and rough drafts.

24.8 Writing a Feasibility Study

Write an individual or group report evaluating the feasibility of two or more alternatives. Explain your criteria clearly, evaluate each alternative, and recommend the best course of action.

1. Is it feasible for a local restaurant to open another branch? Where should it be?

2. Is it feasible to create a program to mentor women and traditionally underrepresented groups in your organization?

3. Is it feasible to create or enlarge a day care center for the children of students?

4. Is it feasible to start a monthly newsletter for students in your program?

5. With your instructor's permission, choose your own topic.

24.9 Writing a Library Research Report

Write an individual or group library research report.

1. **Recommending a Dress Policy.** Your boss asks you to look into "business casual" dress. "Is it time to retire it? And what *is* 'business casual'? Recommend how our employees should dress, and why. Include some photos of what is and isn't appropriate." To start, read Anne Field, "What Is Business Casual?" *Business-Week*, October 30, 2000, 180–90.

   Hint: Choose a business, nonprofit, or government agency you know well and recommend a policy for it.

2. **Evaluating Online Voting.** As an aide to one of your state's members of Congress, you frequently research topics for legislation. "Look into online voting. I want to know what the problems are and whether it's feasible for the next election." Start with Stephen H. Wildstrom, "Click and Be Counted," *BusinessWeek*, April 24, 2000, 22; and Thomas E. Weber, "'Scalable' Ballot Fraud: Why One Tech Maven Fears Computer Voting," *The Wall Street Journal*, March 19, 2001, B1.

3. **Understanding Demographic Changes.** You work for a major political party. Your boss says, "As you know, so-called 'minorities' are increasingly middle class. I want you to analyze one ethnic group in our state. What issues are they interested in? Which party do they favor? What appeals might persuade them to vote for a candidate of the other party?" Depending on the group you pick, read Jonathan J. Higuera, "No Political Pigeonhole," *Hispanic Business*, December 2001, 33; Robert H. Brischetto, "The Hispanic Middle Class Comes of Age," *Hispanic Business*, December 2001, 21–36; or Deborah Kong, "Number Crunch," *aMagazine*, December 2001/January 2002, 38–39, 78.

4. **Evaluating Welfare Reform.** You work for a local foodbank. The director says, "We're serving more people than ever. Lifetime limits for

receiving welfare are going into effect. Yet rising unemployment means that many former welfare recipients are out of work again. And even people who still have jobs may lack health insurance and have trouble making ends meet. Look into the situation. Is the state doing enough in terms of job counseling?

Do people need child care or transportation? Should Washington change welfare reform?" Start with Alexandra Starr, "Welfare Reform's Toughest Test," *BusinessWeek*, December 10, 2001, 52–53.

5. With you instructor's permission, choose your own topic.

24.10   Writing a Recommendation Report

Write an individual or group recommendation report.

1. **Recommending Courses.** What skills are in demand in your community? What courses at what levels should the local college offer?

2. **Improving Sales and Profits.** Recommend ways a small business can increase sales and profits. Focus on one or more of the following: the products or services it offers, its advertising, its decor, its location, its accounting methods, its cash management, or any other aspect that may be keeping the company from achieving its potential. Address your report to the owner of the business.

3. **Improving Customer Service.** Evaluate the service in a local store, restaurant, or other organization. Are customers made to feel comfortable? Is workers' communication helpful, friendly, and respectful? Are workers knowledgeable about products and

services? Do they sell them effectively? Write a report analyzing the quality of service and recommending ways to improve.

4. **Evaluating a Potential Employer.** What training is available to new employees? How soon is the average entry-level person promoted? How much travel and weekend work are expected? Is there a "busy season," or is the workload consistent year-round? What is the corporate culture? Is the climate nonracist and nonsexist? How strong is the company economically? How is it likely to be affected by current economic, demographic, and political trends? Address your report to a college placement office; recommend whether it should encourage students to work at this company.

5. With your instructor's permission, choose your own topic.

Polishing Your Prose

Improving Paragraphs

Good paragraphs demonstrate unity, detail, and variety.

The following paragraph from a sales letter illustrates these three qualities:

> The best reason to consider a Schroen Heat Pump is its low cost. Schroen Heat Pumps cost 25% less than the cheapest competitor's. Moreover, unlike the competition, the Schroen Heat Pump will pay for itself in less than a year in energy savings. That's just 12 months. All of this value
>
> *continued*

comes with a 10-year unlimited warranty—if anything goes wrong, we'll repair or replace the pump at no cost to you. That means no expensive repair bills and no dollars out of your pocket.

A paragraph is **unified** when all its sentences focus on a single idea. As long as a paragraph is about just one idea, a topic sentence expressing that idea is not required. However, a topic sentence makes it easier for the reader to skim the document. (Essays use a *thesis statement* for the central idea of the entire document.) Sentences throughout the paragraph should support the topic sentence or offer relevant examples.

Transitions connect. Common transitions are *and, also, first, second, third, in addition, likewise, similarly, for example (e.g.), for instance, indeed, to illustrate, namely, specifically, in contrast, then,* and *on the other hand.*

Detail makes your points clearer and more vivid. Use concrete words, especially strong nouns and verbs and adjectives and adverbs, that say what you mean. Avoid redundancies.

Variety is expressed first in sentence length and patterns and second in the number of sentences in each paragraph. Most sentences in business writing should be 16 to 20 words, but an occasional longer or very short sentence gives punch to your writing.

The basic pattern for sentences is subject/verb/object (SVO): *Our building supervisor sent the forms.* Vary the SVO pattern by changing the order, using transitions and clauses, and combining sentences.

Also vary paragraph length. First and last paragraphs can be quite short. Body paragraphs will be longer. Whenever a paragraph runs eight typed lines or more, think about dividing it into two paragraphs.

Exercises

Rewrite the following paragraphs to improve unity, detail, and variety.

1. Mr. Walter Pruitt visited our business communication class yesterday. He spoke about the importance of internships. Mr. Pruitt works for the Martin Day Company. The Martin Day Company provides fulfillment services for Internet companies. Mr. Pruitt told us he got his first job because of an internship. An internship is an opportunity for students to work with a company for a period of time to get business experience. Mr. Pruitt went to college and interned with Martin Day. At first, Martin Day only wanted him to work for 10 weeks. Mr. Pruitt did such a good job, they kept him on another 10 weeks and another. Mr. Pruitt was offered a job by Martin Day when he graduated.

2. As a chief petty officer in the U.S. Navy, I supervised dozens of mechanics and technicians aboard both light and heavy cruisers. My many skills and experiences qualify me for a management position at Stokes Construction. I was in the U.S. Navy for 27 years. My other duties included securing munitions, storing hazardous materials, and repairing heavy equipment. Before joining the service, I built houses for Silverstreit & Sons Builders. That was in Baltimore. I retired from the U.S. Navy last year. At Silverstreit & Sons Builders, I learned to read and draft blueprints. I also learned basic and advanced building techniques, including carpentry and roofing. I was with Silverstreit & Sons for four years. The U.S. Navy taught me leadership skills. The Navy also taught me discipline.

Check your answer to the odd-numbered exercise at the back of the book.

Module 25

Using Visuals

Start by asking these questions:

- What are stories, and how do I find them?
- Does it matter what kind of visual I use?
- What design conventions should I follow?
- Can I use color and clip art?
- What else do I need to check for?
- Can I use the same visuals in my document and my presentation?

Charts and graphs help make numbers meaningful and thus help communicate your points in oral presentations, memos, letters, reports, and meetings. This module shows you how to turn data into charts and graphs. See Module 5 for a discussion of designing slides for oral presentations and Module 20 for a discussion of other aspects of good oral presentations.

In your rough draft, use visuals

- **To see that ideas are presented completely.** A table, for example, can show you whether you've included all the items in a comparison.
- **To find relationships.** For example, charting sales on a map may show that the sales representatives who made quota all have territories on the east or the west coasts. Is the central United States suffering a

Use visuals only for points you want to emphasize.

"It looks much worse when you see the big picture."

recession? Is the product one that appeals to coastal lifestyles? Is advertising reaching the coasts but not the central states? Even if you don't use the visual in your final document, creating the map may lead you to questions you wouldn't otherwise ask.

In the final presentation or document, use visuals

- **To make points vivid.** Readers skim memos and reports; a visual catches the eye. The brain processes visuals immediately. Understanding words—written or oral—takes more time.
- **To emphasize material** that might be skipped if it were buried in a paragraph.
- **To present material more compactly and with less repetition** than words alone would require.
- **To focus on information that decision makers need.**

The number of visuals you need depends on your purposes, the kind of information, and the audience. You'll use more visuals when you want to show relationships and to persuade, when the information is complex or contains extensive numerical data, and when the audience values visuals.

Your chart is only as good as the underlying data. Check to be sure that your data come from a reliable source (◀▶ Module 22).

What are stories, and how do I find them?

A story is something that is happening, according to the data.

To find stories, look for relationships and changes.

FYI

Using visuals as well as words more than quadruples the audience's retention rate and makes the audience twice as likely to agree with the speaker's recommendations.

Source: "The Numbers on Why You Need Visuals," www.presentersonline.com/training/pres_fund/visual/train _article_visualnumbers.html; visited site Sept. 29, 2002.

Every visual should tell a story. Stories can be expressed in complete sentences that describe something that happens or changes. The sentence can also serve as the title of the visual.

Not a story: U.S. Sales, 1995–2000

Possible stories: Forty Percent of Our Sales Were to New Customers.
Growth Was Greatest in the South.
Sales Increased from 1995 to 2000.

Stories that tell us what we already know are rarely interesting. Instead, good stories may

- Support a hunch you have.
- Surprise you or challenge so-called "common knowledge."
- Show trends or changes you didn't know existed.
- Have commercial or social significance.
- Provide information needed for action.
- Be personally relevant to you and the audience.

To find stories,

1. **Focus on a topic** (starting salaries, who likes rock music, and so forth).
2. **Simplify the data** on that topic and convert the numbers to simple, easy-to-understand units.
3. **Look for relationships and changes.** For example, compare two or more groups: Do men and women have the same attitudes? Look for changes over time. Look for items that can be seen as part of the same group. For example, to find stories about TV ads, you might group ads in the same product category—ads for cars, for food, for beverages.

When you think you have a story, test it against all the data to be sure it's accurate.

Some stories are simple straight lines: "Sales Increased." But other stories are more complex, with exceptions or outlying cases. Such stories will need more nuanced titles to do justice to the story. And sometimes the best story arises from the juxtaposition of two or more stories. In Figure 25.1, *Business-Week* uses four **paired graphs** to tell a surprising story. Individually, the graphs tell simple stories. Together, however, they tell an interesting story. Often, sales fall when prices rise. But in 2000–02, home sales rose in spite of rising prices. Often all prices rise or fall together. But in this market, prices for consumer goods excluding shelter fell.

Gene Zelazny points out that the audience should be able to *see* what the message *says*:

Does the chart support the title; and does the title reinforce the chart? So if I *say* in my title that "sales have increased significantly" I want to *see* a trend

Figure 25.1

Paired Graphs Tell a Complex Story

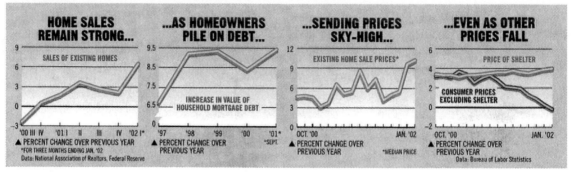

Source: *BusinessWeek*, March 11, 2002, 28.

moving up at a sharp angle. If not, if the trend parallels the baseline, it's an instant clue that the chart needs more thinking.[1]

Almost every data set allows you to tell several stories. You must choose the story you want to tell. Dumps of uninterpreted data confuse and frustrate your audience; they undercut the credibility and goodwill you want to create.

Does it matter what kind of visual I use?

Yes! The visual must match the kind of story.

Visuals are not interchangeable. Choose the visual that best matches the purpose of presenting the data.

- Use **tables** when the reader needs to be able to identify exact values. (See Figure 25.2a.)
- Use a chart or graph when you want the reader to focus on relationships.[2]
  - To compare a part to the whole, use a **pie chart.** (See Figure 25.2b.)
  - To compare one item to another item, or items over time, use a **bar chart** or a **line graph.** (See Figures 25.2c and 25.2d.)

What design conventions should I follow?

Check your visuals against the lists that follow.

Every visual should contain six components:

1. A title that tells the story that the visual shows.
2. A clear indication of what the data are. For example, what people *say* they did is not necessarily what they really did. An estimate of what a number will be in the future differs from numbers in the past that have already been measured.

Figure 25.2

Choose the Visual to Fit the Story

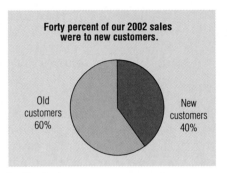

U.S. sales reach $44.5 million.			
	Millions of dollars		
	1998	2000	2002
Northeast	10.2	10.8	11.3
South	7.6	8.5	10.4
Midwest	8.3	6.8	9.3
West	11.3	12.1	13.5
Totals	37.4	38.2	44.5

a. Tables show exact values.

Forty percent of our 2002 sales were to new customers.

Old customers 60%
New customers 40%

b. Pie charts compare a component to the whole.

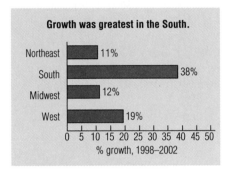

Growth was greatest in the South.

Northeast 11%
South 38%
Midwest 12%
West 19%

% growth, 1998–2002

c. Bar charts compare items or show distribution or correlation.

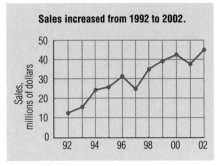

Sales increased from 1992 to 2002.

Sales, millions of dollars

d. Line charts compare items over time or show distribution or correlation.

3. Clearly labeled units.
4. Labels or legends identifying axes, colors, symbols, and so forth.
5. The source of the data, if you created the visual from data someone else gathered and compiled.
6. The source of the visual, if you reproduce a visual someone else created.

Formal visuals are divided into tables and figures. **Tables** are numbers or words arranged in rows and columns; **figures** are everything else. In a document, formal visuals have both numbers and titles, e.g., "Figure 1. The Falling Cost of Computer Memory, 1992–2002." In an oral presentation, the title is usually used without the number: "The Falling Cost of Computer Memory, 1992–2002." The title should tell the story so that the audience knows what to look for in the visual and why it is important. Informal or **spot** visuals are inserted directly into the text; they do not have numbers or titles.

Instant Replay

How to Find Stories

1. Focus on a topic.
2. Simplify the data.
3. Look for relationships and changes.

Tables

Use tables only when you want the audience to focus on specific numbers. Graphs convey less specific information but are always more memorable.

- Round off to simplify the data (e.g., 35% rather than 35.27%; 34,000 rather than 33,942).
- Provide column and row totals or averages when they're relevant.

The Six Components of Every Visual

1. A title that tells the story that the visual shows.
2. A clear indication of what the data are.
3. Clearly labeled units.
4. Labels or legends identifying axes, colors, symbols, and so forth.
5. The source of the data, if you created the visual from data someone else gathered and compiled.
6. The source of the visual, if you reproduce a visual someone else created.

- Put the items you want readers to compare in columns rather than in rows to facilitate mental subtraction and division.
- When you have many rows, screen alternate entries or double–space after every five entries to help readers line up items accurately.

Pie Charts

Pie charts force the audience to measure area. Research shows that people can judge position or length (which a bar chart uses) much more accurately than they judge area. The data in any pie chart can be put in a bar chart.[3] Therefore, use a pie chart only when you are comparing one segment to the whole. When you are comparing one segment to another segment, use a bar chart, a line graph, or a map—even though the data may be expressed in percentages.

- Start at 12 o'clock with the largest percentage or the percentage you want to focus on. Go clockwise to each smaller percentage or to each percentage in some other logical order.
- Make the chart a perfect circle. Perspective circles distort the data.
- Limit the number of segments to five or seven. If your data have more divisions, combine the smallest or the least important into a single "miscellaneous" or "other" category.
- Label the segments outside the circle. Internal labels are hard to read.

Bar Charts

Bar charts are easy to interpret because they ask people to compare distance along a common scale, which most people judge accurately. Bar charts are useful in a variety of situations: to compare one item to another, to compare items over time, and to show correlations. Use horizontal bars when your labels are long; when the labels are short, either horizontal or vertical bars will work.

- Order the bars in a logical or chronological order.
- Put the bars close enough together to make comparison easy.
- Label both horizontal and vertical axes.
- Put all labels inside the bars or outside them. When some labels are inside and some are outside, the labels carry the visual weight of longer bars, distorting the data.
- Make all the bars the same width.
- Use different colors for different bars only when their meanings are different: estimates as opposed to known numbers, negative as opposed to positive numbers.
- Avoid using perspective. Perspective makes the values harder to read and can make comparison difficult.

Several varieties of bar charts exist. See Figure 25.3 for examples.

- **Grouped bar charts** allow you to compare either several aspects of each item or several items over time. Group together the items you want to compare. Figure 25.3a shows sales were highest in the West. If we wanted to show how sales had changed over time in each region, the bars should be grouped by region, not by year.
- **Segmented, subdivided,** or **stacked bars** sum the components of an item. It's hard to identify the values in specific segments; grouped bar charts are almost always easier to use.

Figure 25.3
Varieties of Bar Charts

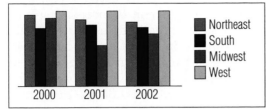

a. Grouped bar charts compare several
aspects of each item, or several items over time.

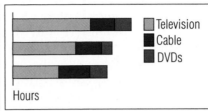

b. Segmented, subdivided, or
stacked bars sum the components
of an item.

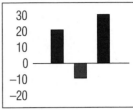

c. Deviation bar charts
identify positive and
negative values.

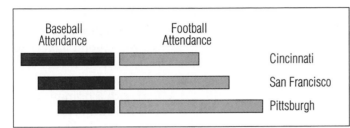

d. Paired bar charts show the correlation
between two items.

e. Histograms or **pictograms** use images to
create the bars.

- **Deviation bar charts** identify positive and negative values, or winners and losers.
- **Paired bar charts** show the correlation between two items.
- **Histograms** or **pictograms** use images to create the bars.

Line Graphs

Line graphs are also easy to interpret. Use line graphs to compare items over time, to show frequency or distribution, and to show correlations.

- Label both horizontal and vertical axes.
- When time is a variable, put it on the horizontal axis.
- Avoid using more than three different lines on one graph. Even three lines may be too many if they cross each other.
- Avoid using perspective. Perspective makes the values harder to read and can make comparison difficult.

Can I use color and clip art?

Use color carefully.

Avoid decorative clip art in memos and reports.

Color makes visuals more dramatic, but it creates at least two problems. First, readers try to interpret color, an interpretation that may not be appropriate.

**Tables and
Figures**

Tables are
numbers or words
arranged in rows
and columns;
figures are
everything else. In a
document, formal
visuals have both
numbers (Figure 1)
and titles. In an oral
presentation, the
title is usually used
without the
number.

Second, meanings assigned to colors differ depending on the audience's national background and profession.

Connotations for color vary from culture to culture (◄ ► p. 53). Blue suggests masculinity in the United States, criminality in France, strength or fertility in Egypt, and villainy in Japan. Red is sometimes used to suggest danger or *stop* in the United States; it means *go* in China and is associated with festivities. Red suggests masculinity or aristocracy in France, death in Korea, blasphemy in some African countries, and luxury in many parts of the world. Yellow suggests caution or cowardice in the United States, prosperity in Egypt, grace in Japan, and femininity in many parts of the world.[4]

These general cultural associations may be superseded by corporate, national, or professional associations. Some people associate blue with IBM or Hewlett-Packard and red with Coca-Cola, communism, or Japan. People in specific professions learn other meanings for colors. Blue suggests *reliability* to financial managers, *water* or *coldness* to engineers, and *death* to health care professionals. Red means *losing money* to financial managers, *danger* to engineers, but *healthy* to health care professionals. Green usually means *safe* to engineers, but *infected* to health care professionals.[5]

These various associations suggest that color is safest with a homogenous audience that you know well. In an increasingly multicultural workforce, color may send signals you do not intend.

When you do use color in visuals, Thorell and Smith suggest these guidelines:[6]

- Use no more than five colors when colors have meanings.
- Use glossy paper to make colors more vivid.
- Be aware that colors on a computer screen always look brighter than the same colors on paper because the screen sends out light.

In any visual, use as little shading and as few lines as are necessary for clarity. Don't clutter up the visual with extra marks. When you design black and white graphs, use shades of gray rather than stripes, wavy lines, and checks to indicate different segments or items.

In memos and reports, resist the temptation to make your visual "artistic" by turning it into a picture or adding clip art. **Clip art** is predrawn images that you can import into your newsletter, sign, or graph. A small drawing of a car in the corner of a line graph showing the number of miles driven is acceptable in an oral presentation or a newsletter, but out of place in a written report.

Edward Tufte uses the term **chartjunk** for decorations that at best are irrelevant to the visual and at worst mislead the reader.[7] Turning a line graph into a highway to show miles driven makes it harder to read: it's hard to separate the data line from lines that are merely decorative. If you use clip art, be sure that the images of people show a good mix of both sexes, various races and ages, and various physical conditions (◄ ► p. 62).

What else do I need to check for?

Be sure that the visual is accurate and ethical.

Always double-check your visuals to be sure that the information is accurate. However, many visuals have accurate labels but misleading visual shapes.

Figure 25.4
**Chartjunk and
Dimensions
Distort Data**

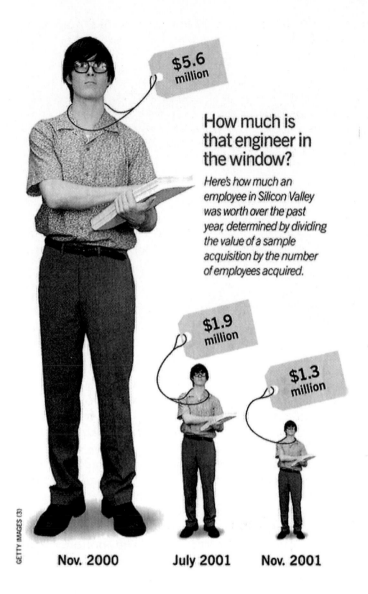

$5.6 million

How much is
that engineer in
the window?

*Here's how much an
employee in Silicon Valley
was worth over the past
year, determined by dividing
the value of a sample
acquisition by the number
of employees acquired.*

$1.9 million

$1.3 million

GETTY IMAGES (3)

Nov. 2000   July 2001   Nov. 2001

Visuals communicate quickly; audiences remember the shape, not the labels. If the reader has to study the labels to get the right picture, the visual is unethical even if the labels are accurate.

Figure 25.4 is distorted by chartjunk and dimensionality. In an effort to make the visual interesting, the artist used a picture of a young man (presumably an engineer) rather than simple bars. By using a photograph rather than a bar, the chart implies that all engineers are young, nerdy-looking white men. Women, people of color, and men with other appearances are excluded. The photograph also makes it difficult to compare the numbers. The number represented by the tallest figure is not quite 5 times as great as the number represented by the shortest figure, yet the tallest figure takes up 12 times as much space and appears even bigger than that. Two-dimensional figures distort data by multiplying the apparent value by the width as well as

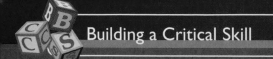

Integrating Visuals into Your Text

Refer to every visual in your text. Normally give the table or figure number in the text but not the title. Put the visual as soon after your reference as space and page design permit. If the visual must go on another page, tell the reader where to find it:

As Figure 3 shows (p. 10), . . .

(See Table 2 on page 3.)

Summarize the main point of a visual *before* you present the visual itself. Then when readers get to it, they'll see it as confirmation of your point.

Weak: Listed below are the results.

Better: As Figure 4 shows, sales doubled in the last decade.

How much discussion a visual needs depends on the audience, the complexity of the visual, and the importance of the point it makes. If the material is new to the audience, you'll need a fuller explanation than if similar material is presented to this audience every week or month. Help the reader find key data points in complex visuals. If the point is important, discuss its implications in some detail. In contrast, one sentence about a visual may be enough when the audience is already familiar with the topic and the data, when the visual is simple and well designed, and when the information in the visual is a minor part of your proof.

When you discuss visuals, spell out numbers that fall at the beginning of a sentence. If spelling out the number or year is cumbersome, revise the sentence so that it does not begin with a number.

Correct: Forty-five percent of the cost goes to pay wages and salaries.

Correct: In 2002, euro notes and coins entered circulation.

by the height—four times for every doubling in value. Perspective graphs are especially hard for readers to interpret and should be avoided.[8]

Even simple bar and line graphs may be misleading if part of the scale is missing, or **truncated.** Truncated graphs are most acceptable when the audience knows the basic data set well. For example, graphs of the stock market almost never start at zero; they are routinely truncated. This omission is acceptable for audiences who follow the market closely.

Since part of the scale is missing in truncated graphs, small changes seem like major ones. The graph in Figure 25.5, from Philadelphia Suburban's 1994 Annual Report, seems to show a healthy growth. But a close look at the numbers shows a different story. The bottom of the glass is 230,000 customers, not zero. The real growth was 6.4%, not the 300% that the visual shows.[9] Another annual report disguised losses by using a negative base.[10] Because readers expect zero to be the base, they're almost certain to misread the visual. Labels may make the visual literally "accurate," but a visual is unethical if someone who looks at it quickly is likely to misinterpret it.

Data can also be distorted when the context is omitted. As Tufte suggests, a drop may be part of a regular cycle, a correction after an atypical increase, or a permanent drop to a new, lower plateau.

To make your visuals more accurate,

- Differentiate between actual and estimated or projected values.
- When you must truncate a scale, do so clearly with a break in the bars or in the background.
- Avoid perspective and three-dimensional graphs.
- Avoid combining graphs with different scales.
- Use images of people carefully in histographs to avoid sexist, racist, or other exclusionary visual statements.

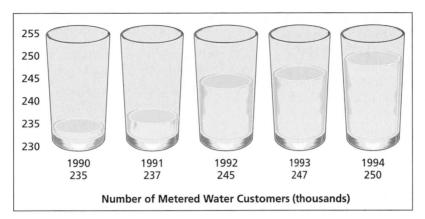

Figure 25.5

Truncated Scales Distort Data

Source: The Wall Street Journal, May 25, 1995, B1.

Can I use the same visuals in my document and my presentation?

Only if the table or graph is simple.

For presentations, simplify paper visuals. To simplify a complex table, divide it into several visuals, cut out some of the information, round off the data even more, or present the material in a chart rather than a table.

Visuals for presentations should have titles but don't need figure numbers. Do know where each visual is so that you can return to one if someone asks about it during the question period. Decorative clip art is acceptable in oral presentations as long as it does not obscure the story you're telling with the visual.

Summary of Key Points

- In the rough draft, use visuals to see that ideas are presented completely and see what relationships exist. In the final report, use visuals to make points vivid, to emphasize material that the reader might skip, and to present material more compactly and with less repetition than words alone would require.

- You'll use more visuals when you want to show relationships and to persuade, when the information is complex or contains extensive numerical data, and when the audience values visuals.

- Pick data to tell a story, to make a point. To find stories,
  1. Focus on a topic.
  2. Simplify the data.
  3. Look for relationships and changes.

- **Paired graphs** juxtapose two or more simple stories to create a more powerful story.

- The best visual depends on the kind of data and the point you want to make with the data.

- Visuals must present data accurately, both literally and by implication. **Chartjunk** denotes decorations that at best are irrelevant to the visual and at worst mislead the reader. Truncated graphs omit part of the scale and visually mislead readers. Perspective graphs and graphs with negative bases mislead readers.

- Summarize the main point of a visual before it appears in the text.
- Visuals for presentations need to be simpler than visuals on paper.
- How much discussion a visual needs depends on the audience, the complexity of the visual and the importance of the point it makes.

Assignments for Module 25

Questions for Comprehension

25.1 How can you find stories in data?

25.2 What is the difference between a table and a figure?

25.3 What is chartjunk?

Questions for Critical Thinking

25.4 Why does each visual need to tell a story?

25.5 Why are charts more memorable than tables?

25.6 When is chartjunk most likely to be acceptable? Why?

25.7 When is a truncated scale most likely to be acceptable?

Exercises and Problems

25.8 **Identifying Stories**

Of the following, which are stories?

1. Computer Use
2. Computer Prices Fall
3. More Single Parents Buy Computers Than Do Any Other Group
4. Where Your Tax Dollars Go
5. Sixty Percent of Tax Dollars Pay Entitlements, Interest

25.9 **Matching Visuals with Stories**

What visual(s) would make it easiest to see each of the following stories?

1. Canada buys 20% of U.S. exports.
2. Undergraduate enrollment rises, but graduate enrollment declines.
3. Population growth will be greatest in the West and South.
4. Companies with fewer than 200 employees created a larger percentage of new jobs than did companies with more than 5,000 employees.
5. America's heads of households are getting older.

25.10 Evaluating Visuals

Evaluate each of the following visuals.
- Is the visual's message clear?
- Is it the right visual for the story?
- Is the visual designed appropriately? Is color, if any, used appropriately?

- Is the visual free from *chartjunk*?
- Does the visual distort data or mislead the reader in any way?

1.
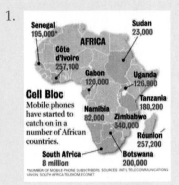

Source: Newsweek, August 27, 2001.

2.
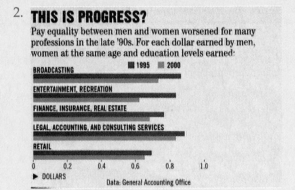

Source: BusinessWeek, March 11, 2002, 10.

3.
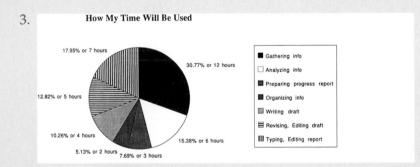

4.
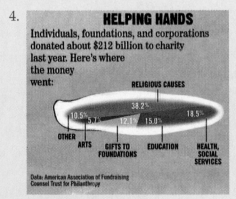

Source: BusinessWeek, July 29, 2002, 14.

5.
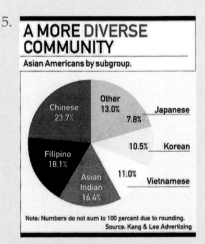

Source: American Demographics, July/August 2002, 40.

6.

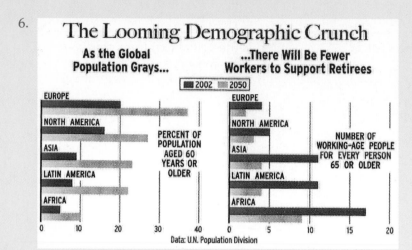

The Looming Demographic Crunch

As the Global Population Grays...

...There Will Be Fewer Workers to Support Retirees

2002 2050

Source: BusinessWeek, August 26, 2002, 140.

7.

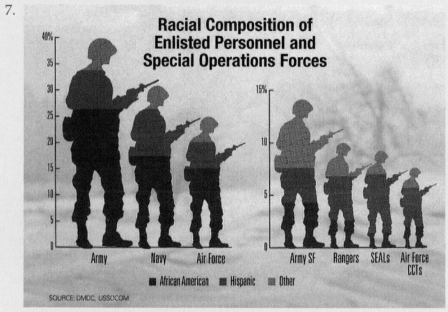

Racial Composition of Enlisted Personnel and Special Operations Forces

Army   Navy   Air Force   Army SF   Rangers   SEALs   Air Force CCTs

African American   Hispanic   Other

SOURCE: DMDC, USSOCOM

Source: Black Enterprise, February 2002, 28.

25.11 Interpreting Data

As Your Instructor Directs,

a. Identify at least seven stories in one or more of the following data sets.

b. Create visuals for three of the stories.

c. Write a memo to your instructor explaining why you chose these stories and why you chose these visuals to display them.

d. Write a memo to some group that might be interested in your findings, presenting your visuals as part of a short report. Possible groups include pet stores, career counselors, and financial advisors.

e. Brainstorm additional stories you could tell with additional data. Specify the kind of data you would need.

1.

Sushi Anyone?
The young and the affluent are the most culturally adventurous.

Q: HOW OFTEN DO YOU FIND YOURSELF EXPLORING AND LEARNING ABOUT CULTURES THAT ARE NEITHER YOUR OWN NOR THOSE OF YOUR ANCESTORS?

Age*	All	18–24	25–34	35–44	45–54	55–64	65+
Very often	24%	29%	23%	18%	29%	19%	24%
Often	21%	23%	27%	22%	17%	21%	19%
Sometimes	31%	29%	27%	36%	30%	32%	30%
Seldom	15%	14%	14%	16%	17%	19%	12%
Never	8%	4%	9%	8%	7%	9%	13%

Annual HH Income*	All	Under $25K	$25K–$34.9K	$35K–$44.9K	$45K–$54.9K	$55K–$64.9K	$65K–$74.9K	$75K–$99.9K	Over $100K
Very often	24%	20%	20%	23%	20%	30%	22%	28%	37%
Often	21%	21%	21%	17%	25%	18%	28%	20%	23%
Sometimes	31%	32%	35%	31%	33%	32%	36%	30%	24%
Seldom	15%	13%	16%	23%	15%	13%	6%	17%	14%
Never	8%	13%	8%	7%	6%	8%	7%	6%	2%

Source: *Maritz Marketing Research*

Numbers may not add up to 100 due to rounding.

Source: *American Demographics*, July 2001, 10.

2.

Projected job growth, by profession, 2000 to 2010	
Computer software engineers	95%
Computer support specialists and systems administrators	92%
Desktop publishers	67%
Systems analysts, computer scientists, and database administrators	62%
Medical records and health information technicians	49%
Public relations specialists	36%
Advertising, marketing, promotions, and sales managers	32%
Biomedical engineers	31%
Financial analysts and personal financial advisers	29%
Management analysts	29%
Environmental engineers	26%
Television, video, and film camera operators and editors	26%
Computer hardware engineers	25%
Economists and market and survey researchers	25%
Environmental scientists and geoscientists	21%
Industrial designers	21%

Source: *Business 2.0*, June 2002, 142.

3.

Generational Thirst
Percent of all dollars spent annually in each beverage category, by life stage

	Carbonated Beverages	Coffee	Juices, Refrigerated	Soft Drinks Non-carb.	Bottled Water	All Remain Carb. Bev/Diet	All Remain Carb. Bev/Reg	Coffee, Liquid
Young singles (age 18–34)	2%	1%	2%	2%	2%	2%	1%	3%
Childless younger couples (two adults, 18–34)	4%	3%	4%	4%	6%	4%	4%	8%
New families (2 adults, 1 or more children <6)	5%	3%	5%	8%	6%	4%	5%	4%
Maturing families (2 adults, 1 or more children, not all <6 or + 12)	26%	19%	22%	36%	22%	21%	30%	19%
Established families (1 or more children, all + 12)	12%	9%	10%	10%	10%	9%	14%	12%
Middle aged singles (35–54)	7%	5%	7%	4%	9%	9%	7%	7%
Middle aged childless couples (2 adults, 35–54)	18%	17%	16%	14%	18%	19%	16%	18%
Empty nesters (2 adults, +55, no children at home)	20%	32%	24%	17%	20%	24%	17%	21%
Older singles (55+)	7%	11%	10%	6%	7%	8%	6%	8%
Total	100%	100%	100%	100%	100%	100%	100%	100%

Source: *American Demographics,* February 2000, 63.

4.

Ruling the Roost
In 2000, pooches made their homes in 39 percent of U.S. households and kitty cats in 34 percent, compared with 37 percent and 30 percent, respectively, in 1988.

Percent of U.S. households that own at least one of the following:

	1988	1992	1996	2000
Dog	37%	38%	37%	39%
Cat	30%	32%	32%	34%
Freshwater fish	n/a	10%	11%	12%
Bird	6%	6%	6%	7%
Small animal	4%	5%	5%	5%
Reptile	n/a	n/a	3%	4%
Saltwater fish	n/a	0.8%	0.6%	0.7%
Any pet	56%	58%	59%	62%

Source: American Pet Products Manufacturers Association, 2001–2002 National Pet Owners Survey

Source: *American Demographics,* May 2002, 36.

For the Birds

Hispanic Americans are 21 percent less likely than the average American to own a dog, but they are 11 percent more likely than average to own a bird.

Index* of pet ownership, by race and ethnicity:

	White	Black	Asian	Hispanic**
Dog	110	44	65	79
Cat	112	24	71	74
Bird	109	33	***	111
Any pet	110	43	72	80

*An index of 100 is the national average. For example, whites are 10 percent more likely to own a dog than the average American, while blacks are 56 percent less likely to own a dog.
**Hispanic can be of any race.
***Sample size too small
Source: Mediamark Research. Inc.

Source: American Demographics, May 2002, 36.

5.

In the Red

Average credit card debt per U.S. household:

2001	*$8,562
2000	$8,123
1999	$7,564
1998	$7,188
1997	$6,900
1996	$6,487
1995	$5,832
1994	$4,811
1993	$3,601
1992	$3,444
1991	$3,223
1990	$2,985

*As of July 2001

Source: American Demographics, January 2002, 56.

6.

Changes in Aggregate Spending by Age, 1990–2000

Still the pig-in-a-python generation. Baby Boomers maintained their economic dominance in the '90s by outspending other age groups by at least two to one. In 2000, Americans between ages 35 and 54 years spent as much as all other age groups combined.

	All Consumers		Generation Y Under 25		Generation X 25–34		Baby Boomers 35–54		Matures Over 55	
	1990	2000	1990	2000	1990	2000	1990	2000	1990	2000
Number of consumer units (000s)	96,968	109,367	7,581	8,306	21,287	18,887	35,858	45,857	32,241	36,316
Average annual expenditure	$28,381	$38,045	$16,525	$22,543	$28,117	$38,945	$72,606	$91,309	$47,814	$65,873
Aggregate spending (billions)	$2,752	$4,161	$125	$187	$599	$736	$1,297	$2,092	$728	$1,144
Share of aggregate spending			4.6%	4.5%	21.7%	17.7%	47.1%	50.3%	26.5%	27.5%
Percent change: 1990–2000			−1.1%	−18.7%	6.7%	4.0%				

Source: Consumer Expenditure Survey, 1990 and 2000.

Source: American Demographics, April 2002, 37.

7.

Consumer Spending by Income, 2000

As incomes rise, Americans spend proportionately more of their budgets on clothes, insurance and going out, with less spent on food, health care and home entertainment. As for spending on housing, the rich and poor spent about the same: one-third of their overall budgets.

	Total Reporting	$20,000–$29,999	$30,000–$39,999	$40,000–$49,999	$50,000–$69,999	$70,000 and over
Number of consumer units (000s)						
	81,454	12,039	9,477	7,653	11,337	15,424
Average annual expenditures						
	$40,238	$29,852	$35,609	$42,323	$49,245	$75,964
Dollar share						
Apparel and services	5.0%	4.7%	4.7%	4.7%	4.8%	5.3%
Men and boy's	1.2%	1.2%	1.1%	0.9%	1.2%	1.3%
Women and girl's	1.9%	1.6%	1.7%	2.0%	1.9%	2.0%
Entertainment	4.9%	4.7%	4.7%	4.7%	5.1%	5.1%
Fees and admissions	1.3%	1.0%	1.0%	1.0%	1.3%	1.8%
Televisions, radios, audio equipment	1.6%	1.7%	1.7%	1.7%	1.6%	1.4%
Food	13.5%	15.1%	14.4%	14.7%	13.3%	11.4%
Food at home	7.8%	9.8%	8.4%	8.4%	7.3%	5.9%
Food away from home	5.7%	5.3%	6.0%	6.3%	6.0%	5.5%
Health care	5.3%	6.8%	5.6%	5.1%	4.7%	3.8%
Drugs	1.1%	1.6%	1.2%	1.0%	0.9%	0.6%
Health insurance	2.4%	3.3%	2.7%	2.4%	2.2%	1.7%
Housing	31.1%	31.4%	31.2%	30.4%	30.3%	30.2%
Owned dwellings	11.4%	8.3%	10.5%	10.6%	12.4%	14.0%
Rented dwellings	5.1%	8.3%	7.1%	6.1%	3.5%	1.8%
Personal insurance and pensions	10.7%	6.4%	8.4%	10.2%	12.3%	15.6%
Life and other personal insurance	1.0%	1.0%	1.0%	0.8%	1.0%	1.2%
Pensions and Social Security	9.7%	5.3%	7.4%	9.4%	11.3%	14.4%
Transportation	18.8%	19.2%	20.5%	20.6%	19.6%	17.6%
Cars and trucks, new	4.0%	3.9%	4.1%	4.5%	4.0%	4.5%
Cars and trucks, used	4.5%	4.5%	5.4%	5.4%	4.7%	3.2%

Source: *American Demographics*, April 2002, 36.

25.12 Graphing Data from the Web

Find data on the Web about a topic that interests you. Sites with data include

American Demographics Archives: www.inside.com/default.csp?entity = American Demo

Catalyst: www.catalystwomen.org/press_room/factsheets.htm

FEDSTATS (links to U.S. government agencies): www.fedstats.gov

Food and Nutrition Information Center: www.nal.usda.gov/fnic/etext/000056.html

U.S. Census Bureau E-Stats: www.census.gov/eos/www/ebusiness614.htm

White House Briefing Room (economic issues): www.whitehouse.gov/fsbr/esbr.html

As Your Instructor Directs,

a. Identify at least seven stories in the data.

b. Create visuals for three of the stories.

c. Write a memo to your instructor explaining why you chose these stories and why you chose these visuals to display them.

d. Write a memo to some group that might be interested in your findings, presenting your visuals as part of a short report.

e. Print out the data and include it with a copy of your memo or report.

Polishing Your Prose

Writing Subject Lines and Headings

Subject lines are the title of a letter, memo, or e-mail message. Headings within a document tell the reader what information you will discuss in that section.

Good subject lines are specific, concise, and appropriate for your purposes and the response you expect from the reader. Subject lines are required in memos, optional in letters.

- Put in good news if you have it.

- If information is neutral, summarize it.

- Use negative subject lines if the reader may not read the message, needs the information to act, or if the negative is your error.

- In a request that is easy for the reader to grant, put the subject of that request or a direct question in the subject line.

- When you must persuade a reluctant reader, use a common ground, a reader benefit, or a directed subject line that makes your stance on the issue clear.

Headings are single words, short phrases, or complete sentences that indicate the topic in a document section. Headings must be parallel—that is, they must use the same grammatical structure—and must cover all the information until the next heading.

The most useful headings are **talking heads,** which sum up the content of the section.

Weak: Problem
               Cause 1
               Cause 2
               Cause 3

Better: Communication Problems
             Between Air Traffic Controllers and Pilots

               Selective Listening
               Indirect Conversational Style
               Limitations of Short-Term Memory

Exercises

For the situations in 1–6, write a good subject line. Make 7–10 into effective headings using parallel form.

1. We're going to raise your insurance rates!

2. Why can't Macefield, Inc., employees stop using the photocopier for personal business?

3. Blood drive.

4. We're thinking about opening a gym for the employees, but we're not sure how everyone feels about it.

5. Making the Most of Undergraduate Years; Making the Most of Graduate School; Now What?

6. Work areas are getting too messy—if something isn't done soon, management will have to write up offending employees.

7. Clemente Research Group's Five-Year Goals; What We Want to Accomplish in Ten-Years; Our Fifteen-Year Goals

8. Career Objective; Things that I Did on the Job; Hobbies; My Education; A List of References

9. Research; Logistics; What's in It for Us

10. Market Challenges in East Asia Over the Next Five Years

   Economic Factors

   What will the political climate be like?

   Recent Trade Agreements and Their Effects—a Projection

   We're trying to understand customers using complex research, and it's hard.

Check your answers to the odd-numbered exercises at the back of the book.

BComm Skill Booster

To apply the concepts in this module, complete lessons 44 and 80 on integrating visuals into your written work and creating effective visuals. You can access the BComm Skill Booster through the text Web site at **www.mhhe.com/bcs2e.**

Cases for Communicators

Dawn of a New Duck

Dawn, the top-selling dishwashing liquid in the United States, is launching a short-term advertising campaign based on emotion, not logic. Dawn, it seems, is highly effective in cleaning the feathers of birds caught in oil spills. In fact, the product has been used in the cleanup of environmental disasters for more than 20 years, most notably in the aftermath of the Exxon Valdez spill.

Procter & Gamble is now poised to leverage this unique application of its product. In its new Dawn campaign, the company communicates its concern for community and environment through touching television and print ads. The television ads, for example, show an oil-covered duck being cleaned, an image that is sure to tug at the heartstrings of even the most stoic consumer.

While it is clearly crafted to elicit strong emotions, the campaign is also designed to promote action. Procter & Gamble has committed to donate 10¢ for each bottle of Dawn redeemed in its "Save-A-Duck" program, to a total of $50,000. The donations will be divided between two wildlife rescue groups, Tri-State Bird Rescue and Research, Inc., and International Bird Rescue Research Center. To participate in the program, consumers just need to input the UPC number from their bottle of Dawn on the Save-A-Duck Web site (**http://www.saveaduck.com**); in return, they will receive a certificate of appreciation for each purchase they register.

If successful, this campaign will strike a chord with environmentally aware consumers, creating an emotional connection with Dawn that they will, either consciously or unconsciously, take with them the next time they go to the store. Only time will tell if the Save-A-Duck campaign has cut through Dawn's competitors as well as Dawn cuts through oil!

Source: Jane L. Levere, "A Dishwashing Liquid Cuts the Grease . . . on Ducks?" *New York Times,* July 31, 2002. Accessed on NYTimes.com (**http://www.nytimes.com**) on August 2, 2002.

Individual Activity

Imagine that you work in the market research department at Procter & Gamble. The redemption program on the Save-A-Duck Web site presents your group with a fantastic opportunity to gather additional information from active, engaged consumers. Write an online questionnaire that will elicit critical data about customer demographics and purchase habits from these respondents.

The questionnaire, which will be put on the Save-A-Duck Web site, will appear immediately after visitors input the UPC number from their Dawn purchase and before they receive their certificate of appreciation. Customers will have the opportunity to opt out of filling out the questionnaire, but they will continue to see it on return visits until they fill it out. Return customers who have completed the questionnaire will not see it a second time.

Your manager has created a list of 10 general questions for the questionnaire:

1. Have these customers seen any of the Save-A-Duck advertisements? If so, which ones (print or television)?
2. How did they learn about the Save-A-Duck Web site?
3. Did the Save-A-Duck campaign convince them to buy Dawn?
4. How many of these people are new Dawn users?
5. How many use Dawn already?
6. If they are new users, which dish-washing liquid do they typically buy?
7. If they are regular Dawn users, how often do they buy the product?
8. Is this campaign hitting the market of a specific competitor?
9. How old are these individuals?
10. Is the campaign more effective with men or women?

Before you begin writing the questionnaire, consider these points:

- What type of questions should I write—open or closed?
- Who is the population for this questionnaire?
- Is my sample a random sample, a convenience sample, or a judgment sample?
- How does the sample type affect my ability to generalize my findings?

As you write the questionnaire, ask yourself the following questions:

- Are my questions phrased in such a way as to be neutral and clear?
- Have I made any inappropriate assumptions in my questions?
- Am I using branching questions where appropriate?
- Have I structured the questionnaire so that easier questions come before harder questions?

- Do my questions cover the necessary points as outlined by my manager?
- Have I used indentations and white space effectively?

Make the questionnaire clear, concise, and easy to tabulate.

Group Activity

The Save-A-Duck campaign—composed of print ads, television ads, and a Web site—is nearing completion, and discussions have already begun about its future. Some marketing executives believe that the campaign should be ended, while others think it should be extend indefinitely as part of the overall advertising approach for Dawn.

You and your colleagues in the marketing department have been asked to present a recommendation report to marketing executives on this very issue. You know that the campaign was successful in meeting its donation goals—in fact, the $50,000 was raised much more quickly than anyone anticipated—but you are not sure if it generated enough additional product sales to warrant its continuation.

With other members of your group, brainstorm the questions to which you'd like to get answers in order to write a report. For each question, brainstorm one or more possible stories the data might tell and which kind of visual would best tell that story.

Unit Seven

Job Hunting

Module 26

Researching Jobs

Start by asking these questions:

- What do I need to know about myself to job hunt?
- What do I need to know about companies that might hire me?
- Should I do information interviews?
- What is the "hidden job market"? How do I tap into it?
- What do I do if I've got a major weakness?

Perhaps you already have a job waiting for you; perhaps your skills are in such demand that employers will seek *you* out. If, however, the job picture is more murky, the modules in this unit will help you find your way.

The most successful job hunting method, claims Richard Bolles, hasn't changed:

> Do thorough homework on yourself. Know your best skills, in order of priority. Know the fields in which you want to use those skills. Talk to people who have those kinds of jobs. Find out whether they're happy, and how they found their jobs. Then choose the places where you want to work, rather than just those places that have advertised openings. Thoroughly research these organizations before approaching them. Seek out the person who actually has the power to hire you for the job that you want. Demonstrate to that person how you can help the company with its problems. Cut no corners; take no shortcuts. That method has an 86% success rate.[1]

What do I need to know about myself to job hunt?

Your knowledge, skills, abilities, interests, and values.

Each person could do several jobs happily. Personality and aptitude tests can tell you what your strengths are, but they won't say, "You should be a _____ ." You'll still need to answer questions like these:

- What achievements have given you the most satisfaction? *Why* did you enjoy them?
- Would you rather have firm deadlines or a flexible schedule? Do you prefer working alone or with other people? Do you prefer specific instructions and standards for evaluation or freedom and uncertainty? How comfortable are you with pressure? Are you willing to "pay your dues" for several years before you are promoted? How much challenge do you want?
- Are you willing to take work home? To travel? How important is money to you? Prestige? Time to spend with family and friends?
- Where do you want to live? What features in terms of weather, geography, and cultural and social life do you see as ideal?
- Is it important to you that your work achieve certain purposes or values, or do you see work as "just a way to make a living"? Are the organization's culture and ethical standards important to you?

Once you know what is most important to you, analyze the job market to see where you could find what you want. For example, Peter's greatest interest is athletics, but he isn't good enough for the pros. Studying the job market might suggest several alternatives. He could teach sports and physical fitness as a high school coach or a corporate fitness director. He could cover sports for a newspaper, a magazine, a TV station, or the Web. He could go into management or sales for a professional sports team, a health club, or a company that sells sports equipment. He could create or manage a sports Web page.

What do I need to know about companies that might hire me?

As much as you can!

To adapt your letter to a specific organization and to shine at the interview, you need information both about the employer and about the job itself. You'll need to know

- **What the job itself involves.** Notebooks at campus placement offices often have fuller job descriptions than appear in ads. Talk to friends who have graduated recently to learn what their jobs involve. Conduct information interviews to learn more about opportunities that interest you.
- **The name and address of the person who should receive the letter.** To get this information, check the ad or the Web or call the organization.

Building a Critical Skill

Choosing Whether to Stay or Go

When you've got a job that's OK, it's often hard to know whether to stay or move. After all, you know all the flaws of your current situation. Any new job will have its own flaws, but you probably don't know them and certainly don't know all of them. To decide on the basis of the pluses and minuses you know, therefore, is illogical. You need a better way to compare the job you know to the one that is only a possibility.

William Morin offers a seven-question quiz. Are the following statements true or false for you?

1. Your boss likes you and advocates for you in the organization.
2. Your boss is doing well.
3. You've been promoted in the last two years.
4. Your pension plan, 401(k), and other benefits are vested (or are near vesting) and growing.
5. The company is doing well and can grow further.
6. You're getting better-than-average raises. (Average for white-collar workers is about 3.5% a year in good years.)
7. Your boss has mentioned within the last year that you are valued and he or she sees where you might be headed in the organization.

If most of these statements are true for you, Morin says, you should stay where you are.

Professor John Sullivan offers a different set of questions to evaluate your current job and new possibilities:

1. Do you love the work? The ideal job is one you'd want to do even if you were rich.
2. Do you have a great mentor? Your career will soar if you do.
3. Do you have opportunities to learn a lot fast? No job is forever. But if you keep learning cutting-edge skills, you'll always be employable.
4. Does the job encourage rapid change? Change encourages growth. And growth keeps you employable and promotable.
5. Is the company an employer of choice (EOC, for whom everyone wants to work) or a fun place to work (FPW)? If you're with an EOC, you get an "impeccable pedigree that will prove invaluable" the next time you're on the job market. And a FPW is its own reward.

The job with the most "yes" responses wins.

Source: Anne Fisher, "Ask Annie," *Fortune,* February 7, 2000, 210; and John Sullivan, "What Makes a Great Job?" *Fast Company,* October 1998, 166.

For Internet job hunting, niche job boards are often more useful than general ones. When telecommunications manager Ross Quam decided to leave the U.S. Marines, he got no nibbles from generalist job boards such as Monster.com and America's Job Bank. But when he posted his résumé on Telecomcareers.net, he got three job offers.

An advantage of calling is that you can find out whether a woman prefers *Ms.* or *Mrs.*

- **What the organization does and at least four or five facts about it.** Knowing the organization's larger goals enables you to show how your specific work will help the company meet its goals. Useful facts include
  - Market share.
  - Competitive position.

- New products, services, or promotions.
- The kind of computer or manufacturing equipment the company uses.
- Plans for growth or downsizing.
- Challenges the organization faces.
- The corporate culture (◀ ▷ p. 32).

The directories listed in Figure 26.1 provide information ranging from net worth, market share, and principal products to the names of officers and directors. Ask your librarian to identify additional directories. To get specific financial data (and to see how the organization presents itself to the public), get the company's annual report on the Web. (Note: Only companies whose stock is publicly traded are required to issue annual reports. In this day of mergers and buyouts, many companies are owned by other companies. The parent company may be the only one to issue an annual report.) Many company Web sites provide information about training programs and career paths for new hires. To learn about new products, plans for growth, or solutions to industry challenges, read business newspapers such as *The Wall Street Journal* or *The Financial Post*; business magazines such as *Fortune, BusinessWeek,* and *Forbes*; and trade journals. Each of these has indexes listing which companies are discussed in a specific issue. A few of the trade journals available are listed in Figure 26.2.

The Internet has much of this information, including information about corporate culture and even anonymous statements from employees. Figure 26.3 lists some of the best sites. Check professional listservs and electronic

Site *to* See

Go to
www.jobhuntersbible.com/
Dick Bolles' useful site identifies five ways to use the Internet, explains how to make contacts (whether you already have the name of a person or not), and offers advice about career and personality tests.

General Directories
Directory of Corporate Affiliations
Dun's Million Dollar Directory
Standard & Poor's Register of Corporations, Directors, and Executives
Thomas Register of American Manufacturers

Specialized Directories and Resource Books
Accounting Firms and Practitioners
California Manufacturers Register
Directory of Hotel and Motel Systems
Franchise Annual: Handbook and Directory
O'Dwyer's Directory of Public Relations Firms
The Rand McNally Banker's Directory
Standard Directory of Advertisers ("Red Book")
Television Factbook

Figure 26.1
Print Sources for Addresses and Facts about Companies

Advertising Age
American Banker
Automotive News
Aviation Week
Beverage Industry
Cable Communication Magazine
Canadian Business

Discount Store News
Financial Analysts Journal
Graphic Arts Monthly
HR Focus
Internal Auditor
International Advertiser
Logging and Sawmilling Journal

Nation's Restaurant News
The Practical Accountant
Software Canada
Television/Radio Age
Today's Realtor
Training & Development
Travel Agent

Figure 26.2
Examples of Trade Journals

Figure 26.3

Comprehensive Web Job Sites Covering the Entire Job Search Process

Archeus WorkSearch www.garywill.com/worksearch	**JobStar Central** jobstar.org
Asia Net www.asia-net.com	**Monster.com** content.monster.com
Black Collegian Online www.black-collegian.com	**Quintessential Careers** www.quintcareers.com/index.html
CareerBuilder www.careerbuilder.com	**The Riley Guide** www.rileyguide.com
College Grad Job Hunter www.collegegrad.com	**The Rockport Institute** www.rockportinstitute.com/main.html
Fast Company www.fastcompany.com/career/	**Saludos.com** www.saludos.com/resume.html
The Five O'Clock Club www.fiveoclockclub.com	**WetFeet.com** www.wetfeet.com/asp/home.asp
JobHuntersBible.com (Dick Bolles) www.jobhuntersbible.com	**Vault** vault.com

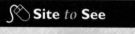

Site to See

Go to
content.monster.com/military/

In addition to more than 380,000 job listings, Monster.com provides general and targeted information for job hunters.

bulletin boards. Employers sometimes post specialized jobs on them: they're always a good way to get information about the industry you hope to enter.

Should I do information interviews?

They'll help any job hunter. They're crucial if you're not sure what you want to do.

In an **information interview** you talk to someone who works in the area you hope to enter to find out what the day-to-day work involves and how you can best prepare to enter that field. You do not ask for a job. However, an information interview can

- Let you know whether or not you'd like the job.
- Give you specific information that you can use to present yourself effectively in your résumé and application letter.
- Create a good image of you in the mind of the interviewer so that he or she thinks well of you when openings arise.

In an information interview, you might ask the following questions:

- Tell me about the papers on your desk. What are you working on right now?
- How do you spend your typical day?
- Have your duties changed a lot since you first started working here?
- What do you like best about your job? What do you like least?
- What do you think the future holds for this kind of work?
- How did you get this job?
- What courses, activities, or jobs would you recommend to someone who wanted to do this kind of work?

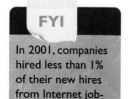

FYI

In 2001, companies hired less than 1% of their new hires from Internet job-posting boards.

Source: The Motley Fool, "The Fool School," *The Columbus Dispatch*, February 24, 2002, F4.

To set up an information interview, phone or write a letter. If you do write, phone the following week to set up a specific time.

What is the "hidden job market"? How do I tap into it?

The "hidden market" is composed of jobs that are never advertised.

Referral interviews and prospecting letters can help you find it.

A great many jobs are never advertised—and the number rises the higher up the job ladder you go. Over 60% of all new jobs come not from responding to an ad but from networking with personal contacts.[2] Some of these jobs are created especially for a specific person. These unadvertised jobs are called **the hidden job market.** Referral interviews, an organized method of networking, offer the most systematic way to tap into these jobs. Schedule **referral** interviews to learn about current job opportunities in your field. Sometimes an interview that starts out as an information interview turns into a referral interview.

A referral interview should give you information about the opportunities currently available in your town in the area you're interested in, refer you to other people who can tell you about job opportunities, and enable the interviewer to see that you could make a contribution to his or her organization. Therefore, the goal of a referral interview is to put you face-to-face with someone who has the power to hire you: the president of a small company, the division vice president or branch manager of a big company, the director of the local office of a state or federal agency.

Start by scheduling interviews with people you know who may know something about that field—professors, co-workers, neighbors, friends. Call your alumni office to get the names and phone numbers of alumni who now work where you would like to work. Your purpose in talking to them is (ostensibly) to get advice about improving your résumé and about general job-hunting strategy and (really) to get **referrals** to other people. In fact, go into the interview with the names of people you'd like to talk to. If the interviewee doesn't suggest anyone, say, "Do you think it would be a good idea for me to talk to _____ ?"

Then, armed with a referral from someone you know, you call Mr. or Ms. "Big" and say, "So-and-so suggested I talk with you about job-hunting strategy." If the person says, "We aren't hiring," you say, "Oh, I'm not asking *you* for a job. I'd just like some advice from a knowledgeable person about the opportunities in banking [or desktop publishing, or whatever] in this city." If this person does not have the power to create a position, you seek more referrals at the end of *this* interview. (You can also polish your résumé, if you get good suggestions.)

Even when you talk to the person who could create a job for you, you *do not ask for a job.* But to give you advice about your résumé, the person has to look at it. When a powerful person focuses on your skills, he or she will

naturally think about the problems and needs in that organization. When there's a match between what you can do and what the organization needs, that person has the power to create a position for you.

Some business people are cynical about information and referral interviewing. Prepare as carefully for these interviews as you would for an interview when you know the organization is hiring. Think in advance of good questions; know something about the general field or industry; try to learn at least a little bit about the specific company.

Always follow up information and referral interviews with personal thank-you letters. Use specifics to show that you paid attention during the interview, and enclose a copy of your revised résumé.

What do I do if I've got a major weakness?

Address the employer's fears, calmly and positively.

Some job hunters face special problems. This section gives advice for six common problems.

"All My Experience Is in My Family's Business."

In your résumé, simply list the company you worked for. For a reference, instead of a family member, list a supervisor, client, or vendor who can talk about your work. Since the reader may wonder whether "Jim Clarke" is any relation to "Clarke Construction Company," be ready to answer interview questions about why you're looking at other companies. Prepare an answer that stresses the broader opportunities you seek but doesn't criticize your family or the family business.

"I've Been Out of the Job Market for a While."

You need to prove to a potential employer that you're up-to-date and motivated. To do that,

- **Understand how work in your field may have changed.** For example, hospital workers now have many more acutely ill patients than they did 10 years ago.
- **Be active in professional organizations.** Attend meetings; read trade journals.
- **Learn the computer programs that professionals in your field use.**
- **Find out your prospective employer's immediate priorities.** If you can show you'll contribute from day one, you'll have a much easier sell. But to do that, you need to know what skills the employer is looking for, what needs the employer has.
- **Show how your at-home experience relates to the workplace.** Dealing with unpredictable situations, building consensus, listening, raising money, and making presentations are transferrable skills.
- **Create a portfolio of your work**—even if it's for imaginary clients—to demonstrate your expertise.[3]

"I Want to Change Fields."

Have a good reason for choosing the field in which you're looking for work. "I want a change" or "I need to get out of a bad situation" does not convince an employer that you know what you're doing.

Think about how your experience relates to the job you want. Jack is an older-than-average student who wants to be a pharmaceutical sales representative. He has sold woodstoves, served subpoenas, and worked on an oil rig. A chronological résumé makes his work history look directionless. But a skills résumé (◄ ► p. 530) could focus on persuasive ability (selling stoves), initiative and persistence (serving subpoenas), and technical knowledge (courses in biology and chemistry).[4]

Learn about the skills needed in the job you want. Learn the buzzwords of the industry.

"I Was Fired."

First, deal with the emotional baggage. You need to reduce negative feelings to a manageable level before you're ready to job hunt.

Second, try to learn from the experience. You'll be a much more attractive job candidate if you can show that you've learned from the experience—whether your lesson is improved work habits or that you need to choose a job where you can do work you can point to with pride.

Third, suggests Phil Elder, an interviewer for an insurance company, call the person who fired you and say something like this: "Look, I know you weren't pleased with the job I did at _____ . I'm applying for a job at _____ now and the personnel director may call you to ask about me. Would you be willing to give me the chance to get this job so that I can try to do things right this time?" All but the hardest of heart, says Elder, will give you one more chance. You won't get a glowing reference, but neither will the statement be so damning that no one is willing to hire you.[5]

"I Don't Have Any Experience."

If you have six months or a year before you start to job hunt, you can get experience in several ways:

- **Take a fast-food job—and keep it.** If you do well, you'll probably be promoted to a supervisor within a year. Use every opportunity to learn about the management and financial aspects of the business.
- **Join a volunteer organization that interests you.** If you work hard, you'll quickly get an opportunity to do more: manage a budget, write fund-raising materials, and supervise other volunteers.
- **Freelance.** Design brochures, create Web pages, do tax returns for small businesses. Use your skills—for free, if you have to at first.
- **Write.** Create a portfolio of ads, instructions, or whatever documents are relevant for the field you want to enter. Ask a professional—an instructor, a local business person, someone from a professional organization—to critique them. Volunteer your services to local fund-raising organizations and small businesses.

Instant Replay

The Hidden Job Market and Referral Interviews

Unadvertised jobs are called **the hidden job market.** Referral interviews, an organized method of networking, offer the most systematic way to tap into these jobs. Schedule **referral interviews** to learn about current job opportunities in your field.

To reach your career goals, define them clearly, understand your strengths, and find information about employers.

Getting experience is particularly important for students with good grades. Pick something where you interact with other people so that you can show that you can work well in an organization.

If you're in the job market now, think carefully about what you've really done. Write sentences using the action verbs in Figure 27.6. Think about what you've done in courses, in volunteer work, in unpaid activities. Especially focus on skills in problem solving, critical thinking, teamwork, and communication. Solving a problem for a hypothetical firm in an accounting class, thinking critically about a report problem in business communication, working with a group in a marketing class, and communicating with people at the senior center where you volunteer are experience, even if no one paid you.

If you're not actually looking for a job but just need to create a résumé for this course, ask your instructor whether you may assume that you're graduating and add the things you hope to do between now and that time.

"I'm a Lot Older Than They Want."

A survey of 2,500 college students and new graduates found that 78% plan to work for their first employers for three years or fewer.[6] You're going to be working at least that long. The employer's real fear is not that you'll retire in just a year but that you won't be flexible, up-to-date, or willing to be supervised by someone younger. To counter these fears,

- **Keep up-to-date.** Read trade journals; attend professional meetings.
- **Learn the computer programs your field uses.** Refer to technology in the résumé, job letter, and interview: "Yes, I saw the specifications for your new product on your Web site."
- **Work with younger people,** in classroom teams, in volunteer work, or on the job. Be able to point to specific cases where you've learned from young people and worked well with them.
- **Use positive emphasis** (◀ ▷ p. 119). Talk about your ability to relate to older customers (who have so much disposable income), the valuable perspective you bring. Focus on fairly recent events, not ones from 20 years ago.
- **Show energy and enthusiasm** to counter the stereotype that older people are tired and ill.

Summary of Key Points

- Informal preparation for job hunting should start soon after you arrive on campus. Formal preparation for job hunting should begin a full year before you begin interviewing.

- Use directories, annual reports, recruiting literature, business periodicals, trade journals, and Web pages to get information about employers and jobs to use in your letter.

- Information and referral interviews can help you tap into the **hidden job market—**

jobs that are not advertised. In an **information interview** you find out what the day-to-day work involves and how you can best prepare to enter that field. **Referral interviews** are interviews you schedule to learn about current job opportunities in your field.

- If you have a major weakness, brainstorm a way to address the employer's fears calmly and positively.

Assignments for Module 26

Questions for Comprehension

26.1 What should you know about yourself before you apply for jobs?

26.2 What information should you try to learn about a company?

26.3 What is an information interview?

26.4 What is the hidden job market?

Questions for Critical Thinking

26.5 Why is it desirable to start thinking about jobs months—even years—before you'll actually be on the market?

26.6 Why is it important to research the companies you want to apply to?

26.7 What is your biggest weakness as you prepare to job hunt? How could you minimize it?

Exercises and Problems

26.8 **Evaluating Career Web Sites***

Evaluate three or more Web sites for job hunters, considering the following questions:

- Is the site easy to navigate?
- Is it visually attractive?
- Are any ads unobtrusive?
- Is its advice good?

- Does it let job hunters specify who may *not* see their posted résumés (e.g., the current employer)?
- Does it have any features that you don't find in other career Web sites?

*Inspired by a problem written by Gary Kohut, University of North Carolina at Charlotte.

26.9 Networking

Write to a friend who is already in the workforce, asking about one or more of the following topics:

- Are any jobs in your field available in your friend's organization? If so, what?
- If a job is available, can your friend provide information beyond the job listing that will help you write a more detailed, persuasive letter? (Specify the kind of information you'd like to have.)
- Can your friend suggest people in other organizations who might be useful to you in your job search? (Specify any organizations in which you're especially interested.)

26.10 Gathering Information about an Industry

Use six recent issues of a trade journal to report on three to five trends, developments, or issues that are important in an industry.

As Your Instructor Directs,
a. Share your findings with a small group of other students.
b. Summarize your findings in a memo to your instructor.
c. Present your findings to the class.
d. E-mail your findings to the other members of the class.
e. Join with a small group of other students to write a report summarizing the results of this research.

26.11 Gathering Information about a Specific Organization

Gather printed information about a specific organization, using several of the following methods:

- Check the company's Web site.
- Read the company's annual report.
- Pick up relevant information at the Chamber of Commerce.
- Read articles in trade publications and *The Wall Street Journal* or *The Financial Post* that mention the organization (check the indexes).
- Get the names and addresses of its officers (from a directory or from the Web).
- Read recruiting literature provided by the company.

As Your Instructor Directs,
a. Share your findings with a small group of other students.
b. Summarize your findings in a memo to your instructor.
c. Present your findings orally to the class.
d. E-mail your findings to the other members of the class.
e. Join with a small group of other students to write a report summarizing the results of this research.

26.12 Conducting an Information Interview

Interview someone working in a field you're interested in. Use the questions listed in the module or the shorter list here:

- How did you get started in this field?
- What do you like about your job?
- What do you dislike about your job?
- Can you give me names of three other people who could also give me information about this job?

As Your Instructor Directs,
a. Share the results of your interview with a small group of other students.

b. Write up your interview in a memo to your instructor.
c. Present the results of your interview orally to the class.
d. E-mail a summary of your interview to other members of your class.

e. Write to the interviewee thanking him or her for taking the time to talk to you.

 Polishing Your Prose

Using Details

Details are especially important in reader benefits (◄|▷ Module 8), reports, résumés, and job application and sales letters. Customers or potential employers look for specific details to help them make decisions, such as what makes your product better than the competition's or how your experience would help the reader. Here's an example:

> I can bring more than ten years of advertising experience to Duncan, Fitzgerald, and Locke, the midwest leader in print and broadcast advertising. My experience includes five years of broadcast sales in Chicago, where I generated more than $19 million in revenue, as well as three years with Alvion and Daye, the leading outdoor advertising company in Indianapolis. For the first four years of my career, I also wrote advertising copy, including hundreds of local and regional radio spots for such diverse products as cookies, cat food, fishing tackle, and children's toys. I also wrote print pieces, including the entire 15-month campaign for Indiana-based "Uncle Bill's Electronics Bazaar," which increased sales by nearly 37% during that period.

Reader Benefits

What features or experiences make your product or service unique? Useful? Cost-effective?

Weak: With the Stereobooster, your car will sound great.

Better: The Stereobooster safely gives your car audio system a full 30 watts per channel of sheer sound excitement, double that of other systems on the market—all for under $50.

The Five Senses

Describe sight, sound, taste, touch, and smell. Some sensations are so powerful that they immediately conjure up thoughts or emotions—the smell of fresh coffee, the sound of ocean waves, the feeling of sunlight against the skin.

Concrete Nouns and Verbs

Concrete nouns and verbs are better than more general nouns and verbs combined with adjectives and adverbs. For instance, *manager* and *15 months* are more concrete than *the person in charge* or *a while*. Concrete words make meaning clear and vivid:

Weak: At my last job, I typed stuff.

Better: As a clerk typist II until July for Hughes and Associates, I typed hundreds of memos, letters, and reports.

Increase your vocabulary by reading a variety of materials. Keep a dictionary and thesaurus handy. Do crossword puzzles or computer word games to practice what you know.

Adjectives and Adverbs That Count

Omit or replace vague or overused adjectives and adverbs: *some, very, many, a lot,* kind/sort of, partly, eventually. Increasingly, novice writers are using *so* as an adjective, as in "He was so happy about the promotion." Exactly how happy is this?

Conversational English, Not Jargon or Obscure Words.

In general, choose the more conversational option over jargon or obscure words: *exit*, *typical*, or *second to last* rather than *egress*, *quintessential*, or *penultimate*.

Exercises

Add details to the following sentences.

1. The person in charge of our department wants some files.

2. We'll be purchasing some new office equipment some time in the upcoming year.

3. It's been a while since I went there.

4. A person at the newspaper wants us to send some information about our latest product for publication.

5. There are lots of reasons why you should hire me.

6. Our profits during the last couple of quarters were up about 20 percent or so.

7. We will have a meeting in the afternoon.

8. My qualifications for the promotion including doing lots of stuff.

9. We plan to travel to a couple of states sometime next month.

10. One of the motorpool people will be bring a car around to one of the building entrances.

Check your answers to the odd-numbered exercises at the back of the book.

BComm Skill Booster

To apply the concepts in this module, complete lesson 63 on creating a network of career contacts. You can access the BComm Skill Booster through the text Web site at **www.mhhe.com/bcs2e.**

Module 27

Résumés

Start by asking these questions:

- How can I encourage the employer to pay attention to my résumé?

- What kind of résumé should I use?

- How do the two résumés differ?

- What parts of the two résumés are the same?

- What should I do if the standard categories don't fit?

- Should I limit my résumé to just one page?

- How do I create a scannable résumé?

A **résumé** is a persuasive summary of your qualifications for employment. If you're in the job market, having a résumé makes you look well organized and prepared. When you're employed, having an up-to-date résumé makes it easier to take advantage of opportunities that may come up for an even better job. If you're several years away from job hunting, preparing a résumé now will make you more conscious of what to do in the next two or three years to make yourself an attractive candidate. Writing a résumé is also an ego-building experience: the person who looks so good on paper is **you!**

Writing a résumé is not an exact science. If your skills are in great demand, you can violate every guideline here and still get a good job. But when you must compete against

Figure 27.1

Allocating Time in Writing Résumé (Your time may vary.)

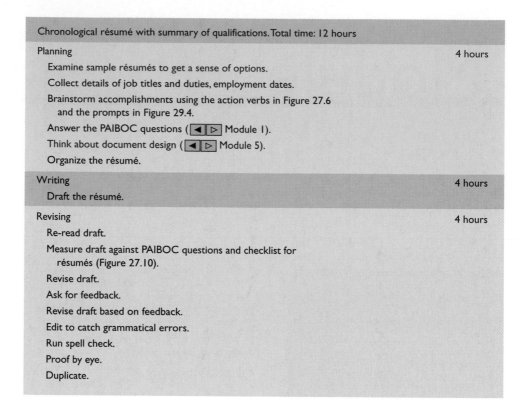

Chronological résumé with summary of qualifications. Total time: 12 hours

Planning	4 hours

Examine sample résumés to get a sense of options.

Collect details of job titles and duties, employment dates.

Brainstorm accomplishments using the action verbs in Figure 27.6 and the prompts in Figure 29.4.

Answer the PAIBOC questions (◀ ▷ Module 1).

Think about document design (◀ ▷ Module 5).

Organize the résumé.

Writing	4 hours

Draft the résumé.

Revising	4 hours

Re-read draft.

Measure draft against PAIBOC questions and checklist for résumés (Figure 27.10).

Revise draft.

Ask for feedback.

Revise draft based on feedback.

Edit to catch grammatical errors.

Run spell check.

Proof by eye.

Duplicate.

many applicants, these guidelines will help you look as good on paper as you are in person.

Figure 27.1 lists the activities required to create a good résumé.

All job communications must be tailored to your unique qualifications. Adopt the wording or layout of an example if it's relevant to your own situation, but don't be locked into the forms in this book. You've got different strengths; your résumé will be different, too.

How can I encourage the employer to pay attention to my résumé?

Show how your qualifications fit the job and the company.

Your résumé can be screened in two ways. If people do the reading, the employer will skim the résumés quickly, dividing the documents into two piles: "reject" and "maybe." In the first round, each résumé may get as little as 2.9 seconds of the reader's attention. Then the reader goes through the "maybe" pile again, weeding out more documents. If there are a lot of résumés (and some companies get 2,000 résumés a week), résumés may get only 10 to 30 seconds in this stage. After the initial pile has been culled to one-half or one-hundredth of the initial pile, the remaining documents will be read more carefully to choose the people who are invited for interviews.

Using a Computer to Create Résumés

Even if you pay someone else to produce your résumé, *you* must specify the exact layout.

Print your résumé on a laser printer on high-quality 8 1/2-by-11-inch paper (never legal size). White paper is standard; a very pale color is also acceptable.

Play with Layout and Design.

Experiment with layout, fonts, and spacing to get an attractive résumé. Consider creating a letterhead that you use for both your résumé and your application letter. (See Figures 27.7 and 28.5.)

Use enough white space to make your résumé easy to read but not so much that you look as if you're padding. Center your name as the title of the document in 14-point (or bigger) type. Use 12-point for headings. To get more on a page, use 11-point type for the text. The default margins and tab settings probably are too big. Especially if you use the indented format, try a 0.8 inch left margin. Set tab settings at 0.3 inch rather than the standard 0.5 inch. Try rules (thin lines) or borders to see if you like their look.

Avoid Templates.

Some services fit every résumé into a single template. Even if you have lots of volunteer work, you have to fit it all into an inch-high space. But if you have no volunteer work, you still have that inch—glaringly empty. Using a standard template defeats the purpose of a good résumé: to make you look as good as possible.

If a placement service requires you to use a template, do so, but also create another résumé that looks good. Take a copy to each interview. Tell the interviewer, "I thought you might like to know a little more about me."

Proofread.

Employers assume that the résumé represents your best work. Proofread carefully to be sure the document is perfect. Especially check

- Spelling of your college, your employers, and your references.
- Parallelism (◀ ▶ p. 86).
- Consistency (spell out all state names or use Postal Service abbreviations for all).
- Dates.
- Phone numbers, e-mail addresses, and URLs.

Alternatively, your résumé may be electronically scanned into a job-applicant tracking system. Then the first set of cuts will be done by computer. The employer specifies the keywords from the job description, listing the knowledge, skills, and abilities that the ideal applicant would have. Sometimes personal characteristics (e.g., *hard worker, good writer, willing to travel*) may also be included. The employer receives the résumés that match the keywords, arranged with the most "hits" first. Then the employer decides who will be invited for interviews.

You need to have both a paper résumé that will look good to the human eye and a scannable résumé that will serve you well in a job-applicant tracking system. To increase the chances that a real human being will pay attention to your résumé,

- Do more than just list what you've done. Show how it helped the organization. If possible, quantify: *increased sales 10%, saved the company $13,000, supervised five people.*
- Emphasize achievements that
  - Are most relevant to the position for which you're applying.
  - Show your superiority to other applicants.
  - Are recent.
- Use the jargon and buzzwords of the industry and the organization.

- Include skills that are helpful in almost every job: ability to use computer programs, to write and speak well, to identify and solve problems, to work with others, to speak a second language.
- Design one résumé to appeal to the human eye and the second to be easily processed by an electronic scanner.
- Consider using a career objective with the employer's name.

These guidelines mean that you may need to produce several different résumés. But the more you adapt your résumé to a specific employer, the more likely it is that you will get a job with that employer.

What kind of résumé should I use?

Choose the kind that makes you look best.

Two basic kinds of résumés exist: chronological and skills. Figures 27.2 and 27.3 show chronological and skills résumés for the same candidate. A **chronological résumé** summarizes what you did in a timeline (starting with the most recent events and going backward in **reverse chronology**). It emphasizes degrees, job titles, and dates. It is the traditional résumé format. Figure 27.4 shows another chronological résumé. Use a chronological résumé when your education and experience show

- A logical preparation for the position for which you're applying.
- A steady progression leading to the present.

A **skills résumé** emphasizes the skills you've used, rather than the job in which or the date when you used them. Figures 27.3, 27.5, and 27.7 show skills résumés. Use a skills résumé when

- Your education and experience are not the usual route to the position for which you're applying.
- You're changing fields.
- You want to combine experience from paid jobs, activities or volunteer work, and courses to show the extent of your experience in administration, finance, speaking, etc.
- Your recent work history may create the wrong impression (e.g., it has gaps, shows a demotion, shows job-hopping, etc.).

Both kinds of résumés omit *I* and use sentence fragments punctuated as complete sentences. Complete sentences are acceptable if they are the briefest way to present information. *Me* and *my* are acceptable if they are unavoidable or if using them reduces wordiness. Both kinds of résumés can use bullet points. Both use details.

How do the two résumés differ?

They handle Experience, Activities, and Volunteer Work differently.

A chronological résumé, like the one in Figure 27.4, uses separate categories for Experience, Activities, and Volunteer Work. Experience is organized by

FYI

Résumé is a French word meaning *summary*. To create the é (e with an acute accent), pull down the "Insert" menu to "Symbol." Never use the apostrophe to replace the accent. However, it is acceptable to type *resume* without the accent marks.

Figure 27.2
A Community College Student's Chronological Résumé

The top margin should be $\frac{3}{4}''$ to $1\frac{1}{2}''$.

Chronological résumés emphasize degrees, dates, and job titles.

Richard A. Douglass *14-point type*

8933 Arbor Village Drive
Columbus, OH 43214 *10-point*
614-555-6437

Construction Education *Education is normally the first category when you're earning a degree.*

1"

Keep side margins fairly small — no more than 1" — to visually fill the page.

Associate of Science Degree in Construction Management, December 2004, Columbus State Community College (Columbus, OH). Certificate in Residential Construction Management.

Construction and Construction Management Experience *12-point*

Start with the most recent job and go backward.

Construction Management Intern, Ryland Homes, Columbus, OH, Summer 2003.
- Calculated material, labor, and equipment needed for projects.
- Analyzed costs and productivity. *11-point*
- Monitored safety and quality assurance

Use past tense for jobs that are over. *Omit "I"; use fragments*

Lead Carpenter, Austen Design & Construction, Columbus, OH 2000-02. Began working with Austen as a subcontractor; hired after 3 months as a subcontractor. Projects ranged from 300 sq. ft. additions and remodeling to 6,000 sq. ft. additions and remodeling. As lead carpenter,

Change the default tab settings.

- Trained 4 employees to run all aspects of remodeling.
- Supervised all aspects of residential foundation, exterior siding and trim, and all interiors.
- Designed and built custom interior trims.

Use details whenever they help you. Numbers are usually good.

Carpenter, Shook's General Services, Columbus, OH, 1999-2000. Built a house in Mansfield, OH.

Use white space to create good visual impact.

Subcontractor to Certified Testing and Plumbing, Cupertino, CA, 1997-99. Tested water systems and installed backflow valves, relief pressure valves, and fire sprinkler systems for industrial clients, including Lockheed, Apple Computer, and San Jose State University.

Carpenter, Brown and Brown, Columbus, OH, 1996-97. Traveled throughout Ohio, Indiana, New York, and Pennsylvania supervising and building Friendly Ice Cream buildings.

Don't repeat hundred when century is the same.

Carpenter, Clausen Builders, Columbus, OH, 1994-05.
- Built the first geothermal house in the Columbus area.

References

If you list references, include at least three. Include at least one employer and one instructor.

Robert Fosnough, Vice President, Ryland Homes, Columbus, OH
robert_fosnough@ryland.com   614-555-0030
Tom Sotak, Department of Construction Sciences, Columbus State Community College, Columbus, OH sotakcon@hotmail.com   614-555-3298
Diana Grogan, Owner, Austen Design & Construction, Columbus, OH
diana@austendesign.com   614-555-7045

Give e-mail addresses and phone numbers so employers can contact your references.

The bottom margin should be $\frac{3}{4}''$ to $1\frac{1}{4}''$.

Figure 27.3
A Community College Student's Skills Résumé

Skills résumés emphasize skills, knowledge, and abilities. Combine experiences from classes, jobs, and volunteer work.

Richard A. Douglass

8933 Arbor Village Drive
Columbus, OH 43214
614-555-6437

Rick listed his cell phone number because that number was the best way to reach him.

Skills in Construction Management

Omit "I."

Here, he combines skills he's learned in class projects and on the job.

Make items in list parallel.

- Analyze and interpret all types of construction drawings and documents.
- Calculate material, labor, and equipment needed for a project.
- Use Gantt bar charts to organize complex construction projects.
- Analyze costs and productivity.
- Monitor safety and quality assurance.

Details and numbers would make this section stronger.

Experience with Construction Supplies and Equipment

Use bold and white space to emphasize points.

- **Sheet Goods.** Well-versed in materials for walls and siding, tile backing, and flooring–ceramic, vinyl, linoleum, hardwood floors.

- **Paint.** Extensive experience with paints, stains, varnishes, lacquers for interior and exterior surfaces, residential and commercial building. Experience with wallpaper and textures; limited experience with faux finishes.

- **Interior Trim.** Experience with all kinds of interior trim, specializing in window design, crown moldings, and fine interior trim.

- **Concrete.** Trouble-shooting residential and commercial problems; improving drainage.

- **Plumbing Supplies.** Thorough experience with backflow valves, pressure relief valves, and fire sprinkler systems.

- **Excavation.** Extensive experience in precision excavating using backhoe and tractors for residential and industrial remodeling and construction.

Construction Work Experience

Nine years of experience as a lead carpenter, crew foreman, and subcontractor. Notable projects include:

Good details

- Remodeling projects from 300 to 6,000 sq. ft.
- Building Friendly Ice Cream stores in Ohio, Indiana, New York, and Pennsylvania
- Testing water systems and installing backflow valves, relief pressure valves, and fire sprinkler systems for industrial clients including Lockheed, Apple Computer, and San Jose State University
- Building the first geothermal house in the Columbus area

Skills résumés are often longer than chronological résumés. To keep the résumé to one page, Rick omits Work History and References.

Construction Education

Associate of Science Degree in Construction Management, December, 2004, Columbus State Community College (Columbus, OH). Certificate in Residential Construction Management.

Figure 27.4
A Chronological Résumé for a Graduate Entering the Job Market

Jerry A. Jackson

Vary font sizes. The name is in 18-point, the main heading in 12-point, and the text in 11-point type.

Campus Address
1636½ Highland Street
Philadelphia, PA 19340
(215) 555-5718
jjackson@ccp.cc.pa.us
hotmail.com/jackson.2495/home.htm

When you have two addresses, set them side by side to balance the page.

Permanent Address
48 East Mulberry
Huntington, NY 11746
(516) 555-7793

If you have a professional Web page, include its URL.

Summary of Qualifications

List 3-7 qualifications. Use keywords.

- **High energy.** Played sports during two years of college. Started two businesses.
- **Sales experience.** Sold both clothing and investments successfully.
- **Presentation skills.** In individual and group presentations, spoke to groups ranging from 2 to 75 people. Gave informative, persuasive, and inspirational talks.
- **Financial emperience.** Knowledgeable about stocks and bonds, especially energy and telecommunication companies.
- **Computer experience.** Microsoft Word, Excel, SPSS, PowerPoint, and Dreamweaver. Experience creating Web pages.

Quantify when possible.

Specify computer programs you have used.

Education

A.A.S. in Finance, May 2005, Community College of Philadelphia, Philadelphia, PA
"B" Average

Sports Experience

CAAD (Colonial Athletes Against Drugs)
Intramural Volleyball Team (Division Champions, Winter 2004)
Two-year Varsity Letterman, Community College of Philadelphia, Philadelphia, PA
Men's NCAA Division II Basketball

(The team did poorly, so he omits its ranking.)

Experience

Use present tense for work you do now.

Financial Sales Representative, Primerica Company, Philadelphia, PA, February 2004-present.
- Work with clients to plan investment strategies to meet family and retirement goals.
- Research and recommend specific investments.

Entrepreneur, Huntington, NY, and Philadelphia, PA, September 2003-January 2004.
- Created a saleable product, secured financial backing, found a manufacturer, supervised production, and sold product—12 dozen T-shirts at $5.25 each—to help pay for college.

Use past tense for jobs that are over.

Ways to handle self-employment

Landscape Maintenance Supervisor, Huntington, NY, Summers 1995-2003.
- Formed a company to cut lawns, put up fences, fertilize, garden, and paint houses.
- Hired, fired, trained, motivated, and paid friends to complete jobs.

Specify large sums of money.

Collector and Repair Worker, ACN, Inc., Huntington, NY, Summers 1995-2001.
- Collected and counted up to $10,000 a day in New York metro area.
- Worked with technicians troubleshooting and repairing electronic and coin mechanisms of video and pinball games, cigarette machines, and jukeboxes.

Figure 27.5

A Skills Résumé for a Graduate Entering the Job Market

A border creates visual variety.

Permanent and campus addresses help readers to locate you.

Allyson Karnes

195 W. Ninth Street
Columbus, OH 43210
(614) 555-3498
karnes.173@osu.edu

6782 Fenwick Drive
Solon, OH 44121
(216) 555-6182

She varies the usual "Summary of Qualifications" to make it specific to the job. This really is Allyson's philosophy— and it's one an agency will appreciate.

Qualifications for Writing Creative Ads That Make People Remember the Product

➢ Created headlines and print ads for a variety of audiences.
➢ Persuaded team members, business owners, and lawyers to accept my ideas.
➢ Self-starter who sees a project through from start to finish.

Education

Skills résumé allows her to combine experience from classes and life.

B.A. in Advertising, June 2005, The Ohio State University, Columbus, OH
   Core courses: Copywriting, promotional strategies, magazine writing, graphics, media planning
   Harvard University Writing Program, Summer 2002, Boston, MA

Experience Creating Ads

Led the team that developed the winning promotional strategy for Max & Erma's Restaurants.
   ➢ Developed idea for theme for a year's campaign of ads.
   ➢ Wrote copy for radio spots, magazine ads, and billboards. One billboard ad had the headline "Multiple Choice" and boxes for burgers, chicken, and salads--with all the boxes checked.
   ➢ Presented creative strategy to Max & Erma's CEO and the Head of Advertising.
   ➢ Strategy won first place from among 17 proposals.

Details, wording demonstrate her ability.

Wrote more than 15 ads for Copywriting class, including
   ➢ Ad for cordless phone: "Isn't It Time to Cut the Cord?"
   ➢ Slogan for Ohio University's Springfest Jamboree: "In Short, It Jams"
   ➢ Billboard for Columbus Boys' School: "Who Said It's Lonely at the Top?"

Allyson chooses unusual bullets rather than the standard dots or squares. In a résumé for an ad agency, the bullets work.

Created ads and revised menu for The Locker Room (restaurant).

Other Writing Experience

Wrote "Commuter Flights" (humor).
Created more than 30 magazine articles as part of courses at Harvard University and Ohio State.
Researched and wrote legal briefs as part of course at Harvard.
Summarized research on $7 million medical malpractice case for Garson and Associates.

Employment History

2002-05   Child care and house management, Worthington, OH. Part-time daily during school year.

Summer   Maid, Harvard Student Agency, Boston, MA. Part-time while attending Harvard
2002   University Writing Program.

Summers   Law Clerk, Garson and Associates, Cleveland, OH. Did independent case research
1998-2001   used by the firm to win $7 million malpractice out-of-court settlement for the client.

Reverse chronology

Portfolio Available on Request *A position of emphasis*

jobs, with the most recent job first. A skills résumé, like the ones in Figures 27.3, 27.5, and 27.7, replaces these three categories with headings of the skills needed for the job for which the job hunter is applying. Within each skill, items are listed in order of importance, combining paid and unpaid work (in classes, activities, and community groups). An Employment History section lists job titles, employers, city, state (no ZIP code), and dates.

Chronological Résumés

In a chronological résumé, include the following information for each job: position or job title, organization, city and state (no ZIP code), dates of employment, and other details, such as full- or part-time status, job duties, special responsibilities or the fact that you started at an entry-level position and were promoted. Include unpaid jobs and self-employment if they provided relevant skills (e.g., supervising people, budgeting, planning, persuading).

Normally, go back as far as the summer after high school. Include earlier jobs if you started working someplace before graduating from high school but continued working there after graduation. However, give minimal detail about high school jobs. If you worked full-time after high school, make that clear.

If as an undergraduate you've earned a substantial portion of your college expenses, say so in a separate sentence either under Experience or in the section on personal data. (Graduate students are expected to support themselves.)

These jobs paid 40% of my college expenses.

Paid for 65% of expenses with jobs, scholarships, and loans.

Use minimal detail about low-level jobs, perhaps not even listing each job separately.

| 1998–2003 | Full-time homemaker. |

| 2001–04 | Various construction jobs to support family. |

Use details when they help you. Tell how many people you trained or supervised, how much money you budgeted or raised. Describe the aspects of the job you did.

Too vague: Sales Manager, *The Daily Collegian*, University Park, PA, 2004–06. Supervised staff; promoted ad sales.

Good details: Sales Manager, *The Daily Collegian*, University Park, PA, 2004–06. Supervised 22-member sales staff; helped recruit, interview, and select staff; assigned duties and scheduled work; recommended best performer for promotion. Motivated staff to increase paid ad inches 10% over previous year's sales.

Instant **Replay**

Chronological Résumés

A **chronological résumé** summarizes what you did in a timeline (starting with the most recent events, and going backward in **reverse chronology**). Use a chronological résumé when your education and experience

- Are a logical preparation for the position for which you're applying.
- Show a steady progression leading to the present.

Verbs or gerunds (the *-ing* form of verbs) create a more dynamic image of you than do nouns, so use them on résumés that will be read by people. (Rules for scannable résumés to be read by computers come later in this module.) In the revisions below, nouns, verbs, and gerunds are in bold type.

Nouns: Chair, Income Tax Assistance Committee, Winnipeg, MB, 2003–04. Responsibilities: **recruitment** of volunteers; flyer **design, writing,** and **distribution** for **promotion** of program; **speeches** to various community groups and nursing homes to advertise the service.

Verbs: Chair, Income Tax Assistance Committee, Winnipeg, MB, 2003–04. **Recruited** volunteers for the program. **Designed, wrote,** and **distributed** a flyer to promote the program; **spoke** to various community groups and nursing homes to advertise the service.

Gerunds: Chair, Income Tax Assistance Committee, Winnipeg, MB, 2003–04. Responsibilities included **recruiting** volunteers for the program; **designing, writing,** and **distributing** a flyer to promote the program; and **speaking** to various community groups and nursing homes to advertise the service.

Note that the items in the list must be in parallel structure (◄ ▷ p. 86). Figure 27.6 lists action verbs that work well in résumés.

Skills Résumés

Skills résumés use as headings the *skills* used in or the *aspects* of the job you are applying for, rather than the title or the dates of the jobs you've held (as in a chronological résumé). For entries under each skill, combine experience from paid jobs, unpaid work, classes, activities, and community service.

Use headings that reflect the jargon of the job for which you're applying: *logistics* rather than *planning* for a technical job; *procurement* rather than

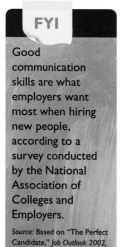

Figure 27.6
Action Verbs for Résumés

analyzed	directed	led	reviewed
budgeted	earned	managed	revised
built	edited	motivated	saved
chaired	established	negotiated	scheduled
coached	examined	observed	simplified
collected	evaluated	organized	sold
conducted	helped	persuaded	solved
coordinated	hired	planned	spoke
counseled	improved	presented	started
created	increased	produced	supervised
demonstrated	interviewed	recruited	trained
designed	introduced	reported	translated
developed	investigated	researched	wrote

Good résumés provide accurate details about what you've done, rather than exaggerate.

purchasing for a civilian job with the military. Figure 27.7 shows a skills résumé for someone who is changing fields. Marcella suggests that she already knows a lot about the field she hopes to enter by using its jargon for the headings.

You need at least three headings related to the job in a skills résumé; six or seven is not uncommon. Give enough detail so the reader will know what you did. Put the most important category from the reader's point of view first.

A job description can give you ideas for headings. Possible headings and subheadings for skills résumés include

Administration	Communication
Alternates or subheadings:	Alternates or subheadings:
Coordinating	Conducting Meetings
Evaluating	Editing
Implementing	Fund-Raising
Negotiating	Interviewing
Planning	Speaking
Keeping Records	Negotiating
Scheduling	Persuading
Solving Problems	Proposal Writing
Budgeting	Report Writing
Supervising	

Instant Replay

Skills Résumés
Use a skills résumé when

- Your education and experience are not the usual route to the position.
- You're changing fields.
- You want to combine experience from paid jobs, activities and volunteer work, and courses.
- Your recent work history may create the wrong impression.

Many jobs require a mix of skills. Include the skills that you know will be needed in the job you want.

In a skills résumé, list your paid jobs under Employment History near the end of the résumé (see Figures 27.5 and 27.7). List only job title, employer, city, state, and dates. Omit details about what you did, since you will have already used them under Experience.

Figure 27.7
A Skills Résumé for Someone Changing Job Fields

On the first page of a skills résumé, put skills directly related to the job for which you're applying.

Marcella G. Cope

370 Monahan Lane
Dublin, OH 43016
614-555-1997
mcope@postbox.acs.ohio-state.edu

Include area code for phone numbers and your complete e-mail address.

Objective

Put company's name in objective.

To help create high quality CD-ROM products in Metatec's New Media Solutions Division

Editing and Proofreading Experience

An extra half space creates good visual impact.

- **Edited** a textbook published by Simon and Schuster, revising with attention to format, consistency, coherence, document integrity, and document design.
- **Proofed** training and instructor's manuals, policy statements, student essays and research papers, internal documents, and promotional materials.
- **Worked with authors** in a variety of fields including English, communication, business, marketing, economics, education, history, sociology, biology, agriculture, computer science, law, and medicine to revise their prose and improve their writing skills by giving them oral and written feedback.

Writing Experience

Use bullets and bold type to add impact.

- **Wrote** training and instructor's manuals, professional papers, and letters, memos, and reports.
- **Co-authored** the foreword to a forthcoming textbook (Fall 2005) from NCTE press.
- **Contributed** to a textbook forthcoming (Fall 2005) from Bedford Books/St. Martin's press.

Computer Experience

- **Designed** a Web page using Dreamweaver (www.cohums.ohio-state.edu/english/People/Bracken.1/Sedgwick/)
- **Learned and used** a variety of programs on both Macintosh and PC platforms:
  Word Processing and Spreadsheets   Dreamweaver
  Microsoft Project   PageMaker
  E-Mail   PowerPoint
  Aspects (a form for online synchronous discussion)
  Storyspace (a hypertext writing environment)

Computer experience is crucial for almost every job. Specify the hardware and software you've worked with.

Other Business and Management Experience

- **Developed** policies, procedures, and vision statements.
- **Supervised** new staff members in a mentoring program.
- **Coordinated** program and individual schedules, planned work and estimated costs, set goals, and evaluated progress and results.
- **Member of team that directed** the nation's largest first-year writing program.

Figure 27.7

A Skills Résumé for Someone Changing Job Fields *(continued)*

Marcella G. Cope

Page 2

If you use two pages be sure to put your name and "Page 2" on the second page. The reader may remove a staple.

Employment History

Most recent job first.

Graduate Teaching Associate, Department of English, The Ohio State University, September 2000-Present. Taught Intermediate and First-Year Composition.

Writing Consultant, University Writing Center, The Ohio State University, January-April 2003

Program Administrator, First-Year Writing Program, The Ohio State University, September 2001-January 2003

Honors

Explain honor societies that the reader may not know.

Phi Kappa Phi Honor Society, inducted 2001. Membership based upon performance in top ten percent of graduate students nationwide.

Letters of Commendation, 2000-03. Issued by the Director of Graduate Studies in recognition of outstanding achievement.

Dean's List, Northwestern University, Evanston, IL

Education

Master of Arts, June 2002, The Ohio State University, Columbus, OH.
  Cumulative GPA: 4.0/4.0

Bachelor of Arts, June 2000, Northwestern University, Evanston, IL.
  Graduated with Honors.

References

Kitty O. Locker
Associate Professor, and Coordinator, Program in Professional Writing
The Ohio State University
421 Denney Hall, 164 W. 17th Ave.
Columbus, OH 43210
614-555-6556
locker.1@osu.edu

Marilyn Duffey
Director, Ohio University Writing Program
Ohio University
140 Chubb Hall
Athens, OH 45701
614-555-9443
duffeymc@ohiou.edu

Choose references who can speak about your skills for the job for which you're applying.

James Bracken
Associate Professor, English and Library Science
The Ohio State University
224 Main Library, 1858 Neil Avenue Mall
Columbus, OH 43210
614-555-2786
bracken@osu.edu

What parts of the two résumés are the same?

Career Objective, Summary of Qualifications, Education, Honors, and References.

Every résumé should have a Summary of Qualifications and an Education section. Career Objective, Honors, and References are optional.

Career Objective

Career Objective statements should sound like the job descriptions an employer might use in a job listing. Keep your statement brief—two or three lines at most. Tell what you want to do, what level of responsibility you want to hold.

Ineffective career objective: To offer a company my excellent academic foundation in hospital technology and my outstanding skills in oral and written communication.

Better career objective: Selling state-of-the-art Siemens medical equipment.

Including the employer's name in the objective is a nice touch.

Often you can avoid writing a Career Objective statement by putting the job title or field under your name.

Joan Larson Ooyen	Terence Edward Garvey	David R. Lunde
Marketing	Technical Writer	Corporate Fitness Director

Note that you can use the field you're in even if you're a new graduate. To use a job title, you should have some relevant work experience.

Summary of Qualifications

A section summarizing the candidate's qualifications seems to have first appeared in scannable résumés, where its keywords helped to increase the number of matches a résumé produced. But the section proved useful for human readers as well and now is a standard part of most résumés. The best summaries show your knowledge of the specialized terminology of your field and offer specific, quantifable achievements.

Weak: Reliable

Better: Achieved zero sick days in four years with UPS.

Weak: Staff accountant

Better: Experience with Accounts Payable, Accounts Receivable, Audits, and Month-End Closings. Prepared monthly financial reports.

Figure 27.8

Keywords for Sample Jobs

Accountant	Hotel Manager	Human Resources Generalist	Marketing Director
Accounts payable	Hospitality management	EEO regulations	Strategic planning skills
Accounts receivable	Banquet sales	ADA	Market research
Audits	Marketing	Applicant screening	New product transition
G/L	Guest relations	Applicant tracking	Trade show management
Microsoft Excel	Employee training	401(K)	Competitive market analysis
Financial reports	Front office management	Merit pay program	Team skills
SEC filings	Occupancy rate	Training and development	Multiple priorities
Budget analysis	Guest services	Compensation	Direct marketing campaigns
Gross margin analysis	Convention management	Recruitment	Business models
Month-end closings	Reservations	Diversity	Marketing business plans

Source: Rebecca Smith, *Electronic Résumés & Online Networking: How to Use the Internet to Do a Better Job Search, Including a Complete, Up-to-Date Resource Guide* (Franklin Lakes, NJ: Career Press, 1999), 192–94.

Weak: Presentation Skills

Better: Gave 20 individual and 7 team presentations to groups ranging from 5 to 100 people.

Your real accomplishments should go in the Summary section. Include as many keywords as you legitimately can. Terms suggested by Rebecca Smith appear in Figure 27.8; see her Web site for even more.

Education

Education can be your first major category if you've just earned (or are about to earn) a degree, if you have a degree that is essential or desirable for the position you're seeking, or if you can present the information briefly. Put Education later if you need all of page 1 for another category or if you lack a degree that other applicants may have.

Include summer school if you took courses to fit in extra electives or to graduate early but not if you were making up a course you flunked during the year. Include study abroad, even if you didn't earn college credits. If you got a certificate for international study, give the name and explain the significance of the certificate.

Highlight proficiency in foreign or computer languages by using a separate category.

Professional certifications can be listed under Education, under or after your name, or in a separate category.

Include your GPA only if it's good. Because grade point systems vary, specify what your GPA is based on: "3.4/4.0" means 3.4 on a 4.0 scale. If your GPA is under 3.0 on a 4.0 scale, use words rather than numbers: "B− average." If your GPA isn't impressive, calculate your average in your major and your average for your last 60 hours. If these are higher than your overall GPA, consider using them.

Site *to* See

Go to
www.eresumes.com

Rebecca Smith's eResumes & Resources provides extensive examples of keywords and Web résumés.

List in reverse chronological order (most recent first) each degree earned, field of study, date, school, city, state of any graduate work, short courses and professional certification courses, college, community college, or school from which you transferred.

B.S. in Personnel Management, June 2005, Georgia State University, Milledgeville, GA

A.S. in Office Management, June 2002, Georgia Community College, Atlanta, GA

To fill a page, you can also list selected courses, using short descriptive titles rather than course numbers. Use a subhead such as "Courses Related to Major" or "Courses Related to Financial Management" which will allow you to list all the courses (including psychology, speech, and business communication) that will help you in the job for which you're applying. Don't say "Relevant Courses," as that implies that all your other courses were irrelevant.

Bachelor of Science in Management, May 2006, Illinois State University, Normal, IL

GPA: 3.8/4.0

Courses Related to Management:

Personnel Administration	Business Decision-Making
Finance	International Business
Management I and II	Marketing
Accounting I and II	Legal Environment of Business
Business Report Writing	Business Speaking

Salutatorian, Niles Township East High School, June 2001, Niles, IL

A third option is to list the number of hours in various subjects, especially if the combination of courses qualifies you for the position for which you're applying.

B.S. in Marketing, May 2005, California State University at Northridge

30 hours in Marketing

15 hours in Spanish

 9 hours in Chicano/a Studies

Honors and Awards

It's nice to have the word Honors in a heading where it will be obvious even when the reader skims the résumé. If you have fewer than three and therefore cannot justify a separate heading, consider using the heading Activities and Honors to get that important word in a position of emphasis. Include the following kinds of entries in this category:

- Listings in recognition books (e.g., *Who's Who in the Southwest*).
- Academic honor societies. Specify the nature of Greek-letter honor societies so the reader doesn't think they're just social clubs.

- Fellowships and scholarships.
- Awards given by professional societies.
- Major awards given by civic groups.
- Varsity letters; selection to all-state or all-America teams; finishes in state, national, or Olympic meets. (These could also go under Activities but may look more impressive under Honors. Put them under one category or the other—not both.)

Omit honors such as "Miss Congeniality" which work against the professional image you want your résumé to create.

As a new graduate, try to put Honors on page 1. In a skills résumé, put Honors on page 1 if they're major (e.g., Phi Beta Kappa, Phi Kappa Phi). Save them till page 2 if Experience takes the whole first page.

References

Including references anticipates the employer's needs and removes a potential barrier to your getting the job. To make your résumé fit on one page, you can omit this category. However, include References if you're having trouble filling the page. Don't say "References Available on Request" since no job applicant is going to refuse to supply references. If you don't want your current employer to know you're job hunting, omit the category in the résumé and say in the letter, "If I become a finalist for the job, I will supply the names of current references."

When you list references, use three to five. Include at least one professor and at least one employer or advisor—someone who can comment on your work habits and leadership skills.

Always ask the person's permission to list him or her as a reference. Don't say, "May I list you as a reference?" Instead, say, "Can you speak specifically about my work?" Jog the person's mind by taking along copies of work you did for him or her and a copy of your current résumé. Tell the person what points you'd like him or her to stress in a letter. Keep your list of references up to date. If it's been a year or more since you asked someone, ask again—and tell the person about your recent achievements.

References the reader knows are by far the most impressive. In a skills résumé, choose references who can testify to your abilities in the most important skills areas.

What should I do if the standard categories don't fit?

Create new ones.

Create headings that match your qualifications: Computer Skills, Military Experience, Foreign Languages, Summer and Part-Time Jobs, Marketing Experience, Achievements Related to Career Objective.

Education and Experience (if you use the latter term) always stand as separate categories, even if you have only one item under each head. Combine other headings so that you have at least two long or three short items under each heading. For example, if you're in one honor society, two social clubs, and on one athletic team, combine them all under Activities and Honors.

FYI

Be honest and accurate. Many employers run a Google search on applicants to find information about them available on the Web. One man discovered that the search engine turned up messages he had posted four years earlier on an anti-Scientology Web site.

Source: Kris Maher, "The Jungle," *The Wall Street Journal,* July 16, 2002, B10.

Instant **Replay**

Summary of Qualifications

In the first section of your résumé, summarize your strengths. Use the specialized terminology of your field and offer specific, quantifiable achievements.

If you have more than seven items under a heading, consider using subheadings. For example, a student who had a great many activities might divide them into Student Government, Other Campus Activities, and Community Service.

Put your strongest categories near the top and at the bottom of the first page. If you have impressive work experience, you might want to put that category first after your name, put Education in the middle of the page, and put your address at the bottom.

Should I limit my résumé to just one page?

Not if you've got lots of qualifications.

A one-page résumé is sufficient, but do fill the page. The average résumé is now two pages, according to career-planning consultant Marilyn Moats Kennedy. An experiment that mailed one- or two-page résumés to CPA firms showed that even readers who said they preferred short résumés were more likely to want to interview the candidate with the longer résumé.[1]

If you do use more than one page, the second page should have at least 10 to 12 lines. Use a second sheet and staple it to the first so that readers who skim see the staple and know that there's more. Leave less important information for the second page. Put your name and "Page 2" or "Cont." on the second page. If the pages are separated, you want the reader to know who the qualifications belong to and that the second page is not your whole résumé.

How do I create a scannable résumé?

Take out all your formatting.

Site *to* See

Go to
www.eresumes.com/tut_
webrezpicks.html

Rebecca Smith posts examples of especially interesting Web résumés.

Figure 27.9 is an example of a scannable résumé.
To increase the chances that the résumé is scanned correctly,

- Use a standard typeface: Helvetica, Futura, Optima, Times Roman, New Century Schoolbook, Courier, Univers, or Bookman.[2]
- Use 12- or 14-point type.
- Use a ragged right margin rather than full justification. Scanners can't always handle the extra spaces between words and letters that full justification creates.
- Don't italicize or underline words—even for titles of books or newspapers that grammatically require such treatment.
- Put the text in bold to make sure letters don't touch each other. Then remove the bold.
- Don't use lines, boxes, script, leader dots, or borders.
- Don't use two-column formats or indented or centered text.
- Put each phone number on a separate line.
- Use plenty of white space.

Figure 27.9
A Scannable Résumé

Jerry A. Jackson

Use 12– or 14–point type in a standard typeface. Here, Times Roman is used.

Keywords: family financial management; investment sales; computer modeling; competitive; self-starter; hard worker; responsible; collegiate athletics; sales experience; willing to travel

In keywords, use labels and terms that employers might use in a job listing.

Campus Address
$1636\frac{1}{2}$ Highland Street
Philadelphia, PA
(215) 555-5718
E-mail address: jjackson@ccp.cc.pa.us
Created a Web page on saving for life goals, such as a home, children's education, and retirement: http://hotmail.com/jackson.2495/home.htm

Permanent Address
45 East Mulberry
Huntington, NY 11746
(516) 555-7793

Don't use columns. Scanners can't handle them.

Summary of Qualifications
High energy. Played sports during two years of college. Started two businesses.
Sales experience. Sold both clothing and investments successfully.
Presentation skills. In individual and group presentations, spoke to groups ranging from 2 to 75 people. Gave informative, persuasive, and inspirational talks.
Financial experience. Knowledgeable about stocks and bonds, especially energy and telecommunication companies.
Computer experience. Microsoft Word, Excel, SPSS, PowerPoint, and Dreamweaver.
Experience creating Web pages.

Education
A.A.S. in Finance, May 2005, Community College of Philadelphia, Philadelphia, PA
"B" Grade Point Average
Comprehensive courses related to major provide not only the basics of family financial management but also skills in communication, writing, speaking, small groups, and computer modeling
Accounting I and II
Business and Professional Writing
Computer Programming
Finance
Economics I and II
Family Resource Management
Family and Human Development Statistics
Public Speaking
Interpersonal Communication

Give as much information as you like. The computer doesn't care how long the document is.

Figure 27.9

A Scannable Résumé *(continued)*

Sports Experience
CAAD (Colonial Athletes Against Drugs)
Intramural Volleyball Team (Division Champions, Winter 2004)
Two-year Varsity Letterman, Community College of Philadelphia, Philadelphia, PA
Men's NCAA Division II Basketball

Don't just justify margins. Doing so creates extra spaces that confuse scanners.

Omit bold and italics. Some scanners can handle bullets, but they aren't needed in a scannable résumé.

Experience
Financial Sales Representative, Primerica Company, Philadelphia, PA, February 2004-present.
Work with clients to plan investment strategies.
Research and recommend specific investments, including stocks, bonds, mutual funds, and annuities.

Entrepreneur, Huntington, NY and Philadelphia, PA, September 2003-January 2004
Created a saleable product, secured financial backing, found a manufacturer, supervised production, and sold product–12 dozen T-shirts at $5.25 profit each–to help pay for college expenses.

Landscape Maintenance Supervisor, Huntington, NY, Summers 1995-2003.
Formed a company to cut lawns, put up fences, fertilize, garden, and paint houses.
Hired, fired, trained, motivated, and paid friends to complete jobs.

Collector and Repair Worker, ACN, Inc., Huntington, NY, Summers 1995-2001.
Collected and counted up to $10,000 a day.
Worked with technicians troubleshooting and repairing electronic and coin mechanisms of video and pinball games, cigarette machines, and jukeboxes.

Willing to relocate
U.S. citizen

- Don't fold or staple the pages.
- Don't write anything by hand on your résumé.
- Send a laser copy. Stray marks defeat scanners.

To increase the number of matches or "hits,"

- Use a Keywords section under your name, address, and phone. In it, put not only degrees, job field or title, and accomplishments but also personality traits and attitude: *dependable, skill in time management, leadership, sense of responsibility.*[3]
- Use industry buzzwords and jargon, even if you're redundant. For example, "Web page design and HTML coding" will "match" either "Web" or "HTML" as a keyword.

- Use nouns. Some systems don't handle verbs well.
- Use common headings such as Summary of Qualifications, Strengths, Certifications, and so forth as well as Education, Experience, and so on.
- Use as many pages as necessary.
- Mention specific software programs (e.g, Lotus Notes) you've used.
- Be specific and quantifiable. "Managed $2 million building materials account" will generate more hits than "manager" or "managerial experience." Listing Microsoft Front Page as a skill won't help as much as "Used Microsoft Front Page to design an interactive Web page for a national fashion retailer, with links to information about style trends, current store promotions, employment opportunities, and an online video fashion show."
- Join honor societies and professional and trade organizations, since they're often used as keywords.[4] Spell out Greek letter societies (the scanner will mangle Greek characters, even if your computer has them): "Pi Sigma Alpha Honor Society." For English words, spell out the organization name; follow it with the abbreviation in parentheses: "College Newspaper Business and Advertising Managers Association (CNBAM)." That way, the résumé will be tagged whether the recruiter searches for the full name or the acronym.
- Put everything in the résumé, rather than "saving" some material for the cover letter. While some applicant tracking systems can search for keywords in cover letters and other application materials, most only extract information from the résumé, even though they store the other papers. The length of the résumé doesn't matter.

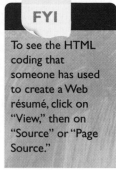

FYI

To see the HTML coding that someone has used to create a Web résumé, click on "View," then on "Source" or "Page Source."

Figure 27.10
Checklist for Résumés

√ ## Checklist for
Asking Readers Questions

Visual Impact

☐ Does the text visually fill the page?

☐ Is your name easy to read (large font, surrounded by white space)?

☐ Are the headings and text easy to skim (bold, rather than underlined or full caps; bullet points)?

Specific Supporting Details

☐ Does a Summary of Qualifications or Keywords highlight your skills and knowledge?

☐ Do recent, relevant, and substantive details show that you are qualified for the job?

☐ Do details interest the reader and set you apart from other applicants?

☐ Are details quantifiable when they help?

Style and Mechanics

☐ Are duties and accomplishments listed in parallel structure?

☐ Does the text omit the word *I*?

☐ Is the writing tight and forceful?

☐ Are jobs listed in reverse chronological order (starting with the most recent)?

☐ If there is a second page, does it contain your name and *Page 2*?

☐ Is the résumé free from typos and other errors?

Summary of Key Points

- A résumé must fill at least one page. Use two pages if you have extensive activities and experience.

- Emphasize information that is relevant to the job you want, is recent (last three years), and shows your superiority to other applicants.

- To emphasize key points, put them in headings, list them vertically, and provide details.

- Résumés use sentence fragments punctuated like complete sentences. Items in the résumé must be concise and parallel. Emphasize verbs and gerunds in a résumé that people will read.

- A **chronological résumé** summarizes what you did in a timeline (starting with the most recent events and going backward in **reverse chronology**). It emphasizes degrees, job titles, and dates. Use a chronological résumé when your education and experience

  - Are a logical preparation for the position for which you're applying.

  - Show a steady progression leading to the present.

- A **skills résumé** emphasizes the skills you've used, rather than the job in which or the date when you used them. Use a skills résumé when

  - Your education and experience are not the usual route to the position for which you're applying.

  - You're changing fields.

  - You want to combine experience from paid jobs, activities or volunteer work, and courses to show the extent of your experience in administration, finance, speaking, etc.

  - Your recent work history may create the wrong impression (e.g., it has gaps, shows a demotion, shows job-hopping, etc.).

- Résumés commonly contain the applicant's name, address, phone number, education, and experience. Activities, honors, and references should be included if possible.

- To fill the page, list courses or list references vertically.

- To create a scannable résumé, create a "plain vanilla" text using industry jargon, buzzwords, and acronyms.

Assignments for Module 27

Questions for Comprehension

27.1 How do you decide whether to use a chronological or a skills résumé?

27.2 In a chronological résumé, in what order do you list your experience?

27.3 Why should you think about dividing a section that has more than seven items?

Questions for Critical Thinking

27.4 Is it ethical to omit information that might hurt you, such as a low grade point average?

27.5 What are the arguments for and against listing references on your résumé?

27.6 Should someone who is having trouble creating a good résumé pay a résumé service to create a document for him or her?

27.7 Suppose that you know that people with your qualifications are in great demand. Is there any reason for you to take the time to write a strong résumé?

Exercises and Problems

27.8   Analyzing Your Accomplishments

List the 10 accomplishments that give you the most personal satisfaction.

These could be things that other people wouldn't notice. They can be things you've done recently or things you did years ago.

Answer the following question for each accomplishment:

1. What skills or knowledge did you use?

2. What personal traits did you exhibit?

3. What about this accomplishment makes it personally satisfying to you?

As Your Instructor Directs,

a. Share your answers with a small group of other students.

b. Summarize your answers in a memo to your instructor.

c. Present your answers orally to the class.

27.9   Remembering What You've Done

Use the following list to jog your memory about what you've done. For each, give three or four details as well as a general statement.

Describe a time when you

1. Used facts and figures to gain agreement on an important point.

2. Identified a problem faced by a group or organization and developed a plan for solving the problem.

3. Made a presentation or a speech to a group.

4. Responded to criticism.

5. Interested other people in something that was important to you and

persuaded them to take the actions you wanted.

6. Helped a group deal constructively with conflict.

7. Demonstrated creativity.

As Your Instructor Directs,

a. Identify which job(s) each detail is relevant for.

b. Identify which details would work well on a résumé.

c. Identify which details, further developed, would work well in a job letter.

27.10   Evaluating Career Objective Statements

None of the following career objective statements is effective. What is wrong with each statement as it stands? Which statements could be revised to be satisfactory? Which should be dropped?

1. To use my acquired knowledge of accounting to eventually own my own business.

2. A progressively responsible position as a MARKETING MANAGER where education and ability would

have valuable application and lead to advancement.

3. To work with people responsibly and creatively, helping them develop personal and professional skills.

4. A position in international marketing which makes use of my specialization in marketing and my knowledge of foreign markets.

5. To design and maintain Web pages.

27.11 Writing a Paper Résumé

Write a résumé on paper that you could mail to an employer or hand to an interviewer at an interview.

As Your Instructor Directs,
a. Write a résumé for the field in which you hope to find a job.

b. Write two different résumés for two different job paths you are interested in pursuing.
c. Adapt your résumé to a specific company you hope to work for.

27.12 Writing a Scannable Résumé

Take the résumé you like best from problem 27.11 and create a scannable version of it.

Polishing Your Prose

Proofreading

Wait until the final draft is complete to edit and proofread. There is no point in proofreading words and passages that might change. (Some writers claim to proofread documents while they're composing; this practice is like trying to mow the lawn and trim the hedges at the same time.)

Editing includes checking for you-attitude and positive emphasis, fixing any sexist or biased language, and correcting grammatical errors.

Proofreading means making sure that the document is free from typos. Check each of the following aspects.

Spelling. Scan for misspelled or misused words that spell checkers don't catch: *not* instead of *now, you* instead of *your, its* instead of *it's, their* instead of *there* or *they're, one* instead of *won,* and so forth.

Consistency. Check abbreviations and special terms.

Names. Double-check the reader's name.

Punctuation. Make sure that parentheses and quotation marks come in pairs. Be on the lookout for missing or extra commas and periods.

Format. Look for errors in spacing, margins, and document design, especially if you compose your document on one computer and print it out at another. Use the correct format for citations—MLA, APA, Chicago, etc.

Numbers and dates. Double-check all numbers to make sure they add up. Make sure page numbers appear where they should and are sequential. Do the same for tables of contents or appendixes. Check dates.

How to proofread is as individual as writing style. Try these methods or invent your own:

- **Read the document from last word to first word** to catch spelling errors.

- **Read the document in stages**—first page, second page, third page—with plenty of "rest" in between so you are fresh for each page.

- **Read pages out of sequence** so you can concentrate on the characters on the page rather than the meaning.

- **Read the document aloud,** listening for awkward or incorrect phrasing.

- **Ask a friend to read the document aloud,** voicing punctuation, while you follow along with the original.

Whatever your approach, build time into the composing process for proofreading. If possible, finish the document a day or two before it's due to allow enough time. (If the document is a 100-page report, allow even more time.) If you're in a hurry, use a spell checker, proof the document yourself, *and* ask a friend or colleague to proof it as well.

Exercises

Proofread the following passages.

1.

> **Resumee for Kathy Jones**
>
> 332 West Long Strt.
> Columbus, OHIO 43215
> (614–555–8188)
>
> **Objection**
> A management position in fullfilament services where my skills, expereince can be best be used to help your company acheeve it's goals.
>
> **Relevent Experience:**
> 2000 to Present Day: Ass. Manager for high-end sports equipment distributor. Responsible for checking new customers out.
>
> 1895–1999: Owned and Operated Jones, Inc., a telephone order procesing company for lady's apparel.
>
> 1997: Received a plague for Must Promising Executive of the Year" from *Columbus* Monthly Magazine.
>
> 1998: Delivery address to local high school seniors on why accuracy is important in business.
>
> **Special Skills**
> Type 7 or more words per minute
> Studied English all my life. Fluent in French.
> Shot at local gun club.

2.

> August 20, 2002
>
> W.W. Lyndhurst INC.
> 10002 Avenue of the Americas
> New York, NY 21211
>
> Mr. Frank Sugarman
> 12o1 North. 5th Stret.
> Detroit, MN
>
> Dear Mrs. Sugar:
>
> Thanx for you're recent enquiry regarding your order of July 17, 2003. AS you know, we at WW Lyndhurt, Ink, value your satisfaction. Rest assure that a replacement part is on it's way.
>
> Should you require anything else, please call me at 1-80-555-1209?
>
> Once again,
>
> Sincerely,
>
> Kevin corcoran

Check your answer to the odd-numbered exercise at the back of the book.

BComm Skill Booster

To apply the concepts in this module, complete lessons 47 and 70 on writing résumés and creating electronic résumés. You can access the BComm Skill Booster through the text Web site at **www.mhhe.com/bcs2e.**

Module 28

Job Application Letters

Start by asking these questions:

- What kind of letter should I use?
- How are the two letters different?
- What parts of the two letters are the same?
- How long should my letter be?
- How do I create the right tone?
- The company wants an e-mail application. What should I do?

The purpose of a job application letter is to get an interview. If you get a job through interviews arranged by a campus placement office or through contacts, you may not need to write a letter. However, if you want to work for an organization that isn't interviewing on campus, or later when you change jobs, you will. Writing a letter is also a good preparation for a job interview because the letter is your first step in showing a specific company what you can do for it.

In your letter, focus on

- Major requirements of the job for which you're applying.
- Points that separate you from other applicants.

- Points that show your knowledge of the organization.
- Qualities that every employer is likely to value: the ability to write and speak effectively, to solve problems, to get along with people.

Note that the advice in this book applies to job hunting in the United States. Conventions, expectations, and criteria differ from culture to culture: different norms apply in different countries. Even within the United States, different discourse communities (◀▶ p. 31) may have different preferences. For example, letters applying for sales jobs should be more aggressive than the examples in this module.

Every employer wants businesslike employees who understand professionalism. To make your application letter professional,

- Create your letter on a computer. Use a standard font (Times Roman, Palatino, Arial, or Helvetica) in 11- or 12-point type.
- Address your letter to a specific person. If the reader is a woman, call the office to find out what courtesy title (◀▶ p. 158) she prefers.
- Don't mention relatives' names. It's OK to use other names if the reader knows them and thinks well of them, if they think well of you and will say good things about you, and if you have permission to use their names.
- Omit personal information not related to the job.
- Unless you're applying for a creative job in advertising or Web design, use a conservative style: few contractions, no sentence fragments, clichés, or slang.
- Edit the letter carefully and proof it several times to make sure it's perfect.

Figure 28.1 lists the activities involved in crafting a strong letter.

> **FYI**
>
> One of the most common mistakes job applicants make, according to Director of Human Resources Director Brenda Melvin, is to fail to change the company name or title in the body of a letter when using a form letter for multiple companies.
>
> *Source:* Brenda Melvin, "The Little Thing Can Mean a Lot in a Tough Job Market," *Chicago Tribune,* July 31, 2002.

What kind of letter should I use?

It depends on whether the company has asked for applications.

Two different hiring situations call for two different kinds of application letters. Write a **solicited letter** when you know that the company is hiring: you've seen an ad, you've been advised to apply by a professor or friend, you've read in a trade publication that the company is expanding. Sometimes, however, the advertised positions may not be what you want, or you may want to work for an organization which has not announced that it has openings in your area. Then you write a **prospecting letter** (as in prospecting for gold.)

Prospecting letters help you tap into the hidden job market (◀▶ p. 519). In some cases, your prospecting letter may arrive at a company that has decided to hire but has not yet announced the job. In other cases, companies create positions to get a good person who is on the market. Even in a hiring freeze, jobs are sometimes created for specific individuals.

Figure 28.1
Allocating Time in Writing a Job Application Letter (Your time may vary.)

Letter responding to an announced job opening. Total time: 12 hours	
Planning	**6 hours**
Read ad carefully.	
Check Web for company facts and culture.	
Identify knowledge, skills, and abilities from the résumé that are particularly relevant to this company and this job.	
Answer the PAIBOC questions (◀ ▷ Module 1).	
Think about document design (◀ ▷ Module 5).	
Organize the message.	
Writing	**3 hours**
Draft the letter.	
Revising	**3 hours**
Re-read draft.	
Measure draft against PAIBOC questions, ad, and checklist for application letters (Figure 28.7).	
Revise draft.	
Ask for feedback on draft.	
Revise draft based on feedback.	
Edit document to catch grammatical errors.	
Run spell check.	
Proof by eye.	
Sign letter; put in envelope with résumé, and mail.	

How are the two letters different?

They begin and end differently.

When you know the company is hiring, organize your letter in this way:

1. State that you're applying for the job (phrase the job title as your source phrased it). Tell where you learned about the job (ad, referral, Web). Briefly show that you have the major qualifications required by the ad: a degree, professional certification, job experience, etc. Summarize your other qualifications briefly in the same order in which you plan to discuss them in the letter. This **summary sentence** or **paragraph** then covers everything you will talk about and serves as an organizing device for your letter.

I have a good background in standard accounting principles and procedures and a working knowledge of some of the special accounting practices of the oil industry. This working knowledge is based on practical experience in the oil fields: I've pumped, tailed rods, and worked as a roustabout.

Let me put my creative eye, artistic ability, and experience to work for McLean Design.

2. Develop your major qualifications in detail. Be specific about what you've done; relate your achievements to the work you'd be doing in this new job. This is not the place for modesty!
3. Develop your other qualifications, even if the ad doesn't ask for them. (If the ad asks for a lot of qualifications, pick the most important three or four.) Show what separates you from the other applicants who will also answer the ad. Demonstrate your knowledge of the organization.
4. Ask for an interview; tell when you'll be available to be interviewed and to begin work. End on a positive, forward-looking note.

Figure 28.2 presents this pattern of organization visually. Figure 28.4 is an example of a solicited letter.

When you don't have any evidence that the company is hiring, you cannot use the pattern for solicited letters. Instead, organize your letter this way:

1. Catch the reader's interest.
2. Create a **bridge** between the attention-getter and your qualifications. Focus on what you know and can do. Since the employer is not planning to hire, he or she won't be impressed with the fact that you're graduating. Summarize your qualifications briefly in the same order in which you plan to discuss them in the letter. This **summary sentence** or **paragraph** then covers everything you will talk about and serves as an organizing device for your letter.
3. Develop your strong points in detail. Be specific. Relate what you've done in the past to what you could do for this company. Show that you know something about the company. Identify the specific niche you want to fill.
4. Ask for an interview and tell when you'll be available for interviews. (Don't tell when you can begin work.) End on a positive, forward-looking note.

Figure 28.3 presents this pattern visually. Figure 28.5 shows a prospecting letter.

Figure 28.2

How to Organize a Solicited Job Letter

Request for Action
Details
Details
Request for Action

Figure 28.3

How to Organize a Prospecting Letter

Attention-Getter
Details
Details
Request for Action

Figure 28.4
A Solicited Letter

1636½ Highland Street
Philadelphia, PA 43201
March 7, 2005

Block format is a standard business format.

Mr. John A. Addison, President and co-CEO
Primerica
116 E. 8th Street
New York, NY 21101

Dear Mr. Addison:

In ¶ 1, show you have the major qualifications listed in the ad.

I am interested in the position of Regional Manager announced in the February 24 issue of *The New York Times*. I will receive an A.A.S. in Finance in May and already have a year's experience as a financial sales representative in Primerica's Philadelphia office.

Be specific about what you've done.

My program in Finance has given me the opportunity to focus on Family Financial Management. I have had the opportunity to take courses not only in investments but also in how families manage their resources and the financial stages that U.S. families typically go through. In one class, I had the opportunity to create an Excel spreadsheet to calculate how much a family needed to save to put two children through college, depending on the age of the children and the anticipated expense of college. Writing the spreadsheet gave me a "hands-on" feel for the need for investments over and above simply looking up figures on a chart.

Show how what you've done relates to what you could do in this job.

Financial selling is a highly competitive field. I am a competitor and have been all my life. While I was in high school, I created a business, hired a staff, and lined up clients. I know the value of training and hard work, and I look forward to the challenge of motivating Primerica's sales staff to do their best. In my landscape business, I delegated work and motivated my employees to do the high-quality jobs that my clients expected. My managerial experience running two businesses could help me become an efficient Regional Manager more quickly.

In the last year, as a financial sales representative for Primerica, I've used my persuasive and sales skills to help clients develop financial plans, choose the best investment products to fit their needs, personalities, and lifestyles, and even recruited two clients to become Primerica representatives themselves. I'd like to continue this record of success in your New York office.

Ask for an interview.

Could we set up an appointment to discuss this possibility? I'll be in New York March 23-27 and would welcome the opportunity to talk about ways that I could put my experience and drive to work for you.

End on a positive, forward-looking note.

Sincerely,

Jerry A. Jackson

Jerry A. Jackson

Encl.: Résumé

Figure 28.5
A Prospecting Letter from a Career Changer

Marcella G. Cope
370 Monahan Lane
Dublin, OH 43016
614-555-1997
mcope@postbox.acs.ohio-state.edu

Marcella creates a "letterhead" that harmonizes with her résumé (see Figure 27.7).

August 23, 2004

Mr. John Harrobin
New Media Solutions
Metatec Corporation
7001 Metatec Boulevard
Dublin, OH 43017

Block format with justified margins lets Marcella get this letter on one page.

Dear Mr. Harrobin:

In a prospecting letter, open with a sentence which
(1) will seem interesting and true to the reader and
(2) provides a natural bridge to talking about yourself.

One way to refer to the enclosed résumé.

Putting a textbook on a CD-ROM saves paper but does nothing to take advantage of the many possibilities the CD-ROM environment provides. Yet it can be a real challenge to find people who write well, proof carefully, and understand multimedia design. You will see from my enclosed résumé that I have this useful combination of skills.

Shows knowledge of the company.

Rita Haralabidis tells me that Metatec needs people to design and develop high-quality CD-ROM products to meet business and consumer deadlines. Most of the writing and editing that I do is subject to strict standards and even stricter deadlines, and I know information is useful only if it is available when clients need it.

Shows she can meet company needs.

When I toured Metatec this spring, members of the New Media Solutions Group shared some of their work from a series of interactive CD-ROM textbooks they were developing in tandem with Harcourt Brace. This project sparked my interest in Metatec because of my own experience with evaluating, contributing to, and editing college-level textbooks.

Relates what she's done to what she could do for this company.

As a program administrator at The Ohio State University, I examined dozens of textbooks from publishers interested in having their books adopted by the nation's largest First-Year Writing Program. This experience taught me which elements of a textbook--both content and design--were successful, and which failed to generate interest. Often, I worked closely with sales representatives to suggest changes for future editions. My own contributions to two nationally distributed textbooks further familiarized me with production processes and the needs of multiple audiences. My close contact with students convinces me of the need to produce educational materials that excite students, keep their attention, and allow them to learn through words, pictures, and sounds.

All of these terms fit Metatec's production of multimedia educational materials.

My communication and technology skills would enable me to adapt quickly to work with both individual clients and major corporations like CompuServe and The American Medical Association. I am a flexible thinker, a careful editor, a fluent writer, and, most importantly, a quick study. I will call you next week to find a mutually convenient time when we can discuss putting my talents to work for Metatec.

Names specific clients, showing more knowledge of the company.

Sincerely,

Marcella G. Cope

Marcella G. Cope

When you're changing fields, learning quickly is a real plus.

Enclosed: Résumé

The First Paragraph of a Solicited Letter

When you know that the firm is hiring, announcing that you are applying for a specific position enables the firm to route your letter to the appropriate person, thus speeding consideration of your application. Identify where you learned about the job: "the position of junior accountant announced in Sunday's *Dispatch*," "William Paquette, our placement director, told me that you are looking for . . . ."

Note how the following paragraph picks up several of the characteristics of the ad:

Ad: Business Education Instructor at Shelby Adult Education. Candidate must possess a bachelor's degree in Business Education. Will be responsible for providing in-house training to business and government leaders. . . . Candidate should have at least six months' office experience. Prior teaching experience not required.

Letter: I am interested in your position in Business Education. I will receive a Bachelor of Science degree from North Carolina A & T University in December. I have two years' experience teaching word processing and computer accounting courses to adults and have developed leadership skills in the North Carolina National Guard.

Good word choices can help set your letter apart from the scores or even hundreds of letters the company is likely to get in response to an ad. The following first paragraph of a letter in response to an ad by Allstate Insurance Company shows a knowledge of the firm's advertising slogan and sets itself apart from the dozens of letters that start with "I would like to apply for . . . ."

The Allstate Insurance Company is famous across the nation for its "Good Hands Policy." I would like to lend a helping hand to many Americans as a financial analyst for Allstate, as advertised in the *Chicago Tribune.* I have an Associate of Applied Science degree in Accounting from Harold Washington College and I have worked with figures, computers, and people.

Note that the last sentence forecasts the organization of the letter, preparing for paragraphs about the student's academic background and (in this order) experience with "figures, computers, and people."

First Paragraphs of Prospecting Letters

In a prospecting letter, asking for a job in the first paragraph is dangerous: unless the company plans to hire but has not yet announced openings, the reader is likely to throw the letter away. Instead, catch the reader's interest. Then in the second paragraph shift the focus to your skills and experience, showing how they can be useful to the employer.

Here are an effective first paragraph and the second paragraph of a letter applying to be a computer programmer for an insurance company:

Computers alone aren't the answer to demands for higher productivity in the competitive insurance business. Merging a poorly written letter with a database of customers just sends out bad letters more quickly. But you know how hard it is to find people who can both program computers and write well.

My education and training have given me this useful combination. I'd like to put my associate's degree in computer technology and my business experience writing to customers to work in State Farm's service approach to insurance.

Last Paragraphs

In the last paragraph, indicate when you'd be available for an interview. If you're free any time, say so. But it's likely that you have responsibilities in class and work. If you'd have to go out of town, there may be only certain days of the week or certain weeks that you could leave town for several days. Use a sentence that fits your situation.

I am available for interviews any Wednesday or Friday.

I could come to Memphis for an interview March 17–21.

Should you wait for the employer to call you, or should you call the employer to request an interview? In a solicited letter, it's safe to wait to be contacted: You know the employer wants to hire someone, and if your letter and résumé show that you're one of the top applicants, you'll get an interview. However, for sales jobs, say that you'll call the employer—and do it! In a prospecting letter, also call the employer. Because the employer is not planning to hire, you'll get a higher percentage of interviews if you're aggressive. Don't, however, be rude. No one owes you a response. And when you do call, be polite to the person who answers the phone.

If you're writing a prospecting letter to a firm that's more than a few hours away by car, say that you'll be in the area the week of such-and-such and could stop by for an interview. Companies pay for follow-up visits, but not for first interviews. A company may be reluctant to ask you to make an expensive trip when it isn't yet sure it wants to hire you.

End the letter on a positive note that suggests you look forward to the interview and that you see yourself as a person who has something to contribute, not as someone who just needs a job.

I will call you on Wednesday, April 25, to schedule a time when we can talk.

Instant Replay

How to Organize a Prospecting Letter

1. Catch the reader's interest.
2. Create a bridge between the attention-getter and your qualifications. Summarize your qualifications in the order in which you plan to discuss them in the letter.
3. Develop your strong points in detail. Relate what you've done in the past to what you could do for this company. Show that you know something about the company. Identify the specific niche you want to fill.
4. Ask for an interview. End on a positive, forward-looking note.

The best job applications give the employer a sample of what you can do. Freelance director Burke Wood shot commercials "on spec" to convince potential clients to hire him.

> I look forward to discussing with you ways in which I could contribute to The Limited's continued growth.

What parts of the two letters are the same?

The body paragraphs discussing your qualifications.

In both solicited and prospecting letters you should

- Address the letter to a specific person.
- Indicate the specific position for which you're applying.
- Be specific about your qualifications.
- Show what separates you from other applicants.
  - Show a knowledge of the company and the position.
  - Refer to your résumé (which you would enclose with the letter).
  - Ask for an interview.

**Go to
www.intel.com**

Many Web pages give you all the information you need to write a good job letter. Follow links to "about Intel" to learn about the company's values, work/family programs, and specific job listings. Both the home page and "pressroom" give information about recent achievements. "Investor relations" has financial information.

Showing a Knowledge of the Position and the Company

If you could substitute another inside address and salutation and send out the letter without any further changes, it isn't specific enough. Use your knowledge of the position and the company to choose relevant evidence from what you've done to support your claims that you could help the company. (See Figures 28.4 and 28.5.)

One or two specific details usually are enough to demonstrate your knowledge. Be sure to use the knowledge, not just repeat it. Never present the information as though it will be news to the reader. After all, the reader works for the company and presumably knows much more about it than you do.

Separating Yourself from Other Applicants

Your knowledge of the company separates you from other applicants. You can also use course work, an understanding of the field, and experience in jobs and extracurricular events to show that you're unique.

Targeting a Specific Company in Your Letter

If your combination of skills is in high demand, a one-size-fits-all letter may get you an interview. But when you must compete against dozens—perhaps hundreds or even thousands—of applicants for an interview slot, you need to target your letter to the specific company. Targeting a specific company also helps you prepare for the job interview.

The Web makes it easy to find information about a company. The example below shows how applicants could use information posted on the United Parcel Service (UPS) Web site on August 25, 2002.

Check for Facts about the Company.

Like most corporate Web sites, www.ups.com has dozens of facts about the company. A computer network administrator might talk about helping to keep the 228,200 PCs working well. A Web weaver could talk about supporting the 66.4 million hits a day that the site gets or about developing even more interactive content, like the Time-in-Transit calculator. Someone in accounting might talk about being able to convert currency from the euro, the pound, or the yen into dollars and back again. Someone in human resources could talk about processing benefits for the 330,000 U.S. employees, keeping the company in *Fortune's* 50 best companies for minorities or encouraging recruits to join what *Fortune* called "The World's Most Admired Company" in its industry.

Check News Releases and Speeches.

A February 11, 2002, release notes that customers in 34 countries now have wireless access to tracking information. A candidate knowledgeable about European languages and culture could talk about the use of cell phones worldwide (the percentage of owners in Finland is twice that of the United States). Several releases discuss UPS's Asian hubs. Anyone in international business could talk about helping UPS expand its Asian base even further in culturally sensitive ways.

In a February 20, 2002, speech, CEO Michael Eskew said that companies need to develop winning teams, create complete supply chain solutions, expand customer focus, streamline operations, and accelerate innovation. Students who have worked in teams, studied supply chains, served customers, improved operations, or demonstrated creativity could discuss their experience.

Check the Corporate Culture.

Under "Employment Opportunities," "Life at UPS" describes the company's facilities, benefits, and commitment to diversity and philanthropy. Reading about the active participation that UPS encourages may remind applicants to talk about their own work tutoring fifth graders or building houses for Habitat for Humanity, activities that demonstrate their fit with UPS. The use of the term *UPSers* for employees suggests another way to identify with the company: Use that term once in the letter to suggest how close one is to being an insider. The ad campaign for brown suggests other ways to adapt a letter to the company: Talk about the "brown" character traits you share or your desire to "bleed brown."

- This student uses summer jobs and course work to set herself apart from other applicants:

A company as diverse as Monsanto requires extensive recordkeeping as well as numerous internal and external communications. Both my summer jobs and my course work prepare me to do this. As Office Manager for the steamboat *Julia Belle Swain,* I was in charge of most of the bookkeeping and letter writing for the company. I kept accurate records for each workday, and I often entered over 100 transactions in a single day. In business and technical writing I learned how to write persuasive letters and memos and how to present extensive data in reports in a simplified style that is clear and easy to understand.

- This student uses her sorority experience and knowledge of the company to set herself apart from other applicants in a letter applying to be Assistant Personnel Manager of a multinational firm:

> As a counselor for sorority rush, I was also able to work behind the scenes as well as with the prospective rushees. I was able to use my leadership and communication skills for group activities for 70 young women by planning numerous activities to make my group a cohesive unit. Helping the women deal with rejection was also part of my job. Not all of the rushees made final cuts, and it was the rush counselor who helped put the rejection into perspective.
>
> This skill could be helpful in speaking to prospective employees wishing to travel to Saudi Arabia. Not all will pass the medical exams or make the visa application deadlines in time, and the Assistant Manager tells these people the news. An even more delicate subject to handle is conveying news of a death of a relative or employee to those concerned. My experience with helping people deal with small losses gives me a foundation to help others deal with more severe losses and deeper grief.

How long should my letter be?

Use a full page.

A short letter throws away an opportunity to be persuasive; it may also suggest that you have little to say for yourself or that you aren't very interested in the job.

Without eliminating content, tighten each sentence (◀ ▷ p. 324) to be sure that you're using space as efficiently as possible. If your letter is still a bit over a page, use slightly smaller margins, a type size that's one point smaller, or justified proportional type to get more on the page.

However, if you need more than a page, use it. The extra space gives you room to be more specific about what you've done and to add details about your experience that separate you from other applicants. Employers don't *want* longer letters, but they will read them *if* the letter is well written and *if* the applicant established early in the letter that he or she has the credentials the company needs.

How do I create the right tone?

Use you-attitude and positive emphasis.

You-attitude and positive emphasis help you sound assertive without being arrogant.

You-Attitude

Unsupported claims may sound overconfident, selfish, or arrogant. Create you-attitude (◄ ▶ p. 106) by describing exactly what you have done and by showing how that relates to what you could do for this employer.

Lacks you-attitude: An inventive and improvising individual like me is a necessity in your business.

You-attitude: Building a summer house-painting business gave me the opportunity to find creative solutions to challenges. At the end of the first summer, for example, I had nearly 10 gallons of exterior latex left, but no more jobs. I contacted the home economics teacher at my high school. She agreed to give course credit to students who were willing to give up two Saturdays to paint a house being renovated by Habitat for Humanity. I donated the paint and supervised the students. I got a charitable deduction for the paint and hired the three best students to work for me the following summer. I could put these skills in problem solving and supervising to work as a personnel manager for Burroughs.

Remember that the word *you* refers to your reader. Using *you* when you really mean yourself or "all people" can insult your reader by implying that he or she still has a lot to learn about business:

Since you're talking about yourself, you'll use *I* in your letter. Reduce the number of *I*'s by revising some sentences to use *me* or *my*.

> Under my presidency, the Agronomy Club . . .

> Courses in media and advertising management gave me a chance to . . .

> My responsibilities as a summer intern included . . .

In particular, avoid beginning every paragraph with *I*. Using prepositional phrases or introductory clauses will avoid beginning a sentence with *I*.

Positive Emphasis

Be positive. Don't plead ("Please give me a chance") or apologize ("I cannot promise that I am substantially different from the lot"). Most negatives should be omitted in the letter.

Avoid word choices with negative connotations (◄ ▶ p. 119). Note how the following revisions make the writer sound more confident.

FYI

Job titles include
- Top Dog: Allpets.com (pet portal)
- Cultural Czar (nurtures corporate culture): Homestead.com (tools for building Web sites)
- Product Evangelist: Adventa (Silicon Valley startup)
- Prince of Pine, Monarch of Mulch, Marquis of Machinery: International Paper

Source: "Job Titles of the Future," *Fast Company,* April 2000, 64, 76; "Talent from the Class of 2000," *Fortune,* May 29, 2000, 100; and "Job Titles of the Future," *Fast Company,* June 2000, 72.

When you job hunt, focus on positives. Show what you've learned and how your skills can meet the employer's needs.

Negative: I have learned an excessive amount about writing through courses in journalism and advertising.

Positive: Courses in journalism and advertising have taught me to recognize and to write good copy. My profile of a professor was published in the campus newspaper; I earned an "A" on my direct mail campaign for the American Dental Association to persuade young adults to see their dentist more often.

Excessive suggests that you think the courses covered too much—hardly an opinion likely to endear you to an employer.

The company wants an e-mail application. What should I do?

Compose a document in a word-processing program. Then paste it into your e-mail screen.

When you submit an e-mail letter (see Figure 28.6) with an attached résumé,

- Tell what word-processing program your scannable résumé is saved in.
- Put the job number or title for which you're applying in your subject line and in the first paragraph.
- Prepare your letter in a word-processing program with a spell checker to make it easier to edit and proof the document.
- Don't send anything in all capital letters.
- Don't use smiley faces or other emoticons.
- Put your name and e-mail address at the end of the message. Most e-mail programs put the "sender" information at the top of the screen, but a few don't, and you want the employer to know whose letter this is!

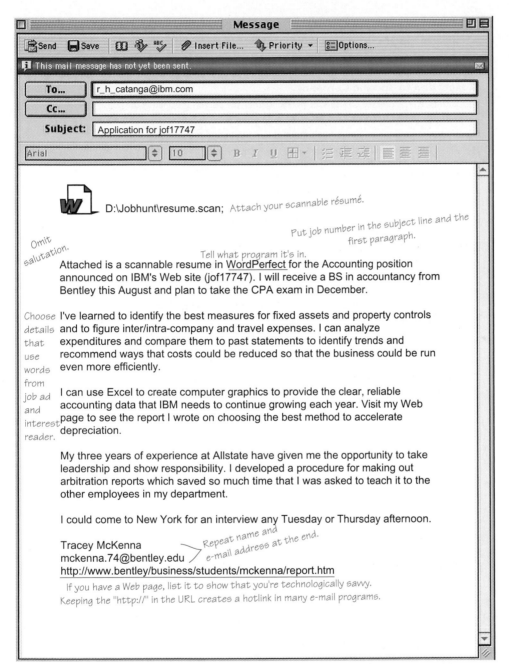

Figure 28.6
An E-Mail Application Letter

Message

Send   Save   Insert File...   Priority ▾   Options...

This mail message has not yet been sent.

To...   r_h_catanga@ibm.com

Cc...

Subject: Application for jof17747

Arial   10   B I U

D:\Jobhunt\resume.scan;   *Attach your scannable résumé.*

Put job number in the subject line and the first paragraph.

Omit salutation.

Tell what program it's in.

Attached is a scannable resume in WordPerfect for the Accounting position announced on IBM's Web site (jof17747). I will receive a BS in accountancy from Bentley this August and plan to take the CPA exam in December.

Choose details that use words from job ad and interest reader.

I've learned to identify the best measures for fixed assets and property controls and to figure inter/intra-company and travel expenses. I can analyze expenditures and compare them to past statements to identify trends and recommend ways that costs could be reduced so that the business could be run even more efficiently.

I can use Excel to create computer graphics to provide the clear, reliable accounting data that IBM needs to continue growing each year. Visit my Web page to see the report I wrote on choosing the best method to accelerate depreciation.

My three years of experience at Allstate have given me the opportunity to take leadership and show responsibility. I developed a procedure for making out arbitration reports which saved so much time that I was asked to teach it to the other employees in my department.

I could come to New York for an interview any Tuesday or Thursday afternoon.

Tracey McKenna
mckenna.74@bentley.edu
http://www.bentley/business/students/mckenna/report.htm

Repeat name and e-mail address at the end.

If you have a Web page, list it to show that you're technologically savvy.
Keeping the "http://" in the URL creates a hotlink in many e-mail programs.

Figure 28.7
Checklist for Job Application Letters

Checklist for

Asking Readers Questions

Adaptation to Specific Company

☐ Is the letter addressed to a specific person (either the person specified in the ad or the person with the power to create a job for you)?

☐ Does the letter show your knowledge of the company and the position?

☐ Does the letter specify the position you're looking for?

Organization

☐ If you know the company is hiring, does the first paragraph indicate that you're applying for the job and list your major qualification(s)?

☐ If, as far as you know, the company is not hiring, does the first paragraph catch the reader's interest and create a bridge to talking about yourself?

☐ Does the last paragraph ask for an interview?

Specific Supporting Details

☐ Do details show that you have the basic qualifications specified in the ad?

☐ Do details show that you can go beyond the basics to contribute to the company?

☐ Do details separate you from other applicants?

Style and Mechanics

☐ Is the writing smooth, tight, and forceful?

☐ Does the text avoid using *I* at the beginning of every paragraph?

☐ Does the text use you-attitude and positive emphasis?

☐ Is the letter free from typos and other errors?

Formal and Visual Impact

☐ Does the letter use a standard letter format?

☐ Is the page visually attractive, with a good mix of paragraph lengths?

Summary of Key Points

- When you know that a company is hiring, send a **solicited job letter.** When you want a job with a company that has not announced openings, send a **prospecting job letter.**

- Organize a solicited letter in this way:

  1. State that you're applying for the job and tell where you learned about the job (ad, referral, etc.). Briefly show that you have the major qualifications required by the ad. Summarize your qualifications in the order in which you plan to discuss them in the letter.

  2. Develop your major qualifications in detail.

  3. Develop your other qualifications. Show what separates you from the other applicants who will also answer the ad. Demonstrate your knowledge of the organization.

  4. Ask for an interview; tell when you'll be available to be interviewed and to begin work. End on a positive, forward-looking note.

- Organize a prospecting letter in this way:

  1. Catch the reader's interest.

2. Create a bridge between the attention-getter and your qualifications. Summarize your qualifications in the order in which you plan to discuss them in the letter.

3. Develop your strong points in detail. Relate what you've done in the past to what you could do for this company. Show that you know something about the company. Identify the specific niche you want to fill.

4. Ask for an interview and tell when you'll be available for interviews. End on a positive, forward-looking note.

- In both letters, you should
  - Address the letter to a specific person.
  - Indicate the specific position for which you're applying.

- Be specific about your qualifications.
- Show what separates you from other applicants.
- Show a knowledge of the company and the position.
- Refer to your résumé (which you would enclose with the letter).
- Ask for an interview.

- Use your knowledge of the company, your course work, your understanding of the field, and your experience in jobs and extracurricular activities to show that you're unique.

- Use you-attitude by supporting general claims with specific examples and by relating what you've done to what the employer needs. Use positive emphasis to sound confident.

Assignments for Module 28

Questions for Comprehension

28.1 How should you organize a letter in response to an announced job opening?

28.2 How should you organize a letter when the company has not announced openings?

Questions for Critical Thinking

28.3 Why is it important for you to separate yourself from other applicants?

28.4 Why should you *not* ask for a job in the first paragraph of a prospecting letter?

28.5 Why is a good writing style particularly important in a job application letter?

28.6 Is it ethical for someone who isn't a good writer to hire someone to "ghostwrite" the letter for him or her?

28.7 Suppose that people with your qualifications are in great demand. Is there any reason for you to take the time to write a strong letter?

Exercises and Problems

28.8 **Analyzing First Paragraphs of Prospecting Letters**

All of the following are first paragraphs in prospecting letters written by new graduates. Evaluate the paragraphs on these criteria:

- Is the paragraph likely to interest the reader and motivate him or her to read the rest of the letter?
- Does the paragraph have some content that the student can use to

create a transition to talking about his or her qualifications?

- Does the paragraph avoid asking for a job?

    1. Ann Gibbs suggested that I contact you.
    2. Each year, the Christmas shopping rush makes more work for everyone at Wieboldt's, especially for the Credit Department. While working for Wieboldt's Credit Department for three Christmas and summer vacations, the Christmas sales increase is just one of the credit situations I became aware of.
    3. Whether to plate a two-inch eyebolt with cadmium for a tough, brilliant shine or with zinc for a rust-resistant, less expensive finish is a tough question. But similar questions must be answered daily by your salesmen. With my experience in the electro-plating industry, I can contribute greatly to your constant need of getting customers.
    4. Prudential Insurance Company did much to help my college career, as the sponsor of my National Merit Scholarship. Now I think I can give something back to Prudential. I'd like to put my education, including a degree in finance from _____ College, to work in your investment department.
    5. Since the beginning of Delta Electric Construction Co. in 1997, the size and profits have grown steadily. My father, being a stockholder and vice president, often discusses company dealings with me. Although the company has prospered, I understand there have been a few problems of mismanagement. I feel with my present and future qualifications, I could help ease these problems.

28.9 Improving You-Attitude and Positive Emphasis in Job Letters

Revise each of these sentences to improve you-attitude and positive emphasis. You may need to add information.

1. I understand that your company has had problems due to the mistranslation of documents during international ad campaigns.
2. Included in my résumé are the courses in Finance which earned me a fairly attractive grade average.
3. I am looking for a position which gives me a chance to advance quickly.
4. Although short on experience, I am long on effort and enthusiasm.
5. I have been with the company from its beginning to its present unfortunate state of bankruptcy.

28.10 Writing a Solicited Letter

Write a letter of application in response to an announced opening for a full-time job that a new graduate could hold. **Turn in a copy of the listing.** If you use option (a), (b), or (d) below, your listing will be a copy. If you choose option (c), you will write the listing and can design your ideal job.

a. Respond to an ad in a newspaper, a professional journal, in the placement office, or on the Web. Use an ad that specifies the company, not a blind ad. Be sure that you are fully qualified for the job.

b. Take a job description and assume that it represents a current opening. Use a directory to get the name of the person to whom the letter should be addressed.

c. If you have already worked somewhere, assume that your employer is asking you to apply for full-time work after graduation. Be sure to write a fully persuasive letter.

d. Respond to one of the listings below. Use a directory or the Web to get the name and address of the person to whom you should write.

1. Pepsi-Cola is hiring an **assistant auditor.** Minimum 12 hours of accounting. Work includes analysis and evaluation of operating and financial controls and requires contact with many levels of Company management. Extensive travel (50%) required through the United States, along with some international work. Effective written and oral communication skills a must, along with sound decision-making abilities. Locations: Los Angeles, Dallas, Atlanta, Philadelphia, Denver, Chicago. Refer to job FA-2534.

2. Roxy Systems (Roxy.com) seeks **Internet Marketing Coordinators** to analyze online campaigns and put together detailed reports, covering ad impressions and click-through rates. Must have basic understanding of marketing; be organized, creative, and detail-oriented; know Microsoft Excel; have excellent communication skills; and be familiar with the Internet. Send letter and resume to mike@roxy.com.

3. Bose Corporation seeks **public relations/communications administrative associate** (Job Code 117BD). Write, edit, and produce the in-house newsletter using desktop publishing software. Represent the company to external contacts (including the press). Provide administrative support to the manager of PR by scheduling meetings, preparing presentations, tabulating and analyzing surveys, and processing financial requests. Excellent organizational, interpersonal, and communication skills (both written and oral) required. Must be proficient in MS Office and Filemaker Pro.

4. The Limited is hiring **executive development program trainees.** After completing 10-week training programs, trainees will become assistant buyers. Prefer people with strong interest and experience in retailing. Apply directly to the store for which you want to work.

5. A local nonprofit seeks a **Coordinator of Volunteer Services.** Responsibilities for this full-time position include coordinating volunteers' schedules, recruiting and training new volunteers, and evaluating existing programs. Excellent listening and communication skills required.

28.11 Writing a Prospecting Letter

Pick a company you'd like to work for and apply for a specific position. The position can be one that already exists or one that you would create if you could to match your unique blend of talents. Give your instructor a copy of the job description with your letter.

Address your letter to the president of a small company, the area vice president or branch manager of a large company. Use directories or the Web to get the name and address of the person with the power to create a job for you.

Polishing Your Prose

Using You and I

You-attitude (◀ ▶ Module 6) means that you'll use lots of *you*'s in business messages. However, use *you* only when it refers to your reader. When you mean "people in general," use another term.

Incorrect: When I visited your office, I learned that you need to find a way to manage your e-mail.

Correct: When I visited your office, I saw the importance of managing one's e-mail.

Incorrect: Older customers may not like it if you call them by their first names.

Correct: Older customers may prefer being called by courtesy titles and their last names.

Omit *you* when it criticizes or attacks the reader.

Not you-attitude: You didn't turn your expense report in by the deadline.

You-attitude: Expense reports are due by the fifth of each month. We have no record of receiving your report.

When you talk about what you've done, use *I*.

Correct: In the past month, I have completed three audits.

In general, keep *I*'s to a minimum. They make you sound less confident and more self-centered.

Weak: I think that we would save money if we bought a copier instead of leasing it.

Better: We would save money by buying a copier instead of leasing it.

Weak: I want to be sure that I understand how I will be affected by this project.

Better: How will this project affect our unit?

When you write a document that focuses on you (such as a progress report or a job application letter), vary sentence structure so that you don't begin every sentence with *I*.

Correct: This job gave me the opportunity to . . .

Correct: As an intern, I . . .

Correct: Working with a team, I . . .

When you use a first-person pronoun as part of a compound subject or object, put the first-person pronoun last.

Correct: She asked you and me to make the presentation.

Correct: You, Kelly, and I will have a chance to talk to members of the audience before the dinner.

Be sure to use the right case. Omit the other part(s) of the compound to see the case you should use:

She asked me.

I will have a chance.

Use the same form when you restore the other words.

Exercises

Revise the following sentences to eliminate errors and improve the use of *you* and *I*

1. I have taken a lot of time and trouble to get a copy of *Using Excel* for each of you.

2. While reading the job description on your Web page, I saw that you need to manage your time well.

3. Please return the draft to me and Mehtap.

4. I spoke with the manager of accounts this afternoon. He said you made several errors that resulted in a loss of nearly $40,000 this quarter. You should correct those errors.

5. I have asked each department head if he or she had information to announce at the meeting, collated the responses, and arranged the topics to cover in an agenda. I have indicated how much time each topic will take. I am herewith distributing the agenda for Friday's meeting.

6. I've been a payroll supervisor for 11 years and, believe me, you get to work with a lot of people during that time.

7. My last job showed me that you have to be able to solve problems quickly.

8. You have got to be kidding! You have written a report that is so difficult to read, only you can understand it.

9. The client asked me and my supervisor to explain our strategy more fully.

10. I expect that you will be pleased to learn that the promotion is going to Sally. After all, you have worked with her for nearly three years. She asked that her old office be offered to me or you.

Check your answers to the odd-numbered exercises at the back of the book.

BComm Skill Booster

To apply the concepts in this module, complete lesson 48 on creating cover letters. You can access the BComm Skill Booster through the text Web site at **www.mhhe.com/bcs2e.**

Module 29

Job Interviews

Start by asking these questions:

- Why do I need an interview strategy?
- What details should I think about?
- Should I practice before the interview?
- How should I answer traditional interview questions?
- How can I prepare for behavioral and situational interviews?
- How can I prepare for phone or video interviews?

Job interviews are scary, even when you've prepared thoroughly. But when you are prepared, you can harness the adrenaline to work for you so that you put your best foot forward and get the job you want.

Today many employers expect you to

- Be more aggressive. One employer deliberately tells the company receptionist to brush off callers who ask about advertised openings. He interviews only those who keep calling and offer the receptionist reasons why they should be interviewed. (However, if you're rejected even after giving reasons, accept the rejection gracefully.)
- Follow instructions to the letter. The owner of a delivery company tells candidates to phone at a

precise hour. Failing to do so means that the person couldn't be trusted to deliver packages on time.[1]

- Participate in many interviews. Candidates for jobs with Electronic Arts, a maker of computer games, first answer questions online. Then they have up to five phone interviews—some asking candidates to solve problems or program functions. Candidates who get that far undergo "the gauntlet": three days of onsite interviewing.[2]

- Have one or more interviews by phone, computer, or video.

- Take one or more tests, including drug tests, psychological tests, aptitude tests, computer simulations, and essay exams where you're asked to explain what you'd do in a specific situation.

- Be approved by the team you'll be joining. In companies with self-managed work teams, the team has a say in who is hired.

- Provide—at the interview or right after it—a sample of the work you're applying to do. You may be asked to write a memo or a proposal, calculate a budget on a spreadsheet, or make a presentation.

Be nice to the receptionists and secretaries you speak to. Find out the person's name on your first call and use it on subsequent calls. "Thank you for being so patient. Can you tell me when a better time might be to try to get Mr. or Ms. X? I'll try again on [date]." Sometimes, if you call after 5 P.M., executives answer their own phones since clerical staff members have gone home.

If you get voice mail, leave a concise message with your name and phone number. Even if you've called 10 times, keep your voice pleasant. If you get voice mail repeatedly, call the main company number to speak with a receptionist. Ask whether the person you're trying to reach is in the building. If he or she is on the road, ask when the person is due in.

T or F "I'd rather do things my way than follow the rules."

T or F "I love to help people cheer up and feel better."

T or F "I am good at taking charge of a group."

Blockbuster Video uses Unicru's online questionnaires with True/False statements to screen for management, dependability, customer-service, and sales potential among hourly workers.

Why do I need an interview strategy?

So that you can be proactive!

Develop an overall strategy based on your answers to these three questions:

1. **What about yourself do you want the interviewer to know?** Pick two to five points that represent your strengths for that particular job. These facts may be achievements, character traits (such as enthusiasm), experiences that qualify you for the job and separate you from other applicants, the fact that you really want to work for this company, and so on. For each strength, think of a specific action or accomplishment to support it. For example, be ready to give an example to prove that you're "hard working." Show how you helped an organization save money or serve customers better.

   Then at the interview, listen to every question to see if you could make one of your key points as part of your answer. If the questions don't allow you to make your points, bring them up at the end of the interview.

2. **What disadvantages or weaknesses do you need to minimize?** Expect that you may be asked to explain weaknesses or apparent weaknesses in your record: lack of experience, so-so grades, or gaps in your record.

3. **What do you need to know about the job and the organization to decide whether to accept this job if it is offered to you?**

What details should I think about?

What you'll wear, what you'll take with you, and how to get there.

Inappropriate clothing or being late can cost you a job. Put enough time into planning details so that you can move on to substantive planning.

What to Wear

Your interview clothing should be at least as formal as the clothing of the person likely to interview you. When the interview is scheduled, ask the person who invites you whether the company has a dress policy. If the dress is "casual," wear a shirt and a good-quality skirt or pants, not jeans.

If you're interviewing for a management or office job, wear a business suit. What kind of suit? If you've got good taste and a good eye for color, follow your instincts. If fashion isn't your strong point, read John Molloy's *New Dress for Success* (men's clothes) and *The New Woman's Dress for Success Book.* Perhaps the best suggestion in the books is his advice to visit expensive stores, noting details—the exact shade of blue in a suit, the number of buttons on the sleeve, the placement of pockets, the width of lapels—and then go to stores in your price range and buy a suit that has the details found on more expensive clothing.

For onsite interviews, show that you understand the corporate culture. Paul Capelli, former public relations executive at Amazon.com and now vice president of public relations at CNBC, suggests that applicants find out what employees wear "and notch it up one step":

> If the dress is jeans and a T-shirt, wear slacks and an open collar shirt. . . . If it's slacks and an open collar shirt, throw on a sport coat. If it's a sport coat, throw on a suit. At least match it and go one step up, but don't go three steps down.[3]

Choose comfortable shoes. You may do a fair amount of walking during an onsite interview.

Take care of all the details. Check your heels to make sure they aren't run down; make sure your shoes are shined. Have your hair cut or styled conservatively. Jewelry and makeup should be understated. Personal hygiene must be impeccable. If you wear cologne or perfume, keep it to a minimum.

What to Bring to the Interview

Bring extra copies of your résumé. If your campus placement office has already given the interviewer a data sheet, present the résumé at the beginning of the interview: "I thought you might like a little more information about me."

Bring something to write on and something to write with. It's OK to bring in a small notepad with the questions you want to ask on it.

Bring copies of your work or a portfolio: an engineering design, a copy of a memo you wrote on a job or in a business writing class, an article you wrote for the campus paper. You don't need to present these unless the interview calls for them, but they can be very effective.

Bring the names, addresses, and phone numbers of references if you didn't put them on your résumé. Bring complete details about your work history and education, including dates and street addresses, in case you're asked to fill out an application form.

If you can afford it, buy a briefcase to carry these items. At the start of your career, an inexpensive briefcase is acceptable.

Note-Taking

During or immediately after the interview, write down

- The name of the interviewer (or all the people you talked to, if it's a group interview or an onsite visit).
- What the interviewer seemed to like best about you.
- Any negative points or weaknesses that came up that you need to counter in your follow-up letter or phone calls.
- Answers to your questions about the company.
- When you'll hear from the company.

The easiest way to get the interviewer's name is to ask for his or her card. You may be able to make all the notes you need on the back of the card.

Some interviewers say that they respond negatively to applicants who take notes during the interview. However, if you have several interviews back-to-back or if you know your memory is terrible, do take brief notes during the interview. That's better than forgetting which company said you'd be on the road every other week and which interviewer asked that *you* get in touch with him or her.

FYI

Raises are usually set as a percentage of your current salary. If you work for 40 years, getting an extra $2,000 in salary on your first job could yield $15,000 of extra income in compounded raises.

Source: Christine Larson, "Why the Wage Gap?" *Executive Female,* April/May 2002, 27.

How to Get There

If you're going to a place you haven't been before, do a practice run at the same time of day your interview is scheduled for. Check out bus transfers or parking fees. On the day of the interview, leave early enough so that you'll get to the interview 15 minutes early. Use the extra time to check your appearance in the restroom mirror and to thumb through the company publications in the waiting room. If an accident does delay you, call to say you'll be late.

Should I practice before the interview?

Absolutely!

Your interviewing skills will improve with practice. Rehearse everything you can: put on the clothes you'll wear and practice entering a room, shaking hands, sitting down, and answering questions. Ask a friend to interview you. Saying answers out loud is surprisingly harder than saying them in your head.

Some campuses have videotaping facilities so that you can watch your own sample interview. Videotaping is more valuable if you can do it at least twice, so you can modify behavior the second time and check the tape to see whether the modification works.

How to Act

Should you "be yourself"? There's no point in assuming a radically different persona. If you do, you run the risk of getting into a job that you'll hate (though the persona you assumed might have loved it). On the other hand, all of us have several selves: we can be lazy, insensitive, bored, slow-witted, and tongue-tied, but we can also be energetic, perceptive, interested, intelligent, and articulate. Be your *best* self at the interview.

Interviews can make you feel vulnerable and defensive; to counter this, review your accomplishments—the things you're especially proud of having done. You'll make a better impression if you have a firm sense of your own self-worth.

Every interviewer repeats the advice that mothers often give: sit up straight, don't mumble, look at people when you talk. It's good advice for interviews. Be aware that many people respond negatively to smoking.

Office visits that involve meals and semisocial occasions call for sensible choices. When you order, choose something that's easy and unmessy to eat. Watch your table manners. Eat a light lunch, with no alcohol, so that you'll be alert during the afternoon. At dinner or an evening party, decline alcohol if you don't drink or are underage. If you do drink, accept just one drink—you're still being evaluated. Be aware that some people respond negatively to applicants who drink hard liquor.

Parts of the Interview

Every interview has an opening, a body, and a close.

In the **opening** (two to five minutes), good interviewers will try to set you at ease. Some interviewers will open with easy questions about your major or interests. Others open by telling you about the job or the company. If this happens, listen so you can answer later questions to show that you can do the job or contribute to the company that's being described.

The **body** of the interview (10 to 25 minutes) is an all-too-brief time for you to highlight your qualifications and find out what you need to know to decide if you want to accept a second interview. Expect questions that allow you to showcase your strong points and questions that probe any weaknesses evident from your résumé. (You were neither in school nor working last fall. What were you doing?) Normally the interviewer will also try to sell you on the company and give you an opportunity to raise questions.

Be aware of time so that you can make sure to get in your key points and questions: "We haven't covered it yet, but I want you to know that I. . . ." "I'm aware that it's almost 10:30. I do have some more questions that I'd like to ask about the company."

In the **close** of the interview (two to five minutes), the interviewer will usually tell you what happens next: "We'll be bringing our top candidates to the office in February. You should hear from us in three weeks." One interviewer reports that he gives applicants his card and tells them to call him. "It's a test to see if they are committed, how long it takes for them to call, and whether they even call at all."[4]

Close with an assertive statement. Depending on the circumstances, you could say: "I've certainly enjoyed learning more about General Electric." "I hope I get a chance to visit your Phoenix office. I'd really like to see the new computer system you talked about." "This job seems to be a good match between what you're looking for and what I'd like to do."

FYI

Replacing an employee costs the company about 1½ times the person's annual salary.

Source: Sue Shellenbarger, "To Win the Loyalty of Your Employees, Try a Softer Touch," *The Wall Street Journal,* January 26, 2000, B1.

Stress Interviews

A **stress interview** deliberately puts the applicant under stress. If the stress is physical (e.g., you're given a chair where the light is in your eyes), be assertive: Move to another chair or tell the interviewer that the behavior bothers you.

Usually the stress is psychological. A group of interviewers fire rapid questions. A single interviewer probes every weak spot in the applicant's record and asks questions that elicit negatives. If you get questions that put you on the defensive, **rephrase** them in less inflammatory terms, if necessary, and then **treat them as requests for information.**

Q: Why did you major in physical education? That sounds like a pretty Mickey Mouse major.

A: You're asking whether I have the academic preparation for this job. I started out in physical education because I've always loved sports. I learned that I couldn't graduate on time if I officially switched to business administration because the requirements were different in the two programs. But I do have 21 hours in business administration and 9 hours in accounting. And my sports experience gives me practical training in teamwork, motivating people, and management.

Respond assertively. The candidates who survive are those who stand up for themselves and who explain why indeed they *are* worth hiring.

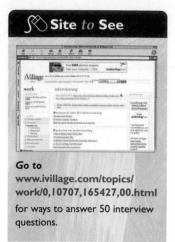
Silence can also create stress. One woman walked into her scheduled interview to find a male interviewer with his feet up on the desk. He said, "It's been a long day. I'm tired and I want to go home. You have five minutes to sell yourself." Since she had planned the points she wanted to be sure interviewers knew, she was able to do this. "Your recruiting brochure said that you're looking for someone with a major in accounting and a minor in finance. As you may remember from my résumé, I'm majoring in accounting and have had 12 hours in finance. I've also served as treasurer of a local campaign committee and have worked as a volunteer tax preparer through the Accounting Club." When she finished, the interviewer told her it was a test: "I wanted to see how you'd handle it."

Increasingly common is the variety of stress interview that asks you to do—on the spot—the kind of thing the job would require. An interviewer for a sales job handed applicants a ballpoint pen and said, "Sell me this pen." (It's OK to ask who the target market is and whether this is a repeat or a new customer.) Candidates who make it through the first two rounds of interviews for sales jobs at Dataflex are invited to participate in a week's worth of sales meetings, which start at 7 A.M. four times a week. The people who do participate—not merely attend—are the people who get hired.[5] AT&T asks some applicants to deliver presentations or lead meetings. Massachusetts Mutual Life asked the finalists for a vice presidency to process memos and reports in a two-hour in-basket exercise and participate in several role plays.[6]

How should I answer traditional interview questions?

Choose answers that fit your qualifications and your interview strategy.

As Figure 29.1 shows, successful applicants use different communication behaviors than do unsuccessful applicants. Successful applicants are more likely to use the company name during the interview, support their claims with specific details, and ask specific questions about the company and the industry. In addition to practicing the content of questions, try to incorporate these tactics.

The following questions frequently come up at interviews. Do some unpressured thinking before the interview so that you'll be able to come up with answers that are responsive, honest, and paint a good picture of you. Choose answers that fit your qualifications and your interview strategy. See Figures 29.2 and 29.3 for examples of the ways recruiters evaluate answers.

1. **Tell me about yourself.**
   Don't launch into an autobiography. Instead, state the things about yourself that you want the interviewer to know. Give specifics to prove each of your strengths.

2. **What makes you think you're qualified to work for this company? Or, I'm interviewing 120 people for 2 jobs. Why should I hire you?**
   This question may feel like an attack. Use it as an opportunity to state your strong points: your qualifications for the job, the things that separate you from other applicants.

Figure 29.1

The Communication Behaviors of Successful Interviewees

Behavior	Unsuccessful Interviewees	Successful Interviewees
Statements about the position	Had only vague ideas of what they wanted to do; changed "ideal job" up to six times during the interview.	Specific and consistent about the position they wanted; were able to tell why they wanted the position.
Use of company name	Rarely used the company name.	Referred to the company by name four times as often as unsuccessful interviewees.
Knowledge about company and position	Made it clear that they were using the interview to learn about the company and what it offered.	Made it clear that they had researched the company; referred to specific brochures, journals, or people who had given them information.
Level of interest, enthusiasm	Responded neutrally to interviewer's statements: "OK," "I see." Indicated reservations about company or location.	Expressed approval of information provided by the interviewer nonverbally and verbally; "That's great!" Explicitly indicated desire to work for this particular company.
Nonverbal behavior	Made little eye contact; smiled infrequently.	Made eye contact often; smiled.
Picking up on interviewer's cues	Gave vague or negative answers even when a positive answer was clearly desired ("How are your math skills?").	Answered positively and confidently—and backed up the claim with a specific example of "problem solving" or "toughness."
Response to topic shift by interviewer	Resisted topic shift.	Accepted topic shift.
Use of industry terms and technical jargon	Used almost no technical jargon.	Used technical jargon: "point of purchase display," "NCR charge," "two-column approach," "direct mail."
Use of specifics in answers	Gave short answers—10 words or less, sometimes only one word; did not elaborate. Gave general responses: "fairly well."	Supported claims with specific personal experiences, comparisons, statistics, statements of teachers and employers.
Questions asked by interviewee	Asked a small number of general questions.	Asked specific questions based on knowledge of the industry and the company. Personalized questions: "What would my duties be?"
Control of time and topics	Interviewee talked 37% of the interview time; initiated 36% of the comments.	Interviewee talked 55% of the total time, initiated subjects 56% of the time.

Source: Based on research reported by Lois J. Einhorn, "An Inner View of the Job Interview: An Investigation of Successful Communicative Behaviors," *Communication Education* 30 (July 1981), 217–28; and Robert W. Elder and Michael M. Harris, eds., *The Employment Interview Handbook* (Thousand Oaks, CA: Sage, 1999), 300, 303, 327–28.

3. **What two or three accomplishments have given you the greatest satisfaction?**
   Pick accomplishments that you're proud of, that create the image you want to project, and that enable you to share one of the things you want the interviewer to know about you. Focus not just on the end result, but on the problem-solving and thinking skills that made the achievement possible.

4. **Why do you want to work for us? What is your ideal job?**
   Even if you're interviewing just for practice, make sure you have a good answer—preferably two or three reasons you'd like to work for that

Figure 29.2

Poor Responses to Behavioral Interview Questions

Source: Adapted from *Fast Company*, January 1999, 156.

Carolyn Murray (cmurray@wlgore.com), 37, a savvy recruiter at W.L. Gore & Associates, developers of Gore-Tex, pays little attention to a candidate's carefully scripted responses to her admittedly softball questions. Instead, she listens for a throwaway line that reveals the reality behind an otherwise benign reply. Herewith, Murray delivers a post-game analysis of how three job candidates whiffed during their interviews.

Question	Response	Evaluation
"Give me an example of a time when you had a conflict with a team member."	" 'Our leader asked me to handle all of the FedExing for our team. I did it, but I thought that FedExing was a waste of my time.' "	"At Gore, we work from a team concept. Her answer shows that she won't exactly jump when one of her teammates needs help."
"Tell me how you solved a problem that was impeding your project."	" 'One of the engineers on my team wasn't pulling his weight, and we were closing in on a deadline. So I took on some of his work. ' "	"The candidate may have resolved the issue for this particular deadline, but he did nothing to prevent the problem from happening again."
"What's the one thing that you would change about your current position?"	" 'My job as a salesman has become mundane. Now I want the responsibility of managing people.' "	"He's not maximizing his current position. Selling is never mundane if you go about it in the right way."

Figure 29.3

Good Responses to Interview Questions

Source: Adapted from *Fast Company*, January 1999, 157.

As CEO of Motley Fool, a wildly popular investment Web site, **Erik Rydholm** (erikr@fool.com), 31, has little time for fooling around with undesirable job candidates. To streamline the interview process, he's come up with three questions that quickly separate the fools from the Fools.

Question	Response	Evaluation
" 'What does Foolishness mean to you?' That's a great first question, one that separates those who get it from those who are clueless."	"One guy emphasized that we give people the power to gather investing information from many sources by visiting a single Web site."	"He understood that we're trying to revolutionize the way people lead their financial lives—by putting a lot of power at their disposal."
" 'Should the Motley Fool consider putting its name on mutual funds and selling a line of financial services?' "	"He encouraged us to consider whether branding a fund would undercut our integrity and whether it even related to our core competencies."	"He understood that there's integrity to the Motley Fool brand, and he recognized the risk of undercutting that integrity."
" 'How does the Motley Fool succeed?' That gets to the heart of how we can continue to capitalize on our current market share."	"One candidate argued that the Motley Fool is not a source—it's a service: We guide people through their investment decisions."	"He understood the difference between a 'source' and a 'service'—which made me confident that he could think distinctively for us."

company. If you don't seem to be taking the interview seriously, the interviewer won't take you seriously, and you won't even get good practice.

5. **What college courses did you like best and least? Why?**
   This question may be an icebreaker; it may be designed to discover the kind of applicant they're looking for. If your favorite class was something outside your program, prepare an answer that shows that you have qualities that can help you in the job you're applying for: "My favorite class was on the American novel. We got a chance to think on our own, rather than just regurgitate facts; we made presentations to the class every week. I found I really like sharing my ideas with other people and presenting reasons for my conclusions about something."

6. **Why are your grades so low?**
   If possible, show that the cause of low grades now has been solved or isn't relevant to the job you're applying for: "My father almost died last year, and my schoolwork really suffered." "When I started, I didn't have any firm goals. Once I discovered the program that was right for me, my grades have all been 'Bs' or better." "I'm not good at multiple-choice tests. But you need someone who can work with people, not someone who can take tests."

7. **What have you read recently? What movies have you seen recently?**
   These questions may be icebreakers; they may be designed to probe your intellectual depth. The term you're interviewing, read at least one book or magazine (regularly) and see at least one movie that you could discuss at an interview.

8. **Show me some samples of your writing.**
   The year you're interviewing, go through your old papers and select the best ones, retyping them if necessary, so that you'll have samples if you're asked for them. Show interviewers essays, reports, or business documents, not poetry or song lyrics.

   If you don't have samples at the interview, mail them to the interviewer immediately after the interview.

9. **Where do you see yourself in five years?**
   Employers ask this question to find out if you are a self-starter or if you passively respond to what happens. You may want to have several scenarios for five years from now to use in different kinds of interviews. Or you may want to say, "Well, my goals may change as opportunities arise. But right now, I want to . . . ."

10. **What are your interests outside work? What campus or community activities have you been involved in?**
    While it's desirable to be well-rounded, naming 10 interests is a mistake: The interviewer may wonder when you'll have time to work.

    If you mention your fiancé, spouse, or children in response to this question ("Well, my fiancé and I like to go sailing"), it is perfectly legal for the interviewer to ask follow-up questions ("What would you do if your spouse got a job offer in another town?"), even though the same question would be illegal if the interviewer brought up the subject first.

11. **What have you done to learn about this company?**
    An employer may ask this to see what you already know about the company (if you've read the recruiting literature, the interviewer doesn't

Instant Replay

What Successful Interviewees Do

Successful applicants

- Know what they want to do.
- Use the company name in the interview.
- Have researched the company in advance.
- Back up claims with specifics.
- Use technical jargon.
- Ask specific questions.
- Talk more of the time.

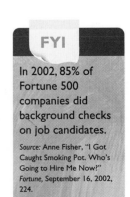

FYI

In 2002, 85% of Fortune 500 companies did background checks on job candidates.

Source: Anne Fisher, "I Got Caught Smoking Pot. Who's Going to Hire Me Now?" *Fortune,* September 16, 2002, 224.

need to repeat it). This question may also be used to see how active a role you're taking in the job search and how interested you are in this job.

12. **What adjectives would you use to describe yourself?**
Use only positive ones. Be ready to illustrate each with a specific example of something you've done.

13. **What is your greatest strength?**
Employers ask this question to give you a chance to sell yourself and to learn something about your values. Pick a strength related to work, school, or activities: "I'm good at working with people." "I really can sell things." "I'm good at solving problems." "I learn quickly." "I'm reliable. When I say I'll do something, I do it." Be ready to illustrate each with a specific example of something you've done.

14. **What is your greatest weakness?**
Use a work-related negative, even if something in your personal life really is your greatest weakness. Interviewers won't let you get away with a "weakness" like being a workaholic or just not having any experience yet. Instead, use one of the following three strategies:

a. Discuss a weakness that is not related to the job you're being considered for and which will not be needed even when you're promoted. End your answer with a positive that *is* related to the job:

[For a creative job in advertising:] I don't like accounting. I know it's important, but I don't like it. I even hire someone to do my taxes. I'm much more interested in being creative and working with people, which is why I find this position interesting.

[For a job in administration:] I don't like selling products. I hated selling cookies when I was a Girl Scout. I'd much rather work with ideas—and I really like selling the ideas that I believe in.

b. Discuss a weakness that you are working to improve:

In the past, I wasn't a good writer. But last term I took a course in business writing that taught me how to organize my ideas and how to revise. I may never win a Pulitzer Prize, but now I'm a lot more confident that I can write effective reports and memos.

c. Discuss a work-related weakness:

I procrastinate. Fortunately, I work well under pressure, but a couple of times I've really put myself in a bind.

15. **Why are you looking for another job?**
Stress what you're looking for in a new job, not why you want to get away from your old one.
If you were fired, say so. There are four acceptable ways to explain why you were fired:

a. You lost your job, along with many others, when the company downsized due to economic reasons.

b. It wasn't a good match. Add what you now know you need in a job, and ask what the employer can offer in this area.

c. You and your supervisor had a personality conflict. Make sure you show that this was an isolated incident, and that you normally get along well with people.

d. You made mistakes, but you've learned from them and are now ready to work well. Be ready to offer a specific anecdote proving that you have indeed changed.

16. **What questions do you have?**

This gives you a chance to cover things the interviewer hasn't brought up; it also gives the interviewer a sense of your priorities and values. Don't focus on salary or fringe benefits. Better questions are

- What would I be doing on a day-to-day basis?
- What kind of training program do you have? If, as I'm rotating among departments, I find that I prefer one area, can I specialize in it when the training program is over?
- How do you evaluate employees? How often do you review them? Where would you expect a new trainee (banker, staff accountant) to be three years from now?
- What happened to the last person who had this job?
- How are interest rates (a new product from competitors, imports, demographic trends, government regulation, etc.) affecting your company?

Benefits, working conditions, and the work itself are just as important as salary in evaluating job offers.

"Of course, we don't have much of a retirement plan."

Negotiating Salary and Benefits

The best time to negotiate for salary and benefits is after you have the job offer. Try to delay discussing salary early in the interview process, when you're still competing against other applicants.

Useful Sites for Negotiating Salary

www.wageweb.com
Detailed salary data for several fields

www.salary.com
Median, high, low salary data, searchable by job and city

www.datamasters.com
Cost of living in various cities

Prepare for salary negotiations by finding out what the going rate is for the kind of work you hope to do. Cultivate friends who are now in the workforce to find out what they're making. If your campus has a placement office, ask what last year's graduates got. Check Web sites and trade journals for salaries, often segmented into entry-level, median, and high salaries and even by city. This research is crucial. As recently as 2000, male students expected salaries in their first jobs that were 14% higher than the salaries female students expected. More than twice as many men as women expected to receive signing bonuses. Men were 16% more likely to expect annual bonuses, and the bonuses men expected were 16% higher than the bonuses women expected.

If the interviewer asks you about your salary requirements before a job offer has been made, try this response: "I'm sure your firm can pay me what I'm worth." Then either ask about pay ranges or go back to your qualifications for the job. If the interviewer demands a response, give a range using specific increments based on your research: "I'd expect to make between $37,300 and $41,900." As you say this, watch the interviewer. If he or she has that blank look we use to hide dismay, you may have asked for much more than the company was planning to offer. Quickly continue, ". . . depending, of course, on fringe benefits and how quickly I could be promoted. However, salary isn't the most important criterion for me in choosing a job, and I won't necessarily accept the highest offer I get. I'm interested in going somewhere where I can get good experience and use my talents to make a real contribution."

The best way to get more money is to convince the employer that you're worth it. During the interview process, show what you can do that the competition can't. Work to redefine the position in the employer's eyes from a low-level, anybody-could-do-it job to a complex combination of duties that only someone with your particular mix of talents could do.

After you have the offer, begin negotiating salary and benefits. You're in the strongest position when (1) you've done your homework and know what the usual salary and benefits are and (2) you can walk away from this offer if it doesn't meet your needs. Again, avoid naming a specific salary. Don't say you can't accept less. Instead, Kate Wendleton suggests, say you "would find it difficult to accept the offer" under the terms first offered.

Remember that you're negotiating a package, not just a starting salary. A company that truly can't pay any more money now might be able to review you for promotion sooner than usual, or pay your moving costs, or give you a better job title. Some companies offer fringe benefits that may compensate for lower taxable income: use of a company car, reimbursements for education, child care or eldercare subsidies, or help in finding a job for your spouse or partner. And think about your career, not just the initial salary. Sometimes a low-paying job at a company that will provide superb experience will do more for your career (and your long-term earning prospects) than a high salary now with no room to grow.

Work toward a win-win solution. You want the employer to be happy that you're coming on board and to feel that you've behaved maturely and professionally.

Source: Kate Wendleton, Through the Brick Wall: How to Job-Hunt in a Tight Market (New York: Villard Books, 1992), 278; and Rachel Emma Silverman, "Great Expectations," The Wall Street Journal, July 25, 2000, B10; Suzanne Koudsi, "You want more," Fortune, April 29, 2002, 177–78.

- How would you describe the company's culture?
- This sounds like a great job. What are the drawbacks?

Increasingly, candidates are asking about work-life balance and about the control they'll have over their own work:

- Do people who work for you have a life off the job?
- If my job requires too much travel, can I change without doing serious damage to my career?
- What support can you offer my significant other?
- Do you offer flextime?
- How much pressure do you have to achieve your projects? How much freedom is there to extend a deadline?[7]

You won't be able to anticipate every question you may get. (One interviewer asked applicants, "What vegetable would you like to be?" Another asked, "If you were a cookie, what kind of cookie would you be?"[8]) Check with other people who have interviewed recently to find out what questions are being asked in your field.

How can I prepare for behavioral and situational interviews?

Think about skills you've used that could transfer to other jobs.

Learn as much as you can about the culture of the company you hope to join.

Many companies are now using behavioral or situational interviews. **Behavioral interviews** ask the applicant to describe actual behaviors, rather than plans or general principles. Thus, instead of asking, "How would you motivate people?" the interviewer might ask, "Tell me what happened the last time you wanted to get other people to do something." Follow-up questions might include, "What exactly did you do to handle the situation? How did you feel about the results? How did the other people feel? How did your superior feel about the results?" In your answer,

- Describe the situation.
- Tell what you did.
- Describe the outcome.
- Show that you understand the implications of what you did and how you might modify your behavior in other situations.

For example, if you did the extra work yourself when a team member didn't do his or her share, does that fact suggest that you prefer to work alone? If the organization you're interviewing with values teams, you may want to go on to show why doing the extra work was appropriate in that situation but that you can respond differently in other situations.

Figure 29.4 lists common behavioral interview questions.

Figure 29.4
Behavioral Interview Questions

Describe a situation in which you

1. Created an opportunity for yourself in a job or volunteer position.
2. Used writing to achieve your goal.
3. Went beyond the call of duty to get a job done.
4. Communicated successfully with someone you disliked.
5. Had to make a decision quickly.
6. Overcame a major obstacle.
7. Took a project from start to finish.
8. Were unable to complete a project on time.
9. Used good judgment and logic in solving a problem.
10. Worked under a tight deadline.
11. Worked with a tough boss.
12. Handled a difficult situation with a co-worker.
13. Made an unpopular decision.
14. Gave a presentation.
15. Worked with someone who wasn't doing his or her share of the work.

Situational interviews put you in a situation that allows the interviewer to see whether you have the qualities the company is seeking. For example, Southwest Airlines found that 95% of the complaints it received were provoked by only 5% of its personnel. When managers explored further, they found that these 5% of employees were self-centered. To weed out self-centered applicants, Southwest now puts several candidates into a room and asks each to give a five-minute speech on "Why I Want to Work with Southwest Airlines." But the interviewers watch the *audience* to hire the people who are pulling for other speakers to do well, as opposed to those who are only thinking about their own performance.[9]

Situational interviews may also be conducted using traditional questions but evaluating behaviors other than the answers. Greyhound hired applicants for its customer-assistance center who made eye contact with the interviewer and smiled at least five times during a 15-minute interview.[10]

How can I prepare for phone or video interviews?

Practice short answers. Retape until you look good.

Try to schedule phone interviews for home, not work, and for a time when things will be quiet. If a company wants to interview you on the spot, accept only if the timing is good. If it isn't, say so: "We just sat down to dinner. Could you call back in 30 minutes?" Then get your information about the company, ask the kids to be quiet, and get your thoughts in order.

To prepare for a phone interview,

- Tape yourself so you can make any adjustments in pronunciation and voice qualities.
- Practice short answers to questions. After giving a short answer in the interview, say, "Would you like more information?" Without a visual

FYI

For a phone interview,

- Keep a copy of your résumé and the job description near the phone.
- Write out in advance a statement about why you're looking for a job.
- Ask the interviewer to spell his or her name; get the title, phone number, mailing address, and e-mail address. You'll need this information for your thank-you note.

Source: Donna A. Ford, "Phone Interviews: New Skills Required," *Intercom,* April 2002, 19.

channel, you can't see the body language that tells you someone else wants to speak.

Two kinds of video interviews exist. The first kind is a live interview using videoconferencing equipment. For this kind of interview, use the same guidelines for a phone interview. In the second kind, the company sends a list of questions, asking the applicant to tape the responses.

If you're asked to prepare a videotape,

- Practice your answers.
- Tape the interview as many times as necessary to get a tape that presents you at your best.
- Be specific. Since the employer can't ask follow-up questions, you need to be detailed about how your credentials could help the employer.

For both interviews, smile when you talk to put more energy into your voice.

Summary of Key Points

- Develop an overall strategy based on your answers to these three questions:
  1. What two to five facts about yourself do you want the interviewer to know?
  2. What disadvantages or weaknesses do you need to overcome or minimize?
  3. What do you need to know about the job and the organization to decide whether or not you want to accept this job if it is offered to you?
- Wear a conservative business suit to the interview.
- Bring an extra copy of your résumé, something to write on and write with, and copies of your work to the interview.
- Record the name of the interviewer, what the interviewer liked about you, any negative points that came up, answers to your questions about the company, and when you'll hear from the company.
- Rehearse in advance everything you can. Ask a friend to interview you. If your campus has videotaping facilities, watch yourself on tape so that you can evaluate and modify your interview behavior.
- Be your best self at the interview.

- Successful applicants know what they want to do, use the company name in the interview, have researched the company in advance, back up claims with specifics, use technical jargon, ask specific questions, and talk more of the time.
- As you practice answers to questions you may be asked, choose answers that fit your qualifications and your interview strategy.
- **Behavioral interviews** ask the applicant to describe actual behaviors, rather than plans or general principles.
- To answer a behavioral question, describe the situation, tell what you did, describe the outcome, and show that you understand the implications of what you did and how you might modify that action in other situations.
- **Situational interviews** put you in a situation that allows the interviewer to see whether you have the qualities the company is seeking.
- For a phone interview, give short answers. Then ask, "Would you like more information?"
- If you answer questions on videotape, retape as many times as necessary to show your best self.

Assignments for Module 29

Questions for Comprehension

29.1 What three questions should form the basis for an interview strategy?

29.2 How do you use your interview strategy during an interview?

29.3 How do successful interviewees communicate?

Questions for Critical Thinking

29.4 What are your greatest strengths? How can you demonstrate them during an interview?

29.5 What are your weaknesses? How will you deal with them if they come up during an interview?

29.6 What are your options if you are asked what you believe is an illegal interview question? Which option seems best to you? Why?

29.7 Is it unethical to practice answering interview questions, so that you come across as very poised at an interview?

Exercises and Problems

29.8 **Interviewing Job Hunters**

Talk to students at your school who are interviewing for jobs this term. Possible questions to ask them include

- What field are you in? How good is the job market in that field this year?
- What questions have you been asked at job interviews? Were you asked any stress or sexist questions? Any really oddball questions?
- What answers seemed to go over well? What answers bombed?
- Were you asked to take any tests (skills, physical, drugs)?
- How long did you have to wait after a first interview to learn whether you were being invited for an office visit?

How long after an office visit did it take to learn whether you were being offered a job? How much time did the company give you to decide?
- What advice would you have for someone who will be interviewing next term or next year?

As Your Instructor Directs,
a. Summarize your findings in a memo to your instructor.
b. Report your findings orally to the class.
c. Join with a small group of students to write a group report describing the results of your survey.

29.9 **Interviewing an Interviewer**

Talk to someone who regularly interviews candidates for entry-level jobs. Possible questions to ask include the following:

- How long have you been interviewing for your organization? Does everyone on the management ladder at your company do some interviewing, or do people specialize in it?

- Do you follow a set structure for interviews? What are some of the standard questions you ask?
- What are you looking for? How important are (1) good grades, (2) leadership roles in extracurricular groups, or (3) relevant work experience? What advice would you give to

someone who doesn't have one or more of these?

- What are the things you see students do that create a poor impression? Think about the worst candidate you've interviewed. What did he or she do (or not do) to create such a negative impression?
- What are the things that make a good impression? Recall the best student you've ever interviewed. Why did he or she impress you so much?
- How does your employer evaluate and reward your success as an interviewer?

- What advice would you have for someone who still has a year or so before the job hunt begins?

As Your Instructor Directs,
a. Summarize your findings in a memo to your instructor.
b. Report your findings orally to the class.
c. Join with a small group of students to write a group report describing the results of your survey.
d. Write to the interviewer thanking him or her for taking the time to talk to you.

29.10 Preparing an Interview Strategy

Based on your analysis for Problems 27.8 and 27.9, prepare an interview strategy.

1. List two to five things about yourself that you want the interviewer to know before you leave the interview.
2. Identify any weaknesses or apparent weaknesses in your record and plan ways to explain them or minimize them.

3. List the points you need to learn about an employer to decide whether to accept an office visit or plant trip.

As Your Instructor Directs,
a. Share your strategy with a small group of other students.
b. Describe your strategy in a memo to your instructor.
c. Present your strategy orally to the class.

29.11 Preparing Answers to Behavioral Interview Questions

Answer the questions in Figure 29.4.

As Your Instructor Directs,
a. Share your answers with a small group of other students.
b. Present your answers in a memo to your instructor, and explain why

you've chosen the examples you describe.
c. Present your answers orally to the class.

29.12 Preparing Questions to Ask Employers

Prepare a list of questions to ask at job interviews.

1. Prepare a list of three to five general questions that apply to most employers in your field.
2. Prepare two to five specific questions for each of the three companies you are most interested in.

As Your Instructor Directs,
a. Share the questions with a small group of other students.
b. List the questions in a memo to your instructor.
c. Present your questions orally to the class.

Polishing Your Prose

Using a Dictionary

Like any tool, a dictionary has many uses. It shows how to spell words, defines them, details pronunciation, and sometimes, like a thesaurus, gives synonyms.

But using dictionaries can be challenging for non-native speakers of English. To look up words, you must first know their spelling, or at least be close enough. Definitions may have words the reader does not know, and several definitions may exist—which is the one you want? Slang terms may be missing, as well as idiomatic expressions.

Two different kinds exist. Most are *descriptive*, meaning they explain how words *are* used, including slang and other non-standard usages. Other dictionaries are *prescriptive*, telling how editors think words *should* be used. For instance, "verbal" in a descriptive dictionary would mean spoken, not written words. "Verbal" in a prescriptive dictionary would mean using words.

The type of dictionary is usually shown in the introduction or preface.

Well-meaning foreign language dictionaries may prescribe words and phrases that are out of date or too formal.

Lastly, dictionaries come in all shapes and sizes. A portable pocket dictionary is unlikely to be as comprehensive as a 700-page college edition, which may be impractical for students to carry around.

Use these questions to evaluate a dictionary:

- Is it descriptive or prescriptive?
- Do the definitions make sense to you?
- Are common and uncommon terms in your field of study defined?
- Does your English instructor find it appropriate for the class?
- If you are using a foreign language dictionary, share some of the definitions with native speakers of English. Do they agree with the definitions?

Exercises

Compare and contrast the definitions of the following words in both prescriptive and descriptive dictionaries. Which definition for each do you prefer and why?

1. Dialogue
2. Input
3. Text
4. Space
5. Position
6. Compose
7. Engineer
8. Document
9. Monitor
10. Champion

Check your answers to the odd-numbered exercises in the back of the book.

BComm Skill Booster

To apply the concepts in this module, complete lesson 49 on preparing for job interview questions. You can access the BComm Skill Booster through the text Web site at **www.mhhe.com/bcs2e.**

Module 30

Follow-Up Letters and Calls and Job Offers

Start by asking these questions:

- What should I say in a follow-up phone call or letter?

- What do I do if my first offer isn't the one I most want?

What you do after the interview can determine whether you get the job. One woman wanted to switch from banking, where she was working in corporate relations, to advertising. The ad agency interviewer expressed doubts about her qualifications. Immediately after leaving the agency, she tracked down a particular book the interviewer had mentioned he was looking for but had been unable to find. She presented it to him—and was hired.[1]

Xerox expects applicants for sales and repair positions to follow up within 10 days. If they don't, the company assumes that the person wouldn't follow up with clients.[2]

If the employer sends you an e-mail query, answer it promptly. You're being judged not only on what you say but on how quickly you respond.

What should I say in a follow-up phone call or letter?

Reinforce positives and overcome any negatives.

Site *to* See

Go to
interview.monster.com/
encore/followup
for a good sample follow-up
letter after an interview.

After a first interview, make follow-up phone calls to reinforce positives from the first interview, to overcome any negatives, and to get information you can use to persuade the interviewer to hire you. Career coach Kate Wendleton suggests asking the following questions:

- "Is there more information I can give you?"
- "I've been giving a lot of thought to your project and have some new ideas. Can we meet to go over them?"
- "Where do I stand? How does my work compare with the work others presented?"[3]

A letter after an office visit is essential to thank your hosts for their hospitality as well as to send in receipts for your expenses. A well-written letter can be the deciding factor that gets you the job.[4] The letter should

- Remind the interviewer of what he or she liked in you.
- Counter any negative impressions that may have come up at the interview.
- Use the jargon of the company and refer to specific things you learned during your interview or saw during your visit.
- Be enthusiastic.
- Refer to the next move, whether you'll wait to hear from the employer or whether you want to call to learn about the status of your application.

Be sure that the letter is well written and error-free. One employer reports,

> I often interviewed people whom I liked, . . . but their follow-up letters were filled with misspelled words and names and other inaccuracies. They blew their chance with the follow-up letter.[5]

Figure 30.1 is an example of a follow-up letter after an office visit.

Figure 30.1

Follow-Up Letter after an Office Visit

405 West College Street, Apt. 201
Thibodaux, LA 70301
April 2, 2004

Single-space your address, date when you don't use letterhead.

Mr. Robert Land, Account Manager
Sive Associates
378 Norman Boulevard
Cincinnati, OH 48528

Dear Mr. Land:

After visiting Sive Associates last week, I'm even more sure that writing direct mail is the career for me.

Refers to things she saw and learned during the interview.

I've always been able to brainstorm ideas, but sometimes, when I had to focus on one idea for a class project, I wasn't sure which idea was best. It was fascinating to see how you make direct mail scientific as well as creative by testing each new creative package against the control. I can understand how pleased Linda Hayes was when she learned that her new package for *Smithsonian* beat the control.

Reminds interviewer of her strong points.

Seeing Kelly, Luke, and Gene collaborating on the Sesame Street package gave me some sense of the tight deadlines you're under. As you know, I've learned to meet deadlines, not only for my class assignments, but also in working on Nicholls' newspaper. The award I won for my feature on the primary election suggests that my quality holds up even when the deadline is tight!

Thank you for your hospitality while I was in Cincinnati. You and your wife made my stay very pleasant. I especially appreciate the time the two of you took to help me find information about apartments that are accessible to wheelchairs. Cincinnati seems like a very liveable city.

I'm excited about a career in direct mail and about the (possibility) of joining Sive Associates. I look forward to hearing from you soon!

Be positive, not pushy. She doesn't assume she has the job.

Refers to what will happen next.

Sincerely,

Gina Focasio

Gina Focasio
(504) 555-2948

Writer's phone number.

Puts request for reimbursement in P.S. to de-emphasize it. Focuses on the job, not the cost of the trip.

P.S. My expenses totaled $454. Enclosed are receipts for my plane fare from New Orleans to Cincinnati ($367), the taxi to the airport in Cincinnati ($30), and the bus from Thibodaux to New Orleans ($57).

Encl.: Receipts for Expenses

Being Enthusiastic

Every employer wants employees who are enthusiastic about their work. Enthusiastic people seem more energetic than others; they're more fun to be around. The more enthusiasm you show, the better you'll do in job interviews and on the job itself.

It's easiest to show enthusiasm when you really feel it. Don't settle for "just a paycheck." In addition to meeting your financial needs, the ideal job would let you

- Use the skills you want to use.
- Work with the kind of people you want to be around.
- Work with a product, service, or idea that interests you.
- Have the level of responsibility you want.
- Build knowledge and skills so that you'll be even more employable in the future.
- Achieve a goal that matters.

While you may not get all of these factors in a single job offer, you probably can get the ones that matter most to you—if you know what they are.

Seeming enthusiastic is easy for some outgoing people. If you're naturally shy or reserved, showing your enthusiasm may feel like "acting" at first. If you're reserved,

- Smile.
- Lean forward as you talk.
- Put lots of energy into your voice. Vary pace, tone, and volume.
- Use energy in body movements. Gesture while you sit still. Walk quickly. (In some company cultures, run.)
- Let your comments show your interest. Show that you've done your homework. Volunteer to work on issues. Talk to people about issues informally as well as in meetings.
- Participate fully in games and activities designed to energize workers. Think of ways to showcase your talents to help energize others.

Dell works to build enthusiasm. Talented people who are excited about what they do give companies a competitive advantage. Here, managers dash to a meeting.

What do I do if my first offer isn't the one I most want?

Phone your first-choice employer to find out where you are on that list.

Some employers offer jobs at the end of the office visit. In other cases, you may wait for weeks or even months to hear. Employers almost always offer jobs orally. You must say something in response immediately, so plan some strategies.

If your first offer is not from your first choice, express your pleasure at being offered the job, but do not accept it on the phone. "That's great! I assume I have two weeks to let you know?" Some companies offer "exploding" job offers that expire in one week or less,[6] but most firms will give you two weeks.

Then *call* the other companies you're interested in. Explain, "I've just got a job offer, but I'd rather work for you. Can you tell me what the status of my application is?" Nobody will put that information in writing, but almost everyone will tell you over the phone. With this information, you're in a better position to decide whether to accept the original offer.

Some applicants have been successful in getting two weeks extended to several weeks or even months. Certainly if you cannot decide by the deadline, it is worth asking for more time: The worst the company can do is say *no.* If you do try to keep a company hanging, be prepared for weekly phone calls asking you if you've decided yet.

Make your acceptance contingent upon a written job offer confirming the terms. That letter should spell out not only salary but also fringe benefits and any special provisions you have negotiated. If something is missing, call the interviewer for clarification: "You said that I'd be reviewed for a promotion and higher

The secret of success

© 1999 Ziggy and Friends, Inc. /Dist. by Universal Press Syndicate

Instant Replay

Follow-Up Phone Calls

After a first interview, make follow-up phone calls to reinforce positives from the first interview, to overcome any negatives, and to get information you can use to persuade the interviewer to hire you.

Instant Replay

Follow-Up Letters

A letter after an office visit should

- Remind the interviewer of what he or she liked in you.
- Counter any negative impressions.
- Use the jargon of the company and refer to specifics from the visit.
- Be enthusiastic.
- Refer to the next move.

Figure 30.2
Letter Expressing Continued Interest in a Position

4531 Sand Hill Dr.
Fullerton, CA 92842
May 14, 2004

Single-space your address, date when you don't use letterhead.

Mr. Adam Phillips
Benner Electronics
1715 Ridgeview Pkwy.
San Diego, CA 91325-5472

Dear Mr. Phillips:

Summarize situation in ¶1.

Four weeks ago, I sent a résumé and job application letter to Benner Electronics for the position of Regional Sales Manager but have not heard from anyone. I wanted you to know I am still interested in the position and am available for an interview.

Since submitting my materials, I was awarded a "Gold Medal of Achievement" from my present employer for outstanding sales in April. I led the Orange County group in semiconductor sales, with more than 45,000 units sold for a total of $81,700.

Add achievements that occurred after you sent your résumé in.

I would like to discuss how I might put my energy and enthusiasm to work as Benner Electronics' next Regional Sales Manager. If you would like to schedule an interview, please let me know.

Sincerely,

Maria Alvarez

Maria Alvarez
714-555-1219   *Writer's phone number*

salary in six months, but that isn't in the letter." You have more power to resolve misunderstandings now than you will after six months or a year on the job.

When you've accepted one job, let the other places you visited know that you're no longer interested. Then they can go to their second choices. If you're second on someone else's list, you'll appreciate other candidates' removing themselves so the way is clear for you.

If you already have a job, you may decide to wait until your desired employer does offer you a job. Figure 30.2 is an example of a letter telling a company that the candidate is still interested.

Summary of Key Points

- Use follow-up phone calls to reinforce positives from the first interview, to overcome any negatives, and to get information you can use to persuade the interviewer to hire you.
- A follow-up letter should
  - Remind the interviewer of what he or she liked in you.
  - Counter any negative impressions that may have come up at the interview.
- Use the jargon of the company and refer to specific things you learned during your interview or saw during your visit.
- Be enthusiastic.
- Refer to the next move you'll make.
- If your first offer isn't from your first choice, call the other companies you're interested in to ask the status of your application.

Assignments for Module 30

Questions for Comprehension

30.1 What should you do in a follow-up phone call?

30.2 What should you do in a follow-up letter?

30.3 What should you do if the first offer you get isn't from your first-choice employer?

30.4 Why should you phone rather than write or e-mail your first-choice employer after you've received another job offer?

Questions for Critical Thinking

30.5 Is it ethical for a quiet, reserved person to try to seem more enthusiastic?

30.6 How could you counter a negative impression that came up during an interview?

30.7 Why is it important to get a job offer in writing before you accept it officially?

Exercises and Problems

30.8 **Writing a Follow-Up Letter after an Onsite Visit**

Write a follow-up e-mail message or letter after an onsite visit or plant trip. Thank your hosts for their hospitality; relate your strong points to things you learned about the company during the visit; allay any negatives that may remain; be enthusiastic about the company; and submit receipts for your expenses so you can be reimbursed.

30.9 **Clarifying the Terms of a Job Offer**

Last week, you got a job offer from your first-choice company, and you accepted it over the phone. Today, the written confirmation arrived. The letter specifies the starting salary and fringe benefits you had negotiated. However, during the office visit, you were promised a 5% raise in six months. The job offer says nothing about the raise. You do want the job, but you want it on the terms you thought you had negotiated.

Write to your contact at the company, Eliza Raymono.

Polishing Your Prose

Who / Whom and I / Me

Even established writers sometimes get confused about when to use *who* versus *whom* and *I* versus *me.* These pronouns serve different functions in a sentence or part of a sentence.

Use *who* or *I* as the subject of a sentence or clause.

Correct: Who put the file on my desk? (*Who* did the action, *put.*)

Correct: Keisha and I gave the presentation at our annual meeting. (Both *Keisha* and *I* did the action, *gave.*)

Correct: John, who just received a Ph.D. in management science, was promoted to vice president. (*Who* is the subject of the clause "who just received a Ph.D. in management science.")

Use *whom* and *me* as the object of a verb or a preposition.

Correct: Whom did you write the report for? (*Whom* is the object of the preposition *for.*)

Correct: She recommended Thuy and me for promotions. (*Me* is an object of the verb *recommend.*)

Though some print sources may use *who* and *whom* interchangeably, stick to the rules until this practice becomes widely acceptable.

If you're not sure whether a pronoun is being used as a subject or object, try substi-

tuting *he* or *him.* If *he* would work, the pronoun is a subject. If *him* sounds right, the pronoun is an object.

Correct: He wrote the report.

Correct: I wrote the report for him.

Exercises

Choose the correct word in each set of brackets.

1. For [who/whom] is this letter intended?

2. This report should be sent to [who/whom] for duplication?

3. Take it from Les and [I/me]: it pays to be prepared in business.

4. Tell the Accounting Department that Tom and [I/me] are on our way up for the meeting.

5. There was only about an hour for Kelly, Maria, and [I/me] to get to the airport.

6. A friend [who/whom] visited our office last week would like to apply for a job here.

7. It is the customer for [who / whom] we make our product.

8. I can't tell from the damaged label [who/whom] the package is for— better call the delivery service and get it traced for [I/me].

9. Trust [I/me]: it's not a good idea to begin a letter with "To [who/whom] it may concern," even if people frequently do.

10. Jenny and [I/me] expect to have the proposal draft finished by noon. Should she or [I/me] call you when it's ready?

Check your answers to the odd-numbered exercises at the back of the book.

BComm Skill Booster

To apply the concepts in this module, complete lesson 50 on following-up on your job interview. You can access the BComm Skill Booster through the text Web site at **www.mhhe.com/bcs2e.**

Cases for Communicators

A Needle in the E-Haystack

The average online job applicant is invisible to potential employers, hidden in the crowd of résumés filling their in-boxes and databases.

Online job boards greatly increased a company's pool of potential applicants. That larger pool of applicants quickly became a sea of résumés flooding human resource departments. In response, many companies have had to rethink their use of these general-purpose job boards. Some now use special software programs with filters to identify only those résumés that contain specific key words. Résumés lacking those predetermined words never make it out of cyberspace and into the company's files, much less onto someone's desk. Other companies now include questionnaires as part of their online application process in an attempt to gauge the "fit" of a candidate, and still other companies have stopped using the general job boards altogether, relying instead on niche job boards that focus on special skills or career areas.

Tailoring résumés to suit specific jobs has always been good practice in an employment search, but it is critical when applying for a position online. Applicants need to take special care to investigate the positions for which they are applying so they can include relevant keywords and details. General-purpose boards help you see the breadth of employment opportunities, but you're more likely to find a job on niche job boards and employment sites operated by companies, colleges and universities, and professional organizations.

The best way for an online job seeker to stand out from the crowd is to make a personal contact within the company. In other words, network, network, and network to land that next job. Of course, you can take advantage of the speed and efficiency of e-mail to make those connections!

Source: T. Shawn Taylor, "With So Many Resumes on the Internet, Many End Up Cyber-Trashed," *The Chicago Tribune,* January 30, 2002. Accessed on Chicago Tribune Online Edition (www.chicagotribune.com) on August 16, 2002.

Individual Activity

Imagine that you are a consultant at an employment services company. In this position, you offer job seekers advice and expertise on targeted job searches, résumés, cover letters, and interviewing.

The company has an extensive database of employment resources, but you and your colleagues must constantly work to keep the information complete and accurate. In addition to your consulting schedule, you must identify one career path per week and do an exhaustive search of placement and informational resources in that field.

Your task is to think of a career in which you are interested and create a list of resources that you could use to find job leads, get information, and identify networking possibilities. Use all information options available to you, including the local library, school resources, and Internet, among others.

Before you being your search, consider the following questions:

- What general directories or resource books could I use?
- What specialized directories or resource books should I investigate?
- What trade journals could I explore?
- Have I identified general online search sites?
- What niche sites could I explore?
- Which professional organizations would have information or resources?
- What major companies in the field should I investigate?
- What are their competitors?
- What additional career information could I find in my campus placement office?
- Do I know anyone who is already in the field?
- Can I access an alumni networks or placement services?
- Have I reviewed local and national papers for job leads?
- What professional listservs or electronic bulletin boards would be relevant?
- What other resources could I explore to find out more about opportunities in this field?

Group Activity

(Note: To prepare for this group activity, find at least three job postings that include detailed descriptions of the position, required skills, and hiring company. These types of postings are relatively easy to find on online job search engines, such as Monster.com. Copy these postings and distribute them to each member of the group.)

As a consultant at an employment services company, you meet regularly with your colleagues to review the quality of the company's offerings and to hone your skills through group training. Last week, in a discussion about client needs, you realized that, as a result in the upswing of employment opportunities in the area, your company has seen an increased number of clients who need help targeting their cover letters and résumés for specific positions.

Review the first job posting. As you read, consider the following:

- What are the key words in this posting?
- What specific information, if any, does the posting highlight about the company, its industry, or its products or services?
- What are the specific skills required for the position?

As a group, discuss the advice that you might give to someone applying for this position. What advice could give to this client on targeting a cover letter or résumé?

Answer the following questions:

- What are the key words you would expect this employer to look for in a résumé?
- What active words should your client try to use in a résumé or cover letter?
- What skills or types of skills should your client emphasize?
- What details about the company could or should the client include in this solicited letter?

Review each job posting. How do you think this type of exercise might benefit you as you prepare your own résumé and cover letters and begin to interview for positions?

Glossary

A

Acknowledgment responses Nods, smiles, frowns, and words that let a speaker know you are listening.

Active listening Feeding back the literal meaning or the emotional content or both so that the speaker knows that the listener has heard and understood.

Active verb A verb that describes the action of the grammatical subject of the sentence.

Adjustment The response to a claim letter. If the company agrees to grant a refund, the amount due will be adjusted.

Analytical report A report that interprets information.

Assumptions Statements that are not proven in a report, but on which the recommendations are based.

B

Bar graph A visual consisting of parallel bars or rectangles that represent specific sets of data.

Behavioral interviews Job interviews that ask candidates to describe actual behaviors they have used in the past in specific situations.

Bias-free language Language that does not discriminate against people on the basis of sex, physical condition, race, age, or any other category.

Blind ads Job listings that do not list the company's name.

Blind copies Copies sent to other recipients that are not listed on the original letter or memo.

Block format In letters, a format in which inside address, date, and signature block are lined up at the left margin.

Blocking Disagreeing with every idea that is proposed in a meeting.

Body The main part of a letter, memo, or report.

Body language Nonverbal communication conveyed by posture and movement, eye contact, facial expressions, and gestures.

Boilerplate Language from a previous document that a writer includes in a new document. Writers use boilerplate both to save time and energy and to use language that has already been approved by the organization's legal staff.

Brainstorming A method of generating ideas by recording everything a person or a group thinks of, without judging or evaluating the ideas.

Branching question Question that sends respondents who answer differently to different parts of the questionnaire. Allows respondents to answer only those questions that are relevant to their experience.

Bridge A sentence that connects the attention-getter to the body of a letter.

Buffer A neutral or positive statement designed to allow the writer to bury, or buffer, the negative message.

Build goodwill To create a good image of yourself and of your organization—the kind of image that makes people want to do business with you.

Bullets Large round dots or squares that set off items in a list. When you are giving examples, but the number is not exact and the order does not matter, use bullets to set off items.

Business slang Terms that have technical meaning but are used in more general senses. Used sparingly, these terms are appropriate in job application letters and in messages for people in the same organization, who are likely to share the vocabulary.

Businessese A kind of jargon including unnecessary words. Some words were common 200 to 300 years ago but are no longer part of spoken English. Some have never been used outside of business writing. All of these terms should be omitted.

Buying time with limited agreement Agreeing with the small part of a criticism that one does accept as true.

C

Case The grammatical role a noun or pronoun plays in a sentence. The nominative case is used for the subject of a clause, the possessive to show who or what something belongs to, the objective case for the object of a verb or a preposition.

Channel   The physical means by which a message is sent. Written channels include memos, letters, and billboards. Oral channels include phone calls, speeches, and face-to-face conversations.

Channel overload   The inability of a channel to carry all the messages that are being sent.

Chartjunk   Decoration that is irrelevant to a visual and that may be misleading.

Checking for feelings   Identifying the emotions that the previous speaker seemed to be expressing verbally or nonverbally.

Checking for inferences   Trying to identify the unspoken content or feelings implied by what the previous speaker has actually said.

Choice or selection   The decision to include or omit information in a message.

Chronological résumé   A résumé that lists what you did in a timeline, starting with the most recent events and going backward in reverse chronology.

Citation   Attributing a quotation or other idea to a source in the body of the report.

Claim letter   A letter seeking a replacement or refund.

Clear   A message whose audience gets the meaning the writer or speaker intended.

Clip art   Predrawn images that you can import into your newsletter, sign, or graph.

Close   The ending of a document.

Closed or defensive body position   Keeping the arms and legs crossed and close to the body. Suggests physical and psychological discomfort, defending oneself, and shutting the other person out.

Closed question   Question with a limited number of possible responses.

Closure report   A report summarizing completed research that does not result in action or recommendation.

Clowning   Making unproductive jokes and diverting the group from its task.

Clustering   A method of thinking up ideas by writing the central topic in the middle of the page, circling it, writing down the ideas that topic suggests, and circling them.

Collaborative writing   Working with other writers to produce a single document.

Collection letter   A letter asking a customer to pay for goods and services received.

Collection series   A series of letters asking customers to pay for goods and services they have already received. Early letters in the series assume that the reader intends to pay but has forgotten or has met with temporary reverses. Final letters threaten legal action if the bill is not paid.

Comma splice or comma fault   Using a comma to join two independent clauses. To correct, use a semicolon, add a coordinating conjunction, subordinate one of the clauses, or use a period and start a new sentence.

Common ground   Values and goals that the writer and reader share.

Communication theory   A theory explaining what happens when we communicate and where miscommunication can occur.

Complaint letter   A letter that challenges a policy or tries to get a decision changed.

Complete   A message that answers all of the audience's questions. The audience has enough information to evaluate the message and act on it.

Complex sentence   Sentence with one main clause and one subordinate clause.

Complimentary close   The words after the body of the letter and before the signature. *Sincerely* and *Cordially* are the most commonly used complimentary closes in business letters.

Compound sentence   Sentence with two main clauses joined by a conjunction.

Conclusions   Section of a report that restates the main points.

Conflict resolution   Strategies for getting at the real issue, keeping discussion open, and minimizing hurt feelings so that people can find a solution that feels good to everyone involved.

Connotations   The emotional colorings or associations that accompany a word.

Convenience sample   A group of subjects to whom the researcher has easy access.

Conversational style   Conversational patterns such as speed and volume of speaking, pauses between speakers, whether questions are direct or indirect. When different speakers assign different meanings to a specific pattern, miscommunication results.

Coordinating   Planning work, giving directions, fitting together contributions of group members.

Coordination   The third stage in the life of a task group, when the group finds, organizes, and interprets information and examines alternatives and assumptions. This is the longest of the four stages.

Correct   Used to describe a message that is accurate and free from errors in punctuation, spelling, grammar, word order, and sentence structure.

Credibility   The audience's response to the source of the message.

Criteria   The standards used to evaluate or weigh the factors in a decision.

Critical incident   An important event that illustrates a subordinate's behavior.

Cropping   Cutting a photograph to fit a specific space. Also, photographs are cropped to delete visual information that is unnecessary or unwanted.

Culture   The unconscious patterns of behavior and beliefs that are common to a people, nation, or organization.

Cycling   The process of sending a document from writer to superior to writer to yet another superior for several rounds of revisions before the document is approved.

D

Dangling modifier   A phrase that modifies a word that is not actually in a sentence. To correct a dangling modifier, recast the modifier as a subordinate clause or revise the sentence so its subject or object can be modified by the now-dangling phrase.

Data   Facts or figures from which conclusions can be drawn.

Decode   To extract meaning from symbols.

Decorative visual   A visual that makes the speaker's points more memorable but that does not convey numerical data.

Defensive or closed body position   Keeping the arms and legs crossed and close to the body. Suggests physical and psychological discomfort, defending oneself, and shutting the other person out.

Demographic characteristics   Measurable features of an audience that can be counted objectively: age, sex, race, education level, income, etc.

Denotation   A word's literal or "dictionary" meaning. Most common words in English have more than one denotation. Context usually makes it clear which of several meanings is appropriate.

Dependent clause   A group of words that contains a subject and a verb but cannot stand by itself as a complete sentence.

Descriptors   Words describing the content of an article. Used to permit computer searches for information on a topic.

Dingbats   Small symbols such as arrows, pointing fingers, and so forth that are part of a typeface.

Direct request   A pattern of organization that makes the request directly in the first and last paragraphs.

Directed subject line   A subject line that makes clear the writer's stance on the issue.

Discourse community   A group of people who share assumptions about what channels, formats, and styles to use for communication, what topics to discuss and how to discuss them, and what constitutes evidence.

Document design   The process of writing, organizing, and laying out a document so that it can be easily used by the intended audience.

Documentation   Providing full bibliographic information so that interested readers can go to the original source of material used in a report.

Dominating   Trying to run a group by ordering, shutting out others, and insisting on one's own way.

E

Early letter   A collection letter that is gentle. An early letter assumes that the reader intends to pay but has forgotten or has met with temporary reverses.

Editing   Checking the draft to see that it satisfies the requirements of good English and the principles of business writing. Unlike revision, which can produce major changes in meaning, editing focuses on the surface of writing.

Ego-involvement   The emotional commitment the audience has to its position.

Elimination of alternatives   A pattern of organization for reports that discusses the problem and its causes, the impractical solutions and their weaknesses, and finally the solution the writer favors.

Emotional appeal   Making the audience want to do what the writer or speaker asks.

Empathy   The ability to put oneself in someone else's shoes, to *feel with* that person.

Encode   To put ideas into symbols.

Enunciate   To voice all the sounds of each word while speaking.

Evaluating   Measuring the draft against your goals and the requirements of the situation and audience. Anything produced during each stage of the writing process can be evaluated, not just the final draft.

Evidence   Facts or data the audience already accepts.

Exaggeration   Making something sound bigger or more important than it really is.

Executive summary   A summary of a report, specifying the recommendations and the reasons for them.

Expectancy theory   A theory that argues that motivation is based on the expectation of being rewarded for performance and the importance of the reward.

External audiences   Audiences who are not part of the writer's organization.

External documents   Documents that go to people in another organization.

External report   Report written by a consultant for an organization of which he or she is not a permanent employee.

Extrinsic benefits   Benefits that are "added on"; they are not a necessary part of the product or action.

Eye contact   Looking another person directly in the eye.

F

Feasibility study   A report that evaluates two or more possible alternatives and recommends one of them. Doing nothing is always one alternative.

Feedback   The receiver's response to a message.

Figure   Any visual that is not a table.

Fixed typeface   A typeface in which each letter has the same width on the page. Sometimes called *typewriter typeface.*

Flaming   Sending out an angry e-mail message before thinking about the implications of venting one's anger.

Focus groups   Small groups who come in to talk with a skilled leader about a potential product.

Forced choice   A choice in which each item is ranked against every other item. Used to discover which of a large number of criteria are crucial.

Form letter   A letter that is sent unchanged or with only minor modifications to a large number of readers.

Formal meetings   Meetings run under strict rules, such as the rules of parliamentary procedure summarized in *Robert's Rules of Order.*

Formal report   A report containing formal elements such as a title page, a transmittal, a table of contents, and an abstract.

Formalization   The fourth and last stage in the life of a task group, when the group makes and formalizes its decision.

Format   The parts of a document and the way they are arranged on a page.

Formation   The second stage in the life of a task group, when members choose a leader and define the problem they must solve.

Freewriting   A kind of writing uninhibited by any constraints. Freewriting may be useful in overcoming writer's block, among other things.

G

Gatekeeper   The audience with the power to decide whether your message is sent on to other audiences. Some gatekeepers are also initial audiences.

Gathering   Physically getting the background data you need. It can include informal and formal research or simply getting the letter to which you're responding.

General slang   Words or phrases such as *awesome, smokin',* or *at the end of my rope* that are sometimes used in conversations and in presentations, but are not appropriate in business and administrative writing since they appear sloppy or imprecise.

Gerund   The *-ing* form of a verb; grammatically, it is a verb used as a noun.

Getting feedback   Asking someone else to evaluate your work. Feedback is useful at every stage of the writing process, not just during composition of the final draft.

Glossary   A list of terms used in a report with their definitions.

Goodwill   The value of a business beyond its tangible assets, including its reputation and patronage. Also, a favorable condition and overall atmosphere of trust that can be fostered between parties conducting business.

Goodwill ending   Shift of emphasis away from the message to the reader. A goodwill ending is positive, personal, and forward-looking and suggests that serving the reader is the real concern.

Goodwill presentation   A presentation that entertains and validates the audience.

Grammar checker   Software program that flags errors or doubtful usage.

Grapevine   The informal informational network in an organization, which carries gossip and rumors as well as accurate information.

Ground rules   Procedural rules adopted by groups to make meetings run smoothly.

Groupthink   The tendency for a group to reward agreement and directly or indirectly punish dissent.

Guided discussion   A presentation in which the speaker presents the questions or issues that both speaker and audience have agreed on in advance. Instead of functioning as an expert with all the answers, the speaker serves as a facilitator to help the audience tap its own knowledge.

H

Headings   Words or short phrases that group points and divide your letter, memo, or report into sections.

Hearing   Perceiving sounds.

Hidden job market   Jobs that are never advertised but may be available or may be created for the right candidate.

Hidden negatives   Words that are not negative in themselves, but become negative in context.

High-context culture   A culture in which most information is inferred from the context, rather than being spelled out explicitly in words.

Histogram   A bar graph using pictures, asterisks, or points to represent a unit of the data.

Hot buttons   Issues to which the audience has a strong emotional response.

I

Impersonal expression   A sentence that attributes actions to inanimate objects, designed to avoid placing blame on a reader.

Indented format   A format for résumés in which items that are logically equivalent begin at the same horizontal space, with carryover lines indented three spaces. Indented format emphasizes job titles.

Independent clause   A group of words that can stand by itself as a complete sentence.

Infinitive   The form of the verb that is preceded by *to.*

Inform   To explain something or tell the audience something.

Informal meetings   Loosely run meetings in which votes are not taken on every point.

Informal report   A report using letter or memo format.

Information interview   An interview in which you talk to someone who works in the area you hope to enter to find out what the day-to-day work involves and how you can best prepare to enter that field.

Information overload   The inability of a human receiver to process all the messages he or she receives.

Information report   A report that collects data for the reader but does not recommend action.

Informational messages   In a group, messages focusing on the problem, data, and possible solutions.

Informative message   Message to which the reader's basic reaction will be neutral.

Informative presentation   A presentation that informs or teaches the audience.

Informative or **talking heads**   Headings that are detailed enough to provide an overview of the material in the sections they introduce.

Initial audience   The audience that assigns the message and routes it to other audiences.

Inside address   The reader's name and address; put below the date and above the salutation in most letter formats.

Interactive presentation   A conversation in which the seller uses questions to determine the buyer's needs, probe objections, and gain provisional and then final commitment to the purchase.

Intercultural competence   The ability to communicate sensitively with people from other cultures and countries, based on an understanding of cultural differences.

Internal audiences   Audiences in the writer's organization.

Internal document   Document written for other employees in the same organization.

Internal documentation   Providing information about a source in the text itself rather than in footnotes or endnotes.

Internal report   Reports written by employees for use only in their organization.

Interpersonal communication   Communication between people.

Interpersonal messages   In a group, messages promoting friendliness, cooperation, and group loyalty.

Interpret   To determine the significance or importance of a message.

Interview   Structured conversation with someone who is able to give you useful information.

Intrinsic benefits   Benefits that come automatically from using a product or doing something.

Introduction   The part of a report that states the purpose and scope of the report. The introduction may also include limitations, assumptions, methods, criteria, and definitions.

J

Jargon   There are two kinds of jargon. The first kind is the specialized terminology of a technical field. The second is businessese, outdated words that do not have technical meanings and are not used in other forms of English.

Judgment sample   A group of subjects whose views seem useful.

Justification report   Report that justifies the need for a purchase, an investment, a new personnel line, or a change in procedure.

Justified margins   Margins that end evenly on the right side of the page.

K

Keywords or descriptors   Words describing the content of an article used to permit computer searches for information on a topic.

L

Late letter   A collection letter that threatens legal action if the bill is not paid.

Letter   Short document using block or modified block format that goes to readers outside your organization.

Letterhead   Stationery with the organization's name, logo, address, and telephone number printed on the page.

Limitations   Problems or factors that limit the validity of the recommendations of a report.

Line graph   A visual consisting of lines that show trends or allow the viewer to interpolate values between the observed values.

Listening   Decoding and interpreting sounds correctly.

Low-context culture   A culture in which most information is conveyed explicitly in words rather than being inferred from context.

M

Main or independent clause   A group of words that can stand by itself as a complete sentence.

Maslow's hierarchy of needs   Five levels of human need posited by Abraham H. Maslow. They include physical needs, the need for safety and security, for love and belonging, for esteem and recognition, and for self-actualization.

Mean   The average. Found by adding up all the numbers and dividing by the number of numbers.

Median   The middle number.

Memo   Document using memo format sent to readers in your organization.

Methods section   The section of a report or survey describing how the data were gathered.

Middle letter   A collection letter that is more assertive than an early letter. Middle letters may offer to negotiate a schedule for repayment if the reader is not able to pay the whole bill immediately, remind the reader of the importance of good credit, educate the reader about credit, or explain why the creditor must have prompt payment.

Minutes   Records of a meeting, listing the items discussed, the results of votes, and the persons responsible for carrying out follow-up steps.

Misplaced modifier   A word or phrase that appears to modify another element of the sentence than the writer intended.

Mixed punctuation   Using a colon after the salutation and a comma after the complimentary close in a letter.

Mode   The most frequent number.

Modified block format   A letter format in which the inside address, date, and signature block are lined up with each other one-half or one-third of the way over on the page.

Modifier   A word or phrase giving more information about another word in a sentence.

Monochronic culture   Culture which treats time as a limited resource and emphasizes efficiency.

Monologue presentation   A presentation in which the speaker speaks without interruption. The presentation is planned and is delivered without deviation.

Myers-Briggs Type Indicator   A scale that categorizes people on four dimensions: introvert-extravert; sensing-intuitive; thinking-feeling; and perceiving-judging.

N

Negative message   A message in which basic information conveyed is negative; the reader is expected to be disappointed or angry.

News release   Messages that package information about a company and that the writer would like announced in local and national media.

Noise   Any physical or psychological interference in a message.

Nominative case   The grammatical form used for the subject of a clause. *I, we, he, she,* and *they* are nominative pronouns.

Nonagist   Words, images, or behaviors that do not discriminate against people on the basis of age.

Nonracist   Words, images, or behaviors that do not discriminate against people on the basis of race.

Nonrestrictive clause   A clause giving extra but unessential information about a noun or pronoun. Because the information is extra, commas separate the clause from the word it modifies.

Nonsexist language   Language that treats both sexes neutrally, that does not make assumptions about the proper gender for a job, and that does not imply that men are superior to or take precedence over women.

Nonverbal communication   Communication that does not use words.

Normal interview   A job interview with some questions that the interviewer expects to be easy, some questions that present an opportunity to showcase strong points, and some questions that probe any weaknesses evident from the résumé.

Noun–pronoun agreement   Having a pronoun be the same number (singular or plural) and the same person (first, second, or third) as the noun it refers to.

O

Objective case   The grammatical form used for the object of a verb or preposition. *Me, us, him, her,* and *them* are objective pronouns.

Omnibus motion   A motion that allows a group to vote on several related items in a single vote. Saves time in formal meetings with long agendas.

Open body position   Keeping the arms and legs uncrossed and away from the body. Suggests physical and psychological comfort and openness.

Open punctuation   Using no punctuation after the salutation and the complimentary close.

Open question   Question with an unlimited number of possible responses.

Organization   The order in which ideas are arranged in a message.

Organizational culture   The values, attitudes, and philosophies shared by people in an organization that shape its messages and its reward structure.

Orientation   The first stage in the life of a task group, when members meet and begin to define their task.

Original or **primary research**   Research that gathers new information.

P

Paired graphs   Two or more simple stories juxtaposed to create a more powerful story.

Parallel structure   Putting words or ideas that share the same role in the sentence's logic in the same grammatical form.

Paraphrase   To repeat in your own words the verbal content of what the previous speaker said.

Passive verb   A verb that describes action done to the grammatical subject of the sentence.

People-first language   Language that names the person first, then the condition: "people with mental retardation." Used to avoid implying that the condition defines the person's potential.

Perception   The ability to see, to hear, to taste, to smell, to touch.

Performance appraisals   Supervisors' written evaluations of their subordinates.

Personal space   The distance someone wants between him- or herself and other people in ordinary, nonintimate interchanges.

Personalized   A form letter that is adapted to the individual reader by including the reader's name and address and perhaps other information.

Persuade   To motivate and convince the audience to act.

Persuasive presentation   A presentation that motivates the audience to act or to believe.

Pie chart   A circular chart whose sections represent percentages of a given quantity.

Pitch   The highness or lowness of a sound. Low-pitched sounds are closer to the bass notes on a piano; high-pitched sounds are closer to the high notes.

Planning   All the thinking done about a subject and the means of achieving your purposes. Planning takes place not only when devising strategies for the document as a whole, but also when generating "mini-plans" that govern sentences or paragraphs.

Polychronic culture   Culture which emphasizes relationships rather than efficiency.

Population   The group a researcher wants to make statements about.

Positive emphasis   Focusing on the positive rather than the negative aspects of a situation.

Positive or good news message   Message to which the reader's reaction will be positive.

Possessive case   The grammatical form used to indicate possession or ownership. *My, our, his, hers, its,* and *their* are possessive pronouns.

Postal service abbreviations   Two-letter abbreviations for states and provinces.

Prepositions   Words that indicate relationships, for example, *with, in, under, at.*

Presenting problem   The problem that surfaces as the subject of disagreement. The presenting problem is often not the real problem.

Primary audience   The audience who will make a decision or act on the basis of a message.

Primary research   Research that gathers new information.

Pro and con pattern   A pattern of organization for reports that presents all the arguments for an alternative and then all the arguments against it.

Problem-solving persuasion   A pattern of organization that describes a problem that affects the reader before offering a solution to the problem.

Procedural messages   Messages focusing on a group's methods: how it makes decisions, who does what, when assignments are due.

Process of writing   What people actually do when they write. Most researchers would agree that the writing process can include eight parts: planning, gathering, writing, evaluating, getting feedback, revising, editing, and proofreading.

Product of writing   The final written document.

Progress report   A statement of the work done during a period of time and the work proposed for the next period.

Proofreading   Checking the final copy to see that it's free from typographical errors.

Proportional font   A font in which some letters are wider than other letters (for example, *w* is wider than *i*).

Proposal   Document that suggests a method for finding information or solving a problem.

Prospecting letter   A job application letter written to companies that have not announced openings but where you'd like to work.

Psychographic data   Human characteristics that are qualitative rather than quantitative: values, beliefs, goals, and lifestyles.

Psychological description   Description of a product or service in terms of reader benefits.

Psychological reactance   Phenomenon occurring when a reader reacts to a negative message by asserting freedom in some other arena.

Purpose statement   The statement in a proposal or a report specifying the organizational problem, the technical questions that must be answered to solve the problem, and the rhetorical purpose of the report (to explain, to recommend, to request, to propose).

Q

Questionnaire   List of questions for people to answer in a survey.

R

Ragged right or **unjustified margins**   Margins that do not end evenly on the right side of the page.

Random sample   A sample for which each person of the population theoretically has an equal chance of being chosen.

Reader benefits   Benefits or advantages that the reader gets by using the writer's services, buying the writer's products, following the writer's policies, or adopting the writer's ideas. Reader benefits can exist for policies and ideas as well as for goods and services.

Recommendation report   A report that recommends action.

Recommendations   Section of a report that specifies items for action.

Reference line   A *subject line* that refers the reader to another document (usually a numbered one, such as an invoice).

Referral interview   Interviews you schedule to learn about current job opportunities in your field and to get referrals to other people who may have the power to create a job for you. Useful for tapping into unadvertised jobs and the hidden job market.

Release date   Date a report will be made available to the public.

Request   To ask the audience to take an easy or routine action.

Request for proposal (RFP)   A statement of the service or product that an agency wants; a bid for proposals to provide that service or product.

Respondents   The people who fill out a questionnaire.

Response rate   The percentage of subjects receiving a questionnaire who agree to answer the questions.

Restrictive clause   A clause limiting or restricting the meaning of a noun or pronoun. Because its information is essential, no commas separate the clause from the word it restricts.

Résumé   A persuasive summary of your qualifications for employment.

Reverse chronology   Starting with the most recent job or degree and going backward. Pattern of organization used for chronological résumés.

Revising   Making changes in the draft: adding, deleting, substituting, or rearranging. Revision can be changes in single words, but more often it means major additions, deletions, or substitutions, as the writer measures the draft against purpose and audience and reshapes the document to make it more effective.

RFP   See *request for proposal*.

Rhetorical purpose   The effect the writer or speaker hopes to have on the audience (to inform, to persuade, to build goodwill).

Rival hypotheses   Alternate factors that might explain observed results.

Run-on sentence   A sentence containing several main clauses strung together with *and, but, or so,* or *for*.

S

Salutation   The greeting in a letter: "Dear Ms. Smith."

Sample   The portion of the population a researcher actually studies.

Sans serif   Literally, *without serifs*. Typeface whose letters lack bases or flicks. Helvetica and Geneva are examples of sans serif typefaces.

Saves the reader's time   The result of a message whose style, organization, and visual impact help the reader to read, understand, and act on the information as quickly as possible.

Scope statement   A statement in a proposal or report specifying the subjects the report covers and how broadly or deeply it covers them.

Secondary audience   The audience affected by the decision or action. These people may be asked by the primary audience to comment on a message or to implement ideas after they've been approved.

Secondary research   Research retrieving data someone else gathered.

Sentence fragment   A group of words that are not a complete sentence but that are punctuated as if they were a complete sentence.

Sentence outline   An outline using complete sentences that lists the sentences proving the thesis and the points proving each of those sentences. A sentence outline is the basis for a summary abstract.

Serif   The little extensions from the main strokes on the *r* and *g* and other letters. Times Roman and Courier are examples of serif typefaces.

Sexist interview   A stress interview in which questions are biased against one sex. Many sexist questions mask a legitimate concern. The best strategy is to respond as you would to a stress question: rephrase it and treat it as a legitimate request for information.

Signpost   An explicit statement of the place that a speaker or writer has reached: "Now we come to the third point."

Simple sentence   Sentence with one main clause.

Situational interviews   Job interviews in which candidates are asked to describe what they would do in specific hypothetical situations.

Skills résumé   A résumé organized around the skills you've used, rather than the date or the job in which you used them.

Slang   See *business slang* and *general slang*.

Solicited letter   A job letter written when you know that the company is hiring.

Spell checker   Software program that flags possible errors in spelling.

Spot visuals   Informal visuals that are inserted directly into text. Spot visuals do not have numbers or titles.

Stereotyping   Putting similar people or events into a single category, even though significant differences exist.

Storyboard   A visual representation of the structure of a document, with a rectangle representing each page or unit. An alternative to outlining as a method of organizing material.

Strategy   A plan for reaching your specific goals with a specific audience.

Stress   Emphasis given to one or more words in a sentence.

Stress interview   A job interview that deliberately puts the applicant under stress, physical or psychological. Here it's important to change the conditions that create physical stress and to meet psychological stress by rephrasing questions in less inflammatory terms and treating them as requests for information.

Structured interview   An interview that follows a detailed list of questions prepared in advance.

Subject line   The title of the document, used to file and retrieve the document. A subject line tells readers why they need to read the document and provides a framework in which to set what you're about to say.

Subjects   The people studied in an experiment, focus group, or survey.

Subordinate or dependent clause   A group of words containing a subject and a verb but that cannot stand by itself as a complete sentence.

Summarizing   Restating and relating major points, pulling ideas together.

Summary sentence or paragraph   A sentence or paragraph listing in order the topics that following sentences or paragraphs will discuss.

Survey   A method of getting information from a large group of people.

T

Table   Numbers or words arrayed in rows and columns.

Talking heads   Headings that are detailed enough to provide an overview of the material in the sections they introduce.

Teleconferencing   Telephone conference calls among three or more people in different locations and video-conferences where one-way or two-way TV supplements the audio channel.

Telephone tag   Making and returning telephone calls repeatedly before the two people are on the line at the same time.

10-K report   A report filed with the Securities and Exchange Commission summarizing the firm's financial performance; an informative document.

Thank-you letter   A letter thanking someone for helping you.

Threat   A statement, explicit or implied, that someone will be punished if he or she does something.

Tone   The implied attitude of the author toward the reader and the subject.

Tone of voice   The rising or falling inflection that indicates whether a group of words is a question or a statement, whether the speaker is uncertain or confident, whether a statement is sincere or sarcastic.

Topic outline   An outline listing the main points and the subpoints under each main point. A topic outline is the basis for the table of contents of a report.

Topic sentence   A sentence that introduces or summarizes the main idea in a paragraph. A topic sentence may be either stated or implied, and it may come anywhere in the paragraph.

Transitions   Words, phrases, or sentences that show the connections between ideas.

Transmit   To send a message.

Transmittal   A memo or letter explaining why something is being sent.

Truncated code   Symbols such as asterisks that turn up other forms of a keyword in a computer search.

Truncated scales   Graphs with part of the scale missing.

U

Umbrella sentence or paragraph   A sentence or paragraph listing in order the topics that following sentences or paragraphs will discuss.

Understatement   Downplaying or minimizing the size or features of something.

Unity   Using only one idea or topic in a paragraph or other piece of writing.

Unjustified margins   Margins that do not end evenly on the right side of the page.

Unstructured interview   An interview based on three or four main questions prepared in advance and other questions that build on what the interviewee says.

V

Verbal communication   Communication that uses words; may be either oral or written.

Vested interest   The emotional stake readers have in something if they benefit from keeping things just as they are.

Visual impact   The visual "first impression" you get when you look at a page.

Volume   The loudness or softness of a voice or other sound.

W

Watchdog audience   An audience that has political, social, or economic power and that may base future actions on its evaluation of your message.

White space   The empty space on the page. White space emphasizes material that it separates from the rest of the text.

Withdrawing   Being silent in meetings, not contributing, not helping with the work, not attending meetings.

Wordiness   Taking more words than necessary to express an idea.

Works cited   The sources specifically referred to in a report.

Writing   The act of putting words on paper or on a screen, or of dictating words to a machine or a secretary.

Y

You-attitude   A style of writing that looks at things from the reader's point of view, emphasizes what the reader wants to know, respects the reader's intelligence, and protects the reader's ego. Using *you* probably increases you-attitude in positive situations. In negative situations or conflict, avoid *you* since that word will attack the reader.

Polishing Your Prose
Answers to Odd-Numbered Exercises

Module 1: Sentence Fragments

1. Margaret faxed the contract to the Legal Department for review.
3. Making our profit margin higher is our main goal for the year.
5. Our first attempt to make the document more readable had mixed results.
7. Tom could have taken the afternoon off but instead completed the report.
9. Lisa is an ideal employee because she meets deadlines and is willing to work overtime to complete projects.

Module 2: Comma Splices

1. We interviewed two people for the accounting position, and we made a job offer to one.
3. The Director of Purchasing went to our Main Street warehouse to inspect the inventory. Chuck called him later to ask how things went.
5. Mr. Margulies gave an audiovisual presentation at our September sales meeting in Terre Haute, and it went very well.
7. Working weekends is tough, but it's part of life in the business world today.
9. Because he joined the department in 1982, Sunil is our most experienced employee.

Module 3: Using Idioms

1. *From A to Z* literally refers to all letters in the English alphabet. In business, it means thoroughly examining a subject.
3. *Catch a plane (or cab)* literally means capturing a vehicle. In business, it means successfully hailing a cab or boarding an airplane for a flight.
5. *Sign on the dotted line* literally means adding a signature to a dotted line. In business, it means formally agreeing to a contract by signing it.
7. *In the black/in the red* literally means the color black and the color red. In business, *in the black* means having a budget surplus or profit. *In the red* means having a deficit.
9. *Slam the competition* would literally mean a physical assault. In business, it means to defeat your competition.

Module 4: Using Spell and Grammar Checkers

1. The project will have been completed by next Thursday.
3. We created the solution in the '90s using a new chemical process. (*Was created* is a passive verb. The passive is acceptable, however, if the writer wants to emphasize when the solution was created, not who created it.)
5. I called your office because we're needed in the mailroom.
7. Tom is looking into buying more property, but it won't happen really soon.
9. This computer's spell checker did a pretty good job.

Module 5: Active and Passive Voice

1. The visitors' arrival is more important than who is expecting them. Therefore, use passive voice.
3. Unless the context for the message is negative, change to active. The mailroom staff collected outgoing correspondence.
5. Passive voice is acceptable, as what should be turned in on time—the form—is the focus of the sentence.
7. In April, we amortized the budgets and created files for the project.
9. Send packages to the mailroom for delivery.

Module 6: *Its / It's*

1. The company projected that its profits would rise during the next quarter.
3. I don't want responsibility for the project unless it's important.
5. I'm not sure whether it's a good idea to offer a conference.
7. It's good that our computer automatically backs up its files.
9. Its cash reserves protected the company from a hostile takeover.

Module 7: Singular and Plural Possessives

1. The winter holiday season can account for one-fourth to one-half of a store's annual profits.
3. In order to sell in another country, you need to understand its people's culture.
5. Two of our computers' monitors need to be repaired.
7. Employees who have worked as Big Sisters have enjoyed seeing the girls' progress.
9. Either is acceptable depending on the number of secretaries involved.

Module 8: Plurals and Possessives

1. We can move your family's furniture safely and efficiently.
3. A memo's style can build goodwill.

5. The company's benefits plan should be checked periodically to make sure it continues to serve the needs of employees.

7. The managers all have open-door policies.

9. Burnout affects a social worker's productivity as well as his or her morale.

Module 9: Making Subjects and Verbs Agree

1. Lakeland and Associates, the leading management consulting firm in the United States, operates offices in all 50 states.

3. Every project team trains for at least 90 days before projects are started.

5. A series of meetings is planned for February.

7. Make it a point to have your report ready by Friday.

9. The offices in Buenos Aries report a 19% increase in employee turnover for the past year.

Module 10: Dangling Modifiers

1. Using the fax machine, we process new orders quickly.

3. We can complete projects quickly by working in teams.

5. As your résumé shows, you had a good deal of experience with computer software before joining our company.

7. You can keep a journal, a simple notebook filled with thoughts and ideas about your business experiences.

9. As a new employee, you can ask your supervisor for answers to questions.

Module 11: Parallel Structure

1. Ask Ms. Liken, Mr. Fitzgerald, Mr. Anderson, and Prof. Timmons to join us for the meeting. (Use professional titles like "Dr." or "Prof." for other members who have them.)

3. Make sure benefits announcements get routed to managers, supervisors, and HR staff.

5. The project's fixed costs include material, salaries, advertising, bonuses, and travel.

7. The selection committee reviews each job applicant based on education, experience, extracurricular activities, awards, and personal statement.

9. Each agency should estimate
   Annual Costs
   Monthly Costs
   • Salaries
   • New Equipment
   • Reserve Funds

Module 12: Expressing Personality

1. Too many exclamation points make this person sound chirpy and immature.

3. This person sounds threatening and inflexible.

5. By speaking "legalese," this person would probably confuse or overwhelm many readers or listeners.

7. All caps, bold, and double-underlining make this person sound angry and defiant.

9. This person sounds insulting and offers no constructive criticism to help the reader understand how to fix the problem.

Module 13: Making Nouns and Pronouns Agree

1. The mayor should give himself or herself credit for doing a good job.

3. Correct.

5. The union votes today on whether it will go on strike.

7. Correct.

9. Every employee is interested in improving his or her technical skills.

Module 14: Matters on Which Experts Disagree

1. The schedule includes new product information, role plays with common selling situations, and awards to top sales people.

3. Prepare to make a brief oral report on a challenging sales situation.

5. I hope that we will have time to work through many of these situations in our role plays. ("Hope" can also be a hidden negative; if the situation has negative connotations, avoid using the word.)

7. We'll feature oral quotes from customers in our radio ads.

9. If the Web page will be live, we can access it during the meeting. (Remember, "hope" can be a hidden negative; in this case, emphasizing that it might not be available during a meeting is negative.)

Module 15: Run-On Sentences

1. All online purchases should be itemized based on type and cost, so remember to include the appropriate shipping confirmation number.

3. We will take a final product inventory on December 1. Managers will report any lost stock, so employees should make sure any broken items are reported. Managers should record this information in their computer databases.

5. John leaves his computer on overnight, but Aaron turns his off. Marilyn leaves hers on, too, and so does Tashi.

7. The Cleveland office is planning a new marketing campaign; the Atlanta office will help with the promotion, but the Detroit office is coordinating the product show.

9. Last week, I went to Montreal and Haj went to Miami. This week, Tony took a trip to Scottsdale, so our travel budget is almost gone.

Module 16: Commas in Lists

1. At the weekly staff meeting we will be joined by Mr. Loomis, Ms. Handelman, Ms. Lang, and Mr. Kim.

3. Buy small, medium, and large paper clips at the office supply store.

5. Applicants should send copies of their resumes to Mr. Arther Bramberger, Human Resource Director; Ms. Tina Ramos, Vice President of Marketing; and Ms. Ellen Choi, Administrative Assistant in Marketing.

7. Interns will be rotated through the receiving, claims adjustment, customer service, and shipping departments.

9. We are open until 9 P.M. on Mondays, Wednesdays, Fridays, and Saturdays.

Module 17: Combining Sentences

1. There are many reasons to choose Armbruster, Locke, Peabody & Associates as your human resources consulting firm. Our company has 140 consultants, more than 75 years in the business, and offices in New York, Chicago, Washington, D.C., Los Angeles, and Seattle.
3. The Development Team members took a plane to Seattle on Friday. It rained that day, so they used umbrellas. They then attended a conference on Saturday and returned on Sunday.
5. In January and February, the sales department plans to push its newest line of replacement toner cartridges. It will also hire two support people from the clerical pool in January. In March, the department will assess the success of the sales push and by April decide whether to repeat it in the fall.

Module 18: Delivering Criticism

1. Please work to improve your spelling skills.
3. Our instructor told us we can only use two fonts in the report.
5. How can we increase this project's chances of getting a passing grade?
7. While creative, this document needs to focus more on the task at hand.
9. Let's make this clip art more diverse.

Module 19: Hyphens and Dashes

1. Our cutting-edge fashions sell best in French-Canadian cities like Montreal.
3. Next Monday, *BusinessWeek* magazine will do a cover story on a thriving new business created by Native Americans. (When used as nouns, terms such as *Native American* need no hyphen.)
5. Our gift certificates come in 5-, 10-, and 15-dollar denominations.
7. We need to work on more cost-effective versions of our best-selling software programs.
9. Kathy gave us four options during the sales meeting on Friday afternoon.

Module 20: Choosing Levels of Formality

1. Starting at 5 P.M., all qualifying employees may begin their vacations.
3. Call to schedule a meeting to talk about your memo.
5. Rick has performed well as manager of our Sales Department.
7. Please contact me if you have questions.
9. In this report, I have assumed that the economy will continue to grow.

Module 21: Mixing Verb Tenses

1. Many of our retirees worked for the company for many years.
3. The phone rang until I answered it.
5. About two hundred résumés came in for the position yesterday.

7. Before you leave for the interview, make sure you have a copy of your employment records. You should also take another copy of your résumé. When you get back, make sure you send a thank-you letter to everyone you meet today.
9. About a quarter of the employees eligible for telecommuting take advantage of this employee benefit. The rest of the employees feel that they are comfortable with their current schedules. We are debating whether to keep the program.

Module 22: Using MLA Style

1. *Environmental Protection Agency.* "An Office Building Occupant's Guide to Indoor Air Quality." 19 July 2001. <http://www.epa.gov/iaq/pubs/occupgd.html>.
3. Locker, Kitty O., and Stephen Kyo Kaczmarek. *Business Communication: Building Critical Skills.* 2nd ed. Boston: McGraw-Hill/Irwin, 2004.
5. Alison Stein Wellner. "The National Headcount." *American Demographics* Mar. 2001. s12.
7. Kaczmarek, Stephen Kyo. "Progress on Proofreading." E-mail to Kitty Locker. 21 Sept. 2003. [Put in your own name as author, the title of the post, the name of the person you're writing to, and the exact date of the posting.]
9. Campbell, Kim Sydow, Saroya I. Follender, and Guy Shane. "Preferred Strategies for Responding to Hostile Questions in Environmental Meetings." *Management Communication Quarterly* 11 (1998): 401–21.

Module 23: Being Concise

1. Our records show that you are responsible.
3. The mainframe is in the basement.
5. We faxed the application.
7. I enjoyed the presentation.
9. The advertising department manager yelled that a delivery truck's headlights were on.

Module 24: Improving Paragraphs

1. Mr. Walter Pruitt, who works in fulfillment for the Martin Day Company, visited our class yesterday to talk about the importance of internships. An internship is an opportunity for students to work with a company to get business experience. Mr. Pruitt got his first job because of an internship with Martin Day. At first, the company only wanted him to work for ten weeks, but then kept him on for another ten weeks, then another. When he graduated, Martin Day offered him a full-time job.

Module 25: Writing Subject Lines and Headings

1. Insurance Rate Increase
3. Help Others by Giving Blood August 10
5. Making the Most of Undergraduate Years; Making the Most of Graduate Years; Making the Most of Post-Graduate Years
7. Clemente Research Group's Five-Year Goals; Clemente Research Group's Ten-Year Goals; Clemente Research Group's Fifteen-Year Goals
9. Research; Logistics; Benefits

Module 26: Using Details

1. The Human Resources Department Manager wants personnel files for all employees.
3. It's been five years since I last went to Antigua.
5. The Martin Day Company should hire me because of my 14 years of experience in transportation and logistics, expert knowledge of Microsoft Office, and strong professional references, such as Mr. Walter Pruitt, Martin Day's Director of Fulfillment Services.
7. The Public Relations Department staff will meet at 2 P.M. in the Board Room.
9. Mr. Jacobs and I will travel to Ohio and Michigan from April 3 through April 12.

Module 27: Proofreading

1.   Résumé for Kathy Jones

332 West Long Street
Columbus, OH 43215
(614) 555-8188

Objective
A management position in fulfillment services where my skills and experience can best be used to help your company achieve its goals.

Experience
2000 to Present: Assistant Manager for high-end sports equipment distributor. Responsible for assisting new customers at checkout.

1995–1999: Owned and operated Jones, Inc., a telephone order processing company for ladies' apparel.

1998: Delivered an address to local high school seniors on why accuracy is important in business.

1997: Received a plaque for "Most Promising Executive of the Year" from Columbus Monthly Magazine.

Special Skills
Type 70 or more words per minute.
Fluent in French.
Member of local gun club.

Module 28: Using *You* and *I*

1. Here is your copy of *Using Excel.*
3. Please return the draft to Mehtap and me.
5. Here is the agenda for Friday's meeting. It includes the meeting's topics and time limits to discuss each.
7. My last job showed me that employees have to be able to solve problems quickly.
9. The client asked my supervisor and me to explain our strategy more fully.

Module 29: Using a Dictionary

1. *Dialogue* can be used as a noun (a conversation) and as a verb (the act of conversing). A prescriptive dictionary will likely favor the first definition.
3. In the noun form, *text* is simply words appearing on a page or screen. A recent verb form means sending messages electronically, as in "Text my PDA later about where to meet for dinner." A prescriptive dictionary will likely favor the first definition.
5. *Position* can be a noun (a place, rank, or viewpoint) and a verb (to put something into place). Prescriptive dictionaries may favor any or all of these definitions.
7. In noun form, an *engineer* is someone who uses tools and mathematical principles to design and build things—or, *engineer* them. Prescriptive dictionaries may favor either or both definitions.
9. *Monitor* can be used as a noun (a computer or video screen or someone or something used to watch) or a verb (the act of watching). Prescriptive dictionaries may favor any or all of these definitions.

Module 30: *Who / Whom* and *I / Me*

1. For whom is this letter intended?
3. Take it from Les and me: it pays to be prepared in business.
5. There was only about an hour for Kelly, Maria, and me to get to the airport.
7. It is the customer for whom we make our product.
9. Trust me: it's not a good idea to begin a letter with "To whom it may concern," even if people frequently do.

Endnotes

Module 1

1. W. B. Johnson and A. E. Packer, *Workforce 2000* (Indianapolis: Hudson Institute, 1987), 99.
2. Anne Fisher, "Ask Annie," *Fortune*, March 1, 1999, 242.
3. Hal Lancaster, "Making the Break from Middle Manager to a Seat at the Top," *The Wall Street Journal*, July 7, 1998, B1.
4. Fisher, "Ask Annie," 244.
5. Elaine Viets, "Voice Mail Converts Boss into a Secretary," *The Columbus Dispatch*, August 10, 1995, 3E; Rochelle Sharpe, "Work Week," *The Wall Street Journal*, September 26, 1995, A1.
6. Henry Mintzberg, *The Nature of Managerial Work* (New York: Harper & Row, 1973), 32, 65.
7. Frederick K. Moss, "Perceptions of Communication in the Corporate Community," *Journal of Business and Technical Communication* 9, no. 1 (January 1995): 67.
8. "1996 Cost of a Business Letter" (Chicago: Dartnell/From 9 to 5, September 30, 1996), 1.
9. Dianna Booher, *Cutting Paperwork in the Corporate Culture* (New York: Facts on File, 1986), 24.
10. Claudia MonPere McIsaac and Mary Ann Aschauer, "Proposal Writing at Atherton Jordan, Inc.: An Ethnographic Study," *Management Communication Quarterly* 3 (1990): 535.
11. Elizabeth Allen, "Excellence in Public Relations & Communication Management," IABC/Dayton Awards Banquet, Dayton, OH, July 12, 1990.

Module 2

1. Audiences 1, 3, and 4 are based on J. C. Mathes and Dwight Stevenson, *Designing Technical Reports: Writing for Audiences in Organizations*, 2nd ed. (New York: Macmillan, 1991), 40. The fifth audience is suggested by Vincent J. Brown, "Facing Multiple Audiences in Engineering and R&D Writing: The Social Context of a Technical Report," *Journal of Technical Writing and Communication* 24, no. 1 (1994): 67–75.
2. Amiso M. George, "Cultivating Effective Internal Communication—Strategies That Work: The Case of USAA Insurance and Financial Services," Association for Business Communication Annual Meeting, Los Angeles, November 3–6, 1999.
3. Isabel Briggs Myers, "Introduction to Type" (Palo Alto, CA: Consulting Psychologists Press, 1980). The material in this section follows Myers's paper.
4. Isabel Briggs Myers and Mary H. McCaulley, *Manual: A Guide to the Development and Use of the Myers-Briggs Type Indicator* (Palo Alto, CA: Consulting Psychologists Press, 1985), 251, 248, respectively.

5. Alan W. H. Grant and Leonard A. Schlesinger, "Realize Your Customers' Full Profit Potential," *Harvard Business Review,* September–October 1995, 65–66.
6. Anne Fisher, "Internet Buyers Are Not What You Think," *Fortune*, January 10, 2000, 190.
7. Jennifer Lach, "Data Mining Digs In," *American Demographics*, July 1999, 42.
8. Daniel Pearl, "UPS Takes on Air-Express Competition," *The Wall Street Journal*, December 20, 1990, A4.
9. Matt Siegel, "The Perils of Culture Conflict," *Fortune*, November 9, 1998, 258.
10. Linda Driskill, "Negotiating Differences among Readers and Writers," presented at the Conference on College Composition and Communication, San Diego, CA, March 31–April 3, 1993.

Module 3

1. See, for example, W. B. Johnson and A. E. Packer, *Workforce 2000* (Indianapolis: Hudson Institute, 1987). The population estimates are unchanged; see Robyn D. Clarke, "The Future Is Now," *Black Enterprise*, February 2000, 99.
2. Bureau of the Census, *Statistical Abstract of the United States 1997*, Table 22, 22–23.
3. Cited in Farai Chideya, *The Color of Our Future* (New York: Morrow, 1999), 17.
4. "Amazing Numbers," *Selling Power*, September 1996, 28.
5. "Harvard Tracking Religious Diversity," *The Columbus Dispatch*, November 13, 1993, 10H.
6. Joel Dreyfuss, "Get Ready for the New Work Force," *Fortune*, April 23, 1990, 165.
7. "All It Takes Is a Little Investigation," *Going Global: Mexico*, brochure published by *Inc.*, October 1993, n.p.
8. Michael J. Marquardt, *The Global Advantage: How World Class Organizations Improve Performance Through Globalization* (Houston, TX: Gulf, 1999), 2.
9. Poppy Lauretta McLeod, Sharon Alisa Lobel, and Taylor H. Cox, Jr., "Ethnic Diversity and Creativity in Small Groups," *Small Group Research* 27, no. 2 (May 1996): 248–64.
10. David A. Victor, *International Business Communication* (New York: HarperCollins, 1992), 148–60.
11. John Webb and Michael Keene, "The Impact of Discourse Communities on International Professional Communication," in *Exploring the Rhetoric of International Professional Communication: An Agenda for Teachers and Researchers*, ed. Carl R. Lovitt with Dixie Goswami (Amityville, NY: Baywood, 1999), 81–109.
12. Christina Haas and Jeffrey L. Funk, " 'Shared Information': Some Observations of Communication in

Japanese Technical Settings," *Technical Communication* 36, no. 4 (November 1989): 365.

13. Thomas Kochman, *Black and White Styles in Conflict* (Chicago: University of Chicago Press, 1981), 44–45.

14. Laray M. Barna, "Stumbling Blocks in Intercultural Communication, in *Intercultural Communication,* ed. Larry A. Samovar and Richard E. Porter (Belmont, CA: Wadsworth, 1985), 331.

15. Marjorie Fink Vargas, *Louder than Words* (Ames: Iowa State University Press, 1986), 47.

16. Michael Argyle, *Bodily Communication* (New York: International University Press, 1975), 89.

17. Jerrold J. Merchant, "Korean Interpersonal Patterns: Implications for Korean/American Intercultural Communication," *Communication* 9 (October 1980): 65.

18. Ray L. Birdwhistell, *Kinesics and Context: Essays on Body Motion Communication* (Philadelphia: University of Philadelphia Press, 1970), 81.

19. Paul Ekman, Wallace V. Friesen, and John Bear, "The International Language of Gestures," *Psychology Today* 18, no. 5 (May 1984): 64.

20. Carmen Judith Nine-Curt, "Hispanic-Anglo Conflicts in Nonverbal Communication," in *Perspectivas Pedagogicas,* ed. I. Abino et al. (San Juan: Universidad de Puerto Rico, 1983), 235.

21. Baxter, 1970, reported in Marianne LaFrance, "Gender Gestures: Sex, Sex-Role, and Nonverbal Communication, in *Gender and Nonverbal Behavior,* ed. Clara Mayo and Nancy M. Henley (New York: Springer-Verlag, 1981), 130.

22. Nine-Curt, "Hispanic-Anglo Conflicts," 238.

23. Brenda Major, "Gender Patterns in Touching Behavior," in *Gender and Nonverbal Behavior,* ed. Clara Mayo and Nancy M. Henley (New York: Springer-Verlag, 1981), 26, 28.

24. "Minor Memos," *The Wall Street Journal,* February 12, 1988, 1.

25. Natalie Porter and Florence Gies, "Women and Nonverbal Leadership Cues: When Seeing Is Not Believing," in *Gender and Nonverbal Behavior,* ed. Clara Mayo and Nancy M. Henley (New York: Springer-Verlag, 1981), 48–49.

26. Robert C. Christopher, *Second to None: American Companies in Japan* (New York: Crown, 1986), 102–03.

27. John Condon and Keisuke Kurata, *In Search of What's Japanese about Japan* (Tokyo: Shufunotomo Company, 1974), 77.

28. Lawrence B. Nadler, Marjorie Keeshan Nadler, and Benjamin J. Broome, "Culture and the Management of Conflict Situations," in *Communication, Culture, and Organizational Processes,* ed. William B. Gudykunst, Lea P. Stewart, and Stella Ting-Toomey (Beverly Hills, CA: Sage, 1985), 103.

29. Argyle, *Bodily Communication,* 90.

30. Mary Ritchie Key, *Paralangauge and Kinesics* (Metuchen, NJ: Scarecrow, 1975), 23.

31. Fred Hitzhusen, conversation with Kitty Locker, January 31, 1988.

32. Lisa Davis, "The Height Report: A Look at Stature and Status," *The Columbus Dispatch,* January 19, 1988, E1, New York Times Special Features.

33. Deborah Tannen, *That's Not What I Meant!* (New York: William Morrow, 1986).

34. Karen Ritchie, "Marketing to Generation X," *American Demographics,* April 1995, 34–36.

35. Thomas Kochman, *Black and White Styles in Conflict* (Chicago: University of Chicago Press, 1981), 103.

36. Daniel N. Maltz and Ruth A. Borker, "A Cultural Approach to Male-Female Miscommunication," in *Language and Social Identity,* ed. John J. Gumperz (Cambridge: Cambridge University Press, 1982), 202.

37. Vincent O'Neill, "Training the Multi-Cultural Manager," Sixth Annual EMU Conference on Languages and Communication for World Business and the Professions, Ann Arbor, MI, May 7–9, 1987.

38. Akihisa Kumayama, comment during discussion, Sixth Annual EMU Conference on Languages and Communication for World Business and the Professions, Ann Arbor, MI, May 7–9, 1987.

39. Muriel Saville-Troike, "An Integrated Theory of Communication," in *Perspectives on Silence,* ed. Deborah Tannen and Muriel Saville-Troike (Norwood, NJ: Ablex, 1985), 10–11.

40. Brenda Arbeléz, statement to Kitty Locker, December 12, 1996.

41. Brad Edmondson, "What Do You Call a Dark-Skinned Person?" *American Demographics,* October 1993, 9.

42. Lisa Tyler, "Communicating about People with Disabilities: Does the Language We Use Make a Difference?" *The Bulletin of the Association for Business Communication* 53, no. 3 (September 1990): 65.

43. Marilyn A. Dyrud, "An Exploration of Gender Bias in Computer Clip Art," *Business Communication Quarterly* 60, no. 4 (December 1997): 30–51.

Module 4

1. See especially Linda Flower and John R. Hayes, "The Cognition of Discovery: Defining a Rhetorical Problem," *College Composition and Communication* 31 (February 1980): 21–32; and the essays in two collections: Charles R. Cooper and Lee Odell, *Research on Composing: Points of Departure* (Urbana, IL: National Council of Teachers of English, 1978), and Mike Rose, ed., *When a Writer Can't Write: Studies in Writer's Block and Other Composing-Process Problems* (New York: Guilford Press, 1985).

2. Rebecca E. Burnett, "Content and Commas: How Attitudes Shape a Communication-Across-the-Curriculum Program," Association for Business Communication Convention, Orlando, FL, November 1–4, 1995.

3. Peter Elbow, *Writing with Power: Techniques for Mastering the Writing Process* (New York: Oxford University Press, 1981), 15–20.

4. See Gabriela Lusser Rico, *Writing the Natural Way* (Los Angeles: J. P. Tarcher, 1983), 10.

5. Rachel Spilka, "Orality and Literacy in the Workplace: Process- and Text-Based Strategies for Multiple Audience Adaptation," *Journal of Business and Technical Communication* 4, no. 1 (January 1990): 44–67.

6. Fred Reynolds, "What Adult Work-World Writers Have Taught Me About Adult Work-World Writing,"

Professional Writing in Context: Lessons from Teaching and Consulting in Worlds of Work, (Hillsdale, NJ: Lawrence Erlbaum Associates, 1995), 18–21.

7. Raymond W. Beswick, "Communicating in the Automated Office," American Business Communication Association International Convention, New Orleans, LA, October 20, 1982.

8. Dianna Booher, *Cutting Paperwork in the Corporate Culture* (New York: Facts on File Publications, 1986), 23.

9. Susan D. Kleimann, "The Complexity of Workplace Review," *Technical Communication* 38, no. 4 (1991): 520–26.

10. This three-step process is modeled on the one suggested by Barbara L. Shwom and Penny L. Hirsch, "Managing the Drafting Process: Creating a New Model for the Workplace," *The Bulletin of the Association for Business Communication* 57, no. 2 (June 1994): 10.

11. Glenn J Broadhead and Richard C. Freed, *The Variables of Composition: Process and Product in a Business Setting,* Conference on College Composition and Communication Studies in Writing and Rhetoric (Carbondale, IL: Southern Illinois University Press, 1986), 57.

12. Robert Boice, "Writing Blocks and Tacit Knowledge," *Journal of Higher Education* 64, no. 1 (January/February 1993), 41–43.

Module 5

1. Linda Reynolds, "The Legibility of Printed Scientific and Technical Information," *Information Design,* ed. Ronald Easterby and Harm Zwaga (New York: Wiley, 1984), 187–208.

2. Once we know how to read English, the brain first looks to see whether an array of letters follows the rules of spelling. If it does, the brain then treats the array as a word (even if it isn't one, such as *tweal*). The shape is processed in individual letters only when the shape is not enough to suggest meaning. Jerry E. Bishop, "Word Processing: Research on Stroke Victims Yields Clues to the Brain's Capacity to Create Language," *The Wall Street Journal,* October 12, 1993, A6.

3. M. Gregory and E. C. Poulton, "Even Versus Uneven Right-Hand Margins and the Rate of Comprehension of Reading," *Ergonomics* 13 (1970): 427–34.

4. Marilyn A. Dyrud, "An Exploration of Gender Bias in Computer Clip Art," *Business Communication Quarterly* 60, no. 4 (December 1997): 30–51.

5. Jakob Neilsen, "Top Ten Mistakes in Web Design," May 1996, http://222.useit.com/alertbox/9605.html.

Module 7

1. Charles Burck, "Learning from a Master," *Fortune,* December 27, 1993, 144; Kathy Casto, "Assumptions about Audience in Negative Messages," Association for Business Communication Midwest Conference, Kansas City, MO, April 30–May 2, 1987; and John P. Wanous and A. Colella, "Future Directions in Organizational Entry Research," *Research in Personnel/Human Resource Management,* ed. Kenneth Rowland and G. Ferris (Greenwich, CT: JAI Press, 1990).

2. Annette N. Shelby and N. Lamar Reinsch, Jr. "Positive Emphasis and You-Attitude: An Empirical Study, *Journal of Business Communication* 32, no. 4 (October 1995): 303–327.

3. Alan Farnham, "Are You Smart Enough to Keep Your Job?" *Fortune,* January 15, 1996, 42.

4. Mark A. Sherman, "Adjectival Negation and the Comprehension of Multiply Negated Sentences," *Journal of Verbal Learning and Verbal Behavior* 15 (1976): 143–57.

5. Margaret Baker Graham and Carol David, "Power and Politeness: Administrative Writing in an 'Organized Anarchy,' " *Journal of Business and Technical Communication* 10.1 (January 1996): 5–27.

6. John Hagge and Charles Kostelnick, "Linguistic Politeness in Professional Prose: A Discourse Analysis of Auditors' Suggestion Letters, with Implications for Business Communication Pedagogy," *Written Communication* 6, no. 3 (July 1989): 312–39.

Module 8

1. See Tove Helland Hammer and H. Peter Dachler, "A Test of Some Assumptions Underlying the Path-Goal Model of Supervision: Some Suggested Conceptual Modifications," *Organizational Behavior and Human Performance* 14 (1975): 73.

2. Edward E. Lawler, III, *Motivation in Work Organizations* (Monterey, CA: Brooks/Cole, 1973), 59. Lawler also notes a third obstacle: People may settle for performance and rewards that are just OK. Offering reader benefits, however, does nothing to affect this obstacle.

3. Abraham H. Maslow, *Motivation and Personality* (New York: Harper & Row, 1954).

4. John J. Weger reports Herzberg's research in *Motivating Supervisors* (New York: American Management Association, 1971), 53–54.

5. Diane L. Coutu, "Human Resources: The Wages of Stress," *Harvard Business Review,* November–December 1998, 21–24; and Charles Fishman, "Sanity, Inc.," *Fast Company,* January 1999, 85–99.

6. Susan Greco, "Hire the Best," *Inc.,* June 1999, 32–52.

7. Kevin Leo, "Effective Copy and Graphics," DADM/DMEF Direct Marketing Institute for Professors, Northbrook, IL, May 31–June 3, 1983.

Module 10

1. Thomas L. Fernandez and Roger N. Conaway, "Writing Business Letters II: Essential Elements Revisited," *1999 Refereed Proceedings,* Association for Business Communication Southwest Region, ed. Marsha L. Bayless, 65–68.

2. In a study of 483 subject lines written by managers and MBA students, Priscilla S. Rogers found that the average subject line was five words; only 10% of the subject lines used 10 or more words ("A Taxonomy for Memorandum Subject Lines," *Journal of Business and Technical Communication* 4, no. 2 [September 1990]: 28–29).

3. Richard C. Whitely, *The Customer-Driven Company* (Reading, MA: Addison-Wesley, 1991), 39–40.

4. Deborah Tannen, *That's Not What I Meant: How Conversational Style Makes or Breaks Your Relations with Others* (New York: Morrow, 1986), 108.

5. An earlier version of this problem, the sample solutions, and the discussion appeared in Francis W. Weeks and Kitty O. Locker, *Business Writing Cases and Problems*, 1984 ed. (Champaign, IL: Stipes, 1984), 64–68.

Module 11

1. Jack W. Brehm, *A Theory of Psychological Reactance* (New York: Academic Press, 1966).

2. Ilan Mochari, "The Talking Cure," *Inc.*, November 2001, 123.

3. Kitty O. Locker, "Factors in Reader Responses to Negative Letters: Experimental Evidence for Changing What We Teach," *The Journal of Business and Technical Communication* 13, no. 1 (January 1999): 5–48.

4. Frederick M. Jablin and Kathleen Krone, "Characteristics of Rejection Letters and Their Effects on Job Applicants," *Written Communication* 1, no. 4 (October 1984): 387–406.

5. John D. Pettit, "An Analysis of the Effects of Various Message Presentations on Communicatee Responses," Ph.D. dissertation, Louisiana State University, 1969; and Jack D. Eure, "Applicability of American Written Business Communication Principles Across Cultural Boundaries in Mexico," *The Journal of Business Communication* 14 (1976): 51–63.

6. Gabriella Stern, "Companies Discover That Some Firings Backfire into Costly Defamation Suits," *The Wall Street Journal*, May 5, 1993, B1.

Module 12

1. For a discussion of sales and fund-raising letters, see Kitty O. Locker, *Business and Administrative Communication*, 6th ed. (Burr Ridge: Irwin/McGraw-Hill, 2003), 252–82.

2. James Suchan and Ron Dulek, "Toward a Better Understanding of Reader Analysis," *The Journal of Business Communication* 25, no. 2 (Spring 1988): 40.

3. Frances Harrington, "Formulaic Patterns versus Pressures of Circumstances: A Rhetoric of Business Situations," Conference on College Composition and Communication, New Orleans, LA, March 17–19, 1986.

4. Min-Sun Kim and Steven R. Wilson, "A Cross-Cultural Comparison of Implicit Theories of Requesting," *Communication Monographs* 61, no. 3 (September 1994): 210–35.

5. Priscilla S. Rogers, "A Taxonomy for the Composition of Memorandum Subject Lines: Facilitating Writer Choice in Managerial Contexts," *Journal of Business and Technical Communication* 4, no. 2 (September 1990): 21–43.

6. Karen Lowry Miller and David Woodruff, "The Man Who's Selling Japan on Jeeps," *BusinessWeek*, July 19, 1993, 56–57.

7. John D. Hartigan, "Giving Kids Condoms Won't Work," *The Wall Street Journal*, December 19, 1990, A16.

8. J. C. Mathes and Dwight W. Stevenson, *Designing Technical Reports: Writing for Audiences in Organizations* (Indianapolis: Bobbs-Merrill, 1979), 18–19.

9. Daniel J. O'Keefe, *Persuasion* (Newbury Park, CA: Sage, 1990), 168; Joanne Martin and Melanie E. Powers, "Truth or Corporate Propaganda," *Organizational Symbolism*, ed. Louis R. Pondy, Thomas C. Dandridge, Gareth Morgan, and Peter J. Frost (Greenwich, CT: JAI Press 1983), 97–107; and Dean C. Kazoleas, "A Comparison of the Persuasive Effectiveness of Qualitative versus Quantitative Evidence: A Test of Explanatory Hypotheses," *Communication Quarterly* 41, no. 1 (Winter 1993): 40–50.

10. "Phoning Slow Payers Pays Off," *Inc.*, July 1996, 95.

11. An earlier draft of this problem and analysis appeared in Francis W. Weeks and Kitty O. Locker, *Business Writing Problems and Cases*, last ed. (Champaign, IL: Stipes, 1984), 96–99.

Module 13

1. Sara Kiesler, Jane Siegel, and Timothy W. McGuire, "Social Psychological Aspects of Computer-Mediated Communication," *American Psychologist* 39, no. 10 (October 1984): 1129. People still find it easier to be negative in e-mail than on paper or person; see John Affleck, "You've Got Bad News," Associated Press, June 19, 1999.

2. Bettina A. Bair, "Teaching Technology," e-mail to Kitty Locker, October 22, 1999.

Module 15

1. Interoffice memo in a steel company.

2. Caleb Solomon, "Clearing the Air: EPA-Amoco Study of Refinery Finds Pollution Rules Focusing on Wrong Part of It," *The Wall Street Journal*, March 29, 1993, A6.

3. Philip B. Crosby, *Quality Is Free: The Art of Making Quality Certain* (New York: New American Library, 1979), 79–84.

4. *News-Gazette*, Champaign-Urbana, IL, January 16, 1979, C-8.

5. Richard C. Anderson, "Concretization and Sentence Learning," *Journal of Educational Psychology* 66, no. 2 (1974): 179–83.

6. Based on Lynn Ashby, "7, 8, Facilitate," *Houston Post*, February 17, 1978.

7. Gretchen Glasscock, "My Favorite Bookmarks," *Fast Company*, October 1999, 62.

8. Mary Ellen Podmolik, "New Rule Raises Stakes for Minority Shop Owners," *Advertising Age*, February 28, 2000, 34; and Hersch Doby, "Changing the Rules," *Black Enterprise*, April 2000, 23.

Module 16

1. Robert L. Brown, Jr., and Carl G. Herndl, "An Ethnographic Study of Corporate Writing: Job Status as Reflected in Written Text," *Functional Approaches to Writing: A Research Perspective*, ed. Barbara Couture (Norwood, NJ: Ablex, 1986), 16–19, 22–23.

2. Linda Flower, *Problem-Solving Strategies for Writing* (New York: Harcourt Brace Jovanovich, 1981), 39.

3. Harris B. Savin and Ellen Perchonock, "Grammatical Structure and the Immediate Recall of English

Sentences," *Journal of Verbal Learning and Verbal Behavior* 4 (1965): 348–53; Pamela Layton and Adrian J. Simpson, "Deep Structure in Sentence Comprehension," *Journal of Verbal Learning and Verbal Behavior* 14 (1975): 658–64.

4. Arn Tibbetts, "Ten Rules for Writing Readably," *The Journal of Business Communication* 18, no. 4 (Fall 1981): 55–59.

5. Thomas N. Huckin, "A Cognitive Approach to Readability," *New Essays in Technical and Scientific Communication: Research, Theory, Practice,* ed. Paul V. Anderson, R. John Brockmann, and Carolyn R. Miller (Farmingdale, NY: Baywood, 1983), 93–98.

6. James Suchan and Ronald Dulek, "A Reassessment of Clarity in Written Managerial Communications," *Management Communication Quarterly* 4, no. 1 (August 1990): 93–97.

Module 17

1. For a full account of the accident, see Andrew D. Wolvin and Caroline Gwynn Coakely, *Listening,* 2nd ed. (Dubuque, IA: William C. Brown, 1985), 6.

2. "Listen Up and Sell," *Selling Power,* July/August 1999, 34.

3. Thomas Gordon with Judith Gordon Sands, *P.E.T. in Action* (New York: Wyden, 1976), 83.

4. Molefi Asante and Alice Davis, "Black and White Communication: Analyzing Work Place Encounters," *Journal of Black Studies* 16, no. 1 (September 1985): 87–90.

Module 18

1. For a fuller listing of roles in groups, see David W. Johnson and Frank P. Johnson, *Joining Together: Group Theory and Group Skills* (Englewood Cliffs, NJ: Prentice Hall, 1975), 26–27.

2. Beatrice Schultz, "Argumentativeness: Its Effect in Group Decision-Making and Its Role in Leadership Perception," *Communication Quarterly* 30, no. 4 (Fall 1982): 374–75; Dennis S. Gouran and B. Aubrey Fisher, "The Functions of Human Communication in the Formation, Maintenance, and Performance of Small Groups," in *Handbook of Rhetorical and Communication Theory,* ed. Carroll C. Arnold and John Waite Bowers (Boston: Allyn and Bacon, 1984), 640; and Curt Bechler and Scott D. Johnson, "Leadership and Listening: A Study of Member Perceptions," *Small Group Research* 26, no. 1 (February 1995): 77–85.

3. Nance L. Harper and Lawrence R. Askling, "Group Communication and Quality of Task Solution in a Media Production Organization," *Communication Monographs* 47, no. 2 (June 1980): 77–100.

4. Rebecca E. Burnett, "Conflict in Collaborative Decision-Making," in *Professional Communication: The Social Perspective,* ed. Nancy Roundy Blyler and Charlotte Thralls (Newbury Park, CA: Sage, 1993), 144–62.

5. Kimberly A. Freeman, "Attitudes Toward Work in Project Groups as Predictors of Academic Performance," *Small Group Research* 27, no. 2 (May 1996): 265–82.

6. Nancy Schullery and Beth Hoger, "Business Advocacy for Students in Small Groups," Association for Business Communication Annual Convention, San Antonio, TX, November 9–11, 1998.

7. Jeffrey A. Fadiman, "Intercultural Invisibility: Deciphering the 'Subliminal' Marketing Message in Afro-Asian Commerce," Sixth Annual Conference on Languages and Communication for World Business and the Professions, Ann Arbor, MI, May 8–9, 1987.

8. Raymond L. Gordon, *Living in Latin America* (Skokie, IL: National Textbook, 1974), 41.

9. Philip R. Harris and Robert T. Moran, *Managing Cultural Differences,* 2nd ed. (Houston: Gulf, 1987), 78.

10. Lisa Ede and Andrea Lunsford, *Singular Texts/Plural Authors: Perspectives on Collaborative Writing* (Carbondale, IL: Southern Illinois Press, 1990), 60.

11. Rebecca Burnett, "Characterizing Conflict in Collaborative Relationships: The Nature of Decision-Making During Coauthoring." Ph.D. dissertation, Carnegie-Mellon University, Pittsburgh, PA, 1991.

12. Kitty O. Locker, "What Makes a Collaborative Writing Team Successful? A Case Study of Lawyers and Social Service Workers in a State Agency," in *New Visions in Collaborative Writing,* ed. Janis Forman (Portsmouth, NJ: Boynton, 1991), 37–52.

13. Ede and Lunsford, 66.

14. Meg Morgan, Nancy Allen, Teresa Moore, Dianne Atkinson, and Craig Snow, "Collaborative Writing in the Classroom," *The Bulletin of the Association for Business Communication* 50.3 (September 1987): 22.

Module 19

1. Cathy Olofson, "So Many Meetings, So Little Time," *Fast Company,* January/February 2000, 48; and Fara Warner, "How Google Searches Itself," *Fast Company,* July 2002, 50.

2. Andrea Williams, "The Rhetoric of Corporate Communications: A Case Study of a Canadian Employee Communications Program in a Global Financial Services Organization," Ph.D. dissertation, The Ohio State University, 2002, Chapter 5.

3. Michael Schrage, "Meetings Don't Have to be Dull," *The Wall Street Journal,* April 29, 1996, A12.

4. Eric Matson, "The Seven Deadly Sins of Meetings," *Fast Company Handbook of the Business Revolution,* 1997, 29.

5. Matson, 30.

6. "There's Something about Mary," *Fortune,* October 25, 1999, 368.

7. H. Lloyd Goodall, Jr., *Small Group Communications in Organizations* (Dubuque, IA: William C. Brown, 1990), 39–40.

8. Roger K. Mosvick and Robert B. Nelson, *We've Got to Start Meeting Like This: A Guide to Successful Meeting Management,* rev. ed. (Indianapolis: Park Avenue, 1996), 2nd ed. 177.

9. M. B., "The New Girls' Club," *Inc.,* March 1999, 88.

10. Cynthia Crossen, "Spotting Value Takes Smarts, Not Sight, Laura Sloate Shows," *The Wall Street Journal,* December 10, 1987, A1, A14; and Joan E. Rigdon, "Managing Your Career," *The Wall Street Journal,* December 1, 1993, B1.

11. Gina Imperator, " 'You Have to Start Meeting Like This,' " *Fast Company,* April 1999, 204–10.

Module 20

1. Dan Gillmor, "Putting on a Powerful Presentation," *Hemispheres,* March 1996, 31.
2. Carol Hymowitz, "When You Tell the Boss, Plain Talk Counts," *The Wall Street Journal,* June 16, 1989, B1.
3. Linda Driskill, "How the Language of Presentations Can Encourage or Discourage Audience Participation," paper presented at the Conference on College Composition and Communication, Cincinnati, OH, March 18–21, 1992.
4. "A Study of the Effects of the Use of Overhead Transparencies on Business Meetings," Wharton Applied Research Center, reported in Martha Jewett and Rita Margolies, eds., *How to Run Better Business Meetings: A Reference Guide for Managers* (New York: McGraw-Hill, 1987), 109–110, 115.
5. Tad Simons, "Multimedia or Bust?" *Presentations,* February 2000, 44, 49–50.
6. Stephen E. Lucas, *The Art of Public Speaking,* 2nd ed. (New York: Random House, 1986), 248.
7. John Case, "A Company of Businesspeople," *Inc.,* April 1993, 90.
8. Edward J. Hegarty, *Humor and Eloquence in Public Speaking* (West Nyack, NY: Parker, 1976), 204.
9. Ray Alexander, *Power Speech: Why It's Vital to You* (New York: AMACOM, 1986), 156.
10. Robert S. Mills, conversation with Kitty O. Locker, March 10, 1988.
11. Phil Theibert, "Speechwriters of the World, Get Lost!" *The Wall Street Journal,* August 2, 1993, A10.
12. Some studies have shown that previews and reviews increase comprehension; other studies have found no effect. For a summary of the research see Kenneth D. Frandsen and Donald R. Clement, "The Functions of Human Communication in Informing: Communicating and Processing Information," *Handbook of Rhetorical and Communication Theory,* ed. Carroll C. Arnold and John Waite Bowers (Boston: Allyn and Bacon, 1984), 340–41.
13. S. A. Beebe, "Eye Contact: A Nonverbal Determinant of Speaker Credibility," *Speech Teacher* 23 (1974): 21–25; cited in Marjorie Fink Vargas, *Louder than Words* (Ames, IA: Iowa State University Press, 1986), 61–62.
14. J. Wills, "An Empirical Study of the Behavioral Characteristics of Sincere and Insincere Speakers" Ph.D. dissertation, University of Southern California, 1961; cited in Marjorie Fink Vargas, *Louder than Words* (Ames, IA: Iowa State University Press, 1986), 62.

Module 21

1. For a useful taxonomy of proposals, see Richard C. Freed and David D. Roberts, "The Nature, Classification, and Generic Structure of Proposals," *Journal of Technical Writing and Communication* 19, no. 4 (1989): 317–51.
2. Christine Peterson Barabas, *Technical Writing in a Corporate Culture: A Study of the Nature of Information* (Norwood, NJ: Ablex Publishing, 1990), 327.

Module 22

1. Janice M. Lauer and J. William Asher, *Composition Research: Empirical Designs* (New York: Oxford University Press, 1986), 66.
2. Frederick F. Reichheld, "Learning from Customer Defects," *Harvard Business Review,* March–April 1996, 56–69.
3. Cynthia Crossen, "Margin of Error: Studies Galore Support Products and Positions, But Are They Reliable?" *The Wall Street Journal,* November 14, 1991, A1, A7.
4. Cynthia Crossen, "Diaper Debate: A Case Study of Tactical Research," *The Wall Street Journal,* May 17, 1994, B8.
5. "Whirlpool: How to Listen to Consumers," *Fortune,* January 11, 1993, 77.
6. Peter Lynch with John Rothchild, *One Up on Wall Street: How to Use What You Already Know to Make Money in the Market* (New York: Simon and Schuster, 1989), 187.
7. Patricia Sullivan, "Reporting Negative Research Results," and Kitty O. Locker to Pat Sullivan, June 8, 1990.

Module 23

1. Michael L. Keene to Kitty Locker, May 17, 1988.
2. Susan D. Kleimann, "The Need to Test Forms in the Real World," Association for Business Communication Annual Convention, Orlando, FL, November 1–4, 1995.

Module 25

1. Gene Zelazny, *Say It with Charts: The Executive's Guide to Successful Presentations,* 4th ed. (New York: McGraw-Hill, 2001), 52.
2. Most of these guidelines are given by Zelazny, *Say It With Charts: The Executive's Guide to Successful Presentations.*
3. W. S. Cleveland and R. McGill, "Graphical Perception: Theory, Experiments, and Application to the Development of Graphic Methods," *Journal of the American Statistical Association* 79, no. 3 & 7 (1984): 531–53; cited in Jeffry K. Cochran, Sheri A. Albrecht, and Yvonne A. Greene, "Guidelines for Evaluating Graphical Designs: A Framework Based on Human Perception Skills," *Technical Communication* 36, no. 1 (February 1989): 27.
4. L. G. Thorell and W. J. Smith, *Using Computer Color Effectively: An Illustrated Reference* (Englewood Cliffs, NJ: Prentice Hall, 1990), 12–13; William Horton, "The Almost Universal Language: Graphics for International Documents," *Technical Communication* 40, no. 4 (1993): 687; and Thyra Rauch, "IBM Visual Interface Design," *The STC Usability PIC Newsletter,* January 1996, 3.
5. Thorell and Smith, p. 13.
6. Ibid., 49–51, 214–15.
7. Edward R. Tufte, *The Visual Display of Quantitative Information* (Cheshire, CT: Graphics Press, 1983), 113.
8. Thophilus Addo, "The Effects of Dimensionality in Computer Graphics," *Journal of Business Communication* 31, no. 4 (October 1994): 253–65.
9. Kathleen Deveny, "What's Wrong with This Picture? Utility's Glasses Are Never Empty," *The Wall Street Journal,* May 25, 1995, B1.
10. Day Mines *1974 Annual Report,* 1; reproduced in Tufte, 54.

Module 26

1. Richard Bolle, "Here's How to Pack Your Parachute," *Fast Company*, September 1999, 242.
2. Walter Kiechel III, "Preparing for Your Outplacement," *Fortune*, November 30, 1992, 153.
3. Carl Quintanilla, "Coming Back," *The Wall Street Journal*, February 22, 1996, R10; Megan Malugani, "How to Re-Enter the Health-Care Job Market," *The Columbus Dispatch*, March 22, 2000, 13.
4. LeAne Rutherford, "Five Fatal Résumé Mistakes," *Business Week's Guide to Careers* 4, no. 3 (Spring/Summer 1986): 60–62.
5. Phil Elder, "The Trade Secrets of Employment Interviews," Association for Business Communication Midwest Convention, Kansas City, MO, May 2, 1987.
6. Anne Fisher, "Ask Annie," *Fortune*, February 7, 2000, 210.

Module 27

1. Timothy D. Schellhardt, "Managing: Pitfalls to Avoid in Drafting a Resume," *The Wall Street Journal*, November 28, 1990, B1; Elizabeth Brockman and Kelly Belanger, "A National Study of CPA Recruiters' Preferences for Résumé Length," *The Journal of Business Communication*, 38 (2001): 29-45.
2. Beverly H. Nelson, William P. Gallé, and Donna W. Luse, "Electronic Job Search and Placement," Association for Business Communication Convention, Orlando, FL, November 1–4, 1995.
3. Rebecca Smith, *Electronic Resumes & Online Networking: How to Use the Internet to Do a Better Job Search, Including a Complete, Up-to-Date Resource Guide* (Franklin Lakes, NJ: Career Press, 1999), 191–96.
4. Taunee Besson, *The Wall Street Journal National Employment Business Weekly: Resumes* (New York: John Wiley and Sons, 1994), 245.

Module 29

1. Thomas Petzinger, Jr., "Lewis Roland's Knack for Finding Truckers Keeps Firm Rolling," *The Wall Street Journal*, December 1, 1995, B1.
2. Bill Breen and Anna Muoio, "PeoplePalooza," *Fast Company*, November 2000, 88.

3. Rachel Emma Silverman, "Why Are You So Dressed Up? Do You Have a Job Interview?" *The Wall Street Journal*, April 17, 2001, B1.
4. Sherri Eng, "Company Culture Dictates Attire for Interviews," *The Columbus Dispatch*, August 25, 1996, 33J.
5. The Catalyst Staff, *Marketing Yourself* (New York: G. P. Putnam's Sons, 1980), 179.
6. Richard C. Rose and Echo Montgomery Garrett, "Guerrilla Interviewing," *Inc.*, December, 1992, 145–47.
7. Julie Amparano Lopez, "Firms Force Job Seekers to Jump through Hoops," *The Wall Street Journal*, October 6, 1993, B1.
8. Sue Shellenbarger, "New Job Hunters Ask Recruiters, 'Is There Life After Work?'" *The Wall Street Journal*, January 29, 1996, B1; and Sue Shellenbarger, "What Job Candidates Really Want to Know: Will I Have a Life?" *The Wall Street Journal*, November 17, 1999, B1.
9. Donna Stine Kienzler, letter to Ann Granacki, April 6, 1988.
10. Joel Bowman, "Using NLP to Improve Classroom Communication," Association for Business Communication Regional Conference, Lexington, KY, April 9–11, 1992.
11. Christopher Conte, "Labor Letter," *The Wall Street Journal*, October 19, 1993, A1.

Module 30

1. The Catalyst Staff, *Marketing Yourself* (New York: G. P. Putnam's Sons, 1980), 101.
2. Claud Dotson, comment at the Association for Business Communication Western Regional Conference, Boise, ID, April 13, 1996.
3. Kate Wendleton, *Through the Brick Wall: How to Job-Hunt in a Tight Market* (New York: Villard Books, 1992), 244.
4. Carol A. Hacker, *Job Hunting in the 21st Century: Exploding the Myths, Exploring the Realities* (Boca Raton: St. Lucie Press, 1999), 154.
5. Ray Robinson, quoted by Dick Friedman, "The Interview as Mating Ritual," *Working Woman*, April 1987, 107.
6. Albert R. Karr, "Work Week," *The Wall Street Journal*, November 16, 1999, A1.

Credits

Cartoons and Figures

Warren Miller Cartoon, Module 1: Copyright © The New Yorker Collection 1993. Warren Miller from cartoonbank.com. All rights reserved.

Mick Steven Cartoon, Module 2: Copyright © The New Yorker Collection 1994. Mick Stevens from cartoonbank.com. All rights reserved.

Far Side Cartoon, Module 3: The Far Side® by Gary Larson © 1984 FarWorks, Inc. All Rights Reserved. Used with permission.

Foxtrot Cartoon, Module 4: FOXTROT © Bill Amend. Reprinted with permission of UNIVERSAL PRESS SYNDICATE. All rights reserved.

Non Sequitur Cartoon, Module 5: NON SEQUITUR © Wiley Miller. Dist. by UNIVERSAL PRESS SYNDICATE. Reprinted with permission. All rights reserved.

Marvin Cartoon, Module 6: Reprinted with special permission of North American Syndicate.

Peanuts Cartoon, Module 7: PEANUTS reprinted by permission of United Feature Syndicate, Inc.

Sally Forth Cartoon, Module 8: Reprinted with special permission of King Features Syndicate.

Peanuts Cartoon, Module 9: PEANUTS reprinted by permission of United Features Syndicate, Inc.

Mother Goose & Grimm Cartoon, Module 10: Copyright © Tribune Media Services, Inc. All Rights Reserved. Reprinted with permission.

Non Sequitur Cartoon, Module 11: NON SEQUITUR © Wiley Miller. Dist. by UNIVERSAL PRESS SYNDICATE. Reprinted with permission. All rights reserved.

Dilbert Cartoon, Module 12: DILBERT reprinted by permission of United Features Syndicate, Inc.

Dilbert Cartoon, Module 13: DILBERT reprinted by permission of United Features Syndicate, Inc.

One Big Happy Cartoon, Module 14: By permission of Rick Detorie and Creators Syndicate, Inc.

One Big Happy Cartoon, Module 15: By permission of Rick Detorie and Creators Syndicate, Inc.

One Big Happy Cartoon, Module 16: By permission of Rick Detorie and Creators Syndicate, Inc.

Frank & Ernest Cartoon, Module 17: FRANK & ERNEST reprinted by permission of Newspaper Enterprise Association, Inc.

For Better or Worse Cartoon, Module 18: Copyright © Lynn Johnston Productions, Inc./Distributed by United Features Syndicate, Inc.

Farcus Cartoon, Module 19: FARCUS © is reprinted with permission from LaughingStock Licensing Inc., Ottawa, Canada. All rights reserved.

Figure 19.2: From Inc.: The Magazine for Growing Companies. Copyright © 1995 by Business Innovator Group Resources, Inc. Reproduced with permission of Business Innovator Group Resources, Inc. via Copyright Clearance Center.

Far Side Cartoon, Module 20: The Far Side® by Gary Larson © 1985 FarWorks, Inc. All Rights Reserved. Used with permission.

Dana Fradon Cartoon, Module 21: Copyright © The New Yorker Collection 1992. Dana Fradon from cartoonbank.com. All rights reserved.

Shoe Cartoon, Module 22: Copyright © Tribune Media Services, Inc. All Rights Reserved. Reprinted with permission.

Rubes Cartoon, Module 23: By permission of Leigh Rubin and Creators Syndicate, Inc.

Peanuts Cartoon, Module 24: PEANUTS reprinted by permission of United Features Syndicate, Inc.

Farcus Cartoon, Module 25: FARCUS © is reprinted with permission from LaughingStock Licensing Inc., Ottawa, Canada. All rights reserved.

Figure 25.5: From Wall Street Journal, Easter Edition. Copyright © 1995 by Dow Jones & Co., Inc. Reproduced with permission of Dow Jones & Co., Inc. via Copyright Clearance Center.

Problem 25.10 (1): From Newsweek, August 27, 2001. Copyright © 2001 Newsweek, Inc. All rights reserved. Reprinted by permission.

Problem 25.10 (2): Reprinted from March 11, 2002 issue of BusinessWeek by special permission. Copyright © 2002 by The McGraw-Hill Companies, Inc.

Problem 25.10 (4): Reprinted from July 29, 2002 issue of BusinessWeek by special permission. Copyright @ 2002 by The McGraw-Hill Companies, Inc.

Problem 25.10 (5): From American Demographics, July/August 2002. Copyright © 2002, Media Central, Inc., a PRIMEDIA Company. All rights reserved.

Problem 25.10 (6): Reprinted from August 26, 2002 issue of BusinessWeek by special permission. Copyright © 2002 by The McGraw-Hill Companies, Inc.

Problem 25.10 (7): From Black Enterprise, February 2002. Copyright © 2002. Reprinted with permission of Black Enterprise Magazine, New York, NY. All rights reserved.

Problem 25.11 (1): From American Demographics, July 2001. Copyright © 2001. Media Central, Inc., a PRIMEDIA Company. All rights reserved.

Problem 25.11 (2): From Business 2.0, June 2002. Copyright 2002 Time, Inc. Reprinted with permission. All rights reserved.
Problem 25.11 (3): Data from AC Nielsen Homescan, American Demographics, February 2000, p. 63.
Problem 25.11 (4): From American Demographics, May 2002. Copyright © 2002, Media Central Inc., a PRIMEDIA Company. All rights reserved.
Problem 25.11 (5): From American Demographics, January 2002. Copyright © 2002, Media Central Inc., a PRIMEDIA Company. All rights reserved.
Problem 25.11 (6): From American Demographics, April 2002. Copyright © 2002, Media Central Inc., a PRIMEDIA Company. All rights reserved.
Problem 25.11 (7): From American Demographics, April 2002. Copyright © 2002, Media Central Inc., a PRIMEDIA Company. All rights reserved.
Zits Cartoon, Module 26: Copyright © Jerry Scott and Jim Borgman/Distributed by United Feature Syndicate, Inc.
Figure 27.8: Reprinted from Electronic Resumes & Online Networking: How to Use the Internet to Do a Better Job Search, Including a Complete Up-to-Date Resource Guide. Copyright © 1999 Rebecca Smith. Published by Career Press.
Frank & Ernest Cartoon, Module 28: FRANK & ERNEST reprinted by permission of Newspaper Enterprise Association, Inc.
Danny Shanahan Cartoon, Module 29: Copyright © Danny Shanahan.
Ziggy Cartoon, Module 30: ZIGGY © ZIGGY AND FRIENDS, INC. Reprinted with permission of UNIVERSAL PRESS SYNDICATE. All rights reserved.

Photos
1.1: © 1995 John Garaventa. All rights reserved. Courtesy Griffin Hospital

1.2: Photo by Bob Day
2.1: Courtesy American Legacy Foundation
2.2: Lifecode®, Photograph by Bob Greenspon
2.3: Lifecode®, Photograph by Bob Greenspon
2.4: Thomas Strand/Courtesy of TEC Interface Systems
3.1: © Ron Ceasar
3.2: Michel Porro/Getty Images
3.3: © Strauss/Curtis/CORBIS
6.1: Photo by Terry Miller
7.1: Kitty O. Locker, by permission of Joseph-Beth Booksellers
8.1: Courtesy Floyd Hurt of the Rousing Creativity Group
8.2: Courtesy Debra Beyers/Commerce Bank
10.1: Courtesy of Siemens AG/ShareNet
12.1: Courtesy of the Arab American Institute
12.2: © Gregg Goldman
13.1: Courtesy of Lumeta Corporation. Patent(s) Pending & Copyright © Lumeta Corporation 2002. All Rights Reserved.
15.1: Courtesy of the California Dried Plum Board
17.1: © Frank Ockenfels
18.1: © Brian Warling
18.2: © Marnie Crawford Samuelson
19.1: Courtesy of The Association for Quality and Participation
20.1: Courtesy Deutsch, Inc.
20.2a–f: © Junebug Clark/Photo Researchers
22.1: © Sian Kennedy
24.1: Photo by Mike Watiker, Courtesy of Medflight of Ohio
25.4: Reprinted with permission of Getty Images.
26.1: © Robert Burroughs
28.1: Burke Wood, Freelance director
29.1a, b, c: © John Clark
30.1: © 2000 Dan Cohen

Index